D0340699

Roget's Descriptive Word Finder

Roget's
Descriptive
word
finder

A Dictionary/Thesaurus
of Adjectives

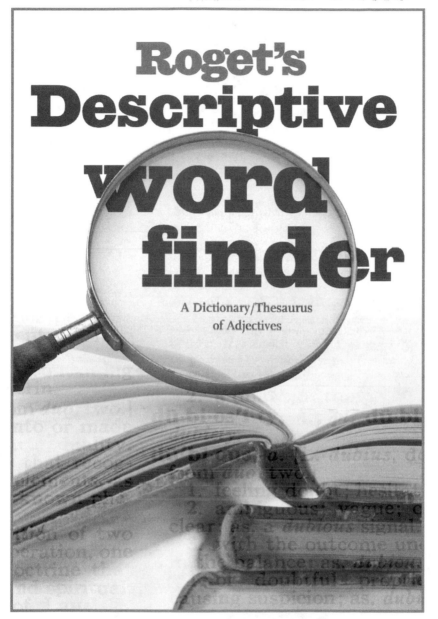

Barbara Ann Kipfer

WRITER'S DIGEST BOOKS
CINCINNATI, OHIO
www.writersdigestbooks.com

Roget's Descriptive Word Finder. Copyright © 2003 by Barbara Ann Kipfer.
Manufactured in the United States of America. All rights reserved. No part of this book
may be reproduced in any form or by any electronic or mechanical means including
information storage and retrieval systems without permission in writing from the publisher,
except by a reviewer, who may quote brief passages in a review. Published by Writer's
Digest Books, an imprint of F&W Publications, Inc., 4700 East Galbraith Road,
Cincinnati, Ohio 45236. (800) 289-0963. First edition.

Visit our Web site at www.writersdigest.com for information on more resources for writers.

To receive a free weekly e-mail newsletter delivering tips and updates about writing and
about Writer's Digest products, register directly at our Web site at http://newsletters.fwpub
lications.com.

07   06   05   04   03   5   4   3   2   1

Library of Congress Cataloging-in-Publication Data

Kipfer, Barbara Ann
    Roget's descriptive word finder : a dictionary/thesaurus of adjectives / by Barbara Ann
    Kipfer.—1st ed.
       p.   cm.
    Includes index.
    ISBN 1-58297-170-6
       1. English language—Synonyms and antonyms. I. Title: Descriptive word finder. II.
    Title.

PE1591.K544   2003
423'.1—dc21   2003041056
                                                                                      CIP

Edited by Kelly Nickell
Designed by Sandy Kent
Cover by Joanna Detz
Production coordinated by Michelle Ruberg

Acknowledgments

Thank you to my husband, Paul Magoulas, who did so much work on this project. You have been a wonderful collaborator. Also, thanks to my children, Kyle and Keir, who inspire me to use many descriptive words!

About the Author

Dr. Barbara Ann Kipfer is the author of more than twenty-five books, including the best-selling *14,000 Things to Be Happy About* (Workman, 1990) and Page-A-Day calendars based on it. She has also authored *The Wish List* (1997), *1,400 Things for Kids to Be Happy About* (1994), and *8,789 Words of Wisdom* (2001) for Workman. Her other books are *Roget's 21st Century Thesaurus in Dictionary Form* (Dell, 1992; Second Edition, 1999), *21st Century Spelling Dictionary* (Dell, 1993), *21st Century Manual of Style* (Laurel, 1993), *The Order of Things* (Random House, 1997), *Dictionary of American Slang* (Third Edition, Harper-Collins, 1995), *Sisson's Word and Expression Locater* (Second Edition, Prentice-Hall, 1994), *Encyclopedic Dictionary of Archaeology* (Kluwer Academic/Plenum, 2000), *The Writer's Digest Flip Dictionary* (Writer's Digest Books, 2000), *Roget's Thesaurus of Phrases* (Writer's Digest Books, 2001), and *Roget's International Thesaurus* (Sixth Edition, HarperResource, 2001).

Dr. Kipfer holds a Ph.D. in linguistics (University of Exeter), a Ph.D. in archaeology (Greenwich University), a master's in linguistics (Exeter), a bachelor's in physical education (Valparaiso University), and a master's in Buddhist studies (Greenwich University).

Dr. Kipfer has worked for such companies as Ask Jeeves, CNET, Dictionary.com and Thesaurus.com, Idealab, Answers.com, Mindmaker, General Electric Research, IBM Research, Wang, Bellcore (now Telcordia), GoTo (now Overture), Cymfony, and Knowledge Adventure. For more information, visit www.thingstobehappyabout.com and click on "About the Author."

Introduction

This book contains thousands of entries for describing people, places, and things with adjectives. It is a combination dictionary and thesaurus exclusively for adjectives and adverbs. Writers can avoid clichés by using fresh, accurate details and by finding the most evocative word or phrase for what they want to describe.

Writers appreciate having different modes of access to words and phrases to elaborate on the descriptions in their own works. This new book offers thousands of descriptive words and phrases in a detailed thematic scheme, providing a comprehensive reference on adjectives and adverbs for writers. As a thematic dictionary, it is based on the ways that people, places, and things are described, and it is all about adjectives and adverbs. As a thesaurus, this treasury of terms for writers depicts the nuances among descriptive words and phrases.

Dictionaries place related words apart in their alphabetical scheme of things, whereas the human mind puts them together in categories or themes. This book contains 572 easily understood categories.

This special reference tool has definitions, and many of the entries have synonyms after the semicolon. But because the entries are arranged thematically, a comparison of the definitions provides the thesaural explanation and differentiation for the writer.

The compiler has included every adjective described in other publications about adjectives—print dictionaries, dictionaries of descriptive terms, thematic dictionaries, dictionaries of obscure words—to provide a wide range of both common and unfamiliar adjectives. The less-familiar adjectives offer the user many colorful terms that can add flavor to one's writings.

Whenever in doubt or for further clarification, do consult an authoritative college or unabridged print dictionary. Sometimes the user will need a more detailed definition to be sure that the chosen word is correct for the intended context.

The addendum to this book is a quick word-finder with no definitions, where writers can get ideas by looking at topical lists.

About Adjectives and Adverbs

Words that express some feature or quality of a noun or pronoun are traditionally known as adjectives. An adjective can occur immediately before a noun: *red house*, the attributive function. An adjective can occur alone after forms of the verb *to be*: *The house was red*, the predicate function. An adjective can be immediately preceded by *very* or other intensifying words: *very red, extremely smart*. An adjective can be compared: *big/bigger/biggest, beautiful/more beautiful/most beautiful*.

Many adjectives have no distinctive ending, but some suffixes typically signal that a word is an adjective:

- *-able* added to a verb; e.g., washable
- *-al* added to a noun; e.g., musical
- *-ed* added to a noun; e.g., ragged
- *-esque* added to a noun; e.g., Romanesque
- *-ful* added to a noun; e.g., hopeful
- *-ic* added to a noun; e.g., heroic
- *-ish* added to a noun; e.g., foolish
- *-ive* added to a verb; e.g., effective
- *-less* added to a noun; e.g., restless
- *-like* added to a noun; e.g., childlike
- *-ly* added to a noun; e.g., friendly
- *-ous* added to a noun; e.g., desirous
- *-some* added to a noun; e.g., bothersome
- *-worthy* added to a noun; e.g., praiseworthy
- *-y* added to a noun; e.g., sandy

Many adjectives permit the addition of *-ly* to form an adverb, such as *sad/sadly*.

The adverb is the most heterogeneous of English parts of speech. Adverbs have two chief uses: as part of a clause structure (1) relating to the meaning of the verb and (2) relating to some other element of the clause or to the clause as a whole. Most adverbs are fairly easy to recognize because they are formed by adding an *-ly* suffix to an adjective, such as *happy/happily*. Other distinctive adverb endings are *-fashion, -style, -ward, -ways,* and *-wise.* Adverbs work along with adverb phrases and clauses to perform their range of functions.

Abandonment—Discontinuance

abandoned: given up; cast-off
abrogated: abolished by authority
cast-off: thrown or laid aside; discarded
derelict: deserted or abandoned
disbanded: turned loose out of their ranks; dispersed; dismissed
discontinued: broken off; stopped
disused: not used
green: inexperienced
jaculative: sporadic; darting
left: abandoned
nonobservant: not observant
premorse: ended abruptly
relinquished: given up; abandoned
relinquishing: surrendering

restoring: giving up
unaccustomed: not accustomed
unappropriated: having no particular application
unculled: not gathered; not selected
unhabituated: not accustomed
unhackneyed: not accustomed
uninured: not accustomed
unowned: not owned; not acknowledged as one's own
unpursued: not pursued or followed
unseasoned: not accustomed
untrained: not accustomed
unused: not accustomed
unusual: not accustomed
unwonted: not accustomed

Aberration—Unconventionality

aberrant: wandering or deviating from the right course
abnormal: not normal
abnormous: not normal
absonant: unnatural
ambagious: talking or doing things in an indirect manner; devious
amorphous: irregular in shape
amphibious: possessing two natures
androgynal: partaking of the nature of a male and a female
androgynous: partaking of the nature of a male and a female

anomalistic: not conforming to a rule
anomalous: not conforming to a rule
arbitrary: depending on no rule
azygous: odd; unpaired
circuitous: roundabout; indirect
crablike: moving sideways
curious: somewhat odd or strange
denaturalized: made unnatural; deprived of citizenship
desultory: jumping from one thing to another, like a circus rider
deviating: varying

devious: straying; wandering; leaving the path of rectitude

diffluent: going different directions; bifurcating; dichotomous; divergent

discursive: passing from one thing to another; rambling

eccentric: not conforming to any rule

egregious: extraordinary

epicene: common to both sexes

errabund: wandering; erratic

errant: wandering; wayward

erratic: wandering; rambling in thought

exceptional: not ordinary

exclusive: not including some things

excursive: desultory; digressive; erratic; roving

exotic: foreign

extraordinary: out of the ordinary course

fantastic: extremely fanciful

farblondzhet: wandering aimlessly; confused or out of it

grotesque: whimsical and uncouth

heteroclite: anomalous

heterogeneous: possessing characteristics of a number of different things

hybrid: produced from the mixture of two species

hypotypic: not typical

indirect: not straight to the point; roundabout

informal: not formal

irregular: not regular

lawless: not restrained by law

misplaced: bestowed in the wrong place

mongrel: of mixed breed

monstrous: very abnormal, so as to be an admonition from the gods

nondescript: not able to be described

nonunion: opposed to trade unions

noteworthy: worthy of observation

odd: not having anything to mate it

original: not imitated or imitating

outlandish: uncouth

peculiar: belonging to one

preternatural: not governed by any known powers of nature

quaint: not conforming to the present manner, style, etc.

qualified: limited

queer: slightly comical

rambling: roving; discursive

rare: occurring not very often; dear

remarkable: extraordinary and noticeable

singular: entirely different from others

strange: not easily explained

stray: straying; irregular

unaccountable: not to be accounted for

unaccustomed: not accustomed

uncommon: not common

unconformable: not conformable

unconventional: not customary

uncustomary: not usual

undescribed: unheard of

undirected: not guided; not knowing the way

unexampled: unprecedented

unusual: not usual

unwonted: not customary

vagrant: wandering; erring

wandering: not guided by anything definite

wanton: free from restraint

wonderful: strange

zigzag: going from side to side; at angles

Absence

absent: not present to

away: not present to

desert: uninhabited

deserted: left; abandoned

devoid: not in possession of

empty: without contents; not filled

exempt from: free from; released as from an obligation or duty

gone from home: away from one's usual place

inexistent: having no existence

lost: gone from the presence or possession of

missing: absent from proper place; lost

nonresident: not residing in

not having: without

not present: absent
nowhere to be found: lost
omitted: left out; not included
tenantless: without a tenant; unoccupied
unhabitable: not suitable for abode
uninhabitable: not suitable for abode
uninhabited: without dwellers

unoccupied: not taken up or occupied
untenanted: not taken up or occupied
vacant: empty
vacuous: empty
void: devoid of matter
wanting: without

Accord—Harmony

accordant: agreeing in a purpose
agreeing: in accord; concurring
allied: akin; joined
apt: quick at understanding; pertinent
at home: in the proper place
at one with: concurring in a given proposition; on good terms
at peace: friendly
banded together: united for a common purpose
becoming: suited to character, position, or disposition
cemented: closely united
commensurate: commensurable
compatible: not repugnant; agreeing
conciliatory: pacific
concordant: agreeing; consonant
conformable: agreeing in form; correspondent
congenial: kindred; sympathetic
congruous: characterized by suitability; agreeable; harmonious
consentaneous: reciprocally acquiescent
consistent: agreeing in reality with profession
consonant: likeness of sound; according
correspondent: having suitability; fit
fraternal: brotherly
friendly: living as friends

harmonious: agreeing in thought or purpose; concordant; peaceable
henotic: harmonizing
in accord: having the idea of agreement, similarity, or harmony; agreeing
in accordance with: having the idea of agreement, similarity, or harmony
in harmony with: having the idea of agreement, similarity, or harmony
in keeping with: having the idea of agreement, similarity, or harmony
in one's proper element: suitable to
in point: under discussion
in still water: free from strife
in unison with: agreeing with
of a piece: of same sort; like
of one mind: agreeing in thought
on all fours: to correspond with exactly
pat: exactly fitting
pertinent: applicable; relevant; suited
proportionate: adjusted in a due proportion
reconciled: brought in harmony; harmonized
suiting: adapting; befitting; agreeing
to the point: suitable
to the purpose: suitable
tranquil: at peace; free from strife
unisonous: being in harmony; agreement; of the same pitch
united: of like views or purpose

Account

accountable: capable of being accounted
anecdotic: pertaining to short stories
cadastral: pertaining to valuation or registration for the purpose of taxation
described: depicted; delineated
descriptive: narrative; pictorial

epic: recitive of heroic exploits
graphic: very clear and pronounced
historic: part of history
hypomnematic: consisting of notes or memoranda
legendary: based on tradition

narrative: pertaining to a logical account of successive events

storied: connected with history

suggestive: calling forth other incidents

traditional: not authentic; based on legends

traditionary: traditional

Achromatism

achromatic: free from color

achromic: without color; achromatic

allagrugous: grim and ghastly

aplanatic: freed from spherical aberration by two lenses

ashy: ash-colored

blond: having a fair skin, light eyes, and fair hair

cadaverous: deathly pale

cold: bluish in tone or effect

colorless: without color

dead: lusterless; dull

dingy: of a dusky color

discolored: having lost its color; changed in color

dull: without luster

dun: of a dull dark-brown color

etiolated: pale and drawn

exsanguine: anemic; bloodless

faint: indistinct in color

fair: having light or clear color

ghastly: having a deathlike appearance

glassy: transparent

hueless: without shade of color

lackluster: wanting luster; dim

leaden: having the color of lead

light-colored: of a faint or pale shade of color

muddy: clouded

pale: lacking in color and freshness

pale as a corpse: unnaturally pale

pale as a ghost: unnaturally pale

pale as a witch: unnaturally pale

pale as ashes: unnaturally pale

pale as death: unnaturally pale

pale-faced: having a pale face

pallescent: growing pale

pallid: of a pale or wan appearance, as from illness

sallow: of an unhealthy yellowish color

tallow-faced: having a tallowy complexion

uncolored: without color

wan: having pale skin, as from sickness or anxiety; blanched; chalky; etiolated; pallid; pasty

white: of the color of snow

xanthochroid: pertaining to those with blond hair and a pale complexion

Acidity

acerb: sour and bitter

acerbic: sour or astringent in taste

acescent: slightly sour; turning sour

acetic: pertaining to vinegar

acetose: causing acetification

acetous: causing acetification

acid: containing acid

acidic: sharp and biting in flavor

acidulated: tinged with acid

acrid: sharp, biting, or bitterly pungent

astringent: harshly biting; especially constrictive to taste buds

biting: sharp; somewhat acidic; producing harsh taste

bitter: having a harsh, disagreeably acrid

taste; being one of the four basic taste sensations

caustic: sharp and acidic

crabbed: rough or harsh to the taste

flinty: of wine, mainly Chablis; having a whiff of gunpowder

hard: acid, as hard cider

piquant: pleasingly sharp, biting, or tart

pungent: biting or acrid; having a sharp effect on the taste organ

rough: astringent, applied to wine

sharp: strongly pungent or biting

sour: tart; acidic; lemony; being one of the four basic taste sensations

sour as vinegar: very sour

sourish: acidulous

styptic: having the quality of restraining bleeding

subacid: slightly tart or biting; moderately acid

tart: sour or acidic; sharp to the taste

Acting

acting: portraying; performing

balatronic: buffoonish

buskined: wearing buskins; pertaining to tragedy

comic: provoking mirth

cothurnal: in the spirit of classical tragic drama

dramatic: pertaining to representation on the stage

farcical: belonging to a farce or burlesque

histrionic: pertaining to actors or acting; dramatic; theatrical

melodramatic: pertaining to a melodrama, a romantic play full of startling incidents

operatic: pertaining to the musical form of the drama

Roscian: pertaining to acting

scenic: dramatic; theatrical

stagey: pertaining to the stage; theatrical

thalian: pertaining to comedy; comic

theatric: of the nature of dramatic representation; befitting the stage

theatrical: of the nature of dramatic representation; befitting the stage

tragic: pertaining to tragedy

tragicomic: partly tragic and partly comic

tyronic: amateurish

Activity

acting: doing

activable: capable of being activated

active: having activity; quick in movement

afoot: on foot

agile: having power of quick movement of body

agoing: in movement

alert: active in watchfulness

alive: in a state of operation or activity

alive and frisking: alive and active

animated: full of vital activity

assiduous: unremitting in activity or effort

astir: on the move

at call: liable to be required at any time

at work: come out of sleep; vigilant; awake

brisk: having life, vivacity, or spirit

brisk as a bee: active

brisk as a lark: very brisk

broad awake: fully awake

businesslike: requiring attention and assiduity

bustling: excitedly stirring about

busy: active at anything

busy as a bee: continuous in application and effort

busy as a hen with one chicken: continuous in application and effort

diligent: continuous in application and effort

doing: carrying out in action

do-it-yourself: pertaining to practice of building or repairing items oneself, especially household objects

eager: keenly desirous to obtain or perform something

enterprising: having boldness and ability in business

eventful: full of important events, hence full of life and activity

expeditious: accomplished with speed

extradictionary: consisting of deeds, not words

fast: moving rapidly; quick

forward: eager to presumptuousness

frisky: inclined to playful activity

full of business: vigorously working; hardworking; hard at it; hard at work

fussy: taking active interest in trivial things
in action: at work
in earnest: at work; in harness
in full swing: in active operation
in harness: in active duty
in operation: in effect
indefatigable: incapable of being exhausted
industrious: working with diligence
intent: having the mind directed to an object
light-footed: quick on the feet
lively: full of vivacity and animation
meddlesome: given to meddling
meddling: participating without permission in the concerns of others
motatorious: constantly active
never tired: never experiencing fatigue
nimble: active in body
nimble as a squirrel: quick-footed; nimble-footed
notable: worthy of observation
nutational: nodding, as a head
occupied: employed in an exclusive manner
officious: unduly participating in others' concerns
on duty: ready; on foot; on one's legs
on the alert: on the lookout
on the anvil: in a state of formation
overofficious: too officious
painstaking: diligent and careful in labor
pantopragmatic: meddling in everybody's business

plodding: laboriously toiling
pottering: working unspiritedly
pushing: to advance with energy
quick: characterized by life or speed
quick as a lamplighter: characterized by life or speed
Rabelaisian: pertaining to an abundance of vigor, humor, caricature, frankness (like Rabelais's work)
resolute: having a steadfast purpose
restless: never resting; eager for variety
restless as a hyena: never resting; eager for variety
sedulous: constant and persevering in effort
sharp: keen and eager; active
smart: quick in thought or action
spirited: having spirit or vim
sprack: brisk; active; alert
spry: inclined to quick movement; nimble
stirring: moving vigorously
strenuous: zealous in anything; ardently eager
tripping: moving lightly and nimbly
undertaking: engaging in
unsleeping: not sleeping
unwearied: not wearied or fatigued
up and doing: active and brisk; up and stirring
vivacious: full of life and activity
wide awake: perfectly awake
workaday: a week day
working: toiling
zealous: earnest in a cause

Addition—Increase

accessory: additional
accrual: increasing
added: brought together to make a whole
additional: supplemental; in the way of an addition; supplementary
additive: allowing to be added
adjectitious: added to
adscititious: supplemental; extrinsic; superfluous
anabatic: augmenting; increasing

ascititious: supplemental
ascriptitious: added to a list; ascribed; attributed
beblubbered: swollen
big: of great size
bigswoln: swelled to a great size
bloated: distended by fluid or gas
blowsy: having a fat, red face
bulbous: having bulbs
distended: spread out in every direction

dropsical: affected with dropsy
edematous: dropsical
epactal: additional
evasé: enlarging gradually, like a funnel; wider at the top
exaggerated: represented in undue proportions
expanded: unfolded
expansive: stretching out to a great distance
extra: beyond what is due
fat: fleshy
flabelliform: spread out like a fan
full-blown: completely expanded
full-formed: completely expanded
full-grown: having completed development
gor-belly: having a protuberant belly; gor-bellied
gravid: pregnant; distended
hypertrophic: overdeveloped; over-grown; hypertrophied
hypertrophied: having an excessive growth; hypertrophic
increased: made larger; augmented
larger: of greater size
obese: large in body
oedematous: dropsical
on the increase: increasing
overgrown: larger than normal growth

patulous: spreading slightly; open; expanded
phlogogenetic: causing inflammation
pinguescent: becoming fat; fattening
planteric: fattened for slaughter
potbellied: having a protuberant belly
puffy: distended by air or something soft
pulvinate: swelling like a pillow or cushion
pursy: fat
scaturient: effusive; gushing forth
subjunctive: joined at the end
sufflated: inflated; blown-up
supervacaneous: needlessly added
supplement: supplying to make up for a deficiency
supplemental: added to supply a correc-tion for a defect
supplementary: serving as a supplement
suppletory: supplying deficiencies
sway-bellied: having a protuberant belly
swelling: inflated; puffed up
swollen: increased in bulk
tumid: swollen by an alteration of the internal structure
turgescent: becoming inflated; swelling
turgid: swollen by something put in; dis-tended; bloated
undiminished: not decreased
wide-open: expanded
widespread: expanded

Admission—Inclusion

absorbent: tending to drink in or suck up
absorptive: that which takes in and incorporates
admissible: worthy or capable of being entertained; allowable
admitted: allowed to enter; received
admitting: granting or ready to grant the privilege of entering
another-guess: of another type or sort
congeneric: included under the same genus or kind

congenerous: belonging to the same genus or kind
constituting: serving to form, compose, or make up
containing: being able to hold
entrant: admitting
included: comprised; enclosed
including: comprising; enclosing
inclusive: comprising; embracing
of the same class: belonging to the same type

Adulation

abject: in a servile condition

adulatory: servilely flattering

base: low and untrustworthy in conduct toward others

beggarly: miserably mean

blandiloquent: in the language of compliment

caressed: treated in a caressing manner

caressing: showing affection by words and actions

come-hither: beckoning in a flirtatious manner

courtierlike: very courteous

courtierly: very courteous

cringing: acting with base humility

crouching: bowing in reverence

dicty: snobbish; conceited; high-class; dickty

down on one's marrow-bones: in an abject condition

fair-spoken: bland in speech

fawning: seeking favor by cringing

fine: nice; artful; subtle

flattering: praising unduly or insincerely

fulsome: offensive from excess of praise; flattering and insincere

gnathonic: deceitfully flattering; sycophantic; gnathonical

going steady: regularly dating one person

groveling: acting in an abject and mean condition

honeyed: sweetly flattering

honey-mouthed: having a flattering mouth

ingratiating: eager to please; accommodating; smarmy

lovesick: in love; sighing like furnace

mealymouthed: speaking in a deferential and insincere manner; euphemistic

mean: of an ignoble and hateful disposition

oily: deceitfully affable in speech or manners

osculant: kissing

parasitical: gaining a living by fawning upon a person

parietal: having to do with rules governing contact between sexes and dating hours, especially at an institution such as a college

plausible: apparently right

pliant: easily influenced

prostrate: showing extreme humility

puzzomous: disgustingly obsequious

servile: meanly obsequious

slavish: like a slave

smooth: suave, often deceitfully

smooth-tongued: deceitfully pleasing in speech

sneaking: acting with servility

sniveling: affecting tender emotions in a hypocritical manner

soapy: using flattery; flattering

specious: appearing well at first sight, but really unsound

spoony: addicted to spooning; enamored in a silly or sentimental way

supple: compliant to the humors of others

sycophantic: like a sycophant; servile in flattery; fawning

unctuous: extremely bland or suave

Advice

admonitory: serving to warn or reprove

advising: counseling

advisory: giving or tending to give advice

consiliary: giving counsel

dehortatory: dissuading

hortative: advisory; encouraging; urging

hortatory: fitted to encourage in a given course

officious: offering unwanted advice; meddlesome; intrusive; bossy

paramuthetic: encouraging; consoling

parenetic: advisory; counseling

proceleusmatic: encouraging; inspiring

recommendatory: having a recommendation

suggestible: that may be suggested; easily influenced by suggestions

Affectation—Arrogance

ad captandum: for the purpose of pleasing or attracting

affected: having assumed what is not real or unnatural

apopathetic: showing-off

aprioristic: innate; presumptive

arbitrary: having no control to limit one's own selfish desire

arrogant: giving oneself undue importance

artificial: unnatural; feigned; affected

assuming: taking upon oneself proudly and without due cause

assumptive: taken for granted

audacious: displaying defiant boldness

aweless: lacking reverential fear

barefaced: shameless

baronial: having the character of a baron; lordly

beauish: foppish; dandyish

big-sounding: bombastic; pompous

bloated with pride: swollen with pride

blown: swollen; distended

bluff: rough but kind in speech

blustering: talking boisterously

boldfaced: impudent

brazen: of hardened impudence

brazen-faced: excessively bold

buckish: foppish; lewd

bumptious: pushy; conceited; self-assertive; brash; brazen; cheeky; impertinent; impudent; nervy

cavalier: slighting

ceremonial: in accordance with form

ceremonious: in accordance with form

conceited: having a high estimation of oneself

consequential: having the air of importance

contumelious: expressing scornful insolence

coxcombical: foppish

dandified: foppish

dashing: boastingly showy

dead to shame: having lost all sense of shame from long association with evil

demure: affectedly modest

devil-may-care: reckless

dictatorial: given to speaking in an overbearing manner

dignified: having a stately impressiveness

disdainful: full of disdain; scornful

domineering: ruling insolently

dramatic: theatrical; showy

egolatrous: self-worshiping

egotistic: egotistical

egotistical: addicted to or manifesting an excessive love of self

en grande tenue: in full dress

endimanche: in Sunday clothes

euphuistic: affectedly elegant in writing

fastuous: stuck-up; arrogant

fine: showy; pretentious

finical: foppish

finikin: foppish

fire-eating: always desirous to fight

flaming: brilliant; shining

flashing: cheaply pretentious and showy

flashy: showy, but empty

flatulopetic: pretentious; pompous

flaunting: make an ostentatious display; showy

flippant: frivolously insolent

flushed: elated; being animated with joy

foppish: vain and overnice in dress and deportment

formal: strictly observing rules of etiquette

forward: not reserved and modest

free and easy: showing little regard for conventionality

fripperous: gaudy; ostentatious

froufrou: fussy; showy; frou-frou

full of affectation: affected

full of sound and fury: ferocious and boastful

garish: extravagantly showy or flashing
gaudy: of brilliant colors; garish
gaudy as a butterfly: showy
gaudy as a peacock: showy
gaudy as a tulip: showy
gay: brilliant; showy
glittering: shining; sparkling
grand: magnificent; wonderful
haughty: disdainful and overbearingly proud
hauteur: being arrogant and haughty
hectoring: domineering over, as a bully
high: conceited
high and mighty: great and powerful in one's own opinion
high-flowing: extravagant
high-flown: bombastic; excessively proud; swelled; pretentious
high-handed: carried on in an overbearing manner
high-mettled: full of mettle or spirit; proud
high-minded: foolish and proud
high-plumed: abundantly decorated
high-souled: magnanimous
high-sounding: ostentatious; boasting
high-toned: aristocratic
hufty-tufty: swaggering
imperious: commanding in an insolent manner
impertinent: insolently presumptuous
impudent: insolently bold
in best bib and tucker: in best clothes
in buckram: in a stiff manner
in Sunday clothes: in best clothes
inflated: puffed up; pompous; bombastic
insolent: haughty and contemptuous toward other
intolerant: not enduring a difference of opinion
janty: in a careless or self-satisfied manner
jaunty: in a careless or self-satisfied manner
la-di-da: suggesting pretentiousness; la-de-da; la-di-dah; lah-di-dah
lofty: elevated in manner or mien; proud

lofty-minded: high-minded; characterized by pride
lordly: like a lord; haughty; domineering
lost to shame: having no sense of shame
magisterial: showing authority in an overbearing manner
magnificent: exhibiting great splendor
majestic: imposing and attractive
malapert: impudent; outspoken; insolent
mimsy: prim; prudish
mincing: spoken imperfectly and with affected softness
namby-pamby: weakly sentimental
niminy-piminy: affected; effeminate
not natural: unnatural
obnoxious: pushy; forward
on one's high horses: haughty
on one's high ropes: haughty
on stilts: pompous; haughty
orgulous: proud; haughty; orgillous
ostensible: declared as genuine; pretended; professed; avowed
ostentatious: fond of making a display from vanity
overacted: performed to excess
overbearing: arrogant and domineering
overdone: exaggerated; too elaborate
overweening: characterized by arrogance; presumptuous pride
overwise: affectedly wise
overwrought: exaggerated; too elaborate
palatial: like a palace; grand
paughty: arrogant; pretentious
pedantic: like a pedant
perked up: being exalted; carrying oneself proudly
pert: insolently forward; malapert; sprightly
pompous: displaying great power or wealth; showy; boastful
pragmatical: self-important
precocious: too forward in displaying one's accomplishments
presumptuous: insolently self-asserting
pretentious: attempting to pass for more than one's real value; affected; artificial; phony

priggish: conceited or affectedly precise in dress and manners

prim: very neat and stiff

proud: having an undue sense of one's importance

proud as a peacock: showy and proud

proud as Lucifer: showy and proud

proud-crested: proudly presumptuous

prudish: affectedly modest

prunk: proud; vain; saucy

puffed-up: inflated with pride or vanity

punctilious: exact in forms of etiquette

puritanical: scrupulously strict in morals or religion

purse-proud: arrogant, due to money; purseproud

Quakerish: scrupulous in dress

rakish: debonair in appearance or manner

recherché: pretentious; overblown

ritual: according to form or ritual

roistering: acting in a blustering manner

rollicking: acting in a careless, swaggering manner

saucy: impertinently bold, so as to give a sauce to his good wit

self-admiring: being pleased with oneself

self-applauding: approving oneself

self-confident: confident in one's own ability

self-conscious: unduly conscious of one's own acts

self-flattering: making complimentary speeches of self

self-glorious: vainglorious

self-opinionated: holding opinions of one's own in a conceited way stubbornly

self-satisfied: self-complacent

self-sufficient: having overweening confidence in one's powers

sentimental: indulging in displays of exaggerated feelings

shameless: insensible to shame

showy: making a great display

simpering: smiling in a silly or affected manner

smug: affectedly nice

solemn: stiff

spectacular: pertaining to a grand scenic display

splendid: fine; excellent

stagey: bombastic in style or manner

starch: stiff and rigid

starched: formal

starchy: stiff and precise

stately: grand; imposing; dignified

stiff: formal and not easy

stiff-necked: unyielding; insubordinate

stilted: artificially elevated in manner

straitlaced: stiff and straight, especially in morals

stuck up: proud; haughty

sumptuous: involving great expenditure

superbious: arrogant; haughty; overbearing

supercilious: haughty with pride; with raised eyebrows

swaggering: acting insolently in public

swollen: inflated or distended, as with one's consequence

theatrical: artificial; pompous

thrasonic: marked by insolent boasting, like Thraso, a braggart soldier in Terence's *Eunuchus*

too-too: pertaining to affectation

turgid: vainly ostentatious

ultracrepidarian: presumptuous; going too far; overstepping the mark

unabashed: not disconcerted or embarrassed

unblushing: having an insolent countenance; not embarrassed; bold

unceremonious: informal

unconstrained: not repressed

unctuous: ingratiating; behaving in an affected manner

unnatural: in an assumed manner

vain: elated with self-admiration

vain as a peacock: proud of one's person or dress

vainglorious: overproud of one's achievements; vaunting

vaporing: boasting vainly

would-be: pretending to be what one is not

Affluence—Enough—Welfare

abounding: plentiful; abundant

absolute: without limitation or condition

abundant: in great excess above what is necessary

adequate: equal to what is required, morally, intellectually, or materially

affluent: rich in worldly goods; abounding in wealth

agreeable: pleasant or grateful to one

all straight: having money affairs in good condition

ample: somewhat more than necessary

arriviste: newly rich; parvenu

at one's ease: without trouble or anxiety

auspicious: giving promise of success or prosperity

banausic: mundanely concerned with making money

Barmecidal: giving the illusion of abundance

big with: fruitful with; teeming with

born under a lucky star: lucky

born with a silver spoon in one's mouth: lucky

buoyant: lighthearted; cheerful

centimillionaire: having more than $100 million

cheap: stingy

choke full: completely full

closefisted: stingy; miserly

commensurate: corresponding in amount or degree

competent: adequate in ability; applied to mental endowments

copious: in great quantities, as if from a rich source

enough: having a quantity that will satisfy the purpose or demand

enough and to spare: more than enough

exhaustless: inexhaustible

flush: abundantly furnished with money

flush of cash: possessing plenty of ready money

flush of money: possessing plenty of ready money

flush of tin: possessing plenty of ready money

fortunate: receiving some unforeseen good or blessings; favored of fortune

frim: flourishing; thriving

full: abounding in; containing all that it can hold

grushie: flourishing

halcyon: calm and peaceful, as the sea while the halcyon broods

in a fair way: having good prospects of success

in cash: having a supply of money on hand

in full feather: having a supply of money on hand

in funds: having a supply of money on hand

in good case: well-circumstanced

in high feather: in full spirits; having plenty of money

in luck: fortunate; unexpectedly successful

inexhaustible: impossible to be used up or consumed

lavish: generous, often extravagant, in giving or spending

liberal: large in quantity, as a gift or supply

loaded: very wealthy

lucky: favored by luck; meeting with success

lucrative: profitable; tending to or likely to make money

lucripetous: money-hungry

luxuriant: producing abundantly

made of money: plenteously supplied with money

measured: regulated; restrained within bounds

moderate: limited in quantity

mondain: worldly; sophisticated; mondaine

moneyed: wealthy; well-to-do; monied
niggardly: stingy; miserly
nummamorous: money-loving
opulent: having large means; rich
out of debt: freed from all encumbrances
palmy: flourishing; prosperous
parvenu: newly rich or powerful; on the way up professionally or socially; arriviste
pecuniary: pertaining to money
pecunious: having abundance of money; wealthy
penny-wise: thrifty and careful over small sums or matters
plenteous: plentiful
plentiful: more than enough; applied to supplies of food, water
plenty: plentiful
plenty as blackberries: very plentiful
propitious: helping to success; having favoring influence or tendency
prosperous: successful in those things that men desire; tending to gain
provided for: taken care of financially beforehand
providential: effected by divine direction
puist: in comfortable circumstances
purse-proud: proud of one's wealth, especially in a showy manner
replete: filled again; completely filled
rhinocerical: wealthy; rich
rich: possessing abundant means to supply wants
rich as a Jew: expression signifying enormous wealth
rich as Croesus: expression signifying enormous wealth
rolling in riches: exceedingly wealthy
rolling in wealth: exceedingly wealthy; rolling in it
satisfactory: answering all desires and requirements
Scotch: frugal; cheap

setup: raised from disaster to a sufficient fortune
solvent: able to liquidate all just debts
sparing: frugal; cautious in spending
stingy: frugal; miserly; spending money grudgingly
stintless: without bounds or limits
sufficient: what is needful to serve a purpose; applied to what is to be used or employed
tangible: capable of being handled or touched
thriving: successful through economy and care
tightfisted: stingy; reluctant to spend
unconditional: limited by no conditions
unexhausted: not exhausted
ungenerous: stingy; reluctant to spend money on others
unmeasure: not measured
unsparing: not sparing
unstinted: not stinted
unstinting: not stinting
unwasted: not wasted
up to the mark: up to the standard
valid: having sufficient soundness, said of arguments
wantless: having no want; abundant
warm: easy and safe in money matters
wealthy: having greater means than the generality of men
welfarist: concerned with welfare
well provided: having a sufficient supply
well provided for: generously taken care of beforehand
well stocked: having a sufficient supply
well-off: prosperous; thriving
well-to-do: prosperous; wealthy
well-to-do in the world: prosperous
wholesale: done on a large scale
without stint: lavish; without limit
worth much: well supplied with worldly goods

After—Following

after: coming behind
apoop: toward the back; astern

back: behind
caudal: pertaining to the tail of an animal

crested: having a tuft or ridge on the head or upper back

dorsal: of or pertaining to the back

echinoproctous: having a spiny or prickly behind, like a porcupine

following: that comes after or next in order or time

future: pertaining to time to come

hind: pertaining to the rear part

hinder: pertaining to the rear part

hindermost: farthest back

hindmost: farthest back

later: longer delayed

lumbar: pertaining to the loins

manback: being carried on a person's back

penultimate: next to last

popliteal: concerning the back of the knee

postdiluvial: happening since Noah's flood

postdiluvian: happening since Noah's flood

posterior: back or behind; later in time or place

postern: rear

posthumous: born after the father's death; published after the death of the author

postical: posterior

postliminious: done subsequently

postnate: subsequent

pretelethal: after death; postmortem

rear: behind

retrocollic: pertaining to the back of the neck

retroverted: back to front; reversed

steatopygous: having a fatty behind; steatopygic

subsequent: coming after in time or in order of place

succeeding: following in the course of time or events

tergant: showing the back

Age

advanced in life: old

advanced in years: old

aged: approaching the term of existence

ancestral: pertaining to an ancestor

anicular: old-womanish; weak; feeble-minded; anile

anile: enfeebled in the intellect by age

annotinous: being a year old

annuated: slightly aged

antiquated: of an old and obsolete style

ayne: eldest

declining: weakening from age

decrepit: enfeebled by age

doited: aged; decrepit

effete: worn out by age and incapable of further production

eigne: firstborn

elder: having lived more years than another

eldest: firstborn

epigonous: of a later generation; imitative

firstborn: eldest

firstling: the firstborn

gerocomical: pertaining to medical treatment for the aged

gray: old

gray-headed: old

having one foot in the grave: having lived to an advanced age

hoar: white from age

hoary: white from age

in years: elderly

insenescible: unable to grow old

juvenescent: growing young

marked with a crow's foot: marked with a wrinkle under the eye, as a sign of age

matronly: advanced in years

mellow: ripened by age

no chicken: having advanced beyond the years of youth

of a certain age: at an age deemed suitable for an activity

old: advanced far in years or life

old as Methuselah: old as the oldest man

older: more advanced in years than another
oldest: born first
past one's prime: going toward old age
patriarchal: old and venerable
quadragenarious: being forty years old
ripe: fully matured
run to seed: grown old and useless
senescent: aging
senile: affected by old age
senior: older in years or office
Silurian: very old

stricken in years: infirm from age
superannuated: incapacitated by age
timeworn: feeble from age
turned of: having passed beyond a certain age
venerable: meriting esteem on account of age
waning: gradually declining, like the old moon
wrinkled: having furrows in the skin from age
years old: of age

Agency

acted upon: having some power exerted upon
acting: operating in any way
agentive: pertaining to agent or agency
at work: laboring
effectual: capable of bringing about a result
efficacious: powerful to produce the effect intended
efficient: marked by energetic and useful activity

in action: engaged in work
in exercise: using physical or mechanical powers
in force: driving; compelling
in operation: exerting power
in play: into use
on foot: doing
operative: having the power of acting
practical: capable of being turned to use or account
wrought upon: having power; acting upon

Aggravation—Agitation—Turbulence

aberrant: departing substantially from standard behavior
abrupt: involving unexpected changes
acute: violent; not chronic
aggravable: inclined to aggravate
aggravated: exasperated; incensed
aggravating: annoying; causing irritation
agitated: overly excited or anxious; disturbed
all of a twitter: highly excited
baffled: confused; confounded
bewildered: extremely confused and disoriented
bizarre: odd, extravagant, or eccentric in behavior
bluff: blustering
blustering: windy; disagreeable; swaggering
boisterous: exhibiting tumultuous violence and fury

brainsick: mentally disordered
broken: completely crushed in mind and spirit
brooding: depressed; moody
brusque: blunt or rough in manner
confounded: baffled or confused
confused: unable to differentiate reality; disturbed in mind or purpose; muddled
convulsive: spasmodic
delirious: suffering from delirium
desperate: without care for danger or safety; without hope
desultory: changeable
detonating: causing to explode with a sudden and loud report
deviant: straying from normal behavior
diabolical: perverse, as though possessed by the devil

disedifying: shocking or disturbing; objectionable

disorderly: lacking due order or arrangement

distracted: confused; unfocused; at loose ends

distraught: extremely agitated

disturbed: showing symptoms of emotional illness and distress

dizzy: mentally confused

ebullient: in a bubbling or boiling condition

erratic: peculiar, inconsistent, or unpredictable in behavior

excited: stirred up

explosive: liable to explode or to cause explosion

extravagant: exceeding just or ordinary limits

fanatic: marked by excessive behavior

fazed: disturbed or disconcerted

feral: wild; untamed

ferocious: of a wild, fierce, or savage nature

fierce: having or showing a furious cruel nature

fierce as a tiger: very fierce

fiery: showing excessive warmth or vehemence of mood or temperament

flaming: tending to excite

flustered: confused, anxious, or agitated

frantic: mentally deranged, out of control, or very nervous

frazzled: in state of extreme nervous fatigue

frenzied: violently agitated

furious: overcome with rage or passion

giddy-paced: moving irregularly

headstrong: not easily restrained

hot: characterized by heat or animation

hysteric: convulsive

imbalanced: mentally disturbed or abnormal

impetuous: rushing with force and violence

importunate: annoying; troublesome

in hysterics: having nervous or convulsive fits of a certain kind

incontrollable: incapable of being controlled, restrained, or governed

infuriate: furiously angry

insuppressible: not to be suppressed or concealed

irrepressible: not capable of being repressed

jangled: tense; irritated; nervous

kamikaze: recklessly self-destructive

maladjusted: poorly adapted to normal society; eccentric

manic: hyperactive; excessively excited or agitated

mental: affected with a disorder of the mind

meteoric: having the nature of meteors

mixed-up: completely confused or emotionally unstable

muddled: confused

neurotic: excessively anxious or indecisive

obsessive: unable to escape some persistent idea or need

obstreperous: making a great outcry or disturbance

off-the-wall: extreme terror or nervous hysteria; jitters

outrageous: heedless of authority or decency

overwrought: extremely anxious or agitated

peculiar: odd or eccentric in behavior

perverse: obstinately unreasonable, willful, or evil

phobic: suffering from exaggerated, illogical fears

pixilated: slightly unbalanced

procellous: stormy; tempestuous

queer: peculiar or eccentric in behavior

raging: acting with passionate or unrestrained violence

ramagious: wild

rampant: exceeding all bounds

rattled: confused, disconcerted, and anxious

ravening: seeking eagerly for prey

red-hot: heated to redness; very enthusiastic

restless: unquiet

retarded: severely mentally deficient

riotous: guilty of riot or tumultuous disorder

rocky: unstable, upset, or unsteady

roiled: turbid; stirred up

rough: characterized by rude or violent action

rude: characterized by abrupt or rough discourtesy

saltatory: moving abruptly or by leaps

saturnalian: unrestrained; wild; licentious

savage: of a wild and untamed nature, like the wild man of the woods

scorching: very hot

shaken-up: disoriented or confused

shaking: vibrating

shambling: unsteady

sharp: impetuous or fiery

shattered: in a state of mental, emotional, or nervous collapse or disintegration

spasmodic: abnormally sudden and irregular

spooked: fearful over imagined threats

stormy: characterized by or proceeding from violent agitation or fury

stressed-out: exhausted or extremely anxious

strung-out: addicted to a drug; in an extreme state of nervous exhaustion

subsultory: bounding

tameless: untamable

tangled: disoriented or bewildered

tremulous: trembling

troublous: marked by commotion or tumult

tumultuary: characterized by tumult

tumultuous: disorderly

turbulent: being in violent agitation or commotion

unappeasable: not to be quieted, calmed, or pacified

unbridled: unrestrained

uncontrollable: ungovernable

unextinguished: uncontrolled

ungentle: wild; turbulent; harsh; refractory

ungovernable: not capable of being governed, ruled, or restrained

unmitigable: not capable of being alleviated

unmitigated: not softened in severity or harshness

unquelled: not quieted

unquenched: not put an end to

unquiet: without rest

unrelieved: without relief; no better

unrepressed: not held in check

unruly: not submissive to rule

unsound: abnormal or disordered, as in the mind

unstable: unable to control one's emotions or behave within accepted norms

uproarious: accompanied by or making an uproar

vehement: acting with great force

violent: characterized by intense force, rudeness, and rapidity

volcanic: resembling a volcano

warm: showing excitement

waspish: irascible; having a nature like a wasp

wild: affected with or originating violent disturbances

worked-up: agitated; unable to contain emotions

worse: more evil

Agriculture

agrarian: pertaining to the land or farmers

agrestic: rural

agriculture: the cultivation of the soil for food products

arable: fit for cultivation

basophile: flourishing in alkaline soil

circumcrescent: growing around

corn-fed: designating beef cattle raised

on diet of corn, believed to improve health and flavor
country: pertaining to the country
everbearing: continuously producing or bringing forth fruit
fallow: designating cultivated land left unsown for one season or more
fertile: rich in resources; fruitful; able to reproduce by seeds or spores
free-range: designating livestock and poultry permitted to graze or forage freely outside a small confinement
friable: describing easily crumbled soil
geogenous: growing on or in the ground
geoponic: having to do with agriculture
hortensial: grown in a garden; hortensian
horticultural: pertaining to the culture of gardens

hortulan: concerning a garden
olitory: pertaining to a kitchen garden
pascual: growing in pastures; pascuous
pastoral: characteristic of the rural life of farmers and shepherds, especially in idealized state
predial: consisting of land or farms
ruminant: cud-chewing, especially cattle and sheep
rural: designating farming and ranching regions with small towns; away from large urban centers
rustic: pertaining to the country
slash-and-burn: of a cultivation technique in which land is made usable by burning trees and undergrowth, thereby clearing as well as nourishing the land
sphagnicolous: growing in peat moss

Aim

aimed: directed or pointed at
aligned with: put in the rank; line
bound for: going in some particular direction
direct: in a straight line
directed: aimed; addressed
directed toward: aimed; addressed
easterly: tending toward the east

point toward: to direct one's attention to something
straight: not crooked; keeping in the same path
straightforward: upright; not deviating
undeviating: not going out of the way
unswerving: unflinching; carrying out one's plans without fear or trembling

Alien

alien: foreign
alienigenate: foreign-born
allochthonous: foreign; allochthonant; autochthonous
exaliotriote: foreign
exceptional: forming an exception
excluded: shut-out
extraneous: not belonging to or dependent upon a thing
foreign: not of one's country

fremd: alien; strange; unfriendly
heterochthonous: foreign
inadmissible: not proper to be allowed, admitted, or received
tramontane: foreign; situated beyond the mountains
ulterior: more remote
ultramontane: situated, done, made, said, or expressed beyond the mountain

Alleviation

acopic: relieving tiredness
alleviating: lightening; mitigating
alleviatory: tending to relieve

anodyne: having the power of allaying pain
assuaging: giving relief

assuasive: tending to soothe

balmy: refreshing, soothing or healing like balm

balsamic: soothing like balsam

balsamical: unctuous; mitigating; soothing; balmy

consolatory: inclined to give comfort

curative: possessing the power to cure

demulcent: softening; soothing

emollient: softening or soothing to the skin

hesychastic: soothing; calming; keeping quiet

lenitive: tending to allay or relieve

palliative: soothing; reducing the bad effects; giving temporary relief

phrontifugic: relieving anxiety

soothing: tending to quiet and calm

Amity

accompanying: going along with as a companion or attendant

acquainted: familiar or conversant with

amiable: likeable and with a natural fondness for others

amicable: showing goodwill

amical: of or pertaining to friends

at home with: intimate

brotherly: showing friendship like brothers

clipsome: fit to be embraced or clasped

cordial: having warmth of heart or feeling

familiar: well acquainted

fraternal: friendly; in a manner befitting a brother

free and easy: friendly without formality

friends with: very friendly

hail-fellow-well-met: on very familiar or cordial terms

hand and glove: very intimate

hand in hand with: closely associated

hearty: proceeding from the heart

in one's good books: favored by someone

in one's good graces: favored by someone

intimate: closely connected by friendship

neighborly: disposed to be sociable

on amicable footing: on a mutual footing of goodwill; on amicable terms

on familiar footing: on terms of familiarity; on familiar terms

on friendly footing: on terms befitting friendship; on friendly terms

on good footing: on a favorable footing; on good terms

on intimate footing: on terms of close companionship; on intimate terms

on speaking terms: friendly enough to speak

on visiting terms: friendly enough to interchange visits

sympathetic: having a fellow-feeling for another

thick: closely associated

unhostile: not unfriendly

warmhearted: sympathetic and cordial

welcome: received in a friendly manner

well at home: thoroughly familiar

well with: on good terms

well-affected: influenced in a good manner

Anachronism

anachronistic: involving anything done or existing out of date

anachronous: out of proper chronological position

behindhand: behind time; out of date

belated: behind date; coming too late

misdated: dated wrongly

old hat: of something considered out of date

out-of-date: not in fashion

overdue: not appearing or occurring at the assigned time

parachronic: out of historical time order; anachronistic

parachronistic: marked by an error in chronology

undated: bearing no date

vieux jeu: out-of-date

Anarchy

anarchic: holding to the principles of anarchy

anarchical: holding to the principles of anarchy

anarchistic: striving to overturn all law and order

communistic: advocating class war

effrenate: ungovernable; unbridled

froward: ungovernable

insubordinate: hard to govern

mondo: unexpected; bizarre; anarchic

nihilistic: following the practice of nihilism

ungovernable: that cannot be ruled

unruly: disposed to violate the laws

Anatomy

abdominal: of or pertaining to the abdomen

abdominous: big-bellied; beer-bellied; gor-bellied; paunchy; ventripotent

acerebral: without a brain

acrocephalic: pertaining to pointed heads

acromegalic: having oversize arms and legs; pertaining to excessive growth

adeniform: glandlike

adipose: of fat in connective tissue

afferent: toward the central motor or nerve system

agomphious: toothless

amanous: having no hands

ambidexter: able to use both hands equally well

anatomical: of anatomy; human form; anatomic

anconal: pertaining to the elbow; anconeal

anisognathous: having differing upper and lower teeth

anorchous: without testicles

anurous: tailless

apellous: circumcised; skinless

apocrine: of glands like the mammary

apodal: having no feet

asthenic: having a lean, frail body

axillary: pertaining to the armpit

baggy: having dark circles or bags under the eyes; bagged

balanic: concerning the penis or clitoris

barrel-chested: having a broad chest

bathycolpian: having an ample bosom with much cleavage; bathycolpous

bimana: having hands unlike the feet

bodily: corporeal; pertaining to the body

brachial: pertaining to the arm

brachiate: having arms

brachycephalic: short- or broad-headed

brevirostrate: having a short nose

buccal: pertaining to the cheek(s)

bucculent: being bulb-cheeked; having a double chin

bucktoothed: having large, protruding upper teeth

bustluscious: having a luscious bust

callicolpian: having shapely breasts

callimammapygian: having shapely breasts and buttocks

callipygian: having shapely buttocks

celiac: pertaining to the belly

cervical: belonging to the neck

chalcenterous: having bowels of brass or bronze; tough

chiropodous: having feet adapted for grasping and climbing

ciliary: pertaining to eyelashes or other hairlike processes

cnemial: pertaining to the tibia, shinbone

cock-throppled: having a very large Adam's apple

costal: pertaining to the ribs
costate: having ribs
creatic: pertaining to flesh
cubital: pertaining to the ulna
cynocephalous: having a head or face like a dog
dactylic: concerning the fingers
dasypygal: having hairy buttocks
dentulous: having teeth; dentate; dentigerous
diastematic: gap-toothed
dilambdodont: having two pointed and crossing ridges on the molar teeth
dolichocephalic: having a head more long than wide
dolichoderous: having a long neck
dolichopodous: having long feet
dolichoprosopic: having a disproportionately long face
drooping: having a loose, slightly open mouth
duck-footed: having turned-out feet
dumpy: having a shapeless, short body
eccrine: of glands that secrete externally, as some sweat glands
ectad: toward the outside or surface
ectal: situated near the surface; exterior; outer
ectomorphic: having a slight, slender body
edentulous: having lost the teeth one once had; toothless; edentate; edentulate
endomorphic: having a short, broad, powerful body
epigastric: pertaining to the upper and anterior part of the abdomen
eumorphous: well-formed; having an athletic body type; eumorphic
eurygnathic: having a wide jaw; eurygnathous
excerebrose: without a brain
femoral: belonging to the thigh
fissilingual: having a forked tongue
fodgel: plump and solidly built; buxom
frontal: belonging to the forehead
funic: pertaining to the umbilical cord

funicle: pertaining to any body structure resembling a cord
gash-gabbit: having a projecting chin
gaunt: having a thin face with sharp features; hollow-cheeked; sharp-faced; sharp-featured
genial: pertaining to the chin
genual: pertaining to the knee
ginglyform: pertaining to or like an anatomical hinge joint
gluteal: pertaining to the buttocks
gnathic: pertaining to the jaw
gor-belly: having a protuberant belly; gor-bellied
gremial: relating to the lap or bosom
gressorial: adapted for walking, as some birds' feet
gubbertushed: having buck teeth
hallucal: concerning the big toe
heterodont: having different kinds of teeth
holocrine: of glands in which cells entirely disintegrate to form secretion, as sebaceous glands
homodont: having all one kind of tooth
hypochondriac: pertaining to hypochondria
hypogastric: relating to the lower part of the abdomen
hypsicephalic: having a high skull
iliac: pertaining to the third division of the lesser intestine
intercostal: lying between the ribs
jecoral: pertaining to the liver; hepatic
jimberjawed: having a lower jaw that projects
jowly: having droopy cheeks or jaw skin; heavy-jowled; meaty
knobby-kneed: having large knees
knock-kneed: having knees that touch
labrose: having large or thick lips
lantern-jawed: having a square jaw
leptochrous: delicate and thin-skinned
leptodactylous: having long slender toes
leptorrhinian: having a long narrow nose; leptorrhine; leptorrhinic
leptosome: having a slender body
longimanous: having long hands

lumbar: pertaining to or near the loins
macrocephalic: very large headed
macromastic: having large breasts
macrosomatous: having an abnormally large body
macrotous: having large ears
malar: pertaining to the cheek
mammiferous: having breasts
mammillary: pertaining to or shaped like breasts
megacephalic: having an abnormally large skull
megapod: having large feet
mentulate: of a penis, well-endowed
merocrine: of glands where the secreting cells remain intact, as in sweat glands
mesial: middle
mesomorphic: having a muscular, big-boned body
metopic: pertaining to the forehead; frontal
monorchid: having one testicle
muscle-bound: muscular; sinewy
muscular: pertaining to the muscles
nanoid: having an abnormally small body
niddle-noddle: having a nodding or wobbly head
nuchal: pertaining to the neck, especially the nape
opisthognathous: having a projecting upper jaw; jutting
orad: toward the mouth
orthognathous: having a straight jaw
palatine: of or belonging to the palate
palmiped: having webbed feet
pancreatic: pertaining to the pancreas
papillate: having or resembling nipples
paradigitate: having an equal number of fingers or toes on each extremity
parenteral: in the body, involving a tract other than the alimentary
parietal: pertaining to the bones of the upper part of the skull
pedal: relating to the foot
pedimanous: having feet shaped like hands, as monkeys; pedimane
penial: pertaining to the penis

petrosal: related to the hard portion of the skull that houses the auditory organs
pigeon-toed: having turned-in feet
piligerous: bearing or wearing hair; piliginous
planisthetic: flat-chested
plantigrade: walking on the soles of the feet
platyopic: having a broad, flat nose
plumiped: having feathered feet
pneumatic: having a full, shapely body; curvaceous; voluptuous
podical: anal
prognathous: having a protruding jaw; jimber-jawed; jutting; prognathic
prosopic: pertaining to the face
pursed: having puckered lips
pyknic: having a stocky, round, often muscular body; pycnic
raw: deprived of skin; galled
renal: of an artery supply blood to the kidneys
retrad: in anatomy, backwards
retromingent: discharging urine backwards
round-shouldered: having the shoulders bent forward; stoop-shouldered
sagittal: relating to the connecting seam between the two large bones in the skull
sarcoid: having the characteristics of flesh
sarcous: pertaining to flesh or muscle tissue
scaurous: having large ankles
sciapodous: having large feet
shad-mouth: having the upper lip sticking out a bit; gate-mouth; satchel-mouth
sialagogic: increasing saliva
sloe-eyed: having soft, dark eyes
snaggletoothed: having a jutting tooth
splanchnic: visceral; intestinal
stomatic: pertaining to the mouth
struthonian: tending to hide one's head in the sand, like an ostrich
stumpy: having short, thick legs; piano-legged; stubby

subcutaneous: of tissue situated just beneath the epithelium
subpalpebral: under the eyelid
sural: concerning the calf of the leg
torose: muscular; tortulous; torulose
totipalmate: web-footed; with fully webbed toes
trochocephalic: very round headed

tut-mouthed: having protruding lips
uletic: pertaining to the gums
umbiliform: like a navel; umbiliciform
ventral: abdominal
walleyed: having outwardly turned eyes; strabismic
wallopy: loose-limbed

Anger

acrimonious: full of bitterness or virulence
angry: moved by violent indignation
begrumpled: displeased
bitter: feel as showing enmity; hate
boiling: greatly angered
boiling over: greatly angered
burning: extremely sharp
cantankerous: given to wrangling and fault-finding
convulsed with rage: in a fit of rage
cross: peevish and angry
diversivolent: looking for trouble or an argument
emporté: very irritated; having lost one's cool
fierce: intensely excited
fiery: easily provoked; passionate
flushed with anger: red with wrath
flushed with rage: inflamed with rage
foaming: raging
foaming at the mouth: raging, so as to foam
fractious: unruly; quick to anger or quarrel
fuming: confused or stupefied with anger
furibund: furious; outraged
furious: in uncontrollable anger
glowering: with an angry look; black; furious; scowling
horn-mad: mad from being made a cuckold
hurt: offended; grieved
indignant: having such anger and scorn

as is aroused by meanness or wickedness
infuriate: furious
iracund: easily angered; quick-tempered
irascent: growing angry
irate: wrathful
ireful: full of strong resentment
mad with rage: furious
mad-brained: hotheaded; reckless
offended: sorely displeased
on one's high ropes: haughty; peeved
rabid: unreasonably excited
rageful: furious
raging: furious
relentless: pitiless
savage: brutal and unfeeling
set against: opposed to
sore: aggrieved
splenetic: ill-tempered; peevish
stomachous: obstinate; angry; disdainful
sulky: showing ill feeling by keeping aloof
surly: hostile; antagonistic; malevolent
thrunched: very angry; displeased
umbrageous: easily offended
up in arms: very angry
violent: marked by force and rapidity
virulent: extremely bitter and hostile
warm: slightly passionate
waxy: enraged
wild: roused to fury
worked up: excited
wrath: being in a state of anger
wrathful: being in a state of anger
wrought: stirred up by anger
zowerswopped: ill-natured

Angularity

acute-angled: having less than a right angle

aduncous: bent like a hook; hooked; adunc

akimbo: having the hands on the hips and the elbows bent sharply outward

angular: having an angle or angles; measured by an angle; geniculate; orthometric; sharp-cornered

aquiline: hooked; curving

arake: at an angle deviating from perpendicular

arcuate: bent or curved like a bow; bandy

bent: turned from a straight line

bifurcate: forked

catawamptious: crooked; diagonal

crinkled: formed with folds, ridges, or wrinkles

crooked: having angles; not straight; askew; awry; oblique

cubical: having the shape or properties of a cube

cuneiform: wedge-shaped

dihedral: having an angle formed by two planes meeting at one edge

dovetailed: interlocked by wedge-shaped tenons and spaces

epinastic: bent out and down

equilateral: triangular with equal sides

falcated: sickle-shaped; scythe-shaped

falciform: falcate; having the shape of a scythe or sickle

forked: divided into diverging parts like a fork

furcated: forked; furcating

geniculate: bent at an angle; having kneelike joints; geniculated; inflexed

gleed: crooked; awry

icosahedral: enclosed or contained laterally by twenty surfaces

icositetrahedral: enclosed or contained laterally by twenty-four surfaces

oblique-angled: having either greater or less than a right angle; obliquangular

obpyramidal: having the shape of an inverse pyramid

obtuse-angled: having greater than a right angle

orthogonal: at a right angle; rectangular

pentahedral: enclosed or contained laterally by five plane surfaces

perpendicular: situated at right angles to the horizon; normal; orthogonal; orthometric; upright

polygonal: having more than four angles; many-sided; multiangular; multilateral; polyangular

repandous: bent upward

retrorse: bent or turned backward or downward

retroussé: turned up, as a nose

rhombic: having four equal sides and opposite angles equal (two acute, two obtuse); lozenge-shaped; rhombical

tetrahedral: enclosed or contained laterally by four plane surfaces

zigzag: having lines at angles in alternating directions; chevroned; cringle-crangle; staggered

Answer

agreeable: answering to the circumstances

answering: making or constituting a reply

catechetical: using questions and answers

conclusive: deciding the question in dispute

correspondent: answering to or agreeing with something

counter: serving to answer

definitive: serving to supply a final answer

fit: answering the purpose

forthcoming: willing to make available; responsive

reciprocal: answering to each other

respondent: giving response

responsive: ready or inclined to answer

Antagonism—Defiance

adverse: opposed or opposing
antagonistic: working against each other
at daggers drawn: in hostile state
at issue: in dispute
at variance: not in agreement
at war with: contending against
averse: antagonistic; hostile; opposing
competitive: characterized by rivalry
contrary: in opposition to
contumelious: insolent; reproachful
cross: adverse to
defiant: bold; insolent
defying: defiant
derf: bold; fearless
emulous: eager to excel another
front to front: directly opposing
harageous: rough and bold
hostile: showing the disposition of an enemy

hubristic: insolent
in hostile array: ready for combat
inimical: at enmity with
obstreperous: stubbornly defiant; boisterous; rambunctious
opposed: working against
opposing: working against
oppugnant: antagonistic; hostile
resistant: in an opposing manner
rivalrous: competitive; given to rivalry
truculent: defiant; aggressive; cruel; pugnacious
unfavorable: contrary; discouraging
unfriendly: not adapted to promote or support any object
unpropitious: not favorable
up in arms: in active opposition
with arms akimbo: to have the elbows turned out; disdainful
with crossed bayonets: in conflict

Antiquity

aboriginal: native to the soil; first; primitive
after age: succeeding time
ancient: of great age
antediluvian: old-fashioned; quite out-of-date
antemundane: before the creation of the world
antiquated: grown old; old-fashioned
antique: old; ancient
archaic: no longer in common use; out of use; obsolete
behind the age: not up with the thought or methods of the day
classic: pertaining to ancient literature or art of the highest type
crumbling: falling to pieces through age
customary: usual; habitual
diluvian: pertaining to the deluge
elder: senior; older
eldest: most advanced in age
exploded: rejected; condemned
firstborn: first brought forth; preeminent

fogram: old-fashioned; passé
fossil: dug out of the earth; that which is antiquated
fusty: stale; musty; old and damp
gone by: omitted
gone out: died away
immemorial: beyond memory; long ago
inusitate: obsolete
inveterate: deep-rooted; obstinate from long continuance
medieval: belonging to the middle ages
obsolete: gone out of use; out-of-date
of long standing: in existence for a long time
of other times: old-fashioned
of the old school: belonging to an earlier time
Ogygian: quite ancient; antediluvian
old: aged; far advanced in years
old as Adam: expression employed to denote time long past
old as history: expression employed to denote time long past

old as Methuselah: expression employed to denote time long past

old as the hills: expression employed to denote time long past

old-fashioned: antiquated; having characteristics of former times

paleocrystic: pertaining to ice-covered regions of the Arctic and Antarctic Oceans

paleozoic: pertaining to the lowest geological strata in which forms of life appear

patriarchal: pertaining to the ruler of a family

preadamite: existing before Adam

preglacial: prior to the glacial period

prehistoric: relating to a period antecedent to written history

preraphaelite: pertaining to a style of art that preceded Raphael

prescriptive: acquired by immemorial use

prime: first in time or order; beginning

primeval: original; belonging to the first ages; primitive

primigenous: first formed; original

primitive: belonging to early times; ancient

primordial: existing from the beginning

primordinate: of earliest origin

protogenal: pertaining to primitive creatures

relict: pertaining to a relic or artifact

rooted: deep; radical

run-out: ended; consumed; spent

secondhand: that which has been used before

senile: affected by old age

stale: having lost freshness

superannuated: made obsolete, especially by old age

time-honored: honored from former times

traditional: transmitted by word of mouth only

venerable: rendered sacred by age

vetust: antique; ancient

whereof the memory of man runneth not to the contrary: immemorial

Apathy

all one to: making no difference to

anesthetic: inducing insensibility; anaesthetic

apathetic: characterized by apathy

blind to: wholly indifferent to

callous: hardened as to sensation or feeling

careless: having no care or consideration; indifferent

case-hardened: made insensible to external influences

chloroformed: under the influence of chloroform; insensible

cold: lacking feeling or sympathy; distant; reserved

cold as charity: very unsympathetic

cold-blooded: unfeeling

coldhearted: unfeeling

comatose: relating to or affected with coma

cool: chilling; apathetic

cool as a cucumber: entirely unaffected by

crustose: thick-skinned

dead: wholly incapable of sensation in any sense

dead to: not affected by; indifferent to

deaf to: paying no heed to

dedolent: callous; feeling no grief

devil-may-care: let the devil care, not I

disconscient: lacking conscience; unconscientious

disinterested: impartial

disregarding: paying no attention to

dull: not keenly felt; lacking in lively sensation

easygoing: reckless; inactive

flat: lacking keen sensibility; dull

frigid: cold; wanting feeling

halfhearted: only partially interested; lacking spirit

hard: unyielding; unsympathetic

hardened: rendered callous or insensible to feeling
heartless: without pity or feeling for
impartial: not favoring one more than another
impassible: incapable of pain or suffering; insensitive; unfeeling
impassive: unaffected by suffering; not exhibiting emotion
impenitible: incapable of remorse, repentance
impercipient: not being able to perceive
imperturbable: incapable of being disturbed
impervious: impenetrable to effect or feeling
inattentive: not giving attention to
indifferent: feeling no interest, anxiety, or care
inert: characterized by inertness
infrunite: senseless; tasteless
insensate: unfeeling; not perceived physically
insensible: devoid of feeling, emotion, or sympathy
insipid: wanting in spirit, life, or animation
insouciant: heedless; jaunty; easygoing
insusceptible: incapable of being influenced or moved
inured: hardened
lackadaisical: indolently sentimental
languid: not easily aroused emotionally; apathetic
leucophlegmatic: relating to or affected with a dropsical feeling or condition
listless: languid; spiritless
lukewarm: not enthusiastic; indifferent; neither for nor against
maudlin: foolishly affectionate
mindless: unmindful; careless
neglectful: full of or indicating neglect
numb: destitute wholly or partially of the power of sensation or feeling
obtuse: not keen; dull in feeling, sensibility
pachydermatous: thick-skinned
palsied: affected with loss of sensation

palsy-stricken: having lost sensation
paralytic: pertaining to or affected with paralysis
passionless: lacking passion or emotion
phlegmatic: dull; sluggish; not easily aroused to feeling
pococurante: caring little
proof: impenetrable, as to sensation or impression
proof against: capable of resisting successfully; impervious to
regardless: exhibiting no regard; neglectful
senseless: lacking the power of sense
sleepy: drowsy; lacking spirit
sluggish: slow of emotion or feeling
soulless: without soul; lacking human feeling
spiritless: lacking spirit or liveliness of feeling
steeled against: having no feeling toward
stupefied: incapable of emotion
stuporific: causes stupor
supine: having no interest or care; indolent
tame: lacking in interest or animation
thick-skinned: incapable of being sensibly affected by external action or influence
torpid: having lost partially or wholly the power of sensibility; sluggish
unaffected: having the feelings unmoved
unalluring: not tempting
unambitious: lacking ambition, energy, or spirit
unanimated: not roused; lacking spirit and life
unaspiring: listless; unprogressive
unattracted: disinterested
unblushing: having no sense or feeling of shame
uncared for: unheeded
unconcerned: not concerned or interested
unconscious: passing without noticing
undesirable: not cared for
undesired: not wanted
undesiring: wishing little for

unexcited: not agitated or deeply stirred in feeling
unfeeling: not conscious of the feelings of others; unsympathetic
unfelt: emotionally unaffecting
unimpressed: not affected by an impression
unimpressible: that cannot have an impression made upon
unimpressionable: that cannot have an impression made upon
uninspired: without emotions
unmoved: not aroused to compassion
unruffled: not agitated

unshocked: not having the emotions deeply stirred
unsolicitous: not anxious for
unstirred: not aroused or agitated
unstruck: not suddenly impressed
unsusceptible: not subject to or liable to be affected
untouched: not having the sympathies or feelings aroused
unvalued: regarding as worthless
unwished: not desirable
vain: worthless; unimportant
vegetative: living in a state of habitual indifference

Aperture

ajar: open
aperient: tending to open the bowels; laxative
apertural: pertaining to an opening
cannular: tube-shaped
cribriform: sievelike; pierced with small holes; coliform; cribral; cribrate; cribrose
fistulous: hollow
follicular: in the form of small tubes
foraminous: full of holes
gaping: displaying an opening
hiant: gaping
honeycombed: full of cells or openings
infundibular: funnel-shaped
lacunulose: having tiny holes or gaps
leachy: absorbent; porous
open: not closed; permitting something to pass through
opening: that opens; that becomes open
oscitant: yawning or gaping; drowsy
patent: open
perforated: having holes; cribriform;

holey; pierced; porous; spongeous; perforate
permeable: capable of allowing liquids to pass through
pervious: capable of being passed through
porous: full of holes
riddled: pierced with holes
ringent: gaping
tubicolous: dwelling in a tube
tubular: having a tubelike form
tubulated: provided with tubes
tubulous: having a tubelike form
unclosed: open
unstopped: not closed
upaithric: open to the air; having no roof; hypaethral
vascular: consisting of tubes or vessels
vermiculated: worm-eaten; with worm holes; resembling the tracks of worms; vermiculate
vesicular: like a cell
wide open: gaping
yawning: standing wide open

Appearance—Visibility

apparent: easily seen
appearing: coming into sight
aspectable: visible; fit to look upon
autoptical: based upon the evidence of one's own eyes

before one: in one's presence
before one's eyes: in one's presence
blatant: brazen and obvious; flagrant; conspicuous; obtrusive
clear: distinct

conspectable: easily seen; obvious

conspicuous: in very plain sight

cutaway: seen as a part or layer is cut away so as to reveal the interior

definite: clear

discernible: capable of being perceived

disclosed: exposed to view

discovered: identified or noticed

distinct: easily perceived

doll-faced: having a small, pretty face

epideictic: impressive; for display; showing off; epidictic

exposed to view: laid open to sight

glaring: reflecting a brilliant light

hardened: having a tense expression; drawn; hard; taut

hedgehoggy: of a forbidding appearance or manner

illusory: based on illusion; not real

in bold relief: giving the appearance of standing out from the background

in focus: giving a sharp image

in full view: entirely in sight

in one's eye: imaginary

in relief: projecting upon a plane

in sight: in view of the eye

in strong relief: distinctly outlined

in view: in the plane of sight

kenspeckle: easily recognizable; conspicuous

masked: having facial markings like a mask

obvious: plainly evident

on view: visible

palpable: that may be touched; obvious

panoramic: pertaining to an extended view

perceivable: capable of being seen, physically or mentally

perceptible: that may be seen

periscopic: viewing on all sides

phanic: obvious or visible

pie-faced: having a flat, round face

plain: clear

recognizable: able to be recognized

seeming: apparent to the mind on reflection

shifting: having restlessly moving eyes; darting

skenchback: remarkable in appearance; easily recognizable; having strong family characteristics

staring: gazing fixedly

stereoscopic: pertaining to the stereoscope

telegenic: that shows well on television

telephanous: visible afar

thick-eyed: looking like one is in deep thought

unclouded: not obscure

under one's eye: under one's direction

undistinguishable: not able to be distinguished

undistinguished: not recognized apart

visible: perceivable by the eye

well-defined: clearly bounded

well-marked: plainly marked

whally: of eyes, showing much white; glaring

xanthomelanous: pertaining to those with dark hair and olive or yellow complexion

Approval—Assent—Consent

acquiescent: disposed to submit quietly

affirmative: answering yes

agreed: of the same mind or opinion

agreed on all hands: unanimous

approved: commended; sanctioned

approving: commending

assenting: admitting or agreeing to anything

at one with: agreed

benedictory: expressing good wishes

beyond all praise: above all praise

carried: carried without opposition

carried by acclamation: passed by a shout of approval

cataphatic: affirmative

commendable: creditable; worthy of approval

commendatory: expressing approbation

complimentary: expressing admiration, approbation, or the like

consensual: made by mutual consent

consentaneous: unanimous; with the consent of all

consenting: giving consent

content: agreeing without examination

creditable: deserving or reflecting credit or approbation

crurophilous: liking legs

deserving: deemed worthy

deserving praise: worthy of commendation and approval

encomiastic: bestowing praise or high approval

estimable: deserving good opinion or approval

eulogistic: bestowing high praise

exemplary: commendable; deserving imitation

favorable: expressing approval or partiality

good: having physical or moral qualities that may be approved

hortatory: giving encouragement; urging on

in favor: favored; approved

in favor of: on the side of; approving

in good order: in favor; approved

in high esteem: respected; highly approved

in high power: dominant, as a political party, and hence approved by the majority

laudatory: praising; eulogizing

lavish of praise: bestowing praise extravagantly

lost in admiration: occupied with admiring so as to be insensible to external things

meritorious: praiseworthy; deserving high approval

of estimation: commendable; estimable

of one accord: unanimous

of one mind: unanimous

of the same mind: unanimous

okay: all right

okeydoke: okay

pactitious: settled or arranged by agreement

panegyrical: praising elaborately

plausible: calculated to win approval or confidence

popular: widely approved of or preferred

praised: commended and approved

praiseworthy: worthy of commendation and approval

squeezable: able to be coerced

unanimous: agreeing in opinion or determination

uncensured: exempt from blame

unchallenged: left to pass without examination

unconditional: without conditions

uncontradicted: without assertion to the contrary

uncontroverted: undisputed

uncritical: approving without judgment

unimpeachable: blameless; free from stain or fault; approved

unimpeached: not called in question; not discredited

unquestioned: not doubted

untouchable: above criticism

willing: received of choice or without reluctance

worthy of praise: worthy of commendation and approval

Aptness—Suitability

appropriate: specially apt

apt: suited; fitted

bating: with the exception of; excepting

certain: established as a fact

characteristic: distinguished by some specialty

definite: known with exactness

deictically: pointedly; specifically

determinate: specially limited

diagnostic: indicating the nature of, as of a disease

endemic: peculiar to a specified country or people

esoteric: fitted only for the enlightened

especial: exceptionable among others of the same kind

exclusive: having a tendency to shut out

hypostatic: constituting a distinct personality or substance

idiomatic: peculiar to a certain language or dialect

individual: pertaining to a particular person or thing

original: belonging to the beginning

partial: favoring one side

particular: peculiar to something specified

party: favoring one party

peculiar: having a character exclusively its own

perjink: being precise or minutely accurate; perjinkety

perqueer: accurate

personal: pertaining to a particular person

pilpulistic: hairsplitting

private: not common or general

proper: specially adapted

respective: having relation to a particular person or thing

several: considered distinctly as an individual or as individuals

singular: consisting of only one part

special: for a particular purpose

specific: possessing a peculiar property

subservient: adapted for an especial use

suitable: fitting; appropriate

typical: pertaining to a class or kind

Architecture

amphistylar: having columns at both ends

architectural: relating to buildings and edifices

arcuate: structurally dependent on arches

astylar: without columns

Beaux Arts: with heavy monumental detail; double or coupled columns

Cape Cod: having a simple rectangular one-and-a-half stories of clapboard, with low central chimney, steep shingled roof

Churrigueresque: of architecture that is of extravagant design; embellished decoration; churigueresque

classical: of the architectural style of ancient Hellenic Greece and imperial Rome, emphasizing columniation

claustral: pertaining to a cloister

cloistered: furnished with cloisters

Colonial Revival: having a prominent pedimented front porch and door with columns or pilasters, also double-hung windows with many panes

columelliform: like a small column

Directoire: noting or pertaining to a style of architecture and decoration in

France similar to Regency style in Britain (late 18th c.)

Dutch Colonial: of a one-story dwelling with a side-gabled or -gambreled roof

Egyptian: of an architectural style prevalent from the third millennium B.C. through the Roman era, characterized by the use of massive pillared stonework with emphasis on religious monuments

enneastyle: in architecture, having nine columns

Federal: designed as a simple box, with semicircular fanlight over the front door, small-paned windows; Adam

flamboyant: of a highly decorative Gothic style (France, 15th–16th c.)

Georgian: of a style incorporating classical, Renaissance, and baroque elements of architecture, emphasizing formal, symmetrical design (U.S. and Britain, 18th c.)

Gothic Revival: imitating elements of Gothic design

Greek Revival: of ancient Greek temple design

half-timbered: relating to exterior walls

with exposed, heavy, wooden members separated by masonry

Hellenic: of a monumental style of religious architecture, characterized by columnar supports of pediment-roofed temples (Greece, 8th–4th c. B.C.)

Hellenistic: of a classical style that influenced imperial Roman architecture (Greece, 4th–2nd c. B.C.)

High Victorian Gothic: eclectic Gothic Revival, using many colors and heavy details

Italian Villa: of asymmetrical dwellings with off-center or corner towers, projecting eaves, flat roofs, windows grouped in twos or threes

Mission: stucco with little sculptural ornamentation; with balconies, towers or turrets, tiled roof

monolithic: constructed of concrete, with all members cast at the same time as a single unit

Moorish: of an architectural style emphasizing overall decoration, carving arabesque design, and intricate stuccowork (Spain, 11th–14th c.)

neoclassical: marked by a return to classical architecture in response to romantic themes (Europe, 18th–19th c.)

New England Farm: having a simple box shape of white clapboard, steep-pitched roof, central chimney

Norman: of an architectural style using massive stonework and rounded arches (Britain, 11th c.)

oecodomic: architectural; oecodomical

Palladian: of an architectural style patterned after northen Italian Renaissance (Britain, 18th c.)

peripteral: with pillars on all sides

peristylar: having columns on all sides; peripteral

postmodern: of an architectural style with eclectic, sometimes whimsical use of a variety of styles, especially classical elements, often large-scale for corporate or institutional use (late 20th c.)

Prairie: of a two-story dwelling with low hipped roof, overhanging eaves, one-story porches, no ornamentation

prefabricated: assembled into complete, standardized, structural units at factory

Queen Anne: of a style of architecture and furnishing characterized by simplicity and restraint, especially using red brick (Britain, 18th c.)

regency: of a style of architecture, furnishing and decoration characterized by simple lines and increasing use of Greco-Roman forms (Britain, early 19th c.)

Regency: informal Colonial Revival, painted brick with hip roof and chimney on one side

Saltbox Colonial: of a simple shingle or clapboard rectangular design with a step roof extending far to the rear

Second Empire: having a high mansard roof, varied dormer windows, chimneys, and ornamental brackets beneath the eaves

Spanish Colonial: stuccoed-adobe or stone with flat or low-pitched red-tile roof

stellate: star-shaped

tilt-up: designating concrete walls cast in horizontal frames, then lifted into vertical position

trabeate: in architecture, constructed with beams; trabeated

trabeated: dependent on upright-and-horizontal or post-and-lintel construction, not on arches

Tudor: in a fortresslike stone-and-brick design with semihexagonal bays and turrets, tall casement windows

Victorian: characteristic of a highly decorative architectural style with Gothic elements (U.S. and Britain, late 19th c.)

zoning: of or pertaining to ordinances regulating type, size, and uses of buildings that may be constructed in a specific area

Arrival

arriving: reaching the destination

due: under contract to arrive at a certain time

entering: that enters; coming or going in

ETA: estimated time of arrival

homeward-bound: returning to one's home or family

intersilient: suddenly emerging in the midst

overdue: delayed in arrival

premature: arriving too soon

prepunctual: arriving before the appointed or precise time

pubescent: arriving at the age of puberty

tardy: late in arrival

Art

annulate: furnished or marked with a ring

anomphalous: without a navel, as in art

aperture-priority: designating semiautomatic exposure system in which aperture is preset and camera selects shutter speed

argyle: having a pattern of different-colored diamonds

artificial: made or contrived by art; unnatural

artistic: pertaining to art

banded: having a horizontal marking; barred; belted

Biedermeier: artistically conventional; bourgeois

botonée: ending in a cluster of balls; botonnée

broché: brocaded; lavishly woven

camera-ready: designating a project that is ready to be photographed for reproduction

checkered: having contrasting pattern of squares; checkerboard; counterchanged; patchwork; tessellated

chryselephantine: made of or adorned with gold and ivory

collared: having neck markings like a collar; ruffed

condensed: designating type that is narrow and elongate in proportion to its height

copied: produced from an original

copper-toning: designating chemical additives that give warm brownish tinge to black-and-white photo

crossbanded: having crosswise stripes or bands

decalcomanic: referring to transferring pictures by tracing

displayed: in heraldry, with wings and talons spread

expanded: designating type that is wider in proportion to its height, having a flattened, oblong appearance

exploded: seen as separate components, retaining their relative positions

fictile: made of earth or clay by a potter

figulate: made of clay

figurative: representing by means of figures or symbols

filigreed: having delicate ornamental openwork design

florid: highly ornate

flowery: abounding in figures

futuramic: advanced in design

graphic: represented visually, especially by drawing or printing

hard: fired at high temperature

ideoplastic: of artistic processes modified by mental impressions

illustrated: made clear by example or figures

illustrative: designed or tending to adorn or make clear

imitative: characterized by imitation

inclave: shaped like a series of dovetails
incuse: stamped
latticed: having a crossed-strip design
lavaliere: concerning something worn around the neck
like: similar
linear: of or pertaining to a line or lines; lineal; lineiform
lineate: having lines, stripes; lined; scored; striped
lineolate: having fine lines
made: produced artificially
malleated: having a hammered design
manufactured: made by hand or machinery
marmoreal: resembling marble or marble statue
matelassé: having a raised pattern like quilting
matte: not shiny; dull; lusterless
mosaic: having an inlaid design of pieces
nonchromatic: designating film that is not sensitive to colors
oil: covering with oil
ornamented: decorated
ornate: finely finished; polished
orthochromatic: designating film that is sensitive to all colors except red
outlined: drawn or traced in outline; delineatory; in profile; outlinear; silhouette
panchromatic: designating film that is sensitve to all colors
Parian: denoting fine, unglazed, marble-like porcelain
pencil: made with a pencil
pictorial: of or characteristic of a picture
picturesque: having the beauty of a picture
plaid: having a tartan or unbalanced checkered pattern
plastic: capable of being shaped, molded, cast, or pressed into different shapes
plateresque: of ornate silverwork; plateresco
pommée: having a ball or disk at the end of each arm, as certain crosses

punctate: marked with points or spots
punctiform: like a point or dot
punctuate: having a number of dots
Queen Anne: of a style typical during the reign of Queen Anne (1702–1714)
raw: unfired
refractory: having high heat resistance
representative: serving to portray or symbolize
represented: serving to portray or symbolize
representing: serving to portray or symbolize
ring-streaked: circularly marked or streaked; ringstraked
roman: designating common, upright style of typeface
rosular: in a pattern of rosettes
scalariform: having bars or stripes in a ladderlike pattern
scrimshaw: engraved and colored ivory or shell
semigloss: designating most common surface of paper for color prints
shutter-priority: designating semiautomatic exposure system in which shutter speed is selected and camera sets aperture, used especially to convey motion
sigillate: decorated with seals or stamps
site-specific: designating a sculpture that is created, designed, or selected for a specific location
soft-core: fired at low temperature
streaked: having irregular stripes
supellectile: pertaining to furniture
tessellated: made of variously colored cubes or squares of glass or tile to form a pattern; formed of mosaic patterns; tessellate
testaceous: made of baked clay; having the color of baked clay
textorial: pertaining to weaving
vermiculate: having a wormlike pattern; vermiculated
vitreous: resembling glass in transparency, brittleness, hardness, or glossiness

vittate: striped or banded; vittated

volant: represented, as in heraldry, as flying

vulned: in heraldry, injured

waffle: having an indented checkered pattern; waffled

washed-out: having poor color reproduction; faded

Ascent

acclivous: ascending; acclivitous; climbing; rising

anabamous: able to climb

armipotent: having a tendency to rise

ascending: rising; climbing

buoyant: tending to rise or float

emersal: rising to the top

eoan: concerning the rising of the sun in the east

ortive: pertaining to rising, as the sun in the east; eastern

rising: having an upward slope or lie

scandent: climbing

scansorial: pertaining to climbing

superfluitant: floating above or on the surface

supernatant: swimming

up: rising, as in a cloud

Assertion

absolute: authoritative; peremptory

affirmatory: having affirmation

asserting: stating positively

assertive: affirmative; positive

broad: plain; open; clear

categorical: without condition; absolute

certain: plain; evident; open

confident: being bold; self-reliant

decided: having a decision; resolute

declaratory: making an affirmation

definitve: final; conclusive

distinct: open; clear

dogmatic: having positive beliefs

emphatic: having force or emphasis

explicit: plainly expressed

express: declared with distinctness

flat: unqualified; positive

formal: done according to form

ipse-dixitish: concerning dogmatic assertion

marked: distinguished by a mark

peremptory: positive in opinion; absolute

philodoxical: fond of one's own opinion; dogmatic

pointed: having sharpness or a point

positive: that which may be asserted

predicable: capable of predication

predicatory: able to be affirmed as a quality

pronunciative: dogmatic

round: unqualified; full

solemn: having gravity; done formally

thetical: dogmatic; prescribed; thetic

trenchant: keen; biting

unretracted: not taken back; still affirmed

Association—Connection

affiliated: closely related

a-gatewards: pertaining to accompanying part of the way home

allied to: bound to, as by treaty; also related by similarity of structure

allusive: pertaining to indirectly

approximating: coming near to in any respect

approximative: tending to, or obtained by, approximation

appurtenant to: relating to something more important

associated: connected in thought

banded together: united together as in a band

belonging to: appertaining

bonded together: held together as with bonds

catenated: chainlike; catenoid; catenular; catenulate

chainlike: having links or connections; catenary; catenate; concatenate; concatenated; festooned
cognate: related by blood
commensal: living, eating together
comparable: allowing of comparison
confederated: leagued together in a common end
connected: conjoined; fastened together
contubernial: living together like a family; cohabiting; sharing the same tent; contubernal
correlative: having a reciprocal relation
dowelled: fastened together by means of headless peg or pin
embattled: marshaled in battle array
factional: pertaining to factions
federative: leagued together
ginglymoid: hingelike
implicated: connected with or involved in, often in a bad sense
in alliance: in union
in common with: having the same part or interest as others
in league: together
in partnership: in union
in relation with: related
in the same category: of the same kind or class
interlaced: woven together; braided; entwined; intertwined; interwoven; plaited; plexiform
joint: united; working together
ligulate: straplike; lorate
like: similar
linked together: associated together as if with links
obvolute: twisted together; coiled
proportionable: varying as something else varies
proportional: varying as something else varies
proportionate: varying as something else varies
referable to: capable of being considered in relation to
related: having mutual connection
relating: pertaining to
relative: having relation; pertaining
relative to: pertaining to
relevant: bearing upon; connected with

Astonishment

abracadabrant: marvelous or stunning
agape: having the mouth wide open, as in wonder or expectation
aghast: stupefied with sudden fright or horror
all agog: all eager
astonished: mentally stunned
awestruck: impressed or struck with solemn dread
breathless: out of breath; intense or eager
consterned: dismayed; amazed
donnered: stupefied; stunned
extonious: astonishing
frappant: striking; impressive
inconceivable: that cannot be imagined; incomprehensible
incredible: impossible to be believed
indescribable: that cannot be described
ineffable: incapable of being expressed in words; unutterable
inenarrable: indescribable; unspeakable
inexpressible: unspeakable; unutterable
inimaginable: incapable of being imagined
like a duck in thunder: struck with consternation
lost in amazement: extremely amazed
lost in astonishment: extremely amazed
lost in wonder: extremely amazed
marvelous: exciting wonder or some degree of surprise
miraculous: manifesting power beyond the forces of nature; supernatural
mirandous: wondrous
monstrous: out of the common course of nature
moonstruck: amazed or confounded
mysterious: not revealed or explained
nefandous: unspeakable; unmentionable

openmouthed: gaping, as in wonder or surprise

overwhelming: irresistible; overpowering

passing strange: exceedingly strange

planet-struck: confounded

prodigious: out of or above the ordinary; excessive

selcouth: wondrous; miraculous; unusual

spellbound: arrested by a spell or charm

stampointed: bewildered; quite astonished

strange: causing surprise; exciting curiosity

striking: impressive; surprising

stupendous: overcoming by its vastness; amazing

surprised: confounded; confused

surprising: of a nature to excite wonder or astonishment

thunderstruck: shocked by surprise

unable to believe one's senses: perplexed; dumbfounded

unexpected: coming without warning; taken by surprise

unheard-of: unparalleled; unprecedented

unimaginable: incapable of being imagined

unspeakable: beyond the power of speech

unutterable: too great for verbal expression; inexpressible

wonderful: having qualities that excite wonder or admiration

wonder-working: accomplishing wonders

wondrous: such as may excite surprise and astonishment

Astronomy—Universe

anomalistic: pertaining to the anomaly or angular distance of a planet from its perihelion

A-OK: all systems go; okay to proceed as planned

astral: pertaining to the stars; starry

astriferous: starry

astronomical: dealing with astronomy

celestial: pertaining to the sky or heaven

circumpolar: about the pole

cometary: pertaining to a comet

cosmical: relating to the universe and all visible nature

cosmopolitan: dwelling in all parts of the world

cosmotellurian: associated with or affecting both the heavens and the earth

earthly: pertaining to this world

extragalactic: outside the Milky Way system

extraterrestrial: not from Earth

geocentric: viewing the universe as though Earth were its center

geotic: belonging to Earth; terrestrial

go/no-go: being the point at which decision to launch or not launch must be made

heavenly: resembling heaven; celestial

heliacal: emerging from or passing into the light of the sun

heliocentric: viewing the universe as though the Sun were its center

intergalactic: existing or occurring between galaxies

intermundane: between stars or planets

interplanetary: being or occurring within a solar system but outside the atmosphere of any planet or sun

intersidereal: interstellar

lunar: pertaining to the Moon

mundane: pertaining to the world; worldly

nebular: of or relating to nebulae

novilunar: pertaining to a new moon

orbific: world-making

orbital: belonging or pertaining to an orbit

planetary: pertaining to the planets

plenilunary: pertaining to the full moon

selenian: pertaining to the Moon

selenitic: influenced by the Moon
sideral: relating to the stars; measured by the apparent motion of the stars
sidereal: relating to the stars; measured by the apparent motion of the stars
solar: pertaining to the Sun
solisequious: following the Sun
sphery: like a sphere or star
starry: adorned with or resembling stars
stellar: of or pertaining to the stars; astral
stellated: star-shaped; ornamented with stars; stellate
stelliferous: containing stars
subastral: beneath the stars or heavens
sublunary: situated under the Moon
telescopic: pertaining to a telescope; small

telluric: pertaining to the earth, or procured from it
terraqueous: consisting of land and water
terrene: pertaining to the earth; earthy
terreous: consisting of earth
terrestrial: of Earth; existing on Earth
terrestrious: earthy; being or living on the earth
tidal: pertaining to tides
under the sun: anywhere on Earth
universal: occurring throughout the universe, the cosmos
uranic: celestial; astronomical
zodiacal: pertaining to the zodiac

Atmosphere—Air—Weather

aerial: belonging to the air; high
aeriform: having the nature or form of air; not solid
airy: light like air; high in the air
anhelous: short of breath; panting
antipluvial: preventing precipitation
atmospheric: pertaining to the atmosphere
billowing: describing bulging masses of high clouds
bioclimatic: relating to effect of climate on living things
blowing: causing the air to be in motion
blustering: exhibiting noisy violence, as the wind
boisterous: acting with noisy turbulence
boreal: pertaining to the north wind; northern
breezy: characterized by or having breezes; airy
cirrus: of detached thin white clouds
clement: pertaining to pleasant, mild weather
cloudy: covered with or resembling clouds
containing air: holding air
cumuliform: like a cumulus cloud
dyspneal: short of breath

effervescent: gently giving off bubbles of gas
eolian: of or caused by the wind; aeolian
favonian: mild, like the west wind
flatulent: windy; affected with gas in the stomach
fogbound: surrounded by fog; unable to navigate because of fog
gusty: subject to gusts or squalls
high-pressure: designating air mass with barometric pressure exceeding atmospheric pressure
innubilous: cloudless; clear
irrespirable: not breathable
low-pressure: designating air mass with barometric pressure less than atmospheric pressure
meteorological: relating to the atmosphere and its phenomena
moazogotl: of a cloud that is created by warm, dry winds on the lee side of a mountain
nebulous: cloudy; indistinct
nepheligenous: producing clouds or smoke
nimbiferous: bringing storm clouds or rain
nubilous: relating to clouds

offshore: blowing from shore to sea
onshore: blowing from sea to shore
oragious: stormy
overcast: covered, as the sky with clouds
pulmonary: of or pertaining to the lungs
pulmonic: of or pertaining to the lungs
seasonable: normal for time of year
semitropical: subtropical
sneaping: of the wind, biting and severely chilling
squally: disturbed often with sudden or violent gusts of wind
stormy: characterized or proceeding from a storm
stoury: like a forceful snowstorm; stourie
subarctic: adjacent to Arctic Circle
subtropical: typical of regions bordering the tropics; semitropical
suspirious: sighing or breathing heavily; suspirant

sussultatory: heaving up and down
temperate: without temperature extremes
tempestuous: of or pertaining to a tempest
thwankin: of clouds, thick and gloomy
tobaccoy: like tobacco; filled with tobacco smoke
unseasonable: abnormal for time of year
weatherproof: protection against rough weather
weatherwise: skillful in foreseeing the changes of the weather
windfirm: sufficiently sturdy and firm to withstand a very strong wind
windy: accompanied or characterized by wind
zephyr: pertaining to a west or light wind
zephyrous: breezy; airy

Atonement—Recompense—Conciliation

absolvable: capable of being freed from the penalty of guilt
atonable: that may be atoned for; atoneable
atoning: reconciling; expiating
compensatory: making amends
composing: being in a state of adjusting or settling
conciliatory: tending to placate or mollify
expiatory: having character of an expiation
munerary: having the nature of a gift
pacified: restored to peace

piacular: atoning
piaculous: atoning
placatory: conciliatory; mollifying; placating
premial: having the nature of a reward
propitiatory: pertaining to propitiation
recompensive: repaying; rewarding
remunerative: affording remuneration
remuneratory: rewarding
reparatory: tending to repair
retributive: involving retribution or recompense
sacrificial: of a sacrifice; pertaining to a sacrifice
sacrificatory: offering sacrifice

Attack

aggressing: commencing the attack
aggressive: disposed to attack unjustly
assailing: attacking; assaulting
assaulting: that attacks
attacking: assailing
batterfanged: beaten and beclawed
battering: that violently assails with blows

ictic: abrupt; caused by a blow
ingruent: assailing; attacking
obsidional: pertaining to a siege
offensive: making the first attack
petulcous: extremely aggressive; like a ram
up in arms: in a state of hostility

Badness

abominable: very hateful

accursed: doomed to utter destruction; detestable

arrant: notoriously bad

as bad as bad can be: very bad

bad: opposed to good; morally perverted

baleful: full of malignity

baneful: having deadly qualities

base: morally mean

below par: lower than the standard

burdensome: harmfully oppressive

confounded: mingled together in confusion

corrosive: eating away

corrupting: turning from good to bad

crapulous: coarse; crapulent

cursed: execrated, or deserving execration

damnable: meriting punishment

damned: declared guilty; adjudged worthy of sentence

deadly: causing death

debased: lowered in estimation; lowered in quality, character

deedeed: damned

deleterious: harmful, morally or physically

demoniacal: like a demon

deplorable: that should be lamented

depraved: morally corrupt

destructive: causing ruin

deteriorated: reduced in quality or value

detestable: deserving abhorrence

detrimental: involving or producing loss

diabolic: having the attributes of the devil; malicious; infernal; nefarious

dire: terribly evil

disadvantageous: not suited to the promotion of success

disastrous: occasioning or accompanied by terrible and ruinous effects

dissentaneous: negative; disagreeable

disserviceable: incapable of being used to advantage

dreadful: causing terror and fear

eldritch: weird; eerie; eldrich

elfin: pertaining to elves

elflike: having the characteristic of an elf

envenomed: infected with poison or malice

evil: contrary to divine law; having morally injurious qualities

exceptionable: liable to objection

execrable: worthy of hate

fiendish: like a fiend

fiendlike: with the qualities of a fiend; devilish

flagrant: notorious; heinous

foul: offensive to the moral sense

full of mischief: full of small pranks; inclined to tease and cut capers

fulsome: offensive from excessive flattery

ghostlike: like a ghost; spectral
ghostly: like a ghost; spectral
grievous: hard to bear
harmful: tending to bring about permanent injury
hateful: exciting dislike
hateful as a toad: regarded as an object of scorn, aversion, and contempt
haunted: frequented by ghosts or apparitions
horrible: causing terror
horrid: suited to arouse terror
hurtful: tending to cause physical or mental pain
hyperphysical: supernatural
ill: productive of harm
ill-conditioned: badly or weakly conditioned
ill-contrived: badly put together; weakly conceived
impish: like an imp
inauspicious: lacking favorable omens
incompetent: not capable
indifferent: without any preference; neither good nor bad
infandous: too horrible to talk about; infand
infernal: evil enough for hell
injured: wronged; deprived of just and natural rights
injurious: that which tends to harm or wrong
irremediable: not to be reclaimed or replaced
lamentable: causing sorrow and regret
lurid: terrible; ghastly; ominous
malefic: occasioning evil or disaster
malign: having an ill disposition toward others
malignant: animated by excessive hatred
mean: low-minded; low in rank; low in character
mischief-making: making trouble or disturbance
mischievous: given to the doing of pranks that injure or harm
nocent: harmful; nocuous
nocuous: pertaining to poison

noisome: very offensive
noxious: productive of harm
obnoxious: liable to censure
onerous: having weight; burdensome
oppressive: pressing on one heavily
peccant: guilty of transgression
pernicious: having a harmful effect; ruinous; thoroughly destructive
picayune: mean; contemptible; paltry
pitiable: meriting compassion
pitiful: calling forth compassion
poisonous: deadly in effects
prejudicial: characterized by bias
rank: strong in a bad sense
reprehensible: deserving reproof
roinous: mean; contemptible
rotten: having become putrid
rotten to the core: morally depraved in every respect
sad: afflicted with grief
scathful: inflicting severe injury
scrofulous: corrupt; degenerate
shammocking: shambling; good-for-nothing
shocking: causing surprise and horror
sinister: left-handed; ill-omened
spectral: having the appearance of a ghost or specter
unadvisable: that which could not be done after deliberation; imprudent
uncanny: strange; weird
unearthly: supernatural; alarming
unlucky: not having fortune; ill-omened
unprofitable: producing no gain; making no improvement; not conducive to progress
unsatisfactory: causing dissatisfaction; failing to gratify
untoward: not easily taught; not docile; perverse; awkward
venomous: having a malign spirit
vile: base in morals
villainous: capable of great wickedness
virulent: strongly poisonous; extremely bitter; malignant
weird: caused by magical influence and awakening superstitious fear

wide-wasting: destroying to a great distance; ravaging far and wide

woeful: afflicted with grief or calamity; causing sorrow or grief

wretched: very unhappy; fallen deep in disaster

wrong: going aside from right; falling in error

Beauty

adonic: unusually handsome

aesthetic: relating to beauty

Apollonian: having classic physical beauty, like Greek and Roman sculpture

artistic: in accord with the rules of art

artistical: in accord with the rules of art

aspectabund: of a pleasantly changing countenance

attractive: having power to attract

beaming: giving forth light

beamy: radiant

beauteous: full of beauty

beautified: made beautiful or ornate

beautiful: possessing great beauty

becoming: fitting; suitable to

bleached blond: having chemically lightened hair; bottled blond; drugstore blond; peroxide blond; platinum

blooming: having beauty and vigor

bonny: possessing homelike beauty

bright-eyed: having brilliant eyes, hence beautiful

brilliant: resplendent with luster

cherry-cheeked: having red cheeks

chiseled: having well-defined features; fine-featured; sculptured

comely: handsome

curious: skillfully wrought

dainty: of delicate structure

dapper: trim in appearance

dazzling: exciting admiration by display

delicate: of refined and gentle nature

elegant: having acquired grace and beauty

enchanting: having power to fascinate

esthetic: relating to beauty; artistic; aesthetic

eyesome: pleasing to the eye

fair: agreeable to the sight

featous: handsome; good-looking; well-proportioned

fine: finished, hence beautiful

fit to be seen: pleasing or fitted to the sight

gimp: smart

glossy: smooth and bright

glowing: shining with intense heat

good-looking: handsome

goodly: of agreeable appearance

gorgeous: making a great show

graceful: exhibiting beauty of action

gracile: graceful and slender

grand: imposing on account of vastness

handsome: admirable; pleasing in appearance

harmonious: symmetrical

in full bloom: at the height of beauty

jaunty: of an affected manner; janty

jimp: handsome

leggiadrous: graceful

lovely: inspiring love

magnificent: of imposing appearance

natty: neat

neat: free from disorder

not amiss: pretty fair

ornamental: serving to ornament

passable: fairly good looking

penciled: having drawn-on eyebrows

personable: having a handsome person

pictorial: like a picture

picturesque: having the kind of beauty that is pleasing in a picture

pretty: possessing delicate or diminutive beauty

proper: of a correct or becoming appearance

quaint: curiously fashioned

refined: having a delicate polish

resplendent: refulgent with bright luster

rich: highly ornate; abounding in beauty

rosy: like a rose in color
rosy-cheeked: ruddy
ruddy: reddish in color, indicating health
sabi: in Zen, having a quality of simple, restrained, mellowed beauty
seemly: becoming in appearance
shapely: having a good form
shining: conspicuous for pleasing qualities
showy: of an appearance that attracts attention
sightly: pleasing to look upon
sleek: smooth; glossy
smart: sprucely dressed; showy
snod: neat; trim; in good order
sparkling: very bright
specious: beautiful; showy; giving a good first impression
splendid: of an imposing appearance
spotless: without blemish
spruce: neat and trim in appearance
sublime: awe-inspiring and elevating

superb: possessing impressive beauty
svelte: slender and graceful; elegant
symmetrical: having symmetry
tempean: beautiful and charming
tidy: distinguished by neatness
tight: neat
tretis: well-proportioned; handsome
tricksy: crafty; artful
trim: nicely adjusted
undefaced: not marred
undeformed: of a good form
unspotted: without spot or blemish
venust: beautiful and elegant
wabi: in Zen, having a quality of simple, serene, solitary, somber beauty
well-composed: of good carriage
well-favored: endowed with beauty
well-grouped: nicely arranged
well-proportioned: having a symmetrical form
well-varied: presenting a pleasing diversity

Before—Preceding

above-mentioned: said or mentioned before
aforesaid: said or mentioned before
antecedaneous: preceding in time
antecedent: prior in time, rank
antecibal: happening before meals; before dinner; anteprandial
antejentacular: before breakfast
antelucan: before dawn
antepaschal: before Passover or Easter
anteprandial: before dinner; antecibal
anterior: in front of; toward the front; preceding in time or place
antevenient: preceding in time
before: toward the beginning
before mentioned: toward the beginning
epiclimactically: after the climax
fore: at the front
foregoing: going before
former: going before
front: to have the front toward
head-on: facing front
inaugural: pertaining to or done at an inauguration

inferoanterior: below and in front
introductory: leading up to something more important; preliminary
isagogic: introductory
preagonal: just before death
precedent: going before; prior; preceding
preceding: going before
precibal: occurring before meals
precursive: going before as a forerunner
precursory: going before as a forerunner
predormient: before sleep
prefatory: of or pertaining to a preface
prelapsarian: before the fall; innocent
preliminary: introductory
preludious: pertaining to a prelude
prelusive: characteristic of a prelude
prelusory: characteristic of a prelude
premundane: existing before the creation of the world
preparatory: having to do with preparation; preliminary
preprandial: before dinner; precibal
prevenient: going before; preventing
prior: preceding in time, rank; previous

probouleutic: concerning preliminary deliberation

prodromous: precursory

proemial: of or pertaining to a proem or an introductory statement

propaedeutic: pertaining to or providing introductory or preliminary instruction; propadeutic

said: as a legal term meaning aforesaid

vanward: at or to the front

wraparound: extending around the front and sides

Beginning—Infancy

aboriginal: indigenous to the soil

aliunde: from a different source; from elsewhere

at the breast: nursing

baby: young or little

babyish: without discretion; like a baby

beginning: commencing

begun: commenced

boyish: full of mischief and sport; like a boy

callow: wanting experience in the world

childish: silly and trifling; like a child

embryonic: in the embryo

first: having the foremost place

foremost: of the first rank

girlish: frivolous; like a girl

in arms: that has to be carried about in the arms

in long clothes: in an infant state

in one's teens: in the years ending with *teen*

in swaddling clothes: in an infant state

in the cradle: in an infant state

inaugural: pertaining to an inauguration

inceptive: marking the beginning

inchoate: just commenced

inchoative: just begun

incipient: coming into existence

infantile: childish

infantine: pertaining to infants; infantile

initial: marking or at the beginning

initiative: relating to initiation

initiatory: suited to introduce

innascible: without a beginning; not subject to birth

introductory: acting as an introduction

just begun: begun now

kittenish: playful and thoughtless; like a kitten

leading: having the foremost place

maiden: initiative

mewling: crying weakly; whimpering

nascent: beginning to exist

natal: dating from one's birth

neonatal: concerning a newborn child

newborn: recently born

new-fledged: having just acquired feathers

paronymous: derived from a common source; conjugate

postnatal: referring to period after birth

postpartum: referring to period following birth, especially mother's depression during this time

primeval: dating from the first ages

primogenial: firstborn

puerile: immature and weak; like a child

puling: whining; whimpering; mewling

rudimental: relating to the rudiments

shardborn: born in dung

tootlish: childish

unfledged: not having attained to full growth

Betterment

all the better for: much improved for

aright: correctly

better: preferable; improved in health

better advised: better informed

better for: improved for

better off: in a better condition

corrigible: that may be set right or amended

emendatory: relating to improvement

improvable: that may be improved

improved: bettered

improving: growing better; turning to best account

progressive: improving

reformatory: tending to produce a change from worse to better

remedial: corrective; affording a remedy

reparatory: amending defects

Bigotry

arbitrary: despotic; fixed; obstinate

bigoted: obstinate and unreasonable

case-hardened: made callous to outside influences

contumacious: rebellious; stubborn

cross-grained: perverse; hard to persuade

deaf to advice: stubborn

dogged: obdurate; persistent like a dog

dogmatic: arrogant; positively sure

hardmouthed: having a hard mouth like a horse, therefore not easily controlled

headstrong: insisting upon one's own way; stubborn

heady: headstrong

hidebound: narrow-minded; fixed in one's opinions

immovable: not to be moved

impersuasible: not to be persuaded

impervious: impenetrable

impervious to reason: unreasonable; stubborn

impracticable: difficult to get along with; unreasonable; headstrong

incorrigible: not to be corrected

inert: without the power to move; slow

infatuated: unreasonably filled with a desire for something

inflexible: not to be turned from an opinion

intractable: unruly; not easily controlled

mulish: like a mule in stubbornness

not to be moved: intractable

obdurate: inexorable; unyielding; stubborn; impenitent

obstinate: irrationally persistent in one's opinions

obstinate as a mule: stubborn as a mule

perverse: unreasonable; wilfully intractable

pervicacious: very obstinate or stubborn; willful

pigheaded: stupidly obstinate

positive: certain of one's opinions

prejudiced: biased

prepossessed: biased; prejudiced

recalcitrant: stubborn; obstinate; defiant; refractory

refractory: not easy to control

restiff: recalcitrant; stubborn

restive: recalcitrant; stubborn

resty: restive

self-willed: headstrong; stubborn

sociocentric: of the attitude that one's group is better than others

stiff-backed: not easily bent; stubborn

stiff-hearted: not easily bent; stubborn

stiff-necked: not easily bent; stubborn

stubborn: inflexible; opinionated

sulky: morose; sullen

sullen: untractable; obstinate

tenacious: holding fast to

unaffected: not to be moved in the feelings

unchangeable: not to be turned away from one's opinions

uninfluenced: not influenced

unmoved: not moved

unpersuadable: not to be persuaded

unruly: not to be governed

untractable: not easily ruled

unyielding: not giving way

wayward: disobedient

willful: determined to have one's own way; obstinate; headstrong

Biology

aerobic: living, growing, or occurring in the presence of oxygen

agamic: asexual; parthenogenic

agrestian: growing wild; living in the wild; agrestal

anaerobic: living, growing, or occurring in the absence of oxygen

archesporial: pertaining to cells from which spore mother cells originate

autacoidal: hormonal

azzardly: poor; not advanced in growth

bacillary: bacterial

basal: at resting level

bimanous: two-handed

biodegradable: capable of being broken down and absorbed in the natural environment

biological: relating to the science of physical life, plants, and animals

bionomic: associated with ecology

biped: two-footed

bicrural: two-legged

blissom: in heat; blissoming

celative: adapted for concealment

crepitous: farting

cryptic: using colors, markings for concealment; protective

dacryopyostic: tear-producing; lachrymal

deglutitious: pertaining to swallowing

diallel: mating in which each female breeds to two or more males

digenous: bisexual

digoneutic: producing young twice a year

ditokous: producing twins

dizygotic: coming from two separately fertilized eggs, as fraternal twins

edentate: toothless

endothermic: warm-blooded; homoiothermic

epigamic: attractive to the opposite sex during mating season

exogenous: originating from outside an organism

gamic: developing after fertilization

haploid: possessing only one set of chromosomes, as in gametes

hematic: pertaining to blood; bloody

hyperosmic: having a keen sense of smell

luxuriant: growing profusely

mammillated: having nipples; mamillate; mammillate

marine: sea-dwelling

metapneustic: having the respiratory apparatus in the butt

microsmatic: having a weakly developed sense of smell

motor: having to do with muscles and movement

multilocular: having many cells

muriform: consisting of flattened cells as to resemble bricks or stones in a wall

myogenic: originating within muscle

nizzertit: stunted in growth

oviparous: producing eggs that hatch outside the body

ovoviviparous: producing eggs that develop in the body and hatch within or immediately after expulsion from the parent

palamate: web-footed

paratonic: retarding growth

parthenic: virginal; unfertilized; parthenian

parturient: pertaining to childbirth; giving birth to

pelagic: dwelling in the open sea

rank: luxuriant in growth

ruttish: horny; in heat

sedentary: living in one place

sphygmic: pertaining to the pulse

spodogenous: pertaining to the production of organic waste matter

stenobathic: relating to aquatic life

totipotent: of a cell, capable of developing into or generating a complete organism

urled: stunted in growth

yeld: not old enough to procreate or give milk

Black

atramental: jet-black
atramentous: inky; black; like ink
black: absolutely destitute of color
black as a shoe: figurative degrees of blackness; expression denoting intense blackness
black as a tinker's pot: figurative degree of blackness; expression denoting intense blackness
black as jet: figurative degree of blackness; expression denoting intense blackness
black as midnight: figurative degree of blackness; expression denoting intense blackness
black as my hat: figurative degree of blackness; expression denoting intense blackness
black as November: figurative degree of blackness; expression denoting intense blackness
black as thunder: figurative degree of blackness; expression denoting intense blackness
brunette: having brown or black hair
coal-black: black as coal or jet; deep-black
dark: absolutely destitute of light
dingy: soiled; tarnished; dirty; dark brown
dusky: not luminous; partially dark
ebon: like ebony in color; black

ebony: black; coal-black; ebon; ink-black; jet; onyx; sable
Ethiopic: applied to the negro race as inhabiting Africa
fuliginous: smoke-colored; sooty
gray: of a white color tempered with black; hoary
inky: of or like ink
jet-black: black as coal or jet; deep-black
jetty: black as jet
murky: that which is at once dark, obscure, and gloomy
nigrescent: growing black; approaching blackness
nocturnal: pertaining to night; nightly
obscure: that from which light is more or less cut off
of the deepest dye: very black
perse: purplish black, like indigo
pitchy: like pitch in color; dark; dismal
raven: having black hair; ebony; jet
sable: of the color of a sable's fur; black
scoriac: pertaining to black basaltic lava; scoriaceous
somber: cloudy; gloomy; melancholy
soot: grayish black; anthracite
sooty: resembling soot; black, like soot
suggilated: beaten black-and-blue
swart: being of a dark hue; moderately black
swarthy: being of a dusky complexion; tawny or black
zibeline: pertaining to sable

Blue

aqua: greenish blue; china blue; Nile blue; Prussian blue; teal; turquoise
atmospheric: resembling the atmosphere in color
azure: having a sky-blue color
blue: having a color resembling that of the clear sky
bluish: rather blue
cerulean: sky-colored
cesious: blue-gray

chalybeous: steel-blue; looking like steel; chalybeus
cold: having a bluish effect
cyaneous: sky-blue
ecchymotic: black-and-blue; ecchymosed
gentian: purplish blue; hyacinth; marine; moonstone; sapphire; violet
indigo: grayish blue; Copenhagen blue;

delft blue; Dresden blue; robin's egg; steel-blue

livid: blue, as in a bruise

mazarine: of a deep rich blue

opalescent: a pearly light, reflecting a play of opaline colors

periwinkle: violet-blue

powder blue: pale blue; aquamarine; azure; baby blue; cerulean; lapis lazuli; Persian blue; sky-blue; Wedgwood blue

royal blue: deep blue; cobalt; electric blue

sky-blue: of the color of the sky

sky-colored: having the color of the sky

sky-dyed: sky-colored

ultramarine: vivid blue; bright blue; sky-blue

watchet: of a light-blue or sky-blue color

Bluntness

auriculate: in botany, having a pair of blunt projections

bluff: abrupt; broad and flat

blunt: having a thick edge or lacking an acute point; not sharp or piercing

bluntish: rather or somewhat blunt

chubbish: blunt and thick

dubby: dull; blunt

dull: not sharp or keen; having a blunt edge or point

hebetate: having a blunt or soft point

morned: having a blunt head

obtundent: blunting or lessening pain

obtuse: blunt or rounded at the extremity, as a leaf

snub: blunt; stubby; stumpy; snubbed

Border—Boundary

arcifinious: in law, having a natural boundary as a defensive frontier

border: lying on the edge

bounded: that has its limits marked

chamfered: having a flattened or beveled edge

coextensive: extending equally; having the same limits

conterminable: with the same limits

conterminate: with the same limits

cultellated: having a knifelike edge

cultrate: having a sharp edge like a knife; cultriform

deckle-edged: having a rough, untrimmed edge

definite: with fixed limits

erose: uneven and irregular, like a chewed edge

fringed: edged with short threads; fimbriate

frontier: pertaining to the limits of a country

indented: having cuts into the edges; nicked; nocked

jagged: with an uneven or sharp edge

labial: having edges or lips

labiated: provided with edges or lips

limbate: bordered; edged

marginal: pertaining to the margin

marginated: provided with margins

notched: having cut-into edges; hacked; nicked

peripheral: along an edge; border; marginal

repand: having a wavy or undulating edge

scalloped: having a regularly curving edge; crenate; invecked; invected

scrolled: having ornamentally curled edging

skirting: lying close to; running along the edge of

terminal: pertaining to a boundary

vallate: having a raised outer edge

Botany

acervate: developing in bunches
acinaceous: consisting of or full of kernels
barbate: bearded
botanical: pertaining to the science of plants
carpogenous: fruit-producing
dealbate: in botany, covered with a filmy white powder
fasciate: in botany, compressed into a bundle, having stems grown together
flagellate: in botany, having runners or runnerlike branches
glaucous: in botany, covered with bloom
imberbe: beardless; uimberbic
phyllogenetic: associated with leaf growth
pullulant: sprouting; budding
soboliferous: creating plant growth close to the ground

Bottom

basad: toward the base
basal: at the bottom; bottommost
based on: resting upon
benthonic: dwelling on the bottom of a body of water; benthic
bottom: pertaining to the bottom
built on: having a foundation
caudad: toward the tail or end of the body
founded on: having a foundation
fundamental: constituting the foundation
grounded on: built upon
nethermost: lowest
undermost: lowest

Bragging

boastful: disposed to boast
boasting: that boasts or brags
braggart: boastful
cock-a-hoop: exulting
elate: puffed up by success
elated: filled with exultation
exultant: given to rejoicing
flaming: very ardent
flushed: glowing with excitement
flushed with victory: excited about success
gasconading: inclined to brag or boast like a gascon
in high feather: exulting in spirit
jactant: boasting; boastful
jubilant: shouting songs of triumph
magniloquent: speaking in a pompous style
on stilts: elevated as if on stilts, hence pompous
pretentious: inclined to claim more than is one's due
stilted: bombastic
thrasonic: pertaining to Thraso, a braggart soldier in Terence's *Eunuchus*, hence boastful
thrasonical: bragging; boastful
triumphant: exultant over victory
vainglorious: possessed of empty pride
vaunted: boasted or bragged of

Bravery

adventurous: inclined to hazard life in adventures
audacious: impudently bold or daring
audaculous: slightly bold

aweless: not affected by awe

bodacious: bold and audacious; complete; thorough

bold: ready to meet danger

brave: not losing heart in the face of living or active opponents

chivalrous: acting like a knight

confident: trusting in oneself or others

courageous: calmly and persistently brave in moral and physical dangers

daring: anxious for adventures

dashing: spirited

dauntless: not easily daunted

determined: not wavering

dogged: stubbornly persistent

doughty: brave

dreadless: not affected with dread

enterprising: acting with a calculated boldness

fearless: not affected with fear

fierce: showing a cruel disposition

firm: fixed

gallant: displaying gallantry

hardy: able to endure

heroic: of a hero

impavid: fearless; brave

indomitable: unconquerable

intrepid: calm in the face of the greatest dangers

lionhearted: very brave

lionlike: bold as a lion

manful: displaying valor and prowess

manly: becoming a man

mettlesome: courageous

penthesilean: brave, like Penthesilea

plucky: possessing spirit

pugnacious: inclined to fight

reassured: encouraged

resolute: uninfluenced by the consequences of his own actions

savage: rejoicing in the pain of others

self-reliant: trusting in one's own abilities

soldierly: acting like a soldier

spirited: possessing ardor

spiritful: spirited

stout: firm; resolute

unabashed: not confused

unalarmed: not alarmed

unappalled: not appalled

unapprehensive: not expecting something fearful or evil

unawed: not affected with awe

unblenched: not having shown fear by paleness of the face

unblenching: not betraying fear by whiteness of the face

undaunted: fearless

undismayed: not frightened

undreaded: fearless

unfeared: not frightened

unshrinking: not shrinking

valiant: unyielding in the face of danger

valorous: unyielding in the face of danger

venturesome: risky

venturous: risky

Breadth

ample: large; making a full supply for every want

breadthways: in the direction of the width or thickness; breadthwise

broad: extended from side to side; wide

discous: like a disk or flat circular plate

dumpy: short and thick

extended: stretched out in length and breadth

fanlike: shaped like a fan

latitudinous: wide

outspread: expanded

outstretched: spread out; extended outside of or beyond

squab: fat; bulky

squat: short and thick, like an animal sitting on its hams or heels

thick: having a great extent or depth from one surface to its opposite

thick as a rope: not very thick; comparatively thin

thickset: having a short, stout body

wide: having great extent between the sides; greatly extended every way
wide as a church door: extremely broad

widening: becoming wider; broadening; dilating; expanding; splayed

Brittleness

arenaceous: made up of sandy, gritty particles; arenoid; arenose
arenarious: sandy
arenose: full of fine sand or grit; gritty
attrite: rubbed; worn by friction
branny: resembling or consisting of bran
brittle: liable to break
brittle as glass: as easy to break as glass
crimp: crumbled easily; brittle
crisp: easily crumbled
crumbly: easily crumbled; friable; brittle
dusty: filled with dust; clouded with dust
efflorescent: forming into white threads or powder
esquillous: splintery
farinaceous: mealy; starchy; consisting of meal
fissile: easily split
flocculent: coalescing in small flocks or flakes
floury: resembling flour; mealy; farinaceous
fragile: easily broken
frail: so constituted as to be broken easily
frangible: capable of being broken; fragile; breakable
friable: easily crumbled or pulverized; fragile; easily destroyed
furfuraceous: made of bran; like bran; scurfy

gimcrack: cheap, showy, and frail
granular: consisting of or resembling grains
gritty: containing sand or grit; full of hard particles
impalpable: extremely fine, so that no grit can be perceived by touch
in pieces: broken up
lacerable: capable of being torn
mealy: soft, dry, and friable
phut: breaking, becoming useless; pfft
powdery: easily crumbling to pieces; dusty
psammous: sandy
pulverizable: that can be reduced to powder
pulverized: reduced to powder
pulverulent: powdery; dusty; easily reduced to powder
sabulous: sandy; gritty; arenaceous; sabulose
sandy: consisting of, abounding with, grains of sand
shivery: easily broken; brittle; easily falling into pieces
short: brittle; friable
splintery: breaking into splinters
splitting: causing to split; bursting
tophaceous: sandy; gritty; rough
triturated: powdery; dusty; comminuted; pulverous; pulverulent

Brown

aithochrous: reddish brown; ruddy
auburn: reddish brown; hennaed
bay: red-brown, inclining to a chestnut color
bronze: metallic brown
brown: of a dark color, inclining to redness
brown as a berry: of the color of a berry

brown as mahogany: of the color of mahogany
brunette: having brown or black hair; a brownish complexion
brunneous: dark brown
butterscotch: golden brown; camel; caramel
café au lait: vivid brown

castaneous: chestnut-colored

chestnut: of the same color as a chestnut

chocolate: dark brown as chocolate; brunet; brunette; deep brown; nut-brown

cinnamon: yellowish brown as cinnamon

coffee: medium brown; cocoa; saddle; saddle brown; saddle tan; walnut

dapple: variegated brown

fawn-colored: of a light brown color, like a young deer

foxy: reddish brown, like a fox

fulvous: tawny in color

fuscous: grayish brown

ginger: yellowish brown

glandaceous: acorn-colored

khaki: light brown; yellowish brown; beige; ecru; fawn; fox; raw sienna; sand; sienna; tan

liver-colored: of a dark brown color; dark or brownish red, like the liver

liverish: having reddish brown skin

mahogany: reddish brown; auburn; bay; burnt sienna; chestnut; cinnamon; copper; henna; oxblood; roan; rosewood; russet; rust; sienna; umber

maroon: brownish crimson

mousy: having grayish brown hair

nut-brown: brown as the shell of a dried hazelnut

nutmeg: grayish brown; sepia

russet: reddish or yellowish brown, like a russet apple

snuff-colored: of a dark yellowish brown color

sunburnt: burnt brown by the sun

tan: of a yellowish brown color tinged with red

tanned: turned to a tan color by the sun

tawny: yellowish brown in color, like tanned leather

tortoiseshell: mottled brown and yellow

whity-brown: brownish with a white tinge

Business

blue-collar: pertaining to factory or manual labor

businesslike: suitable for business or commerce

capital-intensive: requiring large capital investment or expenditure relative to need for labor

cost-effective: producing good results for amount invested; efficient in use of funds

employable: physically or mentally fit for work; meeting minimum job requirements

labor-intensive: requiring large supply of labor relative to need for capital investment

on spec: performed or made without guarantee of payment for work or service

overbudget: describing venture in which costs exceed estimated costs

pink-collar: pertaining to low-paid work usually done by women, especially secretarial work

self-employed: designating a person owning a business or working freelance

undercapitalized: lacking sufficient operating funds

unemployable: designating a person unable to find work because of age, lack of skills, or disability

up-front: invested or paid before service is rendered or product is delivered

white-collar: pertaining to office, sales, or professional work, usually involving people, information, and ideas

Calmness—Inexcitability

anodyne: having the power to allay pain
armed with patience: patient
bearing with: enduring
bland: of a soft and balmy quality
calm: free from disturbance or agitation; unmoved
chastened: subdued; softened
clement: lenient
cold-blooded: heartless
collected: having all powers awake and at command
cool: exercising self-control; not excited
cool as a cucumber: not agitated
cool as custard: not agitated
coolheaded: not easily excited
demulcent: an application soothing to an irritated surface
demure: grave; modest; quiet-looking
dispassionate: calm; free from emotion
easygoing: not easily aroused
enduring: long-suffering
equanimous: of calmness; emotional balance even under stress; even-tempered
gentle: mild in disposition
gentle as a lamb: very gentle
grave: serious in manner
grave as a judge: very grave
halcyon: calm and peaceful, as the ocean, while Halcyon broods
hypnotic: tending to produce sleep
imperturbable: not easily agitated

inexcitable: not easily excited
inirritable: not easily provoked
lamblike: gentle; unoffending
lenient: of merciful disposition
lenitive: having the power or tendency to allay pain or mitigate suffering
long-suffering: very patient
mawkish: having feeble or false sentiment; lacking in robustness
measured: restrained within bounds
meek: not resisting
mild: moderate in action or disposition
mild as mother's milk: very gentle
milk and water: weak and vacillating
moderate: keeping or kept within reasonable limits
oily: pertaining to, containing, or resembling oil
pacative: calming; tranquilizing; pacate
pacific: having a peaceful nature or character
palliative: serving to mitigate or relieve
patient: bearing uncomplainingly
patient as Job: very patient
peaceable: inclined to peace
peaceful: undisturbed; tranquil
philosophic: showing great fortitude
placid: naturally calm
platonic: ideal; devoid of sensual feeling
quiet: temporarily at peace
quiet as a mouse: very quiet

reasonable: characterized by moderation

remollient: having a soothing effect

resigned: submissive

sedate: not buoyant

sedative: having a soothing or tranquilizing tendency

serene: calm, like the night of stars

slow: having no spirit or liveliness

smooth: calm and unruffled

sober: moderate in or abstinent from the use of intoxicating drink

sober-minded: being calm and mild in intellect

soft: expressive of mildness

soft as peppermint: very soft

staid: not fanciful

stayed: not fanciful

still: being at rest

stoical: looking with indifference on pleasure and pain

subdued: having all excitement or passion conquered

submissive: passive

tame: lacking in interest or animation

temperate: observing moderation in the indulgence of the appetites; not passionate

tempered: moderated

tolerant: enduring cheerfully the opinions of others

tranquil: free from and unaffected by agitation or disturbance; at peace

undemonstrative: not expressing emotions by actions

undisturbed: not disturbed

unexcited: not excited

unexciting: not exciting

unimpassioned: not working on the emotions

unirritating: not exciting anger

unoffending: harmless

unpassionate: lacking in passion

unperturbed: unmoved by passion

unresisting: humble

unruffled: not disturbed; tranquil

unstirred: unmoved

unsusceptible: not yielding to influence easily

untroubled: rid of trouble

Carefulness

accurate: truthful

alert: active

Argus-eyed: sharp-sighted

arrect: on the alert; attentive; intent

awake: not asleep

broad-awake: fully roused from slumber

careful: cautious and prudent

considerate: thoughtful and forbearing

guarded: cautious

heedful: regardful of advice and appearances

menseful: considerate; neat; tidy; discreet

painstaking: giving careful and scrupulous attention

particular: careful of details

provident: frugal

prudent: careful to follow the most profitable course

punctilious: attentive to details and conventions

regardful: closely attentive

scrupulous: cautious from conscientious motives

solicitous: taking utmost care or heed

surefooted: not liable to stumble

thoughtful: reflective; disposed to consider matters

tidy: orderly in habits

vigilant: thoughtfully watchful

wakeful: active

watchful: full of caution

way-wise: skilled or talented at not getting lost

wide-awake: thoroughly vigilant

wistful: contemplative

Carelessness

abandoned: forsaken

careless: unconcerned with responsibility

fribble: frivolous

heedless: inconsiderate; rash

improvident: heedless and unwary

imprudent: lacking in proper regard for consequences

inattentive: not heedful or observant

incircumspect: not cautious

inconsiderate: disregardful

inexact: not strictly precise

neglected: not treated with proper attention

neglectful: shiftless in the performance of duty

neglecting: not treating with proper attention

negligent: given to omitting duty

offhand: impromptu

perfunctory: done merely for the sake of performing a duty

reckless: careless; heedless

remiss: slack in duty

shelved: put aside as done

shunted: turned aside

slovenly: habitually careless in personal appearance

supine: inert; indolent

thoughtless: characterized by want of discretion

uncircumspect: not cautious

unexamined: not investigated

unexplored: not searched through

unguarded: left without a guard

unheeded: disregarded

unmarked: without a mark

unmindful: not retaining in mind

unmissed: not wanted

unnoted: not recorded

unnoticed: not observed

unobserved: not perceived

unperceived: not discerned

unregarded: not cared for

unremarked: not observed

unscanned: not scrutinized

unsearched: not explored

unseen: not seen

unsifted: not analyzed

unstudied: natural

unwary: careless

unwatchful: not on the watch

unweighed: not considered carefully

yemeless: negligent

Cause

aboriginal: of or pertaining to the first

agnogenic: of unknown cause

amblotic: causing abortion; ambolic

cacestogenous: caused by an unfavorable home environment

causal: productive of a result

connate: of common birth; cognate

efficacious: producing the desired result

embryonic: rudimentary

embryotic: in the earliest stage of development

germinal: of the nature of a germ

original: first of its kind

originated: arisen or sprung from

primary: earliest

primitive: pertaining to the beginning or first state

primordial: of the first order

princeps: first; original

radical: pertaining to the root or foundation

seminal: pertaining to the seed or first development

subjacent: causative and figuratively underlying

Caution

admonitive: serving to warn or reprove

admonitory: serving to warn or reprove

aposematic: warning away

careful: acting with care

cautelous: wary; crafty

cautionary: conveying a warning

cautious: acting with caution

chary: reluctant or cautious, as in giving a pledge; circumspect; guarded

circumspect: acting with circumspection

cool: not excited

discreet: having good judgment; prudent; not showy or obtrusive

guarded: acting with care and caution

heedful: giving heed

monitory: giving warning or advice

on one's guard: on the lookout for danger or attack; cautious; prepared; ready

overcautious: acting with too great care and consideration

pedetentous: proceeding cautiously

politic: crafty; acting with prudence rather than principle

premonitory: giving previous warning or notice

prudent: careful for the future; possessed of foresight

sematic: serving as a warning

shy of: wary; backward

skillful: with careful and well-trained powers

steady: cool; not impulsive

stealthy: acting with wariness and great secrecy

surefooted: to be depended upon; not given to making mistakes

unadventurous: not wont to take risks or ventures

unenterprising: lacking boldness and energy

warned: made aware; notified; informed

warning: cautioning against danger

wary: always guarding against deceptions and dangers, even to timidity

watchful: full of care and vigilance

Celibacy

celibatarian: favoring or marked by celibacy

celibate: or or relating to celibacy

chaste: celibate; single

single: unmarried

sole: celibate; unmarried

spouseless: without a wife

unmarried: without wife or husband

unwedded: without wife or husband

unwiving: pertaining to celibacy

virgin: relating to or characteristic of a virgin

wifeless: without a wife

Center—Medium—Middle

abstemious: moderate in food and drink intake

adiaphorous: neutral; neither right nor wrong

average: ordinary

axial: around an axis or center

azygous: without a fellow; single

central: relating to the middle; placed in the middle

centrical: centrally located

centripetal: directed toward the center; unifying

commonplace: of not much excellence

concentric: having a common center

entad: inward; toward the center

equatorial: relating to the equator

equidistant: halfway between

focal: pertaining or belonging to the central point or focus

fulcrate: having or acting as a fulcrum

geocentric: having the earth as the center

homocentric: having the same center

intermediate: coming between or being in the middle place

mean: filling a middle place; common

medial: relating to the middle or mean

mediate: between the two extremes; acting as an intervening agent

Mediterranean: closed in or nearly closed in by land

medium: intermediate between two degrees, amounts

mesial: middle; dividing into two equal parts; mean; medium; middlemost; midmost

mesne: between two extremes; intermediate

mesothetic: middle; intermediate

mid: occupying the middle part

middle: halfway between two points; equidistant from extremes

middle-class: intermediate

middlemost: nearest the middle

middling: of medium size or weight

midmost: middlemost or middle

neutral: not acting for or against anything

paracentral: near the center

phallocentric: centered on the penis

straight: having the same direction throughout

tapsell: of a gate turning about a central post

umbilical: pertaining to the navel; hence, in the center

vorticiform: vortexlike

vortiginous: whirling around a center or rushing in eddies; vortical

Ceremonial

after-hours: occurring or operating in early morning hours after regular bars close, when only a few, sometimes private, social clubs are open

baptismal: of or pertaining to baptism

black-tie: designating a formal affair to which a tuxedo is worn

celebrated: marked with particular ceremony

celebrating: honoring

ceremonial: of, pertaining to, or characterized by outward form and ceremony

chic: stylish; elegant; following the latest trends

commemorative: tending to keep fresh in memory

Dionysian: frenzied and orgiastic

dress-up: designating a gathering to which one dresses formally or in costume

eucharistical: pertaining to or of the nature of the Eucharist

immortal: never to die

paschal: of or pertaining to the Jewish Passover or the Christian Easter

ritual: of, pertaining to, or consisting of a rite or rites

ritualistic: adhering to or tending to or favoring ritualism

sociable: friendly; enjoying the company of others

solemnized: celebrated

trendy: fashionable in the latest social mode; faddish

white-tie: designating extremely formal affair to which men wear swallow-tailed coats and white bow ties

Certainty

absolute: self-determined

ascertained: known or established with certainty

assured: made sure or certain

authentic: genuinely accurate

authoritative: positively established

avoidless: not to be escaped

axiomatic: self-evident

categorical: admitting no exceptions or doubts

certain: admitting neither doubt nor denial; fixed; regular

clear: free from doubt or misgiving

conclusive: not able to be refuted or proved false

decided: settled as to doubt

decisive: having the power or quality of deciding

definite: certain

definitive: most authoritative; conclusive; settling something

determinate: having the power of settling or limiting definitely

doubtless: without doubt

evident: easily manifest to both eye and mind

incontestable: not to be denied or contradicted

incontrovertible: too certain to be disputed

indefeasible: that which cannot be undone

indisputable: too obvious to admit of contradiction

indubious: not doubtful

indubitable: plainly certain

inevitable: not to be evaded or resisted

infallible: incapable of erring

insured: assured; guaranteed

irrefutable: that cannot be refuted or disproved

iwis: certainly

known: generally recognized

official: derived from or done by the proper authority

positive: fully convinced or confident

questionless: beyond question

reliable: worthy of belief or dependence

self-evident: producing certainty or conviction from mere consideration

solid: worthy of credence or trust

sure: worthy of dependence; certain to meet expectations

trustworthy: meriting trust and confidence

unavoidable: not to be escaped

unchangeable: fixed in form or substance

uncontested: not denied

undeniable: not to be refuted

undisputed: not contradicted

undoubted: accepted without hesitation or doubt

unequivocal: admitting of but a single, certain interpretation

unerring: accurate

unimpeachable: not to be reproached

unmistakable: not doubted

unqualified: unconditional; absolute

unquestionable: not to be doubted or questioned

unquestioned: not doubted

well-founded: clearly established

ywis: certain; certainly; iwis

Charge

accusable: chargeable with crime

accusative: producing accusations

accusatory: pertaining to or containing an accusation

accused: charged with crime or wrong

accusing: censuring

anapologetical: inexcusable

chargeable: liable to be at fault; liable to be responsible for an ill deed

criminatory: involving accusation

denunciatory: threatening

imputable: chargeable with a fault

imputative: transferred or transmitted by imputation

in custody: under guard

in detention: kept confined or detained

in the house of detention: in prison

in the lockup: in the place where persons are temporarily confined when under arrest

in the watchhouse: imprisoned in the building occupied by the watch or guard

indefensible: not capable of being defended or maintained

inexcusable: not admitting excuse or justification

recriminatory: accusing in return

suspected: under surveillance as a suspicious character

under a cloud: overshadowed by difficulties; having one's reputation injuriously affected

under surveillance: watched or guarded

under suspicion: mistrusted

unjustifiable: not able to be proved to be just

unpardonable: that may not be shown clemency or pardoned

vicious: corrupt in conduct or habits

Charitableness

accommodating: given to doing kindnesses or granting favors

amiable: having a pleasing disposition

beneficent: doing good; kind; charitable

benevolent: possessing a disposition to do good

benignant: kind; helpful in influence

bounteous: characterized by liberality

bountiful: liberal in giving

broad-hearted: generous; liberal

brotherly: having the nature of a brother; hence, kind, affectionate

charitable: good to the poor and the helpless

complacent: self-approved; contented

complaisant: anxious to please

fatherly: having the nature or disposition of a father

fraternal: brotherly

friendly: disposed to help or assist others

good-humored: having a pleasant temper

good-natured: having a disposition to please and be pleased

gracious: showing mercy or grace

humane: disposed to treat man and lower animals with kindness

indulgent: inclined to yield to the desires of those under our care

kind: desirous of the happiness of others

kindhearted: of a sympathetic nature

kindly: sympathetic

largehearted: generous

maternal: motherly

merciful: characterized by pity

motherly: having the disposition of a mother; hence, tender, compassionate

obliging: given to doing favors

paternal: fatherly

sisterly: having the disposition of a sister

spleenless: gentle; kind

sympathetic: given to sympathy

sympathizing: sympathetic

tenderhearted: very sensitive to impressions; affectionate

warmhearted: possessed of strong affection

well-intentioned: having good purposes

well-meaning: of a good intention

well-meant: having had a good intention

well-natured: good-natured

Cheapness

a drug in the market: plenteous with lack of demand; hence, cheap

bargain-basement: markedly cheap

borax: marked by cheapness

brummagem: phony; cheap

catchpenny: cheap and showy

cheap: low in price

cheap and nasty: cheap and filthy; worthless

claptrap: characterized by showiness of a cheap nature

depreciated: sunk in value

discounting: deducting from the sum owing or to be paid

hand-me-down: ready-made; cheap and shoddy; secondhand

pinchbeck: cheap; sham; spurious

slimpsy: sleazy; cheap; of poor quality

tatty: cheap; inferior

Chemistry

acetic: pertaining to vinegar

acidic: describing a solution with pH less than 7

adiabatic: designating a process in which no energy is transferred between a system and its surroundings

amphoteric: capable of acting as an acid or base

anhydrous: having no water of crystallization

aqueous: describing a solution in water

basic: describing a solution with pH greater than 7

bituminous: of the nature of bitumen; containing much volatile hydrocarbon

catalytic: relating to a resolution into parts

chemical: relating to the physical science of elementary substances or forms of matter

decomposed: resolved from existing combinations

dyadic: of a pair; involving two elements

endothermic: absorbing heat energy

equivalent: having the same capacity to combine or react chemically

exothermic: releasing heat energy

ferric: pertaining to iron

ferrous: containing iron; ferruginous

guttatim: in pharmacy, drop by drop

haloid: saltlike

heterogeneous: containing dissimilar elements

hydrated: formed by combination of water and another substance in definite molecular ratio

hydrophilic: attracted to and interacting with water

hydrophobic: not attracted to or interacting with water

hydroxyl: containing the negatively charged OH group

hygroscopic: capable of absorbing water from air

inflammable: that can be set on fire

insoluble: that cannot be dissolved in a fluid

isobaric: occurring at constant pressure

isothermic: occurring at constant temperature

lixiviate: alkaline

molal: denoting a property of weight expressed per mole of a substance

molar: denoting a property of volume expressed per mole of a substance

neutral: describing a compound or solution that is neither acidic nor basic

phosphoric: pertaining to phosphorus

reversible: describing reactions in which products are changed back into original reactants under certain conditions

ruthenic: pertaining to or derived from a rare metallic element

salsuginous: slightly salty; brackish

senary: composed of six elements or sections

spagyric: pertaining to alchemy; alchemical

specific: denoting a property of volume expressed per unit mass of a substance

spontaneous: occurring without outside influence

sulfuric: pertaining to sulfur

synthetic: man-made; not occurring in nature

terebinthine: pertaining to turpentine

thionic: sulfuric

transuranic: having an atomic number greater than uranium's

Choice—Decision

choice: worthy of being chosen

choosing: that chooses

chosen: selected; picked out

conclusive: decisive; ending doubt

decisive: characterized by decision; determining; conclusive

deligible: worthy to be chosen

determinate: fixed or limited definitely

discoursive: passing from one judgment to another

discretional: of or pertaining to a decision

discursive: wandering; drawing conclusions from premises

disposed: inclined; tending toward or against

doxastic: concerning an opinion

eclectic: selecting at will from the productions of others

half-minded: of having made a partial decision

homodox: having the same opinion; homodoxian

in the loop: in the sequence of decision making

judging: inclined or disposed to judge

judicious: having or exercising sound judgment

multivolent: of many minds

optional: depending on choice

peremptory: allowing no contradiction; precluding all debate

perficiently: decisively; effectively

predisposed: inclined in advance, pro or con

preferential: having, showing, or constituting preference

snap: designating judgment reached hastily and without deliberation

unbiased: fair; free from prejudice

Church

abbatial: belonging to an abbey

abbatical: belonging to an abbey

antinomian: pertaining to a belief that Christian faith alone will see one through anything

apostolic: of or pertaining to an apostle or the apostles

apostolical: of or pertaining to an apostle or the apostles

archiepiscopal: pertaining to the archbishop

autocephalous: of a self-governing church body

biblical: pertaining to the Bible

canonical: belonging to the canon of Scripture

capitular: pertaining to an ecclesiastical chapter

churchish: resembling a house of worship; churchy

clerical: pertaining to the clergy

conventual: monastic

denominational: pertaining to a denomination

ecclesiastical: of or pertaining to the church

ecclesiological: belonging to the science or theory of church building and decoration

ecumenical: pertaining to whole Christian church, especially promoting its unity

episcopal: governed by bishops; pertaining to the Anglican Church

episcopalian: relating to the Episcopal Church, its polity

evangelical: of or pertaining to the gospel or the four Gospels

evangelistic: evangelical

hierarchical: pertaining to a hierarchy

hieratic: concerning sacred or priestly activities

His Eminence: title applied to a cardinal

His Grace: title applied to an archbishop

His Holiness: title applied to the pope

homiletic: like a sermon; sermonizing

in orders: belonging to a grade of the ministry

inspired: communicated, imparted, or guided by inspiration

kaaba: pertaining to the Islamic shrine in Mecca that is the goal of pilgrimage

kerygmatic: pertaining to preaching

laical: pertaining to the laity

latitudinarian: referring to tolerance of different religious beliefs; broad-minded

lay: relating to the laity, as distinct from the clergy

litaneutical: pertaining to a litany

ministerial: relating to or characteristic of a minister or the ministry

monachal: of or pertaining to monks; monastic

monasterial: pertaining to monks or nuns; ascetic

monastic: pertaining to monasteries; like monks; recluse; ascetic

monkish: like monks; withdrawn from the world

ordained: invested with ministerial or sacerdotal functions

papable: qualified to become pope

papal: pertaining to the pope or the Roman Catholic system

paparchical: concerning government by a pope

pastoral: relating to a pastor of a church or his duties

pontifical: pertaining to a pontiff or high priest; hence, to the pope

prelatical: relating to prelates or prelacy

presbyterian: governed by elders

priestly: relating to or befitting a priest

priest-ridden: completely under the domination of priests

profane: not sacred or holy; secular

prophetic: of or pertaining to a prophet or prophecy

religious: pertaining to religion

sacerdotal: of or pertaining to the priesthood or priests

sacred: set apart or dedicated to religious use; esteemed especially dear to Deity

scriptural: of or pertaining to biblical revelations

sectarian: attached to the beliefs of a denomination

secular: pertaining to this present world; belonging to the laity

supralapsarian: transcending or predestined to the Creation and Fall of Man

sybilline: like a prophet; mysterious

syncretic: uniting different systems of philosophy or religion

syncretical: uniting different systems of philosophy or religion

temporal: civil or political, as distinguished from ecclesiastical

textuary: contained in the text; serving as a text

the reverend: worthy of reverence; said of a clergyman

the right reverend: said of a bishop

the very reverend: said of a dean

theandric: pertaining to both God and man; divine and human; theandrical

theocentric: having a view that God is at the center

theochristic: anointed by God

theocratic: pertaining to a theocracy; administered directly by God

theological: relating to theology

theopneust: divinely inspired; theopneustic

theopneustic: given by inspiration of the Spirit of God

trayf: unclean or unfit according to religious law

ultramontane: favoring or holding extreme views in regard to the supremacy of the pope

unhouseled: not having had the Eucharist administered; unhouselled

vatic: pertaining to prophets or seers; prophetic; inspired

Circle—Roundness

annular: pertaining to or formed like a ring

beadlike: round, like a bead

bell-shaped: in the form of a bell

belted: having a belt

bulbiform: bulb-shaped; bulbous

bulbous: bulblike in shape or structure

campaniform: bell-shaped; campaniliform; caliciform; campanular; campanulate; campanulous

campaniliform: bell-shaped

campanulate: bell-shaped

circinate: ringlike; annular; cingular

circular: of a perfectly closed curve; annular; cycloid; cycloidal; rotund; round

circumrotatory: turning, rolling, or whirling around

columnar: columnlike; basaltiform; columniform

conic: having the form of a geometrical cone

conical: cone-shaped

coniform: cone-shaped; conic; conical; strobile

cycloidal: pertaining to a cycloid

cyclostomate: having a round mouth

cylindric: having the form of a cylinder

cylindrical: having the form of a cylinder

cylindroid: having the form of a cylinder

egg-shaped: having the shape of an egg

elliptic: pertaining or related to an ellipse

elliptical: pertaining or related to an ellipse

full-orbed: completely round

fungiform: shaped like a fungus or mushroom

gibbous: swelling by a regular curve or surface

gimmal: pertaining to a double ring for the finger; gemel

globated: having the form of a globe; spherical

globose: having the form of a globe; spherical

globous: having the form of a globe; spherical

globular: having the form of a globe; spherical

guttiform: shaped like a drop

gyratory: revolving; whirling around

knobbed: having rounded protuberances

lobed: having rounded projections; lobate; lobular

lumbriciform: resembling an earthworm in form

molendinaceous: like a windmill

moniliform: jointed or constricted, at regular intervals, so as to resemble a string of beads

obconic: pear-shaped

obrotund: of a ball or sphere somewhat flattened; obround

ooid: egg-shaped; pertaining to eggs; ellipsoidal; elliptical; ooidal; oval; ovaliform; oviform; ovoid

orbicular: similar to an orb

oval: shaped like an egg

ovate: egg-shaped

oviform: egg-shaped

ovoid: egg-shaped

ovopyriform: shaped like an egg or pear

pear-shaped: having the form of a pear

penannular: of an almost complete ring; almost circular

peristrephic: turning around; rotatory; peritropal

pyriform: pear-shaped

ringed: having parallel encircling rings

rotary: turning around, as a wheel on its axis

rotating: turning around, as a wheel on its axis

rotatory: turning around, as a wheel on its axis

rotund: round; circular; spherical

round: having every portion of the surface or of the circumference equally distant from the center; round as a ball; round as an apple; round as an orange rounded: made circular

spherical: round; like a sphere; bombous; conglobate; globate; globose; globular; orblike; rotund; round; spheral; spheriform

spheroidal: approximately round; almost a sphere; ellipsoidal

stobic: spinning like a top

strobic: spinning

strombuliform: like a screw or spinning top

trochiform: shaped like a top; turbinate

trochilic: having power to draw out or turn around

vertiginous: turning around; rotary

vortical: of or pertaining to a vortex or vortices in form or motion; whirling

vorticose: vortical; whirling

City

citizenly: pertaining to a citizen

citylike: having the manners of a city dweller

crosstown: located at opposite points of town

genteel: stylish; well-bred

greater: designating metropolitan area surrounding city

interurban: between or connecting cities or towns

megalopolitan: pertaining to a very large city; megapolitan

metropolitan: relating to or characteristic of a city

municipal: restricted to one self-governing locality

oppidan: relating to a town

polished: refined and polite

residential: restricted to or occupied by private homes and apartments

suburban: pertaining to the suburbs of a city

towny: having qualities associated with a town

urban: of, relating to, characteristic of, or constituting a city

urbicolous: living in the city

villageous: pertaining to a village or villages; villagey; villagy

Cleanness

apinoid: clean; dirt-free

besom-clean: clean as a broom can make a floor without washing

clean: free from dirt

cleaned: freed from dirt

cleanly: disposed to be clean

clysmic: washing; cleansing

gimp: dressed in a careful and cleanly manner

immaculate: perfect in purity; without spot

kempt: neatly kept; trim

neat: marked by strict cleanliness

pure: free from defilement

smectic: purifying; detergent

spotless: free from impurity

spruce: neat in dress

stainless: absolutely pure

tersive: detergent; having the power to clean by wiping; detersive

tidy: marked by order and cleanness

trim: perfect in order and neatness

uninfected: free from contagion

unsoiled: free from defilement

unspotted: free from blemishes

unstained: absolutely pure

untainted: not made impure by an admixture of foul matter

well-scrubbed: looking clean

Clearness

clear: distinct; intelligible
definite: clear; unmistakable; unambiguous
distinct: easily understood; clear to the mind
explicit: plainly expressed
expressive: full of meaning
graphic: describing with pictorial effect
illustrative: designed to make clear by means of figures, comparisons
intelligible: capable of being understood; clear
legible: that may be read
lucent: clear; translucent; lucid
lucid: intellectually clear
luminous: light-bearing; radiant; clear; intelligible
obvious: immediately evident

perspicuous: translucent; clear; lucid
plain: that may be readily seen or understood
popularized: made clear and acceptable to the common people
positive: openly and plainly expressed; explicit
recognizable: capable of being recognized
transparent: easy to see through or understand
transpicuous: easily seen through or understood; transparent
unambiguous: not ambiguous; clear; perspicuous
unconfused: not confused; distinct
unequivocal: unambiguous; clear; certain; unmistakable
unmistakable: clear; plain; obvious

Closure

airtight: closed so that air cannot enter
caecal: pertaining to the caecum's closing
closed: shut
hermetically sealed: closed as to make airtight
impassable: not to be passed through
impenetrable: not to be passed through
imperforate: without holes
impermeable: not permitting a passage
impervious: not permitting a passage
imporous: without pores or holes
indehiscent: closed at maturity
invious: trackless; pathless; without roads

operculated: having a lid or cover
pathless: unopened
shut: closed
snug: closely covered
tight: closed
unopened: closed
unpassable: not permitting a passage
unpierced: without holes through
untrodden: without a way
unventilated: closed that air cannot pass through
watertight: impervious to water

Coercion—Force

bold: audacious; striking
coactive: compulsory; obligatory; restrictive; constraining
coercive: intended to coerce
compelled: forced; constrained
compelling: that demands attention
compulsatory: operating with force

compulsive: irresistible
compulsory: by force or constraint
dynamic: pertaining to dynamics; characterized by mechanical force
dynamical: pertaining to dynamics; characterized by mechanical force
elevated: lofty in character; sublime

eloquent: powerfully expressive; stirring; convincing
expostulatory: containing or expressing earnest or kindly protest
forceful: powerful; vigorous; effective
forcible: powerful; effective; accomplished using force
full of point: cogent
glowing: burning; showing intense feeling
impassioned: greatly animated or excited
impressive: holding the attention; exciting admiration
incisive: cutting; penetrating; trenchant
ineluctable: irresistible
inexorable: rigidly severe
intercessory: containing or expressing intercession
irresistible: too strong
lively: vivid; spirited
lofty: stately; noble; elevated
mediatorial: serving to mediate
nervous: manifesting terseness, vigor, and crispness in response to coercion

obligatory: binding in law or duty
peremptory: decisive; compulsory
petulant: fretful; peevish; snappish; exhibiting a type of force or power
piquant: racy; sparkling; lively; exhibiting a type of force or power
pithy: forcible; sententious
pointed: pungent; epigrammatic
powerful: having great effect on the mind; convincing
protested: objected to
pulsive: coercive
pungent: piercing; caustic
racy: lively; piquant; tasting of the stock or family, like certain choice wines
sensational: causing strong feeling
slashing: striking or cutting at random
sparkling: brilliant; vivacious
spirited: full of spirit, life or vigor
stringent: binding strongly
trenchant: effective; penetrating; biting
vehement: carrying all before it; impetuous; passionate; fiery
vigorous: powerful; forcible

Coexistence

associated with: joined
coetaneous: coming into existence at the same time; of the same age
coeternal: equally eternal
coeval: existing from the same time; contemporary
coevous: existing from the same time
coexisting: to exist at the same time
coincident: happening at the same time
concomitant: occurring together at the same time; accompanying
concurrent: agreeing in opinion
contemporaneous: existing or occurring at the same time; contemporary

contemporary: living at the same time
equaeval: of equal age; of the same period
isochronous: occurring at equal intervals of time
simultaneous: occurring at exactly the same time, as two sounds
synchronal: pertaining to events of the same date
synchronical: pertaining to events of the same date
synchronistical: pertaining to events of the same date
synchronous: pertaining to events of the same date

Cold—Cooling

aguish: somewhat cold
algefacient: cooling; algific
algid: very cold; chilly; sharp
algific: that which produces cold; algefacient

arctic: cold; frigid; pertaining to the northern regions
biting: sharp; severe
bitter: characterized by severity
bleak: cold and sweeping

boreal: pertaining to the north or north wind

brumal: pertaining to the winter

chelmaphilic: liking winter and cold

chill: moderately cold

chilly: disagreeably cold

clay-cold: cold as clay or earth

clumpst: having hands stiff with cold

cold: deprived of heat; frigid; not warm

cold as a charity: very cold

cold as a frog: very cold

cold as a stone: very cold

cold as Christmas: very cold

cold as iron: very cold

cold as marble: very cold

cool: moderately cold

cool as a cucumber: expression for moderate coldness

cool as a custard: expression for moderate coldness

cooled: made cool

cooling: that cools or makes cool

cutting: chilling

ectothermic: cold-blooded; poikilothermic

fireproof: not burnable

freezing: becoming congealed by cold

fresh: cool; brisk

frigid: cold; wanting heat

frigolabile: easily affected by cold

frigorific: cold-producing

frore: frozen

frostbitten: injured by freezing

frost-bound: injured by freezing

frost-nipped: injured by freezing

frosty: cold enough to congeal water

frozen out: affected by freezing; ostracized

gelid: very cold; frozen; freezing; frigid; icy

glacial: pertaining to a glacier

hematocryal: cold-blooded

hibernal: wintry; cold

hyemal: pertaining to winter; hiemal

hyperboreal: very cold

hyperborean: very cold; northern

icebound: totally surrounded by ice

iced: cooled by ice

icing: making frozen

icy: cold like ice; frigid

inclement: severe; rigorously cold

incombustible: not destructible by fire

isocheimenal: pertaining to an imaginary line connecting all places of an equal winter temperature

keen: sharp; biting

lukewarm: neither hot nor cold

marmoreal: marblelike; cold and white

nipped: affected by the cold

nipping: checking the growth of, as by frost; biting; piercing

nival: relating to snow; niveous; snowy

niveous: resembling snow

piercing: penetrating

pinching: biting

poikilothermal: cold-blooded; poikilothermic; poikilothermous

raw: piercingly cold and damp

shivering: trembling

Siberian: pertaining to or like Siberia

starved: made cold

subboreal: cold but not freezing

tepid: lukewarm

unflammable: not capable of being ignited

uninflammable: not capable of being ignited

unthawed: not melted

unwarmed: not warmed; chilly

wintry: like winter; chilly

Color

allochroous: multicolored; changing or turning color

bright: of brilliant color

chromatic: colored; pigmented

colored: infused with color; having color

colorific: of or pertaining to the production or sensation of color

crude: having inharmonious colors

Day-Glo™: fluorescent in daylight

deep: of intense or dark hue
deep-colored: dark
discordant: out of harmony
double-dyed: dyed twice over
flaring: shining out in glaring colors
flashy: gaudy
flaunting: gaudy
florid: of a lively, reddish hue
fresh: retaining vividness or distinctness
gairish: garish
garish: displaying a gaudy effect
gaudy: brilliant in color
gay: brilliant in color or appearance
glaring: emitting an excessively bright light
gorgeous: conspicuous by splendor of colors
harmonious: symmetrical
high-colored: having a strong, deep, or glaring color
inharmonious: unsymmetrical
intense: having strength or marked contrast
iridal: like a rainbow, as the iris of the eye

iridian: rainbowlike; having changeable color; iridescent
isochroous: possessing the same color throughout
mellow: agreeable to the senses
multicolored: having many colors; kaleidoscopic; motley; parti-colored; polychromatic; polychrome; polychromic; prismatic; varicolored; variegated; versicolor; versicolored
pavonine: iridescent in color
pearly: resembling pearls in color and luster
polychromatic: exhibiting many colors
prismatic: exhibiting rainbow tints; bright-colored
prismatoidal: resembling a prism; prismlike; prismatic; prismoidal
raw: untempered or without tone
rich: pleasing in color
showy: gaudy
sweet: agreeable to the eye
tinctorial: pertaining to dyeing, coloring
tingent: capable of tingeing
unfaded: not dulled in tint or color
vivid: having intense luminosity or high chroma

Combustible

ardent: combustible; inflammable
burnable: capable of being consumed by fire
carbonaceous: containing carbon; hence, combustible
combustible: capable of being set on fire
combustious: in combustion, burning
empyrical: pertaining to combustion

igneous: pertaining to fire
ignivomous: vomiting fire
incendiary: inflammatory; igniting combustible materials
inflammable: highly combustible
piceous: combustible; inflammable
quick: rapidly combustible

Commonness

barbaresque: barbaric in form or style
barbarian: uncivilized and cruel
barbaric: destitute of refinement
barbarous: wild; brutal; savage
base: of humble or ignoble birth; of low station
baseborn: born out of wedlock
beggarly: miserably poor; mean; sordid
below par: inferior in position or rank

boorish: awkward and rude in manners
born within sound of Bow-bells: having the characteristics of a Cockney
brutish: like a beast; ferocious
churlish: like a churl; rude; sordid
clownish: coarse and ill-bred
Cockney: related to or like a vulgar Londoner

common: commonplace; vulgar; coarse; low

demotic: popular; pertaining to the people

dunghill: sprung from the dunghill; base; mean

earthborn: mean or ignoble

homely: plain; not polished

homespun: plain in manner or style; not elegant

ignoble: of low birth or family; base

loutish: clumsy; awkward

low: mean or humble in rank; unrefined

lowborn: born in humble life

low-minded: mean in mind or disposition

mean: of humble antecedents; worthy of no respect

menial: pertaining to servants; servile

mushroom: resembling a mushroom; upstarting

no great shakes: nothing extraordinary; of little worth

obscure: of humble condition; lowly

of low extraction: of low and humble birth

of low origin: of low and humble birth

of low parentage: of low and humble birth

of mean extraction: of low and humble birth

of mean origin: of low and humble birth

of mean parentage: of low and humble birth

philodemic: fond of the common people

plebeian: relating to the common people

proletarian: pertaining to the lower or lowest classes of society

proletariat: pertaining to the rabble

raffish: resembling the rabble; worthless

risen from the ranks: ascended into prominence from among the lowly

rude: coarse in manners or behavior

rustic: pertaining to the country; plain; untaught

scrubby: small and mean; inferior

snobbish: pertaining to a snob

sorry: poor; mean; worthless

subaltern: inferior; subordinate

uncivilized: lacking refinement; coarse

underling: low; inferior

unknown to fame: not known to the world

unlicked: rough; uncultured

untitled: not having a name of distinction or dignity

vile: of little worth; base; depraved

vulgar: pertaining to common people; inelegant

Compassion

clement: gentle in temper and disposition

compassionate: full of compassion

exorable: that may be moved by pity

forbearing: long-suffering

humane: kind; compassionate

humanitarian: benevolent

lenient: clement; merciful

melting: feeling or expressing tenderness

merciful: having mercy

pitiful: having pity; tenderhearted

pitying: that feels or expresses pity

ruthful: tender; pitiful; sad; woeful

soft: tender; sympathetic

softhearted: having tenderness of heart

sympathetic: inclined to, or produced by sympathy

tender: mild; gentle

tender as a chicken: easily moved

tenderhearted: easily moved

touched: affected mentally or morally

unhardened: not hardened or morally depraved

weak: clement

welwilly: benevolent

Compensation

all straight: paid in full
compensating: serving to make compensation
compensatory: serving to make compensation
countervailing: opposing with a force equal to the opponent's
equivalent: of the same value
in the opposite scale: in the balance

moratory: pertaining to delay in paying a debt or other obligation
never indebted: never going in debt
out of debt: free from obligation
owing nothing: free from obligation
paid: free from claims upon
paying: freeing from debt
unowed: free from debt

Completion—Entirety

absolute: free from limitations
abundant: fully sufficient
all-sided: developed on all sides
araphorostic: seamless; unsewed; arrhaphostic
as full as a vetch: as full as a pea pod
as full as an egg is of meat: filled to the shell
ascititious: not essential; added from without
bodacious: bold and audacious; complete; thorough
brimful: filled to the point of overflowing
brimming: full or filling to the brim
chock-full: choke-full
choke-full: completely full
climactic: pertaining to a climax
complete: having all the needed or usual parts
completed: finished; done
completing: being in the state of completion
concluding: drawing to an end
conclusive: decisive; final
consummate: finished; complete
crammed: filled
crowning: completing; consummating
desinent: terminal; closing
done: completed; finished
done for: used up; destroyed
entire: complete in all its parts
exhaustive: treating thoroughly; attempting all possibilities

final: conclusive; allowing no appeal
fraught: filled; loaded; fully laden
free: not under restraint
full: with as much in as possible
full-charged: carrying as much as possible
full-fraught: fully laden
full-laden: with a full load
good: full or complete in measure
heavy-laden: carrying much
highly wrought: completely worked into shape or condition
indiscerptible: that cannot be destroyed by separation of parts
indissoluble: not to be melted or liquefied; incapable of separation
indissolvable: not to be melted or liquefied; incapable of separation
individual: existing as one entity; not to be divided; single
indivisible: that cannot be divided or separated
integral: comprising all the parts; unbroken parts or numbers
laden: filled up
locuplete: rich and complete; plentifully stocked
maturescent: approaching maturity
napoo: nothing; finished
one: a single number; forming a whole
paulopast: just completed or finished
perfect: without defect or lack
plenary: full in all respects; entire; absolute

radical: carried to the fullest limit

regular: thoroughgoing; complete

replete: full to the uttermost

ripe: most fit for eating or consumption

saturated: filled by absorption

seamless: having no seam; woven throughout

sheer: utter

solid: completely filled

subitary: suddenly or hastily done or made

supplemental: like or pertaining to a supplement

supplementary: supplemental

sweeping: including many in a single act or assertion

terminal: at the end; final

thorough: complete; going through and through

thoroughgoing: going to the bottom of things

topful: brimful

total: complete in amount, used in reference to quantity

unbroken: expressing completeness or entirety

unbruised: expressing completeness or entirety

unclipped: expressing completeness or entirety

unconditional: not limited in any way

uncropped: expressing completeness or entirety

uncut: expressing completeness or entirety

undemolished: expressing completeness or entirety

undestroyed: expressing completeness or entirety

undiminished: expressing completeness or entirety

undissolved: expressing completeness or entirety

undivided: entire

unmitigated: having full force

unqualified: without limitations or restrictions

unsevered: expressing completeness or entirety

unshorn: expressing completeness or entirety

whole: containing all the parts

wholesale: buying and selling in large quantities only

with all its parts: whole

Composition

ambigenal: of two kinds; hybrid

bastard: of mixed breed

bigenerous: of two species; hybrid

combined: bound together

composed: compound; composite

cross: crossbred; hybrid

esemplastic: unifying disparate things; synthesizing

heterogeneous: not uniform in composition

hybrid: composite

impregnated with: filled with

ingrained: fixed deeply

polyhybrid: pertaining to a heterozygous hybrid

synthetic: constructive

Concavity

alveolar: marked by alveoli

arched: having an arch or arches

bell-shaped: shaped like a bell

biconcave: concave on two sides

campaniform: bell-shaped

capsular: like a capsule

cavernous: containing caverns

cellular: containing cells

collabent: collapsing in the middle; sunken

concave: hollowed inward; bowllike; concave; craterlike; depressed; dished; sunken

crateriform: having an inverted center, as a bowl or saucer

depressed: lower than the surrounding surface

engrailed: having concave indentations

funnel-shaped: shaped like a funnel

gibbous: humpbacked; arched

groin-vaulted: arched in intersections

hollow: having a vacant place in the interior

honeycombed: having cells like a honeycomb

infundibular: funnel-shaped

infundibuliform: funnel-shaped

invex: concave

porous: containing pores

retiring: bending toward the rear

retreating: bending toward the rear

simous: concave

spongious: porous

spongy: porous

stove-in: dented

vaulted: arched, as a ceiling; concaved below

Condition—Situation

adventitious: forming only an incidental part

choosehow: under any circumstances (and is placed last in a sentence)

circumstantial: dependent upon indirectly related incidents

conditional: depending on certain modifying terms; subject to conditions

contingent: depending on something else, such as a future event

crisic: critical; pertaining to a crisis

critical: pertaining to the turning point in some event

ectopic: occurring in a place other than the usual one

entopic: occurring in the usual place

exceptional: implying an exception

ferial: referring to a nonfeast day

formal: referring to form in contrast to substance

given: granted

guarded: on condition

hypothetical: assumed for the sake of argument

incidental: occurring along with something else

modal: having the form without the reality; denoting a manner

organic: pertaining to an organ or organs

provisional: provided for present service; temporary

qualifying: having a modifying condition

situational: pertaining to circumstances or conditions

structural: pertaining to structure

Conduct

abnormally: in an irregular manner

accommodately: in a manner suited to

accordingly: agreeably

businesslike: well or precisely done

conducting: that conducts; having the power to guide or direct

executive: possessing the power to control

howgates: in what manner

othergates: in another way or manner; otherways

practical: applying knowledge to some useful end

shabash: well done

strategical: pertaining to or displaying foresight

Confinement

begirt: surrounded as with a band

buried in: absorbed in

cabined: closely restrained; cribbed; confined

circumscribed: confined within bounds

coactive: serving to constrain

cohibitive: restraining

confining: bounding; limiting; restricting

constrained: chained; secured with bonds

determinate: definitely limited or numbered

embedded: deposited in a partly enclosing mass

embosomed: received into one's bosom

encysted: enclosed in a membranous sac

enwreathing: surrounding

fenced: secured

hapteric: fastening; holding fast

hedged in: surrounded

hidebound: closely confined

icebound: totally surrounded by ice

immersed in: dipped in

immuring: enclosing

imprisoned: confined in prison

in a ring fence: surrounded by a ring fence

in custody: under guard

in Lob's Pound: held playfully between the legs and feet of an adult; said of a child

in swaddling clothes: in the band wrapped around infants

in the bloom of: covered with; in a flourishing condition

jammed in: wedged in

laid by the heels: fettered; shackled

landlocked: enclosed by land

lapt: wrapped around

mewed up: shut up

nidulant: nestling; embedded

obvallate: walled in

on parole: bound by one's word of honor

put up: imprisoned

restrained: held in check; hindered

restringent: restrictive

stiff: rigid; inflexible

straitlaced: having the bodice or stays tightly laced

under hatches: confined belowdecks

under lock and key: under restraint or in prison

under restraint: deprived of freedom

weather-bound: detained by unfavorable weather

wedged-in: fastened in tightly

wind-bound: delayed by contrary winds

Conservation

conservative: wishing to preserve ancient customs or institutions

hygienic: pertaining to hygiene; relating to the care and preservation of the health

intact: untouched; unhurt; safe

preservative: serving to keep from harm

preservatory: preservative

preserved: kept safe; protected

preserving: keeping safe; protecting

prophylactic: tending to ward off disease

safe: out of danger

safe and sound: unharmed; having been preserved

unhurt: without hurt or damage

unimpaired: not lessened in value

uninjured: not injured

unmarred: not injured or disfigured

unsinged: not even slightly burned

with a whole skin: unhurt

Constituent

clastic: having separable pieces
compartmentalized: in parts or sections
constituent: that makes a thing what it is; that which is essential; formative
discrete: individual; distinct; detached
divided: parted; separated; distributed
forming: give form to
fractional: comprising a part or the parts of a unit
fragmentary: composed of broken pieces

in compartments: composed of distinct parts or divisions
inclusive: enclosing
meristic: pertaining to or divided into segments
multifid: having many clefts or divisions
ort: leftover tidbit
scissile: easily split or divided; scissible
sectional: made up of several distinct parts
subsicive: leftover

Continuance—Duration

abiding: continuing
accrescent: growing continuously; ever-increasing
chronic: lingering; lasting
consecutive: following in regular order
constant: unchangeable
continued: having but slight pauses or intervals
continuing: that continues; abiding; lasting
continuous: absolutely without intervals or breaks
curtate: comparatively short in time
diuturnal: having a long duration; lasting
durational: lasting
entire: having all its parts
evergreen: always green; fresh
fugacious: fleeting; of short duration; ephemeral
gradual: proceeding by regular steps
immediate: coming after with the loss of little time
in a line: following one after another; linear; in a row
inconvertible: not capable of being changed into something else
intransient: remaining; permanent
intransitive: not passing over; constant
intransmutable: unchangeable
lasting: enduring; perpetual
lifelong: lasting for life

linear: continuous like a line
lingering: protracted
livelong: entire
longeval: capable of living long
longevous: long-lived
long-lived: capable of living long
long-pending: lingering
long-standing: enduring
long-winded: prolonged
macrobian: long-lived
macrobiotic: long-lived
nisi: pending
perdurable: everlasting; permanent; unusually durable
perennial: continuing for many years
permanent: durable
perpetual: lasting; unceasing
progressive: advancing regularly
prolonged: extended in space or time
protracted: extended; prolonged
serial: arranged in a series
slow: not quick
spun-out: greatly extended
successive: following in order
supernaculum: to the last drop
sustained: upheld; continued
unbroken: not broken
undying: that does not end or die
unintermitting: unceasing
uninterrupted: unbroken in connection
unremitting: not relaxing
unreversed: unchanged

unrevoked: not annulled
unshifting: stable
unstopped: not checked

unvaried: unaltered
unvarying: constant

Contract

ad idem: in agreement on a point
agreed: arranged or settled by common consent
benami: made, held, done, or transacted in the name of another person; benamee
contractual: pertaining to a mutual agreement or compact
conventional: pertaining to convention
innominate: of a certain type of contract that is real but has no special name; of a commutative contract
mediatory: pertaining to mediation or a mediator
negotiable: that may be negotiated
nominate: being a contract involving delivery of property for which the actual property was to be returned
under hand and seal: ratified

Contraposition

antarctic: pertaining to the south
antipodal: on the opposite side of the earth
arctic: northern
austral: southern; austrine
boreal: northern
broadside: facing sideways
catercorner: diagonally opposed at an intersection; kitty-corner
contraposed: set in opposition; set against each other
diametrically opposite: extremely opposed
facing: with the face or front in a given direction

fronting: with the face or front in a given direction
heterochiral: having the sides reversed, as in a mirror
heterolateral: concerning opposite sides
inverse: opposite in order
kitty-corner: catercorner
meridional: south; southern
northern: toward the north
opposite: in front of
reverse: turned backwards
septentrional: northern
southern: toward the south
subcontrary: somewhat contrary

Contrast—Opposition—Reversal

á contrecoeur: against the wishes of the heart
adverse: opposing; opposite; averse
antagonistic: opposing; acting against; contending
antipodean: relating to the opposite side of the world
antithalian: against enjoyment
antithetical: strongly contrasted; directly opposite
apotropaic: pertaining to turning aside or averting
as opposite as black and white: directly opposite

as opposite as fire and water: directly opposite
as opposite as light and darkness: directly opposite
as opposite as the poles: directly opposite
at cross purposes: having opposite purposes
bottom upwards: reversed
conflicting: opposing; contending
contraconscientious: against conscience; contraconscient
contradictory: contradictory statements cannot be both true

contranitent: struggling in opposition
contrapletal: polar; complementary
contrariant: opposed; antagonistic
contrarious: showing oppositeness; repugnant
contrary: opposite; adverse
contrasted: opposed; placed in comparison
contrasty: showing great contrasts in visual qualities
converse: turned about so that opposite parts are changed about
counter: opposing
counteracting: action in opposition
countervailing: acting to an equal extent in the opposite direction
dead against: vigorously opposed to
diametrically opposite: opposite as the two extremities of a diameter
differing: directly opposite
hostile: opposed
Hyperion to a satyr: opposing like beauty and ugliness
inconsistent: self-opposing; not agreeing with each other
inside out: reversed
inverse: opposed in order or effect; inverted
inverted: turned in a contrary direction
just the other way: exactly opposite
keel upwards: overturned
negative: opposite of positive

no such thing: not this, but the opposite or the other
not to be thought of: contrary to reason
obverted: turned to show a different surface
on one's head: upside down
opposed: contrary; opposite; adverse
opposing: contrary; antagonistic
opposite: standing, situated, or placed in front of, over, or against
quite the contrary: quite the opposite
quite the reverse: quite the opposite
reactionary: tending to act in an opposite direction; tending to react rashly
recalcitrant: kicking back or against; repugnant
repercussive: reverberated; repellent
retroactive: having reverse action; retrospective
retrorse: turned backwards
reverse: opposite; turned backwards
reverting: turning back
revulsive: tending to cause a sudden change
rovescio: reversed
supine: lying on the back
top-heavy: having the top or upper part too heavy for the lower part; hence, liable to turn or tip over
topsy-turvy: upside down
upside down: with the upper side down
withershins: contrary; against the grain
wrong side out: with the inside out
wrong side up: with the bottom up

Conventional

canonical: pertaining to the canon of scripture
common: to be noticed everywhere or often
conventional: conformity to a fixed standard
exemplary: worthy to be taken as an example
formal: inclined to the observance of forms
habitual: settled by frequent practice
illustrative: serving to illustrate

naturalized: accepted as a citizen of a foreign country; accommodated to new surroundings
nomic: conventional; ordinary
normal: conforming to the general rule of nature
orderly: nicely arranged
ordinary: not above the average
orthodox: in accordance with the established belief
positive: laid down arbitrarily
procrustean: violently forcing into con-

formity, as did Procrustes, an Athenian highwayman who made travelers fit his bed by stretching them or cutting off their legs

regular: following some rule
rigid: not varying
sound: well grounded
strict: rigorous

technical: pertaining to the principles of some profession
typical: marked by the principal characteristics of a group
uncompromising: not conceding anything
usual: customary
vernacular: of usual or typical style

Conversation

alloquial: addressing others; not conversational
chatty: loquacious; gossipy
colloquial: conversational
confabular: conversational
conversable: qualified for conversation; free in discourse
conversational: pertaining to conversation
conversing: holding conversation; interchanging thoughts and opinions in a free, informal manner
discoursive: inclined to converse; containing dialogue or conversation
discursive: passing from one subject to another; wandering away from the point
interlocutory: consisting of or pertaining to dialogue; conversational

Conversion

aliened: converted into a foreigner
born-again: enthusiastically and newly converted
conversible: capable of being converted or transposed
conversive: capable of being converted or changed
converted into: changed into something else
convertible: easily converted
impromptu: converted to use in emergency
naturalized: admitted to citizenship in a nation
reconstructed: converted from a belief
resolvable into: able to be analyzed into
transitional: involving transition

Convexity

arched: shaped like or provided with an arch
bellied: having the shape of a belly
biconvex: convex on two sides; amphicyrtic
bloated: swollen from water or gas
bold: projecting out prominently
bombous: convex; rounded
bossed: ornamented or strengthened with knobs or studs
bosselated: knobbed
bossy: of a bossed nature
bowed: bulged out
bulbiform: bulb-shaped; bulbous
bulbous: swelling like a bud
bunchy: gathered in bunches
clavated: like a club or nail in appearance; clavate
convex: rounded and bulging outward; curved; cupped; cupriform; protuberant
corniform: horn-shaped; cornute
cornute: horn-shaped
gibbous: irregularly round
hemispheric: like a hemisphere
hummocky: rising up like a little hill

in relief: raised or projecting
lenticular: like a lens
lentiform: shaped like a double convex lens
maniform: shaped like a hand
nodular: shaped like nodules
odontoid: toothlike
papulose: marked by papulae
papulous: marked by papulae

projecting: sticking out
prominent: easily noticeable
protuberant: rising up gradually
raised: higher than the surrounding surface
salient: jutting; projecting; protruding; standing out
tuberculous: having tubercles
tuberous: bearing tubers
tumorous: like a tumor

Cooking

à bleu: of meat, very rare
à la carte: designating foods priced and chosen separately by dish
à la Dieppoise: with mussels and shrimp
à la grecque: with olive oil and lemon
à la king: served with cream sauce
à la mode: in the style of; served with ice cream
à l'ail: with garlic
à point: of meat, well done
à saignant: of meat, rare
abroach: of a beverage, tapped or on tap
acetarious: pertaining to plants used in salads
aioli: of a rich sauce of garlic, egg yolk, lemon juice, and olive oil
al burro: served with butter
al dente: of pasta, toothy or firm to the bite
alfresco: eaten outdoors
amandine: served with almonds
amygdalate: made of almonds
anacardic: pertaining to the cashew nut
anglaise: boiled
antipastic: pertaining to appetizers, hors d'oeuvres
arachidic: from the oil of peanuts
argenteuil: with asparagus
au bleu: poached instantly upon being killed
au fromage: with cheese
au gratin: with cheese or a bread crumb crust, often toasted
au jus: served with natural juices
au naturel: uncooked or cooked simply

azymic: pertaining to unleavened bread; azymous
back: designating nonalcoholic drink served on the side with a shot of spirits
baveuse: of cheese and egg dishes, runny
béarnaise: of hollandaise sauce seasoned (as with minced shallots, tarragon, and chervil)
béchamel: with white cream sauce
Bercy: with shallots and parsley
blinky: on the edge of sourness, as milk
bolognese: with meat sauce
boned: without bones, as a fish filet
bourguignon: with red wine, onions or shallots, bacon, and parsley
brut: designating very dry champagne
cacciatore: hunter's style; containing tomatoes, mushrooms, herbs, and other seasonings
carnous: fleshy
caseous: cheeselike; caseic
cenal: referring to the midday meal
cenatory: pertaining to dinner or supper
cereal: pertaining to edible grains
cervisial: pertaining to beer
charpenté: of wine, smooth and fat
chasseur: with brown sauce usually containing tomatoes, mushrooms, shallots, and white wine
chewy: of wine, with a lot of body; densely textured; fleshy; meaty
cibarious: pertaining to food; edible
Clamart: with peas
classically sculptured: of wine, having a well-balanced vintage

closed: of wine, being young and years away from full character

cooking: in the process of being prepared for eating

corked: of wine, smelling of its own cork

corsé: of wine, hard and tannic

Crécy: with carrots

creole: spicy sauce or dish, usually with rice

culinary: pertaining to cooking

dauphine: with straw potatoes

depascent: feeding; eating

devorative: capable of being swallowed whole

dietetic: designating low-calorie food eaten to lose weight

elongated: of wine, having water added; distended; elliptical; extended; lengthened; oblong; oblongitudinal; prolongated; protracted; stretched

en brochette: cut into chunks and broiled on a skewer

en crôte: baked in a crust

espagnole: with brown sauce

estragon: with tarragon

étouffée: smothered

farci: of food that is stuffed

fat: of wine, having an intense, rich quality

flambé: designating a dish served in flaming brandy or other liquor

Florentine: with spinach

forestière: with wild mushrooms, bacon, and potatoes

franconia: of food, browned, as whole potatoes are browned with a roast

frumentaceous: concerning wheat or another grain

full-tilt boogie: of pizza, with everything

Hogen-Mogen: of drink, strong or heady

humming: of a drink, strong

Indienne: with curry

jardiniere: with variety of fresh vegetables

jentacular: pertaining to breakfast

julienne: of food, cut in narrow strips

kosher: prepared according to Jewish dietary laws

lingible: meant to be licked

long-neck: designating beer bottle with a long neck

low-cal: designating cuisine or a dish that is low in calories; lo-cal

lush: full of juice

lyonnaise: with onions

magiric: pertaining to the art of cooking

maigre: of food, containing neither meat nor blood

malic: pertaining to apples

manducable: chewable; edible

marengo: with tomatoes

marinière: cooked in white wine, especially fish

market-ripe: of fruits and vegetables picked before they are ripe

mellisugent: honey-sucking

meunière: with browned butter, lemon, and parsley

Milanese: with cheese

mit Schlag: with whipped cream; mit

Montmorency: with cherries

Mornay: designating a dish served with a white cheese sauce

neat: straight up

Nesselrode: with chestnuts

Newburg: with cream, egg yolk, butter, and paprika sauce

nicoise: with olives or olive oil, capers, anchovies, etc.

normande: cooked with cider and cream

nucal: pertaining to nuts

O'Brien: of vegetables, sauteed with pimentos and diced green peppers

omphacine: pertaining to unripe fruit

over-easy: describing a fried egg that is flipped over and cooked briefly before serving

panary: pertaining to bread

papillote: wrapped and cooked in greased paper or foil

parmentier: with potatoes

Perigord: with truffles

piccata: with lemon and parsley, also sometimes with capers

popinal: pertaining to bars, restaurants

postcibal: after dinner; postcenal, postprandial

postprandial: after a meal, especially dinner; postcenal, postcibal

pricked: of wine that has turned to vinegar

Provençale: with tomatoes, garlic, onions, and herbs

racked: of wine or beer that has been separated from its lees

rare: cooked briefly, especially meat

ripieno: stuffed

rissole: browned by frying in deep fat

riziform: like a grain of rice

rosorial: persistent, repeated biting, chewing, or nibbling

savory: piquant and not sweet

sec: dry, designating wine, usually white

seeded: with seeds removed

self-service: designating restaurant in which one takes food from serving area to table

semese: half-eaten

short: crisp, flaky, and crumbling, especially pastry

soft: designating wine and beer, as opposed to hard liquor

stiff: strong, in describing drink; high in alcoholic content

straight up: designating an alcoholic drink without mixer or a chilled drink without ice, such as a martini; neat

stroganoff: with sour cream and mushrooms

subgum: prepared with mixed vegetables in Chinese style

succulent: pertaining to thick, fleshy, juicy plants

sunnyside up: describing an egg fried on one side only

sweet: describing fruity wines, opposite of dry

sweet-and-sour: designating a Chinese-style dish of meat, seafood, etc., cooked in a sugar and vinegar sauce

tandoori: baked in a clay tandoor oven

tenellous: somewhat tender, as meat

to go: describing food bought at a restaurant to eat at home

ullaged: of a bottle or cask's spilled, consumed, or evaporated contents

vacuum-packed: sealed in a jar or can with nearly all air evacuated before sealing to preserve freshness

vapeur: of food, steamed

vegetarian: describing meals or cuisine without meat, chicken, or fish

Véronique: garnished with white grapes

vindemial: pertaining to vintage

well-done: thoroughly cooked until all redness is gone, especially meat

well-succeeded: of wines that have fulfilled the expectation of their vintage

worn: of wine that has been too long in the bottle

Cooperation

at one with: agreed

banded together: confederated

coadjutant: working together

coadjuvant: working together

concurrent: occurring or acting together

concurring: coming together in opinion or action

cooperating: working together

favorable to: inclined to

in alliance with: in agreement with

in cooperation: helping; assisting

in league: in cooperation

of one mind: agreed

propitious: favorably inclined; boding well

unopposed: without opposition

Costliness

avanious: extortionate
costly: paid for with a big price
dear: sold for a high price
dearbought: bought at a high price
dispendious: expensive
exorbitant: marked by a desire to get more than is reasonable
expensive: costing much

extortionate: oppressive
extravagant: immoderately high
high: costing more than usual
impretiable: invaluable; priceless
precious: having great inherent value
priceless: worth a great deal
sumptuous: luxurious; costly
unreasonable: too high in price

Country

agrestic: unpolished; uncouth; rustic
arcadian: ideally rural or simple; pertaining to a simple, untroubled existence
bucolic: pastoral; rustic; rural
country: of, or pertaining to, the region outside a city
georgic: agricultural and rural; rustic
pastoral: pertaining to the life of shepherds and rustics

poimenic: pertaining to pastoral care
rural: rustic
rurigenous: born or living in the country; rustic
rustic: rude; country
rusticated: rendered rustic in appearance
villatic: rural; rustic

Cover

antipudic: covering one's genitals
apatetic: camouflaged
armor-plated: faced with armor plate
barbellate: hairy; covered with bristles
conchiferous: producing or characterized by shells
conchitic: made of shells; having numerous shells
conchological: pertaining to conchology (shells)
cortical: pertaining to the bark
covered: having a covering
covering: over the top of
cutaneous: pertaining to the skin
cuticular: pertaining to the outer coat of the skin
cyanotic: having bluish skin
decorticated: deprived of bark; flayed; skinned
deric: pertaining to skin
dermal: pertaining to the lower layer of the skin
desquamate: shedding scales

dough-faced: having a mask or false face
echinulate: covered with small bristles or spines
enameled: covered with gloss
encrusted: covered with crust
encuirassed: covered with a hard surface or hard plates
flue: fluffed; flocked; covered with down
furfuraceous: covered with dandruff or small scales
galericulate: covered with a hat
imbricate: having overlapping pieces; imbricated; obvolute
imbricated: covered with overlapping scales
incanous: covered with soft white hair
ironclad: covered with iron
lanuginous: downy; covered with soft downy hair
lepidote: covered with flaky scales
lined: covered with a lining
loricated: covered with a shell or plates
lutose: covered with mud

overlaid: covered with another substance
pastose: covered with thick paint
plumulaceous: downy; covered with small feathers
procryptic: camouflaged
rorulent: covered with dew
scaled: having overlapping circles or semicircles; perulate
scaly: covered with scales
scurfy: pertaining to or covered with dandruff
skinny: lacking in flesh to make the form plump; covered with skin
squamaceous: having scales, like a reptile; squamous
squamate: having scales; squamose; squamous

squamous: covered with scales
stegocephalic: having a covered head, capped; stegocephalous
stimulose: covered with stinging hairs
strigillose: covered with stiff hairs; bristly; strigose
stupulose: covered with fine, short hairs
superincumbent: lying or pressing on; atop
superjacent: lying above; superincumbent
tegumentary: resembling a tegument
tomentose: covered with densely matted hair
under cover: covered

Cowardice

caitiff: mean; cowardly
chicken: having lost one's nerve
chickenhearted: cowardly as a chicken
cowardly: wanting in courage; proceeding in fear
cradden: cowardly; craddon
dastardly: cowardly
feigning: shirking; cowardly

hilding: mean; cowardly
imbellious: unwarlike; cowardly
milk-livered: cowardly; fainthearted
niddering: cowardly
recreant: cowardly; afraid
with feet of clay: displaying cowardice

Craft—Cunning

acute: quick to see and understand
arch: roguish
artful: full of art
artificial: affected; unnatural
astute: characterized by acuteness and finese
Byzantine: underhanded; of complicated scheming
cagey: shrewd; especially cautious not be entrapped
calculated: carefully thought out to accomplish an end
callid: cunning; crafty
canny: clever, calculating, or shrewd; cautious
captious: designed to confuse or ensnare, especially in argument
cautelous: crafty; sly

circuitous: indirect or evasive in deeds or language
cloak-and-dagger: pertaining to melodrama, intrigue, and espionage
contriving: planning
convoluted: tortuously involved, complex, or confusing
crafty: displaying craft
crooked: deceitful and dishonest
cunning: possessing cunning
deceitful: full of deceit
deep: not easily seen into
designing: laying artful plans for the future
diplomatic: marked by diplomacy
disingenuous: artful; scheming; deceptive
feline: sly like a cat

insidious: practicing underhandedness
while appearing friendly
intriguing: practicing intrigue
knowing: possessing more knowledge of
some kinds than is desirable
leery: shrewd and sly
lubricious: slippery; tricky
Machiavellian: devious, cunning, or
unscrupulous
pawky: cunning; shrewd; arch
politic: self-seeking
political: adept at influencing and ma-
nipulating allies and adversaries
profound: deep
sharp: quickness to perceive
shrewd: astute; keen; clever
skillful: using skill
slippery: untrustworthy, devious, or
tricky

sly: observing and acting in a furtive
manner
sneckdrawing: sly; crafty
sportive: playful or mischievous
stealthy: sly
strategic: marked by strategem
subdolous: somewhat crafty; sly
subtle: exhibiting subtlety
surreptitious: sneaky; sly
tactical: strategic
thick: in an intimate, often secret, association with someone
tricksy: given to playing tricks
tricky: given to playing tricks
underhand: private; secret
unwholesome: corrupt
vafrous: shrewd; cunning
venal: open to corruption and bribery
vulpine: foxlike; crafty; cunning; sly
wily: showing guile

Creation

autofuctiferous: self-productive;
parthenogenic
big with: pregnant
biparous: bearing twins
brought to bed with: confined to bed
with childbirth
creative: having the power to create or
produce
Daedalian: ingeniously made; cunningly
contrived; daedal
double-ribbed: pregnant
enascent: being born
enceinte: pregnant
formative: having power to form or
shape
fraught with: laden or charged with
genetic: pertaining to creation or
generation
genetical: genetic
genital: pertaining to the reproductive
organs of animals
gestant: pregnant
gonemous: bearing many children

in the family way: soon to give birth to
a child
in the straw: in childbed
inchoate: recently begun; not completely
formed
indigenous: originating in a place or
country
ingenious: cleverly contrived; clever
novitious: new; just invented
parous: having borne a child
parturient: bringing forth young
parturifacient: inducing childbirth
poietic: creative; productive; active
pregnant: big with child; fruitful
produced: generated; brought into
existence
producing: generating; bringing into
existence
productive of: having the power of
producing
prolific: producing abundantly
puerperal: pertaining to childbirth
puerperous: bearing children
teeming: prolific; produced in
abundance

Credit

accredited: credited with

auctorizate: accredited; autorizate

bailable: admitting of bail

chalked up: ascribed; credited

credential: accrediting

credible: deserving of credit; reputable

creditable: deserving of credit; bringing esteem

credited: placed to one's credit

crediting: giving credit

honest: bringing honor; creditable

respectable: of a superior kind; creditable

Credulousness

childish: believing like a child

confiding: trusting one's secrets or opinions to another

credulous: ready to believe

green: inexperienced, so as to be easily imposed upon

gullible: easily cheated

infatuous: easily drawn to

overconfident: too confident

overcredulous: too credulous

silly: acting so as to show lack of judgment or experience

simple: trusting because of lack of knowledge

soft: simple

stupid: easily deceived

superstitious: given to superstition

unfledged: inexperienced

Crossing

areolar: having interstices like the areolae

barred: marked with lines drawn across

cancellated: like a lattice

compital: pertaining to a crossroads

crisscross: having crossed lines; cancellate; crisscrossed; crosscut; reticulate; reticulated

cross: not in the same direction

crossed: placed crosswise

crosshatched: having crossing sets of parallel lines

crossing: running in different directions through or near

crucial: intersecting

decussate: intersected; crossed like an X; chiasmal; decussated

grated: made like grates

matted: twined together

reticular: having a netlike pattern; reticulated

retiform: net-shaped; reticular

strabismic: cross-eyed

streaked: marked with streaks

strigose: streaked

textile: capable of being woven

transverse: crosswise

Crudeness

abrupt: breaking off suddenly

affected: having assumed something not one's own

artificial: not natural

barbarous: violating the rule of purity in rhetoric

cramped: limited

crude: not skillfully finished

dry: not interesting

euphemistic: describing an unpleasant fact by a softened expression

formal: marked by the observance of form or style

graceless: lacking grace

grotesque: ridiculously odd

halting: hesitating

harsh: unpleasant to the ear

inelegant: not elegant

labored: not proceeding easily
mannered: practicing bad manners
offensive to polite ears: inelegant or offensive of speech
ponderous: lacking in animation; weighty

rude: unskilled in make or action
stiff: not elastic
turgid: bombastic
uncouth: not gracefully developed
ungraceful: not graceful

Cry

clamant: urgent in the call for help
clamorous: making a great disorderly shouting
conclamant: shouting together; calling out in unison
conjubilant: shouting together in joy
crying: wailing; weeping
gemebund: incessantly moaning
hinnible: able to whinny or neigh
hylactic: like barking

latrant: barking
mugient: bellowing; lowing
openmouthed: clamorous
pipient: piping; chirping
plangorous: wailing
remugient: shouting again; resounding
stentorian: extremely loud, like Homer's Stentor
vagient: crying like a child
vociferous: vehement in shouting

Curvation

aquiline: like an eagle; curved or hooked like an eagle's beak
barrel-vaulted: arched and rounded; cylindrically vaulted
bell-shaped: shaped like a bell
bombé: with an outward swelling
bowed: bent over
bowlegged: having the legs bent in an outward curve
cardioid: heart-shaped
circular: like a circle
concamerated: vaulted
concavo-convex: more curved on the concave than the convex side
conchoidal: in the form of a conchoid
convexo-concave: more curved on the convex than the concave side
cordate: heart-shaped; cordated
cordiform: heart-shaped
crescentic: crescent-shaped
crump: crooked
curvate: having a curve or curves; arciform; arcing; bowed; curviform; curvilineal; curvilinear
curved: in the shape of a curve
curviform: in the shape of a curve

curvilineal: in the shape of a curve
curvilinear: in the shape of a curve
curvulate: slightly curved
cusped: of two branches curving to a point
devex: bending down
devious: departing from the regular course
downcurved: curved downward; decurvate; decurved; downturned
excurved: curved outward; excurvate
falcate: curved like a sickle; crescent-shaped; falcated; falcicular; falciculate; falciform
ficiform: fig-shaped; caricous; ficicoid
fig-shaped: shaped like a fig; ficiform
heart-shaped: in the form of a heart
hooked: curving back toward itself
incurved: curved inward; aduncous; hooked; incurvate; involute
involute: curled or coiled inward
lenticular: in the form of a double convex lens; lentiform; lentoid
lentiform: in the form of a double convex lens
looped: curved and almost closed
lunette: shaped like a half-moon

luniform: moon-shaped

lunular: moon-shaped

meniscal: crescent-shaped; crescentic; crescentiform; meniscate; menisciform; meniscoid

meniscoid: crescent-shaped; concavo-convex

oblique: slanting

obpyriform: shaped like an upside-down pear

pear-shaped: shaped like a pear

procurved: curved forward

recurved: curved backward; recurvate

recurvous: curved back

reniform: kidney-shaped; nephroid

retroflex: bent or curled back; cacuminal

saber-legged: curved

semicircular: of the form of a half-circle; hemicyclic

semilunar: of the form of a half-moon

sigmoidal: curved in two directions

sweeping: having a long curving outline or contour

upcurved: curved upward; arched; arcuate; concamerated; upturned; vaulted

vaulted: in the form of a vault

Dampness

dabbled: moistened by little dips
damp: between dry and wet
dank: moist; damp; imbrued; roral; rorid
dewy: moist with dew
dripping: falling in drops
humectant: retaining moisture
humid: somewhat wet
irriguous: watery; moist
juicy: full of juice
lipper: wet
lopper: slushy
madescent: growing damp
moist: slightly wet
muddy: turbid with mud
muggy: damp; moist
ombrophilous: able to withstand a lot of rain
reeking: emitting vapor
roral: dewy; roric
roric: creating dew
rorid: bedewed
roscid: containing dew
sammy: clammy; damp
saturated: penetrated with moisture
sloppy: wet; muddy; especially wet so as to spatter easily
soaking: completely wet
sodden: saturated or heavy with moisture; very wet; suffused
soft: made to yield to pressure by the presence of moisture
soggy: soaked with water
swampy: like a swamp; low and wet
swashy: soft, like overripe fruit
undried: not dried
uvid: moist or wet
watery: full of water
wet: moistened by water
wet through: thoroughly wet
wet to the skin: thoroughly wet
wringing wet: thoroughly wet
xerophilous: drought-resistant

Dance

assoluta: extraordinary
couru: running
dancing: related to rhythmical movements
en arrière: to the back; backwards
en avant: to the front; forward
en dedans: moving arms or legs inward, toward body
en dehors: moving arms or legs outward, away from body
en face: facing body directly forward
en l'air: performed off the ground

en seconde: performed in second position
heel-and-toe: pertaining to locked-knee step in which the heel of one foot touches ground before the toe of other foot leaves it
orchestic: pertaining to dancing
par terre: performed on the ground
penché: leaning forward
saltatory: pertaining to dancing
soutenu: sustained, especially of battement rising into fifth position demi-pointe with equal weight on both legs
tendu: stretched and extended straight, especially a leg
terpsichorean: pertaining to dancing
tripudiary: pertaining to dancing

Darkness

Acherontic: dark; gloomy; forbidding
aphotic: lightless
benighted: shrouded in darkness
black: destitute of light
blae: dismal; sunless
caliginous: obscure; dark; veiled
cimmerian: dark; gloomy; forbidding
cloudy: dim; not clear
cockshut: pertaining to twilight
crepuscular: pertaining to morning twilight
dark: destitute of or not radiating or reflecting light
dark as a pit: very dark
dark as Erebus: very dark
dark as pitch: very dark
darkened: made dark
darkling: without light
darksome: gloomy; obscure
dingy: of a dark or dusky color
dusky: dark; gloomy; almost black
gloomy: dark
lightless: without light
lurid: gloomy; dismal
melanic: of dark hair or complexion; melanotic
murksome: dark, obscure, and gloomy
murky: gloomy, dark, and obscure
noctivagant: wandering about at night
noctivagous: wandering about at night
nocturnal: pertaining to the night
obscure: darkened; imperfectly illuminated
overcast: covered with gloom; darkened
phaeochrous: dark skinned
pitch-dark: very dark
pitchy: black; dark; dismal
shady: abounding with shade; overspread with shade
sombre: dull; gloomy; dark; under a shade
sombrous: dull; gloomy; dark; under a shade
subfusc: dark; dusky; subfuscous
sunless: shaded; destitute of the sun's rays
swarthy: having dark skin; swart
tenebrious: gloomy; dark; tenebrous
tenebrous: dark; obscure; gloomy; tenebrious
thestral: dark; dim
umbrageous: shady; obscure
unilluminated: not lighted up

Deafness

deaf: lacking the sense of hearing
deaf as a beetle: entirely deaf
deaf as a post: entirely deaf
deaf as a trunk-maker: entirely deaf
deafened: made deaf
dull of hearing: lacking some power of hearing
earless: without ears; deaf
hard of hearing: having one's hearing powers impaired
inaudible: without sound
out of hearing: too far away to be heard
stone-deaf: totally deaf
stunned: overpowered as to one's sense of hearing
surd: deaf

Death

amort: at the point of death; as if dead; lifeless

anabiotic: apparently dead but capable of being revived

antemortem: preceding death

asleep: dead; into the state of death

at death's door: close to death

at peace: dead

at the last gasp: close to death

at the point of death: close to death

booked: doomed to die

burial: pertaining to a funeral or burial

buried: interred; put into the grave

cinerary: pertaining to ashes

commorient: dying together

condemned: sentenced to death for crimes committed

dead: deprived of life; inanimate; not living

dead and gone: quite dead

dead as a doornail: quite dead

deadly: causing death; fatal; likely to cause death

deathlike: deadly; fatal; resembling death

deceased: dead; departed from this life

defunct: dead; deceased

defunctive: pertaining to death

demised: pertaining to the death of a distinguished person

departed: having left; gone; dead

departed this life: dead

dying: about to die; approaching death; pertaining to death; perishing

eclipsed: having died

eighty-sixed: dead, especially killed

elapsed: having died

elegiac: expressing sorrow or lamentation

encharnelled: buried

exanimate: deprived of animation

extinct: no longer living, especially of a species

fey: fated to die

funebrial: pertaining to burial; mournful

funerary: associated with burial

funereal: pertaining to burial; mournful

gathered to one's fathers: dead

given over: given to death

going: dying

going off: dying

gone: departed; dead

Hippocratic: pertaining to the change produced in the face by death, long illness, or the like

iced: dead, especially from unnatural causes

in extremis: at the point of death; in grave circumstances

in the agony of death: in the death struggle

in the jaws of death: at the point of death

inanimate: not living; deprived of animation

infernal: relating to or inhabiting the eternal inferno of hell

intestate: without a valid will at time of death

late: recently deceased, used as reference with person's name

launched into eternity: suddenly killed; dead

lethal: deadly

lifeless: without life; deprived of life

lost: dead

moribund: at the point of death; at the point of coming to an end; dying

morient: dying

mortal: causing or liable to cause death

mortuary: belonging or pertaining to the burial of the dead

mortuous: deathlike

near one's end: close to death

no more: dead; departed

numbered with the dead: dead

on one's deathbed: dying

on one's last legs: near death

out of the world: dead

peace-parted: having left the world in peace

posthumous: occurring after one's death

post-obit: effective after particular person's death

pretelethal: after death; postmortem

released: dead; freed from life

sepelible: ready for burial

smabbled: killed in battle; snabbled

stillborn: dead at birth

taken off: having died

terminal: dying, especially from fatal illness

testate: having made and left a valid will

thanatoid: deathlike; apparently dead

tottering on the brink of the grave: at the point of death

with one foot in the grave: close to death

Debt

bankrupt: unable to pay one's debts

beggared: reduced to a beggar; impoverished

behindhand: in arrears

chargeable: liable to be made responsible for some debt

debtable: under pecuniary obligation

due: payable because of the expiration of the time agreed upon

gazetted: officially announced as a debtor

gratis: freely

in arrears: in debt

in debt: owing

in the gazette: publicly announced as a debtor

incumbered: burdened with debts; encumbered

indebted: owing

insolvent: unable to pay debts when due

involved: burdened, as with debt

liable: responsible

minus: lacking

not paying: defaulting

outstanding: unpaid

owing: to be paid

pecuniary: pertaining to money matters and obligations

sperate: of debts, likely to be paid

unable to make both ends meet: to be in debt

unpaid: not paid

unremunerated: without pay

unrequited: not repaid

unrewarded: not rewarded

worse than nothing: worthless

Deceit—Fraud

ad captandum: to catch; for catching

adulterated: rendered counterfeit

artificial: produced by art to imitate nature

babyshed: deceived by childish tales

barefaced: unscrupulous; not concealing one's vices

bastard: not genuine; false; spurious

bogus: counterfeit; fraudulent; spurious

brummagem: cheap and showy; spurious; bogus

calophantic: pretending or deceiving with a show of excellence

catchpenny: cheap; poor; showy; deceptive in appearance

catchy: clever and beguiling, often tricky

colorable: specious; plausible; deceptive

contraband: falling under public edict

counterfeit: made to resemble something else; pretended

covinous: collusive; fraudulent

cunning: having or exercising craft or shrewdness

deceitful: characterized by deception

deceived: misled by falsehood or deceit

deceiving: misleading

deceptious: calculated to deceive

deceptive: having power or tendency to deceive

delusive: misleading; deceptive

delusory: tending to mislead; deceptive

devious: scheming, cunning, or deceptive

disguised: changed in appearance by unusual arrangement of hair, by mask, or by dress

double-dealing: marked by duplicity; deceitful

elusive: fallacious; using deception to escape

ersatz: artificial; fake; synthetic; simulated

factitious: proceeding from or created by art as opposed to nature; artificial

fair-weather: loyal only during good times

faithless: disloyal; deceitful

faulted: having deficiencies, lack, defects

feigned: simulated; pretended

fraudulent: based on, proceeding from, or characterized by fraud

fucatory: counterfeit; deceitful

illegitimate: spurious; not genuine

ill-gotten: acquired by improper or evil means

illicit: prohibited by law or custom; not permitted or authorized

illusive: deceiving or misleading by allusion or false appearance

illusory: deceiving or tending to deceive, as by false appearance

insidious: designed to draw another into a trap or fraud; treacherous

make-believe: pretended; imagined

meretricious: deceitfully and artfully attractive

mock: merely imitating the reality; counterfeit; assumed

parlous: dangerously shrewd and cunning

pawky: cunning or crafty

pinchbeck: made of pinchbeck; not genuine; cheap

predatory: preying upon or living off others

prestigiatory: juggling; delusive

prestigious: of or pertaining to sleight of hand; deceptive

pretended: making a false appearance; affected

pseudo: false

rotten at the core: apparently good but bad in reality

scamped: made dishonestly

sham: not genuine or real; pretended

simulated: assumed; having a false appearance

so-called: called, but perhaps doubtfully so

sophisticated: obscure with specious reasoning

spurious: not proceeding from the proper source or from the source pretended; not genuine; counterfeit

supposititious: imaginary; unreal; counterfeit; false; phony

surreptitious: accomplished by secret and improper means

tinsel: superficially brilliant

tricky: deceitful; knavish

trumped-up: invented for a fraudulent purpose

two-faced: double-dealing; inconstant in allegiance; hypocritical

unconscionable: unscrupulous; done without conscience

unscrupulous: lacking principles; willing to do anything to achieve one's goal

unsound: not sound; defective; unreal

unsupported by evidence: seemingly untrue

untrue: lacking truth; false

wildcat: financially reckless and conducted in violation of normal business practices

Decrease

ablatitious: lessening; diminishing; subtractive

astringent: causing flesh to draw together

compact: placed close together

compressible: able to be compressed

contracted: drawn together

contractile: having the quality of contraction

contracting: drawing together

deaccessioned: removed from an exhibit

or the records of a museum, library, etc., usually in order to sell the item

decreased: lessened; diminished

decreasing: diminishing; lessening

decrescent: decreasing gradually; waning as the moon

epitomistic: condensed; quite cogent

on the wane: waning; decreasing in size, brightness, or importance

pungled: shrunken or shriveled

smaller: of less size

strangulated: constricted

stunted: checked in growth

subtracted: taken away from

subtractive: having power to subtract

unexpanded: undeveloped

waning: decreasing

Deepness

abysmal: deep; profound; pertaining to an abyss

ankle-deep: reaching to the ankle

bottomless: without a bottom

buried: covered up; deep in the earth

catachtonian: underground; catachthonic; subterranean

deep: extending far below the surface

deep as a well: having the same depth as a well

deep-seated: having the seat far down

ebbless: not decreasing in depth

fathomless: not to be measured

hypogeal: subterranean; underground, especially pertaining to living or constructing underground

knee-deep: deep enough to extend to the knee

profound: deep in meaning

soundless: that can not be sounded

subaqueous: adapted for use under water

subliminal: below the threshold of consciousness

submarine: relative to the lower part of the sea, like submarine divers

submerged: sunk down so as to be covered

subterranean: under the surface of the earth

subterrene: under the surface of the earth

sunk: fallen down; in

underground: below the surface of the earth

unfathomable: not to be measured for depth

unfathomed: not measured

unplumbed: very deep

Defamation—Derision—Scorn

abusive: coarse and rude in reproach

black-mouthed: foul and abusive

bumptious: full of offensive self-conceit

calumniatory: containing a false, malicious report or accusation

calumnious: containing a false, malicious report or accusation; insulting; abusive

cavalier: haughty; slighting; supercilious

contemptible: worthy of scorn or disdain

contemptuous: showing contempt or disdain

contumelious: haughtily reproachful; insolent

cynical: contemptuous of others's doings and opinions

defamatory: tending to bring disrepute upon

derisive: mocking; ridiculing

derogatory: disparaging; contemptuous

despicable: that should be despised; contemptible

despised: considered as mean or worthless

detracting: lessening the estimation of

detractory: tending to lessen the estimation of

disdainful: full of disdain; scornful

disparaging: tending to injure by unfavorable comparison

downtrodden: abused by superior power; treated with contempt

foulmouthed: using obscene and abusive language

foul-tongued: using obscene and abusive language

haughty: proud and disdainful

libelous: containing anything damaging to character

maledicent: addicted to vicious, abusive speech

opprobrious: insulting; abusive

pejorative: derogatory; disparaging

pilgarlicky: pitiable

pitiable: contemptible; paltry

pitiful: contemptible; paltry

sarcastic: exhibiting contemptuous language

sardonic: having a forced, sneering laugh or smile

satirical: containing irony

scorned: treated or regarded with contempt

scornful: full of scorn or contempt

scurrile: gross or vile in speech

scurrilous: abusive; insulting; derisive

slanderous: containing false tales or reports

sniffy: disdainful; haughty

supercilious: haughty; scornful; with an air of superiority; condescending; haughty; stuck-up; superior; overbearing; arrogant

thersitical: insulting; abusive in language

turpid: foul; nasty; vile

unenvied: contemptible

vilipendious: insulting; abusive; vilipensive

vituperative: insulting; abusive

wanky: contemptible

withering: blighting

Defense

alleged: asserted to be true

apagogic: pertaining to a proof by reductio ad absurdum (indirect demonstration of proof)

apologetic: said or written in defense of

armed: furnished with weapons

armed at all points: completely armed

armed cap-a-pie: armed from head to foot

ballproof: invulnerable to balls from firearms

casemated: furnished with a bombproof covering

castellated: built in the style of a castle

defended: guarded; protected

defending: guarding; protecting

defensive: serving to protect or defend

gas-operated: using some of the exhaust gases to operate action

ironclad: protected or covered with iron

iron-plated: covered with iron

loaded: containing ammunition or explosive charge

loopholed: provided with loopholes

machicolated: having holes through the floor for discharging weapons

magnum: designating a cartridge equipped with a larger charge than other cartidges of comparable size

mural: resembling a wall

panoplied: dressed in complete armor

proof against: able to resist

pump-action: designating manually operated repeating shotgun or rifle; slide-action

single-action: designating firearm that requires cocking of hammer before firing each shot

slide-action: designating rifle or shotgun with mechanism that ejects shell case and cocks and reloads firearm when slid back and forth quickly; pump-action

smoothbore: having a grooveless, unrifled bore

to the teeth: in open opposition

Deficiency—Lack

anaphrodisiac: tending to reduce sexual desire

anaphroditious: lacking sexual desire

at a low ebb: in a low condition

at the end of one's tether: at the end of one's resources

bare: without ornament, as bare walls

crude: unfinished

defective: lacking a part

deficient: below the standard, or less than there ought to be

denuded of: stripped of its covering or appendages

destitute of: without that which is necessary or desirable

devoid of: without that which naturally does or may belong there

docked: curtailed

drained: empty of wealth, resources

dry: free from moisture; lacking interest

empty: containing nothing

empty-handed: without help or resources

extravasated: drained or pumped out

failing: wanting

famine-stricken: suffering from famine; said of a people or land

famished: suffering or dead from lack of nourishment, especially food

garbled: to pick out parts to serve a purpose

going on: in process of completion

half-and-half: being half one thing and half another

half-starved: deprived of food

hollow: containing an empty space

hungry: feeling pain from want of food

ill-furnished: not well fitted out

ill-off: poor or unfortunate

ill-provided: not having much on hand, or not in a state of readiness

ill-stored: poorly supplied

imperfect: not complete in all its parts

in arrears: unpaid though due

in debt: owing something

in default: incompleted

in hand: in process of being made

in progress: unfinished

in want: lacking

inadequate: not adequate

incompetent: not competent

incomplete: not finished

insufficient: not sufficient

jejune: devoid of life, point, or interest

lacking: wanting; not sufficient

lame: imperfect; unsatisfactory

lopped: cutoff

manqué: unrealized; unfulfilled

meager: deficient in quantity or quality

mutilated: crippled

not enough: lacking

not to be had: scarce

not to be had at any price: very scarce

not to be had for love or money: very scarce

out of: without

perfunctory: done without interest or zeal

poor: lacking the means of a comfortable subsistence

proceeding: in the process

scant: scarcely enough

scarce: not abundant enough for the need or demand

scrimp: short; scanty

scurvy: vile; mean; low; vulgar

short: defective

short of: incomplete; lacking

sketchy: containing only an outline

slack: lacking diligence, promptness, speed

spare: scanty; thin; lean

sparing: slight

starved: suffering or dead from hunger

starveling: failing to meet the needs or requirements

stingy: meanly ungenerous

stinted: limited

thin: not crowded, abundant, or thick

too little: not enough

truncated: cut short

uncompleted: not finished

unequal to: inadequate for the purpose

unfed: without proper nourishment

unfinished: incomplete

unfulfilled: in a manner that is not fulfilled

unfurnished: not fitted up

unprovided: not in a state of readiness; with nothing on hand

unreplenished: without being filled up again

unstored: not collected together

unsupplied: without supplies

untreasured: despoiled of treasure

vacant: to be unoccupied

wanting: deficient

weighed in the balances and found wanting: lacking a necessary qualification

without resources: without that which can be turned to aid

Deformity

askew: obliquely

awry: turned to one side

bandy: crooked outward at the knees

bandy-legged: crooked outward at the knees; bowlegged

bloated: morbidly enlarged

bloodshot: red and inflamed

bobtailed: having a short tail or a tail cut off

bow-kneed: having the legs bent in an outward curve

bowlegged: having the legs bent in an outward curve

bunchbacked: having a bunch on the back; crookbacked

claudicant: limping; lame

clubfooted: having a congenital distortion of the feet

couped: cutoff; with just the head showing

cratered: having bowllike depressions

crooked: considerably bent

crooked as a rainbow: having a long curve or bend

crookbacked: stooped; croocked

crump: crooked

curtailed of one's fair proportions: deformed

decollated: cut off at the neck

deformed: marred or distorted in form

discolored: having an unnatural color

distorted: twisted out of shape

foveate: pitted; pockmarked

freckled: covered with spots

gaunt: lean, as with fasting or suffering

gnarled: having bent, knobby, or deformed fingers

grotesque: ludicrously misshapen

hipshot: having one hip lower than the other; sprained or dislocated in the hip

hip-skeltered: askew, crooked, or irregular

humpbacked: crookbacked

hunchbacked: crookbacked

ill-made: not well made

ill-proportioned: not well proportioned

imperfect: not complete

injured: hurt; not perfect

irregular: not consistent throughout; not according to the usual rule

knock-kneed: having the legs bent inward at the knees

kyphotic: humpbacked

mammoxed: seriously mangled; injured

misbegotten: irregularly or unlawfully begotten

misproportioned: badly proportioned

misshapen: badly shapen

not straight: crooked

not true: not precisely right or accurately adjusted

on one side: obliquely set

out of shape: deformed

pitted: marked with hollows

pouty: having the lower lip sticking out a bit; truculent

round-shouldered: having an unnatural turn of the shoulders

scalene: having no two sides equal; said of triangles

skew-jawed: having a crooked jaw; agee-jawed

snub-nosed: having a short and slightly turned-up nose

splayfooted: having the foot turned outward

stumpy: short and thick

taliped: clubfooted

uloid: scarlike

unsymmetric: misshapen

wapper-jawed: having a crooked jaw

warped: bent or twisted off its plane; buckled

wry: bent to one side; distorted

wry-rumped: deformed in the lower back

Dejection

a cup too low: not to have drunk enough to be in good spirits

a prey to melancholy: melancholic

at a low ebb: in the lowest or weakest condition

atrabilious: melancholic; morbid; atrabiliar

bearish: like a bear; ill-tempered

bilious: ill-natured

black-browed: sullen

borne-down: oppressed by sorrow or disappointment

bowed-down: overcome by sorrow or disappointment

broken-down: overcome by sorrow or disappointment

brokenhearted: overcome by sorrow or disappointment

careworn: tired and worn with care

cheerless: without cheer or comfort

chopfallen: chapfallen; disheartened; discouraged

clouded: gloomy

clouded over: made gloomy

comfortless: in want or distress

crestfallen: dispirited

cross-grained: hard to please

crusty: curt in manner or speech

cut-up: badly used; broken in spirit

dark: gloomy

dashed: disappointed

dejected: depressed or humbled; low-spirited

demure: having a grave or sober bearing

depressed: held down

depressing: causing depression or low spirits

desolate: forsaken; sad and lonely

despondent: with a despairing look; hopeless

desponding: gloomy

disaffected: discontented; disloyal or un-friendly to authority

disappointing: that frustrates an expectation or desire

disconsolate: not to be comforted or consoled; hopelessly sad

discontented: not contented

discouraged: having lost heart

disheartened: having lost all spirit and courage

dismal: very gloomy

disquixotted: disillusioned

dissatisfied: displeased

dissentient: not agreeing

doleful: mournful

dolent: sad

dolesome: mournful

dorty: bad-tempered; sullen

dour: gloomy; stern; obstinate

down in the mouth: dejected

down on one's luck: disappointed

downcast: downhearted

downfallen: dejected

downhearted: somewhat discouraged

downtrodden: entirely disheartened

dreadful: full of fear or dread

dreary: lonely and cheerless

dull as a beetle: cheerless and gloomy

dull as ditchwater: cheerless and gloomy

dumpish: given to have the dumps

dyspeptic: malcontent; disgruntled
dysthymic: chronically sad or depressed
epicedian: sad; mournful; funereal; edpicedial
exacting: too severe in making demands
exigent: requiring immediate help
farouche: sullen; shy; antisocial
flat: dull; spiritless
forlorn: without help or friends in time of need
frowning: gloomy; disapproving
funereal: sad; mournful
gloomy: taking a sad view of matters
glum: sullen and silent
grave as a judge: sober
grave as a mustard pot: serious and solemn
grave as an undertaker: serious and solemn
grim: having a worried or depressed expression; of stern countenance; gloomy; grave; long-faced; saturnine; solemn; unsmiling
grim-faced: stern and forbidding in aspect
grim-visaged: stern and forbidding in aspect
grum: morose; sour
hangdog: sad
heartsick: extremely depressed in spirits; very despondent; deeply grieved
heart-stricken: overwhelmed with grief
heavyhearted: sad; despondent
hipped: melancholy; depressed
hypercritical: excessively critical
hypochondriacal: having morbid melancholy
hyppish: depressed; low in spirits
ill at ease: restless
in bad humor: in an ill temper
in despair: utterly hopeless
in doleful dumps: like Witherington in Chevy Chase who, when his legs were smitten off, fought upon his stumps
in low spirits: disheartened; discouraged
in tears: weeping
in the doldrums: gloomy
in the dumps: gloomy; glum

in the suds: in trouble or distress, as on washing day
in the sulks: in a state of ill humor
inconsolable: not to be comforted
infelicific: causing unhappiness
insatiate: never satisfied
jaundiced: envious
jawfallen: dejected; chapfallen
joyless: dull and solemn
lackadaisical: listless
lacrymose: sad; ready to shed tears
lamentable: sorrowful
latrant: snarling; complaining
liversick: heartsick
long-faced: despondent
lost: bewildered; perplexed
lowering: sullen; angry
low-spirited: depressed
luctiferous: bringing sorrow
luctual: mournful; sorrowful
lugubrious: dismal; mournful; gloomy; doleful
malcontent: dissatisfied
melancholic: given to melancholy
melancholy as a gib-cat: despondent
moanworthy: pitiful; lamentable; sad
moody: out of humor; sullen
moping: dejected; dull; spiritless
mopish: given to gloomy feelings
morose: sullen; crabby
mournful: calling forth sorrow or grief
mumpish: sullen; sulky
oppressed with melancholy: melancholy
out of heart: discouraged
out of humor: angry
out of sorts: not feeling good
out of spirits: discouraged
overcome: crushed; prostrated; as with grief
pensive: thoughtful; sad
prostrate: helpless; overcome
querent: complaining
regretful: full of regret
repining: complaining to oneself
rueful: causing sorrow or regret
sad: in a condition or subdued sorrow

saturnine: gloomy; melancholic; blue in disposition
sedate: sober; serious
serious: of a sober, earnest disposition
sick at heart: disappointed
sober: not given to jesting
solemn: of an extremely serious and grave disposition
somber: somewhat melancholy
sore: distressed
soul-sick: hopeless
sour: having an unfriendly disposition
soured: made sour
spiritless: without life or spirit
spleenful: peevish; melancholy
splenetic: fretful and ill-tempered
staid: of a steady, sober disposition
stayed: of a steady, sober disposition
subtrist: a bit sad

sulky: obstinate
sullen: of a gloomy, obstinate disposition
sullen-sick: sick from gloominess, moroseness
triste: sorrowful
tristful: sad; gloomy
uncheerful: not bright or lively
uncheery: not bright or lively
unconsolable: not to be comforted
ungratified: not gratified
unhappy: sorrowful
unlively: not spirited
unmanned: deprived of courage
unnerved: discouraged
unsatisfactory: not satisfactory
unsatisfied: not satisfied
unsonsy: causing unhappiness
wan: haggard; pale
weary: worn; tired
wobegone: wretched

Denial

at issue upon: in controversy
cashiered: dismissed from position of command or authority; deposed
contradictory: tending to deny; affirming the opposite
deniable: that can be denied
denied: declared untrue

denying: declaring untrue
negative: opposed to positive
negatory: belonging to negation
recusant: obstinately declining to conform
refused: denied; declined
rejected: cast-out; refused

Departure

abducent: carrying or drawing away; abducting
abductive: carrying away
apopemptic: pertaining to a farewell
departing: taking leave; vanishing
dimissory: sending away; permitting departure
effused: poured out; shed
fled: having departed suddenly
nidifugous: leaving the nest soon after birth

outgoing: issuing out
outward bound: going away from
rebarbative: repellent; revolting; off-putting
repellent: driving back by force
repelling: causing to be driven back
repulsive: resisting
stolen away: having departed stealthily
valedictory: suitable for an occasion of leave-taking

Derision

burlesque: in the style of burlesque
derisible: deserving of mockery
derisive: scoffing; mocking; derisory

flarting: mocking; jeering
hudibrastic: coarsely satirical like Hudibras

ironical: mockingly sarcastic
mock: containing derisive mimicry
mordant: biting; caustic; sarcastic; corrosive

sarcastic: containing covert, bitter, personal satire
sardonic: derisive and mocking
scurrilous: low and indecent

Descent

deciduous: falling off at a certain season
declivous: descending; declivitous
decurrent: extending downward
decursive: running down
defluous: falling off; flowing down
demersal: sinking to the bottom, especially of fish eggs

descendent: falling
descending: moving downwards
downgyred: falling into circular wrinkles
labent: sliding; gliding
nodding to its fall: having the top bent forward
stillatitious: falling in drops

Desire

agog: in eager desire
all agog: all eager
ambitious: desirous of power, honor, preferment
anadipsic: pertaining to excessive thirst
anxious: concern about the outcome of certain events
appetent: eagerly desirous
appetizable: able to excite an appetite
appetizing: exciting appetite
ardent: glowing; warm
aspiring: longing for; hoping
at a loss for: in need of
athirst: in need of drink
avid: eagerly longing for
belly-pinched: starved; hungry
bent on: inclined; leaning in that way
bent upon: inclined; leaning in that way
breathless: overanxious; very desirous
bulimic: voracious; constantly hungry
burning: earnest; eager
concubitant: concupiscible; lustful; desirous
covetous: desiring the property of another
craving: with an intense appetite for
curious: eager to find out
desirable: profitable to have
desired: wished for

desiring: longing; desirous
desirous: wanting something
devoured by desire: overcome with passion
drouthy: thirsty
dry: needing drink
dying for: giving up one's life for
eager: excited by desire in the pursuit of anything
enviable: desirable and arousing envy
envious: displaying envy
esurient: greedy; voracious in disposition; hungry
exacting: unreasonably severe in making demands
exoptable: extremely desirable
extortionate: oppressive; hard
fain: glad; willing
famished: overcome with hunger
fervent: hot; zealous
gair: eager; greedy
grasping: miserly; greedy
greedy: gluttonous; rapacious
greedy as a hog: very greedy
hungry: desirous for food
hungry as a church mouse: very hungry
hungry as a hawk: very hungry
hungry as a horse: very hungry
hungry as a hunter: very hungry

impatient: restless in desire or expectation

in demand: desirous of possessing

inclined: in the mood or mind for something

ingordigious: greedy

insatiable: not able to be satisfied

intent on: eager in the pursuit of

intent upon: eager in the pursuit of

keen: eager

lickerish: eager to taste; craving

mad after: overcome by passion

meatwhole: having a healthy appetite

openmouthed: gaping; clamorous

optative: expressing desire

orectic: pertaining to appetite, desire

overeager: too eager

parched with thirst: very thirsty

partial to: biased in favor of

peckish: hungry

phagomanic: extremely hungry

pinched with hunger: very hungry

pleasing: that gives pleasure or satisfaction

quenchless: inextinguishable

rabid: mad, as a mad dog

rapacious: gluttonous; greedy

ravening: greedily devouring

ravenous: voracious

ravenous as a wolf: very ravenous

salacious: lascivious; arousing sexual desire

sarcophilous: fond of flesh

sedulous: constant in attendance to business

set on: adhering to closely

set upon: adhering to closely

sharp-set: eager in appetite or desire of gratification

should-be: desiring or attempting to be; would-be

sitient: thirsty

sky-aspiring: extravagant in ambition

solicitous: concerned; care for

sordid: meanly avaricious

tantalizing: tormenting by exciting desires that cannot be satisfied

thirsty: in need of water

tibialoconcupiscent: having a lascivious interest in watching a woman put on stockings

unquenchable: inextinguishable

unsated: not satisfied

unsatisfied: not satisfied

unslaked: unquenched

vaulting: leaping unrestrained

venerean: pertaining to sexual desire or intercourse

voracious: rapacious; greedy

wishful: having the desire to gain

wistful: longing; desirous

with an empty stomach: grasping; hungry

yiver: eager; greedy

Destiny

about to be: coming to pass almost immediately

about to happen: coming to pass almost immediately

at hand: coming to pass almost immediately

brewing: in preparation

close at hand: about to happen in a very short time

coming: going to be present at some future time

destined: determined for the future

forthcoming: about to appear

going to happen: about to take place

hanging over one's head: almost ready to happen

imminent: likely to befall very soon

impending: almost sure to happen at some uncertain time

in embryo: in its earliest stage

in prospect: contemplated

in reserve: retained for future use

in store: ready or prepared for future use

in the wind: astir

in the womb of futurity: getting ready to appear at a future time

in the womb of time: getting ready to appear at a future time

instant: about to occur at once

looming in the distance: giving remote indications of happening

looming in the future: giving remote indications of happening

looming on the horizon: giving remote indications of happening

near: not far off in time

near at hand: not far off in time

on the cards: likely to happen

overhanging: imminent

pregnant: about to appear

preparing: getting ready to happen

that is to be: thought of as being in the future

that will be: thought of as being in the future

to come: future

unborn: having not yet occurred

Destruction

baneful: having poisonous or deadly qualities; pernicious; poisonous; deadly

deadly: causing death; sure to destroy

deletory: blotting out

destroyed: ruined

destroying: destructive

destructive: causing destruction; fitted to destroy

detrimental: capable of causing damage, loss

disintegrous: not cohesive; falling apart

dislimning: rubbing or blotting out

exitious: destructive; deadly; exitial

extinct: being at an end; quenched

fatiferous: destructive; deadly

fricative: rubbing or blotting out

incendiary: destroying by maliciously setting fire to

internecine: mutually destructive or deadly

irrefragable: indestructible; stubborn

kafkaesque: having a nightmarish quality

lethiferous: deadly; destructive; lethiferal

marcescent: withered; decayed

marcid: withered; decayed

mundicidious: world-destroying

nocuous: harmful; hurtful; venomous; poisonous

nodding to its fall: tottering

perishing: that goes to destruction

phthartic: destructive; deadly

poisonous: having the qualities of a poison

putrescent: rotting; decaying

ruinous: tending to ruin; gone to decay

saprogenic: causing rot or decay; pertaining to decay; saprogenous

slighted: leveled; razed

subversive: tending to subvert or overturn

suicidal: pertaining to suicide; destroying one's own interests

symphoric: accident-prone

tottering to its fall: about to fall

trembling to its fall: about to fall

venene: poisonous; venenose

veneniferous: bearing poison

virose: poisonous, rank, and unwholesome

vorpal: keen; deadly

wasted: passed away

Deterioration

all the worse for: injured on account of

altered: changed

altered for the worse: changed so as to be worse than before

at a low ebb: in a low condition

battered: beaten so as to be bruised or deteriorated

blighted: blasted; marred

broken-down: enfeebled; dilapidated

cankered: affected with canker; ill-natured

contabescent: wasting away; atrophied

crumbling: falling into decay or ruin; deteriorating

decadescent: beginning or tending to decay

decayed: deteriorated as to physical or social condition; rotten

deciduous: falling off; subject to be shed periodically

decrepid: worn-out; enfeebled

decrepit: worn-out; enfeebled

degenerate: deteriorated in worth or goodness

deleterious: hurtful; pernicious

depraved: morally corrupt

deteriorated: having become worse

dilapidated: decayed; partially ruined

discolored: altered in color; stained

done for: tired out; destroyed

effete: not able to produce any longer; exhausted; sterile

faded: deteriorated in color, freshness, or brightness

far gone: very much deteriorated

fatigued: worn-out; tired

finewed: moldy

fit for the dust hole: valueless; useless

fit for the wastepaper basket: valueless; useless

fracid: rotten; overripe

imperfect: defective

in a bad way: badly situated

injured: damaged; hurt; harmed

jizzicked: of something so far gone that it cannot be repaired

manky: rotten; inferior

marasmic: withering; wasting away

mildewed: tainted with mildew

moldering: crumbling into small pieces

moldy: covered over with or containing mold

moss-grown: grown over with moss

moth-eaten: eaten by moths

murled: crumbling; disintegrating

nodding to its fall: perishing

on one's last legs: on the brink of ruin

on the decline: declining; deteriorating

on the wane: decreasing

ossifragous: bone-breaking

out of repair: in bad condition

out of tune: discordant; inharmonious

past cure: impracticable; past mending

past work: useless

reduced: diminished in size, value

reduced to a skeleton: fleshless; emaciated

retrograde: declining toward a worse state

rotten: decomposed naturally; putrid

rusty: covered with rust; deteriorated from disuse

secondhand: not new; of inferior grade

seedy: like a plant run to seed; shabby

shabby: ragged; paltry; despicable

shaken: injured, as by a shock

spoiling: corrupting

spotted: stained with spots

sprung: strained, cracked, so as to be useless

stale: deteriorated from standing

tabescent: wasting away

tabid: deteriorated gradually by the complaint called tabes

tainted: deteriorated by being imbued with something odious, harmful, or poisonous

the worse for: impaired by

the worse for wear: impaired or deteriorated by wear

threadbare: worn out to the threads

timeworn: worn out or deteriorated by time

tottering: broken; unsteady

undermined: secretly deteriorated

unimproved: deteriorated

used-up: consumed; exhausted

wasted: needlessly deteriorated

weather-beaten: deteriorated by exposure to the weather

weathered: worn away by exposure to the atmosphere

wilted: deteriorated by exposure to heat

withering: tending to fade or wilt

worm-eaten: deteriorated by being eaten by worms
worn: deteriorated; impaired
worn-out: wholly deteriorated
worn to a shadow: expression denoting degree of deterioration
worn to a thread: expression denoting degree of deterioration
worn to rags: expression denoting degree of deterioration
worn to the stump: expression denoting degree of deterioration
worse: less good

Determination

bent upon: determined
decided: unwavering
definitive: bringing to an end; conclusive
determined: resolved; strong-willed
earnest: serious in purpose
firm: settled; unshaken
game to the backbone: thoroughly resolved
indomitable: unyielding
inexorable: not to be moved by entreaty or prayer
inflexible: not to be turned from a purpose; firm
intent upon: having the mind set upon
iron: unyielding; not to be bent
not to be put down: immovable
not to be shaken: immovable
obstinate: stubborn; firm to the extreme
peremptory: very positive in opinion or judgment; dogmatic
pertinacious: persistent; determined; resolute; obstinate
proof against: capable of resisting successfully
relentless: unmoved by pity
resolute: having a fixed purpose and constant in carrying it out
resolved: strong-willed; determined
self-possessed: full of self-control
serious: earnest
set upon: bent upon
staunch: standing firm; determined; unwavering; stanch
steady: constant; unwavering
steeled against: immovable
strong-minded: inflexible
strong-willed: resolute
trenchant: effective
unflinching: resolute
unhesitating: with readiness of judgment or action
unshrinking: resolute

Devotion

avid: enthusiastic; fervid
chauvinistic: excessively patriotic
chivalric: devoted to one's country
devotional: of or pertaining to devotion
devout: earnestly attentive to religious duties; pious
fanatical: controlled by intemperate zeal
fervid: burning with religious zeal or eagerness
hallelujatic: pertaining to hallelujahs
loyal: constant in one's affection to one's country
patrial: relating to one's fatherland
patriotic: loving one's fatherland
prayerful: given to prayers
pure: free from everything that can debase or render unclean
religiose: excessively religious
reverent: expressing reverence; profoundly respectful
solemn: marked with religious gravity or pomp
worshipping: paying divine honors to; devout
zealotic: more zealous than zealous
zealous: full of enthusiasm, devotion; diligent

Diaphaneity

clear: free from opacity or obscurity
clear as crystal: absolutely transparent
crystalline: resembling crystal in clearness
diaphanous: of anything insubstantial or thin; transparent
glassy: resembling glass in transparency; fishlike; glazed; glazy; hyaline; luster-less; vitreous; vitriform
gossamer: light and somewhat transparent
hyaline: glassy; crystalline
limpid: marked by clearness or trans-parency; simple and clear
lucid: clear; transparent
pellucid: permitting the maximum amount of light to pass through; clear; transparent
relucent: throwing back light; clear; bright
serene: clear; placid
tralucent: transmitting rays of light; transparent; clear
translucent: transmitting rays of light; allowing light to pass through but not transparent
transparent: having the property of transmitting rays of light so that bod-ies can be seen through; diaphanous
transpicuous: transparent; pervious to the sight
vitreous: having the quality of glass

Difficulty

accomplished with difficulty: hard to do
aerumnous: full of trouble
aground: checked
arduous: laborious; toilsome
at a loss: uncertain
at a nonplus: in a fix; quandary
at a standstill: aground
at bay: cornered up, as a hunted boar
at cross-purposes: having different intentions
at one's wit's end: puzzled
at the end of one's tether: having come to the end of the rope or string
awkward: clumsy; unskillful
beset with difficulties: in trouble
between Scylla and Charybdis: danger-ous; difficult to pass without suffering destruction
between two stools: pertaining to trying to do two things at once and failing in both
complicated: intricate; tangled
crabbed: perplexing; difficult
critical: careful in passing judgments
delicate: not easy
desperate: hopeless
difficult: perplexing; hard to deal with
difficult to deal with: perplexing
driven from post to pillar: much embarrassed
driven into a corner: much embarrassed
driven to extremity: much embarrassed
driven to one's wit's end: much embarrassed
driven to the wall: much embarrassed
embarrassing: obstructing; rendering difficult
encompassed with difficulties: perplexed
entangled by difficulties: perplexed
farpotshket: all fouled up, especially as the result of trying to fix it
fashious: troublesome
feisty: difficult; troublesome
formidable: dreadful; fearful
full of difficulties: difficult
graveled: checked; run aground
hard: difficult
hard put to it: in straits
hard to deal with: difficult
hard up: poor
hard-earned: earned with difficulty
hard-fought: contested vigorously

hard-pressed: pressed vigorously
hard-set: firmly resolved
herculean: like Hercules, first in strength and labors for mankind
ill-conditioned: not fit for the contest
implex: complex; intricate
impracticable: not feasible
in a clever stick: caught
in a fine pickle: in a sorry plight; smarting in the acid of pickle
in a fix: in trouble
in a scrape: in trouble
in deep water: puzzled
in difficulty: in trouble
in hot water: in trouble
in the suds: in worry; in difficulty
in the wrong box: in a wrong position
intractable: hard to govern
intricate: difficult to understand, follow, or arrange
invious: untrodden
irksome: tiresome; burdensome
knotted: made difficult
laborious: arduous
labyrinthine: convoluted
more easily said than done: hard to do
nonplussed: confused; puzzled
not easy: difficult
not feasible: impossible
not made with rose water: not easy
not out of the woods: more difficulties to be overcome
not to be handled with kid gloves: not easily managed
onerous: burdensome
operose: wrought with labor
out of one's depth: out too far to touch bottom
pathless: without a way or guide to get out of
perplexing: puzzling

perverse: intractable; obstinate
pinched: put into a tight place
plaguy: troublesome; tiresome
plexiform: complicated, like a network
put to it: tested; tried
put to one's shifts: make use of every expedient
puzzled: baffled; put in a quandary
quisquous: perplexing; difficult to deal with or handle; ticklish; quiscos; quisquose
reduced to straits: pinched; pressed
refractory: unruly; disobedient
rugged: stiff; hard
run hard: abused; overworked
set fast: unmovable; unflinching
sooner said than done: hard to do
sorely pressed: in narrow straits
straitened: confined; hampered
stranded: run aground
stubborn: unmanageable; perverse; obstinate
stuck fast: caught
surrounded by breakers: in difficulties
surrounded by difficulties: in difficulties
surrounded by quicksand: in difficulties
surrounded by shoals: in difficulties
thorny: rough; hard to travel
thrown out: disabled; disqualified
ticklish: delicate; difficult
toilsome: burdensome; cumbersome
tough: very intricate; complicated
trackless: untrodden
troublesome: bringing trouble
trying: straining
under a difficulty: in trouble
unmanageable: hard to manage
unwieldy: bulky; awkward
up a tree: in difficulty, from which the dogs prevent escape

Digest

abridged: shortened
analectic: made up of selections
compendiarious: concise; abridged

compendious: containing the substance in a narrow compass
condensed: compressed; contracted

contract: condensed
corrept: abridged; contracted; shortened
curtailed: cutoff; reduced
decurtate: shortened; abridged; curtailed
digested: reduced; condensed
miniature: designed on a smaller scale

minified: lessened
potted: condensed; summarized
synoptic: arranged for giving general view
truncated: shorter in one dimension; foreshortened; shortened; stunted

Dimension—Direction

aberrant: wandering
actinoid: in the shape of a star; rayed
aligned: arranged in a straight line; set in order
allover: extending over an entire surface
ascending: moving upward from lower to higher level
back-and-forth: backward and forward; from side to side; to-and-fro
bidirectional: capable of moving in two, usually opposite directions
bilateral: having or concerning two sides
bilevel: divided horizontally into two usually equal parts
broad: extending to a great range or width
centrifugal: moving away from center or axis
centripetal: moving toward center or axis
chockablock: crowded together; extremely full
circuitous: following an indirect path
circumambient: lying on all sides
clockwise: in the direction in which clock hands rotate
coast-to-coast: extending across an entire nation or continent
counterclockwise: in the direction opposite that in which clock hands rotate; backward
cross-country: extending across an entire country
dangling: hanging loosely
descending: moving downward from higher to lower position
dextral: on or leaning to the right

diagonal: running in an oblique direction from a reference line
dimensional: having measurements or measurable parts
direct: from point to point by shortest course; straight
directional: designating direction in space
divergent: separating at a point
diverging: branching out
ectad: toward the exterior
edgewise: sideways
encircling: running completely around in a circle
equiangular: having all angles equal
equilateral: having all sides equal
extensive: covering a great area or scope
falling: descending freely, usually straight downward
forrit: forward
frontal: located at or moving against the front
geocentric: having Earth as center
geodesic: pertaining to the geometry of curved surfaces
high: reaching upward, especially to great extent; elevated from a surface
horizontal: parallel to the horizon or level ground; level; at right angles to vertical
inclined: at an angle with another surface
indirect: deviating from straight line or path
infinite: boundless in all directions; immeasurable
isometric: having equality of measure
isosceles: having two sides equal and nonparallel

latitudinal: having side-to-side extent, especially as measure of distance from Earth's equator

left: located toward the west when facing north

level: flat; horizontal; having all parts at equal height

linear: consisting of or moving in a straight line; having a single dimension

long: of a considerable extent; extending to greater length than breadth; far; distant

long-distance: situated at or extending a great distance

longitudinal: placed or moving lengthwise; having top-to-bottom extent

multilateral: having many sides

nationwide: extending across an entire country

oblique: neither perpendicular nor parallel to another surface; slanting or sloping

obtuse: designating an angle greater than 90 degrees but less than 180 degrees

out-of-bounds: outside designated limits or boundaries

outward: directed away from the center; situated on the outside

patulous: spreading widely from the center

pervasive: spread throughout every part

prolate: extended in a line joining the poles

protracted: extended in space, especially forward or outward

quaquaversal: turning or pointing in every direction; going off in all directions

radial: extending from a center; moving along a radius

radiant: tending in different directions from a center

radiating: extending in a direct line away from or toward a center

rectilinear: moving in or forming a straight line

retroflex: turned sharply backward

retrograde: directed or moving backward; against the general direction

reverse: moving opposite to the regular direction; having backside forward

right: located toward the east when facing north

ringed: encircled; formed of rings

rising: moving to a higher position

rotary: turning on an axis

sinistral: on or leaning to the left

statewide: extending throughout an entire state

straight: moving or extending continuously in one direction without turning

straightforward: moving in a direct line

stratified: forming layers in a graded series

symmetrical: corresponding in size, form, and relative position on opposite sides of a line, plane, point, or axis

syntropic: turning or pointing in the same direction

tabular: arranged in vertical and horizontal rows

tangential: digressing suddenly from one course and turning to another

three-dimensional: having height, width, and depth

to-and-fro: back-and-forth

two-dimensional: having height and width only

ubiquitous: existing everywhere

uniaxial: having one axis

unidirectional: moving in one direction only

unilateral: arranged on one side

universal: existing everywhere; distributed throughout space without limit or exception

unsymmetrical: asymmetrical

up-and-down: moving alternately upward, then downward

upright: having main axis perpendicular or vertical

vertical: perpendicular to horizon or level surface; upright; designating an extent to the highest point; at right angles to horizontal

wide: of specific extent from side to side; covering a large area

worldwide: extending throughout the world

Dimness

auroral: pertaining to dawn
cloudy: lacking clearness or brightness
confused: rendered indistinct
crepuscular: pertaining to twilight; dimness
dark: not light; without brightness
darkish: somewhat dark
dim: obscure; indistinct; not clear
dingy: of a dark color
dirty: not clean or clear; indistinct
dull: not bright; indistinct
dun: dark; obscure
fading: becoming dim
faint: not bright; dull
fuliginous: dark; dusky
glassy: having a fixed, staring appearance
lackluster: wanting brightness
leaden: of a dull appearance like lead
looming: shining

lurid: gloomy; dismal
misty: obscure; dim
muddy: turbid; dull; not clear
muggy: moist and close
nebular: cloudy; hazy; dim
nebulous: cloudy; hazy; dim
obnubilated: clouded; obscure
overcast: darkened; clouded
pale: faint or light in color
scialytic: creating shadows
shadowed forth: indicated dimly
shady: overspread with shade
shorn of its beams: deprived of its light
spissatus: in meteorology, having a density that blocks or dims the sun
thestral: dark; dim
umbrageous: shady
umbral: shadowy; umbrageous
umbriferous: shady

Dim-sightedness

astigmatic: pertaining to astigmatism
blear: having bloodshot appearance
blear-eyed: with bloodshot eyes
blind: without sight
blind as a bat: very blind
blind as a beetle: entirely blind
blind as a buzzard: sightless
blind as a mole: not able to see
blind as an owl: able to see little
blind of one eye: being without sight in one of the visual organs
blinded: made blind
bloodshot: having reddened eyes; red-eyed
dark: not to be seen
dim-sighted: having poor sight
eyeless: without the organs of sight
gravel-blind: nearly stone-blind; worse than half-blind; sand-blind

half-blind: partially able to see
monoculous: one-eyed
moon-eyed: having an eye affected by the moon
mope-eyed: shortsighted
myopic: nearsighted
one-eyed: having one good eye
pop-eyed: having eyes wide open
presbyopic: longsighted; farsighted
purblind: nearsighted
sand-blind: half-blind
sightless: without the sense of sight
stark-blind: entirely without sight
stone-blind: sightless
transfixed: having motionless eyes; glazed; staring; unblinking
undiscerning: not able to distinguish
visionless: without ability to see

Disagree—Disapprove

abusive: prone to ill-treat by coarse, insulting words

adverse: unfavorable; opposed to one's interest

ajar: out of harmony

answerable: obliged to account for

aristarchian: extremely critical

at a discount: poorly esteemed

at cross-purposes: acting counter to one another without intending it

at daggers drawn: ready to fight

at feud: at enmity

at high words: strongly enraged

at issue: in controversy

at loggerheads: quarreling, as thick heads

at odds: at variance

at sixes and sevens: disagreeing

at variance: disagreeing

bad: unfavorable or offensive

biting: cutting or sarcastic

blameworthy: deserving blame

blown upon: brought into discredit

captious: apt to catch at faults

carping: faultfinding

censorious: severe in making remarks on others

chid: scolded

clamorous: complaining in noisy language

condemnatory: containing censure

controversial: pitted against in defending some cause

contumacious: obstinately disobedient or rebellious

critical: inclined to criticize or find fault

cutting: severe; sarcastic

cynical: given to sneering at rectitude and the conduct of life by moral principles

damnatory: expressing the highest condemnation

defamatory: injurious to reputation

denominational: sectarian; characterized by different opinions

denunciatory: accusing; threatening

disagreeing: differing in opinion

disapproved: regarded with disfavor

disapproving: scandalized

discontented: dissatisfied

discordant: clashing; opposing

disgruntled: discontented; having ill humor

disparaging: undervaluing

disputatious: ready to argue

dissentient: dissenting; withholding approval; disagreeing in feeling, thought, or view

dissenting: disagreeing; refusing adherence

dissident: differing; dissenting

disunited: separated; put apart

dry: severe, grave, or hard; withering

embroiled: entangled in a broil or quarrel

exceptionable: objectionable

exploded: rejected with open contempt

extorted: obtained violently from an unwilling person

factious: pugnacious; quarrelsome; opposed to law

fastidious: difficult to please

gladiatorial: eager for a combat

grudging praise: praising with envy

hard upon: severe

hostile: critical; antagonistic toward; opposed

hypercritical: unreasonable or unjustly critical; censorious

illaudatory: not praising or complimentary

in bad odor: out of all favor

in hot water: in trouble; in difficulties

inconsequential: unimportant; insignificant

inexcusable: incapable of being justified

intropunitive: blaming oneself rather than others or external events; intrapunitive

judgmental: tending to pass moral judgment

litigant: contending in law

litigious: given to the practice of contending in law

negative: characterized by contradiction or dissent

noncontent: dissatisfied

nonjuring: refusing to swear allegiance

objurgatory: expressing reproof; rebuking; scolding

on bad terms: unfriendly; jangling

opposed: contrary; set in contrast to

out of the question: not worthy of thought or consideration

out of tune: out of harmony; discordant

pejorative: tending to disparage or devalue

pettifogging: subject to artful tricks, as in law

polemic: disposed to argue or dispute

protestant: protesting; formally dissenting

quarrelsome: easily provoked to contest

rabulistic: carping; quibbling; rabulous

recusant: obstinately refusing conformity; dissenting; nonconforming

rejectaneous: not chosen or received

rejected: denied

rejectitious: implying or necessitating rejection

reprehensible: worthy of blame

reproachful: abusive

sarcastic: scornfully severe

sardonic: derisive; mocking

scandalized: disgraced

schismatic: of or pertaining to schism or dissent

sectarian: devotedly attached to the tenets of a denomination; dissenting from all but one sect

severe: very strict in judgment

sharp: cutting in language

snooty: showing disdain and snobbishness

sparing of praise: not giving full credit

stuck-up: self-important; snobbish

supercilious: patronizing and haughtily disdainful of others

taboo: forbidden; banned as evil

to blame: guilty

together by the ears: quarreling

tongue-whaled: severely scolded

torn: divided by violent measures

trenchant: keen; biting

unacknowledged: not confessed or avowed

unapproved: unfavorable

unavowed: not openly acknowledged

unbewailed: not mourned for

unblest: accursed; unblessed

uncommendable: not worthy of praise

uncomplimentary: unfavorable; derogatory

unconsenting: not agreeing

unconverted: not agreeing with the Christian religion; not changed in opinion

unconvinced: not persuaded by argument; unsatisfied by evidence

underrated: valued at less than true worth

undeserving: not worthy of consideration, respect, or assistance

unfavorable: adverse; contrary; not propitious

unflattering: unfavorable; derogatory

unlamented: unwept for

unpacific: not peaceful

unpacified: fighting

unplausive: not approving

unpopular: disapproved of or disliked in general or by a particular group

unpromising: appearing unlikely to succeed

unreconciled: at variance

unsatisfactory: inadequate; worthy of disapproval or rebuke

unsung: insufficiently praised

unwilling: unconsenting

unworthy: lacking in value; undeserving

up in arms: fighting against

verboten: forbidden; prohibited by law

wrong: incorrect; judged to be false

Disappearance

deciduous: disappearing after having served its purpose

disappearing: vanishing

evanescent: passing away by degrees; fleeting; impermanent

evanid: evanescent; fleeting; transient

forfeited: lost by default

gone: moved away

lost: not to be found; wasted

lost to sight: disappeared; vanished

lost to view: disappeared; vanished

missing: lost to sight

obsolescent: gradually disappearing, especially in biology

vanishing: disappearing from sight or existence

Disappointment

aghast: terrified

anticlimatic: disappointing expectation

balked: disappointed; checked

chagrined: vexed; mortified; disappointed

choked: disappointed; annoyed

crestfallen: disappointed; crushed; dejected; disheartened

disappointed: without one's hopes realized

frustrated: thwarted or defeated in purpose

gutted: bitterly disappointed

out of one's reckoning: not to find conditions just as expected

Discord—Fighting—Hostility

agonistic: combative; strained for the sake of effect; agonistical

airborne: designating ground forces carried in aircraft

alienated: having love or affection withdrawn from

antipersonnel: designating weapons intended to maim or kill human beings rather than to damage property and equipment

antitank: designating missile or artillery designed for use against armored vehicles

armed: furnished with weapons for fighting

armed to the teeth: entirely equipped with arms

armigerous: bearing arms

astrive: energetically struggling

at daggers drawn: at enmity with each other

at enmity: cherishing resentment

at issue: disputing

at loggerheads: quarreling

at odds: in disagreement; at enmity

at open war with: hostile to

at variance: in disagreement; at enmity

at variance with: in disagreement; at enmity

at war: engaged in fighting

at war with: fighting; contending

barratrous: habitually causing fights

battailous: ready for battle; warlike

bellicose: inclined to war

belligerent: carrying on war; waging war

bristling with arms: conspicuously covered with arms

cankered: embittered

cantankerous: ill-natured; contrary

chivalrous: pertaining to chivalry; warlike

coldhearted: lacking sympathy

combative: disposed to fight

competitive: marked by competition

contending: defending; fighting

contentious: relating to strife; fond of contention

cool: lacking cordiality

cornobbled: hit with a fist

crabbed: sour-tempered

cross: unkind in speech or manner

curst: ill-tempered; cross-grained; cursed

disaffected: filled with discontent

disagreeing: lacking harmony

discordant: clashing

discrepant: different

disproportionate: unsuitable to something else in bulk, form

disproportionated: unsuitable to something else in bulk, form

divergent: receding farther and farther from each other

embattled: furnished with embattlements; ready for battle

estranged: on less intimate terms than formerly

exceptional: unusual; anomalous; unconformable

fighting: ready for combat; warlike

gladiatorial: pertaining to gladiators

hostile: repugnant; disagreeing strongly

ill-assorted: badly arranged

ill-sorted: badly selected; ill-fitted

ill-timed: done at an unsuitable time

improper: not proper; not fit

in arms: ready or prepared to fight

in bad odor with: out of favor with

in battle array: equipped and waiting for battle

in open arms: at war

in the field: out for warlike purposes; looking for battle

inadmissible: not allowable

inapplicable: not fit

inapposite: not suitable or pertinent

inappropriate: not suited; not fitted

inapt: unfit

incompatible: not consistent; not consonant

incongruous: not well mated; having dissimilar natures

inconsistent with: not agreeing at all times with itself

inimical: adverse; injurious or harmful; hostile

internecine: mutually destructive, especially due to conflict within a group

intrusive: forcing itself in without permission

irreconcilable: not being made able to agree

irreducible: not resolvable into something else

knock-down-drag-out: describing an especially violent and prolonged fight

laquearian: armed with a noose, as a gladiator

manubiary: pertaining to the spoils of war

martial: pertaining to war; military

militant: of a warlike disposition; engaged in warfare

military: relating to soldiers, arms, or warfare

misjoined: not fittingly united and suited

mismatched: not fittingly united and suited

mismated: not fittingly united and suited

misplaced: not fittingly united and suited

not on speaking terms: not friendly

on bad terms: unfriendly

out of character: unfitted for, or disagreeing with

out of its element: unfitted for, or disagreeing with

out of joint: unfitted for, or disagreeing with

out of keeping: unfitted for, or disagreeing with

out of place: unfitted for, or disagreeing with

out of proportion: unfitted for, or disagreeing with

out of season: unfitted for, or disagreeing with

out of time: unfitted for, or disagreeing with

palestric: pertaining to wrestling

palestrical: pertaining to wrestling

pugilistic: pertaining to pugilism

pugnacious: disposed to fight

quarrelsome: inclined to quarrel
repugnant to: opposed; antagonistic
rival: having opposing interests
soldierlike: brave
soldierly: like or characteristic of a real soldier; heroic
stipendiarian: mercenary
strategic: pertaining to overall military power and goals
strategical: brought about by artifice
stratonic: pertaining to an army
sword in hand: ready for the fray
tactical: pertaining to battlefield operations or any immediate military objective
tauromachian: relating to bullfighting
together by the ears: struggling
top secret: pertaining to security
triphibian: designed or equipped to operate on land, on water, or in air
unaccommodating: not suiting and fitting

unapt: inapt; unsuited
unbecoming: not suited to rank or character
unbefitting: unsuited
uncommensurable: unproportionate
unconformable: not correspondent; not compliant
uncongenial: having a similar nature
unconsonant: inharmonious
under arms: drawn up fully armed and equipped
unfit: not fit; incompetent
unfitting: making unsuitable
unfriendly: not kind or favorable
unharmonious: not the same; discordant
unpacific: not inclined to conciliation
unpeaceful: not peaceful
unsuitable: improper; incongruous
unsuited: unfitted; discordant
up in arms: eager for war; in a warlike attitude
up in arms against: actively hostile to
warlike: eager to carry on war

Discredit

abject: sunk to a very low condition
arrant: notoriously bad; shameless
at a discount: of questionable reputation
base: of low moral character
beggarly: of little or no standing or worth
blown upon: having a tainted or impaired reputation
dedecorous: disgraceful
degrading: tending to injure or lower
derogatory: defamatory or injurious
despicable: mean; contemptible
dirty: of low reputation
discreditable: injurious to reputation; disgraceful
discredited: brought into disrepute
disgraced: in bad repute
disgraceful: bringing disgrace; shameful
disreputable: causing ill repute
down in the world: disgraced
downtrodden: dishonored

humiliating: dishonored
ignominious: marked with ignominy; shameful
in bad repute: disgraced
in the background: in ill favor
in the shade: in ill favor
indign: unbecoming; undignified
infamous: of exceeding bad repute
inglorious: without glory; disgraceful; shameful
loaded with shame: disgraced
low: having poor reputation; of base reputation
mean: of contemptible reputation
nameless: without fame or distinction
notorious: widely known as or bad reputation
opprobrious: offensively reproachful
out at elbows: in bad circumstances
out of contenance: abashed; confounded
out of fashion: deprived of rank or honor
out of favor: deprived of rank or honor

out of repute: not favored

outrageous: shocking; extremely disgraceful

overcome: surpassed; outrivaled

pitiful: awakening pity

pudendous: shameful

questionable: of suspicious or doubtful character

renownless: without renown

ribald: coarsely indecent or obscene

scandalous: disgraceful

scrubby: of an inferior kind; low; mean

shabby: low; contemptible

shameful: bringing reproach or disgrace

shocking: extremely surprising or offensive in conduct or character

shorn of its beams: deprived of honor

shorn of one's glory: deprived of honor

unable to show one's face: disgraced

unbecoming: unbefitting

under a cloud: in ill favor

under an eclipse: in ill favor

unglorified: without glory or worship

unhonored: disgraced

unknown to fame: not honored

unmentionable: too shameful to mention

unnoted: unhonored

unnoticed: neglected

unworthy: base; low

vile: base; of the lowest character or reputation

Dishonesty

abject: sunk to a mean condition; groveling

any-lengthian: unscrupulous

arrant: very bad; notoriously depraved

base: low in rank or character; mean

base-minded: low in thoughts; ignoble

beneath one: unworthy of

blackguard: suited to a blackguard; low; vile

contemptible: worthy of disdain; despicable

corrupt: of an impure character; depraved

crooked: not straight in character or morals; dishonest

dark: concealed; mysterious

dead to honor: debased

debased: lowered in character or purity

degraded: made mean; lowered in moral purity

derogatory: detracting; injurious to one's reputation

dirty: morally filthy; vile

disgraceful: full of disgrace; causing disgrace

dishonest: wanting in honesty; deceptive

dishonorable: bringing dishonor; discreditable

disingenuous: not frank, sincere, or candid

disloyal: lacking loyalty; faithless

double-faced: deceitful

double-tongued: having duplicity of speech

emptitious: corruptible; capable of being bought

faithless: not observing one's obligations; untrustworthy

false: not true or faithful; deceptive

false-faced: hypocritical

falsehearted: false in character or disposition

fishy: doubtful; improbable; foul

foul: offensive to the moral sense; unfair

fraudulent: practicing fraud; deceitful

groveling: crawling on the earth; mean; base

ignominious: deserving ignominy or public disgrace

indign: unworthy

infamous: having a bad reputation; having no honor

inglorious: without glory or honor

insidious: lying in wait to do harm; stealthy in doing harm

knavish: like a knave; roguish; dishonest

little: small in dignity; contemptible

lost to shame: utterly depraved
louche: devious; dishonest; shady; disreputable
low-minded: entertaining low sentiments and base motives
low-thoughted: having low thoughts
Machiavellian: relating to Machiavelli; unscrupulous
mean: ignoble in character; without honor
mongrel: of mixed breed; ofttimes used as an epithet of contempt
of bad faith: having a bad reputation
one-sided: having only one side; partial; unfair
paltry: trifling; contemptible
perfidious: violating one's obligations; faithless
perjured: having sworn falsely
pettifogging: conducting in a mean and tricky manner
rascally: worthy of a rascal; base
recreant: apostate; crying for mercy; craven
scabby: full of scabs; mean; vile
schlenter: dishonest; counterfeit; fake
scrubby: stunted; small and mean
scurvy: covered with scabs; contemptible
shabby: ill-dressed; despicable
slippery: evading one; tricky
sneaking: acting with cowardice; cringing
timeserving: complying to the demands of the times without regard to principle
tortuous: having twists; hence, erratic

treacherous: having good appearance, but bad by nature
trothless: without good faith; not keeping a pledge
trustless: not worthy of trust; faithless
truthless: faithless
unauthenticated: not shown to be trustworthy
unbecoming: not befitting; not suitable
unbefitting: not befitting; not suitable
unbeseeming: not becoming or proper
unchivalric: unbecoming an ideal knight; ungallant
unconscientious: not governed by conscience
unconscionable: unscrupulous; outrageous
undignified: without dignity
unfair: marked by dishonesty or fraud
unfaithful: manifesting absence of faith
ungentlemanlike: unbefitting the manner of a gentleman
ungentlemanly: unbefitting the manner of a gentleman
unhandsome: ungenerous; ungracious
unknightly: without gallant or noble qualities
unmanly: without gallant or noble qualities
unscrupulous: without any scruple or caution
untrustworthy: that cannot be depended on
venal: capable of being bribed
vile: low; mean
wicked: evil in principle; sinful

Disjoined

abjunct: disconnected; severed
abjunctive: exceptional; isolated; disconnected
abstract: general; abstruse
adrift: in a drifting state
apart: separate; aside
asunder: apart
demountable: capable of being taken apart for later reassembly

discerptible: divisible; breakable
discontinuous: not continued
discrete: disconnected; distinct
disjoined: separated; disunited
disjunctive: helping to disjoin
disparate: dissimilar
dissilient: bursting apart
distinct: separate from all others

divellent: causing to come apart or separate
divisible: capable of division
far between: much space intervening
free: exempt; possessing liberty
insular: pertaining to an island
isolated: set apart; alone
loose: not fastened tightly
multipartite: having many parts
partable: separable
reft: torn apart
rift: split open

schiztic: characterized by separation; separating
scissile: capable of being cut
separate: disjoined; apart
shuked: of wine casks that have been taken apart; shooked
straggling: wandering aimlessly
sundered: set or kept apart; separate; separated
unannexed: not joined to anything else
unassociated: alone
unattached: separate

Disobedience

contumacious: perverse; refractory; insubordinate; disobedient
disobedient: resistant
factious: creating factions; divisive
froward: perverse; obstinate
impatient of control: hard to govern
insubordinate: disobedient
insurgent: rebelling
iscariotic: traitorous
lawless: not subject to law
mutinous: revolting
proditorious: traitorous
recalcitrant: kicking; opposing
recusant: dissenting
refractory: resisting authority or control; not yielding; unruly; unmanageable
resisting: offering resistance
restiff: obstinate; stubborn

restive: obstinate; stubborn
riotous: wanton; unrestrained
seditious: stirring up contention; tending to turbulence
sequacious: obsequious; given to following others
unbidden: uncommanded; unrequested
uncompliant: not submitted to established laws, rules
uncomplying: not submitting to established laws, rules
ungovernable: not able to be controlled
unobeyed: not obeyed
unruly: factious; disobedient
unsubmissive: not subjective; not compliant
untoward: unruly; perverse; unmanageable

Disorganization

aflunters: in a state of disorder
chaogenous: arising out of chaos
deranged: unbalanced; disordered
disconcerted: confused
disorganized: without order, connection, or arrangement
farmisht: confused; mixed up

fartumlt: disoriented; confused
indiscriminate: not systematic
mixty-maxty: muddled; confused
mommixed: disorderly; confused
nebulochaotic: chaotic; confused; hazy
raddled: fuddled; confused
wopsy: tangled; disheveled; disordered

Disproof

anapodictic: undemonstrable
anatreptic: defeating; refuting
capable of refutation: able to be refuted or to be replied to

condemned on one's showing: proved guilty by one's own admission
condemned out of one's mouth: condemned by one's own evidence

confutable: capable of being shown false

confuted: replied to; answered

confuting: opposing in argument

disproved: proved untrue or erroneous

eristic: pertaining to controversy or an argument; argumentative

philopolemic: fond of argument or controversy

reconfutable: able to be overcome in argument

refragable: capable of being refuted

Disregard

absent: inattentive; tending to wander from the present surroundings

absentminded: having the mind away from the present

abstracted: drawn off for a time by the consideration of weightier matters

bemused: dazed or muddled as with liquor

blind: incapable of seeing; unwilling to attend or understand

blithe: carefree; without thought or regard

brainsick: mentally deranged

careless: having no concern; thoughtless

cursory: rapid; superficial; careless

deaf: incapable of hearing; obstinately inattentive

disconcerted: deranged as to mind; thrown into confusion

disregarded: treated without respect or attention; slighted

distrait: preoccupied with worry; absent-minded; lost in thought; abstracted; distracted

dizzy: thoughtless; heedless

dreaming on other things: not attentive to the subject in hand

dreamy: characteristic of dreams; absentminded

engrossed: wholly absorbed

giddy: thoughtless

giddy as a goose: very unsteady and flighty

giddy-brained: without thoughtfulness or stability

hand over head: without thinking

harebrained: reckless and foolish

harum-scarum: in careless haste

heedless: having no heed or care

high-flying: having extravagant aims or views

in a reverie: in a musing mood

in the clouds: in the place of the unreal or superficial

inadvertent: careless and heedless

inattentive: not fixing the mind upon a thing

inconsiderate: having no consideration or thought

listless: having no activity

lost: wandered away; bewildered

lost in thought: inattentive to everything save one's mental operation

mindless: not regarding with attention; heedless

musing on other things: careless of what one is doing

muzzy: absentminded

napping: careless

off one's guard: unawares; incautious

offhand: without preparation or attention

percursory: very cursory

preoccupied: having the attention occupied before

put-out: inconvenienced; deprived

rantipole: rakish; reckless

rapt: carried out of oneself, as with love or admiration

regardless: having no regard or respect

respectless: without regard

scatterbrained: giddy; careless

thoughtless: wanting in thought; rash

undiscerning: lacking power to discriminate

unheeding: not heeding

unmindful: not keeping in mind; inattentive

unobservant: neglect of observance; careless
unreflecting: not thinking or considering

wild: not cultivated; reckless
wrapped in thought: wholly absorbed in thought

Disrespect

affrontive: insulting
aweless: void of respectful fear
contumelious: rude and sarcastic in speech
derisive: mocking; ridiculing
disparaging: belittling
disregarded: intentional neglect
disrespected: treated or regarded with contempt
disrespectful: wanting in respect
insulting: conveying an insult
irreverent: wanting in respect to superiors
rude: characterized by rough discourtesy; impolite

sarcastic: bitterly ironical; taunting
scurrile: grossly offensive or vulgar
scurrilous: grossly offensive or vulgar
subderisorious: mildly ridiculing; mocking
supercilious: exhibiting haughty contempt or indifference
unenvied: exempt from the envy of others
unregarded: slighted; deemed unworthy of notice
unrespected: not honored or esteemed
unsaluted: not greeted
unworshiped: not worshiped or adored

Dissonance

absonant: discordant; not consonant
acute: shrill and piercing
cacophonous: having a disagreeable sound; inharmonious
coarse: loud and harsh
cracked: harsh and imperfect
creaking: grating; squeaking
discordant: not in harmony or musical concord
dissonant: inharmonious
ear-piercing: sharp and penetrating in the highest degree
grating: having an irritating voice; ear-splitting; piercing; screechy; squeaky; twittery
gruff: rough and repulsive
grum: harsh and guttural
harsh: grating on the ear; displeasing
high: relatively acute
hoarse: having a rough grating sound

horrisonant: terrible-sounding
horrisonous: producing a terrible sound
immelodious: not melodious
inharmonious: out of harmonious accord
out of tune: not in harmony or concord
piercing: sharp and pentrating
rough: loud and hoarse
scrannel: harsh; grating; unmelodious
sepulchral: grave and low
sharp: piercing and high in pitch
shrill: intensely sharp
singsong: in a drawling or monotonous manner or tone
stridulous: harsh and grating
trumpet-toned: very loud and harsh
tuneless: unmusical
unharmonious: discordant
unmelodious: not musical
untunable: not able to be tuned

Dissuasion

averse: turned away or aside in mind

dehortatory: arguing or advising against

diallelous: arguing in a circle; diallelus

dissuaded: advising or attempting to change from some course or action

dissuading: arguing against

dissuasive: tending to dissuade

expostulatory: arguing earnestly to convince a person of an error

monitive: advising; giving friendly counsel

monitory: advising; giving friendly counsel

repugnant: repulsive to the feelings or taste

uninduced: not to be influenced

unpersuadable: not to be persuaded; obstinate

Distaste

abhorrent: detestable; repugnant

adverse: opposed

adverse to: turned from; hostile to

disagreeable: not to one's liking

disgusting: offending the taste

disinclined: alienated; indisposed

disliking: regarding with distaste or aversion

distasteful: disagreeable to the taste; nasty

dogsick: very sick

fulsome: offensive from excess

heartsick: despondent; pained in mind

insufferable: unendurable

loathful: hating; abhorring

loathsome: exciting disgust

loth: odious; hateful; loath; loathe

offensive: distasteful

out of conceit with: not having a favorable opinion of

queasy: ticklish; squeamish

repellent: tending to drive back

repugnant: combative

repulsive: bitter; arousing disgust

shy of: afraid of

sick: affected by disease

sick of: disgusted with

uncared for: neglected; unloved

unpopular: disliked; despised

District

amphigean: found or occurring throughout the world

Antarctalian: of the region south of a line where mean temperatures are about 44 degrees Fahrenheit

Arctalian: of the region including all northern seas and as far south as icebergs travel

azonic: of anything not local; not confined to a particular zone

civil: pertaining to the city or state

classical: suggestive of ancient Greece or Rome; neoclassical

costumbrista: depicting local customs, art

districtual: belonging to a marked-off territory

gerontogeous: pertaining to the Eastern Hemisphere, Old World

holarctic: pertaining to arctic regions

illocal: not restricted to a particular place

local: pertaining to some particular or definite place

Manx: pertaining to the Isle of Man

Novanglian: pertaining to New England

orarian: pertaining to the seashore

parochial: pertaining to or relating to a parish

provincial: pertaining to or relating to a province

sympatric: dwelling in overlapping regions

tedesco: Germanic

territorial: pertaining to a territory

topopolitan: limited to a certain area
transpadane: living north of the Po
River; beyond the Po River (from
Rome)

Diversity

a hundred: expression meaning in great
numbers; numerous
a million: expression meaning in great
numbers; numerous
a myriad: expression meaning in great
numbers; numerous
a thousand: expression meaning in great
numbers; numerous
a thousand and one: expression meaning
in great numbers; numerous
a world of: a great many
all kinds of: widely differing examples of
all manner of: every sort of; all the different kinds of
all manners of: widely differing examples
of
all sorts of: widely differing examples of
allogeneous: different in kind
and heaven knows whatnot: a great
many things besides
and whatnot: having very many different
things; much besides
anidian: lacking differentiation
briarean: hundred-handed
characteristic: showing the distinctive
qualities of
crowded: having or being filled with
great numbers
daedal: intricately made, like the work of
Daedalus
decuple: tenfold
dedal: intricately made, like the work of
Daedalus
desultory: jumping or passing from one
thing to another without order or rational connection
different: of various or contrary nature,
form, or quality; unlike
differing: being unlike
dioristic: distinguishing; distinctive
discriminating: making or seeing a
difference

discriminative: making sharply defined
differences
disparate: different in kind; unrelated
distinctive: expressing distinction or difference; distinct
distinguishable: capable of being
differentiated
divers: different in kind or species
diverse: distinct; different
diversified: made different; variegated;
varied; differing in an essential way
diversiform: having a different form;
variform
eclectic: borrowing from diverse sources;
broad in matters of taste or opinion
endless: without limit or end
epicene: common to both sexes
ever so many: very many
full many: very many
half a dozen: six
half a hundred: fifty
heterogeneous: made up of different
kinds
in profusion: in great numbers
indiscriminate: not making any
distinction
irregular: departing from the usual or
proper form
manifold: various in kind or quality
many: composed of or constituting a
great number
many-sided: versatile
modified: slightly altered or varied
more than one can tell: in countless
numbers
mosaic: composed of various materials
motley: heterogeneously made or mixed
up
multifarious: existing in many forms or
varieties
multifold: many times doubled; manifold; numerous

multiform: having many forms; multi-farious; multiplex
multigenerous: having many kinds
multinominal: having many terms
multiple: consisting of more than one
multiplied: increased by itself
multispiral: having several whorls
multitudinous: consisting of great numbers
multiversant: infinitely variable
multivious: having many paths, roads, ways
myriad: innumerable; composed of numerous diverse elements
nice: apprehending slight differences or delicate distinctions
no end of: numberless
no end to: numberless
not a few: many
not the same: different
numberose: in great numbers
numerous: in great numbers
numerous as the hairs on the head: multitudinous; in great or countless numbers
numerous as the sands on the seashore: multitudinous; in great or countless numbers
numerous as the stars of the firmament: multitudinous; in great or countless numbers
of all sorts and kinds: of all known forms, shapes, styles
of every description: of all known forms, shapes, styles
of various kinds: of many different shapes, forms, styles
omnifarious: of all kinds or forms; dealing with all kinds of things

omniform: having many forms; omnifarious
omnigenous: of all kinds
omnigruous: consisting of all kinds
other: different
peopled: filled with inhabitants
plenty as blackberries: in great numbers
pluripotent: pertaining to numerous potentialities
polymorphic: having many forms; polymorphous
populous: having many inhabitants
profuse: superabundant; in great numbers
proletaneous: having many children
protean: variable; versatile; having many forms
rough: characterized by a lack of uniformity in surface
several: more than one, but not a great number
some forty or fifty: an uncertain quantity
something else: something different
studded: thickly set, as with gems
sundry: a small number; various
teeming: full with or of
thick: dense; containing a great number
thick as hops: very numerous
thick coming: coming in great numbers
unequal: of different magnitudes
uneven: not uniformly plane
unmatched: having no equal or match
varied: made different in form, position, or state
variform: having different shapes or forms
various: of different kinds or species; divers; diverse
very many: a great many
widely apart: very different

Divinity

angelic: of or pertaining to angels
believing: having firm faith
catholic: universal
Christian: pertaining to Christ or Christianity

consecrated: declared sacred
converted: persuaded to adopt a faith
Cytherean: pertaining to the goddess Venus or the planet Venus

deiparous: giving birth to a god or goddess

deipotent: having divine power

devoted: showing strong attachment to religion

devout: devoted to religion or religious duties

divine: of or pertaining to a god; religious; sacred

elected: selected as an object of special mercy and favor

fairylike: having the qualities of a fairy

faithful: strong in faith or belief

God-fearing: devout

godly: pious; conformed to the law of God

heavenly-minded: devout

hilasmic: propitiatory

holy: morally excellent; pure in heart

humble: thinking lowly of oneself

inspired: guided by divine influence

justified: proven right or valid

not of the earth: heavenly

omnipotent: all-powerful; attribute of God in Christianity

omnipresent: all-present; attribute of God in Christianity

omniscient: all-knowing; attribute of God in Christianity

pietistic: making an ostentatious display of religion

pious: having piety; religious

pure: free from moral defilement or guilt; innocent

regenerated: reformed spiritually

religious: having religion; godly

reverent: showing due respect to religion

sacred: pertaining to religion or religious services

saintlike: resembling a saint

saintly: like a saint

sanctified: made holy

seraphic: having the nature or character of a seraph; pure; sublime

solemn: connected with religion; characterized by seriousness

spiritual: controlled by the Divine Spirit; holy

sylphic: like a sylph or fairy

sylphlike: with qualities suggesting a sylph

theomorphic: having a godlike form or aspect

unearthly: supernatural

Domestication

bucolic: pertaining to herdsmen or shepherds

domestic: tame

domesticated: made domestic or familiar; tamed; naturalized

dumb: pertaining to a domesticated animal

enchorial: native; endemic

familiar: pertaining to animals, domesticated and tame

gentle: pertaining to fruit or tree, domesticated and cultivated

homemade: of domestic manufacture

indigenous: native to some place

pastoral: pertaining to the life of shepherds and rustics

rangé: domesticated; settled; rangée

tame: having lost native or ancestral wildness

zootechnic: of or relating to improving domesticated animals

Dominance

dominant: exercising a ruling influence

hegemonical: pertaining to leadership or supreme command

herile: pertaining to a master

important: of great influence

in the ascendant: having influence superior to all others

influential: exercising control over others

predominant: possessing superiority in influence

prepollent: superior in influence, power, weight
prevailing: predominant
prevalent: having widespread and effectual influence

rampant: influential beyond all bounds
regnant: reigning; dominant
rife: abundant in number and quantity
weighty: of great practical influence

Doubt—Misgiving

abroad: uncertain, as in calculation
adrift: aimless; without occupation
afraid to say: not certain enough to say
ambiguous: double in meaning
ancipitous: doubtful
apocryphal: of doubtful authenticity; spurious
astray: wandering, as in reasoning
at a loss: unable to decide
at a nonplus: puzzled
at fault: embarrassed
at one's wit's end: entirely at a loss
at sea: ignorant of how to proceed; puzzled; confounded
casual: occurring without premeditation
changeable: liable to change; capricious
confused: being unable to think clearly
contingent: dependent on unknown circumstances
contingent on: dependent on
controvertible: admitting of debate; deniable
debatable: disputable
deceptive: misleading
dependent on: determined by
dependent on circumstances: determined by circumstances
disputable: that may be called in question
distracted: unsettled in reason
distraught: confused
distrustful of: uncertain about
doubtful: subject to doubt
doubting: tending to disbelieve
dubious: calling forth doubt
enigmatic: not easily solved
equivocal: questionable; suspicious
evasive: avoiding by artifice or sophistry
experimental: undergoing a test
fallacious: involving fallacies

fallible: liable to be incorrect or false, as an argument
false: contrary to truth; sometimes designedly intended to deceive
finespun: worked out with too much subtlety
hard to believe: seemingly doubtful
hypothetical: taken as an unproved premise from which to deduct proof
ignorant: lacking knowledge
illusive: deceiving
illusory: illusive
in a cloud: not knowing how to proceed
in a maze: in a state of confusion
in a state of uncertainty: doubtful
in question: doubtful
in suspense: in a state of uncertainty
inconceivable: not capable of being explained by the human intellect
incredible: not admitting of belief
incredulous as to: doubtful about
indecisive: not bringing to a definite end
indefinite: not established or determined
indeterminate: not precise
jesuitical: given to subtle sophistries
lost: bewildered
mebby-scales: wavering between two opinions
minimifidian: having the least faith possible; close to faithlessness
misgiving: feeling a loss of confidence; feeling mistrust
mystic: secret
not to be believed: seeming false or impossible
occasional: pertaining to or occurring at irregular times or periods
open to discussion: debatable
open to doubt: uncertain
open to suspicion: uncertain

oracular: doubtful, like lying oracles
out of one's reckoning: wrong in calculation
overrefined: too subtle
paradoxical: seemingly absurd, but possibly true
perplexing: troubled with uncertainty
pettifogging: characteristic of a pettifogger
plausible: seeming to be true
plausive: specious; ostensibly okay
precarious: not to be relied upon for certainty; unsteady
problematical: involving doubt
puzzled: baffled or confused
questionable: liable to be doubted or suspected
quibbling: given to quibbles
shy of: avoiding with suspicion
skeptical as to: doubtful about
slippery: elusive; tricky
sophistical: characterized by or given to sophistry
specious: having only the appearance of truth
staggering: causing great amazement
subject to: liable to
suspect: doubtful

suspicious: admitting of mistrust
suspicious of: distrustful
ticklish: not fixed; easily affected
unascertained: not definitely known
unauthentic: not genuine; not reliable
unauthenticated: not supported by sufficient authority
unauthoritative: not derived from creditable sources
unbelieving: doubtful
uncertain: not sure or definite
unconfirmed: not assured or verified
uncounted: of uncertain number
undecided: not settled upon
undefinable: not to be described
undefined: not clear
undemonstrable: not admitting of demonstration or proof
undemonstrated: not made certain
undeserving of belief: doubtful
undetermined: not fixed upon
unreliable: not to be depended upon
unsettled: not steady or fixed
untold: secret
untrustworthy: not worthy of trust or confidence
unworthy of belief: false; incredible
vague: dim; unfixed

Dryness

aneroid: without liquid
anhydrous: lacking water
arid: devoid of moisture
dried: free of liquid or moisture
dry: not wet or moist
dry as a biscuit: extremely dry
dry as a bone: extremely dry
dry as a mummy: extremely dry
dry as a stick: extremely dry
dry as dust: extremely dry
exsuccous: sapless; dry
fine: clear and bright
gizzen: dried or shriveled
husky: dry and harsh
juiceless: destitute of juice; dry

rainless: devoid of rain
sapless: without sap; hence dry, withered
sear: dried up or withered, as leaves in autumn
sere: without moisture
siccaneous: dry
siccative: drying
undamped: not moistened or wet
waterproof: impervious to water
watertight: so close or tight as not to leak
without rain: dry and harsh
xeric: having little moisture
xerophobous: unable to withstand drought
xerotic: dry

Dueness

absolute: free from control
allowable: permitted
allowed: permitted; granted
authorized: given power to act
becoming: fit; appropriate
befitting: seemly; in place
chartered: having written legal authority
claiming: asserting a right to
condign: worthy; suitable
constitutional: consistent with the supreme law of the land
correct: right; legal
creditable: worthy of commendation
decorous: becoming; fit
deserved: merited; worthy
deserving: worthy of praise or honor
due: owed
due to: owed to
enfranchised: given free citizenship
entitled to: earned; won
equitable: correct; consistent
fit: adequate
fitting: becoming
having a right to: due to receive
imprescriptible: not capable of being lost or acquired by usage
inalienable: not able to be alienated
indefeasible: not able to be defeated or set aside
inviolable: intact; not to be injured
just: rendering what is due
just the thing: exactly right

lawful: according to law
legal: according to law
legalized: sanctioned by law
legitimate: authorized; lawful
licit: lawful
meet: appropriate; becoming
merited: deserved
meriting: deserving
ordained: appointed; set apart
peremptory: demanding; dictatorial
prescribed: appointed; directed
prescriptive: gained by long possession
presumptive: giving ground for belief
privileged: accorded special rights
proper: decent; becoming
quite the thing: exactly right
richly deserved: very worthy
right: correct; consistent
right as a trivet: not unstable
sanctioned: approved of
seemly: becoming; befitting
square: upright; honest
unalienable: not to be taken away; inalienable
unchallenged: exercising authority without opposition
unexceptionable: choice; select
unimpeachable: not to be questioned
up to the mark: meeting with approval; superior
warranted: given authority or power to do
worthy of: meriting

Dullness

commonplace: neither new nor striking; ordinary
dry as dust: dull and prosy
dull: without spirit; slow of understanding; not cheerful
dull as ditchwater: stupid and inactive
flat: lacking spirit or interest; dull; insipid
flat-brained: dull
gaumless: unaware; stupid

hebetudinous: stupid; dull
humdrum: monotonous; commonplace; stupid
inficete: without wit; not amusing; deadly serious
insulse: dull; insipid; tasteless; flat
matter-of-fact: treating of facts or realities; ordinary
melancholic: depressed in spirits; dejected

monotonous: continued with dull uniformity; unvaried
plodding: diligent but slow
pointless: without any sharpness or
keenness
prosaic: resembling prose; dull;
uninteresting
prosing: dull and tedious minuteness in
speech or writing
purblind: lacking understanding, insight
slow: dull, as in understanding; not lively
stolid: heavy; lacking liveliness; calm and
unmoved; plodding

stumpf: dull
stupid: deficient in understanding; sluggish; foolish
unasinous: equally stupid or asinine
unentertaining: not amusing; giving no
delight
unimaginative: dull; stupid
uninteresting: not capable of exciting or
attracting the mind
unlively: not lively; dull
vapid: dull; uninteresting; tedious;
insipid
weary, flat, stale, and unprofitable: tiresome; irksome

Duty

accountable: answerable
affianced: engaged to marry
amenable: liable to be punished
answerable: able to be replied to
beholden to: indebted
behooving: proper
binding: holding firmly
bound: constrained by a legal or moral
obligation
bound by: held by
bound to: under obligation to
casuistical: pertaining to casuistry
chargeable on: liable to be laid at one's
door
committed: devoted; pledged; bound
compromised: pledged to
conscientious: bound by conscience
due to: owing to
dutiful: rendering services or regard that
is due
ethical: pertaining to ethics
ethological: pertaining to the science of
character
imperative: mandatory
in duty bound: held by duty

in for it: committed to a given course
incumbent on: falling to one's lot
indebted to: beholden
liable: responsible; answerable
meet: fulfilling
moral: bound to exercise right conduct
obligatory: imposing duty or obligation
obliged to: put under obligation to do
peremptory: positive; decisive
pledged: deposited as a security
promised: committed; assured
promising: committing; assuring
promissory: of the nature of a promise
responsible: answerable; liable to requite
right: conformable to the will of God
saddled with: under a burden, as a horse
stringent: binding strongly
tied by: bound to do
tied down: bound to do
under hand and seal: under one's signature and certification of legality
under obligation: bound
upon oath: upon the most sacred
promise
votive: dedicated or given on account of
a vow

Earliness

anticipatory: acting beforehand or in expectation of something

early: in good time; soon

forward: in the lead

immediate: at the same instant

in time: not too late

near: not far off

near at hand: not far off

precipitate: without due forethought; headforemost

precocious: developed before the usual time

premature: ripened or done before the proper time

prepunctual: overly prompt; arriving earlier than the appointed time

prevenient: previous

prime: of the best quality; being in the best period of growth or strength

prompt: ready at short notice

punctual: observing exactly appointed times of action

rath: early; rathe

sudden: coming without warning

summary: regardless of the usual methods; quickly

timely: happening at right time

unexpected: not foreseen

Economics

accounting: computing; reckoning up

antitrust: pertaining to policies or laws designed to curb monopolies

at risk: denoting the amount an owner or investor stands to lose should business go bankrupt

bankrupt: designating a person or entity whose total property and assets are insufficient to pay debts

bearish: pessimistic about security prices; causing or describing a fall in stock prices

black: showing a profit; in the black

broke: bankrupt; having little or no available cash

bullish: optimistic about security prices; causing or expecting a rise in stock prices

capital-intensive: designating production using more capital than labor

cash-and-carry: sold for cash payment with no delivery included

cheap: low-priced; reluctant to spend money

comp: complimentary

cut-rate: at reduced price

dear: expensive

deductible: designating an amount or type of expense that may be used to reduce adjusted gross income before calculating tax

disadvantaged: deprived of decent standard of living by poverty or lack of opportunity

door-to-door: selling by calling at each house or apartment in an area; shipped directly from point of pickup to point of delivery

down-and-out: poor; destitute

economic: pertaining to economics and finances

expensive: high in cost or price

free: available at no cost

full-service: offering broad range of services in one basic line of business

gilt-edged: designating highest quality securities and bonds

gratis: at no cost; free

half-price: reduced to half of original price

hand-to-mouth: relating to bare existence with nothing to spare

hard up: lacking resources

high-pressure: pertaining to sales effort involving insistent arguments, forceful persuasion, or refusal to take no for an answer

in stock: available for sale at the present time

in the black: operating at a profit; black

in the red: operating at a loss; red

labor-intensive: designating production using more labor than capital

listed: designating a security traded on one of the exchanges

low-pressure: pertaining to sales effort involving subtle persuasion and soft-spoken arguments

low-price: available at little cost

Malthusian: pertaining to the theories of T. R. Malthus regarding dichotomy between geometric population growth and arithmetic increase in means of subsistence, causing shortages unless war or famine intervenes to eliminate the imbalance

marketable: fit for sale

mom-and-pop: designating small family-owned business, usually retail

monetary: of or pertaining to money or finance

nonpartisan: describing items on which the payer bank deducts exchange charge before paying them to the collecting bank

nonrefundable: final and not subject to return or refund

nontaxable: not liable to taxation

on time: purchased on credit with payments to be made over fixed period of time

on-demand: pertaining to note payable immediately upon receipt

OTC: over-the-counter

out-of-pocket: owed or paid out in cash

outstanding: of securities, publicly issued and in circulation

overinsured: having coverage beyond value of insured objects

overpriced: designating securities priced above true value with potential to decline in price

over-the-counter: OTC; designating stocks not listed on any exchange; sold directly to buyers

partisan: describing items that the payer bank remits without charge

point-of-purchase: relating to a place where sales are made or purchases paid for

postal: relating to or conducted by postal service

postpaid: having postage prepaid by sender

preenactment: designating property acquired or activities begun prior to tax reform act of October 23, 1986

red: showing a loss; in the red

reduced: at less than original price

steep: expensively priced

storewide: throughout all departments of store, used especially of a sale

subordinated: designating debt obligation whose holder is placed in precedence below preexisting creditors

tax-exempt: not liable to taxation

uncovered: unprotected under insurance policy

underinsured: having insufficient insurance

underpriced: priced below true value with potential to increase in price

uninsured: having no insurance

unsecured: not guaranteed by collateral

worthless: lacking monetary value

Education

abecedarian: relating to the alphabet

abiological: pertaining to the study of inanimate things

academic: relating to an institution of higher education

accredited: issuing degrees recognized as valid

acroatic: pertaining to profound learning

apt: quick to learn

basal: fundamental, especially of a reading book

brought up at the feet of Gamaliel: having had the advantages of an excellent education

chrestomathic: devoted to useful learning

coeducational: being an institution for male and female students

collegiate: of or relating to college

communicatory: imparting information

decanal: pertaining to a dean

didactic: characterized by giving instruction; instructive

didascalic: didactic; moralistic; pertaining to a teacher

disciplinal: pertaining to discipline

docile: easily taught

doctrinal: pertaining to teaching or to doctrine

donnish: professorial in manner or disposition

educable: capable of being educated

educational: pertaining to education

educative: imparting education

emeritus: designating retired college professor holding honorary title

expository: serving to explain

extracurricular: designating student activities not receiving academic credit; engaged in outside classroom

extramural: relating to extension courses

fledged: mature; trained; experienced

heuristic: encouraging learning, investigation; promoting discovery

in leading strings: figurative expression for having much to learn

inkhorn: pedantic; learned

instructive: serving to teach

intercollegiate: designating contest or activities conducted among or between colleges

interscholastic: designating contest or activities conducted among or between schools

intramural: designating contests or activities conducted within a single university or school

learned: trained and informed by study

misteaching: instructed erroneously

nod-crafty: nodding to give an air of wisdom

Pierian: concerning poetry or learning

polytechnic: relating to instruction in technical arts and applied sciences

postdoctoral: designating work and study undertaken after receipt of doctorate

postgraduate: designating study leading to postgraduate degree

predoctoral: designating student or course of study leading toward doctoral degree

professorial: pertaining to a professor

question-and-answer: designating a test

given in the form of interrogation of student by teacher

remedial: designating courses intended to correct poor study habits or improve skills in specific field

scholarly: like a scholar

scholastic: relating to schools or students

school-age: old enough to begin school, generally six years old

self-paced: designed so that student can learn at his or her own rate

self-taught: having acquired learning or skills without formal education

semiliterate: barely able to read and write

studious: given to learning

tardy: late for beginning of class

taught: provided with knowledge or instruction

teachable: capable of learning

teaching: instructive; involving or used for teaching

tenured: designating college professor holding permanent employment

unedifying: not improving the mind

Elasticity

blubbery: elastic; rubbery; springy

buoyant: not sinking in a liquid

elastic: having the quality of returning to the former conditions when forced from it

frisky: jumping with lightness

leaping: jumping

renitent: having the quality of returning to the former conditions when forced from it

resilient: having the quality of returning to the former conditions when forced from it

saltatorial: fond of leaping

saltatory: leaping; springing

springy: having the quality of returning to the former conditions when forced from it

supersalient: leaping upon

taut: tight on the surface

tensile: stretchable; able to be drawn out; extensible

Electricity

analog: designating electronic process in which data is represented by physical quantities that correspond to the variables involved

diamagnetic: designating materials in which induced current field opposes applied magnetic field

digital: designating an electronic process that defines frequencies and other data as discrete, binary bits of information

electric: describing any device that uses or produces a charge of electricity

electrostatic: describing effects caused by charges at rest, such as electric charge on an object

faradic: operating on inductive electricity

ferromagnetic: designating materials that retain magnetism

paramagnetic: designating materials that have slight magnetic susceptibility

solid-state: designating electronic device that utilizes properties of semiconductor materials, not electron tubes

thermoelectric: describing production of electric current directly from heat

transient: designating an instantaneous peak

Embellishment

adorned: decorated; ornamented

auriphrygiate: fringed or ornamented with gold embroidery

beautified: embellished; made beautiful

becoming: suitable

bedight: adorned; covered; dressed

begilt: covered with gilt

behounc'd: fancied up; made fine

chased: having hammered indentations

decorative: ornamental; pertaining to a decoration

dressed to advantage: well-dressed

embellished: beautified; adorned

festooned: decorated

fine as a carrot fresh scraped: very splendid

fine as a Mayday queen: very splendid

fine as fivepence: very splendid

flashy: having a cheap and showy appearance

floriated: having flower-shaped ornaments; floral; floreted

flowery: overadorned

garish: having a gaudy effect

gaudy: flashy

gay: brilliant in appearance

gilt: golden

glittering: shining; sparkling

goffered: having ornamental curls or plaits

gorgeous: conspicuous on account of brilliant colors

in best bib and tucker: in best appearance

in full dress: in formal attire

in Sunday best: in best dress

inaurate: gilded

new-gilt: newly covered with gold

new-spangled: newly decorated with spangles

ornamental: decorative

ornamented: having ornaments added

ornate: highly decorated

piped: having tubelike trimming

pointillé: ornamented with a sharp-pointed tool

pranked out: dressed with showy ornaments

rich: composed of precious materials

showy: gaudy; dressed in cheap ornaments

smart: well and carefully dressed

splendiferous: unusually splendid; magnificent

tasselated: adorned with tassels

toreutic: relating to wrought metalwork, especially highly finished

tricksy: neat

Emotion

absorbing: engrossing

acute: keenly affecting the senses or sensibilities

affected: regarded with affection; beloved

affected with: somewhat influenced by

anxiolytic: serving to reduce anxiety

ardent: intensely passionate; impassioned

attempered: regulated

boiling: raging

boiling over: raging

breathless: indicative of fear, surprise

burning: vehement

captious: difficult to please; upset by trivial defects

cast: formed

caustic: bitterly sarcastic

characterized: distinguished by peculiar marks or traits

clairsentient: perceiving what is normally unperceivable

conscious: aware of an action, influence, or effect upon the organs of sense; knowing any state of mind

cordial: warm in feeling

cutting: sharp; sarcastic

deep: profound; heartfelt

deep-felt: heartfelt

deep-mouthed: ready to express feeling

deep-rooted: firmly implanted

devoured by: completely absorbed by

disposed: inclined

eager: impatiently desirous for action

earnest: having a deep, resolute desire to accomplish

eaten up with: of deep affection

ecstatic: extremely delightful

electric: spirited; thrilling

emotional: of, having, or pertaining to emotion

emotive: tending to excite emotion

enraptured: filled with rapture

enthusiastic: filled with enthusiasm

essentic: showing emotion naturally

esthetic: with the artistic sense well cultivated

exsensed: out of one's senses

fanatical: extravagantly zealous

feeling: emotionally affected by

fervent: showing intensity of feeling

fervid: ardent; showing intensity of feeling; fervent

feverish: excitable and uncertain

fiery: vehement; passionate

flaming: intensely excited; vehement

flexanimous: mentally flexible; able to change others' minds

formed: modeled by discipline

framed: regulated

glowing: fervent; intense

gushing: exuberant; abundant

having a bias: feeling strongly in one way

heart-expanding: largehearted; generous in praise

heartfelt: most sincere

hearty: warm and sincere

home-felt: inward; private

hysterical: fitfully emotional

imbued with: impressed; filled with

impassioned: full of feeling; passionate

impetuous: acting with great vehemence or violence

impressed with: very sensible of

impressive: likely to fix on the mind

in a quiver: shaking with emotion

inborn: implanted by nature

inbred: bred within

incisive: cutting; penetrating

inclined: having a tendency or leaning toward

indelible: not able to be blotted out or forgotten

ineffaceable: incapable of being blotted out

ingenuous: open; sincere

ingrained: worked into the mental or moral constitution of

inveterate: fixed and settled by long continuance

keen: quick to perceive or apprehend; eager and sharp

keen as a razor: extremely keen

lively: gay; animated; brisk; making a striking effect upon the sense or perception

molded: given a certain training

moved with: roused to action by

passionate: characterized by passion

pathematic: pertaining to or caused by emotion

pathoscopic: indicative of the passions

penetrated with: deeply affected by

penetrating: powerful to pierce or sink deep

perceptive: having power to become aware of through the medium of the senses

perfervid: passionate; zealous

pervading: permeating every part

piercing: sharp and penetrating like a needle

piquant: agreeably sharp or severe

poignant: severely painful, cutting, or severe

profound: deep and intense

psychosensory: pertaining to sense perception

psychosexual: referring to the link between sex and the mind, emotions

pungent: very piquant

quick: irritable; hasty; easily angered

rabid: raging mad, like a mad dog

racy: strikingly and vigorously original

rapt: carried away from oneself into raptures

rapturous: extremely and deeply joyful

raving: pertaining to irrational or furious talk

rectopathic: easily hurt emotionally

red-hot: raging; furious; fiery

seized with: entirely overcome by

sensible: capable of being affected by outside influences

sensificatory: producing sensation; sensific

sensitive: easily affected by outside influences; relating to the senses

sensorial: pertaining to the nervous system

sensory: pertaining to the nervous system

sensuous: keenly alive to pleasures derived through the senses; pertaining to the senses

sentient: having sensation or feeling

sharp: having strong or quick powers of sensibility; keen

sincere: in reality what it appears to be

smart: emphatic and sharp

soul-stirring: passionate and profoundly impressive

squeasy: readily nauseated; easily upset

strong: marked by force or strength

struck all of a heap: affected suddenly

swelling: pompous; increasing in intensity

thin-skinned: easily affected

thrilling: causing a thrill

touched with: moved to compassion

trenchant: cutting deeply and quickly

vivid: producing a lively effect

warm: slightly passionate

warmhearted: cordial

wistful: with longing or desire

with feeling: with emotion

wrought up: roused into a passion

zealous: enthusiastically devoted

Entertainment

aleiptic: pertaining to physical or gymnastic training

amused: entertained

amusing: entertaining

closed: restricted as to permissible time, place, and game that may be hunted

corybantic: pertaining to wild noisy dancing

diverting: entertaining through distraction

entertaining: pleasing

espiègle: playful

festal: joyous; gay

festive: joyous; gay

jocund: cheerful

jolly: full of life and mirth

jovial: mirth-inspiring

laughable: provoking laughter or derision

ludibrious: ridiculous

ludibund: playful

lusory: playful; lusorious

mute: of a hound, following scent of fox without crying out

piscatory: relating to fishing or fishermen

playful: sportive

pleasant: giving enjoyment

psyllic: pertaining to snake-charming

recreative: giving relief after labor

rompish: given to rude play

scacchic: pertaining to chess

sphairistic: tennis-playing

sporting: engaging in or related to open-air sports such as hunting and fishing

toxophilite: pertaining to archers or archery

venatic: of or pertaining to hunting

warrantable: of legal age for being hunted, especially deer

wicketed: in croquet, halfway through the hoop

witty: funny; jocular

zugzwang: in chess, being obliged to move but unable to do so without disadvantage; in zugzwang

Equality

all one: the same
all the same: equal
ana: in equal parts, especially in regard to pharmacy prescriptions
as broad as long: equal in all directions
balanced: having equal weight on each side
coequal: of the same rank, value
convertible: easily made equal to; exchangeable with
coordinate: of the same order
drawn: indeterminable
equable: equal and uniform at all times
equal: exactly the same as; just; equitable
equalized: made equal to
equipollent: equal in power, validity
equiponderant: having equal weight; counterpoised; counterweighted
equiponderous: having equal weight
equisized: of the same size
equitable: distributing equal justice; fair; just
equivalent: of the same significance as
even: equally distributed

homologous: existing in the same relation in corresponding objects
isochronous: concerning equal time or timing; recurring regularly
level: parallel to the horizon
libratory: balancing; moving like a balance
monotonous: the quality of being all or much alike
much at one: alike
much the same as: alike
neither more nor less: exactly alike
on a footing with: like; equal to
on a level with: like; equal to
on a par with: like; equal to
poised: self-confident and balanced
quits: on even terms
resolvable into: capable of being made into or like something else
symmetrical: having parts arranged so as to balance
synonymous: having nearly the same meaning
tantamount: equal in one's own estimation
the same thing as: like; identical
up to the mark: up to the standard

Erectness

bolt upright: boldly erect
erect: in a perpendicular posture
erigible: able to be erected
freestanding: standing unsupported or alone
hunched over: not erect in stature; slumped
ithyphallic: penilely erect; indecent; obscene
normal: forming a right angle
perpendicular: exactly upright
plumpendicular: perpendicular to the ground

pritchkemp: standing erect and alert; armed and ready; locked and loaded
rampant: standing upright upon the hind legs
rectangular: right-angled
sejant: in a sitting posture
standing up: being erect
statant: upright; standing; of an animal, standing with four feet on the ground
straight: direct
upright: in an erect position
vertical: upright; up-and-down; perpendicular to plane of the horizon; perpendicular; plumb; true

Error

aberrant: wandering into error
all in the wrong: wholly in error
apocryphal: of doubtful authenticity; spurious
astray: wandering into error or evil
at cross-purposes: in disagreement
beside the mark: away from the mark or in error
controvertible: not too evident to exclude difference of opinion
deceitful: tending to mislead or ensnare
delusive: apt to lead into error
devoid of truth: not possessing truth
erroneous: marked by error
exploded: having had the falsity or error of shown
fallacious: of, pertaining to, or involving a fallacy or error
false: contrary to truth or fact; erroneously believed to exist
faulty: characterized by solecisms
groundless: without foundation in truth
heretical: at variance with or subversive of accepted views or beliefs
ideal: consisting of, pertaining to, or existing in ideas
illogical: of erroneous reasoning
illusive: deceiving by false show
illusory: tending to lead into error by false appearances
in error: wrong
in the wrong box: erroneously placed
inaccurate: not accurate; erroneous

incorrect: in error; faulty
indefinite: not definite, determinate, or precise
inexact: not precisely true
mistaken: wrong in judgment
mock: false; counterfeit
on a false scent: tracing anything erroneously
on the wrong scent: tracing anything erroneously
out: mistaken
out in one's reckoning: mistaken
perverted: turned to error
refuted: proved in error
spurious: not genuine; false
tripping: blundering
unauthenticated: not shown to be genuine
under an error: mistaken
unexact: not correct or accurate
ungrounded: without foundation in truth
unreal: not real
unsound: not founded on truth or correct principles
unsubstantial: not real; not having substance
unsustainable: not capable of being sustained or supported
untrue: not according to truth
untrustworthy: not worthy of being trusted
wide of the mark: far from being true

Establishment

at anchor: fastened with an anchor
domesticated: made domestic
embosomed: hidden or half concealed
ensconced: sheltered; protected
established: made permanent; fixed
imbedded: deposited, as in a bed; embedded
moored: fastened, as a vessel

placed: to set or put in a particular position
posited: firmly placed
rooted: firmly fixed
situate: permanently fixed
unremoved: not taken away
vested in: placed in

Eternity

aeonian: everlasting; eonian
amaranthine: never fading
ceaseless: without a stop or end
coeternal: equally eternal
continual: without interruption; unceasing
deathless: not subject to death; immortal
endless: without end
eternal: having neither beginning nor end
ever-flowing: unceasing
evergreen: remaining unwithered throughout the year
everlasting: having no end
ever-living: living always
having no end: continuing forever
immarcescible: indestructable; imperishable; immarcessible
immortal: not subject to death; undying

imperishable: exempt from liability to decay; not destructible
incessant: going on without interruption
indesinent: perpetual
interminable: having no termination or limit; endless
never dying: continuing always
never ending: continuing always
never fading: continuing always
olamic: infinite; eternal
perpetual: continuing without intermission; everlasting
sempiternal: with a beginning, but without end; everlasting
Sisyphean: endless and ineffective, like Sisyphus's toil
unceasing: never ceasing
undying: imperishable; immortal
unending: having no end
unfading: not fading; everlasting
uninterrupted: ceaseless

Ethnology

ambosexual: of sexual traits or characteristics common to both sexes; ambisexual
androgynous: exhibiting both masculine and feminine characteristics
anthropoid: manlike
anti-ethnic: anti-Gentile
civic: pertaining to a city, citizen, or citizenship
congeneric: of the same race or origin
consanguine: of the same lineage, descent, origin; having a common ancestor; consanguineous
cosmopolitan: common to all the world
deivirile: both divine and human
ecdemic: of foreign origin
epicene: pertaining to both sexes; rather indeterminate sexually; androgynous
ethnic: pertaining to race; ethnological
ethnocentric: convinced that one's own race is superior

ethnological: pertaining to the divisions of mankind
genealogical: showing the descent from a common ancestor
gynaecocoenic: having women in common
historic: important in history; momentous; making history
historical: pertaining to or concerned with history
homophylic: of the same race
human: having the qualities or attributes of man
individual: characteristic of a single person
infra-angelic: human
isogenous: having a common origin
mortal: belonging to humans
national: common to a whole people or race
neanthropic: concerning modern man

nonliterate: preliterate

paleoanthropic: pertaining to the earliest humans

personal: pertaining to a particular person

pithecological: concerning the study of apes

polyphyletic: derived from more than one ancestor

preliterate: designating culture or people who lack any writing system; nonliterate

primitive: pertaining to preliterate or tribal people with strong cultural and physical similarities to their early ancestors

prosopoeic: imbued with human qualities

public: belonging to the people

simian: apelike; monkeylike; pithecian; pithecoid; simioid; simious

social: relating to the public as an aggregate body

sociocultural: of or pertaining to interaction of social and cultural elements

sociological: pertaining to the origin and history of human society

xanthous: pertaining to the yellow type of mankind

Evasion

avoiding: tending to flee from

elusive: tending to slip away or escape

escaped: fled from

escaping: in the act of getting away

evasive: tending or seeking to evade; escaping ready apprehension

fugitive: escaping or escaped; runaway

lucifugous: avoiding daylight

neutral: refraining from interference in a contest of any kind

runaway: escaping or escaped from restraint or control

shy: easily frightened or startled

unattempted: not attempted or tried

unsought: not searched for

wild: unrestrained

Evening

eveninglike: like late afternoon or early night

night-tripping: going lightly in the night

noctambulous: walking at night, either awake or asleep

noctilucent: glowing at night

noctilucous: shining at night; phosphorescent

noctivagant: wandering at night

nocturnal: active during the nighttime

nowanights: during these nights

pannychous: lasting all night

thestreen: last night

vespertine: pertaining to twilight, evening

yestreen: last night

Evidence

adminicular: corroborative

autoptic: pertaining to evidence based on observation

based on: having as a foundation

confirmatory: strengthening

corroborative: strengthening

deducible: capable of being inferred

evident: distinctly visible; quite obvious

evidential: based on a display or proof

evidentiary: pertaining to proof

founded on: based on

grounded on: based on

indicative: serving to show

indicatory: serving to show

showing: pointing out

Evil

agathokakological: composed of good and evil

agley: awry

awry: in an evil course

bad: marked by evil

cacodemonic: possessed by an evil spirit; cacodaemonic

deprecatory: serving or tending to avert evil

devilish: having the qualities of the devil

diabolic: pertaining to the devil; satanic

disastrous: occasioning or accompanied by evil

energumenical: possessed of an evil spirit; demoniacal

evil: morally bad; wicked

execrable: very bad; detestable

goetic: invoking evil spirits

hellborn: born of hell

infernal: pertaining to the lower regions or hell

lenocinant: lewd; tempting to evil

malefic: mischievous; harmful; creating evil; maleficent

maleficent: causing evil or harm

malominous: portending evil

Manichaean: believing the world is divided into good and evil

out of joint: gone wrong

peccable: susceptible or liable to temptation, sin; peccant

peccant: sinning; morally wrong

qued: evil; bad

satanic: having the qualities of Satan; devilish

scelerate: extremely wicked

tortious: injurious; wrongful

venal: able to be bribed or corrupted

Exaggeration

bombastic: pompous speech or writing

egregious: surpassing in rascality

exaggerated: beyond what is strictly true

extravagant: going beyond proper bounds

fabulous: not true; invented

high-flying: lofty; extravagant

hyperbolical: given to exaggeration; hyperbolic

on stilts: above people's heads

overwrought: overworked; overdone

preposterous: absurd; monstrous; outrageous

supercalifragilisticexpialidocious: fantastic; fabulous

Excess

adscititious: supplemental; additional

a-go-go: all you want

crammed to overflowing: gorged

dangwallet: abundantly; excessively; plentifully

drenched: wet from being poured or sprinkled on

dropsical: resembling dropsy

duplicate: exactly copied

excessive: passing beyond what is ordinary, required, fit

exorbitant: excessive in degree or amount

expletive: inserted or added for emphasis

extravagant: exceeding reasonable bounds

exuberant: copious and rich

filled to overflowing: gorged

gorged: filled by eating greedily

in excess: more than sufficient

inordinate: not limited; said of human desires; excessive; immoderate; intemperate

lautitious: sumptuous

lavish: characterized by extravagance or profusion

luxurious: sumptuously enjoying; supplied with luxuries
needless: unnecessary
obese: encumbered with flesh or fat
on one's hands: not to be used or sold
opiparous: sumptuous
outré: excessive; extreme; bizarre; unconventional or improper
over and above: being more than required
overcharged: exaggerated; excessive in price
overflowing: running over
overfond: fond to excess
overmuch: more than necessary
overweening: of opinion or desire, excessive and exaggerated
plethoric: evincing plethora
prodigal: wastefully extravagant
profuse: richly abundant
ready to burst: gorged
redundant: repetitive; superfluous
replete: completely full or supplied

running down: going to waste
running over: more than full
running to waste: having more than is sufficient
spare: over and above what is necessary
superabundant: more than can be used or controlled
supererogatory: nonessential; superfluous
superfluous: superabundant; said of things material
supernumerary: beyond the number stated
supersaturated: being more concentrated than normal
supervacaneous: needless
to spare: more than enough
too many: more than enough
too much: more than enough
turgid: swollen
uncalled for: unnecessary
unnecessary: needless
woundy: excessive

Exchange

acting: taking the part of another
commercial: pertaining to commerce
exchangeable: that may be bought and sold or exchanged
for sale: offered to those who want to buy
fungible: interchangeable
in the market: offered for sale
interchangeable: capable of being exchanged
marketable: fit to be sold; in demand
mercantile: pertaining to buying and selling

retail: concerned in selling goods in small quantities
staple: established in trade, as an article of commerce
subdititious: secretly substituting
substituted: put in place of another
trading: employed in commerce
vicarious: of emotions experienced imaginatively through others' experience; based upon the substitution of one person for another
vice: in the place of
wholesale: concerned in selling goods in large quantities

Excitement

afflated: inspired
agacant: exciting; provocative
agonizing: causing agony; wrestling
appetizing: stimulating desire
astir: active

boiling: in a state of intense emotion
boisterous: noisy
burning: producing an intense feeling
chafing: fretful
clamorous: making a great outcry

delirious: raving

demoniac: frenzied; quite energetic; demoniacal

demoniacal: devilish; crazy

demonstrative: making a great show

distracted: mentally disordered; torn asunder

ebullient: bubbling over with excitement; exuberant

effervescent: lively; energetic; animated; bubbly; perky; pert; spry; vivacious

electric: thrilling

entheal: divinely inspired; entheate

enthusiastic: filled with enthusiasm

estuous: excited; passionate

excitable: easily roused up

excited: stirred up

exciting: stirring up the spirits

fanatical: showing unreasonable enthusiasm

febrile: feverish; fevered

fervid: burning with zeal

feverish: highly excited

fidgety: nervous

fidgin fain: eager; excited; restless with excitement

fierce: unrestrained

fiery: easily wrought up

fisselig: flustered or nagged to the point of incompetence

flaming: bursting forth with passion

flushed: to be overcome by excitement

foaming: furious

fuming: exhibiting fretful passion

furious: raging

fussy: paying too much attention to trifles

glowing: hot

gomphipothic: sexually excited by good teeth

haggard: desperate

hasty: quickly aroused to anger

hot: highly excited

hurried: excited

hurry-skurry: confused; in a bustle

hysterical: liable to uncontrollable outbursts of emotion

impassioned: expressing great emotion

impatient: restless

impetuous: acting spontaneously

imposing: impressive

impulsive: acting without forethought

inextinguishable: uncontrollable, like the laughter of the gods at Vulcan

intolerant: not enduring difference of opinions

irrepressible: not to be checked

irritable: easily provoked

kedge: lively

lost: bewildered

mad: raving; crazy, as with wrath; raging

madcap: acting in a rash or giddy manner

magazinish: sensationalized; magaziny

mercurial: sprightly; lighthearted; like the god Mercury or quicksilver

mettlesome: high-spirited

moody: variable in humor

overpowering: depriving of self-control

overwhelming: depriving of self-control

passionate: subject to suffering from overpowering feeling

piquant: hurting the feelings

provocative: arousing ill-temper

rabid: inordinately excited

raging: in a violent state of emotion

rampant: unbridled

raving: speaking in a frenzied manner

restless: fidgety

rouncy: fidgety; fussy

seething: violently agitated

sensational: stirring up excitement

simmering: gently moved by emotion

sirenic: fascinating and dangerous, like a siren; sirenical

skittish: easily frightened

sparkling: lively

spicy: marked by zest

stanchless: not able to be stopped

startlish: timid

swelling: stirred up by anger

tantalizing: teasing by disappointing continually, as Tantalus

telling: effective

tempestuous: stormy

thrilling: sending quivers through the body

tumultuous: disorderly
turbulent: in great commotion
uncontrollable: not to be controlled
ungovernable: not to be governed
unquiet: disturbed
unroarious: making a great disturbance
up: excited

vehement: marked by impetuous animation
violent: intense
volcanic: bursting out with violence, like the chimney of the forge of Vulcan
warm: stirred by passion or excitement
wild: greatly excited

Exculpation—Pardon

acquitted: freed from the charge of crime
conciliated: freed from resentment
conciliatory: tending to make peace; pacific
drawing the nail: absolving oneself of a vow
exculpable: capable of being freed from blame
forgiving: prone to forgive
pardonable: that can be forgiven

placable: capable of being appeased
unavenged: permitted to pass without seeking satisfaction for
unchastised: not punished
uncondemned: not found guilty
unpunished: not having a penalty inflicted
unresented: permitted to pass without seeking satisfaction for
unrevenged: permitted to pass without seeking satisfaction for

Exemption

devoid of: wanting; lacking
exempt from: free from
not having: not possessing
unacquired: not having possession of
unblest with: not endowed with; unblessed with
unobtained: not having gained possession of

unpossessed: not owning
unpossessed of: not owning
untenanted: not leased or occupied by a tenant
without: devoid of; wanting
without an owner: belonging to nobody

Expectation

abeyant: being in suspense
agape: having the mouth open, showing a state of expectancy
astonished at nothing: immovable
common: often met with; customary
curious: eager to examine everything
expectant: waiting for something
expected: looked for; anticipated
expecting: looking forward to; waiting for
foreseen: seen or known beforehand

gaping: holding the mouth open, expressive of expectancy
impending: likely to happen
lochetic: waiting in ambush
ordinary: customary; usual
proleptic: expecting; anticipating
prospective: looking toward the future
ready: at hand
spectabundal: eager to see
speratory: expected or hoped for
unamazed: not confounded or bewildered

Expulsion

deciduous: shedding; falling off
ejected: expelled from a place
emitted: given or sent out
emitting: giving or sending out
eructed: belched; burped; eructated
evolved: rolling off
evolving: rolling off

expellable: liable to expulsion
expulsatory: that expels, drives out
exsputory: ejected; spit out
extracted: drawn or pulled out
fugitated: expelled; put to flight
secluded: excluded; expelled

Extension

aforcing: stretching a food dish to accommodate more people
ample: great in extent
amplivagant: large or wide in scope; extensive; amplivagous
boundless: limitless; unbounded
capacious: spacious; extended
digitate: like spread fingers
expansive: very wide; wide-extending; panoramic
exsertile: protruding
extensive: having a wide extent
pathless: untrodden; having no path
protractile: capable of extending; protrusile

roomy: spacious; wide
shoreless: of unlimited extent
spacious: vast in extent
tensional: pertaining to tension
tensive: causing tension
trackless: untrodden
tractile: capable of being drawn out
transverse: extended crosswise; athwart
uncircumscribed: not circumscribed
vast: immense; very great
wide: having great extent
widespread: spread over great extent
worldwide: extended through the whole world

Extravagance

dissipated: scattered; squandered
extravagant: carelessly expending in excess of income
full-handed: having hands full
improvident: lacking foresight; careless
lavish: bountifully extravagant
losel: slothful and wasteful
Lucullan: lavish; sumptuous; Lucullean; Lucullian
nimious: extravagant
overliberal: more generous than one can afford

penny-wise and pound-foolish: economical in small matters, extravagant in large things
prodigal: given to extravagant expenditures; wasteful
profuse: liberal or abundant to excess
thriftless: having no foresight or prudence in management of resources
unthrifty: not thrifty or careful in management of money affairs
wasteful: inclined to waste; causing waste and loss; prodigal

Facility

accessible: within reach
at ease: calm; composed
at home: skillful
disburdened: relieved
disembarrassed: freed from
　encumbrance
disencumbered: freed from
　encumbrance
ductile: easily led; yielding
easily accomplished: not hard to do
easily managed: not hard to manage
easy: not hard
easy of access: not hard to get to
exonerated: freed from blame or
　responsibility
facile: not difficult
feasible: doable; possible
for the million: anyone can do the work
glib: smooth-tongued
in one's element: what one is best fitted
　to do
in smooth water: no opposition
light: easily handled

manageable: docile; able to be controlled
on friction wheels: on smooth surfaces
on velvet: soft; pliable
open to: accessible
pliant: yielding readily to influence
quite at home: well acquainted with the
　work
slippery: smooth; glossy
smooth: with no obstruction or difficulty
submissive: obedient
towardly: willing to do or learn
tractable: easy to deal with; manageable
unburdened: relieved of difficulty
unembarrassed: free from difficulty
unencumbered: not weighed down by
　difficulty
unloaded: relieved of something
　oppressive
unobstructed: unimpeded
unrestrained: free of constraint
untrammeled: not hampered
wieldy: controllable
within reach: attainable
yielding: giving in; docile

Failure

abortive: unsuccessful; fruitless; failing
　before maturity
addle: good for nothing; weak; idle
aground: at a standstill
all up with: without hope or resource

at fault: having the fault
bankrupt: unable to pay one's debts;
　having broken one's bank
befooled: swindled; cheated; gulled
bootless: without profit or advantage

borne-down: having sunk, as if under a great weight
broken: crushed in feeling or spirit
broken-down: ruined or wrecked, financially or physically
capsized: upset, as a boat
castaway: wrecked; wasted
crossed: hindered; obstructed
dashed: checked or discouraged
dead beat: thoroughly defeated
defeated: beaten; overcome
deficient: lacking in necessary qualities
destroyed: overthrown; torn down; knocked to pieces
disconcerted: confused so as to falter
dished: ruined; cheated; badly used
done for: useless; wrecked; ruined
done up: tired out; badly used
downtrodden: oppressed
failing: wasting away
flambé: singed; blazed
foiled: rendered ineffectual by counteraction
foundered: wrecked
fruitless: without results
frustrated: having failed in attainment
grounded: at a standstill
hobbling: limping
hoist by/on/with one's own petard: injured by one's own act
in a sorry plight: in a complicated situation
ineffective: not producing a decided effect
ineffectual: not producing the result intended
inefficacious: not producing or doing any good
inefficient: lacking in ability or skill or power
insufficient: lacking in quantity or degree
knocked on the head: defeated; destroyed
lame: having a halt in the gait
left in the lurch: left in an embarrassing situation, as a ship

lost: not won, gained, or enjoyed
minus: deprived of
nonsuited: having one's suit dismissed in court
oligophrenic: severely deficient mentally
out of one's depth: beyond one's power
out of one's reckoning: not according to one's plan
overborne: crushed
overwhelmed: overpowered
perfunctory: done carelessly; negligent
played out: worn-out
ruined: irretrievably injured
ruined root and branch: thoroughly ruined
sacrificed: lost in pursuing an object
shipwrecked: ruined
short: deficient in
short of: deficient in
stillborn: doomed from the start
stranded: helpless; without resources
struck down: suddenly wrecked, ruined, or killed
stultified: given an appearance of foolishness
successless: without success
swamped: overturned, as a boat
thrown away: wasted
thrown off one's balance: confused; discomposed; disconcerted
thrown on one's back: in a well-nigh hopeless position
thrown on one's beam ends: in a serious or hopeless predicament
tripping: almost falling
unattained: not attained
unavailing: not availing
uncompleted: not finished
undone: ruined; brought to grief
unfortunate: unsuccessful
unhinged: unsettled
unhorsed: defeated; repulsed
unreached: unattained
unsuccessful: not successful
victimized: swindled or duped
wide of the mark: far from correct or from one's object or purpose
wrecked: disabled; nearly ruined

Faintness

dulcet: sweet to the ear; melodious

dull: low; not clear

faint: scarcely audible

floating: sounding quietly and gently

flowing: sounding smoothly

gentle: low; soft; not loud

hoarse: having a rough or grating voice

husky: rough in tone

inaudible: incapable of being heard

just audible: almost inaudible

low: not loud

muffled: wrapped with something that renders sound inaudible

purling: softly murmuring

scarcely audible: hardly audible

soft: gentle; not loud

soothing: tending to calm or console

stifled: deadened

susurrant: murmuring; whispering; gently rustling

whispered: lowly spoken

Faith

accredited: having trust reposed in

acroamatic: esoteric and revealed only to chosen disciples orally

alterocentric: believing that life revolves only around oneself or only around another person

aniconic: opposed to using idols

antediluvian: before the Flood

assured: made certain

autocephalous: having its own chief bishop but in communion with other Orthodox churches

believed: held to be true

believing: accepting as true

blessed: consecrated; holy; enjoying bliss; state prior to sainthood

born-again: designating person who has experienced spiritual awakening and new religious commitment to Christ as personal savior; reborn; saved

Brahmanical: relating to Brahmanism

certain: not admitting of doubt

cleocentric: believing that fame is everything

cocksure: very certain

collegial: marked by sharing of authority among Roman Catholic bishops

commanding belief: producing belief

confident: fully assured

confiding: having faith in

convinced: fully satisfied by proof

credible: worthy of being believed

credulous: apt to believe on slight proof; gullible

defrocked: describing minister or priest who has been removed from office or excommunicated

deserving of belief: worthy of belief

doctrinal: pertaining to doctrine

epideistic: zealous about religion

faithful: believing; steadfast in belief

faithworthy: worthy of trust

fidimplicitary: completely trusting someone

fiducial: indicative of faith

fiduciary: pertaining to one in a position of trust

filiopietistic: concerning ancestor worship, especially to a foolish extreme

God-fearing: deeply fearful or respectful of God

goyish: non-Jewlike

hagiolatrous: concerning worship of saints

hallowed: blessed; made or kept holy

heliolatrous: concerning sun worship

holy: sacred; saintly; pure; whole

imbued with: deeply impressed with

impressed with: strongly influenced by

impressive: touching the conscience

interdenominational: common to or involving different religious denominations

Judaical: relating to the Jews; Judaic

kosher: fit to eat under Jewish dietary laws; proper; legitimate

Mohammedan: relating to the Mohammedan religion; Muhammadan

mystical: involving direct communion with God or the divine

numinous: inspiring awe and fascination; pertaining to mysterious aspect of divine power and religious experience

penetrated with: believing thoroughly in

persuasive: having power to persuade

piacular: making atonement

pistic: pertaining to faith

positive: very decided in opinion

prelapsarian: before the Fall

probable: with more evidence for than against

profane: irreverent; unholy; defiling what is sacred

putative: commonly supposed

reborn: born-again

recreant: failing to keep faith

relating to belief: doctrinal

reliable: worthy of confidence

sacred: consecrated; holy

sacrosanct: extremely sacred or holy

satisfactory: removing doubt from the mind

satisfied: convinced beyond a doubt

saved: having accepted Christ as one's personal savior; born-again

secure: firm in opinion; free from care

sure: deserving to be depended on; free from doubt

suspectless: not having any suspicion

to be depended upon: worthy of belief

trustworthy: worthy of confidence

ultrafidian: extremely gullible

under the impression: having a particular judgment

unhesitating: without hesitation

unholy: lacking in purity

unsuspected: not suspected

unsuspecting: not mistrusting

unsuspicious: not inclined to suspect

venerable: blessed; honorable; state prior to sainthood

void of suspicion: satisfied

wedded to: firmly attached to

worthy of belief: credible

Faithlessness

antichristian: opposed to Christianity

atheistic: denying the existence of God

bigoted: unreasonably devoted to a creed, opinion, or party

blasphemous: sacrilegious in the use of God's name

canting: affectedly pious

carnal: relating to the body or its appetites

deistical: pertaining to deism

desecrating: violating sacredness

devoutless: wanting devotion

earthly: belonging to this world; not spiritual

faithless: not believing in God or religion

fanatical: moved by intemperate zeal

freethinking: denying revealed religion

godless: without belief in the existence of God

graceless: gone away from divine grace

hardened: fixed in error or vice

hypocritical: false in religious pretensions

idolatrous: pertaining to idolatry; given to the worship of false gods

impious: wickedly and boldly defiant of God and his law

incredulous: not disposed to admit or believe

indevout: not attentive to religion

irreligious: indifferent to things sacred

irreverent: lacking in due regard for the Supreme Being

lacking faith: not believing in God or religion

mammon worship: devoted to money-getting

mundane: worldly as opposed to spiritual

overrighteous: affectedly righteous

perverted: corrupted; led astray

pharisaical: resembling the Pharisees, hence hypocritical; self-righteous

pietistical: ostentatiously religious

priest-ridden: governed or controlled by priests

profane: not sacred; given to swearing

reprobate: morally depraved

righteous overmuch: overrighteous

sacrilegious: violating or profaning sacred things

sanctimonious: hypocritically or affectedly pious or saintly

skeptical: inclined to question the grounds for belief

unbelieving: not believing

unchristian: not believing in Christ

unconverted: not turned to God

unctuous: insincerely fervid

undevout: irreligious

ungodly: without faith in God

unhallowed: not consecrated; unholy

unholy: without reverence for God

unregenerate: not renewed in heart

unsanctified: not cleansed from sin

without God: irreligious

worldly: relating to this world or life; temporal

worldly-minded: ungodly

Falsehood

affected: assumed falsely or in outward semblance only; not genuine in manner

artful: produced or characterized by craft or cunning

backhanded: indirect and devious

bogus: not genuine; counterfeit

canting: said in a hypocritical way

chimerical: wildly improbable and imaginative

collusive: fraudulently concerted or devised

collusory: plotting secretly with evil design

counterfeit: bogus; fake; imitation; phony

covinous: fraudulent; collusive; deceitful; conspiring

crooked: insincere, indirect, or dishonest

deceitful: characterized by deception; tricky

dishonest: destitute of integrity or good faith; untrustworthy

disingenuous: wanting in openness and honesty

double-dealing: treacherous; deceitful

double-faced: deceitful; hypocritical

double-handed: deceitful; deceptive

double-hearted: false; deceitful

double-minded: unsettled; unstable

double-tongued: characterized by duplicity of speech; lying

elusory: tending to deceive one's expectations

evasive: tending to deceive

exorbitant: exceeding the bounds of what is proper or customary

fabricated: contrived without ground or reason

fabulous: belonging to fables; fictitious

factitious: created by art as opposed to nature

faithless: untrue to promise or obligation; deceptive; unfaithful

fake: counterfeit

false: contrary to truth; erroneous; artificial; counterfeit

false as dicer's oaths: very false

falsidical: suggesting something to be true that is false

falsified: misrepresented

far from the truth: false

fictitious: false, assumed, or imaginary

fishy: questionable or suspicious

flannelmouthed: speaking in a shifty, ingratiating way

forged: made in false and fraudulent imitation of something that if genuine would be legal

forsworn: perjured

fraudulent: based on, proceeding from, or characterized by fraud

hollow: insincere; empty or vacant, as if containing nothing

hypocritical: characterized by hypocrisy

illusory: deceiving or intending to deceive

imitation: counterfeit

indirect: tending to evade or misrepresent what really is; backhanded

insincere: acting, speaking, or appearing falsely to deceive

invented: fabricated in the mind; concocted

ironical: disguising the real meaning

Janus-faced: double-faced

jesuitical: using crafty or insidious arts or methods

Machiavellian: crafty or cruel in politics; treacherous

mealymouthed: speaking with insincerity

mendacious: addicted to lying; falsifying

pecksniffian: hypocritical; gutless

perfidious: violating good faith

pharisaical: observing the form but neglecting the spirit of religion

phony: false; counterfeit

plausible: seeming likely to be true though open to doubt

prodigal: reckless, extravagant, or excessive

pseudo: false or spurious

quasi: resembling or seeming

questionable: doubtful or suspicious; likely to be false

sanctimonious: hypocritical in displaying righteousness

shadowy: unreliable, doubtful, or illicit

shifty: given to deception, evasion, and fraud

smooth-faced: having a bland expression to deceive

smooth-spoken: using plausible and flattering speech

smooth-tongued: using easy speech

so-called: misrepresented as such

soi-disant: so-called

spurious: lacking validity; false; not genuine

supposititious: put in the place or made to represent the person of another, to deceive or defraud

surreptitious: accomplished by secret and illegitimate or improper means

synthetic: contrived as a substitute for the real thing

tartuffish: hypocritical; tartuffian

tortuous: characterized by indirect tactics; tricky, crooked, or devious

trothless: faithless; treacherous

trumped-up: to make up or invent for a fraudulent purpose

truthless: not agreeing with fact

uncandid: not frank

unfair: not honest

unfounded: resting on no solid foundation of truth or reason

uningenuous: not free from reserve, disguise, equivocation, or dissimulation

untrue: not corresponding with fact

unveracious: not habitually disposed to speak the truth

void of foundation: without any element of truth

without foundation: without any element of truth

Fancy—Imagination

air-built: chimerical; fanciful

air-drawn: imaginary

bucolic: pastoral; rural

chimerical: imaginary; visionary; wildly fanciful

chthonic: pertaining to the underworld

commentitious: imaginary; fabricated

creative: having the imaginative faculty

demiurgic: creative

enthusiastic: filled with enthusiasm; highly imaginative

excogitous: inventive; excogitative

extravagant: immoderate in imagination; fantastic

fabulous: being the product of imagination

fairy: produced by the fairies, as fairy rings, fairy gold

fairylike: like a fairy

fanatic: extravagant in opinions

fanciful: imaginative

fancy: extravagant; imagined

fantastical: conceived by unrestrained imagination

fertile: inventive

fictive: imaginary; fictitious

flighty: given to flights of fancy

haptic: denoting one who draws primarily on the sense of touch

high-flown: extravagant

ideal: reaching an idea above the forms of the senses

illusory: deceiving

imaginary: existing only in imagination

imaginative: creative or constructive

imagined: fancied

imagining: supposing

implicit: unexpressed but essential to the nature of something

in the clouds: in the realm of fancy

inventive: imaginative

legendary: consisting of legends

mythic: imaginary

mythological: pertaining to the myths

notional: existing only in imagination

oneiric: dreamlike; pertaining to dreams; oniric

oneirotic: concerning erotic dreams

original: imagined for the first time; not imitated

pastoral: pertaining to idealized, peaceful, simple, and natural life of farmers and shepherds

pretend: make-believe or imagined

quixotic: like Don Quixote; romantically mad; impractical; visionary

romantic: imaginative

supermundane: ideal; fantastic; chimeral; supramundane

unreal: existing in imagination only

unsubstantial: lacking in substance; visionary

utopian: pertaining to Utopia or imaginary perfection

visile: denoting one who draws primarily on visual data and input

visionary: existing in imagination only

whimsical: fanciful; freakish

Fashion

à la mode: of fashionable attire; chic; stylish

acid-washed: describing denim processed with bleach to fade color

aesthetic: pertaining to the science of taste

after one's fancy: to one's taste

allover: describing a fabric with a single repeating design motif

artistic: pertaining to art

Attic: marking such elegance of taste as characterized Attica in Greece; classic; elegant

banded: having narrow cloth strips for decoration and to prevent raveling

bardocucullated: wearing a cowled cloak

bonded: made of two layers of the same fabric, or of a fabric and a lining material, attached to each other by a chemical process of adhesive

bruffed: thickly clothed

camisated: wearing a shirt over other clothing

capistrate: hooded

castorial: pertaining to a hat

chaste: showing good taste by freedom from extravagance

clad: dressed; covered with clothing

classical: in correct and refined taste; conforming to ancient Greece or Rome

colorfast: describing fabric with permanent color dyed into its yarn, so that it will not fade or run

cultivated: cultured; refined by good taste

custom-tailored: designed, manufactured, or fitted to individual specifications

dainty: of exquisite taste

damassé: woven in reversible, figured pattern like damask

designer: created by or carrying label of specific fashion designer, but often mass-produced

diaphanous: transparent or translucent and gauzy

dight: dressed; arrayed; adorned

dighted: dressed; arrayed; adorned

discinct: worn loosely; unbelted or ungirt

dizened: decked out

dressmaker: having soft lines or elaborate detail

elegant: refined; pleasing to good taste

endimanché: dressed in one's best or festive clothes

euphemistic: using fair words

fashionable: having good appearance; having up-to-date dress or behavior

figured: ornamented, marked, or formed into repeating pattern

fin: subtle; elegant; polished

frayed: worn or ragged from use or age, especially collars and cuffs

full: having ample folds and abundant material

habited: clothed; dressed

in court dress: in full uniform or levee dress

in evening dress: in full dress

in good taste: refined

invested: covered with a garment; clothed

jimpricute: fashionable

long-waisted: having greater than average length between shoulders and waistline

low-necked: having neckline cut low to leave neck and shoulders bare

missy: designating young girls' clothing sizes

motley: of variegated material, like Renaissance fool's outfit

nubby: having rough, knotted weave

ocreate: wearing leggings or boots

off-the-rack: ready-made; not made to individual specifications

paletoted: clothed in a loose garment, as a muumuu or toga

peekaboo: made of sheer and revealing material

preshrunk: designating a cotton garment shrunk to fit before sale

prewashed: designating garments washed before sale, usually to produce faded or worn look or soft texture

pure: refined; classic

raveled: unwoven, untwisted, or unwound

ready-to-wear: designating mass-produced apparel, especially synthetics

refined: cultivated

reversible: being a garment that may be worn with lining side out

sartorial: of or pertaining to a tailor or his work

sericeous: downy or silky in finish or appearance

shod: furnished with a shoe or shoes

short waisted: having less than average length between shoulders and waistline

soigné: showing sophistication, elegance; fashionable; polished; soignée

standaway: designed to stand upright or outward from the body

stonewashed: washed prior to sale with pebbles or stones to give worn appearance

strapless: designating dress or woman's top made without shoulder straps

subvestimentary: concerning clothing worn under a vestment or robe

tasteful: displaying good taste

tasty: in conformity to good taste

threadbare: designating fabric having nap worn so that threads show

to one's mind: agreeable to one

to one's taste: agreeable to one

tonnish: fashionable; chic; tonish

two-ply: designating fabric woven with two sets of warp thread and two of filling

unaffected: natural

unisize: made to fit all sizes or types in normal range

vestiary: pertaining to clothing

waterproof: designating fabric treated so water will not penetrate it

water-repellent: designating fabric treated to resist water absorption

water-resistant: designating fabric sometimes slightly more absorbent than that which is water-repellent

yclad: clothed

youthy: pertaining to an older person trying to dress or act like a much younger person

Faultiness

admissible: worthy of being admitted; allowable

average: of middle size, quality, or ability

bearable: that can be endured

below its full complement: deficient in quantity, number, or amount

below par: at a discount

cracked: having a crack; broken

crude: not mature or perfect

decent: moderate; fairly good

defective: lacking something

deficient: wanting; incomplete

fair: middling; average

faulty: having faults or defects

found wanting: deficient

frail: easily broken or destroyed

funest: fatally flawed; portending doom

good enough: passable

imperfect: wanting in some of its parts

inadequate: not equal to the purpose

incomplete: deficient in some of its parts

indifferent: neither very good nor very bad

inferior: poor or mediocre

injured: impaired in excellence or quality; damaged

inobjectionable: not deserving of disapproval; not offensive

lame: disabled in limb; crippled

leaky: allowing water or other fluid to leak in or out

mediocre: having a middle quality

middling: of middle rank or quality

milk-and-water: weak and vacillating

moderately good: of the average

not amiss: not wrong or out of order

not bad: a little below the average

not perfect: faulty

only better than nothing: faulty

ordinary: of common rank or ability; inferior

out of order: disarranged; in confusion

out of tune: discordant; not in agreeing temper

passable: such as may be allowed to pass; mediocre

peccant: guilty of sin or transmission

pretty good: in some degree good

pretty well: in some degree good

rather good: in some degree good

secondary: not of the first order or rate

second-best: next to the best

second-rate: of the second class, rank, quality, or value

shorthanded: lacking in the regular number of helpers

so-so: neither very good nor very bad

sprung: said of a spar that has been cracked or strained

tainted: corrupted

tolerable: moderately good

under its full complement: deficient in number

under its full strength: imperfect

unsound: not sound

warped: twisted out of its true shape

well enough: in a tolerable degree

wonky: amiss; faulty

Faultlessness

best: having the highest degree of excellence

beyond all praise: best

consummate: of the highest quality

divine: godlike; excellent in the highest degree

faultless: free from blemish

finished: polished in the highest degree

free from imperfection: perfect

harmless: free from the disposition to harm; innocent

immaculate: without spot or blemish

impeccable: not liable or subject to sin; flawless

in perfect condition: faultless

indefectible: not liable to defect or failure

indefective: not wanting in anything

indeficient: full

inimitable: surpassingly excellent

intact: untouched by anything harmful

model: worthy to be imitated

perfect: having all that is needful to its nature and kind

right as a trivet: standing firm

scatheless: unharmed

seaworthy: in condition to go on a voyage

sound: perfect of its kind

sound as a roach: perfectly sound

spotless: free from spots; pure

standard: having a permanent value

superhuman: above that which is human

unblemished: without blemish or defect

uninjured: not injured or harmed

unparagoned: without an equal

unparalleled: having no parallel or equal

unwemmed: unblemished

Fauna

acalephan: pertaining to jellyfish

acaridal: pertaining to mites, ticks; acarine

acaudal: not having a tail; acaudate

accipitrine: like a hawk's beak; pertaining to hawks

actinal: belonging to the mouth of a radiate animal, such as a starfish, from which its arms symmetrically extend

aestivating: passing the summer in a lethargic, low-metabolic state

agnine: pertaining to lamb

alcine: pertaining to elk

alopecoid: like a fox; vulpine

anadromous: of fish, migrating up rivers from the sea to spawn in fresh water

anatine: ducklike

anguineous: snakelike

angustirostrate: having a narrow beak or nose

animal: having the nature of a brute

anserine: pertaining to a goose

apian: related to bees

apiarian: pertaining to beekeeping or bees

aprine: pertaining to wild boars

arachnoid: concerning spiders; cobweb-like; araneiform

arctoid: like a bear

arietine: concerning rams

asinine: pertaining to asses

asteroidal: concerning starfish

australopithecine: pertaining to apes; anthropoid

avian: pertaining to birds; avine; volucrine

bactrian: of a two-humped camel

batoid: concerning rays

batrachoid: froglike; batrachian

bausond: of an animal, having a white spot or streak on the forehead or face

biform: sharing characteristics with two animals or with plant and animal life

bisontine: pertaining to bison; bisonic

blattoid: like a cockroach

boopic: ox-eyed

bovine: related to or resembling a cow or ox

braccate: having feathered legs

branchiate: having gills

brockle: of cattle, apt to break a fence

buteonine: pertaining to buzzards

caballine: horselike

cameline: pertaining to camels

canine: of a dog; relating to a dog; cynoid

capric: goatlike

carcinomorphic: crablike; arthropodal; arthropodous

caridoid: pertaining to shrimp

casteroid: pertaining to beavers

catadromous: migrating from fresh water to the sea to spawn

cebocephalic: monkey-headed

cercopithecan: pertaining to monkeys

cervicorn: having antlers

cervine: pertaining to deer

cetacean: pertaining to whales; cetaceous

chelonian: pertaining to turtles, tortoises

chevaline: horselike

chimopelagic: pertaining to deep-sea organisms that surface only in winter

ciconine: storklike; herodian; herodionine

clicking-fork't: of a sheep, having its ears marked by having two triangular-shaped pieces cut out

clupeoid: pertaining to herring

cobriform: pertaining to cobras

coleopterous: pertaining to beetles; coleopteral

colubrine: snakelike

columbine: pertaining to doves, pigeons, or dodo birds

corvine: crowlike

crotaliform: resembling a rattlesnake

crotaline: pertaining to rattlesnakes

crustacean: pertaining to lobsters; homarine; homaroid; macrural

cuculine: pertaining to cuckoos

culicine: pertaining to mosquitos; culicid

cunicular: concerning rabbits

cuniculous: full of rabbits

cygnine: concerning swans

delphin: pertaining to dolphins

didine: dodolike

dinosaurian: pertaining to dinosaurs; dinosauric

discophoran: like a jellyfish

draconic: dragonlike

dragonate: having qualities of a dragon; fierce; fire-breathing

ecaudate: without a tail; acaudal; acaudate

echinoid: like a sea urchin

elephantine: pertaining to elephants; pachydermoid; proboscidian

entomologic: pertaining to insects; insectean; insectival

epimeletic: denoting the care of young animals by their parents and other members of the same species

epithelial: pertaining to the outer layer of the mucous membrane in animals, such as lips, nipples, etc.

epizootic: pertaining to an animal epidemic

equine: pertaining to horses; caballine; chevaline

erinaceous: concerning the hedgehog

falconine: pertaining to falcons; falconoid

faunal: pertaining to animals or animal life

feliform: catlike; feline

feline: like a cat; characteristic of cats; feliform

ferine: like a wild beast

fishy: like a fish

fissiped: cloven-hoofed

fleshly: pertaining to the animal nature; corporeal; carnal

frampold: of a horse, spirited

gadoid: pertaining to cod

gallinaceous: like a chicken or pheasant; galline

gastropodous: concerning snails

gibbed: concerning a castrated cat

giraffine: pertaining to giraffes; camelopardine

gliriform: resembling a rodent; glirine; rodential

gorilloid: pertaining to gorillas; gorillian; gorilline

grallatorial: pertaining to long-legged wading birds, as crane and heron; grallatory

grillid: pertaining to crickets; grilline
hamirostrate: having a hooked beak
harpactophagous: predatory, especially
insects
herpestine: pertaining to the mongoose
herpetiform: in the character or shape of
a reptile
herpetine: reptilian; snakelike
heterocerous: pertaining to moths
hibernating: passing the winter in a lethargic, low-metabolic state
hippiatric: pertaining to horse doctors
hippic: relating to horses or horse racing
hippocampine: concerning sea horses
hippopotamic: pertaining to the
hippopotamus
hirudinoid: like a leech; bdelloid
horned: of cattle, with horns removed
hyenic: pertaining to the hyena; hyaenic
hystricine: concerning porcupines;
hystricoid
ichthyoid: pertaining to fish; piscial;
piscine
implumous: without feathers
insectiform: insectlike
jubate: having a mane or long fringed
hair
lacertilian: pertaining to lizards; lacer-
tian; lacertine; saurian
lagotic: having rabbitlike ears
larine: pertaining to gulls; laridine
lemurine: concerning lemurs; lemuroid
leonine: pertaining to lions
leporine: pertaining to hares or rabbits;
lagomorphic
limaceous: pertaining to slugs; limacine
limacine: sluglike
limuloid: pertaining to the king crab
longicaudal: having a long tail
loricate: pertaining to alligators; croco-
dilian; emydosaurian
lumbricoid: pertaining to earthworms
lupine: pertaining to wolves
lutrine: otterlike
lyncean: like a lynx; sharp-sighted
macropodine: pertaining to kangaroos;
macropoid
macruran: pertaining to crustaceans with

well-developed abdomens, as lobster,
crayfish, shrimp, prawn
manatine: pertaining to manatees
manxome: like a manx cat
marsupial: concerning pouched animals;
didelphian
meline: badgerlike
mephitine: pertaining to skunks
milch: of domestic animals, giving milk
molluscous: of or pertaining to a mollusk
murine: concerning mice or rats; murid
muscid: pertaining to the fly; musciform
musteline: pertaining to weasels
myoxine: pertaining to the dormouse
myriapodous: concerning centipedes;
myriapodan
myrmecoid: antlike
nasicornous: having a horn on the nose,
like a rhinoceros
nematode: pertaining to roundworms;
nematoid
nidicolous: of young birds that linger for
some time in the nest
ocellated: having eyespots
octopean: pertaining to octopuses; ceph-
alopodous; octopine
odonatous: pertaining to dragonflies;
libelluloid
ophic: pertaining to snakes; anguiform;
anguine; anguineous; ophidian; serpentine; sincrous
orthopterous: pertaining to grasshop-
pers, crickets
oscine: relating to songbirds
ostreiform: concerning oysters; oyster-
shaped; ostreoid; ostreophagous;
ostriform
ovine: sheeplike
pagurian: concerning the hermit crab
pantherine: concerning a panther
papilionaceous: butterfly-like
pardine: pertaining to leopards
parotoid: of certain glands forming
warty masses near the ears of some ba-
trachians, as toads
pelargic: storklike
percoid: resembling a perch
peristeronic: concerning pigeons

philhippic: fond of horses
phocaenine: concerning porpoises
phocine: concerning seals or walruses
phoenicopterous: pertaining to flamingos
piciform: pertaining to woodpeckers; picine
pinniped: relating to aquatic carnivores, as seals and walruses
piscatorial: pertaining to fishes
piscatory: pertaining to fishes
plumaged: having feathers; plumose
porcine: resembling a pig or swine; suine
porpentine: concerning porcupines
precocial: independent or nearly independent when hatched
proboscidate: having a long nose for grasping, like an elephant's trunk; proboscidiform
procyanine: concerning raccoons
psittaceous: parrotlike; psittacine
pulicous: pertaining to fleas; pulicid
pythonic: concerning pythons
queenright: having a queen bee in the hive
rampant: of beasts, rearing or holding forepaws in the air
rangiferine: concerning reindeer
ranine: pertaining to frogs; batrachian; raniform
rasorial: scratching the ground in search of food, as domestic fowl
reptilian: concerning reptiles; herpetiform; reptiloid
ring-tailed: having a tail with colored bands
rostrate: having a beak; rhamphoid
rostrated: having a beak
runcinate: saw-toothed; with teeth curved toward the base
salamandrine: like a salamander in being able to resist fire or live in it
saurian: lizardlike; lacertilian
scaroid: concerning parrot fish
sciaenid: relating to flesh-eating fish of the croaker family
sciurine: squirrellike; sciuroid; spermophiline

sciuroid: like a squirrel's tail or a squirrel
scolopendrine: concerning centipedes
scombroid: resembling the mackerel; scombrid
selachian: sharklike
silurid: concerning catfish; siluroid
sinorous: snakelike; sinerous
sirenian: pertaining to the dugong, manatee, sea cow
soricine: shrewlike; soricoid
spermophiline: pertaining to chipmunks, gophers, squirrels
spheniscine: concerning penguins; impennate
sphragistic: pertaining to seals; otarine; phocine; pinnipedian
sphyraenoid: pertaining to barracuda
strigine: owllike
struthious: like an ostrich, cassowary, emu, or moa; struthionine
suilline: relating to hogs, swine
suoid: relating to hogs
taeniid: concerning tapeworms; taenial
talpoid: molelike; talpine
tarantulous: pertaining to tarantulas
teiid: relating to lizards with forked tongues
telarian: spinning a web
thanatophidian: concerning poisonous snakes
theroid: like a wild beast
thooid: pertaining to the division of the genus *Canis* including wolves, jackals, hyenas, dogs
tigerish: concerning tigers; feline; tigerine; tigrine
trichechine: pertaining to walruses
truttaceous: pertaining to trout
turdiform: thrushlike
ungual: pertaining to hoof, nail, or claw
unguiculate: having hooks, nails, or claws
ungulate: having hoofs; hoof-shaped
unguligrade: walking on hoofs
urinatorial: pertaining to diving birds
ursine: bearlike; arctoid; ursal
vaccine: relating to cows; pertaining to cowpox

vermicular: pertaining to a worm

vermiform: like a worm; vermian; vermicular

vermilinguial: pertaining to anteaters or chameleons

verpertilian: pertaining to bats

vespertilian: batlike

vespine: pertaining to wasps; vespoid

viperine: concerning vipers

vituline: pertaining to calves or veal

volucrine: pertaining to birds

vulpecular: pertaining to foxes; alopecoid; vulpine

vulturine: pertaining to vultures; vulturial

xenarthral: resembling a sloth, anteater, or armadillo

xiphosuran: pertaining to the king crab

zebrine: concerning zebras; hippotigrine

zoological: of the animal kingdom; pertaining to zoology

Female

catamenial: menstrual

effeminate: soft, unmanly, or womanish

enate: related on the mother's side; enatic

female: denoting persons or animals of the female sex

feminine: having the qualities of a woman

gemelliparous: pertaining to a woman who has given birth to twins

gynecic: concerning women; feminine

gynecocentric: pertaining to domination by women

gynecomorphous: characterized as female

ladylike: suitable to a well-bred woman; gentle; delicate

maidenly: befitting a maiden; gentle; modest

matricentric: dominated by the mother or mother's side

matripotestal: pertaining to the authority of a mother

matronly: advanced in years; elderly

matronymic: using the mother's name

muliebral: pertaining to women

muliebrous: effeminate

nulliparous: pertaining to a woman who has never given birth

Sardanapalian: luxuriously effeminate

she: denoting a female

thelytokous: producing only females

unfeminine: acting like a man

unwomanly: not suited or becoming to a woman

womanly: having the qualities becoming to a woman

Fertility

barren: unable to conceive or produce offspring; infertile

congenital: describing a trait derived or inherited from parents through genes

contraceptive: tending to prevent conception

expecting: pregnant

fecund: fertile; prolific

feracious: fruitful; productive

fertile: producing in abundance; able to conceive children

frugiferous: fruit-bearing

fruit-bearing: having fruit in distinction from vegetables

fruitful: fertile; productive

fruitive: capable of producing fruit

generative: having power to generate or produce

gravid: heavy with child; pregnant

illegitimate: born out of wedlock; misbegotten

in utero: in the womb or uterus

in vitro: in glass; artificially inseminated and maintained, as in a test tube

legitimate: lawfully begotten and born in wedlock

life-giving: giving life or animation

luxuriant: producing in superabundance

misbegotten: illegitimate
multiparous: producing many at one birth
natal: relating to or associated with birth
omnific: all-creating
parturient: giving birth to a child
pregnant: having unborn child in one's body; expecting; gravid; with child
prenatal: before birth
pro-choice: advocating legalized abortion
procreant: generative; productive
procreative: having power to generate
productive: having the power of producing; yielding in abundance

profitable: bringing profit; lucrative
pro-life: opposing legalized abortion
prolific: producing young, with the idea of frequency and numbers
propagable: capable of being spread, continued, or multiplied
spermatic: relating or pertaining to semen
stillborn: describing infant dead at birth
teemful: prolific
teeming: productive
uberous: rich; plentiful; productive
unfertile: physiologically unable to conceive and reproduce
unpregnant: not prolific
viparious: life-renewing

Fiber

capilliform: formed like a thread or filament
cilicious: of haircloth
fibrillous: pertaining to fibers
fibrous: like or pertaining to a fiber
filaceous: consisting of threads; filamentous
filamentous: like a filament or thread
filar: having threads or lines across the field of vision, as a gun sight
filiform: formed like a filament
fimbricate: fringelike; fimbriate; fimbrillate; laciniform
flagelliform: formed like a flagellum; long, narrow, and slender

funicular: consisting of or pertaining to a fiber
magged: frayed
ropy: having the capability to be drawn out into a thread
scopate: like a brush; scopiferous
stringy: having an appearance like a string
sutile: sewn
threadlike: having the form of a thread
towy: having short broken fibers; flaxlike
wire-drawn: drawn out into a wire
wiry: thin and flexible, like a wire
xilinous: pertaining to cotton

Filthiness

abominable: very loathsome and filthy
amurcous: stinking; filled with dregs
Augean: utterly filthy
bad: foul and inedible
beastly: having foul habits
bloody: smeared with blood
camarine: mucky; stinking with decayed matter
carious: rotten; decayed
coarse: vile in manners
colluvial: pertaining to massive filth
conspurcated: corrupted; defiled
corrupt: spoiled by decay

crapulous: diseased from overindulgence in drink
dirty: made foul with dirt
dowdy: vulgar-looking
draggletailed: dirty in personal appearance
dreggy: full of grounds
duddie: shabby; tattered; duddy
dusty: covered with fine, dry dirt
effete: worn out by decay
excrementitious: disgustingly filthy, like excrement
fecal: pertaining to animal excrement

feculent: foul from animal excrement
fetid: giving out an evil odor
filthy: repulsively foul
fimetic: excremental
flothery: slovenly though attempting to look fine
flyblown: tainted with the eggs of flies
foul: offensive to the senses
frowzy: slovenly
fusty: rank from moldiness
gory: smeared with thick and clotted blood
grimy: filthy with dry dirt
gross: marked by coarseness and impurity
gurry: relating to the guts or slimy part of something
high: slightly tainted, as meat
immund: filthy; dirty
impetiginous: having a skin made unclean by impetigo
impure: having lost purity
inquinated: polluted; contaminated
maculate: stained; defiled
maggoty: infested with the larvae of flies
meraculous: slightly dirty
mildewed: decayed by the action of a kind of fungus
moldy: covered with a growth of minute fungi
moth-eaten: eaten into by moths
mucid: dirty from a slimy mold
musty: having a rank smell due to decomposition
nasty: nauseous and filthy
offensive: exciting a feeling of displeasure
peccant: corrupt and repulsive from disease
pedicular: pertaining to lice; lousy
pulicose: infested with fleas
purulent: filthy from the formation of pus
putrefied: having a filthy smell as a result of decay
putrescent: beginning to putrefy
putrid: in a state of decay with a fetid odor

pythogenic: coming from garbage
quisquilian: consisting of trash or rubbish; quisquiliary; quisquilious; quisquillous
rancid: foul in smell and taste from decay
reasty: rancid, as salt meat
reechy: reeking, as with sweat
reeky: foul from smoke
rotten: offensive from decomposition
rotting: decomposing; fallen into decay
ruderous: filled with garbage
rusty: dirty with rust
scumbered: fouled with dung
scurfy: dirty from a scalelike affection of the skin
slimy: dirty with wet filth
slovenly: careless in one's personal habits and/or attire
sluttish: disgustingly filthy; like a slut
smoky: dirty from smoke
smutty: stained with soot or smoke
snuffy: soiled with snuff
soiled: having the surface dirtied by contact
sooty: blackened with soot
stercoraceous: dirty; like dung; excremental; stercoral
sterquilinian: pertaining to a dunghill or filth; sterquilinous
tainted: impregnated with foulness
tatterdemalion: ragged; disheveled; sloppy; in tatters; ragtag
thick: dirty and muddy, as water
touched: slightly affected with decay
turbid: dirty from having the sediment stirred up
tuzzimuzzy: disheveled
unclean: dirty
uncleanly: unclean
uncombed: not combed
unkempt: not tidy, neat, or clean
unpurified: remaining dirty
unscoured: remaining dirty
unstrained: containing sediment
unswept: not swept free of dirt
untidy: not neat or clean
unwashed: remaining dirty
unwiped: not wiped free of dirt

Five or More

centenary: pertaining to a hundred
centennial: pertaining to a hundred years
centuple: increased a hundredfold
centuplicate: a hundredfold
centurial: pertaining to a century
decimal: founded upon ten
decuple: tenfold
denary: containing ten
duodenal: relating to musical groups of twelves
duodenary: relating to twelve; twelvefold
eighth: next after seventh
eleventh: next after tenth
fifth: next after fourth
five: of one more than four
hundredth: next after ninety-ninth
in one's teens: but a youth; thirteen to nineteen years old
ninefold: nine times
ninth: next after eighth
octuple: multiplied by eight
pentomic: organized into five groups; pertaining to an army division with five battle groups
quinary: arranged in fives; fifth in order
quinquarticular: consisting of five articles
quinquefid: five-cleft
quinquepartite: consisting of five parts
quintuple: fivefold
secular: observed once in a century
senary: containing six
seventh: next after sixth
sextuple: sixfold; multiplied by six
sixth: next after fifth
tenfold: ten times
tenth: next after ninth
thirteenth: next after twelfth
thousandth: last in a series of one thousand
twelfth: next after eleventh
twentieth: next after nineteenth
twenty-fourth: next after twenty-third
vicesimal: twentieth
vigesimal: pertaining to twenty

Flatness—Levelness

accumbent: leaning or reclining, as the ancients at meals; recumbent
aclinal: horizontal
agroof: flat on one's face
alluvial: relating to the deposits of sand, clay, or gravel made by river action
applanate: flattened out; complanate; planiform
calm: undisturbed
calm as a mill pond: perfectly serene
campestral: pertaining to or thriving on level ground
champaign: pertaining to level country
couchant: lying down
decubital: pertaining to lying down
decumbent: lying down; stretched out
discoid: disklike
even: level, smooth, or equal in surface
flat: having an even and horizontal surface
flat as a billiard table: level
flat as a board: expression for degree of flatness or levelness
flat as a bowling-green: even
flat as a flounder: expression for degree of flatness or levelness
flat as a fluke: expression for degree of flatness or levelness
flat as a pancake: expression for degree of flatness or levelness
flat as my hand: expression for degree of flatness or levelness
flush: even; in the same plane or on the same level
horizontal: parallel to the horizon; level; plane; transverse
jacent: lying at length; recumbent
level: not having one part higher than another
lying: being prostrate
oblate: flattened at the poles
planar: on a plane; having a flat unbro-

ken surface; applanate; even; flattened; homaloidal; level; tabular

plane: without elevations or depressions;
exactly flat

procumbent: lying down or on the face;
prostrate

prone: flat on the face

prostrate: stretched out; lying flat on the
ground

raxed: stretched

rectiserial: having vertical ranks

recumbent: leaning

smooth: having an even surface

smooth as glass: having a polished
surface

supine: lying on the back or with the face
upward

ventricumbent: lying face down or
prone

Flora

ananthous: having no flowers

apocynaceous: of the tropical family that
includes oleander, periwinkle

arborary: pertaining to trees

arborescent: like a tree

avenaceous: oatlike

biform: sharing characteristics with two
animals or with plant and animal life

broad-leaved: describing a plant having
leaves that are not needles

caricous: figlike

cauline: growing on a stem, especially on
the upper part

ceduous: of a tree, ready to be felled

cepaceous: of or like an onion

cespitose: pertaining to turf; growing in
clumps; matted; caespitose

crinoid: pertaining to the sea lily

dasyphyllous: having thick or thickly set
leaves

deciduous: designating any plant that
sheds all its leaves once each year

dendroid: treelike in form

effloriate: blooming; flowering

emarcid: wilted

everbearing: producing fruit throughout
growing season

floral: pertaining to plants and plant life;
pertaining to flowers

floriferous: bearing or producing flowers

floriform: flowerlike; floral

foliaceous: leaflike; leafy

fucoid: pertaining to seaweed

gemmiform: budlike

grassy: having grass; resembling grass

hardy: designating a plant with high resistance or tolerance to cold or freezing temperatures

hederaceous: pertaining to ivy

hempen: pertaining to hemp; pertaining
to a hangman's noose

herbaceous: designating nonwoody
plant

hordeaceous: concerning barley

inflorescent: blossoming

inrooted: deeply rooted

juglandaceous: pertaining to walnuts
and hickories

lichen: a cryptogamous plant that grows
on trees, rocks, often as a fungus

ligneous: like wood; woody

menthaceous: minty

monoecious: hermaphroditic; with uni-
sex flowers or the ability to fertilize
itself

mossy: covered with moss; of moss

musaceous: concerning bananas,
plantains

nuciferous: nutlike

ombrophobous: of a plant that cannot
survive continuous rain

orchidaceous: resembling an orchid

orchideous: concerning or resembling an
orchid

organic: designating plants grown with
animal or vegetable fertilizers only

papaverous: pertaining to poppies

pecky: having discolored or shriveled
grains

phytoform: shaped like a plant

quercine: pertaining to the oak
ramiferous: bearing branches
remontant: flowering again, as roses
root-bound: designating potted plant whose roots have no room to grow
runcinate: saw-toothed; with teeth curved toward the base
sempervirent: evergreen
serotine: flowering late
serotinous: flowering later than other related species
stag-headed: of a tree with dead branches, especially at the top
sylvan: pertaining to the woods or forest; silvan

topiary: pertaining to trimming and clipping of trees and shrubs
unifoliate: having one leaf
variegated: designating a plant with patterned or bicolored leaves and petals
vegetable: having the nature of plants or vegetables
vegetal: pertaining to plants
vegetous: pertaining to plants
verdant: green; like foliage
verdurous: of or pertaining to greenness or green foliage
vimineous: pertaining to twigs or woven twigs
woody: of the nature of wood; covered with wood

Flowing

affluent: flowing abundantly
amnic: pertaining to a river
circumfluent: flowing around or surrounding
confluent: flowing together
diffluent: flowing apart or off
ebbless: not flowing back
effluent: of fluids and waterways, flowing out from a source
emanant: flowing from a source
flowing: proceeding without hesitation; running along, as a stream
fluent: proceeding without hesitation; flowing or capable of flowing
fluvial: belonging to rivers
fluviatile: belonging to rivers
forced: not flowing easily
liquid: flowing smoothly

meandering: flowing in windings
meandrous: flowing in windings
mellifluous: flowing smoothly
potamic: pertaining to rivers, river navigation
profluent: flowing onward or going ahead
refluent: flowing back; ebbing
riparian: pertaining to the banks of a river or stream; riparial; riparious; ripicolous
riparicolous: dwelling in rivers, streams; riparial; riparian; riparious; riverine
riverain: of or relating to a riverbank
riverine: of or relating to a river; amnic; fluvial
streamy: abounding with streams or with running water
tychopotamic: occurring in or near rivers

Foam

afoam: foaming
bubbling: giving off bubbles
effervescent: in a state of effervescence
foamy: consisting of, pertaining to, or resembling an aggregation of bubbles
frothy: covered or filled with froth
nappy: strong; effervescent; foaming

sparkling: effervescent
spumeous: frothy; spumy; spumous
spumescent: like foam; foaming; frothy
spumid: frothy or foamy
spumous: foamy; frothy; spumy
vaporous: full of or resembling vapor
yeasty: light and frothy

Fold

accordion: folding like an accordion
biplicate: twice folded
contortuplicate: twisted back upon itself
corrugated: formed into folds or furrows
crimped: folded into minute ridges or
plaits; frizzed; frizzy

folded: bent over or doubled up
invaginated: turned or folded inside out
pleached: pleated; folded over
plicate: folded like a fan
retrorse: turned, bent, or directed
backward

Forgetfulness

buried in oblivion: forgotten for all time
bygone: long past and forgotten
clean forgotten: entirely forgotten
forgetful: liable to let slip out of mind
forgotten: slipped from the memory
gone out of one's head: not remembered
gone out of one's recollection: not
remembered
insensible: lacking an impressible
memory

insensible to the past: forgetful of the
past
lethean: producing forgetfulness
mindless: having no recollection of
oblivial: causing unawareness
oblivious: forgetful
out of mind: forgotten for the time being
past recollection: that cannot be recalled
sunk in oblivion: forgotten for all time
unremembered: not retained in the
memory

Formlessness

amorphous: having no determinate
shape
anidian: shapeless
asymmetrical: having an axially unbalanced shape; irregular in shape or outline; dissymmetrical
barbarous: rude, as if done by a
barbarian
formless: without due order of parts
Gothic: rude; barbaric
rough: lacking the finish of art

rude: exhibiting but the least of art
rugged: steep and rocky
shapeless: without shape or form
unfashioned: not shaped
unformed: not molded or fashioned
unhewn: in its virgin state
unscorified: not formed into dross
unshaped: having no shape; amorphous;
formless; inchoate; shapeless;
unformed
unshapen: not shaped; misshapen

Four

four: composed of one more than three
fourfold: taken four times
fourth: next after the third
gridlike: having uniformly spaced
squares; graticulated; graticule;
graticuled
parallelogrammatic: having four sides,
with two pairs being parallel and
equal; parallelogrammic
preantepenultimate: fourth from last

quadrable: in math, that which can be
squared
quadratic: like a square
quadrible: capable of being squared
quadrifarious: arranged in four rows or
ranks
quadrifid: deeply cleft into four parts
quadrigeminal: having four similar parts
quadrilateral: having four sides and four

angles; quadrangled; quadrangular; tetragonal
quadripatite: composed of four parts
quadrirotal: having four wheels
quadrivial: where four roads meet
quadruple: of four parts; made four times as great
quadruplicate: twice double
quartered: divided into four parts
quartile: having four equal sides
quaternal: fourfold

quaternary: consisting of four or occupying fourth place
rectangular: having four sides and four right angles
rhomboid: having four sides with unequal not-right angles; rhomboidal
square: having four equal sides and four right angles; foursquare; quadrate; sausage-fingered; stubby
tessaraglot: written or spoken in four languages
tetractic: having four rays

Frequency

constant: without irregularity
continual: always happening; continuing over a long time with no breaks or short breaks
crebrous: frequent
frequent: occurring often at short intervals
habitual: constant
incessant: without perceptible pause
many times: occurring often

nonan: occurring every ninth day
not rare: occurring often
octan: occurring every eighth day
passim: throughout; frequently
perpetual: never ceasing
quartan: occurring every fourth day
quinquagesimal: occurring in a fifty-day season; consisting of fifty days
repeated: done or said more than once
thick-coming: coming close together

Frugality

careful: provident; giving good heed
chary: not liberal
economic: managing with frugality
economical: managing with frugality; avoiding waste; thrifty
frugal: saving unnecessary expense
Lenten: pertaining to Lent; sparing

parsimonious: excessively frugal
penny-wise and pound-foolish: economical in small things, extravagant in large things
saving: frugal; economical
spare: frugal; economical
sparingly: in a sparing manner

Future

aforehand: prepared or provided for the future
augural: significant for the future
close at hand: near
coming: approaching
contingent: liable to happen in the future
eventual: happening as a final or remote consequence

future: that is to be or come hereafter
futuristic: predicted for or pertaining to the future
in prospect: likely to happen
near: approaching
near at hand: approaching
next: the one following
to come: of the future
ulterior: later in time

Gain

acquired: gained; won

acquiring: gaining by one's own exertions

acquisitive: having the power to acquire

advantageous: gainful; profitable

advectitious: imported

gainful: producing gain

lucrative: making increase of money or goods

lucriferous: profitable; lucrative

paying: yielding a return for money expended

proficuous: profitable; useful

profitable: bringing profit or gain

remunerative: affording an ample return for industry or an investment

tontine: referring to the survivor taking all

Gas

aerial: consisting of air; found in the air

aeriform: of the nature of air

airy: consisting of air

carminative: pertaining to expelling gas from the bowels

ethereal: pertaining to ether

evaporable: capable of evaporating

flatulent: pertaining to intestinal gas

fumacious: smoky; fond of smoke

gaseous: having the state or properties of gas

physagogue: expelling gas; flatulent

vaporous: of or like vapor

volatile: disposed to evaporate

Gathering

accumulable: capable of being accumulated

aggregable: collectible into one mass

agminate: bunched together

all of a heap: piled together without any arrangement

allemang: mixed together

as thick as hops: as thick as possible

assembled: brought or called together

chockablock: crowded together

closely packed: gathered in a mass

coacervate: in a crowd; piled up

crowded to suffocation: so dense as to have little air for breathing

cumulative: piled up; gathering volume by addition

dense: having its parts close together

fasciculated: grouped in a fascicle or bunch

gathered: collected together; drawn together
pily: concerning a pile
populous: thickly inhabited
ramé: crowded; bustling; chaotic

serried: crowded in rows; compact
styptic: contracting; pulling in together
swarming: thick like a hive of bees
teeming: produced in great numbers

Generosity

allowable: that may be given
allowed: that is given
bounteous: liberal in bestowing gifts or favors
bountiful: liberal in bestowing gifts or favors
caritative: charitable
charitable: generous; liberal in giving to the poor
communicable: that may be given by intercourse
concessional: yielding
eleemosynary: pertaining to charity or living on charity or giving alms
free: liberal
freehanded: liberal; generous
freehearted: liberal; generous
full-handed: liberal
generous: giving freely and abundantly
given: bestowed without expectation of return

giving: bestowing without expectation of return
gratis: given absolutely for nothing
handsome: large and liberal, of a gift
hospitable: treating strangers with kindness and without reward
largehearted: generous
lending: giving as a loan
lent: given as or pertaining to a loan
liberal: bestowing with a free hand
munificent: very liberal in giving or bestowing
openhanded: giving freely
openhearted: frank; generous
overpaid: paid very generously
princely: munificent
sportulary: dependent on donations; subsisting on handouts
tributary: pertaining to giving tribute
unborrowed: not borrowed
ungrudging: freely giving; liberal
unsparing: liberal
xenial: pertaining to hospitality

Gentility

aldermanic: dignified; stately
aristocratic: very dignified; haughty; connected with the upper classes
courtly: elegant in manners; befitting a court
exalted: elevated in position or rank
genteel: well-bred or refined
gentilitial: well-born
gentlemanlike: befitting a gentleman; courteous
high-born: of lofty descent
high-caste: of patrician birth

highly respectable: worthy of esteem and honor
noble: exalted in rank; most worthy
of gentle blood: descended from noble stock
of rank: of eminence or dignity
patrician: of noble or aristocratic lineage
princely: like a prince; royal; dignified
sri: of a title indicating holiness, venerableness; shree; shri
titled: having a title, as of nobility
well-born: not of mean or common birth

Geography

abyssal: pertaining to dark, cold, lifeless ocean depths

alluvial: pertaining to earth laid down by means of water

bipolar: involving both North and South Poles

bosky: wooded; covered or shaded by brush or trees

campestrian: growing in or pertaining to plains

circumpolar: surrounding or near either pole

conformal: designating a map or projection in which scale and angles are preserved

continental: pertaining to the continent

earthy: like earth; pertaining to the earth

fallow: designating cultivated land left unsown for one season or more

geographical: pertaining to the physical science of the earth's surface, including natural and political divisions

glebous: earthy; full of clods; gleby

insular: of or relating to an island

lallan: pertaining to lowland

landed: having or owning land

landlocked: having no border on or outlet to the sea

littoral: designating the intertidal zone along a shore

marine: of or at the sea or ocean

maritime: concerning the sea or ocean

midland: pertaining to the interior country

offshore: designating area of sea lying a short way from beach

paludal: marshy; swampy

pelagic: of or on the open sea

pratal: pertaining to meadows

predial: consisting of land

riparian: pertaining to the riverbank

subantarctic: bordering on the Antarctic

subarctic: bordering on the Arctic

subtropical: bordering on the tropics

supralittoral: of a shore that is moist but above water

sylvan: covered with woods or groves of trees

tellurian: pertaining to the earth; terrestrial

terrene: pertaining to the earth

terrestrial: of or relating to land

territorial: pertaining to a territory

transcontinental: reaching from one ocean coast to another

Geology

amorphous: not crystallized

cismontane: pertaining to this side of a mountain or mountain range

clivose: hilly; steep

cretaceous: chalky; grayish white; pertaining to the geological period when chalk beds were laid down

crystalline: in the form of a crystal

eolian: carried, deposited, or eroded by the wind

eremic: pertaining to sandy land or deserts

geological: pertaining to the science of the earth's crust and its strata

geomagnetic: relating to magnetic properties of the earth

geomorphic: pertaining to the shape of the earth and its topography

geotectonic: concerning the structure, distribution, movement of the earth's crust

gyroidal: pertaining to nonsymmetrical forms of crystals in which the planes appear to be twisted in respect to each other

isomorphous: crystallizing in forms identical to those of some other substance

meizoseismal: pertaining to the maximum destructive force of an earthquake

montane: pertaining to mountains

montiform: shaped like a mountain

petrescent: turning to stone

petrous: rocky; stony

rostrocarinate: of flint objects resembling a beak

rupestrian: made of rock; inscribed on rock; rupestral

rupicoline: living or growing on rocks; rupestrine; rupicolous

saxatile: pertaining to rocks; saxicoline; saxicolous; saxigenous

saxicolous: growing on rocks

stratal: relating or belonging to the earth's layers

subrecent: of the last part of the Pleistocene period

succussive: shaking violently, especially from below like an earthquake

tectonic: relating to geological changes in the earth's crust; tectonical

terraqueous: consisting of or pertaining to both land and water; amphibious

terremotive: seismic

thalamic: in archaeology, concerning an inner or secret chamber

transmontane: pertaining to the area beyond any mountain or mountain range; tramontane

Zingg: of pebbles classified according to shape

Gluttony

adephagous: gluttonous

autophagous: self-consuming

crapulent: sick from intemperance in eating or drinking

cropsick: sick from overeating, overdrinking

edacious: eating to excess

epithymetic: pertaining to a large appetite for something

farctate: stuffed to the gills

feedy: overfed

gluttonous: grossly indulging in eating

gormandizing: devouring gluttonously

greedy: having an escessive appetite for food or drink

gulous: greedy for food; gluttonous

holus-bolus: in one gulp; altogether

ingluvious: gluttonous

lickerish: fond of delicious food; greedy; lickerous; liquorish

lust-dieted: feeding gluttonously

omnivorous: eating food of all kinds

overfed: fed to excess

overgorged: having eaten excessively

pampered: reared on luxurious food

pantophagous: eating all kinds of food; omnivorous

pleonectic: greedy; grasping

ravening: voracious; greedy

slobberchops: one who slobbers when eating

swinish: like a swine; greedy; beastly

trenching: feasting; pigging out

ventripotent: fat-bellied; gluttonous

voracious: greedy; insatiable

voraginous: very hungry; devouring; voracious

Goodness

above par: better than the usual quality

admirable: excellent in a high degree

advantageous: affording advantage; favorable

agathokakological: composed of good and evil

beneficent: resulting in good; kindly or charitable

beneficial: conducive to well-being; producing an advantage

benignant: beneficial; salutary

best: of the highest degree of excellence

better: of a higher degree of excellence than usual

bosker: very good

capital: of the first quality

cardinal: of prime or special importance

choice: having special excellence

commendable: to be praised for goodness

costly: of great value

crack: of superior excellence; first-class

edifying: tending to moral or spiritual improvement

eellogofusciouhipoppokunurious: very good or very fine

elect: deserving to be chosen among many

estimable: deserving of good opinion

eumoirous: lucky or happy from being a good person

excellent: having good qualities in a high degree

eximious: select; excellent

exquisite: fitted to excite great pleasure

fair: pleasing to the eye or mind

favorable: affording means to aid or benefit

fine: excellent or superior in character, form, or appearance

first-class: of the best quality

first-rate: of the best quality

fresh: having undiminished excellence

genuine: not false or spurious

good: desirable or excellent in any respect

good as gold: of high value

harmless: without hurt or loss

high-wrought: skillfully or finely made

hurtless: harmless

in fair condition: moderately good

in good condition: unimpaired

inestimable: above price; very excellent

inimitable: surpassingly excellent

innocent: free from qualities that can harm or injure

innocuous: producing no bad effects

inoffensive: not displeasing

invaluable: beyond price; very excellent

Manichaean: believing the world is divided into good and evil

nice: pleasing to the senses

of great price: valuable or desirable

of the first water: of the highest excellence or purity

of value: desirable

par excellence: being the best or truest of a kind; exemplary; quintessential

picked: highest-rated

pleasing: agreeable to the senses

praiseworthy: deserving of praise

precious: highly prized

precious as the apple of the eye: of the highest value to a person

priceless: above price; very excellent

prickmedainty: goody-goody

prime: of the first quality

profitable: yielding gain or benefit

propitious: attended by favorable prospects or circumstances

rare: highly valued because of infrequency

salutary: producing a beneficial effect

satisfactory: fulfilling every desire

select: taken as being most excellent

serviceable: such as does serve a useful purpose

sound: free from defect or injury

standard: of a very high type or kind

superexcellent: of superior excellence

superfine: of the very best quality

superlatively good: of the very highest degree of goodness

tidy: fairly well and comfortable

tip-top: best of its kind

tolerable: passably or moderately good

unexceptionable: as good as any

unobjectionable: without defect

unobnoxious: without harmful qualities

unparagoned: matchless

unparalleled: without an equal

up to the mark: satisfactory

useful: serving a good purpose

valuable: costly

very best: of the highest degree of excellence

worth its weight in gold: of the highest value

Gray

ash gray: pale gray
ash-colored: gray as ashes
ashen: gray like ashes
ashy: gray like ashes
charcoal: dark gray; field gray
cinerescent: ashen; grayish; cinereous
cineritious: of a gray resembling ashes
cinerous: of a gray resembling ashes
cool: of a dull color
dingy: of a soiled gray color
dove gray: purplish gray; gunmetal; zinc
drab: a yellowish gray
dun: of a dull, dark-gray color
favillous: ashlike
fuscous: brownish gray in color
gray: of the color of white and black mixed
grey: of the color of white and black mixed
grizzled: having gray or partly gray hair; hoary; silvery
grizzly: grayish

iron gray: gray like iron
leaden: gray like lead
livid: gray like bruised flesh
lyart: streaked with gray
mouse-colored: gray as a mouse
pearly: having a gray luster, like a pearl
platinum: medium gray; metallic gray
plumbaceous: lead-colored
roan: dark with spots of gray thickly interspersed
russet: reddish or yellowish gray
sad: of a dark color
sand: yellowish gray
shistaceous: slate-colored; livid
silver: gray as silver
silvered: gray as silver
silvery: gray as silver
slate: bluish gray; battleship gray; pearl; smoke; steel gray
somber: dusky gray
stone-colored: gray as stone
taupe: brownish gray; resembling a mole; dun; fuscous; mouse gray; smoke

Greed

avaricious: eagerly craving for money
chary: very careful and cautious
cheeseparing: miserly; scrimping
churlish: like a churl; sordid
close: not open or liberal; stingy
closefisted: not inclined to give; mean
closehanded: mean; illiberal
covetous: desirous of getting something from its possessor
extortionate: oppressive
fast-handed: parsimonious
greedy: wishing to have or enjoy everything oneself
griping: grasping; seizing
grudging: envying one the possession of
hardfisted: avaricious in disposition; closefisted
hidebound: narrow-minded; penurious
illiberal: not liberal; ungenerous
mean: miserly in expenditure

mercenary: governed by a sordid love of gain; able to be hired
mingy: mean and stingy
miserly: like a miser; given to hoarding
near: inclined to be penurious; close
niggardly: acquiring by mean and petty savings
parsimonious: close in the expenditure of one's money
peddling: occupying oneself in small affairs
penny-wise: economical in small matters
penurious: very sparing in the expenditure of money; mean; stingy; cheap
rapacious: acquiring by violence, as a robber; eagerly grasping
scrubby: like a scrub; stunted; sordid
shabby: dressed in rags; paltry
sneckdrawn: mean; stingy
sordid: meanly avaricious

sparing: refraining from using; illiberal
stingy: extremely close and desirous of keeping others from getting
strait-handed: closehanded
tight: close and careful in expending
tightfisted: stingy

ungenerous: not generous; illiberal
usurious: practicing usury; eager to increase one's wealth rapidly even though illegally
venal: purchasable or purchased; working for money without principle

Greenness

apple green: light green; celadon; willow green
avocado: blackish green
bottle green: of the color of green glass bottles
caesious: pale blue-green
chartreuse: bright yellowish green
earth-tone: brownish or brownish green
eau-de-nil: light green, like the Nile River
emerald: vivid green; bright green; Kelly green; leaf green; smaragdine; verdant green
festucine: of a yellow-green straw color
filemot: having the color of a dead leaf; fillemot
glaucous: of a grayish-blue green; sea green
grass green: of the color of grass
green: having the color of growing grass
green as grass: of the color of grass
greenish: slightly green

hunter: dark green; bottle green; evergreen; forest; loden; marine green
olive: dull yellowish green; ocher; olive green
olive drab: dull grayish olive
pea green: of the color of green pea pods; yellowish green; absinthe green; leek green; malachite; moss green; Nile green; pistachio; sea green; verdigris
porraceous: leek green
sage: grayish green; celadon
sea green: of the color of seawater
smaragdine: pertaining to emeralds; emerald green
turquoise: bluish green; aquamarine; jade
verdant: green with vegetation; verdurous
vert: green
virent: verdant; green
virescent: greenish; growing green
viridescent: growing green

Groove

bisulcate: having the hoof divided by two grooves
bisulcous: having the hoof divided by two grooves
canaliculated: furrowed longitudinally; canaliculate
cannelured: grooved
corduroy: a kind of ribbed cotton cloth
corrugated: having rows of grooves; plicate
dadoed: having rectangular grooves
fluted: ornamented with parallel grooves; beveled; cannellated; chamfered; channeled; grooved; rutted

foiled: having curled indentations
furrowed: marked with grooves or furrows
glyphic: resembling an ornamental vertical groove; hieroglyphic; pictographic
gouged: having divotlike indentations; chiseled
lirate: having ridges
rabbeted: having a notch or groove near the edge
ribbed: having ribs or ridges; costate
rifled: having spiral grooves
rugulose: having small wrinkles
striate: grooved; furrowed; striped

striated: covered with minute grooves

sulcated: having long, deep grooves; canaliculate; sulcate

trisulcate: having the hoof divided by three grooves

vandyked: having deep indentations

Guilt—Vice—Wrong

abandoned: extremely wicked

accursed: worthy of the curse; detestable; damned

adulterine: illegal

apostate: guilty of desertion from one's party

atrocious: full of enormous wickedness

bad: wanting in good qualities, whether physical or moral

base: low in morals

black: without moral light or goodness

blameworthy: worthy of being treated with disapproval

censurable: deserving of blame

compunctious: feeling guilt, remorse, unease

condemned: sentenced, especially to death

corrupt: changed from good to bad

criminal: pertaining to crime

criminogenic: producing or leading to a crime or criminality

culpable: deserving condemnation or blame

deep in iniquity: sunk low in wickedness

degrading: causing loss in estimation, character, or reputation

demoniacal: pertaining to or resembling evil spirits

demoralized: having suffered a loss of moral principles

demoralizing: causing a loss of morality

depraved: corrupted

desertless: without merit

diabolic: pertaining to the devil; devilish

diabolical: pertaining to the devil; devilish

discreditable: injurious to reputation

disgraceful: causing shame

disorderly: not regulated by the restraints of morality

disreputable: injurious to the reputation

dissolute: given up to vicious pleasures

doli incapax: incapable of guilt

dolose: having criminal intent

evil-disposed: disposed to wickedness

evil-minded: disposed to mischief or sin

exceptionable: open to objection

facinorous: very wicked; atrocious

false: marked by bad faith

fedifragous: treacherous; deceitful

felonious: criminal; miscreant; naughty

fiendlike: like an infernal being

flagitious: very wicked; criminal; atrocious

flagrant: notorious

foul: loathsome; impure

frail: not able to withstand temptations to evil

graceless: depraved

grave: serious

gross: obscene; impure

guiltsick: sick with guilt

guilty: justly charged with and convicted of the commission of a crime; conscious of wrongdoing

heartless: cruel

heinous: odious; enormous

hellborn: born in hell

hellish: fit for hell; detestable

hit-and-run: guilty of leaving the scene of an auto accident to avoid responsibility for injuries and damage caused

hot: stolen

illaudable: worthy of disparagement

ill-conditioned: not well-circumstanced

illegal: not according to law

immoral: inconsistent with rectitude, purity, or good morals

imperfect: morally defective

improper: indecent; not proper; unfit

in fault: in the wrong

in the wrong: holding a wrong or unjustifiable position as regards another person

in the wrong box: in error

incarnate: having the nature of flesh

incorrect: not according to morality

incorrigible: bad beyond correction

indecorous: unbecoming

indefensible: not capable of being justified

indiscreet: wanting in discretion

inequitable: not according to equitable principles; unfair

inexcusable: not able to be justified

inexpiable: not able to be softened or appeased by atonement

infamous: of the worst reputation

infernal: resembling hell

infirm: weak; feeble

iniquitous: unjust; wicked

irreclaimable: incapable of being reclaimed

irremissible: unpardonable

lawless: not held in check by moral law or the laws of man

lax: easy or indulgent in principles

lost in iniquity: hardened by wickedness

lost to virtue: ruined morally

mala fide: acting in bad faith

malevolent: wishing evil

Mephistophelian: fiendish

misbegotten: begotten out of wedlock; despicable

miscreated: created amiss

mutinous: engaged in mutiny

naughty: guilty of improper conduct

nefarious: wicked; iniquitous; reprehensible

nefast: wicked

obdurate: persistent in sin

objectionable: liable to objection because of wrong

of a deep dye: deeply impregnated with, usually in a bad sense

one-sided: pertaining to, having, or considering only one side

partial: favoring one party or side

past praying for: lost in sin

peccable: liable to sin

peccaminous: sinful

penal: pertaining to or constituting legal punishment

perfidious: treacherous; double-crossing; traitorous

piacular: wicked; sinful

poison-pen: written with malice, usually anonymously

profligate: lost in vice

recidivous: relapsing into a former behavior, often criminal; recidivistic

recreant: unfaithful to one's duty

reprehensible: worthy of blame

reprobate: lost to all sense of duty

satanic: devilish

scampish: rascally

scandalous: shocking to morality

scurvy: mean, low, or contemptible

seditious: stirring up insurrection

shameful: disgraceful; infamous

sinful: contrary to the laws of God

sinister: evil; malevolent; left-handed

sinning: transgressing divine law

steeped in iniquity: impregnated with wickedness

stygian: infernal; from the river Styx

sunk in iniquity: lost in sin

supercilious: patronizing; haughtily disdainful

thelyphthoric: that which corrupts women

to blame: at fault

too bad: wrong

transgressive: faulty; liable to transgress

treacherous: practicing treachery

unallowable: not to be allowed

uncommendable: unworthy of praise

unconscionable: inordinately excessive

unduteous: not rendering the respect or obedience due

undutiful: not submissive to superiors

unequal: not equal; inequitable; unjust

unequitable: not equitable, fair, or just

unfair: showing partiality or prejudice

unfit: not fit; improper; wanting in suitable qualifications, physical or moral

unjust: not acting or disposed to act according to justice

unjustifiable: not capable of being justified or proved to be right

unjustified: not according to justice

unpardonable: that may not be pardoned

unprincipled: destitute of conscientious scruples

unrighteous: wicked; sinful

unseemly: not becoming

unwarrantable: not justifiable; unjust; improper

unworthy: improper; wrong

vicelike: partaking of wrong

vicious: addicted to immorality

vile: morally base, despicable, or loathsome

villainous: very wicked or vile

virtueless: destitute of moral excellence

weak: lacking in moral vigor

wee-wow: wrong; in an unsettled state

weighed in the balance and found wanting: guilty

wicked: given to vice or sin

wired: carrying a concealed microphone or recording device in order to collect evidence

worthless: without virtue

wrong: not physically or morally right; not according to moral or divine law

wrongful: injurious; unjust

Habit

accredited: given credit for	**household:** commonly known
accustomary: customary	**ingrafted:** developed by training
accustomed: used to a state or action	**ingrained:** firmly set by instinct
acknowledged: admitted as genuine	**inveterate:** habitual; firmly established
admitted: accepted as true	**jog-trot:** commonplace
besetting: constantly troubling	**naturalized:** made familiar by custom
common: general	**ordinary:** not exceptional
commonplace: ordinary	**permanent:** enduring
conformable: showing external agreement with anything	**prescriptive:** acquired by immemorial use
conventional: agreeing with any arbitrary standard	**prevailing:** most generally found
current: generally accepted	**prevalent:** widely spread, as a disease
customary: according to custom	**received:** accepted
devoted: strongly attached to	**recognized:** acquainted with
established: made stable or constant	**regular:** accordingly to law or custom
everyday: usual	**rooted:** deep-seated
familiar: well-known	**seasoned:** adapted
fashionable: according to some arbitrary and temporary way	**set:** fixed
fixed: established	**stereotyped:** distinctly marked off
frequent: happening often	**stock:** continually used
general: found widely practiced	**trite:** worn out from frequent use
habitual: done involuntarily because of frequent repetition	**understood:** established by belief
hackneyed: worn-out	**usual:** ordinary
	vernacular: native
	wont: using or doing habitually
	wonted: accustomed

Habitation

allopatric: dwelling in different regions	**amphiscian:** dwelling in the torrid zone
American: dwelling in America	**arboreal:** dwelling in trees

arenicolous: dwelling in sand

as is: designating property to be purchased in its present condition with no guarantee of its future state

aularian: pertaining to a hall

autochthonous: native; indigenous; allochthonous; autochthonant; autochthonic

board-and-batt: constructed from wide boards in conjunction with narrow battens; board-and-batten

British: dwelling in Great Britain

castellated: built like a castle; having castles

castrensian: pertaining to a camp or campsite

cavernicolous: dwelling in caverns

collocal: found in or belonging to the same place

cosmopolitan: common to the whole world

cubicular: pertaining to the bedroom

deserticolous: pertaining to living in a desert

domestic: pertaining to the home

domesticated: made domestic

domiciled: provided with a home

domiciliated: settled in a home

English: dwelling in England

epigeal: dwelling near the ground's surface

epigean: living close to the ground; epigeal

estuarine: dwelling in estuaries

exulant: living in exile

fimetarious: growing or living in excrement; fimicolous

garrisoned by: manned with troops

habitable: capable of being inhabited

helobious: living in marshy areas

hypaethral: open to the sky; not roofed; upaithric

hypogeous: dwelling underground; subterranean

in the occupation of: holding in possession

indigenous: born or produced naturally in a country or place

inquiline: dwelling in the nest of another species

labtebricole: living in holes

lapidicolous: living underneath rocks, like grubs or beetles

limicoline: dwelling along a coast; littoral; orarian

limicolous: living in mud or slime

limnophilous: living in freshwater ponds

lithodomous: burrowing or dwelling in a rock

lotic: dwelling in active, moving water

lutarious: pertaining to or living in mud

matrilocal: of a husband living with his wife's family

montigenous: native of mountains

natal: pertaining to one's birth

native: pertaining to the place of one's birth

naturalized: having obtained the rights and privileges of citizenship

nemoral: living in a grove

nesiote: living on an island

occupied by: held in possession by a tenant

palatial: pertaining to or becoming a palace; grand in style

patrilocal: of a wife living with her husband's family

petricolous: dwelling in rocks; lithodomous

practicolous: dwelling in meadows, fields; arvicoline

pratincolous: living in meadows

projicient: concerned with an individual's perception of his surroundings

provincial: pertaining to a province

ruderal: growing in garbage dumps

rural: pertaining to the country

rustic: belonging to the country

saprophilous: living in rotting waste or decaying matter

sepicolous: living in hedges

silvicolous: dwelling in woodlands

spelaean: living or occurring in a cave; spelean

stercoricolous: living in dung

terricolous: dwelling on the ground; terrestrial

trabeated: with horizontal beams

transpontine: living south of the Thames River; on the other side of the bridge

triphibious: living or operating on land, sea, and air

troglodytic: cave-dwelling; troglodytical

uxorilocal: living with one's wife's family

vernacular: originating in one's native land

Hair

achaetous: hairless

acomous: bald

aurocephalous: blond

balding: having little hair left; scant; sparse; thin; thinning; tonsured

barbatulous: having a small beard

barbigerous: bearded; hairy

bushy: having thick eyebrows; beetle-browed; beetling

calvous: bald

capillary: hairlike; threadlike; very fine and slender

capillose: hairy

clean-shaven: free of facial hair

comate: hairy

comose: hairy; tufted

crinal: hairy; crinatory; crinitory

crinicultural: pertaining to hair care, hair growth

crinigerous: overgrown with hair

crinose: hairy; hirsute; shaggy

cymotrichous: having wavy hair

depilous: hairless; bald; glabrous; hairless

euthycomic: having straight hair

glabrous: smooth; hairless

grizzled: unkempt; unshaven

hairy: covered with hairs; like hair

highlighted: of hair with strands that are bleached or tinted; chunked; fronted; streaked

hirsute: hairy all over

hirsutorufous: red-haired

hispid: rough with bristles, spines, or stiff hair

layered: of hair cut at differing lengths for a fuller look

leiotrichous: smooth-haired; having straight hair

lissotrichous: having straight hair

man-browed: with hair growing between the eyebrows

marcelled: of hair curled into soft waves

melanocomous: dark-haired; melanotrichous

mop-topped: having a thick head of hair; leonine; luxuriant

mustached: having a mustache; mustachioed

mystacial: like a mustache; moustachial; mystacal; mystacine; mystacinous

peach fuzz: having adolescent facial hair

philocomal: pertaining to hair care

pilar: hairy

piliform: thread-shaped; hairlike; capilliform

pilose: having soft downy hair; hairy

processed: of hair that is chemically treated

ropy: having hair in thick strands

smarmy: of hair, smooth and sleek

strawberry blond: having reddish blond hair

stubbly: needing a shave; bristly

teased: of hair fluffed out by back-combing; combing toward the scalp; back-combed

towheaded: having very light-colored hair

tweezed: having thin eyebrows from tweezing; plucked

ulotrichous: having woolly hair

unshaven: having some growth of beard

upswept: of hair combed or pinned up on the head; swept-back

Happiness

abderian: pertaining to foolish or excessive laughter; given to idiotic laughter

airy: buoyant; as light as air

all alive: full of life

allegro: cheerful; lively

animated: displaying happiness; lively

blithe: characterized by gladness and mirth

blithesome: imparting gladness and mirth; blithe

bonny: sweet and fair; comely

bright: full of happiness, gladness

brisk: acting or moving quickly

brisk as a bee: lively

buoyant: resisting or easily recovering from depression

buxom: having health and vigor combined with gaiety and liveliness

canty: brisk; glad; lively

cardiacal: invigorating the spirits; giving strength and cheerfulness; cardiac

cheerful: full of cheer

cheering: tending to cheer

cheerly: cheerful

cheery: spontaneously cheerful

cock-a-hoop: elated; on the high horse

convulsed with laughter: moved by uncontrollable laughter

elate: exalted in spirit

elated: having the spirits raised by success

essorant: having a soaring spirit

exhilarating: causing mental and physical liveliness

exultant: rejoicing greatly

exulting: feeling delight on account of victory

flushed: slightly excited

free and easy: having little regard for conventionality

frisky: playful in action

frolicsome: full of prankish sport

full of play: frolicsome

full of spirit: frolicsome

gamesome: playful; sportive

gay as a lark: cheerful and showy

gelastic: pertaining to laughing

gelogenic: provoking laughter

gleesome: marked by glee

happy: joyful

happy as a king: very happy

happy as the day is long: very happy

heartsome: merry; lively

hilarious: mirthful from social pleasure

hopeful: inspiring hope; promising

in good spirits: lively

in high feather: in very good spirits

in high spirits: in very good spirits

in spirits: in a favorable frame of mind

inspiriting: instilling courage or life

janty: gay, easy, and showy; affecting a careless ease

jaunty: gay, easy, and showy; affecting a careless ease

jocose: done or said in jest; in the nature of a joke

jocular: quite funny

jocund: merry or lively

jolly: mirthful and lively

jolly as a sandboy: merry

jolly as a thrush: lively

jovial: good-naturedly mirthful and gay, as one born under the planet Jupiter

joyful: very glad, especially at a particular thing

joyous: joyful, but as a general or continued feeling

jubilant: manifesting joy with shouts or songs

laughable: tending to cause laughter

laughing: making a joyful noise; showing amusement

laughter-loving: lighthearted

light: cheerful

lighthearted: cheerful; free from care

lightsome: light, gay, or cheerful in character or mood

lively: full of energetic action

merry: noisily and laughingly gay

merry as a cricket: cheerful

merry as a grig: cheerful

merry as a marriage bell: very cheerful

mettlesome: spirited; fiery
mirthful: full of mirth
mirth-loving: gay
of good cheer: cheerful
ovant: triumphant, as an ovation
palmy: marked by prosperity or
triumph
playful: fond of play
playful as a kitten: frolicsome
playsome: playful
pleasing: giving pleasure
rattling: lively; surprising
ready to burst with laughter: extremely
amused
ready to die with laughter: extremely
amused
ready to split with laughter: extremely
amused
rejoicing: expressing joy
rident: laughing or smiling broadly
ridibund: laughing easily
risible: pertaining to laughter; causing
laughter
risorial: pertaining to laughter

rollicking: mirthful and frolicsome
smiling: having a pleased facial
expression
sparkling: brilliant; vivacious
spirited: full of spirit, life, or vigor
spiritful: spirited
sportive: fond of play; having a playful
habit
sprightful: sprightly
sprightly: cheerful in disposition and
brisk in manner
spry: quick and active in movement
subrident: smiling; subrisive; subrisory
subrisive: smiling; subrident; subrisory
sunny: bright; genial
tricksy: fond of tricks or pranks
triumphant: full of rejoicing because of
success
unsoulclogged: not weighed down in
spirit
vivacious: having vivacity
waggish: given to tricks or witty hits
winsome: having a winning appearance
or manner

Hardness

adamantean: hard as adamant
adamantine: unyielding; not movable;
adamantean
bony: like a bone; consisting of bone
cartilaginous: consisting of cartilage
concrete: forming a hard mass
corneous: horny; hard
file-hard: unable to be cut with an ordinary file
firm: solid; unyielding
glyptic: concerning gem or stone
engraving
granitic: composed of granite
gritty: consisting of grains or grit
hard: solid; inflexible
hard as stone: denoting a degree of
hardness
horny: like horn
indurate: hardened
indurated: hardened
inflexible: not capable of being bent

insecable: unable to be cut with a knife;
indivisible
osseous: bony; like bone
ossific: forming bone
proof: impenetrable; able to resist
pressure
rigescent: growing stiff or numb
rigid: stiff; unbending
starch: stiff
starched: stiff with starch
stark: inflexible; stiff; rigid
stiff: not easily bent
stiff as a poker: expression denoting degree of hardness or stiffness
stiff as buckram: expression denoting
degree of hardness or stiffness
stony: hard; like a stone
stubborn: intractable; unyielding
tense: drawn; stretched; rigid
tentiginous: stiff; strained
unbending: not deflected

unlimber: not pliant; stiff
unyielding: unpliant

vitreous: like glass in hardness

Harshness

absolute: with no restriction
arbitrary: unreasonable; harsh
arrogant: assuming too much authority
austere: severe or grave in manner or
judgment
austerulous: somewhat harsh
coercive: serving or intending to coerce
cruel: fitted to cause pain or grief
dour: obstinate; hard
draconian: relentless; severe
exigent: demanding immediate action;
exacting
extortionate: given to extortion;
oppressive
grinding: oppressing by exactions, as in
a mill or with a grindstone
hard: stern and unsympathetic
harsh: severe and abusive
haughty: contemptuously overbearing
and oppressive
imperative: demanding obedience
inclement: lacking mildness or
kindliness
inexorable: not to be moved from adherence to a rule
inflexible: firm in will; unchangeable;
inexorable
ingravescent: growing worse or more
severe
inquisitorial: like an inquisitor

ironhanded: rude; harsh
noli-me-tangeretarian: rigid; unbending
obdurate: opposing all sympathetic
influences
oppressive: unreasonably severe
peremptory: not admitting of
remonstrance
positive: confident and overbearing
relentless: insensible or unyielding to
appeals
rigid: not indulgent or yielding; severe
rigorous: characterized by rigor
searching: severe and critical in
investigation
severe: characterized by severity
stern: severe in aspect, judgment, or
manner
stiff: unyielding; harsh
straitlaced: rigid in opinion and manners
strict: governing or governed by rigid
rules
stringent: making rigid, severe
requirements
torvous: stern; severe
tyrannical: like a tyrant
uncompromising: making no
concessions
unsparing: not considerate
withering: causing to shrink or be
abashed

Hate—Malevolence

abhorrent: repugnant; detestable
abominable: detestable; loathsome
acrimonious: exhibiting bitterness of
temper
antisocial: hostile or averse to society
at daggers drawn: at enmity
atrocious: extremely wicked
averse from: repugnant; disliking
barbarous: marked by coarseness and
brutality, especially of speech
belluine: brutal

bitter: severe; harsh; cruel
bloodthirsty: anxious to shed blood
bloody-minded: bloodthirsty; cruel
brutal: having the characteristics of a
brute
brutish: resembling a brute; coarse;
sensual
caustic: burning; sarcastic
churlish: like a churl; hence, rude, surly
cold-blooded: unsympathetic
coldhearted: wanting in feeling

crossed in love: thwarted in love

cruel: disposed to inflict pain, mental or physical; bloody

demoniacal: characteristic of a demon; devilish

despiteful: full of hatred or malice

devilish: possessed of the qualities of the devil

diabolic: like the devil; i.e., the prosecutor of man in the court of God; nefarious

diabolical: like the devil; i.e., the prosecutor of man in the court of God; nefarious

disgusting: sickening; repugnant

disliked: not liked

disobliging: not disposed to oblige or do a favor

draconian: inhumanly severe; cruel

egotistical: referring to self often

envenomed: poisoned with hatred or malice

evil-disposed: inclined toward evil

evil-minded: wicked; atrocious

fell: cruel; savage

ferine: untamed; malignant

ferocious: savage or ravenous in disposition

fiendish: acting like a fiend; i.e., one hating mankind

fiendlike: acting like a fiend; i.e., one hating mankind

flinthearted: hard-hearted; unsympathetic

forsaken: abandoned; left alone

galling: irritating; vexing

grinding: very oppressing; pressing to the grindstone

hard of heart: lacking in feeling; unsympathetic

hard-hearted: lacking in feeling; unsympathetic

harsh: abusive; disagreeable

hateful: malevolent; abhorrent

hellish: like hell; diabolical

ill-conditioned: in bad or unfavorable circumstances

ill-contrived: poorly planned or designed

ill-disposed: badly inclined

ill-intentioned: having an evil purpose

ill-natured: having a bad temper; surly

implacable: inexorable; unrelenting

incendiary: kindling hate or factions

infernal: suitable for hell or its inhabitants

inhuman: void of human qualities; hence, brutal, cruel

inhumane: void of the feelings of humanity

inimical: hating others

inofficious: indifferent to obligation

insulting: abusive; contemptuous

invidious: hateful; likely to incur hatred or ill will

irritating: exasperating; annoying

jaundiced: feeling resentment, envy, jealousy; sallow; waxen

jealous: filled with jealousy

jealous as a Barbary pigeon: very jealous

jilted: discarded after having been encouraged as a lover

lasslorn: forsaken by one's sweetheart; jilted

lovelorn: forsaken by one's love

maleficent: causing harm or evil to others

malevolent: disposed to harm or injure others

malicious: exercising malice; malevolent

malign: evilly disposed toward others

malignant: virulently bent upon doing harm or evil

marblehearted: unsympathetic; stonyhearted

misanthropic: hating mankind

misopolemical: hating war

mordacious: biting; severe

morose: having a sour temper or sullen disposition

not on speaking terms: mutually angry

obnoxious: hateful; offensive; odious

odious: deserving hate; detestable; disgusting; hateful; offensive

offensive: causing anger to a certain degree; displeasing

provoking: arousing resentment; irritating

rancorous: characterized by rancor; intensely malignant

rejected: discarded; cast away from

relentless: void of pity or tenderness

repulsive: inclined to repel; unattractive

ruthless: having no pity

satanic: possessed of the qualities of Satan

set against: opposed

shocking: horrible; disgusting

spiteful: filled with mean and petty hatred

stonyhearted: unsympathetic

sullen: habitually sulky or morose

surly: crabbed; rough

tameless: not capable of being tamed

truculent: ferocious; cruel

unamiable: not friendly; ill-natured

unbeloved: not loved

unbenevolent: lacking benevolence

uncandid: not candid

uncared for: displeasing

uncharitable: wanting in charity

undeplored: not mourned for

unendeared: not loved

unfriendly: void of kindness or benevolence

ungracious: not gracious

unkind: lacking in sympathy or gratitude

unlamented: uncared for

unloved: not attached to

unmourned: not cared for

unnatural: contrary to nature

unpatriotic: not patriotic; having no love of country

untamed: not tamed

unvalued: not wanted

venomous: poisonous; mischievous

virulent: very active to do injury

wlatsome: loathsome; detestable

yellow-eyed: disposed to be jealous

Health

ambulatory: designating a patient able to move from bed

antephialtic: preventing nightmares; antiephialtic

as well as can be expected: as healthy as possible under the circumstances

benign: propitious; mild

bracing: giving strength or vigor

brave: splendid in appearance

cacogastric: having poor digestion

circadian: pertaining to bodily cycles

clean-run: healthy; vigorous

concoquent: digestive

dinic: concerning dizziness

errhine: provoking a sneeze; pertaining to the nose or nasal discharge

florid: blooming; in a healthy condition

flush: full of vigor

for-profit: designating any medical care facility or program owned by investors

fresh: full of original vigor and health

fresh as a daisy: in good health; blooming

fresh as a rose: in good health; blooming

fresh as April: in good health; blooming

good for: beneficial to

green: full of vigor and life

hale: sound; robust; healthy; vigorous

hardy: strong; firm

harmless: incapable of doing harm

healthful: wholesome; tending to produce health

healthy: having good health; sound; prosperous

hearty: firm; sound; not weak

hearty as a buck: figurative expression for perfection of health

hemagogue: promoting blood flow

hematose: full of blood

hygeian: relating to health or hygiene

hygienic: pertaining to hygiene

in fine feather: in good health

in full bloom: in entire strength and vigor

in good case: in good health

in health: not ill; well

in high feather: in good health
innocent: harmless
innocuous: having no injurious qualities
innoxious: not liable to injure
invigorating: imparting vigor
lipothymic: tending to faint or swoon
low tar: containing less tar than usual or standard, therefore less unhealthy
macrosmatic: having a very sensitive nose
micturient: needing to urinate
not-for-profit: designating health facility or program owned by educational institution, foundation, or other non-profit group
nutritious: able to build up animal tissue
on one's legs: well; recovering
on-call: available for consultation in person or by telephone during off-duty hours
pretty bobbish: in good spirits
prophylactic: having power to prevent disease
pruritic: producing itching
psychosomatic: pertaining to interaction of mind and body
ptarmic: causing sneezing; errhine
restorative: having power to restore
revalescent: recovering from illness or injury
roborant: strengthening; restorative
robust: strong, sound, and vigorous in health
rough and ugly: well in health
safe and sound: perfectly unharmed

salubrious: wholesome; healthful; health-giving; salutary
salutary: promoting health
salutiferous: producing good health
sanative: tending to heal or cure
sanatory: conducive to health
sanitary: pertaining to the preservation of health; sanative
sound: free from imperfections or decay
sound as a bell: figurative expression for healthiness
sound as a roach: figurative expression for healthiness
sound of mind and body: well in soul and body
sound of wind: free from weakness of breathing
stanch: sound and firm
staunch: sound and firm
stenotic: pertaining to a narrowing of bodily orifices
terminal: designating incurably ill and dying patient
tolerably well: fairly well
tonic: having power to give bodily strength
uninfectious: not able to cause disease
uninjured: unharmed; whole; sound
unmaimed: not disabled
unmarred: not hurt, injured, or spoiled
unscathed: not harmed or damaged
untainted: not corrupted or diseased
useful: producing good health
vigorous: strong and healthy
well: healthy; sound in body
whole: well; sound
wholesome: producing and advancing good health

Hearing

acoustic: pertaining to the sense of hearing
audible: capable of being heard
auditory: relating to hearing
aural: of or related to the sense of hearing
aurated: having ears
auricular: aural; pertaining to the ear
clairaudient: able to hear things not actually present

deaf-mute: lacking hearing and ability to speak
hard-of-hearing: having defective hearing
hearing: pertaining to the sense of hearing
oculauditory: combining the sense of sight and sense of hearing
otacoustic: aiding hearing

otic: pertaining to the ear; auricular
subaudible: having a frequency below the limit of hearing; scarcely perceptible

Heat—Heating

ablaze: on fire
adiaphoretic: pertaining to sweat prevention
afire: burning
alight: lighted up
anhidrotic: tending to inhibit sweating
ardent: burning; having the appearance of fire
baking: being heated and dry
blazing: emitting flame or light
blood-hot: of the temperature of normal blood, about 98.5 degrees Fahrenheit
blood-warm: of the temperature of normal blood, about 98.5 degrees Fahrenheit
buldering: hot and muggy
burning-hot: extremely hot
burnt: set on fire; consumed by fire
calefacient: producing a feeling of warmth
calorific: causing or producing heat
candent: glowing white with heat
canicular: pertaining to the dog days
close: oppressive and stifling
coctile: baked, as bricks
combustible: easily destroyed by fire
deflagrable: pertaining to a sudden bursting into flame or fast burning
diaphoretic: producing sweat; increasing sweat
diathermal: easily permeable by radiant heat
diathermanous: possessing the property of transmitting radiant heat
ebullient: boiling over
estiferous: producing heat; aestiferous
estival: pertaining to the summer; aestival
euthermic: causing warmth
fervent: hot; glowing
fervid: very hot; burning
fiery: like fire; burning
genial: comfortably warm

glowing: shining with intense heat
heated: made hot
heating: creating heat
hidrotic: causing sweating
hot: having sensible heat; excessively warm
hot as fire: expression denoting degree of heat
hot as pepper: expression denoting degree of heat
hot enough to roast an ox: expression denoting degree of heat
igneous: pertaining to or resembling fire
ignescent: producing sparks; scintillating
in a blaze: hot
in a fever: hot
in a glow: hot
in a heat: hot
in a perspiration: hot
in a sweat: hot
in flames: on fire; burning
incalescent: increasing in heat; growing warm
incandescent: white with heat
inflamed: burning; set on fire
inflammable: easy to become kindled
isotheral: running through places of equal summer heat
isothermal: pertaining to an isotherm, or line of equal heat
isothermic: having the nature of an isotherm
kindling: creating fire; igniting
like a furnace: very hot
like an oven: very hot
lukewarm: moderately warm
mild: neither hot nor cold
molten: changed to a fluid state by heat
on fire: burning
oppressive: overwhelming; heavy
piping-hot: boiling; simmering
plutonic: burning; fiery

pyretic: pertaining to fever; feverish; febrile
red-hot: heated to redness
reeking: emitting a warm, moist vapor
scumfished: smothered; suffocated
semiustulate: half-burned
smoking: emitting a visible vapor as a result of combustion
smoking-hot: almost emitting vapor from its heat
smoldering: burning slowly
sodden: poorly baked
stifling: very hot and close so as to make breathing difficult
stuffy: close; ill-ventilated; stifling
sudoriferous: sweaty; sweat-producing; sudorific
sudorific: causing sweat
suffocating: stopping respiration; stifling
sultry: hot and moist

sunny: exposed to the rays of the sun
sweltered: oppressed with heat
sweltering: oppressively hot
sweltry: abnormally hot and humid
swullocking: very sultry
tepid: moderately warm
thalpotic: pertaining to feeling warmth
thermal: pertaining to heat
thermic: pertaining to heat
torrid: violently hot
tropical: pertaining to the tropics
unextinguished: not put out
unfrozen: not frozen
unquenched: not extinguished
ustulated: singed; scorched; ustulate
volcanic: of or pertaining to a volcano
warm: possessing a moderate degree of heat
warm as toast: hot
warm as wool: moderately warm
white-hot: incandescent

Heaven

airy: placed high in the air; ethereal; heavenly
beatific: happy; blessed; heavenly
celest: heavenly; celestial
celestial: pertaining to the material heavens; of a heavenly nature
celical: heavenly; celestial
elysian: like Elysium; happy
empyrean: of the highest heaven

ethereal: heavenly; celestial; etherial
from on high: from heaven; from above
heavenish: celestial; heavenly
heavenly: like heaven; blessed
paradisiacal: like paradise; supremely blissful
supernal: from above; heavenly; ethereal
unearthly: unlike the earth; heavenly

Heaviness

beefy: heavy and ponderous
burdensome: hard to bear on account of weight
cumbersome: moving heavily
cumbrous: unwieldy
heavy: weighing a lot
heavy as lead: of great gravity
incumbent: weighing upon something
lumpish: heavy like a lump
lumpishy: heavy
massive: of great weight and bulk
plumbeous: leaden; dull; heavy

ponderable: having appreciable weight
ponderous: having unusually great weight and mass
rhinocerial: very heavy, like a rhinoceros
superincumbent: lying upon something else
teemful: pregnant; fruitful; heavy
top-heavy: heavier or larger on top
unwieldy: not easily handled on account of great weight and bulk
weighting: that may be used to measure gravity
weighty: having great gravity

Heed

absorbed: having the attention wholly engaged

alive to: in full action; attentive to

askance: with a sidelong look

attentive: having the mind firmly fixed on one object

audient: listening; paying attention

awake to: attentive

beseeching: with an expectant or hopeful look; imploring

breathless: not breathing from excitement or interest

cognizant: aware

come-hither: with a beckoning or inviting look

deprecatory: with a disapproving look; glaring

distraught: with a troubled look

engaged in: earnestly employed in

engrossed in: absorbed in

excubant: on guard; keeping watch

expergefacient: awakening

fleeting: with a glance; flitting

furtive: with a sly look

heedful: full of care and attention; mindful

intent on: bending the mind to a purpose

levisomnous: watchful

measured: with a watchful look

mindful: attentive

observant: watchful; careful in viewing

observing: quick to notice; observant

occupied with: busy with; employed in

on the watch: watchful

open-eyed: having open eyes; watchful

preoccupied: absorbed in thought

rapt: wholly absorbed

regardant: observant; watchful; contemplative

regardful: having regard or respect for

steadfast: fixed on one place

taken up with: engrossed in

undistracted: not drawn aside from the pursued object

upon the stretch: making a persistent effort

vultured: watched with anticipation

watchful: on the watch; vigilant

wrapped in: so attentive as to disregard all other things

Height

aerial: pertaining to the upper air

alpine: like the Alps

altitudinarian: aspiring to great heights

altitudinous: high or tall

altivolant: flying high

attollent: lifting

beetling: jutting; prominent

bird's-eye: seen from high above

cloud-capped: high as the clouds

cloud-topped: high as the clouds

cloud-touching: high as the clouds

elevated: raised from a lower to a higher level; raised up

eminent: surpassing; very high

exalted: raised to a position of prominence

gigantic: of great size

hanging: suspended in the air

heaven-kissing: as high as heaven; very high

high: elevated; lofty; tall

highest: topmost; crowning

hilly: rugged; like hills

incumbent: placed above or leaning upon something

lanky: thin and tall

lofty: very high

moorland: like the moorland

mountainous: hilly; elevated; like the region of mountains

overhanging: jutting out over or appearing to, as rocky cliffs

overlying: placed above

Patagonian: like an inhabitant of Patagonia; very tall

prominent: in bold relief

rampant: leaping
soaring: floating on high
stilted: bombastic
subalpine: under the Alps
superimposed: placed above
superincumbent: resting on something
superior: situated over
supernatant: floating or swimming above

tall: of great height
tall as a Maypole: very tall
tall as a poplar: very tall
tall as a steeple: very tall
terraced: having different horizontal levels
towering: very high
upland: high in situation
upper: above

Hell

chthonian: pertaining to underworld gods; infernal; beneath the earth; chthonic
damned: consigned to hell
diabolic: suggestive of hell; diabolical
hell-bound: headed for hell
hellish: like hell; fiendish
in limbo: on the border of hell

infernal: pertaining to the lower regions
stygian: pertaining to hell; hellish; infernal; caliginous; fuliginous; tenebrous
sulfurous: pertaining to hellfire, brimstone, and sulfur of hell
Tartarean: pertaining to hell or purgatory

Help

adjutorious: helpful
adjuvant: helpful; auxiliary; contributory
ancillary: subordinate; helping; subsidiary
at one's beck: close at hand
auxiliary: helping; assisting
cataskeuastic: constructive
coadjuvant: assisting; aiding
favorable: inclined toward; friendly
friendly: kindly disposed toward

helpful: giving help
ministrant: attendant; serving, as a minister
neighborly: living close by; friendly
obliging: having the disposition to do favors; eager to help
propitious: fortunate; lucky; favorable
subservient: serving; subordinate
subsidiary: serving to help; assistant
succursal: auxiliary; subsidiary
well-disposed: favorable

Heterodoxy

antichristian: opposed to Christianity
antiscriptural: opposed to scripture
apocryphal: pertaining to the fourteen books contained in the Vulgate Bible, but held uncanonical by Protestant churches
bigoted: stubbornly attached to a creed
cacodoxical: heretical
dissident: not agreeing with; differing from
ethnic: pagan; pertaining to nations neither Christian nor Jew

ethnical: pagan; pertaining to nations neither Christian nor Jew
fanatical: moved with excessive and intemperate zeal
gentile: pertaining to a person who is not a Jew
heathen: irreligious; a dweller on the heath
heathenish: like a heathen
heretical: at variance with accepted religious views
heterodox: differing from accepted doc-

trines or religious opinions; unorthodox

iconoclastic: pertaining to iconoclasm or image breaking

idolatrous: pertaining to the worship of heathen gods

pagan: heathen; not Christian; pertaining to the worship of heathen gods; a dweller in a village

painim: pagan

pantheistic: pertaining to the belief that the universe and God are identical

polytheism: pertaining to the belief in many gods

recusant: refusing to conform to accepted doctrines

schismatic: pertaining to a schism or a division in a church

sectarian: excessively devoted to a sect

secular: pertaining to the present life

superstitious: pertaining to credulous belief in the supernatural

uncanonical: not according to canon

unchristian: not Christian

unorthodox: not firm and sound in doctrine

unscriptural: not in accordance with Scriptures

visionary: pertaining to dreams or apparitions

Homogeneity

clear: free from mixture or obstruction

elementary: with but one constituent element; not compounded

exclusive: tending to exclude or shut out

exempt from: free from

free from: without

homeostatic: remaining essentially the same regardless of external circumstances

homogeneous: having the same nature or similar parts

immiscible: not capable of being mixed

neat: free from uncleanness or disorder

of a piece: of the same sort or kind

pure: free from mixture or extraneous matter

sheer: unmingled; being what it seems to be

simple: uncompounded; plain

single: consisting of but one

unadulterated: not adulterated

unalloyed: not reduced in purity by mixture

unblended: not commingled

uncombined: separate

uncompounded: not formed of different ingredients or elements

undecomposed: not dissolved or broken up

unfortified: not strengthened or confirmed

uniform: being the same throughout

unmingled: not blended or mixed

unmixed: separate; distinct

unsophisticated: unadulterated; pure

untinged: unaffected by mixture

Honesty—Virtue

above all praise: superlatively good

admirable: having qualities to excite approbation, esteem, or reverence

angelic: of the nature of angels

as good as one's word: reliable

beyond all praise: surpassing praise

candid: free from bias or prejudice

chivalrous: having the qualities of an ancient knight; gallant

coeliginous: heaven-born

commendable: deserving of approbation or praise

conscientious: governed by conscience or by the sense of right and wrong

constant: steady in purpose; faithful

constant as the Northern Star: always steady

correct: free from wrong or error; consonant with what is right

creditable: deserving or possessing reputation or esteem

desertful: meritorious

deserving: being entitled to

duteous: performing that which is due

dutiful: controlled by a sense of duty

equitable: characteristic of equity; conforming to the principles of equity

evenhanded: impartial

excellent: excelling or surpassing others in virtue or the like

exemplary: serving as a pattern or model

fair: showing no partiality; just

fair and aboveboard: impartial and open

faithful: trusty in any duty or position

frank: candid and sincere

gentlemanlike: suited to a gentleman; honorable

godlike: of superior excellence

good: possessing moral excellence or virtue

heaven-born: born in heaven

high-minded: magnanimous

high-principled: furnished with good principles

high-spirited: full of spirit

honest: fair and straightforward in dealings with others; free from deceit

honest as daylight: very honest

honorable: conforming to what honor would demand; having excellent motives

impartial: showing no favors; disinterested

impravable: incorruptible

incorruptible: incapable of being corrupted or defiled

innocent: without fault; not tainted by sin

inviolable: not to be injured or profaned

inviolate: not violated

jealous of honor: earnestly guarding honor

just: conformable to the principles of law or justice

laudable: worthy of praise; commendable

loyal: constant and reliable in the performance of duties

matchless: having no equal

meritorious: deserving of reward or honor

moral: relating to duty or obligation

nice: refined in habits or manner

noble: above whatever is low, mean, degrading, or dishonorable

open and aboveboard: dealing fair

openhearted: disclosing one's thoughts; candid and kind

overscrupulous: scrupulous to excess

peerless: matchless

praiseworthy: commendable

punctilious: very nice in regard to etiquette

punctual: exact in respect to the appointed time

pure: free from corruption or moral depravity

religious: given to religion; pious; strict

reputable: having a good reputation; honorable

respectable: deserving respect; having fair excellence

right: according with truth and duty

righteous: according with or performing that which is right

right-minded: having a right or honest mind

saintlike: resembling a saint

saintly: becoming a holy person

scrupulous: hesitating to violate conscience

seraphic: angelic

square: rendering justice; just

stainless: without stain or crime

staunch: firm and steadfast in principle

sterling: of excellent quality

straightforward: going in a straight path; frank

strict: conforming scrupulously to a principle

supramundane: situated above our world; celestial
tender-conscienced: having a sensitive conscience
to be depended upon: honorable
true: conformable to fact; steady in respect to principles and friendships
true as the needle to the north: upright
true to one's colors: uncompromisingly loyal
true to the core: honorable to the heart
true-blue: of inflexible principles; loyal
truehearted: of a true and loyal heart
trustworthy: worthy of trust or confidence
trusty: faithful to duty
unbetrayed: having no trust or confidence violated
unbought: uncorrupted
unbribed: not corrupted with money or rewards
unbroken: not having lost credit
uncorrupt: free from bribery

uncorrupted: free from bribery
undebauched: not corrupt in morals
undefiled: not polluted or filthy
undepraved: not made worse; uncorrupted
unperjured: not swearing to what one knows is untrue
unstained: not stained; untouched by crime
unsullied: untarnished; unspoiled
untainted: not infected by a physical or moral taint
untarnished: not tarnished; without its purity destroyed
unviolated: not broken; unprofaned
unworldly: not worldly; spiritual
upright: correct in morals or conduct
veracious: disposed to speak the truth from habit
virtuous: possessing or exhibiting virtue
well-intentioned: having upright intentions or honorable purposes
worthy: having worth or excellence

Hopefulness

auspicious: favorable; hopeful
bright: cheerful; encouraging
buoyant: lively; cheerful
buoyed up: kept from despondency
cheering: encouraging
confident: having trust; trustful
elated: filled with confidence and hope
encouraging: furnishing grounds to hope for success
enthusiastic: eager and zealous in the pursuit of an object
exultant: triumphant
fearless: without fear
flushed: elated; animated with joy
full of promise: likely to fulfill expectations
hopeful: full of expectation
hoping: having confidence or a desire for something good
in good heart: in a state of confidence or kindliness
in hopes: hoping

inspiriting: encouraging; animating
looking up: hoping
of good omen: propitious; favorable
of promise: tending to cause hope
on the high road to: on the way to success or completion
Panglossian: having an excessively optimistic view
probable: likely
promising: affording hopes
propitious: favorable; hopeful
reassuring: restoring confidence to
roseate: full of roses; blooming; promising
rose-colored: alluring
sanguine: full of hope; not desponding; hopeful; optimistic; confident
secure: free from care, anxiety, or the like; confident
self-reliant: having confidence in oneself
undespairing: not despairing; hopeful
unsuspecting: not distrusting

unsuspicious: not suspicious
utopian: involving imaginary perfection
within sight of land: in a hopeful condition

within sight of shore: in a hopeful condition

Hopelessness

at one's last gasp: deprived of all hope
beyond remedy: not capable of being remedied
brokenhearted: crushed with grief or despair
cureless: beyond all hope of living
despairing: being without hope
forlorn: abandoned; lost
given over: completely abandoned
given up: ceasing from effort
hopeless: despairing; without hope
ill-omened: unfortunate
immedicable: incurable
impracticable: incapable of being practiced
in despair: without hope
inauspicious: unfavorable; unlucky
inconsolable: grieved beyond comfort
incorrigible: beyond correction
incurable: not to be cured
irreclaimable: incapable of being reclaimed
irrecoverable: not capable of being restored or remedied

irredeemable: incapable of being redeemed or recovered
irremediable: incapable of being cured
irreparable: not capable of being recovered
irretrievable: incurable
irreversible: irrevocable
irrevocable: incapable of being recalled
not to be thought of: not to be considered
out of the question: not worthy of consideration
past cure: with no chance of recovery
past hope: with no chance of recovery
past mending: with no chance of recovery
past recall: with no chance of recovery
remediless: not capable of being remedied
ruined: seriously damaged or impaired
threatening: menacing
undone: ruined in reputation or morals
unpromising: not affording a favorable aspect
unpropitious: unfavorable

Humanitarianism

chivalric: pertaining to chivalry; knightly
cosmopolitan: free from local prejudices
generous: having nobleness of mind or kindness in disposition and action
humane: disposed to treat other human beings or animals with kindness
humanitarian: relating to humanitarianism
largehearted: kind; generous

patriotic: unselfishly devoted to one's country and its interests
philanthropic: characterized by philanthropy
public-spirited: disposed to advance the public interests or those of the community
utilitarian: pertaining to utilitarianism

Humbleness

abashed: deprived of self-possession
affable: courteous and ready to converse
ashamed: feeling shame; abashed by guilt

bowed down: caused to stoop, as with grief or shame

browbeaten: intimidated by rough manner or address

chapfallen: having the lips or jaw drooping

condescending: courteous to inferiors

crestfallen: having the crest lowered; dejected

dashed: checked; confounded

down in the mouth: chapfallen; depressed in countenance

down on one's knees: in humble attitude

down on one's marrowbones: down on one's knees

dumfounded: confused with astonishment

flabbergasted: struck with wonder

hontous: ashamed; shameful

humble: not thinking highly of oneself

humbled: lowered in one's self-esteem

humbled in the dust: greatly humbled

humble-minded: having a humble mind

ignominious: characterized by shame, disgrace; despicable

lowly: having low rank

meek: gentle and submissive in disposition

modest: unwilling to push oneself forward unduly

out of countenance: downcast

resigned: submissive to superiors

servile: having the spirit of a slave; cringing

shorn of one's glory: deprived of one's occasion of glory

sober-minded: serious and grave

submissive: willing to obey or conform to the will of another

unoffended: not offended

verecund: modest; shy

Hurry

boisterous: rough; blustery

booming: rushing violently

breathless: so quickly as to be unable to breathe

brusque: short; sharp; quick

cursory: rapid; hasty

festinate: hasty

feverish: impatient; very desirous

furious: frantic; very great, as furious speed

fussy: fidgety

hard-pressed: chased

hasty: with haste

headlong: hasty; precipitous

hotheaded: quick-tempered

hurried: in haste

impelled: driven; urged

impelling: driving; urging

impetuous: doing without thought

impulsive: having the power of driving or impelling

in a hurry: hasty; speedy

in all haste: hurriedly

in haste: hasty; speedy

in hot haste: hurriedly

partito in quarta: in a rush

precipitate: headlong; rushed; rash; sudden; quick

precipitous: headlong; rushed; rash

preproperous: overly hasty; precipitate

pressed for time: in need of time

pushing: hasty

rudderish: hasty; passionate

saccadic: twitching; jerky

scrambling: hurriedly

spoffish: fussy and bustling

umbeer: impatient

urgent: demanding immediate action

Hypothesis

allusive: mentioning in an obscure or indirect manner; suggesting something similar in another book

assumed: adopted as a basis of reasoning

conjectural: consisting of conjectures

given: stated; admitted as a fact

gratuitous: given without claim or consideration, as money, advice

guessive: conjectural
hypothetical: of the nature of or based on hypotheses
mooted: under consideration
postulatory: assumed without proof
presumptive: founded on presumption
putative: commonly thought or supposed
speculative: consisting of speculation
stochastic: pertaining to conjecture, guesswork

suggestive: fitted or likely to suggest
supposable: likely or possible to suppose
supposing: that supposes
suppositious: supposed; hypothetical; conceptual
supposititious: supposed
suppositive: consisting of or implying supposition
theoretical: consisting of theory

Ignorance

a stranger to: ignorant of

absent: of wandering mind

addle-headed: dull-witted; stupid; with brain like an addled egg

addlepated: dull-witted; stupid; with brain like an addled egg

anile: old-womanish; imbecile

apish: apelike; silly

asinine: like an ass; stupid; obstinate

at fault: mistaken and worthy of blame

at sea: in a quandary

at the end of his tether: having exhausted his stock of knowledge

babbling: talking idly

babish: childish

babyish: childish; simple

beefheaded: having a head like a cow's; stupid

beef-witted: having the intelligence of a cow

beetleheaded: dull; stupid

behind the age: not versed in present knowledge

belated: slow of intellect

benighted: unenlightened; ignorant

bewildered: greatly perplexed

bigoted: obstinately and blindly attached to some creed, opinion

blatant: noisy; blustering

blinded: prevented from knowing

blindfold: having the intellect darkened; heedless

blockish: deficient in understanding; stupid

blunderheaded: blundering; stupid

blunt: slow of wit; dull

blunt-witted: dull; stupid

boeotian: dull; obtuse, as the Athenians esteemed the natives of Boeotia to be; boeotic

bookless: unscholarly

bovine: sluggish; dull, as a cow

brainless: without understanding

caught tripping: found blundering

childish: like a child; puerile

childlike: like a child

clodpated: stupid; dull

concealed: hidden from investigation

dansey-headed: giddy; thoughtless

desipient: foolish; silly

dim-sighted: lacking clear perception

diverted: turned away from labor or study, as by amusement

doltish: stupid; dull

driveling: silly; weak; speaking twaddle

dull: slow of perception; sluggish

dull as a beetle: figurative degree of dullness

dull-brained: stupid; doltish

dull-witted: stupid

eccentric: peculiar; erratic

empty: having no intelligence
empty-headed: senseless; foolish
extravagant: immoderate; fantastic
fatheaded: dull of apprehension
fatuous: feeble in mind; weak; silly; stupid
fat-witted: dull; stupid
featherbrained: weak; giddy
feebleminded: weak in intellectual power
foolish: wanting in judgment
frivolous: trivial; silly
giddy: characterized by foolish levity or imprudence
glaikit: thoughtless; foolish; giddy; glaiket
gratuitous: done without good reason; uncalled-for
green: having no knowledge from experience, and hence liable to blunder
gross-headed: thickskulled; stupid
half-baked: immature; inexperienced; callow; sophomoric; wet behind the ears
half-learned: partially educated
half-witted: weak in intellect; silly
having no head: having no knowledge
heavy: sluggish of mind
hoodwinked: easily deceived
idiotic: like an idiot; imbecile
idle: slothful; sluggish
ignorant: having no knowledge
ill-advised: injudicious
ill-devised: not well planned
ill-imagined: not well imagined
illiterate: knowing nothing of literature; unable to read
ill-judged: injudicious; foolish
imbecile: having feeble mental faculties
impalpable: intangible; not easily grasped by the mind
improper: not proper or right under the circumstances
in the dark: uncertain
inapprehensible: unintelligible
inapt: unsuitable
incogitable: not capable of being known
incogitant: thoughtless

inconsiderate: thoughtless; heedless
inconsistent: incongruous; contradictory
indocible: unteachable; indocile
inept: silly; useless; absurd
inexpedient: unwise; inadvisable; indiscreet
infantile: childish
infantine: childish
injudicious: wanting in sound judgment; indiscreet
insensate: destitute of sense; stupid
insipient: unwise; foolish
insulse: insipid; dull; stupid
irrational: not possessed of reasoning powers; absurd
lack-brained: deficient in understanding; witless
lean-witted: having little sense
maggoty-headed: capricious
mindless: not imbued with intellectual powers; unthinking
misinformed: wrongly informed
muddleheaded: stupid
muddyheaded: dull; stupid
narrow-minded: of confined views; illiberal
nescient: ignorant
nonsensical: without sense; absurd; foolish
not bright: dull of intellect
not to be thought of: impossible
novel: not previously known; strange
obtuse: dull intellectually; stupid
off one's mind: free from care
parviscient: uninformed
pedantic: given to pedantry
philistine: narrow-minded; from the Philistines of the Bible
pigheaded: stupidly obstinate
prosaic: dull; uninteresting
puerile: boyish; childish; silly
puzzleheaded: having the head full of confused notions
rash: overhasty in counsel or action
reasonless: destitute of reason; unreasonable
ridiculous: unworthy of consideration; absurd and laughable

rude: uncultured, and hence lacking in manners
sappy: silly
senseless: without sense; foolish
shallow: with only superficial knowledge; lacking intellectual depth
shallow-brained: weak in intellect; foolish
shallow-pated: shallow-brained
shortsighted: unable to understand things deep; of limited intellect
short-witted: having little wit; not wise
silly: destitute of ordinary good sense; simple; foolish
simple: not wise or clever
sleeveless: unreasonable; profitless
sottish: very foolish from habitual drunkenness
spoony: weak-minded
stolid: impassible, dull, or stupid
stupid: very slow of apprehension or understanding; dull-witted
superficial: able to know or characterized by only what is very easily understood
thickskulled: stupid
thoughtless: heedless
unacquainted: not acquainted
unapprehended: not acquainted
unapprised: not acquainted
unascertained: not acquainted
unaware: not acquainted
unbookish: not acquainted
unconscious: not acquainted
unconsidered: not considered or regarded
unconversant: not acquainted
uncultivated: not acquainted
undiscerning: wanting in discernment
undreamed of: not thought of
uneducated: not acquainted
unendowed with reason: without the faculty of reason
unenlightened: lacking knowledge or intelligence
unexplained: not acquainted
unexplored: not acquainted

ungifted: being without native gifts or endowments
unguided: not acquainted
unheard-of: not acquainted
unideal: destitute of ideals
uninformed: not acquainted
uninitiated: not acquainted
uninstructed: not acquainted
unintellectual: lacking intellect
unintelligent: lacking intelligence; ignorant
uninvestigated: not acquainted
unknowing: not acquainted
unknown: not acquainted
unlearned: not acquainted
unlettered: not acquainted
unoccupied: not possessed
unperceived: not acquainted
unphilosophical: not rational; unwise
unread: not acquainted
unreasonable: irrational; not agreeable to reason
unschooled: not acquainted
untaught: not acquainted
unteachable: not teachable; indocile
unthinking: lacking thought
unthought of: not thought of
untutored: not acquainted
unversed: not acquainted
unweeting: not acquainted
unwise: not wise; injudicious; foolish
unwitting: not acquainted
useless: having or being of no use
vacant: empty of thought; stupid
vacuous: empty-headed; inane; expressionless
wanting: absent; lacking; soft
wantwit: idiotic
weak: feeble of mind; foolish
weak in the upper story: figurative expression for weak-headed
weak-headed: not possessing intellectual strength
weak-minded: feebleminded; foolish; idiotic
weetless: witless
without reason: lacking the faculty of reason
witless: without thoughtfulness; foolish

Imitation

apographal: pertaining to a copy or transcript

echopractic: mimicking

epigonous: of a later generation; imitative

faithful: conformable

imitable: that can be imitated

imitated: copied

imitative: inclined to copy

lifelike: like or resembling life

literal: exactly translated or transcribed; unimaginative

mimetic: imitative

mimic: inclined to imitate for sport or ridicule

mock: merely imitative

modeled after: copied after; imitating

molded on: shaped or formed after

paraphrastic: of the nature of a paraphrase

secondhand: not from the original source; being a poor imitation

Impenitence

acolastic: incorrigible

graceless: lacking in grace; depraved

hardened: wanting in feeling; confirmed in error

impenitent: not penitent

incorrigible: beyond hope of reclaiming

indurate: physically or morally hardened

irreclaimable: not able to be reclaimed

lost: hardened beyond recovery

obdurate: stubbornly impenitent

recusant: obstinate in refusal

relentless: unyielding

remorseless: wanting in remorse

seared: hardened

shriftless: without absolution

unatoned: not expiated

uncontrite: not having deep sorrow for sin

unreclaimed: not reformed

unreformed: not improved morally

unrepentant: not repentant

unrepented: not sorry for sin

Impoliteness

abusive: uttering harsh language against a person

acrimonious: exhibiting bitterness in speaking

austere: very serious

bearish: snarling and gruff in conduct

biting: indiscriminately censorious and unfeeling

bitter: marked by sharpness or severity

blackguard: characteristic of a blackguard

bluff: somewhat rude or abrupt, but kindly

blunt: abrupt in manner

boorish: awkward and rude from want of training

brusque: blunt; abrupt

brutal: treating others with brutality

caustic: marked by a sharp and penetrating spite

cavalier: easy; gay

churlish: wanting in kindness and courtesy

contumelious: full of unmerited disrespect and insolence

cool: not allowing much intimacy

crabbed: morose

dedecorous: unbecoming

discourteous: uncourteous

forward: immodest

foulmouthed: using indecent language habitually

foul-spoken: using indecent language habitually

grim: surly

gruff: stern

harsh: sour and unpleasant
ill-behaved: impolite; rude
ill-bred: impolite; rude
ill-conditioned: impolite; rude
ill-mannered: impolite; rude
immorigerous: rude
impolite: not polite
imprudent: lacking prudence
inaffable: not easy of approach
obtrusive: inclined to make one's company unwelcome
peevish: unreasonably cross or querulous
pert: regardless of the respect due superiors
perverse: inclined to do the opposite of what is required
precocious: forwardness
repulsive: forbidding
rough: lacking in politeness
rude: very rough, so as to be offensive
rugged: crabbed
sarcastic: unjustifiably bitter and personal
saucy: marked by sharp impertinence
sharp: cutting in speech
short: petulant
snarling: talking in a surly, growling manner
sour: unpleasant in countenance
stern: stiff or unsympathetic in manner or conduct
sullen: discontented and morose

surly: quarrelsome; cross
surly as a bear: very surly
tart: slightly pungent
trenchant: cutting
unaccommodating: not disposed to please
unbred: not trained
unceremonious: not according to rite or ceremony
uncivil: impolite
uncivilized: rude and barbarous
uncomplaisant: disagreeable
uncourteous: impolite
uncourtly: impolite
ungainly: not attractive
ungallant: impolite
ungenteel: ill-bred
ungentle: ill-mannered
ungentlemanlike: impolite
ungentlemanly: impolite
ungracious: unkind
unladylike: not like a lady
unmannered: without training or manners
unmannerly: without training or manners
unneighborly: not social
unpolished: rude
unpolite: discourteous
venomous: malignant
virulent: moved by a desire to injure
vulgar: indicating a low state of taste and manners

Importance

all-absorbing: so important as to absorb all the attention
capital: of chief importance
cardinal: fundamental and important; like the hinge to the door
chief: highest in importance; head
commanding: dominant and important
considerable: worthy of regard; important
critical: important with reference to consequences
earnest: important and serious

ecbatic: indicating the possible importance of an event
egregious: extraordinary and important
emphatic: forcible and important
essential: indispensable and important
eventful: full of important events
first-rate: of the highest importance and excellence
foremost: most important in time or place
grand: transcendent in importance and impressiveness
grave: serious or weighty, and important

important: having weight or consequence

imposing: impressive and important

impressive: producing an impression on the feelings

in the front rank: leading and important

instant: urgent and important

leading: chief

main: most important; principal

marked: noticeable

material: of importance and consequence

memorable: very remarkable and worthy of remembrance

momentous: of great weight and importance

monsterful: wonderful; extraordinary

never to be forgotten: so important as to always be remembered

noble: magnificent; grand

not to be despised: important

not to be overlooked: worthy of notice

not to be sneezed at: not to be despised

notable: worthy of notice; remarkable

of importance: important

of note: of distinction and importance

of vital importance: of essential consequence

overruling: having a controlling influence

paramount: superior and preeminent

pregnant: having great weight or importance

pressing: urgent and important

primary: first in importance

prime: chief in importance

principal: highest in importance

prominent: eminent; marked in importance

radical: thoroughgoing and important

rare: extraordinary and important

remarkable: worthy of notice; extraordinary

salient: prominent and noticeable

serious: weighty and important

signal: noticeable and memorable

significant: having meaning and importance

solemn: sacredly impressive and important

stirring: arousing; exciting

substantive: lasting; relating to what is essential

superior: better or more important than others

telling: effective and important

trenchant: cutting; severe

urgent: pressing and important

vital: affecting life; essential to life

weighty: convincing and important

worthy of notice: noticeable

worthy of remark: worthy of particular notice

Impossibility

absurd: contrary to reason; opposed to common sense

beyond one's control: impossible to be done

beyond one's depth: impossible to be done

beyond one's grasp: impossible to be done

beyond one's power: impossible to be done

beyond one's reach: impossible to be done

beyond the bounds of possibility: impossible to be done

beyond the bounds of reason: impossible to be done

contrary to reason: impossible to be done

desperate: heedless or careless of safety

from which reason recoils: unreasonable

hygogical: unattainable; next to impossible

impassible: not affected by feeling

impervious: not permitting entrance or passage through

impossible: not capable of happening

impracticable: incapable of being put into practice

inaccessible: not easy of being reached

incompatible: not congruous; not existing together

inconceivable: not conceivable; not imaginable

incredible: not believable

inextricable: not capable of being freed from difficulties

infeasible: not practicable

inimaginable: unimaginable

innavigable: not capable of being sailed

insuperable: not surmountable

insurmountable: not to be overcome or conquered

not possible: not to be done

not to be had: impossible to be accomplished

not to be thought of: impossible to be accomplished

out of one's depth: impossible to be accomplished

out of one's grasp: impossible to be accomplished

out of one's power: impossible to be accomplished

out of reach: impossible to be accomplished

out of the question: impossible to be accomplished

prodigious: enormous; unusual

too much for: beyond one's power

unachievable: not to be accomplished

unattainable: not to be acquired

un-come-at-able: not to be reached

unfeasible: not to be done

unimaginable: not imaginable

unobtainable: not to be secured

unreasonable: against reason

unsurmountable: not to be passed or overcome

visionary: dreamy; impracticable

Impropriety

awkward: ungainly in movement

clumsy: lack of gracefulness in appearance

contraindicated: inadvisable

cumbersome: burdensome

cumbrous: burdensome

disadvantageous: not benefiting

discommodious: incommodious

hulky: clumsy

ill-advised: not based on good judgment

ill-contrived: not well contrived

impedient: hindering

improper: not proper

improprious: lacking proper form

in the wrong place: misfitting

inadmissible: not to be admitted

inadvisable: not advisable

inappropriate: not suitable to the time

inapt: not suited by nature

incommodious: not convenient

inconvenient: causing annoyance

ineligible: not qualified

inexpedient: not expedient

inopportune: happening at the wrong time

lumbering: moving as if heavily burdened

objectionable: worthy of disapproval

out of place: unsuitable

unadvisable: not advisable

undesirable: not to be wished for

unfit: not right or proper

unmanageable: not easily directed

unnecessary: not necessary

unprofitable: not producing gain

unsatisfactory: not satisfactory

unseemly: not in good taste

unsubservient: not servile

unwieldy: ponderous

Impurity

adulterous: given to adultery; illicit
Anacreontic: erotic; convivial
bawdy: obscene; filthy; unchaste
bestial: brutish; sensual; depraved
broad: loose; indelicate; bold
carnal: sensual
carnal-minded: fleshly; lustful; sensual
coarse: not refined or modest; low; vulgar
concupiscent: lustful; carnal; sensual
cyprian: lecherous; lewd
debauched: corrupted in morals; made unchaste
dissipated: pursuing pleasure to excess
dissolute: abandoned; lewd; profligate
equivocal: ascribable either to good or bad motives; questionable
erotic: amorous; amatory
fornicatory: concerning fornication
frail: deficient in moral strength; liable to be led away
free: unduly familiar; indelicate; immodest
fulsome: coarse; indelicate
gallant: polite and attentive to ladies
gay: loving pleasure; wanton
gross: coarse in meaning
immodest: wanting in modesty; impure; sensual
impure: foul; defiled by sin; unchaste
incestuous: guilty of incest; of the nature of incest
incontinent: exercising no restraint over the passions
indecent: immodest; gross; obscene
indecorous: contrary to recognized rules of good breeding; unseemly; rude
indelicate: coarse; immodest
lascivious: having, denoting, or tending to produce wanton desires; lustful; lewd
lecherous: given to or characterized by lewdness or lust
lewd: characterized by lust; libidinous
libidinous: characterized by lewdness
licentious: wanton; lascivious; lewd

lickerish: tempting or tempted by appetite; lustful
light: characterized by moral laxity
loose: dissolute; lewd
lupanarian: lewd; pertaining to a brothel
lustful: having carnal or sensual desire
meretricious: vulgar and tawdry; pertaining to a harlot; wanton
nerotic: sexually psychotic
no better than she should be: unchaste
not to be mentioned to ears polite: indecent; indecorous
obscene: offensive to chastity, decency, or modesty
of easy virtue: easily seduced
of loose character: lewd; dissolute
on the loose: obtaining one's living by prostitution
on the streets: being a prostitute
on the town: being a prostitute
pornerastic: licentious; whoremongering
pornographic: pertaining to licentious painting or literature; lascivious
profligate: immoral; dissolute; recklessly licentious
prurient: having lewd thoughts
rakish: dissolute; profligate
rampant: unbridled; unrestrained
randy: lustful; lecherous
ribald: indulging in or manifesting coarse indecency
riggish: wanton; licentious
ruttish: inclined to rut; lustful
salacious: lustful; lecherous
scortatory: pertaining to lewdness, fornication
sensual: lewd; unchaste; indulging in physical pleasures; full; ripe
sexotropic: constantly thinking about sex
shameless: wanting in modesty; indecent
smutty: obscene; not modest or pure
subagitatory: pertaining to copulation
supinovalent: able to have intercourse only when supine

unchaste: not continent; lewd

unclean: foul; dirty; filthy; morally impure

voluptuous: exciting sensual desires; sensual

wanton: loose; dissolute; lustful

Independence

adrift: unmoored; floating; hence, without relation or connection

alien: of different nature; foreign

arbitrary: without logical connection

away from the point: not connected with the point

away from the purpose: not connected with the point

away from the question: not connected with the point

away from the transaction: not connected with the point

beside the mark: not connected with the point

beside the point: not connected with the point

beside the purpose: not connected with the point

beside the question: not connected with the point

beside the transaction: not connected with the point

detached: disconnected

disconnected: separated; disunited

discordant: contradictory; disagreeing

episodic: out of the regular course of events; as an episode of an epic poem; not directly connected

exotic: foreign; of another kind or nature

extraneous: having no essential relation; irrelevant

far-fetched: studiously sought; not natural or obvious

forced: not arising from natural causes or relations

foreign: not native; having no relation

foreign to the point: not pertinent

foreign to the purpose: not pertinent

foreign to the question: not pertinent

foreign to the transaction: not pertinent

heterogeneous: dissimilar in structure or kind

impertinent: having no bearing on the subject; irrelevant

inapplicable: not suited to the matter in hand

inapposite: not pertinent

incidental: happening by chance; without regularity or design

incommensurable: not comparable in magnitude or value

independent: separate or disconnected; having no connections

insular: standing alone; isolated

irrelative: without mutual connection; unconnected

irrelevant: foreign to the subject; impertinent

irrespective: lacking relation

isolated: detached or insular

misplaced: placed out of natural relations

multifarious: having great diversity or variety

neither here nor there: foreign to the subject under discussion

not comparable: not allowing of comparison

not pertinent: not to the point

not to the purpose: irrelevant

out of the way: foreign

outlandish: not according to usage; uncouth

parenthetical: not essentially a part

quite another thing: an entirely different matter

remote: having slight relation or connection

segregate: separate; select

strange: not related; belonging elsewhere

unallied: not bound to; not similar in form or structure

unconformable: unwilling to conform

unconnected: not logically or naturally related

Indifference

adiaphoral: indifferent in the eyes of the church

adiaphoristic: theologically indifferent

apathetic: indifferent to feelings and emotions; unemotional

betwixt: of an intermediate feeling

callous: insensitive; unsympathetic; indifferent; hardened

Gallionic: indifferent; careless; irresponsible; galleonic

impassive: not feeling emotion; apathetic

incurious: not curious

indifferent: not concerned

insensible: incapable of perceiving or feeling; unmoved; unaffected

Laodicean: lukewarm; indifferent in religious beliefs

lukewarm: having little depth of feeling; indifferent

nonchalant: lacking in interest; wanting in warmth of feeling

noncurantist: characterized by indifference

pococurante: indifferent; nonchalant

unconcerned: devoid of interest; unmoved; uninterested

uninquisitive: not inquisitive

uninterested: not interested; indifferent

Inequality

disequal: unequal

disequilibriate: not in balance

disparate: not conforming to the common standard

disproportionate: having unharmonious dimensions in relation to another; disproportional

heterogeneous: consisting of different parts or different kinds

impar: unequal; unequally matched

inequal: not equal in amount, size, quality, etc.

lopsided: heavier on one side than on the other

overbalanced: heavier on one side than on the other

partial: favoring one more than another

top-heavy: too heavy in the upper parts in proportion to the remaining part

unbalanced: not in a state of balance

unequal: not equal

uneven: not even

unmeet: unevenly matched

Inertia

blunt: dull

doless: lacking in energy or ambition

dormant: possessing inherent activity in a quiescent state

dull: lacking in quickness of mental powers

exanimous: lifeless; exanimate

flat: not interesting

heavy: sluggish

inactive: not active

inert: not changing its condition

latent: undeveloped

lifeless: lacking in energy

listless: lacking energy; effete; sluggish

passive: not active

shiftless: lacking in resourcefulness; idle; lazy

slack: moving in a sluggish manner

sloomy: sluggish; spiritless; dull

slow: not moving fast

sluggish: showing a lack of energy

smoldering: in a latent state

tame: spiritless

torpid: continuously inactive from cold; numb; paralyzed; lethargic

unexerted: not exerted

Infinity

boundless: having no bounds
countless: that cannot be counted
endless: without end
exhaustless: that cannot be exhausted
illimitable: that cannot be limited
illimited: not limited or bounded
immeasurable: that cannot be estimated by comparison with something else
immense: incapable of measurement
incalculable: so great that an estimate cannot be formed
incomprehensible: that cannot be grasped mentally
indefinite: so large as to have no precise limits
infinite: having no bounds or limits; absolute and unconditioned
innumerable: so numerous as not to be counted
interminable: having no limit or end

limitless: without limits
measureless: having no standard great enough to be measured by
numberless: not to be counted
olamic: infinite; eternal
perpetual: infinite in duration
sumless: not to be computed
termless: boundless
unapproachable: that may not be reached
unbounded: having no known bounds
unfathomable: infinite in depth
unlimited: having no limits
unmeasured: not measured
unnumbered: indefinitely numerous
untold: not numbered
without end: infinite
without limit: infinite
without measure: infinite
without number: infinite

Inherentness—Nativeness

bred in the bone: intrinsic; inherent
characteristic: distinguishing; marking
congenital: born with one; existing from birth
congenite: inborn; congenital
connate: existing from birth
derived from within: inborn
essential: important in the highest degree; containing the essence of a substance
fixed: settled; established; unalterable
fundamental: indispensable; basal; primary
hereditary: deriving by inheritance; passing naturally from parent to child
immanent: inherent; intrinsic; subjective
implanted: deeply fixed; instilled
in the grain: infixed deeply
inborn: implanted by nature; innate
inbred: developed from and in the nature; innate
incarnate: embodied in flesh
incurable: remediless

indigenous: native; inherent
ineradicable: incapable of being rooted out
ingenerate: generated within; inborn
ingrained: worked into the mental or moral constitution of; infixed deeply
inherent: permanently existing in something; innate
innate: inborn; natural; native
instinctive: derived from or prompted by instinct; natural
internal: inward; inherent
intrinsic: inward; inherent; essential; genuine; real
intrinsical: intrinsic
invariable: not given to variation or change; always uniform
inward: seated in the mind, heart, spirit, or soul
inwrought: worked into any fabric so as to form a part of its texture
longanimous: patiently enduring, suffering

native: belonging to someone or something by nature; natural to a person, place, or thing

natural: pertaining to the constitution of a thing; essential; characteristic

normal: according to an established rule or principle; natural

radical: original; fundamental; thoroughgoing

running in the blood: inherited

subjective: proceeding from or taking place within the thinking subject

thoroughbred: bred from the best blood through a long line; hence, high-spirited, courageous

to the manner born: familiar with something from birth

virtual: being in essence or effect, but not in form or appearance

Innocence

above suspicion: too innocent to be suspected

arcadian: simple and innocent

artless: not given to the practice of artifices

blameless: free from anything worthy of censure

bloodguiltless: free from guilt of murder

blunt: purposely rough in speech or conduct

candid: characterized by candor

clear: free from guilt

direct: not ambiguous

dovelike: inoffensive and innocent

downright: undisguised

faultless: free from even a slight offense

frank: free from restraint in expressing thoughts and feelings

guileless: free from guile

guiltless: free from wrongdoing

harmless: not inflicting injury

harmless as doves: harmless in an extreme degree

honest: not exhibiting any deceit

immaculate: without moral blemish

impeccant: sinless

inartificial: natural

inculpable: that cannot be charged with wrongdoing

indefectible: not capable of being faulted

inerrable: not able to go astray morally

ingenit: innate; inherent; native; natural; ingenite

ingenuous: not acting or speaking in disguise

innocent: not having done wrong

innocent as a lamb: very gentle and innocent

innocent as the babe unborn: incapable of doing wrong

innocuous: having no injurious qualities; harmless; innocent

innoxious: having no injurious qualities

inoffensive: doing no harm

irreprehensible: that cannot justly be blamed

irreproachable: that cannot be found fault with

irreprovable: that cannot be censured with justice

lamblike: gentle and innocent

naïve: innocent; artless; guileless

native: simple; sincere

natural: without affectation

not guilty: having done nothing wrong

open: not reserved

pauciplicate: simple; uncomplicated

plain: free from anything that will hide the nature or meaning of anything

pure: free from moral corruption

salvable: capable of being saved

Saturnian: marked by simple innocence, as in the golden age, when Saturn ruled the gods and men

simple: acting as without a knowledge of the world

sincere: marked by sincerity

sinless: perfectly innocent

spotless: free from any blemish on moral character

stainless: free from every moral taint
straightforward: honest
unaffected: not affected
unblamable: that cannot be found fault with
unblemished: not marred by guilt
unculpable: that cannot be censured
undefiled: not made impure
undesigning: not designing
unerring: not going astray morally
unexceptionable: that cannot be taken exception to
unflattering: not flattering
unguilty: not guilty
unhardened: not made indifferent to sin

unimpeachable: faultless
unimpeached: not accused of guilt
unobjectionable: that cannot be found fault with
unpoetical: plain
unreproached: not found fault with
unreproved: not censured
unreserved: frank
unsophisticated: simple
unspotted: not tainted with guilt
unstudied: natural; spontaneous; not affected
untutored: uneducated
venial: excusable
virtuous: characterized by moral excellence

Insecurity

adventurous: full of risk
alarming: causing alarm
at bay: without way of escape
at stake: attended with risk
at the last extremity: in the greatest danger
between Scylla and Charybdis: surrounded by great peril
between the hammer and the anvil: liable to meet violent death
between two fires: in very great danger
built upon sand: having no foundation
critical: attended by peril
crumbling: going to decay
dangerous: accompanied by danger
defenseless: without means of defense
endangered: placed in danger
explosive: liable to explode
exposed: without protection
expugnable: capable of being taken by storm
fenceless: undefended
fraught with danger: very dangerous
guardless: without a guard
guideless: without a guide
hanging by a thread: in great peril
harborless: without place of refuge
hazardous: exposed to risk
helpless: without means of help
ill-omened: foretelling danger

in a bad way: in a critical condition
in danger: liable to injury
in question: uncertain
in the lion's den: in the midst of the greatest peril
insecure: lacking security
naufragous: in danger of a shipwreck
nightfoundered: distressed from being lost in the night
nodding to its fall: about to perish
not out of the wood: still in danger
off one's guard: not on the lookout for danger
ominous: portending evil
on a lee shore: near the rocks
on a sandy basis: without a firm foundation
on slippery ground: in a perilous position
on the brink: dangerously situated
on the edge: in the greatest danger
on the rocks: almost certain to be destroyed
on the verge of a precipice: in a very dangerous position
on the verge of a volcano: in a very dangerous position
on the wrong side of the wall: in danger, as from a falling wall
open to: exposed to

parlous: perilous
periculant: being in danger
periculous: perilous
perilous: attended by peril
precarious: subject to risk or danger
ramshackle: going to pieces
reduced to the last extremity: about to be destroyed
shaky: uncertain and fraught with danger
slippery: liable to prove dangerous; risky
slippy: slippery
threatening: portending evil
ticklish: involving risk
top-heavy: heavy at top and liable to fall
tottering: going to ruin
trembling in the balance: uncertain and fearful
tumbledown: gone to ruin

unadmonished: not forewarned
unadvised: not advised
under fire: in danger of being shot
unprepared: not ready for danger
unprotected: exposed to danger
unsafe: not safe or protected
unshielded: unprotected
unstable: not characterized by certainty
unsteady: shaky
untrustworthy: not to be risked
unwarned: not knowing of danger ahead
vertiginous: dizzy; revolving; vacillating; unstable
vulnerable: capable of being wounded or destroyed by attack
waterlogged: soaked with water; liable to sink
with a halter around one's neck: in imminent danger of death

Inside

deep-seated: permanent; intense
domestic: not pertaining to outsiders
enclosed: limited
endemic: prevalent among a certain people
endosmic: osmosing inwardly
home: arising from or pertaining to the home
immanent: dwelling inside; remaining within
indoor: inside
inland: at a distance from the coast
inmost: farthest in
inner: farther in
innermost: inmost
inside: within

interior: inside
internal: on the inside
interstitial: situated within the tissues of an organ
intestinal: pertaining to the intestines
intestine: domestic
intramural: situated within the walls of a city
intraregarding: looking within oneself
inward: directed toward the inside
inwrought: worked in
subcutaneous: situated just beneath the skin
subtegulaneous: indoor
vernacular: belonging to one's native country

Insignificance

airy: unreal; visionary
banal: not fresh; commonplace; trite
beggarly: without important and necessary means of comfortable living; like a beggar
beneath consideration: unimportant
beneath notice: unimportant
beneath regard: unimportant

catchpenny: cheap and unimportant; made to sell
cheap: being of a low price; mean
common: occurring often and hence unimportant
commonplace: ordinary and hence unimportant
contemptible: worthy only of contempt

extrinsic: not essential or inherent; extraneous

fair: only moderately satisfactory

farcical: absurd and of no consequence

feckless: weak; worthless; lacking purpose

fiddle-faddle: nonsensical

fingle-fangle: trifling

finical: overnice or fastidious in unimportant things

finikin: fastidiously precise in unimportant matters

flimsy: weak and ineffective

floccinaucinihilipilification: categorizing something as worthless trivia

footy: worthless; unimportant

fribble: of little importance

frivolous: without significance; trivial

frothy: empty; artificial

gimcrack: trivial and unimportant

idle: useless and unimportant

immaterial: without weight or significance

inane: empty and unimportant

inconsiderable: unworthy of notice

indifferent: exciting no concern

insignificant: without weight or importance

junkettaceous: frivolous; worthless

light: slight and unimportant

meager: poor in quality

mean: of little account or efficiency

mediocre: ordinary; unimportant

mere: this and nothing else

milk-and-water: without character

minutiose: concerned with minute details

miserable: worthless and unimportant

namby-pamby: finical

niggardly: stingy; miserly

niggling: trifling

nonessential: unnecessary and unimportant

not worth a curse: expression denoting degree of unimportance

not worth a straw: expression denoting degree of unimportance

not worth a thought: expression denoting degree of unimportance

not worth mentioning: expression denoting degree of unimportance

not worth speaking of: expression denoting degree of unimportance

not worth the pains: expression denoting degree of unimportance

not worthwhile: expression denoting degree of unimportance

of little account: not important

of little importance: not important

of no account: not important

of no importance: not important

of small account: not important

of small importance: not important

ordinary: usual; regular

paltry: having no important worth or value; trifling

passable: good but not exceptional; fairly good

peddling: insignificant

petty: trifling; unworthy of consideration

piddling: trivial; frivolous

pitiful: paltry; mean

poor: having little value or worth

powerless: devoid of power

puerile: trivial

putid: worthless

respectable: moderately excellent; to be respected

ridiculous: unworthy of serious attention; laughable

scrannel: slight; poor

scrubby: worthless; unimportant

scurvy: mean; contemptible

shabby: not worthy of an important or honorable person; mean

shallow: without depth of intellect

shilpit: worthless; feeble

slender: inconsiderable; meager

slight: insignificant; unimportant

sorry: paltry; poor

so-so: indifferent; passable

subordinate: belonging to inferior rank

tolerable: moderately good; passable

trashy: useless; worthless

trifling: of small importance or value

trivial: commonplace; unimportant; like corner gossip
trumpery: valueless in character
twopenny-halfpenny: cheap; unimportant; petty
unessential: unnecessary
uneventful: marked by no important events
unimportant: lacking importance
unworthy of consideration: unimportant

unworthy of notice: unimportant
unworthy of regard: unimportant
vain: devoid of significance
vile: mean and worthless
weak: having deficient character
weedy: of no more importance or value than a weed
wishy-washy: forceless as a weak, diluted beverage; unimportant
worthless: valueless
wretched: paltry; mean

Instantaneity

abrupt: without notice to prepare the mind for the event
forthwith: without delay; immediately
hasty: done in a hurry; quick
instant: closely pressing in time
instantaneous: happening after an imperceptible period of time
momentary: lasting a very short time
momently: lasting only a moment

quick as lightning: as quickly as possible
quick as thought: as quickly as possible
rapid as electricity: as quickly as possible
skelp: quickly, suddenly, often violently
subitaneous: hasty
sudden: happening unexpectedly
tantivy: quickly; fast; headlong
yarely: quickly; promptly
yeply: quickly; briskly

Instinct

absonant: not concordant; inconsistent
absonous: absonant
anterior to reason: arrived at without the use of the reasoning powers
feeble: weak; as a feeble argument
flimsy: of little strength or force
foolish: void of reason
frivolous: insufficient; lacking weight
gratuitous: without sufficient warrant
groundless: with no basis of reason
hazarded: taken chances on
illogical: without sound reasoning
impulsive: acting without due thought
inconclusive: not warranting a conclusion
inconsequent: not following according to the laws of reason
inconsequential: inconsequent
inconsistent: not agreeing with the rules of logic
incorrect: not following the laws of reasoning

independent of reason: intuitive
instinctive: discerned by instinct
intuitive: known by intuition
invalid: not sound
irrational: not according to reason
irrelevant: not pertaining to the subject
loose: not connected
nonsensical: void of reason
not following: inconsequent
poor: weak
unconnected: not logically related
unproved: not supported by reason
unreasonable: contrary to or exceeding reason
unscientific: not according to the principles of science
unsound: not based on sound reasoning
untenable: not to be defended by good reasons
unwarranted: lacking evidence or authority
vague: unauthorized
weak: lacking force

Intemperance

addicted to drink: drinking habitually

addled: drunk; confused by drink

after-hours: designating establishment serving alcohol after normal bar hours

beery: affected by beer

besotted: stupefied by drink

bibacious: addicted to alcohol; bibulous

bibulous: addicted to alcohol; excessively fond of drinking; bibacious

blasted: very drunk

bleezed: concerning a state when intoxicating liquor begins to affect someone

blind drunk: extremely inebriated

blotto: very drunk

bombed: drunk

bungfu: drunk

canned: drunk

capernoited: tipsy; nimptopsical; pifflecated

cheeping-merry: half-drunk

cherubimical: drunk

clean: not in possession of drugs

cockeyed: drunk

crapulous: sick from overindulgence in liquor

crispy: hungover

crocked: drunk

Dionysian: drunken and orgiastic, after Greek god Dionysus

drunk: intoxicated by alcoholic drink; temporarily impaired, excited, or stupefied by alcoholic drink; under the influence

drunken: under alcoholic influence

dry: designating locale or time in which sale and consumption of alcohol is forbidden; describing wine that is opposite of sweet

dusted: under the influence of PCP, or angel dust

ebrious: tending to get drunk; slightly drunk

flustered: befuddled with drink

fried: very drunk

fuddled: confused with liquor

gambrinous: full of beer

giddy: somewhat inebriated

given to drink: drinking habitually

groggy: stupid or unsteady from drink

high: intoxicated

holding: carrying drugs on one's person

hooked: physically dependent on drug

hungover: feeling unpleasant aftereffects of too much drink

in a state of intoxication: drunk

inebriate: drunken

inebriated: drunk

inebrious: drunken or producing drunkenness

intemperate: excessive; extreme in appetite

intoxicated: made drunk

lit up: drunk

loaded: drunk or high on drugs

market-peart: exhilarated by drink, but not intoxicated

maudlin: made foolish by drinking

muckibus: drunk

muddled: confused by drink

muzzy: muddled or confused, especially by drink

nimtopsical: drunk

oiled: drunk

pickled: drunk

pie-eyed: very drunk

pinned: having constricted eye pupils due to narcotics use

pissed: very drunk

pixilated: pleasurably bewitched; intoxicated; tipsy; led astray

plastered: very drunk

polluted: drunk; intoxicated

potatory: pertaining to drinking or addiction to alcohol

potted: drunk

pot-valiant: feeling brave or courageous from being drunk; potvaliant

refraining: practicing temperance

ripped: very intoxicated; drunk

shitfaced: very drunk

shnockered: drunk

sick: suffering from drug withdrawal
skunk drunk: extremely inebriated
sloshed: very drunk
smashed: very drunk
sober: not drunk, especially habitually temperate in use of alcohol
sotted: drunk
sottish: like a sot
soused: drunk
sozzled: very drunk
spaced-out: feeling floating sensation or numbing effects of drug use
squiffed: very intoxicated; drunk
stale-drunk: having been drunk overnight and having taken too much to remedy the condition
stewed: drunk
stinking: very inebriated
stinko: drunk
stoned: intoxicated by drugs or drink
straight: not using illicit drugs and not intoxicated
strung out: severely addicted to drugs
swacked: very drunk
tanked: drunk

temulent: extremely drunk
temulentive: extremely drunk
the worse for liquor: drunk
tiddly: slightly drunk
tight: drunk
tipsy: slightly intoxicated
toping: habitually drinking
under the influence: in an intoxicated condition
unintoxicated: abstinent; free of alcohol
using: taking drugs; addicted to drugs
wasted: intoxicated; very high
wet: designating locale or time in which consumption of alcoholic drinks is permitted
wiped out: drunk to the point of unconsciousness
wired: very high on drugs, especially stimulants
woozy: intoxicated; slightly dizzy
wrecked: drunk
zoned out: very intoxicated; nearly senseless from drug use
zonked: extremely intoxicated; drunk
zonked out: very intoxicated; nearly senseless from drug use

Interdependence

alternate: one following the other in turn
codependent: of feeling equally needy of another person
commutual: mutual
consectaneous: having a logical consequence; corollary
correlative: reciprocally related
derivative: not original
interchangeable: capable of being transposed

interdependent: mutually dependent
international: pertaining to the mutual relations of nations
misculate: mingled
mutual: affecting both of two persons, parties, or objects
philosophicopsychological: both philosophical and psychological
reciprocal: done or given by one, to or for the other in turn

Interpretation

cosignificative: having the same signification
epexegetic: pertaining to further explanation
equivalent: equal in force or meaning
exegematic: explanatory
exegetical: serving to explain or interpret

explanatory: serving or tending to explain
explicative: explanatory
explicatory: explicative
exponible: needing further explanation
expository: pertaining to or containing exposition; explanatory; illustrative

glozing: interpreting and commenting on

idiographic: involving study or explication of individual cases or events

interpreted: translated; explained

literal: according to the letter; following the exact words, as translation

metaphrastic: close or literal

paraphrastic: of the nature of a paraphrase; explaining or translating; not literal

polyglot: containing several languages

synonymous: having the character of a synonym; expressing the same thing

Interruption

alternate: following one after the other

broken: having spaces or interruptions

desultory: skipping from one to another; random; haphazard; disconnected

disconnected: not united

discontinuous: not continuous

fitful: marked by great irregularity

intermittent: ceasing at times

intermitting: ceasing at times

interrupted: broken in upon

Porlockian: intrusive; interrupting

recurrent: occurring again at stated times

spasmodic: acting by starts

unconnected: not connected

unsuccessive: not successive

Interspace

alveolate: with many small cavities, like a honeycomb

alveoliform: cavitylike

betwixt: between

broken: having spaces or interruptions

cavernous: having an open mouth, as in surprise; agape; gaping

chasmophilous: liking nooks, crannies, chasms, crevices

clathrate: latticelike; clathroid; clathrose

cortinate: cobweblike

crackled: having cracks; cracked; craquelé

embolismal: pertaining to intercalation

episodic: pertaining to an episode

ethmoid: sievelike

far between: occurring at long intervals

fatiscent: cracked

faviform: honeycomb-like; favaginous; alveolate; faveolate

fretted: eaten or worn into holes

geodesic: concerning the shortest distance between two points on a spherical surface

interamnian: between rivers

interaural: between the ears

intercalary: inserted or intruded into the midst of others

intercalated: inserted or placed between layers

intercolline: between hills

intercurrent: coming or running among or between

interjacent: lying or being between; intervenient

interlineal: between two lines; interlinear

interlinear: situated between lines

intermediary: that which lies between

intermediate: lying or being in the middle place

interspatial: belonging to areas between

interstitial: in a space, opening; interspatial

intervenient: coming or being between

intervening: separating

intrusive: entering without right or welcome

machicolated: gap-toothed or having apertures

mediterranean: enclosed by land

merged: to cause to disappear into

parenthetical: thrown in

rictal: pertaining to a gaping mouth; agape

rimose: full of cracks, fissures; rimulose

sandwiched: placed in between, among; intercalated
slit: having a cut opening or openings; gashed; incised; scissored; slashed

vuggy: full of cavities; vughy
with an interval: being open

Investigation—Question

agape: gaping
all-searching: thorough
analytic: resolving into first principles
burning with curiosity: very curious
catechetical: pertaining to instructions by questions and answers
curious: showing curiosity
disquisitionary: of a formal or systematic inquiry; disquisitional
doubtful: open to question
erotetic: interrogatory
ichneutic: concerning tracking, trailing
in course of inquiry: under investigation
in dispute: debated about
in full cry: in eager chase; said of hounds that have caught the scent and give tongue together
in hot pursuit: pursuing eagerly
in issue: debated about
in pursuit: pursuing
in quest of: searching; seeking
in question: under investigation
in search of: seeking after something
inexorable: unable to be persuaded; relentless in pursuit
inquiring: seeking the truth
inquisitive: given to ask many questions
inquisitorial: inclined to ask cruel or rigorous questions
interrogative: denoting inquiry
investigative: inclined to find out and investigate
maieutic: in logic, pertaining to the question-and-answer technique of Socrates
moot: open to discussion
nonplussed: with a questioning look; quizzical
on the lookout for: searching
on the scent: on the track of discovery
overcurious: too curious
peery: curious; suspicious
perquesting: searching through
proposed: offered for consideration
prying: disposed to pry
pursuing: persistently following with the purpose of seizing or securing
pysmatic: pertaining to questions; always asking questions
pytacorian: pertaining to questions
quizzable: that may be quizzed
quizzacious: bantering; given to quizzing
quizzatorial: of a quizzing character
quizzical: characterized by quizzes
requisitive: expressing demand
requisitory: sought for or demanded
rogatory: gathering knowledge about an incident or condition; having authorization to question witnesses to learn facts
undecided: not yet adjudged
under consideration: subject to investigation
under discussion: subject to investigation
under investigation: being tracked
undetermined: not settled by investigation
untried: not yet found out by being tested
zetetic: questioning; asking

Invisibility

adumbered: overshadowed
behind the curtain: in secret
behind the scenes: where one has inside
    information
blurred: indistinct
confused: mixed
covert: secret
dark: not easily seen
dim: shadowy
eclipsed: cast into the shadow
ill-defined: badly outlined
ill-marked: with indistinct marks
imperceptible: not to be seen
inconspicuous: so as not to attract
    attention
indefinite: with uncertain boundaries
indiscernible: not capable of being
    discerned
indistinct: not clearly perceptible
indistinguishable: incapable of being
    separated by the eyes

invisible: not to be seen
misty: made indistinct, as if by mist
mysterious: obscure
nonapparent: not evident
not in sight: out of sight
obscure: less bright
out of focus: not in focus
out of sight: out of the field of vision
shadowy: lacking clearness
sightless: without sight
unapparent: not apparent
unconspicuous: not conspicuous
undefined: not defined; with uncertain
    boundaries
under an eclipse: overshadowed
undiscernible: not capable of being
    discerned
unseen: not visible
veiled: shielded from sight
viewless: invisible

Irregularity

anarchical: lawless; confused; disordered
anomalous: irregular; out of regular
    matter
by planets: irregularly; capriciously
capricious: apt to change suddenly, as a
    goat moves
chaotic: like chaos; disordered; jumbled
complex: consisting of various parts;
    involved
complexed: confused
complicated: woven together
confused: disordered; indiscriminately
    mixed
deranged: put out of order
desultory: jumping from one thing or
    subject to another; not coherent or
    connected
disjointed: out of proper order or
    sequence
dislocated: disordered
disorderly: out of the normal or regular
    way

entangled: confused so as to make extri-
    cation difficult
fitful: marked by fits; irregularly variable
flickering: wavering unsteadily
heteroclite: abnormal; irregular; hetero-
    clitic; heteroclitical
immethodical: out of order
indiscriminate: confused; mingled
inextricable: involved in such a manner
    as to make disentanglement difficult
intricate: complicated; complex
involved: intricate; entangled
irreducible: not to be restored to normal
    order or condition
irregular: not according to usual forms
    or rules
knotted: difficult to loosen; intricately
    intertwined
orderless: out of order; confused;
    disordered
out of gear: irregular
out of joint: irregular

out of order: irregular

out of place: irregular

out of sorts: ill-humored; indisposed

perplexed: confused; complicated; difficult to unravel

promiscuous: consisting of parts confusedly mingled

rambling: wandering; discursive

raveled: intricately and confusedly involved

rhapsodical: unconnected; confused

riotous: pertaining to turbulent and boisterous conduct

shapeless: chaotic; formless

slovenly: disorderly in dress

spasmodic: convulsive; intermittent

straggling: striving; struggling

tangled: intertwined in a confused mass

topsy-turvy: disordered; confused; upside down

troublous: tumultuous

unarranged: disordered

uncertain: inconstant; variable

unmethodical: without method

unpunctual: not done at the exact time

unsymmetric: out of harmonious proportion

unsystematic: out of orderly arrangement and combination

untidy: lacking tidiness

Joining

adhering: sticking to

adhesive: tending to cling

adnate: joined to another part

amplectant: entwining; clasping

biunial: combining two in one

clinging: cleaving

close: nearly attached; compact

coadunate: joined; united

cohering: that cleaves together

cohesive: tending to cohere in homogeneous bodies

coinonomic: pertaining to joint enterprise or management

compact: closely joined

conflate: blended; consolidated

conjoint: associated

conjunct: joined together

corporate: collective

coupled with: united

fast: held firmly; secure

firm: solid; closely united

hand in hand: united by clasping hands

hand-tight: of a fastener tightened as much as possible by hand

indissoluble: impossible of being dissolved

inextricable: incapable of being disunited

infrangible: incapable of being broken

insecable: not capable of being cut

inseparable: not capable of being disjoined

inseverable: not capable of division

intervolved: involved one within another

joined: brought together

joining: bringing together

joint: involving the combined action of two or more; brought together

polymicrian: compact

secure: fastened

sessile: sedentary; immobile; closely attached

set: fixed in position

sticky: adhesive

taut: secure; tight

tenacious: holding fast

tight: firmly held together

tough: not easily parted or broken

united: made into one

unseparated: not parted

Justification

apologetic: expressing regret for fault or failure

defensible: capable of being defended, maintained, or justified

exculpatory: tending to or resulting in
exculpation

excusable: admitting of excuse or pardon

justifiable: capable of being justified

palliative: extenuating

pardonable: that may be pardoned or
shown clemency or indulgence

plausible: seeming likely to be true
though open to doubt

specious: appearing right or correct at
first sight

veniable: excusable

venial: that may be pardoned, forgiven,
overlooked, or tolerated; pardonable

vindicated: justified

vindicating: that proves true, right, or
real

vindicative: contributing to vindication

vindicatory: bringing vindication

Killing

bloodstained: marked with blood; guilty of murder
bloodthirsty: cruel; murderous
bloody: having a cruel disposition
bloody-minded: cruel in disposition; inclined to shed blood
carnificial: pertaining to a butcher or executioner
cruentous: bloody
cynegetic: related to hunting
deadly: causing or liable to cause death
deathly: causing or liable to cause death
ensanguined: bloody; covered with blood
fatal: causing death; deadly; mortal
gory: bloody
halieutic: relating to fishing
homicidal: pertaining to homicide; murderous
internecine: mutually destructive; deadly

killing: slaying; murdering
lethal: deadly; mortal
lethiferous: bearing oblivion; deadly
mortal: causing death; deadly
mortiferous: death-bearing; deadly
murderous: bloody; sanguinary; fond of murder
piscatorial: pertaining to fishing
piscatory: pertaining to fishing
red-handed: taken in the act of homicide
sanguinary: bloodthirsty; eager to shed blood; sanguisugous
sanguinolent: bloody
sicarious: murderous
slaughterous: murderous
sporting: pertaining to sport
suicidal: partaking of the nature of suicide
unhealthy: not healthy
venatic: pertaining to hunting

Knowledge—Intelligence

acataleptic: incomprehensible
accomplished: endowed with accomplishments
acquainted with: having familiar knowledge of
acromatic: difficult to understand
acuminous: sharp in intellect

acute: having fine and penetrating discernment
alive: sensitive to; easily impressed
alive to: in a position to know; readily understanding
aposterioristic: inductive; pertaining to empirical knowledge

apprized of: possessed of information concerning

arch: cunning or sly

argute: sagacious; subtle; shrewd

ascertained: investigated and understood with certainty

astute: critically discerning; sagacious

at home in: thoroughly familiar with

autodidactic: self-taught

awake: in a state of action or vigilance

aware of: knowing about

behind-the-curtain: having knowledge of things generally hidden

behind-the-scenes: having knowledge of things generally hidden

blue: very much devoted to literature

bookish: fond of books

book-learned: possessed of knowledge obtained from books

bright: possessing or showing quick intelligence; quick-witted

calculating: given to contrivance or forethought

canny: shrewd; prudent

clear-eyed: seeing clearly; having a clear mental vision

clearheaded: having a clear understanding; intelligent

clear-sighted: discerning

clear-witted: understanding; intelligent

clever: possessing quickness of intellect; expert

cognitive: having the power to understand a fact or truth

cognizable: capable of being perceived or known; perceptible; recognizable

cognizant of: having apprehension of

cognoscible: capable of being ascertained

commonplace: easily understood by all

commonsensible: having common sense; commonsensical

conscious of: knowing that anything exists

considerate: thoughtful; reflective

conversant with: familiar with

cool: self-controlled; self-possessed

coolheaded: not easily excited; free from passion

declaratory: making clear or manifest

deep: of penetrating intellect; sagacious

deep-read: versed in literature

discerning: acute; shrewd

educated: having the benefits of an education

eleatic: referring to the philosophy that the unchangeable is the only knowable reality and change is subjective

enlightened: possessed of knowledge that enables to see clearly

equitable: characterized by fairness

erudite: characterized by erudition

esoteric: for those with special knowledge; designed for an inner circle

expedient: tending to promote a proposed object

fair: characterized by frankness, honesty, candor, or impartiality

familiar: characterized by intimate knowledge

familiar as household words: very familiar

familiar to every schoolboy: very familiar

familiar with: having intimate knowledge of

farsighted: of good judgment regarding the remote effects of actions; sagacious

forward in: advanced in an understanding of

foxlike: cunning; artful

gnomic: commonly known; aphoristic

hackneyed: oft repeated, and hence common; known to everybody

hardheaded: having sound judgment; shrewd

heaven-directed: directed by divine power

impartial: unbiased; fair

in advance of one's age: farsighted

in one's right mind: sane

in the secret: having an insight into

informed: made known

informed of: having information concerning

inscient: having insight

instructed: put in possession of knowledge

intelligent: distinguished for intelligence; discerning

judicious: proceeding with discretion; wise; prudent

keen: acute of mind; penetrating

keen-eyed: having a keen mental vision

keen-sighted: discerning

keen-witted: intelligent; sharp

knowing: characterized by knowledge; shrewd

known: recognized as the truth

learned: possessed of much learning

let into: permitted to know about, as a secret

lettered: versed in literature

longheaded: having unusual sagacity

longsighted: having great foresight

made acquainted with: informed of

metempirical: pertaining to ideas or concepts outside of human experience; intuitive

needle-witted: sharp-witted

nimble-witted: quick to discern

no stranger to: informed of

noted: famous on account of some accomplishment, as learning or wisdom

notorious: famous; renowned

of unwarped judgment: impartial

omnilegent: reading everything

omniscient: characterized by omniscience

oracular: authoritative; dogmatical

palpable: easily perceived; able to be touched or felt

pancratic: having mastery of all subjects; having universal mastery

panoptic: all-seeing

pedantic: affectedly learned

penetrating: acute; discerning; sagacious

percipient: capable of perceiving; discerning

perspicacious: insightful; discerning

piercing: penetrating; keen

politic: sagacious in promoting a policy; discreet

prehensible: graspable; seizable

privy to: sharing a secret knowledge of

proficient in: knowing well how to do; expert in

profound: characterized by deep, exhaustive knowledge or intelligence

proverbial: having the characteristics of a proverb

provident: prudent in preparing for future exigencies

prudent: practically wise; discreet

quick: animated; ready; brisk

quick of apprehension: of an active mind

quick-eyed: quick to discern

quick-sighted: having acute discernment

quick-witted: having ready wit

rational: endowed with reason; judicious

read in: versed in the literature of

reasonable: governed by reason; agreeable to reason

received: perceived; understood

recognized: accepted as the truth

reflecting: contemplative

reported: publicly known

sagacious: of keen penetration and judgment; shrewd; farsighted; wise

sage: prudent; grave; sagacious

sapient: wise; discerning

scholastic: pertaining to or characterized by schools or scholars

scient: knowing; knowledgeable

scious: possessing knowledge

scrutable: comprehensible through scrutiny, close observation

self-taught: educated by private study

sensible: possessing sense or reason; intelligent

sententious: full of intelligence or wisdom

sharp: marked by keenness of perception or discernment

sharp as a needle: very keen of intellect

sharp-eyed: having acute perception or discernment

sharp-sighted: having acute perception or discernment

sharp-witted: having a nicely discerning mind

shrewd: quick to comprehend; artful; astute

sober: self-possessed; staid

solid: characterized by sound learning or judgment

sound: having all the faculties complete and in normal action or relation

staid: of a steady and sober character

strong in: having especially thorough knowledge of

strong-headed: having strength of mind

strong-minded: having a firm and vigorous intellect

supraliminal: conscious

thoughtful: given to thought; meditative

trite: frequently repeated; commonplace

unbiased: impartial

unbigoted: unprejudiced; tolerant

undazzled: unconfused

undeceived: informed of the truth

unperplexed: free from perplexity

unprejudiced: free from prejudice

unprepossessed: free from prepossession

up to: thoroughly conversant with; equipped with knowledge of

versed in: educated in; knowing considerable about

watchful: circumspect; observant

well-advised: intelligent

well-conned: carefully studied

well-educated: having a good education

well-grounded: having a good fundamental knowledge

well-informed: having a good general knowledge of things

well-judged: intelligent

well-known: famous

well-read: having a good knowledge from reading

wide-awake: keen; alert

wise: having knowledge; prudent

wise as a serpent: an expression denoting degree of wisdom

wise as Solomon: an expression denoting degree of wisdom

wise as Solon: an expression denoting degree of wisdom

wise in one's generation: wise in comparison with others

Language

allophylian: referring to Asiatic and European languages other than Indo-European or Semitic; allophylic

analytic: designating a language that uses function words and changes in word order, rather than inflected forms, to express grammatical relations

aphoristic: containing short, pithy statements

argotic: pertaining to slang

aureate: distinguished by flowery rhetoric

axiomatic: self-evident

belletristic: pertaining to belles lettres or fine literature

bilingual: fluent in two languages

colloquial: designating language characteristic of or suitable to familiar, casual conversation

conditional: designating clause, word, mood, or sentence that expresses a condition or hypothetical state

conjugate: applied to words from the same root

copulative: designating a verb functioning as a copula; designating a conjunction that connects words or clauses of equal rank or function

coradicate: derived from the same linguistic root

current: passing from mouth to mouth

cursive: designating handwriting or printing in which letters are joined together in flowing style

derivative: taken or formed from another word

diachronic: relating to study of a language as it changes over time

dialectic: pertaining to a dialect

diglot: bilingual

effable: able to be expressed

elliptical: tending to be ambiguous, unclear, or roundabout

emphatic: designating a form used to add emphasis, such as *do* in *I do like it*

epicene: designating a noun or pronoun capable of referring to either sex

euphemism: softened in expression or rendered less offensive

euphuistic: relating to euphuism

expressed: uttered in words

factitive: pertaining to verb expressing process of making or rendering in a certain way

feuilletonistic: of a newspaper section devoted to literary trivia

flowery: ornate, excessive, or showy in expression

formal: referring to language use typical of impersonal and official situations, characterized by complex vocabulary and sentences, careful grammar, and avoidance of colloquial expressions

fustian: pompous; inflated

gazooly: pertaining to constantly uttering laments

glottogonic: pertaining to the origin of language

grammatical: relating to grammar

grandiloquent: using pompous or boastful language

heteroclite: irregular in inflection

hieratic: designating simplified form of hieroglyphics used by priests in ancient Egypt

highfalutin: pertaining to pretentious language

hippopotomonstrosesquipedalian: pertaining to a very long word

holocryptic: incapable of deciphering without a key

holophrastic: pertaining to a whole idea expressed in one word

homoglot: of the same language

idiomatic: conforming to idiom

impersonal: being a verb with only third-person singular forms and having an unspecified subject

imsonic: onomatopoeic

inaccurate: not exact in grammar

incorrect: not according to the rules of grammar

informal: referring to language use suitable to or typical of casual or familiar speech or writing

interlingual: using two or more languages, as some dictionaries

irregular: not conforming to the usual pattern of inflection in a language

laconic: concise; using few words

lexical: pertaining to the words or vocabulary of a language

lexicologic: pertaining to the defining of words; lexicological

lexiphanic: using pretentious language

lingual: pertaining to the tongue in speech

linguished: skilled in languages

linguistic: pertaining to language

literal: according to the letter or exact words

literary: pertaining to literature

literose: affectedly literary

logofascinated: fascinated by words

macaronic: made up of Latin words mixed with vernacular words often given Latin endings

monepic: consisting of one word; one-word replies

monoglot: fluent in only one language

multilingual: able to speak several languages

neologic: introducing new words or new meanings of words

neological: introducing new words or new meanings of words

nominal: pertaining to a name or term; giving the meaning of a word

nonstandard: designating grammar, word choice, etc., used and considered acceptable by most educated native speakers

ornate: florid, overly embellished, or high-flown

paradigmatic: referring to a relationship among linguistic elements that can substitute for each other in a given context

paronomastic: playing on the sound of words; punning

paronymous: of like derivation; kindred

pauciloquent: using the fewest words possible to make the point

periphrastic: using two or more words instead of an inflected word to express a grammatical function

phatic: designating speech used to express goodwill or sociability rather than to impart information

pleonastic: pertaining to repetitive speech or writing; redundant

polyglot: multilingual; composed of numerous linguistic groups

polysemous: having many meanings

polysynthetic: designating language that uses long words with many affixes to express grammatical relations and meanings

preterpluperfect: in grammer, past perfect; pluperfect

properispomenon: of a word having a circumflex on its next to last syllable

proverbial: well-known

regular: conforming to usual pattern of inflection in a language

rhematic: derived from a verb

sesquipedal: measuring a foot and a half; applied to long words

sesquipedalian: using very long words

sonorous: of language, high-flown or grandiloquent

standard: designating relatively unified, institutionalized form of language accepted as norm to be spoken and taught

substandard: designating colloquial usage differing from standard dialect and deemed incorrect

suppletive: describing inflected form of word entirely different from stem, such as past tense of go

synchronic: relating to study of a language as it exists at one point in time

syntactic: pertaining to syntax

syntagmatic: referring to relationship among linguistic elements that occur sequentially

synthetic: designating language that uses affixes, rather than separate words, to express grammatical relationships

tautegorical: saying the same thing with different words

titular: existing in name or title only

togated: dignified, stately in language; Latinized; togate

tralatitious: figurative; metaphorical

Tudesque: German, especially of language

ungrammatical: marked by solecisms

verbal: not written; relating to words only

vernacular: belonging to one's native land

volitive: pertaining to verb expressing a wish or permission

vulgar: designating the popular or informal variety of a language, especially Latin

Largeness

ample: of great dimensions or capacity

amplitudinous: of great extent

big: of great or considerable size or amount, relatively or absolutely

bouncing: large and active

brawny: having or characterized by great muscular strength

Brobdingnagian: gigantic; enormous

bulky: of great magnitude and unwieldy

burly: large of body

capacious: able to contain much

capitose: large-headed

chopping: strong and active

chubby-faced: having a full, round face

chub-faced: having a full, round face

colossal: of immense size

comprehensive: large in scope

considerable: somewhat large

corpulent: very fleshy

cyclopean: gigantic

decuman: enormous, especially of waves

enormous: far exceeding the usual size

fat: having excessive flesh

fat as a pig: very fat

fat as a quail: very fat

fat as bacon: very fat

fat as brawn: very fat

fat as butter: very fat

fine: of good size

fleshy: of much flesh

full: ample in extent or volume; well-filled

full-grown: as large as it is likely to become

gargantuan: incredibly big

gaunt: tall and thin

gawsie: large and jolly; well-fed and healthy; gawcie; gawsy

giant: of very great size
giantlike: like a giant
gigantic: unusually great in dimensions
goodly: rather large
gotch-gut: corpulent; gotch-gutted
great: relatively or unusually large
huge: having great bulk or unusual size
hulking: unwieldy; bulky
hulky: unwieldy; bulky
immeasurable: indefinitely extensive
immense: very great in size
infinite: so great as to be immeasurable
jolly: most remarkable
large: exceeding most other things of like kind in bulk or size
large as life: of life-size
lubberly: big and clumsy
lumpish: large and inert
lusty: big and strong
macro: large; numerous; highly developed
magnificent: imposing in appearance
massive: of great bulk and weight
massy: having much bulk or weight
megatherian: very large; Brobdingnagian
mighty: of unusual size or power
monster: extraordinary in size
monstrous: of extraordinary and unnatural size
monumental: grandiose; massive
overgrown: grown beyond the fit or natural size

plump: extended to the full
plump as a dumpling: an expression denoting degree of size
plump as a partridge: an expression denoting degree of size
portentous: extraordinary; marvelous; amazing
portly: somewhat stout or corpulent
prodigious: impressive in size, force, extent; extraordinary
pudding-faced: having a fat, expressionless face
pudgy: plump
puffy: swelled with air or anything soft
pursy: fat; puffy; pussy
Rubensian: pleasingly plump; zaftig
spacious: of very great extent
spanking: uncommonly large
squab: fat and thick
stalwart: large and powerful
stout: having full measure
strapping: large and strong
stupendous: astonishing in magnitude
thumping: of extraordinary size
thundering: very great
towering: very high
unwieldy: difficult to handle on account of size
vast: of great or immeasurable extent
voluminous: of great bulk or size
well-fed: fat
whacking: very large
whopping: unusually large
zaftig: plump and curvaceous

Latency

allusive: having reference to something not fully expressed
by implication: shown or proved to be in connection with
by inference: shown or proved to be in connection with
concealed: hidden
constructive: not directly expressed, but derived from
covert: covered over
crooked: not straightforward in conduct

dark: without light or not easily understood
delitescent: hidden; inactive; latent
dormant: not shown
impenetrable: not to be entered by light
implicit: fairly understood though not expressed in words
implied: contained or included, though not directly stated
in the background: almost out of view
indirect: not in direct relation

indiscoverable: not to be brought to light or knowledge
inferential: deducible by inference
invisible: not able to be seen
latent: hidden
lurking: hiding for an evil purpose
muffled: wrapped up so as to conceal or deaden sound
not expressed: not told or shown
occult: hidden from observation or knowledge
secret: unknown to all but a few
steganographic: written in characters that are not intelligible except to persons who have the key
tacit: done or made in silence
unapparent: not easily seen
unbreathed: not told
underground: secretly
underhand: secretly
understood: made clear or plain
undeveloped: not known or developed
undisclosed: kept from view

undiscovered: hidden from knowledge
unexplained: not made known to the intellect
unexplored: not investigated
unexposed: not brought to light
unexpressed: not shown or told
uninvented: not in existence
unknown: hidden from the mind
unproclaimed: not known to the public
unpublished: not generally known
unsaid: known to but one
unseen: hidden from the eye
unsolved: not clear to the mind
unspied: hidden from the eye
unsung: not celebrated in song or poetry
unsuspected: not regarded as having done an evil act; not brought into light
untalked of: not discussed
untold: not related or recounted
untraced: not marked out or made known
untracked: not known by following
unwritten: not written

Lateness

backward: retiring
behindhand: late
belated: kept back past the proper time
cunctative: tardy; dilatory; cunctatious
delayed: hindered so as to arrive late
dilatory: acting slowly
in abeyance: not in force; not vested, as the title to land wanting its heir
late: after the usual or appointed time for something

posthumous: occurring after death
slow: backward
tardive: tending to or characterized by lateness
tardy: late
unpunctual: not observant of the exact time

Laterality

bilateral: having two sides
collateral: being alongside
contralateral: on the opposite side (of the body)
dextral: on the right; right-handed
eastern: toward the east
flanked: with something on either side
flanking: posted on the side
Hesperian: western; occidental

ipsilateral: on the same side; homolateral; ipselateral
lateral: at or to the side; flanking
Levantine: of the east
many-sided: having many sides
multilateral: having many sides
occidental: western
occiduous: western; occidental
orient: eastern

LAW

oriental: eastern
parallel: running side by side in same direction; similar
parietal: pertaining to a wall
ponent: western; occidental
quadrilateral: having four sides
right-handed: on the right side
sideling: with a sidelong position

sidelong: tending to one side
skirting: being on a side or border
synallagmatic: bilateral; affecting both
sides equally; requiring mutual obligation; sinalagmatic
trilateral: having three sides
western: toward the west

Law

accountable: answerable; responsible for
some action
administrative: administrating;
executive
admissible: allowable in court; being
pertinent to case, especially with regard to evidence
amerciable: lawfully punishable, particularly by fine
ancillary: supplementary; subordinate,
especially such evidence
appellate: capable of being appealed to a
higher tribunal
arcifinious: in law, having a natural
boundary as a defensive frontier
at the bar: before court
bastard: not genuine; illegitimate
capax: legally competent
causidical: pertaining to an advocate or
the maintenance and defense of suits
chartered: enjoying the privileges of a
charter
collateral: incidental or additional to
matter being discussed
condemned: sentenced to death for
crime
consensual: existing or made by mutual
consent but usually unwritten
constitutional: in accordance with or authorized by constitution
coram judice: before the judge; still under consideration
curule: pertaining to those Roman offices
the incumbents of which sat in a certain kind of a chair
darrein: in law, last or final
disentitled: deprived of right or title

disfranchised: deprived of citizenship
executive: pertaining to the execution of
the laws or the conduct of affairs
foraneous: concerning a court of law
forensic: belonging to courts, legal
proceedings
guilty: found justly responsible for of
fense and liable to punishment
heteronomic: functioning under a different law or mode of operation
inquisitorial: pertaining to inquisition
intestate: having died without a will
judicatory: pertaining to the administra-
tion of justice
judicial: pertaining to courts of justice or
to a judge
judiciary: of or pertaining to courts of
judicature or legal tribunals
jural: pertaining to legal matters
juramental: pertaining to an oath
juridical: pertaining to a judge or to
jurisprudence
justiciable: capable of being settled in
court
law-abiding: obedient to the law
lawful: in accordance with established
law; permitted by law
lawless: not regulated or restrained by
law
leal: lawful; just; fair
learned in the law: versed in law
legal: conforming to rules of law; related
to practice of law
legislative: pertaining to the enactment
of laws
legislatorial: of or pertaining to a
legislature

leguleian: concerning petty questions of law

litigious: involved in or pertaining to litigation

municipal: of or pertaining to a city or corporation having the right of administering local government

presiding: designating judge who directs court proceedings, including assigning cases to be heard by other judges

proprietary: having exclusive legal right to use, make, or market

qui tam: who so; a term applied to an action for a penalty given by statute to the person who sues for it

relevant: logically connected to case, especially evidence

rhadamanthine: uncompromisingly just

senatorial: of, relating to, or befitting a member of the higher house of the legislature in the United States

statutable: proceeding from a legislative act

statutory: designating crime or law enacted by legislature

sub judice: before the judge

substantive: having a bearing on fundamental rights and merits as opposed to procedural aspects of case

tortious: pertaining to a tort, personal or civil wrong

ultra vires: beyond strength; designating acts beyond scope of corporate charter

ultroneous: of a witness who testifies voluntarily

unattested: unsupported by evidence

void: having no effect; without legal force to bind

Lawfulness

according to law: lawful; legal

allowable: not forbidden; permissible

chartered: established by charter

ennomic: within the law; lawful

indulgent: yielding to the wishes or humor of those under one's care

lawful: permitted by law

legal: relating to law

legalized: made lawful

legitimate: according to law

licit: lawful

patent: protected by a special privilege

permissible: that may be permitted or allowed

permissive: granting leave

permitted: allowed

permitting: allowing

unconditional: made without conditions; absolute

unforbid: not forbidden; allowable

unforbidden: not forbidden; allowable

Lawlessness

actionable: admitting a suit

arbitrary: despotic; absolute in control

contraband: prohibited by law or treaty

despotic: unrestrained by laws or constitution

despotical: unrestrained by laws or constitution

exlegal: lawless

exlex: bound by no law; not being bound by legal authority

extrajudicial: out of the course of ordinary legal process

illegal: unlawful

illegitimate: not according to law; unlawful

illicit: not legal; unlawful

informal: not according to established forms

infract: broken; violated

injudicial: not according to the forms of law

irresponsible: not to be relied on

lawless: without regard for law

not allowed: forbidden

nothous: illegitimate
null and void: having no legal binding force
prohibited: forbidden by authority
spurious: not legitimate; not genuine
summary: quickly executed
unaccountable: not responsible
unallowed: not allowed; not authorized
unanswerable: not to be answered
unauthorized: not allowed; not authorized
unchartered: not chartered
unconstitutional: not according to the constitution; not authorized
undue: not allowed; not authorized
unlawful: not allowed; not authorized; contrary to law
unofficial: not authorized by official action
unsanctioned: not allowed; not authorized
unwarrantable: not justifiable
unwarranted: not justified
usurped: seized unlawfully
violating: apt to violate

Layer—Scale

discoid: like a disk in form
esquamate: scaleless
filmy: like a film
flaky: like flakes
foliaceous: like a leaf
foliated: reduced to a leaf
ganoid: having scales with a bony core covered with a shiny enamel-like material
lamellar: having thin plates
lamellate: having thin plates or scales, as gills; lamellated
lamellated: having thin plates
lamelliform: like a thin plate in form
laminated: having thin plates
laminiferous: bearing laminae
layered: divided into or covered with layers
membranous: like membrane
micaceous: of the nature of mica
overlayed: coated
scaly: with a covering of scales
schistose: of the nature of schist
schistous: with the quality of being schistose
scutiferous: covered with scales, like a reptile
squamous: covered with scales, like a fish
squamulose: covered with minute scales, like a snake
stratified: arranged in strata
stratiform: of the form of a stratum
tabular: of the nature of a table
tegulated: having overlapping plates or tiles

Laziness

balmy: soft; soothing
desidious: slothful; desidiose
dilatory: delaying; lingering
dreamy: in a state of reverie
dronish: like a drone; doing nothing
drony: like a drone
drowsy: heavy with sleepiness; dull
dull: not sharp; not animated
exanimate: not animated
faineant: lazy; indolent
heavy: dull; inactive
idle: not active
inactive: wanting activity
indolent: lazy by habit
inert: devoid of the power of moving
lackadaisical: languid and halfhearted
laggard: falling behind
lagging: inclined to move slowly
languid: becoming spiritless
lazy: indisposed to work
lazy as Ludlam's dog: very lazy
leaden: like lead; heavy; dull
lethargic: being in a lethargy or a drowse
lethargical: being in a lethargy or a drowse
listless: without active interest

logily: sluggishly; lazily; dully
lumpish: like a lump; inert
lusk: lazy
motionless: without motion
pottering: moving without spirit
remiss: careless in performance of duty
rusty: affected with rust; impaired by inactivity
sedative: soothing in effects
sedentary: lacking in activity
shilly-shally: in an irresolute manner
slack: relaxed and careless in activity; slacking

slothful: inclined to indolence
slow: having little speed
sluggish: inclined not to move; lazy
soulless: without a soul; spiritless
stay-at-home: pertaining to a person always staying at home
subfocal: not completely conscious
supine: lying on the back; careless; indolent
torpescent: becoming torpid
unbusied: not occupied at anything
unoccupied: not possessing time of

Length

appaumé: with the palm outstretched
armshot: at arm's length
as long as my arm: an expression denoting comparative degree of length
as long as today and tomorrow: an expression denoting comparative degree of length
cap-a-pie: from head to foot
interminable: without limit or end
latitudinal: pertaining to geographical latitude, the lines from north to south
lengthened: made long; extended
lengthy: having length; very long
lineal: pertaining to a line or measure of length
linear: pertaining to a line or measure of length

long: extended; stretched out
longitudinal: lengthwise; pertaining to geographical longitude, the lines from east to west; axial
longsome: extended in length
no end of: without limit
oblong: having one principal axis longer than the other
outstretched: expanded
prolate: lengthened in the direction of the polar diameter
sesquipedalian: a foot and one-half long, said especially of long words
unshortened: not shortened
wiredrawn: stretched out like wire

Letter

abecedarian: formed of or pertaining to the letters of the alphabet
adscript: printed or written immediately to the right of another letter and aligning with it
alphabetical: arranged in the order of, pertaining to, or furnished with the letters of the alphabet
alphanumeric: consisting of both letters and numbers; alphanumerical
calligraphic: relating to elaborate or ornamental writing

cuneiform: wedge-shaped; used to describe a kind of letter used in Mesopotamia
digraphic: of two successive letters
hieratic: priestly; used to describe a kind of hieroglyph
hypsiloid: V-shaped; like the Greek letter upsilon; hypsiliform; ypsiliform
lettered: composed of a number of letters
literal: consisting of letters
syllabic: according to or pertaining to syllables
uncial: pertaining to a capital letter

Liberty

absolute: free from any limitation
adespotic: not despotic
allodial: absolutely free of rent or service
anarchical: without government; confused
at ease: free from pain or discomfort
at large: at liberty
at one's ease: unembarrassed
autogenous: self-generating; produced without outside help
autonomous: pertaining to autonomy
discretionary: left to one's own judgment
exempt: free from that to which others are subject
free: not under restraint
free and easy: having little regard for conventionality
free as air: absolutely free
freeborn: free by birth
freed: set at liberty
freehold: of full legal tenure
going a-begging: without an owner
gratis: without reward

in full swing: in unrestrained liberty
independent: without restraint by or dependence upon others
irrepressible: not to be kept back
lax: loose; not firm
left alone: unmolested; forsaken
left to oneself: unmolested; forsaken
liberated: set free
licensed: allowed to do or perform with authority
loose: not confined; dissolute
out of harness: free from restraint
quite at home: free to act
rampant: wild; excessively prevalent
reinless: without reins or checks
relaxed: made loose
remiss: not attending to one's duties
scot-free: free from payment; unhurt
slack: loose; careless
spontaneous: acting of one's own accord
unassailed: not assailed; not biased
unauthorized: unsanctioned
wanton: without proper moral restraints
weak: yielding to influence; not strong

Life

above ground: unburied; alive
alive: filled or imbued with life; not dead
all alive and kicking: full of life
animated: having the vital principle
biomorphic: free-form; shaped as a living form
breathing: respiring
diurnal: living one day
in life: alive
in the flesh: alive
in the land of the living: alive
indefatigable: untiring
lively: quick; active; animated
living: having life
mercurial: animated; lively

on this side of the grave: living
Promethean: having a life-giving quality
quick: alive; animated; living
recuperated: restored to strength
refreshed: recovered
refreshing: strengthening
tenacious of life: hard to kill
untired: not worn-out
unwearied: not worn-out
vegete: alive; flourishing
vital: relating or belonging to life
vivacious: lively; animated
vivified: made alive
vivifying: making alive
zoetic: pertaining to life; living; vital

Light

ablaze: in a blaze; on fire

actinic: pertaining to that power of the sun's rays that produces chemical changes

anacamptic: reflecting or reflected

beaming: emitting light

beamy: shining

blazing: burning with a brilliant flame

bright: shedding much light; luminous

bright as day: light; very bright

bright as noonday: light; very bright

bright as silver: light; very bright

bright as the sun at noonday: light; very bright

burnished: rendered bright or resplendent

circumfulgent: shining around

clear: free from obscurity

cloudless: clear; free from clouds

effulgent: diffusing a flood of light

epipolic: fluorescent

flimmering: flickering and glimmering

fluorescent: luminous with electromagnetic radiation

fulgent: shining; dazzling; glittering

fulgid: shining; dazzling

fulgurant: flashing; fulgurating

fulgurous: flashing like lightning; fulgurant

gairish: gaudy; showy; vulgarly bright

garish: gaudy; showy; vulgarly bright

glassy: having a fixed, staring appearance

glossy: smooth and shining

guttering: flashing weakly; fluttering; sputtering

heliographic: pertaining to the art of taking pictures on any prepared material by means of the rays of the sun and a camera obscura

in a blaze: blazing

incandescent: glowing with intense heat, light

inenubilable: incapable of being made cloudy; intensely uncloudy; inenubilous

interlucent: shining between others

irradiated: lighted; lit up

lambent: shining softly; flickering

light: not dark; clear; bright

light as day: very bright

light as noonday: very bright

light as the sun at noonday: very bright

lightsome: luminous; not dark

lit: having light; filled with light

lucent: shining; resplendent

lucid: bright; clear

luciferous: giving light; illuminating

lucific: producing light

luculent: clear; luminous; lucid

luminiferous: producing light

luminous: emitting light; bright

lustrous: shining; luminous

meridian: pertaining to noonday

meteoric: pertaining to or consisting of meteors

nitid: bright; lustrous; shining; nitidous

noonday: pertaining to midday

noontide: pertaining to midday

orient: rising; east; bright; glittering; shining

phosphorescent: luminous without combustion or heat

photic: relating to light

photoelastic: of or pertaining to certain materials that are capable of double refraction when under stress

photogenic: producing light

photographic: pertaining to photography

plenilunar: full and abundant, like the light of the full moon

radiant: emitting rays of light

refractive: showing deflected light, distorted images; refracted

refulgent: casting a bright light; shining

resplendent: shining very brightly

rutilant: shining

scintillant: sparkling

self-luminous: possessing the power to emit light

sheen: shining; glistening

sheeny: shiny

shining: emitting a strong light; bright
shiny: bright; luminous
splendent: glossy; beaming with light
splendid: very bright
stroboscopic: flashing regularly
sunny: pertaining to the sun or exposed to its rays

transplendent: exceedingly bright
unclouded: free from obscurity
unobscured: clear; bright
vivid: brilliant; bright; clear

Lightness

airy: light as air
astatic: under the influence of no directive agent
buoyant: so light as to float
ethereal: light as ether
floating: hanging free in the air or on the top of some liquid
imponderable: so light as to have no perceptible weight
imponderous: so light as to have no perceptible weight
light: having little weight
light as a feather: an expression denoting degree of lightness

light as air: an expression denoting degree of lightness
light as thistledown: an expression denoting degree of lightness
portable: light enough to be easily carried
sublimated: vaporized by heat
subtile: delicately constituted
uncompressible: impossible to be compressed on account of levity
volatile: so light as to be easily vaporized
weightless: extremely light

Likelihood

apparent: plain to sight; seeming in distinction from real
colorable: having an appearance of right or fact
credible: able to be believed
easy of belief: very probable
hopeful: promising success
in a fair way: of great likelihood
likely: having probability; plausible
ostensible: offered as a reason, real or professed
plausible: apparently true though it may be false; seemingly reasonable

presumable: capable of being presumed; reasonable
presumptive: offering grounds for belief
probable: having more evidence for than against
reasonable: based on reason; just
specious: having the appearance of truth, ofttimes without the reality
to be expected: having strong likelihood of occurring
well-founded: supported by good evidence

Liquid

affluent: of liquids or waterways, flowing into something
colliquative: melting
deliquescent: becoming liquid in the air
fluid: having properties of a fluid
juicy: full of juice
liquefiable: capable of being liquefied

liquefied: changed to a liquid state
liquescent: inclined to liquefy
liquid: having properties of a liquid
lubricated: offering poor or no traction
miscible: mixable in liquid
sappy: full of sap
serous: watery; like serum; fluid

soluble: capable of being dissolved, usually in water
sorbile: drinkable; liquid
sputative: characterized by excessive spitting, salivation
succiferous: creating sap

succulent: having a juicy and soft pulp
uncongealed: in a liquid state
viscous: of liquid, thick and not pouring easily
volatile: of a liquid, evaporating quickly

Littleness

atomic: extremely minute
corpuscular: small and insignificant in size
cramp: contracted in form
cramped: contracted in form and action
dapper: little and active
diminutive: of relatively small size
dumpy: short and thick
duodecimo: of twelve pages of small size, as a book
dwarf: smaller than others of its species
dwarfed: kept or made to become smaller
dwarfish: below the normal size
embryonic: not yet developed
evanescent: gradually passing away
exiguous: small and slender
granular: small and fine, like grains
homeopathic: very small in quantity
impalpable: too small to be felt by the touch
imperceptible: too small to be perceived
inappreciable: too small to be taken into account
inconsiderable: small in quantity or importance
infinitesimal: infinitely small
intangible: imperceptible to the touch
invisible: incapable of being seen
lilliputian: abnormally and ridiculously small
limited: confined to certain bounds

little: below normal size; smaller than other like things
microscopic: visible only under a microscope
miniature: much smaller than reality
minikin: of small size and delicate form
minute: exceedingly small
molecular: of or pertaining to extremely small particles
petty: of little importance
pygmy: very small for its kind
pocket: small enough to go into a pocket
pollard: shorn of the head
portable: small enough to carry
portative: easily carried
puny: small and weak
rudimental: only partially developed
rudimentary: in an incomplete state of development
scant: scarcely enough
scraggy: lean and bony
scrubby: of stunted growth
short: of little stature or length
shrunk: made smaller by contraction
small: comparatively less than another or than a standard
squat: short and thick
stunted: checked in growth
thin: lacking plumpness of figure
tiny: very small
undersized: below normal size
weazened: shrunken and withered
wee: very small

Looseness

dégagé: relaxed; casual
detached: unconnected
disheveled: loosely disordered
flaccid: limp; baggy; droopy; loose; slack
flapping: waving loosely

immiscible: not capable of being mixed
incoherent: not attached
lax: not in a close or firm state
loose: unbound
nonadhesive: not sticking

relaxed: in a loosened condition
segregated: separated
slack: loose
streaming: hanging loosely

uncombined: disunited
unconsolidated: uncombined
withy-cragged: of people, having a loose
neck

Loss

bereaved: deprived of something highly
valued
bereft: poetical form for *bereaved*
cutoff: parted from
denuded: deprived of all covering
deprived of: divested of
dispossessed: to be put out of possession
imperdible: incapable of being lost
irretrievable: not to be recovered
long-lost: having been lost for some time

losing: that loses or results in loss
lost: that has perished
minus: without positive value
not having: not possessing
off one's hands: out of one's possession
or care
out of pocket: having expended more
money than one has received
quit of: deprived of the care of
viduous: widowed; bereaved; viduate

Loudness

big-sounding: having a pompous sound
callithumpian: boisterous; noisy
clamorous: noisy; loud; turbulent
clangorous: sharp or harsh in sound
deafening: very loud in sound
deep: low in sound
ear-deafening: loud; sharp in sound
ear-rending: loud; sharp in sound
earsplitting: loud; sharp in sound
enough to wake the dead: loud to an
excessive degree
enough to wake the seven sleepers: loud
to an excessive degree
fremescent: of a growing murmur; becoming noisy
full: abundant in quantity
high-sounding: noisy
hypnopompic: causing one to wake up
loud: making a great sound
megalophonic: having a loud voice
multisonous: sounding much
noisy: making a loud sound
obstreperous: loud; clamorous
perstreperous: noisy

piercing: shrill
polyphloisboian: making a huge racket;
polyphloesboean; polyphloisbic
powerful: having a full, loud sound
rackety: making a tumultuous noise
randan: noisy; disorderly
raucous: harsh-sounding; hoarse
routous: uproarious; noisy
shrill: sharp and piercing in sound
sonorous: loud-sounding
stentophonic: extremely loud
stentorian: extremely loud; booming;
commanding; robust; resonant
stertorous: pertaining to snoring or loud
breathing
strepent: loud; noisy; boisterous; streper-
ous; strepitant; strepitous
thundering: loud and full in sound
tonant: making loud, deep noise
tonitruous: thundering
trumpet-tongued: having a tongue as
vociferous as a trumpet
uproarious: making a great noise or
tumult

Love

adorable: lovable; worthy of adoration

affectionate: having great love

after one's fancy: pleasing to one

after one's mind: pleasing to one

after one's own heart: pleasing to one

after one's taste: pleasing to one

amative: inclined to love and lust

amatory: pertaining to love

amiable: lovable; pleasing

ammophilous: sand-loving

amorous: full of love; feeling sexually aroused

ardent: passionate; affectionate; eager

attached to: bound to; won over to by moral or other qualities

attractive: pleasing; alluring; having moral qualities that please

beloved: dear to the heart; loved

bewitching: charming; fascinating

bitten: smitten with love

bloten: fond, as children are of caregivers

brokenhearted: rejected in love

captivating: charming; very pleasing; alluring

charmed: fascinated; delighted

charming: pleasing; fascinating

congenial: allied in nature

darling: very dearly beloved; little dear

dear: much esteemed; beloved

dear as the apple of one's eye: very dear

dearly beloved: very dear

dendrophilous: tree-loving; living in trees

devoted: given up to; attached to; consecrated to

enamored: deeply in love; captivated

enchanting: charming; pleasing; agreeable

engaging: tending to draw the affection; attractive

erotic: pertaining to love; amatory

fascinating: pleasing; enchanting

favorite: best beloved; most cared for

fond of: tender; affectionate

glutolatrous: worshipping the buttocks

heartsick: extremely unhappy in love

in love: under the influence of love

in one's good graces: in one's favor

interesting: exciting the emotions or holding the attention

lexicomanic: loving dictionaries

like an angel: lovely

little: small; slight; slender; a term of endearment

lovable: worthy of love

loved: attracted to by some pleasing quality

lovelorn: heartsick, rejected, or unhappy in love

lovely: possessing qualities that are worthy of love

lovesick: anxious or emotionally unbalanced from love

loving: affectionate

moonstruck: dreamily romantic; in love

motherly: like a mother in manner and action

mulierose: extremely fond of women

nearest to one's heart: dearest; most cared for

nemophilous: loving the forest

ornithophilous: bird-loving

over head and ears in love: very much in love; infatuated

Pandemic: pertaining to sensual love

Paphian: erotic; concerning illicit love or wanton sex

passionate: moved to strong feeling, as love, desire, or the like

pet: fondled; indulged

philogynous: fond of women

philophilosophos: fond of philosophers

philoprogenitive: fond of the production of offspring; loving one's offspring

photophilous: light-loving; photophilic

plagose: fond of flogging

popular: well-liked; beloved by the people

potamophilous: river-loving

precious: valuable; dear

pygal: pertaining to the buttocks; loving buttocks
pygophilous: buttocks-loving
rapturous: ravishing; transporting
romantic: pertaining to sexual love; inspiring emotions of romance
sapid: interesting; lively
seductive: tending to lead astray; enticing
smitten: affected with love; enamored; infatuated
struck with: impressed by
sweet: mild; kind; pleasing
sweet upon: in love with
sympathetic: having common feelings or compassion
taken with: pleased with; in love with

tender: gentle; soft
tid: affectionate; fond
to one's fancy: pleasing
to one's mind: pleasing
to one's own heart: pleasing
to one's taste: pleasing
true: faithful
unfaithful: betraying a lover or spouse by taking another
uxorious: too much devoted to one's wife
veneficial: relating to Venus, goddess of love
wedded to: much attached to
well-beloved: much or dearly beloved
winning: attracting; charming
zoophilic: animal-loving

Lowness

below: in a low condition
crouched: in a cringing condition
debased: lowered
flat: not elevated
level with the ground: in the same plane as the ground
low: having little upward elevation
lying low: resting in a low condition
neap: low or lowest

nether: lower
nethermost: lowest
prostrate: fallen low or flat
squat: crouching; short and low
subjacent: lying underneath
sublunar: beneath the moon, i.e., between the orbit of the moon and earth; sublunary
underhung: underhanging

Luck

accidental: happening by chance; not designed or planned
adventitious: not essential; casual
aimless: without aim
aleatory: pertaining to or relying on chance; aleatoric
casual: occurring by chance
causeless: self-originating; uncreated
contingent: likely to occur
designless: happening without intention
driftless: having no drift or direction; purposeless
fortuitous: happening by chance; accidental
fortunate: lucky; prosperous
habnab: hit or miss; at random
haply: happening perhaps by good luck

incidental: coming without regularity
indeterminate: not determined or precise
indiscriminate: confused; promiscuous
lucky: having good luck
never thought of: seemingly impossible
not meant: contrary to intention
possible: capable of happening or not
promiscuous: confused; mingled indiscriminately
purposeless: having no purpose or result
random: done at hazard; left to chance
uncaused: having no cause or reason
undesigned: not intended
undetermined: not settled or established
undirected: not guided
unintended: not designed

unintentional: happening without design
unpremeditated: not done by design

unpurposed: not intentional
unwitting: unintentional
without purpose: aimless

Ludicrousness

awkward: ungraceful in action
baroque: fantastical in style
bizarre: odd in manner or appearance
bombastic: marked by bombast
burlesque: having the qualities of burlesque
comic: adapted to produce mirth
comical: adapted to produce mirth
contemptible: worthy of contempt or ridicule
doggerel: weak, trivial, or absurd; said of verse
droll: laughable and odd
drollish: laughable and odd
eccentric: departing from the ordinary modes and customs
extravagant: beyond the limits of truth
fanciful: irregular and extravagant in opinion or taste
fantastic: absurdly fanciful
farcical: absurdly exaggerated
funny: laughable
gimcrack: cheap and showy
grotesque: misshapen or ludicrously odd
inflated: bombastic; pompous

ironical: characterized by irony
laughable: very ludicrous
ludicropathetic: ludicrous and pathetic
ludicrous: tending to produce laughter
mock heroic: burlesque in heroic style
monstrous: greatly exaggerated
odd: unmatched; not common
out-of-the-way: uncommon
outlandish: strange and uncouth
preposterous: utterly absurd
quaint: pleasingly odd
queer: out of the common way
quizzical: absurd and puzzling
ridiculous: contemptible and funny
risible: mirthful
rum: odd; queer; used contemptuously
seriocomic: combining mirth and gravity
stilted: artificial and elevated in manner or style
strange: new or foreign to the observer
tragicomic: of a mixture of grave and comic scenes
whimsical: producing laughter
whimsical as a dancing bear: producing laughter

Lunacy

amok: in a murderous frenzy; raging violently
ape: crazed, nuts, or wildly overactive; apeshit
apeshit: ape
arreptitious: given to raptures; possessed; mad
balmy: crazy
bananas: crazy; deranged
barmy: balmy
batty: crazy; demented
bent: abnormal, especially somewhat crazed or perverse

bereft of reason: crazy
berserk: crazy; mad; frenzied; crazed
beside oneself: not in usual mental condition
bewildered: confused or uncertain in mind
bonkers: crazy; mentally unbalanced
cachetic: mentally depraved; cachexic
committed: required to enter and remain in mental hospital
corybantic: frenzied, like the priests of Cybele
crackbrained: weak-minded

cracked: having mental defects; insane

crazed: distracted; overexcited; slightly nuts

crazy: mentally deranged or demented; insane

cuckoo: crazy

daffy: nutty; screwy

daft: weak-minded

delirious: in a state of delirium

demented: lacking power to reason; perversely insane

demoniac: behaving as though possessed by the devil

deranged: insane

distracted: wildly confused

distraught: distracted

dithyrambic: passionately or wildly lyrical

doting: characterized by dotage

eccentric: very peculiar in thought and ideas

fanatical: characterized by fanaticism

far-gone: almost hopelessly insane

feebleminded: mentally deficient; moronic

flighty: slightly delirious

frantic: wildly distracted, as by fear or grief

frenetic: frenzied; frantic

frenzied: marked by violent agitation; berserk

giddy: light-headed

gone: lost in madness; outside reality

goofy: nutty; silly

haggard: weakened by great anxiety of mind

haywire: out of control; disordered

homicidal: having murderous intent or making threats

hypped: marked by worry, depression, or hypochondria; hipped

hyppish: tending to worry, depression, or hypochrondria; hippish

hyte: insane

imbecile: weak-minded

incoherent: talking aimlessly

infatuated: filled with an uncontrollable passion

insane: mentally disordered or deranged; suffering from insanity

insensate: showing a lack of sense

kooky: eccentric or peculiar

light-headed: wanting in soundness of mind

loco: insane

lunatic: subject to lunacy; moonstruck

mad: mentally disturbed or deranged; insane; completely senseless or disordered

mad as a hatter: very mad

mad as a March hare: very mad

mad-brained: crazy

maddened: made insane

maniacal: affected with mania

mazed: bewildered

mental: affected with a disorder of the mind

moonstruck: mentally deranged; lunatic

moronic: feebleminded

not in one's right mind: crazy

not right: mentally wrong

not right in one's head: mentally deranged; crazy

not right in one's mind: mentally deranged; crazy

not right in one's upper story: mentally deranged; crazy

not right in one's wits: mentally deranged; crazy

nuts: crazy; insane

nutty: ecentric; mildly crazy; daffy

odd: having peculiar or strange ideas

of unsound mind: crazy

off: slightly crazy; abnormal

out of one's mind: unable to control one's will and judgment

out of one's senses: unable to control one's will and judgment

out of one's wits: unable to control one's will and judgment

overdrawn: oddball; nuts

phrenetic: frenetic

phrensied: frenzied

possessed: behaving as though controlled by supernatural power or powerful subconscious impulse; beyond self-control

possessed with a devil: mad

potty: slightly insane or eccentric

psycho: psychopathic; insane

psychopathic: exhibiting amoral and antisocial behavior, including the inability to tell right from wrong

rabid: frenzied; raging uncontrollably, as if affected by rabies

rambling: uttering incoherent words

raving: past reason or being reasoned with

reasonless: bereft of reason

scatterbrained: with little brains

schizoid: suffering from schizophrenia or multiple personality; schizy

schizy: schizoid

screwy: slightly insane; daffy

shatter-brained: disordered in mind

shatterpated: disordered in mind

sick: mentally ill

silly: lacking good common sense

stark staring mad: wholly and completely destitute of all power of rational thought or action

touched: mentally unbalanced; slightly crazy

touched in one's head: slightly insane

touched in one's mind: slightly insane

touched in one's upper story: slightly insane

touched in one's wits: slightly insane

twisted: perverse; diabolical

unbalanced: mentally disordered; deranged

unglued: mentally unstable or upset

unhinged: not mentally sound

unsane: not sane

unsettled in one's mind: deranged

vecordious: senseless; insane

vertiginous: affected with dizziness

wacko: insane; crazy

wacky: slightly crazy or eccentric

wandering: without control of one's mental faculties

whacked-out: strung out, agitated, or slightly insane

wigged-out: agitated, anxious, or slightly insane

wild: mad beyond control

wowf: crazy; mad

wrong in one's head: mentally weak

wrong in one's mind: mentally weak

wrong in one's upper story: mentally weak

wrong in one's wits: mentally weak

zany: eccentric or mildly abnormal in behavior

Magic

adumbrative: vaguely foreshadowed, with sketchy sense of future

acacae: pertaining to magic

apocalyptic: forecasting or suggesting end of world; pertaining to or like the Apocalypse or any prophetic revelation

apotropaic: intended to guard against evil

attuned: in harmony with or responsive to spiritual life

beatific: marked by sheer bliss; saintly; angelic

blessed: enjoying spiritual contentment; hallowed; consecrated; highly favored

blissed-out: experiencing a continual trancelike state of bliss or euphoria

cabalistic: containing or conveying an occult meaning

celestial: heavenly; suggesting divine inspiration

Chaldean: pertaining to astrology or mysticism

charmed: enchanted; protected by charms

chimerical: visionary and improbable; existing only in fantastic imagination

deep: possessed of heightened consciousness; perceptive beyond the norm

devoid: empty; blank; lacking sensibility

disembodied: lacking substance or reality normally present; having spirit separated from corporeal substance

divine: proceeding from God; devoted to God; supremely good or admirable

eerie: spooky; filling one with dread of the unknown

elevated: exalted in mood or feeling; with a sublime nobility, moral rectitude, or higher consciousness

ethereal: celestial; heavenly; airy; nonmaterial

evanescent: tending to vanish like vapor; fragile; airy; imperceptible

exalted: marked by purity or nobility of thought and manner

existential: relating to, grounded in, or based on human existence, as distinguished from essence

extrasensory: beyond one's normal sense perceptions

fatidic: prophetic

hagborn: born of a witch or hag

hermetic: occult; magical

holy: spiritually whole, sound, or perfect; infinitely good, righteous, or selfless; godlike; sacred

hypnotic: suggesting hypnosis, trance, or detachment from consciousness

imaginary: inexplicable by reason; distinct from three-dimensional reality of senses

incantatory: dealing by enchantment; magical

integrated: characterized by united and harmonious coordination of parts into whole

magic: possessing supernatural powers, like the Magi or the East

magical: pertaining to magic

mantic: prophetic; divinatory

mystic: remote from human observation; secret

mystical: possessing spiritual reality separate from senses and intellect; involving direct communion with God or spirits

numinous: inspiring awe or religious feelings

occult: beyond ordinary knowledge or understanding; mysterious or supernatural

oneiric: of or relating to dreams

orphic: mystic; oracular

pacific: peaceful; harmonious; tranquil

paranormal: supernatural; scientifically inexplicable

phylacteric: pertaining to any charm or amulet worn as a preservative against danger or disease

preternatural: extraordinary; existing outside nature

psychedelic: describing abnormal psychic state of heightened awareness, often produced by drugs and accompanied by hallucinations

psychic: sensitive to nonphysical, supernatural forces

Pythian: relating to the oracle at Delphi, noted for giving ambiguous answers

realized: spiritually enlightened; in harmony with oneself

sacred: hallowed; consecrated; worthy of veneration; holy

sensitive: aware of spiritual and mystical matters beyond information offered by senses

sibylline: prophetic; occult; mysterious

spellbound: in state of enchantment

stoicheiotical: pertaining to magic

sublime: spiritually exalted and noble

supernal: having spiritual character; coming from above

supernatural: beyond nature; miraculous

supersensible: beyond the realm of the senses; spiritual

supreme: loftiest; ultimate; highest

surrealistic: having bizarre, dreamlike quality

talismanic: having the properties of a preservative against evils by occult influence

telestically: mystically; magically

thaumaturgical: wonder-working; miraculous

touched: having received divine revelation, inspiration, or supersensible powers

transcendental: beyond limits of ordinary experience, reality, and comprehension; supernatural

tuned-in: spiritually aware or enlightened

unbelievable: impossible to explain by reason or senses

uncanny: eerie; mysterious; of supernatural origin or power

unfamiliar: strange; difficult to explain

unimaginable: beyond powers of imagination and intellect

unreal: fantastic; beyond normal senses and dimensions

vatic: prophetic; oracular

weird: pertaining to the world of witches; supernatural

Magnitude

above par: of greater value than the face

absolute: great without limitation

abundant: of great frequency in occurrence

ample: of great dimensions
arch: preeminently great
arrant: great in doing evil
astonishing: wonderfully great
at its height: at the point of greatest importance
beyond expression: too great for words
big: great in size
complete: of entire extent
considerable: worthy of regard as being great
consummate: perfectly great
crass: coarse
decided: great without uncertainty
deep: great in depth
desperate: without hope
enormous: excessive in size
essential: absolutely requisite
excessive: too great
exorbitant: too great in price
extensive: of large dimensions
extraordinary: out of the common order
extravagant: beyond bounds or limits
extreme: the highest degree of anything
fabulous: exceedingly great
fair: moderately great
far-gone: advanced
finished: having reached its largest extent
flagrant: notoriously bad
full: complete in measure
gey: very; quite
glaring: plainly evident
goodly: great in proportion or numbers
grave: of great importance
great: of considerable degree
greater: larger than
gross: very large; coarse
heavy: of great weight
high: of great height
huge: having great bulk
immense: very great in extent
important: of great consequence
in the zenith: at the culminating point of greatness
incredible: too greatly improbable to admit of belief
indescribable: that cannot be represented in words

ineffable: too good to be represented in words
inexpressible: not to be expressed
inordinate: great beyond the prescribed bounds
intense: very great in degree
large: great in size
magnitudinous: involving greatness of scale
many: constituting a great number
marked: distinguished for greatness
marvelous: inspiring wonder
mighty: having great power
monstrous: varying greatly from the natural
noble: distinguished for good qualities
noteworthy: deserving attention
of mark: of great distinction
outrageous: great to excess
overgrown: developed beyond the normal
passing: greater than
perfect: complete in all parts
plenary: complete in all requisites
pointed: direct
positive: inherent in a thing by itself
precious: of great value
preposterous: not admitting of the slightest belief
prodigious: great beyond all usual limits
profound: of great intellectual depth
rank: strong in a bad sense
red-hot: intense in a degree beyond the usual
remarkable: so much out of the usual as to demand attention
roaring: large and noisy
serious: of great importance because of attendant danger
signal: large
sound: strong; complete
stark: complete
starkstaring: complete; sheer
strong: having great physical power
stupendous: so great as to overcome the senses with astonishment
swinging: free
thoroughgoing: efficient in everything

thorough-paced: trained to perfection, as a racehorse
thumping: heavy; large
towering: rising higher
unabated: not diminished in strength
unapproachable: thoroughly inaccessible
unco: remarkably; extremely; very
unconscionable: not influenced by mental restraint
undiminished: not decreased in size
unequivocal: not admitting of doubt
unlimited: having no bounds
unmitigated: not lessened in severity
unreduced: not lessened in size or amount

unrestricted: not limited by the usual bounds
unspeakable: that cannot be expressed in words
unsuitable: not fitting
unsurpassed: unexcelled
unutterable: such that it cannot be expressed in words
utter: complete; entire
uttermost: that beyond which there is nothing
vast: immeasurably great
veriest: in the most eminent degree
wholesale: done on a large scale
widespread: extended over a great area
worldwide: of universal importance

Male

agnatic: related on the father's side
andric: involving males
androcentric: pertaining to domination by men
androgenous: pertaining to the production of exclusively male offspring
anthropic: of or pertaining to a man
arrhenotokous: blessed with only boys
fatherbetter: surpassing one's father in some respect
he: denoting persons or animals of the male sex
male: denoting persons or animals of the male sex

manly: possessing qualities characteristic of a true man
masculine: denoting persons or animals of the male sex
patrilineal: pertaining to male descent
patripotestal: pertaining to the authority of a father
Priapean: phallic; overly concerned with masculinity; priapic
unmanly: unbecoming a man; base; cowardly
virile: having the characteristics of mature manhood
womanish: characteristic of a woman; chiefly in a disparaging sense

Manifestation

apparent: clearly seen or easily understood
arrant: unmitigated
autoptical: seen with one's own eyes
bare: devoid of covering
barefaced: impudent
beamish: of a face that is cheerful or optimistic
capable of being shown: that may be proved
cherubic: having a babyish face

clear: free from anything that dims or keeps off the light
clear as day: an expression denoting figurative degree of clearness
clear as daylight: an expression denoting figurative degree of clearness
clear as noonday: an expression denoting figurative degree of clearness
conspicuous: clearly visible on account of prominence
craggy: having a face expressive of experience; rugged

defined: made clear or plain by marking
the limits or outlines
definite: known with exactness
demonstrative: showing clearly or
plainly
disclosed: brought into view by
uncovering
distinct: standing apart, or clearly seen as
standing apart from other things
downright: without doubt; positive
evident: plain to the mind or senses
exoteric: capable of being readily or fully
seen
explicit: expressed plainly
express: set forth or declared with the utmost distinctness
flagrant: openly wicked
frank: open in manner and disposition
freehearted: open; unreserved;
generous
fresh-faced: having an open, sweet face;
fresh-complexioned
glaring: open and bold
glowing: having a very happy expression;
sunny
hard-bitten: having a face expressive of
long suffering; pinched
horse-faced: having a long face; horsey
in the foreground: near the eye
inconcealable: not able to be hidden
from the light
intelligible: capable of being made clear
knitted: having contracted eyebrows, as
in a frown
literal: exact or plain as to fact or detail
manifest: clear and open
manifested: plain

naked: exposed to light
not to be mistaken: unmistakable
notable: clearly seen; conspicuous
notorious: publicly known and the subject of general remark, especially
unfavorable
obvious: easily seen or understood
open: uncovered to the light
open as day: plain and clear as sunlight
ostensive: proper or intended to be
shown
overt: open to view
palpable: readily perceived and detected
patent: open to everybody
plain: readily seen or understood
plain as a pikestaff: very plain
plain as the nose on one's face: plain as
it can be
plain as the sun at noonday: plain as it
can be
plain as the way to parish church: plain
as it can be
redolent: giving off something, such as
an odor; aromatic; suggestive; reminiscent of
rubicund: having a reddish or flushed
face; florid; rosy-cheeked; rubescent;
ruddy; suffused
striking: impressive
unconcealable: not to be hidden from
the light
undisguised: not hidden or concealed
unmistakable: that cannot be taken for
something else
unreserved: not withheld in part
unshaded: allowed to come to the full
light

Marriage

affianced: pledged to marry
affinal: related by marriage
antenuptial: premarital
apopemptoclinic: inclined toward
divorce
betrothed: promised to marry
bridal: pertaining to a bride or a wedding
conjugal: pertaining to marriage or the

relationship between husband and
wife; connubial; marital; nuptial
connubial: pertaining to the married
state; conjugal
cornuted: cuckolded; cornuto
desponsate: married a second time
digamous: married a second time
disespoused: divorced or left behind

dotal: pertaining to woman's marriage dowry

eligible: single; available for marriage

endogamous: pertaining to interbreeding or marriage within one's group

engaged: bound by promise to marry

extramarital: describing that which occurs outside the bonds of marriage

hitched: married

horn-mad: enraged at being cuckolded

hymeneal: relating to marriage; virginal

levirate: relating to a brother-in-law

marital: pertaining to marriage; conjugal; connubial; nuptial

maritorious: excessively devoted to a husband, in a submissive way

marriageable: fitted by age, physical condition, and mental capacity for marriage

married: joined in marriage; conjugal

married all over: of women who let their appearance go after the marriage commences

matrimonial: pertaining to marriage or the married state

morganatic: pertaining to marriage of an aristocratic male to an untitled female

nubile: of marriageable age, especially a young girl

nuptial: relating to marriage, especially to the marriage ceremony

one: said of a man and woman after union by marriage

one bone and one flesh: of a single person by the union of marriage

pentapopemptic: divorced five times

polyandrous: having more than one mate at a time

preternuptual: pertaining to one who commits adultery

spousal: pertaining to marriage

unmarried: single; not married

uxorial: wifely in behavior

wedded: married

Materiality—Entity

absolute: unconditional

actual: existing as the result of antecedents

afloat: not having disappeared

bodily: having a body or material form

corporal: consisting of a material body or substance

corporeal: consisting of a material body or substance

current: in vogue

effective: actual; existing; operative; in effect

existent: having being

existing: having being

extant: not lost or destroyed

impersonal: without the attributes that make up the nature of a person

in esse: in actual existence

in existence: not lost

material: consisting of matter

materialistic: of the nature of materialism

neuter: neither matter nor spirit

not potential: real

objective: having the nature of an object

on foot: in action

ontic: pertaining to or having real being or existence; ontal

palpable: capable of being touched and felt

physical: cognizable by the senses

ponderable: capable of being weighed

positive: not admitting of doubt

prevalent: superior; customary

real: in its true essence

self-existent: having being by its own power

self-existing: having being by its own power

sensible: capable of being perceived by the senses

somatic: pertaining to the body

somatoscopic: physical

substantial: having real existence; actual

substantive: pertaining to what is essential

tangible: perceptible to the touch
true: according to facts
under the sun: in existence
undestroyed: not destroyed
unideal: not ideal

unimagined: not merely fanciful
unspiritual: not of spirit, but matter
well-founded: originated with good reasons or grounds

Materials

aeneous: brassy; like brass; aeneus
aerose: brassy; coppery
air-dried: designating lumber stacked out of doors so that air circulates between boards to remove moisture
ansate: having a handle
banausic: of a mechanic or mechanic's workshop
biodegradable: capable of being easily broken down by natural decomposition
cardiform: resembling a wool card
castellated: designating upward projection with battlements, like a castle
chadless: not possessing chads, the small pieces of punched paper from data cards
chartaceous: paperlike
close-grained: designating wood having fine, compact grain
cretated: rubbed with chalk
druxy: of wood, semirotten; having decayed or knothole spots; druxey
edge-glued: designating flat-edged lumber bonded by gluing
edge-matched: designating lumber with tongue-and-groove edges
electromechanical: designating a device activated electrically, as by a solenoid, and also working mechanically
end-matched: designating lumber with tongue-and-groove ends
factitious: artificial and man-made rather than natural
flat-grained: designating wood having smooth, consistent grain
half-timber: of construction in which the timbers are partly visible; half-timbered

half-timbered: of a wall with wooden beams alternating with masonry
high-gloss: designating very bright, lustrous surface finish, especially of enamel paint
hooked: designating rug made by drawing loops through coarse fabric with a hook
instrumental: serving as an instrument
kiln-dried: designating lumber dried in kiln using regulated steam and hot air
knocked-down: consisting of something delivered to job with parts cut to size but not assembled
knotty: designating lumber with cross-grained, rounded areas, or knots, formed by lump where branch grew out of tree trunk
laniferous: having or creating wool
ligniperdous: destructive to wood
machinal: relating to machines
maduro: of cigars, strong and dark
material: composed of matter
mechanical: pertaining to mechanics
mechanomorphic: having the characteristics of a machine; described in terms of a machine
merdurinous: composed of dung and urine
mixed-grain: designating wood with both closed and open grains
nailsick: of a board with too many nail holes in it
open-grained: designating wood having irregularly patterned grain, usually wide
out-of-plumb: not in proper vertical alignment
pergameneous: like parchment

plumb: in true vertical position

pressure-treated: designating wood compressed under great heat to increase hardness and resistance to moisture and decay

quartersawed: designating lumber cut at a 90-degree angle to tree's growth rings; quartersawn

rabbeted: designating board or plank with a groove cut in the edge to accept another piece of wood to form a joint

raw: in the natural state

semidetached: designating pair of residences joined by common wall

semigloss: designating paint that dries to a finish more lustrous than matte and less lustrous than high-gloss

spring-loaded: designating machine part held in specific position by spring

stramineous: strawlike; straw-colored; (figuratively) valueless

sumpter: pertaining to baggage

systatic: synthetic

tongue-and-groove: designating lumber, especially paneling and flooring, in which boards interlock along edges

treen: wooden

triple-expansion: designating power source using same fluid to do work at three successive stages of expansion

true: precisely or accurately formed, fitted, placed, or calibrated, especially to conform to pattern or form

vertical-grained: designating lumber with grain running lengthwise

wooden: made of wood

Mathematics—Number

algebraic: pertaining to algebra

aliquot: contained in another number without remainder

analytic: resolving into first principles

any: to an indefinite extent or degree

arithmetical: pertaining to arithmetic

bilinear: involving or formed by two lines; linear relative to each of two variables

binary: designating system of numbers having two as its base

calculable: that may be calculated

centesimal: based on hundredths

commensurable: having a common measure

commensurate: proportional

complementary: supplying a deficiency

computable: that can be computed

concentric: designating two or more figures having a common center

conjugate: having the same or similar properties, such as two lines

decadic: pertaining to the decimal system

decimal: founded on the number ten

denary: pertaining to ten

differential: pertaining to differentials

divisible: admitting of division without remainder

duodecimal: based on twelve

exponential: of or pertaining to exponents

factorial: of, relating to, or being factors of a continued product

figurative: containing figures

fingerfull: a pinch; tiny quantity

fluxional: pertaining to fluxions

fractional: pertaining to fractions

geodesic: describing shortest line between two points on surface, especially curved surface

hundredth: being last in a series of one hundred; pertaining to one of a hundred parts

icosian: pertaining to twenty

impossible: pertaining to an imaginary quantity

incommensurable: having no standard of comparison or common measure

incommensurate: not admitting of a common measure

integral: pertaining to an integer
irrational: not equal to the quotient of any two entire quantities
logarithmic: consisting of logarithms
logometric: denoting a scale to ascertain chemical equivalents
mathematical: pertaining to mathematics
millesimal: pertaining to thousandths
more or less: about
more than one: many
negative: less than zero
not alone: being with others
numerable: that may be numbered
numeral: pertaining to numbers
numerical: consisting in number
oblique: neither perpendicular nor parallel; without a right angle
octifid: eighth
parallel: constantly equidistant and in the same plane
perpendicular: at right angle to plane or line
plural: containing more than one
positive: greater than zero
prime: condition of being divisible by no whole number except itself and unity
proportional: pertaining to proportion
quadragesimal: pertaining to the number forty; pertaining to Lent
quadratic: relating to or resembling a square
quadrille: marked or ruled with squares for making graphs

quantitative: relating to differences of quantity
radical: pertaining to the root of a number
rational: expressible as the ratio of two whole numbers
real: not imaginary
reciprocal: used to denote different kinds of mutual relation
sesquialteral: having a ratio of one and a half to one
sexagenary: composed of sixty parts
sexagesimal: based on the number sixty
some: considerable in number or of indeterminate quantity
statistical: pertaining to statistics
surd: irrational
tabular: computed by the use of tables
tenth: being last in a series of ten; pertaining to one of ten parts
three-dimensional: having length, breadth, and thickness
tithe: tenth
transfinite: designating number larger than any finite positive integer
truncated: designating geometric figure, such as cone, having its apex or vertex end cut off by plane
twelfth: being last in a series of twelve; pertaining to one of twelve parts
two-dimensional: having height and width only
upwards of: more than; above
variable: having no fixed value
vicenary: based on the number twenty; containing twenty; vigesimal
vigesimal: having a base of 20

Maturity

adolescent: growing from childhood to manhood
adult: pertaining to mature life
adultoid: resembling an adult
beardless: too young to have a beard
brephic: young; concerning the early stage of growth
budding: developing during youth
callow: without experience in the world
ephebic: entering manhood

full-grown: having reached the normal size of complete development
green: of an unripe youth
grown-up: arrived at full growth or stature
hebephrenic: concerning adolescent silliness
impuberal: not having reached puberty; immature; impubic; prepubescent

in one's prime: in the period of full perfection in life
in one's teens: in adolescence
junior: belonging to youth or earlier life
juvenile: characteristic of youth
manly: worthy of a man
marriageable: of an age suitable to be married
matronly: becoming a mother
mature: having reached full development
middle-aged: between thirty and fifty years of age
nascent: being born or brought forth; immature
neanic: immature; youthful
neotelnic: pertaining to a prolonged adolescence
neotenic: relating to attainment of sexual maturity during the larval stage
nubile: of an age suitable for marriage

of age: having attained majority
of full age: mature in age
of ripe age: of a fully developed age
out of one's teens: twenty years or older
pedomorphic: childlike
prepubescent: designating child just before age of puberty, about twelve years old
pubescent: having arrived at the age of puberty
sappy: immature in age
seasoned: mature; experienced
underage: in one's nonage
virile: pertaining to a man in his mature state
viripotent: of a man, sexually mature; nubile
womanly: becoming a woman
yeanling: young or newborn
young: pertaining to youth
youthful: having youth

Meaning

alike: having likeness in any respect
allegorical: belonging to or pertaining to an allegory
allusive: figurative; containing an allusion
ambiguous: obscure in meaning
amphibological: ambiguous
amphibolous: pertaining to amphiboly
anagogical: having a spiritual or mystical meaning; mysterious; ephemeral; spiritual
antonymous: having nearly opposite meanings
catachrestical: twisted from its natural sense or meaning; far-fetched
colloquial: used in familiar conversation
correspondent: alike in meaning
corresponding: alike in meaning
declaratory: making clear or manifest
delphic: ambiguous
dilogical: ambiguous
equipollent: having equal power or force
equivalent: having equal power or force

equivocal: having two meanings, each of which may be taken
exact: scrupulously careful to conform to a rule or standard
explicit: set forth in the plainest language, so that it cannot be misunderstood
expressive: vividly representing the meaning intended to be conveyed
figurative: employed in a sense not literal
full of meaning: expressing everything that is intended
hermeneutic: interpretive
homonymous: similar in sound, but different in meaning
identical: exactly the same
intelligible: capable of being understood
interchangeable: capable of being used the one for the other
ironical: characterized by irony
jussive: expressing command
linsey-woolsey: being neither one thing nor the other
literal: following the letter or exact words

literatim: literally
lucid: clear; easily understood
meaning: having a particular purpose or intention
metaphorical: relating to metaphor; figurative
of similar meaning: expressing the same thought
of the same meaning: expressing the same thought
parabolic: having the nature of a parable
perspicuous: clearly expressed; easy to comprehend
pithy: forceful
pregnant with meaning: weighty

same: not different
significant: expressive
significative: having a meaning or purpose
significatory: expressive
similar: alike in respect to certain aspects of the meaning of a word
suggestive: conveying a suggestion
synonymic: of or pertaining to synonyms
synonymous: conveying the same or nearly the same idea
tantamount: equivalent in signification or effect
tralatitious: handed down or transmitted
typical: representing by form or resemblance; symbolical

Meaninglessness

fiddle-faddle: trifling
incommunicable: incapable of being told or imparted to others
inexpressible: not capable of utterance in language
inexpressive: without meaning; inexpressible
insignificant: without sense or import
meaningless: without sense or purpose
nonsensical: foolish or without sense
not expressed: implied or left to inference
not significant: without meaning
quibbling: evasive

senseless: deficient in sense
tacit: implied but not expressed
trashy: good for nothing
trivial: trifling
trumpery: deceptive
twaddling: silly
undefinable: not capable of being explained
unexpressive: without meaning; inexpressible
unmeaning: having no signification
unmeant: not intended
vacant: empty of thought
void of sense: wanting in sense
washy: weak or lacking depth

Measure

comparative: thought of as greater or less than something else
geodetical: determined by the operations of geodesy
gradual: proceeding or marked by degrees
inchmeal: gradually; by inches or small degrees
measurable: capable of being measured

measured: determined by measure
measuring: that measures; ascertaining the quantity or magnitude of
metric: proceeding by measurement
metrical: pertaining to measure
poisable: weighable
scalar: pertaining to a numbered scale
shading off: differing by a slight degree
sidereal: measured by means of stars
unmeasured: not measured

Menace

abusive: containing abuse or insulting
  words
baleful: menacing
black-browed: threatening
comminatory: threatening punishment;
  comminative
defiant: bold; insolent
intense: having a fierce look; ferocious;
  menacing

menacing: threatening
minacious: threatening; minatory
minatory: threatening; minacious
minitant: threatening
ominous: presaging or foreboding evil;
  inauspicious
threatening: portending impending evil

Mildness

attemperate: temperate; equable
balmy: mild and soothing
benign: mild; salubrious
clement: characterized by clemency
easygoing: mild-tempered
facile: gentle; mild
forbearing: treating with consideration
  and indulgence
gentle: refined; amiable; tender

indulgent: prone to indulge
lenient: not severe in punishment
low-level: mild
marlish: easygoing
mild: not harsh in disposition
mild as milk: very mild
nesh: tending to be mild, tender, gentle
soft: expressing gentleness or sympathy
tolerant: allowing what one has the
  power to prevent

Mind

branular: pertaining to the brain;
  cerebral
cacophrenic: pertaining to an inferior
  intellect
cerebral: pertaining to the cerebrum;
  mental
conative: pertaining to mental processes
  or behaviors leading to action or
  change
endowed with reason: furnished with
  the faculty of reason
ghostly: relating to the soul
hyperactive: abnormally animated or active, especially in relation to children
ideogenous: of mental origin
immaterial: not consisting of matter;
  spiritual
intellectual: pertaining to the intellect;
  possessing intellect or intelligence
mental: pertaining to the mind or the
  entire rational nature

meshuga: crazy, mad, or nuts; meshugah;
  meshugga; meshuggah; meshuge;
  meshugge
metaphysical: relating to metaphysics;
  treating of or devoted to metaphysics;
  transcendental
mind-altering: changing of the mind
minded: having a particular tendency or
  disposition toward something
mindful: taking thought or care of
multanimous: having a many-sided
  mind
nooscopic: concerning a mental
  examination
philonoetic: intellectual
preconscious: referring to mental activity that is not immediately conscious
  but can easily be recalled
primal: having to do with basic, primitive urges and emotions
psychagogic: inspiring to the mind, soul

psychal: relating to the mind

psychical: of or pertaining to the mind or soul

psychogenic: originating in the mind or in emotional conflict

psychological: of or pertaining to psychology

psychotropic: altering one's mental functions, used especially of tranquilizers and hallucinogenic drugs

rational: pertaining to the reason; having reason; agreeable to reason

self-conscious: awkward and embarrassed in presence of others due to excessive concern with others' opinions

spiritual: of or pertaining to spirit; marked by the highest qualities of the human mind

spirituel: mentally refined

strung out: debilitated from addiction to drug or alcohol; extremely anxious

subconscious: existing in mind beyond conscious level

subjective: proceeding from or taking place within the thinking subject

subliminal: involving stimuli intended to take effect below level of consciousness

unbalanced: having disturbed or uneven mental functions

unstable: emotionally unsettled or unpredictable

wud: mentally ill

Misfortune

adverse: opposed; antagonistic

ambsace: pertaining to bad luck, misfortune

badly off: unfortunate

behindhand: behind in progress

born under an evil star: unlucky

born with a wooden ladle in one's mouth: unlucky

calamitous: full of calamity

clouded: unfavorable

decayed: declined or failed

deplorable: lamentable

devoted: doomed to evil

dire: extremely calamitous

disastrous: causing disaster

down in the world: unfortunate

hapless: having no luck; luckless

ill-fated: unfortunate; calamitous

ill-off: unfortunate; calamitous

ill-omened: unfortunate; calamitous

ill-starred: unfortunate; calamitous

improsperous: not prosperous

in a bad way: unfortunate; having ill fortune

in adverse circumstances: unfortunate; having ill fortune

in an evil plight: unfortunate; having ill fortune

in one's utmost need: unfortunate; having ill fortune

in trouble: unfortunate; having ill fortune

infaust: unlucky

luckless: having no luck

misfortunate: unfortunate

on its last legs: on the point of ruin or disaster

on the road to ruin: failing

on the wane: decreasing in prosperity, power

out of luck: unfortunate

planet-struck: affected by the influence of the planets; moonstruck

poor: without money or resources

quisby: bankrupt; down-and-out

random: determined by chance or luck

ruinous: tending to ruin; calamitous

seismic: of or relating to earthquakes

stygian: extremely gloomy and foreboding

unblessed: not blessed; accursed; unblest

under a cloud: unfavorable

undone: ruined; brought to grief

unfortunate: having ill fortune

unhappy: not happy

unlucky: not lucky

unprosperous: not prosperous
untoward: inconvenient; unfortunate

widdershins: inauspiciously; unlucky; in an unfortunate direction; withershins

Misinterpretation—Misjudgment

bathetic: falsely sentimental
besotted: enslaved; infatuated
bigoted: stubbornly attached to an opinion
borne: narrow-minded and provincial
conceited: having a great opinion of self
confined: within limits; too narrow; mean
credulous: apt to believe without enough evidence
crotchety: full of conceits or fancies
dogmatic: arrogant; overbearing
euhemeristic: interpreting myth as history
fanatical: moved by intemperate zeal
fussy: inclined to make much ado about nothing
illiberal: stingy; niggardly
ill-judging: not judging well
impracticable: not to be practiced; not to be managed
inexplicable: unexplainable
infatuated: excited to misjudged passion
intolerant: narrow-minded; bigoted
jaundiced: affected with prejudice or envy
malentendu: misunderstood

misinterpreted: interpreted wrongly or falsely
misjudged: falsely judged
misjudging: forming false opinions
narrow-minded: bigoted; illiberal
one-sided: having but one side; partial; unfair
opinionated: too much attached to one's opinion
opinionative: opinionated
opinioned: conceited
partial: favoring one party
positive: overconfident; dictatorial
prejudiced: biased with a premature like or dislike
purblind: nearsighted
self-opinioned: self-conceited
shortsighted: unable to understand deep things
stupid: lacking understanding
superficial: comprehending only the obvious
tendentious: biased; opinionated; partial
unreasonable: beyond reason
unreasoning: lacking reason
untranslatable: that cannot be translated
untranslated: not translated
wedded to an opinion: attached closely by prejudice to an opinion
wrongheaded: having the head filled with false notions
yeasty: superficial; frivolous

Mixture

composite: made up of separate or distinct parts
farraginous: mixed; heterogeneous
half-and-half: composed of equal parts of different substances
heterogeneous: consisting of ingredients of various kinds
hybrid: produced by the mixture of two species

implex: intricate; complex
indiscriminate: lacking discrimination; confused
linsey-woolsey: made of linen and wool
macaronic: of a jumble or medley
miscellaneous: consisting of different kinds of things
miscible: that may be mixed
mixed: put together

mongrel: of mixed breed

motley: made up of different colors or various parts

promiscuous: commingled without order or distinction

Moderation

abstemious: eating and drinking temperately

abstinent: totally abstaining, as from intoxicants

encratic: self-controlled; abstinent

equable: even-tempered

frugal: marked by economy

measured: moderate; temperate

moderate: keeping within temperate limits

sober: moderate in or abstinent from the use of intoxicants; not under the influence of liquor

sober as a judge: perfectly sober

sparing: frugal

teetotal: of total abstinence

temperate: observing moderation and self-control, particularly in the case of intoxicants

vegetarian: relating to vegetarianism

within compass: within moderation

Modification—Change

afloat: unfixed; uncontrolled

agitating: stirring up

alterable: capable of being changed or varied

alterative: causing change

alternating: happening in turns or between opposites

capricious: characterized by whim

changeable: liable to change

changed: caused to be different

changeful: uncertain

changing: causing to be different

chatoyant: changing in luster or color, such as fabric

checkered: diversified

desultory: passing from one thing or subject to another without logical connection, as a circus rider leaps from horse to horse

erratic: wandering aimlessly

ever-changing: changing constantly

fickle: wavering in opinion or purpose

fitful: irregular; unstable

fluctuating: varying irregularly

gerful: changeable; gereful; gerie; gerish

inconsonant: subject to change

interchangeable: capable of interchange

interchanged: switching two things into the place of the other

irresolute: wavering; vacillating

labile: changeable, especially chemically, physically, biologically; slippery

mobile: capable of being aroused or excited

modifiable: capable of being diversified by various forms and differences

mutable: liable to change or alteration; fickle; variable

newfangled: disposed to change frequently

plastic: creative; easily molded

protean: pertaining to Proteus; changeable; versatile; infinitely variable

proteiform: protean

restless: uneasy; discontented

spasmodic: occurring at intervals

tittuppy: unstable; unsteady; shaky

touch-and-go: precarious; stopping and then starting

transient: remaining in place only a brief time

transilient: pertaining to abrupt change

transitional: containing, denoting, or involving change

tropophilous: adapted to seasonal changes

unfixed: not fixed

unsettled: not settled

unstable: not steady or firm
unstayed: not sustained; fickle
unsteady: unfixed; variable
vagrant: unsettled; moving with uncertain direction
variable: subject to sudden change

versatile: changeable
vibratory: moving or causing to move to and fro
vicissitudinary: pertaining to change, mutation
wayward: full of whims; perverse

Money

aerarian: fiscal
auriferous: producing or bearing gold; aurific
chrematistic: pertaining to business or moneymaking; preoccupied with getting rich
crumenal: pertaining to a purse
economic: pertaining to money matters or wealth
expended: paid out
expending: being paid out
financial: pertaining to or concerning money matters
fiscal: pertaining to the government treasury
mercenary: serving for pay

monetary: pertaining to money
monied: having a great deal of money; moneyed
numismatical: pertaining to the science of coins
pecuniary: referring to money
pecunious: having a great deal of money
priced: having the price fixed
quaestuary: profit-seeking; undertaken for money
sterling: of accepted value; genuine
sumptuary: pertaining to regulating expenditure or to an expense
to the tune of: at that price
venal: capable of being bought; purchasable

Movement

brachiating: moving by swinging the arms
catabatic: abating; moving downward; katabatic
circumambient: moving around (something)
coxinutant: having a seductive sway of the hips when walking
cursorial: adapted or built for running
dextrosinistral: naturally left-handed, but trained to use the right hand
digitigrade: walking on tiptoes
drawing: moving forward
erratic: wandering
feirie: capable of walking
formicating: crawling like an ant
gestic: relating to gestures, body movement
glad-warbling: singing or walking joyfully

gressible: able to walk
in motion: moving; changing position
irpe: of a grimace or bodily contortion; irp
irreptitious: creeping stealthily
laterigrade: walking sideways
left-handed: capable of using the left hand better than the right
manuductory: leading by the hand
mercurial: quickly moving or changing, like mercury
mobile: moving; changing
motile: moving spontaneously, as microorganisms
motive: possessing the power to move
motory: having the power to produce motion
movable: possessing the power to produce motion
moving: changing position

murgeoning: contorting; writhing

nomadic: wandering from one place to another

paradromic: running side by side; collimated

pedestrious: going on foot; walking; pedestrian

pinnigrade: walking on fins or flippers

proal: having a forward motion of the lower jaw when chewing

projectile: impelling forward

pronograde: walking with the body almost horizontal

propelled: driven forward

propelling: driving forward

propulsive: having the power to propel

recoiling: moving back

rectigrade: moving in a straight line

reptant: crawling; creeping; repent

restless: in a state of motion

shanks' pony: on foot; shank's pony; shanks' mare; shank's mare

shifting: going from place to place

sinistrodextral: moving from left to right

subsultive: moving in an irregular way

surefooted: walking confidently

taligrade: walking on the outer side of the foot

transitional: moving from one place or state to another

unquiet: restless

vermigrade: creeping like a worm

viaggiatory: on the move; traveling frequently

wandle: lithe; nimble

Music

a cappella: without instrumental accompaniment

accelerando: gradually faster

adagio: slowly, gracefully; between largo and andante

agitato: restless or hurried in manner

allegretto: light and moderately fast; faster than moderato, slower than allegro

allegro: brisk or rapid; faster than allegretto, slower than presto

andante: moderately slow and flowing; faster than adagio, slower than moderato

andantino: slightly faster than andante

animato: with spirit; lively

appassionato: with emotion or passion

assonant: pertaining to or having a resemblance to sound

atonal: without reference to key or mode; using all twelve tones of chromatic scale at random

calando: in music, dying away

canorous: melodious

choral: relating to or composed for a chorus or choir

chromatic: containing all twelve half steps in octave

classical: denoting music of the European tradition marked by sophistication of structural elements and embracing vocal, symphonic, chamber, and solo music

clear: easily heard; distinct; entirely musical

clear as a bell: very distinct in sound

concentual: possessing harmony

contrapuntal: based on counterpoint

crescendo: gradually increasing in volume

diatonic: designating major and minor scales; designating eight-tone scale without chromatic deviation

diminuendo: decreasing in volume

dolce: soft and sweet

dulcet: sweet or pleasing to the ear

enchanting: fascinating; very pleasing to the ear

enharmonic: designating tones that have same pitch but different notation, such as C-sharp and D-flat

euphonic: pertaining to sounds that are pleasing to the ear

euphonical: pertaining to sounds that are pleasing to the ear

euphonious: agreeable or pleasing in sound

fidicinal: concerning stringed instruments

fine-toned: excellent or pure in tone

forte: loud; forceful

fortissimo: very loud

full-toned: clear or distinct in tone

funky: dirty, down-home, bluesy, or unsophisticated

go-go: describing style of pop music fashion, origin 1960s

grave: serious; slower than lento, faster than largo

grazioso: graceful; flowing

harmonical: pertaining to harmony or music

harmonious: musically concordant

hip: knowledgeable about current trends in pop culture, especially music

homophonous: having the same pitch

in concert: in unison

in concord: in harmony

in tune: harmonious

instrumental: pertaining to or made by musical instruments

isotonic: having equal tones

larghetto: slow; faster than largo, slower than grave

largo: very slow; slower than grave

legato: in music, smoothly

lento: somewhat slow; faster than larghetto, slower than adagio

lyric: pertaining to or like the lyre or harp; suitable for music

lyriform: shaped like a lyre

lyrophorous: song making, as on a lyre

maestoso: majestic

marcato: accented; stressed; marked

martellato: detached, strongly accented, or hammered with stroke of bow on stringed instrument

measured: regulated; uniform

melismatic: ornate or florid in melody

mellifluous: softly or sweetly flowing

mellow: soft; rich; not harsh

melodious: containing or pertaining to music or melody

melomaniac: loving music

modal: of or relating to a diatonic eight-tone scale other than major or minor; pertaining to mode, as distinguished from key

moderato: at moderate speed; faster than andante, slower than allegretto

modern: designating music composed in classical forms during the twentieth century

modulaminous: melodious

musical: pertaining to or inclined toward music

operatic: pertaining to or like an opera

parlando: delivered or performed as though speaking or reciting; parlante

pedaliter: to be played on a pedal keyboard

pentatonic: designating five-tone scale, especially one arranged like a major scale with the fourth and seventh deleted

pianissimo: very soft

piano: soft; subdued

pizzicato: played with plucked strings

plagal: describing a religious melody with a keynote on the fourth step of a scale

playing: performing on musical instruments

presto: very fast; faster than allegro

rallentando: gradually slowing

rhythmical: regularly recurring in beats or accents

ripieno: in music, accompanying others

ritardando: with gradual slowing of tempo

romantic: designating music of the late nineteenth century marked by free expression of imagination and emotion, virtuosic display, and some experimentation with form

rubato: having variation in speed within musical phrase, especially juxtaposed against steady rhythm

scherzando: lively; brisk; playful

semiclassical: designating composition combining classical and contemporary, popular elements

semplice: simple; straightforward

silver-toned: clear and ringing in tone

silvery: having a clear, tinkling sound

soft: gentle; low; not harsh

sostenuto: sustained in time value of tones

spiccato: performed with short, rapid bow stroke that allows bow to rebound between notes, giving detached effect to tones

staccato: with abrupt, distinct breaks between notes

subito: in music, suddenly

sweet: mild; soft; pleasing

symphonious: harmonious in sound; concordant

symphonizing: harmonizing; agreeing with in sound

tenuto: designating note or chord held to full extent of its time value

tunable: possessing the power to be tuned or put in harmony

tuneful: harmonious; melodious

tutti: all; performed by all voices or instruments together

twelve-tone: pertaining to serial composition using all twelve chromatic tones

unisonant: being in unison

unplugged: performed without electronic amplification or effects

vigoroso: vigorous or spirited in manner

vocal: pertaining to music made by the voice

zoppa: in music, having a shifting, accented beat

Muteness

aphonous: affected with or characterized by aphony; aphonic

breathless: intense or eager, as if holding the breath

croaking: harsh; guttural

deaf and dumb: without ability to hear or speak

deaf-mute: dumb in consequence of deafness

dry: uninteresting; unattractive

dumb: unable to make articulate sound

hoarse: harsh and rough in sound

hoarse as a raven: with a croaking voice

hollow: resembling sound reverberated from a cavity

husky: not clear; hoarse

inarticulate: not produced in distinct intelligible syllables

inaudible: that cannot be heard or is very difficult to hear

mum: saying nothing; silent

mute: uttering no word or sound

mute as a fish: voiceless

mute as a mackerel: dumb

mute as a stockfish: without utterance

muzzled: put to silence

sepulchral: unnaturally low and hollow in tone

silent: not making any sound or noise

sourdine: muted; muffled

speechless: being without faculty of speech

taciturn: habitually silent or reserved

tongueless: speechless; silent

tongue-tied: having the speech impeded by tongue-tie

voiceless: having no voice or speech

wordless: having no words; dumb

Name

anonymous: bearing no name

cognominal: pertaining to the surname

disquiparant: having a different name from one's own, as a father and son's first names

eponymous: giving one's name to something, such as an organization

euonymous: named aptly

having no name: possessing no designation or appellation

hight: called; named

innominate: without a specific name; unnamed

known as: recognized; called by name of

misnamed: wrongly named

named: nominated; mentioned; spoken of

nameless: having no name; inexpressible

né: born; used to indicate former name under which one was born

née: female form of né

nominal: pertaining to a name; existing only in name

nuncupative: declaratory; existing only in name

nuncupatory: nuncupative; oral

onymatic: pertaining to names

onymous: not anonymous; having a name; known

orismological: pertaining to orismology

polyonymous: having many names

pseudepigraphous: signed with a fake name

pseudonymous: bearing a false name or signature

scilicet: namely; that is to say

self-called: named without outside aid

self-christened: self-named

self-styled: called or styled by oneself

so-called: generally styled thus; called as stated

soi-disant: self-styled; so-called

surnominal: pertaining to a surname

theophoric: having the name of a god

titular: existing in title only; nominal

unnamed: not having received a name

veritable: truthful; real; genuine; correctly called or named

videlicet: namely; to wit; viz.

what one may fairly call: expression pertaining to degree of naming

what one may fitly call: pertaining to degree of naming

what one may properly call: pertaining to degree of naming

what one may well call: pertaining to degree of naming

without a name: nameless; possessing no name

yclept: called; named

Narrowness

angustate: narrowed; narrowing

attenuated: made thin or rare

barebone: so thin or lean that the bones show their forms

brawn-fallen: thin; with shrunken muscles

cannulate: hollow and narrow

close: narrow; closely confined

contracted: drawn together or lessened

décharné: emaciated; skeletal; without flesh

delicate: slight or slender

emaciated: wasted away in flesh

extenuated: drawn out or made thin

fastigiate: narrowing at the top

fine: not coarse; thin

finespun: drawn out to a fine thread

gaunt: lean; wasting

gracilescent: growing slender, slim

hatchet-faced: having a sharp visage

herring-gutted: thin in the waist

incapacious: narrow; small

lank: slender; poorly filled out

lanky: somewhat lank or thin

lantern-jawed: thin-jawed or thin-visaged

lean: lacking flesh; thin

lean as a rake: very thin

long-limbed: having a tall, thin body; gangling; gangly; rangy; slab-sided; spindly

macilent: lean; emaciated

marcid: lean; thin

meager: deficient in flesh; thin

narrow: of little distance from side to side

narrowing: becoming narrower; tapered; tapering

peened: beaten thin with a hammer

rawboned: with but little flesh on the bones

scant: meager; less than is needed for the purpose

scanty: lacking in extent; narrow; small

shriveled: drawn into wrinkles; shrunken

skin and bone: having a delicately thin body

skinny: wanting in flesh

slender: narrow in proportion to the length or height

slender as a thread: very slender

slight-made: slim or slender

slim: thin in proportion to the length or height

spare: lean; lacking flesh

spectral: having a deathly thin body; cadaverous; consumptive; skeletal

starved: reduced in flesh by hunger

starveling: lean; emaciated with want

tabid: affected by a progressive wasting away of the body

taper: gradually narrowed toward the end

thin: of little thickness or distance from one surface to its opposite

thin as a lath: extremely thin

thin as a wafer: extremely thin

thin as a whipping post: extremely thin

threadlike: thin like a thread

unexpanded: not spread out or diffused

weedy: like a weed, especially of a rank but weakly growth

worn to a shadow: thin

Nature

artless: honest; frank

characteristic: showing the distinctive qualities or traits of a person or thing

consistent with nature: natural

constitutional: inherent in the structure of the body or mind

created: brought into being; caused to exist

essential: belonging to that which makes a thing what it is

from nature: natural

genuine: belonging to the original stock

indigenous: produced or existing naturally in a country or climate

ingenuous: plain; candid

intrinsic: innate; inward

legitimate: authorized; not false

lifelike: appearing as though possessing life

native: conferred by birth; born in the region in which one lives

natural: constituted by nature; taking place as ordinary; not unusual

normal: conformed to a standard or nature

ontological: of or pertaining to the nature of something; of the science of essence or being; metaphysical

original: pertaining to the origin; first in order

real: actual in being or existence

regular: according to nature

simple: open; not obscure; not complex

spontaneous: arising from internal impulse or natural law

true: in accordance with the actual condition of things

unregenerate: not changed from a natural to a spiritual state

Nearness

accolent: living nearby; neighboring

adjacent: contiguous

adjoining: lying next; bordering

affluent: flowing to

approaching: coming toward; nearing

approximative: coming to without coinciding

asymptotical: approaching but never meeting

at hand: close to

cheek by jowl: next to; apposite; conterminous; coterminous

close: nearby

close at hand: near

convergent: turning toward one point

converging: turning toward one point

equidistant: equally far or near

handy: convenient; close at hand

imminent: jutting toward

impending: hanging over

inby: nearby; beside; inbye

intimate: confidential; familiar

limitrophe: adjacent

near: close by

near at hand: not remote; neighborly

near the mark: close to

neighboring: closely associated

neolocal: not living near one's or one's spouse's family

nigh: near; being close by

penadjacent: next to adjacent

propinquant: near; immediate; nigh; propinquous; proximal; proximate; vicinal

proximal: situated toward the point of origin or attachment; near to; next

proximate: near to; next; very near

subcontiguous: nearly touching

vicinage: neighboring; nearby

vicinal: relating or belonging to a neighborhood; neighboring

youward: toward you

Need

absorbing: fully occupying; requiring one's whole time or attention

called-for: needed; required

crying: calling for

destitute: entirely bereft or lacking

equinecessary: needful to the same degree

essential: of the very basis or essence, and without which a thing cannot exist

exigent: demanding immediate aid or action; pressing

imperative: absolutely required or necessary

in demand: necessary

in request: sought after

in want of: needing or desiring

indispensable: not capable of being omitted; not so strong as essential

inopious: financially needy
instant: pressing; urgent
necessary: of such a nature that it cannot be given up
needful: necessary to the purpose
prerequisite: necessary beforehand

pressing: urgent
required: made a necessary condition
requisite: necessary from the nature of things
urgent: of pressing need

News

afloat: in motion or circulation; used of rumor
all over the town: pertaining to rapidly spreading news
current: circulating; general
currently reported: an account or statement, circulating in general
currently rumored: an unverified report, spreading widely
floating: temporary or fluctuating news
going about: circulating in general
in circulation: going around

in every one's mouth: widespread
many-tongued: ready with the tongue to circulate anything
newsful: full of tidings
newsworthy: of something worth being publicized; of interest to the general public
publicly reported: something noised about openly
publicly rumored: rumor spreading in an open manner
rife: prevalent; current
rumored: generally spoken of

Noncompletion

going on: in an unfinished state
in hand: under way
in one's hands: not finished
in progress: under way
incomplete: lacking fullness
incondite: unfinished; crude; badly constructed
not completed: not finished

proceeding: advancing
sketchyaddle: confused; wanting the power to progress
unaccomplished: not accomplished
uncompleted: not completed
unexecuted: left in an unfinished state
unfinished: not done
unperformed: not performed

Nonentity—Nullity

absent: not present
airy: unsubstantial; fanciful
annihilated: entirely destroyed
azoic: inorganic; without life; lifeless
baseless: without foundation
blank: free from writing or printing; empty
defunct: dead; extinct
departed: dead
diriment: nullifying; making void
dreamy: indistinct; appropriate to dreams
empty: having nothing in it

ethereal: having the nature of ether; spiritlike
eviscerated: deprived of the entrails
exhausted: having lost its vital force
extinct: quenched; put out
fabulous: unreal
gone: ruined; deceased
groundless: without cause, reason, or proper support; false
having no foundation: baseless
hollow: having a cavity within
ideal: not practical
imperscriptible: unrecorded

inane: displaying mental vacuity

inanimate: without life

inorganic: devoid of systematic physical structure

leaving no trace: leaving no mark

lost: gone beyond recovery

mineral: inorganic; pertaining to or like a mineral

missing: not to be found; departed

negative: not active; tending to go in the opposite direction

nominal: in name only; trivial

nonentitive: that is nonexistent

nonexistent: not having existence or being

not any: none

not one: none

null: of no legal force or effect

nullibiquitous: nonexistent

obliterated: wiped out; destroyed

omitted: left out

perished: decayed; passed from life

potential: possible, but not yet existing

shadowy: unreal; unsubstantial

supposititious: only imagined

toom: empty; empty-sounding

unbegotten: not yet brought forth

unborn: not yet born

unconceived: not yet conceived or thought of

uncreated: not yet created

ungrounded: groundless

unmade: not yet made

unproduced: not yet produced

unreal: not having reality

unsubstantial: without substance

vacant: empty or unengaged

vacuous: containing no matter

vain: profitless; unreal

virtual: efficacious without the agency of the material

visionary: impracticable; existing in imagination only

without foundation: having nothing to rest upon

Nonpreparation

abortive: in want of full development

caught napping: unprepared

coarse: composed of rough parts; unrefined

crude: not having reached full development

dismantled: stripped of equipment

disqualified: not having the necessary qualifications

embryonic: pertaining to the embryo

extemporaneous: presented without preparation

fallow: uncultivated

green: unripe; immature

happy-go-lucky: improvident; confiding in luck

ill-digested: badly digested

immature: not full grown

imprompt: unready; unprepared

improvident: not preparing for the future; reckless

in a state of nature: not prepared by artificial means

in dishabille: in a state of undress

in the rough: unworked

incomplete: not fully developed

indigested: not digested; crude

natural: not artificial

out of gear: not suited for working

out of order: not suited for working

precocious: premature development

premature: ripening or happening before the proper or normal time

raw: not prepared by cooking; unprepared

rough: lacking finish or completeness

roughcast: cast without attention to detail

rough-hewn: roughly shapen

rudimental: as yet undeveloped

shiftless: incapable of providing for oneself; thriftless

surprised: caught unprepared, off-guard

thoughtless: without thought; manifesting no preparation

unarranged: not placed in order
unbegun: not started
unblown: not blown
unboiled: not boiled
unconcocted: unmixed
uncooked: not prepared for eating
uncultivated: unprepared for planting
undigested: not properly acted upon by the digestive organs
undressed: not covered; not trimmed
undrilled: not trained
uneducated: without bringing up; without education
unequipped: not fitted with equipment
unexercised: not trained
unfashioned: not shaped
unfitted: not adjusted to
unfledged: not provided with feathers; immature
unformed: without shape
unfurnished: without furniture
unguarded: open; not protected
unhatched: not yet produced; not having chipped the shell

unhewn: not cut
unlabored: not worked upon
unleavened: without leaven
unlicked: not licked into shape
unmellowed: unripe
unnurtured: not nourished up
unorganized: not arranged in order
unpolished: rough
unpremeditated: thoughtless
unprepared: not ready
unprovided: without supplies
unqualified: not fitted for
unready: not prepared
unripe: green
unseasoned: not suited to
unsown: without seed
untaught: ignorant; unlearned
untilled: not prepared for planting
untrained: lacking exercise
untrimmed: without ornament; unpruned; shaggy
untutored: untaught
unwrought: not worked
without preparation: not ready

Nonsense

absurd: contrary to good reasoning
egregious: greatly exceeding, usually in a bad sense
extravagant: immoderate
foolish: wanting in judgment
inconsistent: self-contradictory
macaronic: jumbled
nonsensical: of no importance

preposterous: impracticable
punning: using a word in two senses
quibbling: evading the point and speaking trifles
ridiculous: laughable and comical
senseless: meaningless
sophistical: false
unmeaning: unintelligible

Nourishment

adipsous: quenching thirst
alible: nutritive; nourishing
alimentary: pertaining to aliment
alimonious: nourishing
amophagous: eating animal flesh; carnivorous; creophagous
amphivorous: eating both vegetables and meat
androphagous: man-eating
anthophilous: eating flowers; anthophagous

anthropophagous: eating human flesh
apivorous: bee-eating
arachnivorous: eating spiders
baccivorous: eating berries
batrachivorous: frog-eating; batrachophagous
bibulous: fond of drinking
biophagous: eating living organisms
cannibalistic: eating its own kind
carnivorous: eating meat; zoophagous
cepivorous: onion-eating

coenaculous: dinner-loving
comestible: suitable to be eaten
coprophagous: waste-eating
creophagous: carnivorous
dietetic: relating to diet
dipsetic: causing thirst
eatable: in a condition suitable for eating
edacious: pertaining to eating; voracious
edible: fit to be used as food
entomophagous: eating insects
equivorous: eating horsemeat
esculent: edible; pertaining to food
euryphagous: eating a wide variety of foods; pantophagous
eutrophic: nutritional
foisoned: nourished; foysoned
frugivorous: fruit-eating; fructivorous
fucivorous: seaweed-eating
galactophagous: milk-drinking
geophagous: eating dirt
graminivorous: feeding upon grass
granivorous: feeding upon grain
hematophagous: wanting to suck blood; sanguivorous
herbivorous: eating seeds or other vegetable parts
hippophagous: eating horseflesh
hylophagous: eating wood
ichthyophagous: eating fish; piscivorous
insectivorous: eating insects
lactivorous: drinking milk as one's diet
lacto-ovo-vegetarian: eating vegetarian plus dairy products and eggs
lacto-vegetarian: eating vegetarian plus dairy products
limivorous: eating mud
lithophagous: eating stones, gravel
lotophagous: lotus-eating
mellivorous: eating honey
merdivorous: eating dung
monophagous: eating only one kind of food
myrmecophagous: eating ants
necrophagous: eating carrion, dead animals; scavenging
nourished: fed; having eaten

nucivorous: nut-eating
nutritious: nourishing
nutritive: nourishing
oligophagous: eating only a few or certain kinds of foods
omnivorous: living upon food of all kinds
oophagous: eating eggs
ophiophagous: eating snakes
oryzivorous: rice-eating
ossivorous: eating bones
ovivorous: egg-eating
panivorous: bread-eating
phthirophagous: eating lice
phyllophagous: eating leaves
phyticorous: herbivorous
phytivorous: vegetable-eating; phytophagous
phytophagous: eating plants
piscivorous: fish-eating
pleophagous: eating a variety of food; polyphagous
poculent: drinkable
poltophagic: chewing thoroughly
polyphagous: eating a moderate variety of foods
porcipophagic: pig-eating
potable: fit for drinking
potulent: fit for drinking
predaceous: eating other animals; predatory; raptorial
ranivorous: frog-eating
sanguinivorous: bloodsucking; sanguisugent; sanguivorous
saprophagous: eating decaying or dead matter
sarcophagic: flesh-eating; sarcophagous
scatophagous: eating excrement
scolecophagous: eating worms
seminivorous: eating seeds
subruminative: digesting
trophic: pertaining to nutrition
vegan: eating vegetarian and no animal products in any form
vegetarian: eating no meat; herbivorous
xerophagous: eating dry food
xylophagous: eating wood

Novelty

brand-new: bright and fresh

evergreen: retaining greenness; always fresh

fresh: newly prepared or produced

fresh as a daisy: bright and cheerful

fresh as a rose: ruddy and beautiful

fresh as paint: recently grown, made

green: immature; unripe

immature: undeveloped; imperfect

inchoate: undeveloped; brand-new

just out: appearing at this moment

late: recent; coming after a suitable time

modern: pertaining to the present

neoteric: new; recent in origin; modern

new: lately come into existence

newborn: lately born

newfangled: new-made or new-fashioned

new-fashioned: made in new style

new-fledged: newly feathered; newly initiated

novel: unusual; strange

of yesterday: recent

raw: newly done; fresh

recent: pertaining to time not long past

renovated: made new and vigorous

spick-and-span: bright; quite new

unbeaten: not trodden down; new

unhandled: not previously used

untried: not yet experienced

untrodden: unfrequented; not marked by feet

vernal: belonging to the spring

virgin: pertaining to a virgin; first

young: not long born

Obedience

at one's beck and call: ready to respond to a nod of the head and a call

at one's call: ready to come without previous notice

at one's commands: ready to obey

at one's orders: ready to obey

compliant: willing to do something

complying: assenting; agreeing

devoted: closely attached; worshipping God

faithful: attendant; true to duty

henpecked: dominated by some petty authority, as the husband by the wife

loyal: faithful to one's government or trust

morigerous: obedient; obsequious

obedient: disposed to obey

passive: inactive; unresisting; indifferent

pliant: yielding to influence

resigned: submissive; compliant

restrainable: able to be held in check; able to be controlled

ruly: obedient

submissive: yielding readily to influence

under beck and call: ready to cringe to the biddings of authority

under control: obedient; docile

unresisted: unopposed

woman-tired: henpecked

Objectiveness—Nonessentialness

accidental: nonessential; not necessarily belonging

adscititious: supplemental; additional

adventitious: added extrinsically; not essentially inherent

ascititious: supplemental; not inherent

derived from without: acquired; not natural

extraneous: not belonging to or dependent upon a thing; not essential

extrinsic: not contained in or belonging to a body; external; unessential

extrinsical: extrinsic

implanted: planted for the purpose of growth; inculcated

incidental: happening, as an occasional event; accidental; casual

ingrafted: introduced; set deeply

modal: characterized by form or manner, irrespective of matter or substance

nonessential: not essential

objective: pertaining to an object; outward; external

outward: pertaining to the exterior of an object; external

Obligation

by stress of: under compulsion

if need be: should it be necessary

necessarily: by inevitable consequence

obligated: expected or required

obliged: bound by duty

of course: by consequence

of necessity: by necessary consequence; by compulsion

perforce: by force

reciprocal: given in return, under obligation, or as a result of

rote: done in an automatic way

syntrophic: mutually dependent for nutritional needs

will he, nill he: whether he will or will not; without choice

willing or unwilling: compelled by force

Obscurity

abstruse: hard to understand

ambiguous: having a double meaning

brumous: misty; foggy

confused: rendered indistinct or obscure

crabbed: obscure; perplexing

dark: obscure; mysterious; hidden

dim: indistinct; obscure

enigmatic: obscure; puzzling

enigmatical: obscure; puzzling

hidden: concealed; secret

illegible: incapable of being read

impenetrable: abstruse

inapprehensible: unintelligible; inconceivable

incognizable: incapable of being recognized, known, or distinguished

incommunicable: incapable of being communicated

inconceivable: incapable of being conceived by the mind

inconceptible: inconceivable

indefinite: not explicit; uncertain

inexplicable: not explainable

inexpressible: not capable of expression in language; indescribable

inscrutable: impossible to understand; obscure; mysterious; baffling

insoluble: not to be solved or explained; inexplicable

insolvable: insoluble

involved: made intricate or complicated

larvate: hidden; obscure

latent: hidden; invisible

latitant: hidden; hibernating

loose: vague; rambling

macroscian: casting a long shadow, literally or figuratively

metagnostic: unknowable

misty: lacking clearness; obscure

muddy: confused; cloudy in mind; vague

mysterious: involved in mystery; obscure

mystic: secret; dark; betokening a hidden meaning

mystical: secret; dark; betokening a hidden meaning

nebulous: cloudy; hazy; vague

nubilous: vague

obscure: not easily understood; indistinct

occult: hidden; mysterious

paradoxical: seemingly contradictory

perplexed: confused; of a complicated character

puzzlepated: having or based on confused attitudes or ideas

puzzling: bewildering; perplexing

recondite: not easily understood; perplexing; complicated; obscure

searchless: inscrutable; impenetrable

sphingine: sphinxlike; enigmatic; inscrutable

tenebrific: creating darkness; obscuring

transcendental: vaguely and ambitiously extravagant in speculation, imagery, or diction

turbid: murky; muddy; unclear; obscure

unaccountable: inexplicable; strange

unconceived: not understood

undeciphered: undiscovered

undefinable: not capable of being made clear or of being defined by a definition

undetermined: not defined; indeterminate

undiscernible: not to be seen through; obscure

undiscoverable: that cannot be discovered or found out

unexplained: not explained

unfathomable: incapable of being fathomed or sounded

unintelligible: not intelligible; not capable of being understood

unknowable: incapable of being known

vague: hazy; uncertain; doubtful

Observance

as good as one's word: truthful; true to one's promise

faithful: trustworthy in the observance of promises

honorable: in accordance with the principles of honor

literal: exact as to details

loyal: constant; faithful

observant: watchful; paying close attention to one's duty

punctilious: exact in regard to the forms and usages of society

punctual: observant in regard to an appointed time

true: in conformity with fact; not false

true as the dial of the sun: exact as the sundial

true as the needle to the pole: as true as the magnetic needle is to the pole

Obstruction

alone: apart from others

athwart: lying in the path of

burdensome: oppressive; heavy to be borne

cumbersome: hindering; burdensome; heavy

cumbrous: serving to hinder or obstruct

deserted: forsaken; left alone

hard-pressed: in a difficult position

heavy-laden: weighed down heavily

hindered: opposed; obstructed

hindering: opposing

impedient: hindering

impeditive: obstructive; causing hindrance

in the way of: obstructing

incommodious: inconvenient

intercipient: stopping; intercepting

obstaculous: having the nature of an obstacle

obstructive: hindering; tending to obstruct

obstruent: obstructing; blocking up

obtrusive: inclined to intrude uninvited

onerous: burdensome; oppressive

prophylactic: defending from disease

single-handed: alone; without assistance

unassisted: without help or assistance

unfavorable: not favorable

waterlogged: rendered heavy and clumsy, like a log

wind-bound: prevented from sailing by an opposing wind

Occupation

acting: doing duty in place of another

afoot: in active operation

bureaucratic: businesslike; officious

businesslike: according to right business methods

busy: occupied with work or serious affairs

clerical: pertaining to clerks

functional: pertaining to a duty or function

going on: doing or proceeding

in hand: in the course of transaction

in one's hand: in one's possession or at one's risk

industrial: pertaining to industries or trade

mercative: pertaining to trade, commerce

occupational: belonging to an occupation or business

official: relating to an office or public trust

on foot: in operation

on hand: in immediate possession

on one's hands: in one's care

on the anvil: in a formative or immature state or condition

professional: relating to a profession or calling

workaday: pertaining to a weekday or workday

Occurrence

afloat: in circulation

at issue: undecided

bustling: characterized by confused activity

current: in circulation

doing: taking place

eventful: rich in events or incidents

full of incident: full of events

going on: happening

happening: taking place

in question: under examination

in the wind: rumored; impending

incidental: occurring as minor to something else

occurring: happening; taking place

on foot: astir; begun

on the tapis: under consideration

Ocean

abyssal: of the ocean zone from 13,000-feet to 20,000-feet depth

aequorial: oceanic; marine

autopelagic: dwelling in the deep sea

bathyal: deep-sea; bathypelagic

bathybic: pertaining to the deep sea

benthic: of or relating to the ocean depths; benthonic

benthopelagic: inhabiting the deep ocean

cisatlantic: on the speaker's/writer's side of the Atlantic Ocean

cotidal: simultaneity in tides

epeiric: of a shallow sea that covers a large part of a continent yet remains connected with the ocean

euxine: concerning the Black Sea

grayslick: of a still, glassy-looking sea

hadal: of the ocean zone from 20,000-feet depth and deeper

halimous: pertaining to salt; marine

hydrographic: relating to maritime maps or charts

maricolous: living in the sea

marigenous: produced in or near the sea

marine: pertaining to the ocean; oceanic; pelagic; thalassic

oceanic: pertaining to the ocean

pelagic: pertaining to the deep sea

pelagian: pertaining to the deep sea

seagoing: pertaining to a vessel going out on the ocean or deep sea

sea-surrounded: encircled by the sea

spanipelagic: dwelling in deep sea but surfacing at times

sublittoral: of the ocean zone from the low-water line to the edge of the continental shelf; neritic

tidal: of or pertaining to tides

transmarine: existing across the sea; coming from or going across the sea

Oiliness

adipose: fatty

butyraceous: having the qualities of butter

butyric: pertaining to butter

cereous: waxy

fat: oily; greasy

fatty: consisting of, containing, or having the qualities of fat; fat

greasy: smeared with grease; like grease or oil

lardaceous: like lard; fatty

liparoid: fatty

oily: pertaining to or containing oil; greasy

oleaginous: oily; greasy; fatty in appearance or manner or both; oily

pinguid: fat; unctuous; greasy

pinguidinous: fatty; greasy; pinguid

pinguinitescent: shining with grease

pomadig: able to slip easily through, as though oiled

saponaceous: having the nature or quality of soap

sebaceous: fatty; oily; containing, secreting, or consisting of fat matter

slick: of hair oiled with a hair product; greased; pomaded

slippery: smooth so as to be hard to hold

soapy: resembling, containing, or consisting of soap; smeared with soap

unctuous: like a salve; greasy; soapy to the touch

unguinous: oily; greasy; oleaginous

waxy: like wax; plastic; yielding

Omission

cutoff: exluded; shut out

destuted: omitted; left out

disbarred: excluded; prevented; stopped

excluded: kept out

excluding: debarring

exclusive: shutting out or desiring to shut out

exempt: excluded

inadmissible: such as should be rejected

not included in: not embraced in

omitted: left out; excluded

unrecounted: not considered

Opalescence

hydrophanous: made transparent by wetting

margaritaceous: pearly; margaric; margarite

milky: like milk; turbid

nacreous: pearly

opalescent: reflecting a milky or pearly light

opalescine: reflecting a milky or pearly light

pearly: reflecting an almost clear light

perlaceous: pearly

semidiaphanous: half or imperfectly transparent

semiopacous: semiopaque

semiopaque: half transparent

semipellucid: imperfectly transparent

semitransparent: half or imperfectly transparent

Opportuneness

auspicious: favorable; fortunate

critical: momentous; perilous

favorable: advantageous; propitious

fortunate: happy; lucky

happy: fortunate; lucky; opportune

lucky: auspicious; fortunate

opportune: timely; fortunate; lucky

propitious: auspicious; favorable

providential: brought about by the providence of God

seasonable: timely; done at the proper time

soncy: lucky; thriving; sonsie; sonsy

suitable: fitting; appropriate

timeful: seasonable; timely

timely: opportune; seasonable

well-timed: done or said opportunely

Orange

apricot: having the color of an apricot or an orange color

brass: of the color of brass

copper: like copper in color

flame-colored: having the color of a flame of fire

glowing: exhibiting a strong bright color

hot: having a warm or yellowish red color

melon: deep pink or medium orange

ocherous: resembling ocher in color

orange: of the color of an orange or reddish yellow

orange-colored: possessing the color of an orange

rust: brownish orange; tawny

tangerine: reddish orange; carrot

tawny: brownish orange

terra-cotta: brownish orange; auburn; tawny; titian

Organization

apportioning: divided and assigned according to a plan

arranged: put together in order

cut-and-dried: arranged beforehand, like hay or firewood

embattled: arranged in order for battle

in battle array: drawn up in lines of battle

methodical: having arrangement and regularity

orderly: having order; systematic

organized: ordered and arranged

platted: laid out, arranged, as a city plan

pragmatic: treating things systematically; concerned with practical consequences

raisonné: arranged systematically; logical

regular: going according to rule

rubric: pertaining to a heading or category

systematic: acting according to a comprehensive plan

Originality

aboriginal: first or earliest; primitive

authentic: with original authority

inimitable: that cannot be copied

original: not imitated or copied

sui generis: one of a kind; unique

uncopied: not imitated

unfellowed: unmated; unmatched

unimitated: not copied

unique: without a like

unmatched: not of the same character, form, size, or quality

unparalleled: having no equal; unmatched

Orthodoxy

catholic: not heretical; in accordance with the adopted faith

Christian: of or pertaining to Christ and his doctrine

divine: pertaining to or of God

evangelical: pertaining to the fundamental Protestant doctrines

faithful: full of faith; strong in one's convictions

monotheistic: believing in one God

orthodox: sound or correct in religious doctrine

Protestant: opposed to the Roman Catholic Church

reformed: corrected or amended in religious doctrine

Romish: belonging to the Roman Catholic Church

schismless: without division in a church

scriptural: according to Scripture

sound: correct in creed

strict: observing exactly

true: correct

Outside

advenient: due to outside causes

alfresco: to the open air

ectal: exterior; external; outside

excentric: away from the center

exterior: helping to form the outside

external: closely connected with the outside

extimate: most distant; outermost; uttermost

extraforaneous: outdoor

extramundane: situated outside our world or universe; remote

extramural: outside the walls

extraregarding: looking at what is beyond us

extrinsic: unnatural; foreign

frontal: situated in the front

in the open air: outside

outdoor: in the open air

outer: farther out

outermost: farthest out

outlying: adjacent to

out-of-doors: outside

outside: pertaining to the outside

outstanding: located on the outside

outward: directed toward the outside

round about: surrounding

skin-deep: not going in far

superficial: lying on the surface

Ownership—Property

allodial: pertaining to the absolute ownership of land in distinction from feudal lands

at one's command: in one's ownership or control

at one's disposal: in one's ownership or control

blessed with: in possession of

by one: in one's possession

charged with: entrusted with or having the care of

copyhold: pertaining to tenure of land held by copy of court roll

dominial: pertaining to ownership

embosomed: taken to the bosom

endowed with: enriched or furnished with something of the nature of a gift

feodal: relating to a fee or feud

feudal: relating to a fee or feud

fraught with: laden or filled with

freehold: held by a full legal tenure

in hand: holding

in mortmain: in that state of lands and tenements held by a dead hand, that is one that cannot alienate them; in inalienable possession

in one's grasp: holding

in one's hand: holding

in one's possession: holding

in possession of: holding

in stock: in hand

in store: in hand

in strict settlement: in limitation of lands to the parent for life, and after his death to his several children successively in tail with trustees interposed to preserve contingent remainders, thus tying up the descent to the utmost limit permitted by law

inalienable: that cannot be rightfully taken away

incommunicable: that cannot be revealed to others

instinct with: imbued or alive with

laden with: loaded or burdened with

landed: consisting of real estate or land

latifundian: rich in real estate

manorial: pertaining to a manor

master of: in control of

on hand: ready

one's own: belonging to one

owning: having legal possession

possessed of: having in possession; possessed

possessing: owning

predial: consisting of lands; belonging to real estate

profectitious: pertaining to inherited property

retaining: keeping; holding

retentive: having the ability or power to retain

seized of: possessed of

tenacious: strongly disposed to keep what is in possession

uncommunicated: not communicated or bestowed

undeprived: not dispossessed of anything

undisposed: not disposed; not appropriated

unforfeited: not forfeited; kept

unseated: of land, unsettled or unoccupied

unshared: not shared

unsold: still in possession

walk-in-walk-out: in real estate, buying real estate as is

worth: having possessions or wealth equal to

Pain

a prey to: stricken by

a prey to grief: stricken by

abhorrent: detesting; repugnant to

accursed: doomed to misery or destruction

aching: painful; paining continually

acute: sharp; keen; intense

affecting: moving the emotions; pathetic

afflicted: troubled grievously

afflicting: causing suffering

afflictive: causing pain or grief; distressing

aggravating: making more heinous; provoking

agonizing: causing intense pain

algedonic: pleasingly painful; painfully pleasing

amyctic: irritating; abrasive

annoying: disturbing

anxious: troubled; very worried

aponic: pertaining to painlessness

appalling: making pale with fear

awkward: embarrassing

between hawk and buzzard: in great anxiety

biting: causing intense mental or physical suffering

bitter: having an acrid, biting taste; distressing; painful

bothering: causing trouble

brokenhearted: having the spirits broken by grief or despair

burdensome: grievous to be borne

calamitous: producing distress or misery; unhappy

careworn: burdened with care

carking: distressing; corroding

causing pain: hurtful

caustic: burning; severe; sharp

chagrined: vexed or annoyed

cheerless: without joy or comfort

comfortless: wanting comfort; in distress

concerned: anxious or solicitous for any person or thing

consuming: destroying; wasting

corroding: gnawing; wasting away

cruel: having pleasure in giving pain to others; bloody

crushed: grievously oppressed

crushing: that crushes or oppresses grievously

cumbersome: burdensome; vexatious

cumbrous: making action difficult

cut-up: injured or wounded

cutting: paining

deplorable: worthy of being lamented; causing grief

depressing: casting a gloom upon

depressive: tending to cast down

desolating: making desolate; ruining

devoted: doomed to evil

dire: evil in a degree; very calamitous
disagreeable: not agreeable; unpleasant
disastrous: attended with suffering or disaster
discontented: uneasy in mind
disgusting: sickening
disheartening: depriving of courage and hope
dismal: gloomy; depressing to the feelings
displeased: not pleased; offended; vexed
displeasing: disagreeable to
distasteful: unpleasant to the taste; offensive to the feelings
distressing: causing pain or trouble
disturbed: agitated in mind
dolorific: causing pain, anguish, grief
dolorous: full of grief; sorrowful
doomed: destined to calamity or ruin
dreadful: inspiring dread or great fear
dreary: arousing cheerless sensations or associations
enough to drive one mad: being a cause of irritation or anger
enough to make a person swear: being a cause of irritation or anger
enough to provoke a saint: being a cause of irritation or anger
envenomed: tainted with bitterness or hatred
excruciating: inflicting agonizing pain upon
execrable: very hateful; abominable
fashed: bothered; inconvenienced
fearful: inspiring fear or awe
frightful: exciting alarm or terror
full of pain: causing pain or trouble
fulsome: disgusting by excess or grossness
galling: causing pain or bitterness
grating: making a harsh sound
grave: weighty; solemn
grievous: causing grief; afflictive
grim: having a fear-inspiring aspect
grinding: oppressing by severe exactions
griped: distressed
hagridden: tormented; obsessed; overburdened

harassing: troubling continually
hard: not easy; cruel
harrowing: inflicting pain
harsh: repulsive to the sensibilities
hateful: exciting great dislike or disgust
heartbreaking: causing overpowering sorrow
heartbroken: deeply grieved
heart-corroding: causing overpowering sorrow
heartrending: causing overpowering sorrow
heart-scalded: greatly distressed
heartsickening: causing overpowering sorrow
heart-stricken: dismayed
heart-wounding: causing overpowering sorrow
heavy-laden: weighed down with care or grief
hideous: exciting terror
horrible: exciting horror or fear
horrid: suited to excite horror
horrific: causing horror
horrified: stricken with horror
horrifying: frightening
horror-stricken: struck with an excessive degree of fear with a shuddering
hurtful: causing loss or injury
hurting: causing pain or suffering
ill at ease: uneasy; anxious
ill-used: badly treated
importunate: overpressing in demand
in a state of pain: suffering
in a taking: in a fit of sickness
in a way: perplexed; discomfited
in despair: hopeless
in grief: weeping
in limbo: in confinement or imprisoned
in pain: suffering
in tears: very sorrowful
infelicitous: unhappy or unfortunate
insufferable: offensive beyond endurance
insupportable: that cannot be borne or endured
intolerable: that cannot be tolerated
invidious: likely to produce ill will

irksome: causing uneasiness by long continuance

irritating: causing trouble

joyless: without joy; not causing joy

kedogenous: brought about by worry or anxiety

lamentable: sorrowful; suited to awaken lament

loathful: hating; disgusting

loathsome: exciting loathing or disgust

lost: perplexed; bewildered

melancholy: depression of spirits, as by black bile

Melpomenish: tragic

miserable: extremely unhappy

more than flesh and blood can bear: overcoming by pain or sorrow

mortifying: disheartening; death-making

mournful: full of sorrow; saddening

nasty: disgusting; offensive

nauseating: sickening

nauseous: causing nausea or seasickness; loathsome

not to be borne: unbearable

not to be endured: unbearable

obnoxious: exposed to censure; blameworthy

odious: provoking hatred or disgust

offensive: causing pain or unpleasant sensations

on the rack: suffering torture

onerous: oppressive

oppressive: unjustly severe or harsh

out of humor: in pain; in a bad mood

pained: hurt physically or mentally

painful: full of pain; causing pain or distress

past bearing: painful or irritating, as to be unbearable

pathetic: moving to pity or grief

pestering: paining by continuous annoyance

piteous: miserable; fitted to excite pity

pitiable: worthy of pity

plaguing: worrying

plaguy: troublesome; tormenting

plunged in grief: sorrowing

poor: deserving of pity or sympathy

provoking: teasing

racking: unfeeling

rending: tearing asunder; bursting

repellent: able or tending to repel

repulsive: serving to repulse

revolting: causing gross offense to

rueful: mournful; sorrowful

ruinous: causing ruin; pernicious

sad: affected with grief; calamitous

searching: penetrating; trying

severe: sharp; distressing

sharp: keen; biting; violent

shocking: causing to recoil with horror or disgust

sickening: making sick

sore: painful; sensitive; distressing

sorrowful: full of sorrow; distressed

sorrowing: feeling pain or grief on account of evil experienced

sorry: feeling regret

steeped to the lips in misery: in a state of utter hopelessness or misery

stinging: inflicting sharp pain

stranded: left helpless or perplexed

stricken: afflicted; smitten; wounded

suffering: in pain

teasing: annoying

terrific: causing terror or great fear

thankless: ungrateful

thrilling: penetrating; feeling a tingling sensation through the body

tiresome: tending to tire; tedious

to be pitied: poor and suffering

tormenting: troublesome

torminous: pertaining to an acute, colicklike pain; torminal

torturous: causing torture or suffering

touching: affecting; pathetic

tragical: expressive of the loss of life or of sorrow

tremendous: suited to excite terror or fear; terrible

troublesome: causing trouble or anxiety

unacceptable: not acceptable

unaccommodating: not disposed to please

unbearable: that cannot be endured

uncomfortable: unpleasant
undesirable: disagreeable
undesired: disagreeable
undone: ruined
uneasy: disturbed by pain or anxiety
unendurable: not to be borne
unfortunate: not fortunate; unhappy
unhappy: sorrowful
uninviting: not wished for
unlucky: unhappy
unpalatable: not pleasant to the taste
unpleasant: not pleasant
unpleasing: not pleasant
unpopular: not pleasing to the people
unsatisfactory: unable to cause a feeling of satisfaction

untoward: perverse; troublesome
unwelcome: not desired
vexatious: causing annoyance or trouble
victimized: made a victim of; duped
vile: mean; morally impure
vulnerative: wounding; vulnific; vulnifical
wearisome: making weary or tired
weary: exhausted in patience; tired
withering: causing to languish or pass away
wobegone: steeped in grief or sorrow
woeful: causing calamity or distress
worried: harassed with care and anxiety; annoyed
worrying: causing mental pain to
wretched: sunk in affliction and distress

Painting

abstract: designating reliance on pure form rather than representation of subject matter for effect
architectonic: controlled, linear, geometric in rendering
Byzantine: designating a style with Oriental and Occidental elements and strong religious content
color-field: characteristic of abstract minimal styles without representation, line, form, or modeling, in which color is the sole element (mid-20th c.)
eclectic: composed from disparate elements in many styles
elydoric: of painting with oils and watercolors
encaustic: designating painting done with pigment mixed with beeswax and blended with heat
farded: painted; embellished
figurative: designating identifiable representation of human figure or object
hard-edge: characteristic of a style with geometric abstraction, a flat picture plane, perfection of surface, and graphic precision (U.S. mid-20th c.)
Hellenic: of the classical style of Greek antiquity

Hellenistic: of the postclassical Greek style before the Roman conquest (4th c. B.C.)
hieratic: designating a style characterized by prescribed religious content
high-toned: in painting, brilliant coloring
historiated: having human or animal figure ornament
Italianate: conforming to the style of the Italian Renaissance masters
Kamakura: denoting high classical period (Japan, 13th–15th c.)
low in tone: in painting, not very brilliant coloring
low-toned: in painting, a softened or less pronounced effect
malerisch: painterly; emphasizing form over outline
Ming: characteristic of a highly academic classicism, especially in porcelains (China, 14th–17th c.)
monochromatic: having a one-hued color scheme
monumental: indicating scale, grandeur, and nobility of form or content
nonobjective: characteristic of a style in which emotional, formal values are

emphasized over representation of objects (20th c.)

painterly: like a painter; artistic

painting: created with colors and colorful media

pastoral: designating painting that depicts rural life, often in idealized manner

plein air: pertaining to a style of painting that represents luminous effects of natural light and open-air atmosphere as contrasted with artificial light and the atmosphere of work produced in a studio (France, 19th c.)

polychromatic: painted in many colors

pre-Columbian: of or pertaining to native American art before the arrival of Columbus (pre-16th c.)

prehistoric: pertaining to cave painting and other forms of Paleolithic art

pre-Raphaelite: designating a style modeled on romanticized vision of medieval, pre-Renaissance styles (19th c.)

Renaissance: pertaining to humanistic art that is classical in form and content

representational: designating tasting art concerned with accurate, naturalistic depictions of reality

sfumato: using softening outlines or hazy forms as a painting technique

stippled: painted or designed with dots

tinctorial: relating to colors, dyes, and stains

Palatableness

alliaceous: smelling or tasting like onions or garlic

ambrosial: divinely flavored

appetizing: tending to increase or please the appetite

bigarade: flavored with orange

brackish: having a slightly salty or briny flavor

briny: salty in flavor

complex: of wine, having a variety of tastes and scents

congustable: having a similar flavor or taste

dainty: having a refined, delicate taste

delectable: delicious or appetizing

delicate: refinedly pleasing to the taste

delicious: very pleasing to taste

dry: of wines, not sweet or fruity

dulcet: sweet to the taste

eupeptic: having a good appetite and digestion

exquisite: characterized by a very delicate flavor

ferruginous: having a taste like water with high iron content

flavorful: possessing strong flavor; tasty

fruity: tasting of fruit; of wines, sweet

full-bodied: at full strength or flavor, especially of wines

gamy: having the tangy, tainted flavor of uncooked game

geusioleptic: having a pleasant flavor

gustable: pleasant to the taste

gustatory: pertaining to taste or tasting

gustful: having a good taste

honey: sweet

hot: sharply pungent or peppery

jammy: of wine, with a concentrated fruity taste

juicy: succulent; mouth-watering

lickerish: tempting the appetite

long-in-the-mouth: tough; taking a long time to chew

luscious: exceedingly delightful to the sense of taste

migniard: dainty; delicate

mouthwatering: appetizing

nectareously: excessively sweetly

nice: having a pure, refined taste

oaky: of wine, having a toasty vanilla smell and taste from aging in oak barrels

orexigenic: whetting the appetite

palatable: agreeable to the taste

peppery: hot and pungent; tasting of pepper

pickled: preserved in and tasting of brine

rich: having many qualities that are pleasant to the taste
saccharine: very sweet; artificially sweet
saline: salty
salt: producing that one of the four basic taste sensations that is not sweet, sour, or bitter
salty: tasting of salt
sapid: affecting the taste
saporific: imparting or producing flavor
saporous: tasty; flavorful
savory: having a pleasing flavor
scrumptious: delicious
sec: of wine, dry, not sweet
sipid: tasty; flavorful
spicy: piquant or pungent; seasoned with spices
strong: having a powerful, dominant, specific flavor

succulent: juicy and full of good flavor
sugary: sweet like sugar
sweet: tasting of sugar or honey; being one of the four basic taste sensations
sweet-and-sour: combining the tastes of sugar or honey and vinegar or lemon juice
syrupy: very sweet, especially of viscous liquids
tasteless: having no distinct flavor
tasty: good-tasting; delicious; savory
toothful: eaten with enjoyment
toothsome: agreeable to the taste; palatable
treacly: extremely, sometimes sickly, sweet
uranic: pertaining to the palate
well-tasted: with a good taste
zesty: agreeably piquant

Parentage

adopted: taken by adoption
adoptive: relating to adoption
agnate: having the same male ancestor
akin: of the same family
allied: bound by common family ties
ampherotokous: blessed with boys and girls
ancestral: pertaining to an ancestor
aval: pertaining to grandparents
avunculocal: pertaining to a maternal uncle
biparental: relating to or derived from both parents
close-knit: bound together by intimate social or familial ties
cognate: having common blood
collateral: indirectly descended from the same ancestor
congenital: existing at birth
connate: congenitally united; born together
consanguineous: lineally descended from a common ancestor
familial: of or relating to the family
family: of or belonging to a family

filial: of or pertaining to a son or daughter
full-blooded: of pure, unmixed ancestry
hereditary: passing naturally from parent to child
kindred: of the same family
linear: descendant in a direct line
maternal: characteristic of, related to, or inherited from mother
matrilineal: pertaining to the mother's side of a family
matrilocal: designating extended family in which husband joins household of wife's parents; uxorilocal
matroclinous: resembling the mother; matroclinal; matroclinic
neolocal: living away from both husband's and wife's relatives
nerled: ill-treated, as by a stepmother
novercal: relating to one's stepmother
orbate: parentless; childless
parental: characteristic of a father or mother
paternal: characteristic of, related to, or inherited from father

patriarchal: pertaining to the head of a family

patricentric: dominated by the father or father's side

patrilineal: tracing descent through father's line

patrilocal: characteristic of, related to, or inherited from the father; virilocal

patroclinous: resembling the father; patriclinous

philoprogenitive: producing offspring; having deep affection for one's children

spoiled: designating child overindulged by parents and lacking restraint or responsibility

unfathered: raised by mother only

unfilial: not befitting child's relations with parents

unilineal: having descent traced through either male or female line

uxorilocal: matrilocal

virilocal: patrilocal

Particularness

censorious: given to censuring or faultfinding

dainty: very refined or particular in taste

delicate: very refined; dainty

difficult to please: fastidious

fastidious: overdelicate; very hard to please

finical: overnice or fastidious in matters of dress or manners

hard to please: fastidious

hypercritical: extremely or unduly critical

jimp: dainty; well-formed; well-fitting

lickerish: having a keen relish; lustful

nice: very refined; overparticular in tastes or habits

particular: separate and distinct from others in a group

pleasing: agreeable to the tastes or habits

queasy: very particular in matters of eating; squeamish

querulous: given to finding fault

scrupulous: very particular and careful in matters of right and wrong

squeamish: easily disgusted or shocked in matters of taste or conscience

straitlaced: strict in morals or manners

thin-skinned: sensitive; easily offended

Passiveness

anthropurgic: done or acted upon by humans

fallow: untilled; neglected

impassive: devoid of passion; unsusceptible to feeling

inactive: idle; inert

lethargic: of a slowness to react or respond

out of employ: without work

passive: not active, but acted upon

pathic: passive; suffering

phlegmatic: undemonstrative; phlegmatical

undone: not worked upon; neglected

unemployed: not engaged to work

unoccupied: not working

Past

ancestral: pertaining to ancestors

archaeological: relating to the study of ancient cultures

blown over: dropped and forgotten

bygone: past

ci-devant: has-been, of a notable; former, erstwhile

elapsed: passed away

expired: terminated

exploded: suddenly come to an end

extinct: no longer existing, said of species of animals
foregoing: preceding
foregone: decided beforehand
forgotten: not held in mind anymore
former: past
gone: past
gone by: past
hesternal: pertaining to yesterday
irrecoverable: not to be regained or restored
lapsed: passed away slowly
last: final in order of time
late: recent; coming after the appointed time
latter: the following of two things mentioned
looking back: thinking about the past
never to return: finished; not happening or returning again
no more: past
nudiustertian: pertaining to the day before yesterday
obsolete: gone out of use

over: past
overnight: during the night
passed away: elapsed
past: gone
preterite: past; bygone; former
preteritial: concerned with past events; praeteritial
preterlapsed: past and gone
preterperfect: the perfect tense in grammar
preterpluperfect: pluperfect
pridian: pertaining to the day before yesterday
pristine: belonging to the earliest period or state
quondam: former; onetime
recent: happened lately
retroactive: affecting past acts
retrospective: looking back
run-out: expired; worn-out; ended
sometime: former
that has been: now no longer existing
thenadays: in those days; in time past
whilom: former or formerly; once but no longer
yestern: pertaining to yesterday

Peace

bloodless: not attended by the shedding of blood
calm: free from violent agitation or noise
composed: calm
halcyon: calm; in an interval among storms
incruental: bloodless; incruent
irenic: conducive to peaceful relations

pacific: disposed to make peace
pacificatory: pacifying
pacifist: opposing war or violence
peaceable: not disposed to engage in quarrels; peaceful
peaceful: exempt from commotion
tranquil: not agitated
untroubled: not troubled

Performing Arts

black-and-white: displaying monochrome reproduction of television images
boffo: highly successful, especially as designating a box office hit
CC: closed-captioned
cinematic: characteristic of films or the art of filmmaking
closed-captioned: CC; designating programs having subtitles for hearing-

impaired viewers, with captions appearing only on specially equipped television sets
dark: description of theater on night without performance
featured: designating an actor with a significant part, often named in opening credits
hard-core: pruriently explicit, as in pornography that vividly depicts sex acts

in-the-can: designating a completed program or material that has been shot

live: broadcast as event or performance occurs, as opposed to prerecorded

OC: on camera

off book: designating rehearsal for which actors must have lines memorized

off-camera: designating activity unseen by viewers

offscreen: OS; taking place away from the screen, as a character's voice

OS: offscreen

performing: that does something, such as acting

prerecorded: taped or filmed prior to broadcast

quadraphonic: designating transmission of FM signals using four channels

recurring: occurring regularly, especially of characters on program

rolling: indication that cameras are shooting scene

soft-core: sexually stimulating, as in pornography that features nudity but not explicit sex acts

stagestruck: infatuated with performing and the theater

stand-up: designating comedy in form of monologue delivered while standing alone before audience

stereophonic: designating transmission of FM radio signals using two channels

strawhat: pertaining to summer theater

taped: prerecorded; not live

wide-screen: denoting panoramic dimension in film projection

wild: designating recording of sound separately from picture

X-rated: rating designating sexually explicit film not to be viewed by persons under seventeen, now replaced by NC-17; still used in reference to pornography

Perfume

ambrosial: divinely fragrant

antibromic: deodorant

aromatic: having a pleasing scent or odor

balmy: fragrant like aromatic balm

euodic: aromatic

fragrant: having a sweet or pleasing odor

libanophorous: scented; producing incense

muscadine: having the fragrance of the Southern fox grape

olent: fragrant; having an odor

perfumatory: yielding a pleasant odor

perfumed: sweet-scented

redolent: diffusing a pervasive odor; fragrant

rose: sweetly scented like a rose

rosewatered: delicate; sentimental; perfumed

savory: agreeable in smell; especially fragrant

scented: smelling

spicy: having a pungent odor

suaveolent: sweet-smelling

sweet: fragrant, perfumed, or fresh to the smell

sweet-scented: pleasing to the smell

sweet-smelling: pleasing to the smell

thuriferous: producing or bearing frankincense

Permanence

conservative: disposed or tending to maintain existing conditions

established: made firm; well-founded

intact: left entire

inviolate: unbroken; unhurt

monotonous: kept up with wearying uniformity

permanent: lasting

persistent: inclined to remain firm

persisting: staying; holding firm

stable: resistant to change
stationary: not moving; fixed
unchanged: not changed
uncheckered: undiversified

unfailing: incapable of being exhausted
unrenewed: the same as before
unrepealed: not canceled
unsuppressed: not subdued

Persistence

constant: unchangeably fixed; continuous
game to the last: unyielding to the end
indefatigable: unremitting in labor or effort
indomitable: that cannot be subdued
industrious: assiduously occupied in some work or pursuit
never-tiring: always at work
persevering: continuing
persistent: inclined to remain firm
persisting: tenacious of purpose
pertinacious: stubbornly persistent
plodding: working laboriously
sedulous: diligent; persistent; persevering
solid: firm
staunch: constant and zealous
steadfast: firm in devotion to duty
steady: constant in purpose
steady as time: constant
strenuous: eagerly pressing; zealous

sturdy: resolute in a good sense; having an unyielding quality
true to oneself: unchangeable in purpose
unchangeable: not subject to change
unconquerable: indomitable
undeviating: not deviating or turning aside from its course
undrooping: not to be dispirited or depressed
unfaltering: not hesitating or trembling
unflagging: not languishing or drooping
unflinching: not failing in persevering or doing
unintermitting: not being interrupted
unremitting: incessant
unsleeping: vigilant
unswerving: not departing from a rule of duty
untiring: never becoming weary or fatigued
unwavering: fixed in opinion
unwearied: persistent; indefatigable

Persuasion

attractive: possessing the power to allure or win over; pleasing
disposed: inclined toward
fascinating: charming; enchanting; very pleasing
hortative: inciting; encouraging
hortatory: inciting; encouraging
impulsive: moved by feeling rather than reflection
induced: influenced as by persuasion to do some act
inspired by: stimulated; influenced
instinct with: animated with; imbued with
inviting: pleasing; attractive
motive: having the power to incite to action

persuadable: open to influence or persuasion
persuasive: having the power to persuade or influence
protreptic: persuasive
protreptical: hortatory
provocative: having the power to incite or influence
seductive: having the power to seduce or lead astray
smitten with: overcome with; very much attracted by
spellbound: influenced or fascinated, as by a magic charm
suasive: persuasive
swasivious: agreeably persuasive
tempting: attractive; seductive

Petition

cap in hand: submissive or servile

clamorous: making or made with any loud, repeated outcry

importunate: persistent in entreaty

mendicant: reduced to beggary

on one's bended knees: in an attitude of supplication

on one's knees: in an attitude of supplication

on one's marrowbones: in an attitude of supplication

petitioning: humbly begging

precatory: given to entreaty

requesting: asking with authority

suppliant: asking or entreating fervently; supplicant

supplicatory: expressing supplication

urgent: eagerly importunate or insistent

Philosophy

a fortiori: even more certain, for an even stronger reason

a posteriori: from what comes later; derived from experience; based on empirical data; from a particular instance to a general law

a priori: from what precedes; independent of and prior to experience; based on reason or inherent logic; independent of empirical data; from a general law to a particular instance

analytic: being of a type of proposition or statement inherently true by virtue of its terms' meanings

antiestablishment: working against existing power structure

biconditional: designating a proposition that asserts the mutual interdependence of two things or events

card-carrying: firmly identified with one party or group, especially Communist party

centrist: being party of moderate views positioned at middle of one's own party

circular: describing reasoning in which apparently proved conclusion has been assumed as premise

corporeal: relating to the body or physical matter

discursive: characterized by analysis

domestic: relating to political affairs carried on within one's own country

empirical: pertaining to the senses dependent on experience and direct observation

heuristic: characterized by ability to persuade or reveal rather than to convince logically

immanent: existing within the mind only

indisputable: incontestable; self-evidently true

invalid: incorrectly argued; not logically based on premises

irrefragable: irrefutable; undeniable

irrefutable: not capable of being refuted or disproved

maieutic: pertaining to the Socratic method for clarifying ideas

middle-of-the-road: moderate

nonpartisan: holding views and policies without regard to party

partisan: advocating or based on views of one party

philosophical: pertaining to the love, study, or pursuit of wisdom or knowledge

poetic: apprehended by the emotions

political: of or relating to elections and government functions

rational: having reason; capable of reasoning

reactionary: holding ultraconservative political views that firmly support status quo and advocate suppression of those favoring change

sound: having premises that are true and a conclusion that is valid

transeunt: producing an effect outside the mind

ultraconservative: reactionary; right-wing; extremely conservative

undemocratic: lacking in adherence to democratic principles

valid: correctly argued as a conclusion based on premises

vice versa: expressed as contrary of original statement

zetetic: seeking by inquiry

Physics

adiabatic: designating process in which no energy is transferred between a system and its surroundings

amorphous: describing a solid without crystalline structure

diamagnetic: describing substances containing only paired electrons in which a magnetic field is induced in the opposite direction to that of an applied field

electronegative: having the ability to attract electrons in a molecule and form negative ions; nonmetallic

electropositive: tending to migrate to the negative pole in electrolysis; basic, as an element or group

endothermic: absorbing heat energy

exothermic: releasing heat energy

ferromagnetic: designating a metal strongly capable of modifying a magnetic field and in which magnetization persists after removal of an applied field

immiscible: designating two liquids that will not dissolve in each other

insoluble: incapable of being dissolved in specific solvent

isobaric: occurring at constant pressure

isoelectronic: possessing same number of valence electrons

isothermic: occurring at constant temperature

miscible: designating two liquids that are mutually soluble in all proportions

neutral: having neither positive nor negative electric charge

nonpolar: describing a covalent bond between two atoms with equal electron attraction, or a molecule with no charged ends

paramagnetic: describing substances containing one or more unpaired electrons, in which a magnetic field is induced in the same direction as that of an applied field

physical: pertaining to the properties of matter and energy

polar: describing a covalent bond in which one atom has a stronger electron attraction than the other, or a molecule with oppositely charged ends

spontaneous: occurring without outside influence

Plan

accessory: aiding the principal design or assisting subordinately the chief agent

doctrinaire: applying theories without regard for practical considerations; theoretical; speculative

in course of preparation: during planning

moot: undecided; doubtful; under consideration

on the carpet: under consideration

on the tapis: on the table or under consideration

planned: prepared for action

planning: preparing for action

schematic: having a planned design

strategic: pertaining to strategy or effected by strategy

strategical: pertaining to strategy or effected by strategy

Pleasure

acceptable: worthy of being accepted with pleasure

agreeable: pleasing to the mind or senses

alluring: attractive

anhedonic: incapable of experiencing happiness or pleasure

apolaustic: fond of pleasure; self-indulgent

appetizing: exciting any physical craving or desire

at ease: without care

attractive: drawing by moral influence or pleasing emotion

beatic: happy

beatific: having power to impart blissful enjoyment

beatified: made happy

beneplacit: pleased; satisfied

bewitching: charming

blessed: enjoying happiness

blest: enjoying happiness

blissful: full of joy and felicity

captivated: charmed or fascinated

captivating: charming

causing pleasure: delighting

charming: attractive

cheerful: of a naturally contented disposition

cheering: comforting

cloudless: clear; bright

comfortable: giving comfort or consolation

conciliatory: tending to conciliate

content: completely satisfied

contented: completely satisfied

cordial: sincere; affectionate; giving strength or spirits

dainty: delicate; elegant in manner or breeding

delectable: very pleasing

delicate: pleasing to the senses

delicious: affording great pleasure; charming

delightful: highly pleasing

dulcet: sweet to the ear

ecstatic: immeasurably delightful

elysian: relating to the abode of the blessed after death; pleasing in the highest degree

empyrean: pertaining to the highest and purest region of heaven

enchanted: under the power of enchantment

enchanting: charming

engaging: attractive

enjoying: deriving pleasure from

enraptured: transported with pleasure

enravished: delighted beyond measure

enravishing: delighting

enticing: having power to entice or allure

entranced: ravished with delight

entrancing: charming

evancalous: pleasant to embrace

exquisite: of surpassing quality; delightfully excellent

fallback: less satisfactory but acceptable

fascinated: operated on by an irresistible charm

fascinating: having an irresistible power over

favorite: regarded with particular affection or preference

felicific: producing happiness

felicitous: delightful; prosperous

gemutlich: cozy; comfortable; homey

genial: sympathetically cheerful and happy

glad: moderately joyful

gladsome: pleased; causing joy

gled: glad

grateful: willing to acknowledge favors; affording pleasure

gratifying: satisfying a desire

haimish: homey; cozy

halcyon: calm; peaceful

happy: enjoying good of any kind

happy as a king: an expression denoting degree of enjoyment

happy as the day is long: an expression denoting degree of enjoyment

heartfelt: sincere; hearty

in a blissful state: happy

in a transport of delight: delighted

in ecstasies: in a state or condition of overcoming pleasure

in paradise: in a state or condition of overcoming pleasure

in raptures: in a state of agreeable excitement

inviting: alluring; tempting

joyful: full of joy

killing: captivating; irresistible

leef: pleasing; agreeable

lepid: pleasant; charming

lief: pleasing; agreeable

lovely: charming; amiable

luscious: pertaining to luxury

nice: delicate; dainty

not sorry: glad

overjoyed: extremely gratified

painless: without pain

palatable: agreeable to the taste; acceptable

palmy: prosperous; flourishing

pleasant: agreeable to the mind or senses

pleased: enjoying

pleased as punch: very much pleased

pleasing: giving pleasure

pleasurable: capable of giving pleasure

pleasure-giving: pleasing

prepossessing: attracting confidence, esteem, or love

queme: agreeable; pleasant; suitable

raptured: enraptured

rapturous: ecstatic; transporting

ravished: delighted to ecstasy

ravishing: transporting

refreshing: reviving

resigned: submitting cheerfully

satisfactory: giving satisfaction

satisfied: pleased

Saturnian: distinguished for peacefulness, as the reign of Saturn

seducing: enticing from the right

sensual: given to the pleasures of sense and appetite

seraphic: sublime; angelic

serene: of a calm mind

suant: agreeable; placid; demure

suboptimal: less desirable or satisfactory than hoped for

sweet: pleasing to the senses or mind; amiable; winning

sybaritic: devoted to pleasure; hedonistic

taking: attracting

thrice happy: very happy

thrilling: producing a tingling or exquisite sensation

to one's liking: pleasing

to one's mind: pleasing

to one's taste: pleasing

tolerable: bearable

transported: carried away with pleasure

unafflicted: not suffering from injury

unalloyed: not mixed with misfortune

unmolested: not vexed

unplagued: not teased

unrepining: not discontented

unvexed: not irritated

voluptuous: ministering to sensual gratification or given to the enjoyment of luxury and pleasure

welcome: received gladly; grateful

welcome as the roses in May: delightful

welcomed: received or saluted with kindness

wilcweme: satisfied

winning: suited to gain favor

winsome: charming; endearing

with a joyful face: delighted

with sparkling eyes: happy

without alloy: with unrestrained pleasure

Poetry

acatalectic: said of a verse having the required number of feet

acromonogrammatic: applied to a passage or verse in which each line begins with the letter with which the preceding line ended

alcaic: of or like the poetry of Alcaeus; having the meter of Alcaeus

anapestic: having for its principal foot an anapest

catalectic: incomplete; having one or two syllables lacking to make a complete verse

dithyrambic: passionately lyrical; rhapsodic; wild and irregular

elegiac: pertaining to or having the characteristics of an elegy

epic: having the characteristics of an epic poem

iambic: having its principal foot an iambus

idyllic: having the qualities of a pastoral poem

Ionic: pertaining to Ionia, or its poetry or literature

lyric: pertaining to lyric poetry

lyrical: pertaining to lyric poetry

melic: lyric, as song or poetry

metrical: put in poetical measure; relating to meter

Pierian: concerning poetry or learning

Pindaric: relating to Pindar, a Greek lyric poet

poetic: relating or pertaining to poetry

poetical: relating or pertaining to poetry

sapphic: relating to Sappho, a writer of amatory poems and lyrics

sdrucciola: having a triple rhyme that accents the third syllable from the end

tragicomipastoral: of pastoral tragicomic poetry

trochaic: having principal foot a trochee

tuneful: harmonious; musical; poetical

Politeness

affable: courteous in intercourse

bland: having a pleasantness of talk or manners

civil: observing slight courtesies

civilized: advanced in civilization

complacent: agreeable; courteous

complaisant: agreeable; courteous

conciliatory: tending to gain the goodwill of another

cordial: hearty

courteous: gracefully respectful

cultivated: refined

fair-spoken: having grace of speech

familiar: closely acquainted

fine-spoken: speaking politely

gallant: very attentive to women

gentle: quiet and refined in manners

gentlemanlike: becoming a gentleman

good-humored: of a friendly and easy disposition

good-mannered: well-bred

gracious: disposed to do good to those who have deserved ill

Grandisonian: gentlemanly; heroic

honey-mouthed: sweet or persuasive of speech

honey-tongued: sweet or persuasive of speech

ingratiating: making oneself acceptable by one's pleasing manners

mannerly: showing good manners

mild: having the qualities of harshness and severity subdued

neighborly: social

obliging: disposed to do services for others

obsequious: striving to gain another's favor by consulting his pleasure and making personal sacrifice

off-capped: having taken off caps or hats as form of courtesy

oily: deceitfully complaisant

polished: having all roughness of manner and speech removed
polite: showing proper respect according to the rules of society
refined: freed from everything coarse, low, vulgar, or inelegant
soft-spoken: having a soft or gentle voice
urbane: having polite manners; polite; suave

well-behaved: polite and gentlemanly
well-bred: polite and gentlemanly
well-brought-up: polite and gentlemanly
well-mannered: polite and gentlemanly
winning: attractive

Position

abaxial: off the center line; eccentric
abutting: touching at border, especially ending at contact point
adaxial: on the same side as or facing the axis
adjacent: nearby; just before or facing; adjoining
adjoining: connected at point or along line
advance: located before others
akimbo: with the elbows projecting outward, usually by placing hands on hips
aknee: on one's knee or knees
ambient: encompassing on all sides
anterior: located toward the front; before
antipodal: at the opposite side of the globe
apical: at the highest point
apposed: placed side by side or in proximity
arrayed: lined up; aligned; ranged
at hand: in close proximity
axial: along a central line
back-to-back: facing in opposite directions from a common point
balanced: in equilibrium due to even distribution of weight on all sides
bordering: located or in contact at the edge
catercorner: located diagonally opposite; kitty-corner
caudal: at or toward the tail or posterior end
central: at or near the center; in the middle

centric: in or at the center; central; focused on a center
chirognostic: able to distinguish right from left
circumambient: being on all sides
circumferential: pertaining to the circumference
circumjacent: bordering on all sides
close: being near; having little space between elements
coaxial: having a common axis
coextensive: having identical spatial extent or boundaries
coincident: filling the same space
colinear: having corresponding parts arranged along the same straight line
collateral: parallel or conforming in position or order; running side by side
collinear: lying in or sharing the same straight line
concentric: having a common center
confocal: having a common focus
consecutive: following one another in unbroken order
conterminous: having a common boundary; lying within one common boundary
contiguous: touching along one side or at some point; adjacent
convenient: close at hand; accessible
convergent: coming together in a line; converging; intersecting
converse: reversed
coplanar: occupying the same plane
coterminous: having the same boundary
covering: entirely enclosing or overlaying

crisscross: intersecting; having a number of crossing lines or paths

crossed: intersecting at a specific point

deasil: toward the right; clockwise; deiseal

decussate: crossed or intersected

deep: extending far from surface or edge, especially downward

detached: not connected; separate

discontinuous: not continued; discrete; out of or without sequence

discrete: consisting of separate, unattached elements; constituting a distinct individual or entity

distal: farthest from the point of attachment or origin; terminal

distant: far away; separated by a wide space

distinct: separate; clearly differentiated from others

dorsal: near or on the back

dorsolateral: on both the back and sides

encircling: forming a circle around

enclosed: surrounded on all sides

enclosing: surrounding on all sides; encircling

encompassing: enclosing; forming a border around

enveloping: completely enclosing

equidistant: equally spaced from a fixed point

equitant: overlapping, as leaves

erect: in upright or vertical position

even: at the same level or point

exterior: situated on or outside a surface; beyond the bounds of

external: outside; beyond the surface of

face-to-face: in direct contact, with front sides directed toward each other

facing: with front surface directed toward

far: at a great distance

farther: more distant; more remote

farthest: at the greatest possible distance

first: situated at the beginning or in front

flanking: lying beside, often on both sides

flush: even with the edge of; directly in contact

fore: toward the front; forward

forward: situated at or toward the front

fringe: at the edge

fronting: lying before; facing

gardant: positioned so that one sees the full face and a side view of the body

grufeling: closely wrapped and comfortable in a lying posture

guardant: shown full-face

halfway: at the midpoint

hanging: suspended from a point

hindmost: nearest the rear position

hithermost: nearest on a specific side

immediate: present; near at hand; without intervening space

indoors: situated or occurring within a roofed structure

infradig: below or unworthy of one's position, dignity, character

inner: situated farther within; being closer to the center

innermost: farthest inward

insessorial: perching

interior: located within fixed boundaries

intermediate: in the middle; between two points

interposed: placed between; intervening

intersecting: crossing at a point

interspersed: scattered at intervals among

intervening: lying or placed between

inverted: with top and bottom parts reversed

kitty-corner: catercorner

last: situated farthest to the rear; after all others

lateral: situated at or directed to the side

leeward: facing away from the source of wind

levitated: elevated into the air in apparent defiance of gravity

local: pertaining to or existing in a locality

long-distance: located at a great distance

low: lying close to or at the bottom point

lower: situated below; in a lesser position than another

malposed: badly placed

medial: in the middle

median: being in the middle or in an intermediate position

mid: situated in a middle position; amid; amidst

middle: halfway between extremes; intermediate

midway: halfway; in the middle of a distance

nearby: close at hand

next: immediately before or following nearest

obverse: facing the observer, often in opposition

one-way: designating roadway for movement in one direction only

opposite: situated across from or at the other side of an intervening space

outdoors: situated or occurring outside any enclosure or beneath open air

outer: situated relatively farther out or distant from center

outmost: farthest from the center

outside: located beyond a boundary or outer surface; external; outdoors

overlying: situated directly above and entirely covering

padmasana: in a cross-legged position; lotus position

parallel: extending in the same direction, at all points equidistant, and not converging

pendent: suspended; hanging

peripheral: situated at the external boundary or surface

perpendicular: exactly at right angles to a flat surface or plane

plumb: perpendicular; exactly vertical

point-blank: direct; at very close range

polycentric: having more than one center

port: located on the left side, especially of a vessel

positioned: placed or situated in a certain location; occupying a position

posterior: located toward the rear; behind

prone: having front surface facing downward

prostrate: lying facedown on the ground

proximal: near; especially close to the center

proximate: next to; very near

quincunx: of an arrangement of five things so that four occupy the corner and one is in the center of a square or rectangle

rear: toward or at the back

reclining: leaning backward from vertical position

rectilinear: lying in or forming a straight line; lineal; linear; rectilineal

recumbent: lying down; reclining; leaning

remote: far or distant

retral: located at or toward the back; posterior

ringside: located around a ring

rolled: turned around itself

separate: disconnected in space; distinct from others

sinistral: toward the left

situate: having a fixed or relative position

situated: having or designating a specific location

square: exactly aligned; straight; level

starboard: located on the right side, especially of a vessel

stationary: fixed in position

stoss: facing in the direction of a glacial impact

suburban: of or pertaining to a suburb

suburbicarian: belonging to suburbs

successive: following one after another

superior: located higher up or above

superjacent: overlying

supine: on back with front surface facing upward

surrounding: going completely around

suspended: hanging freely from a point

topical: belonging to a place; local

topographical: pertaining to topography or, in general, to relative position

transverse: reaching across, especially at right angles to front-back axis of object

ulterior: lying on the far side; more remote

ultimate: farthest, especially most remote; last in series

uppermost: located at the highest position

ventral: situated on the front side of a body

windward: facing toward the source of wind

zonal: pertaining to or having the shape of a zone

Possibility

accessible: capable of being reached or attained

achievable: capable of being done

apt to: likely to

at the mercy of: completely in the power of

attainable: that which can be attained or acquired

compatible: able to exist together

compossible: pertaining to coexistence being possible

conceivable: able to be conceived; apprehensible

contingent: liable but not certain to occur; dependent on another event

credible: possible to be believed

dependent on: subject to; inferior to

exposed to: rendered accessible to anything

feasible: able to be executed or done

in danger: in a state of exposure to peril, pain, or any other evil

in posse: potentially but not actually

incident to: apt to occur

incidental: happening as an accidental event

liable: likely possible

magari: odd, if only it were so; perhaps

obnoxious to: exposed; liable

obtainable: possible of being attained or acquired

on the cards: likely to happen

on the dice: possible to happen

open to: accessible to

peradventure: perhaps

performable: able to be accomplished

possible: likely or liable to come to pass or happen

practicable: able to be practiced; feasible

subject: exposed to; liable

superable: able to be overcome

surmountable: rising above; able to conquer

tessarian: pertaining to dice; gambling

unexempt from: not free from

within range of: within reach

within reach: capable of being attained or done

within the bounds of possibility: liable to happen

Poverty

badly off: unfortunately situated; not well-off

barefooted: having the feet bare; poor

beggarly: miserably poor; mean

bereaved: made destitute, as by the death of a relative

bereft: deprived of something as of hope and strength

depauperate: poor; impoverished

destitute: lacking comforts or necessaries of life

distressed: painfully losing what is useful or desirable

dowerless: without a dowry

egestuous: very poor; needy

embarrassed: involved in pecuniary difficulties

fleeced: robbed or plundered

fortuneless: without a fortune; luckless

hard up: in want of money; needy

ill off: unfortunately situated; not well-off

impecunious: without money; poor

in want: very destitute in means of subsistence; needy

indigent: without the means of subsistence

insolvent: unable to pay debts

involved: entangled financially

moneyless: without money

necessitous: pressed with poverty; very needy

needy: very poor; lacking the means of living

not worth a rap: of little account or value

obolary: extremely poor

out at elbows: in a poverty-stricken condition

out at heels: in a poverty-stricken condition

out at pocket: in a poverty-stricken condition

out of money: destitute of money; lacking funds

penniless: without money

pinched: in a starved or distressed condition

poor: having small means

poor as a church mouse: destitute of material riches or goods

poor as a rat: destitute of material riches or goods

poor as Job: destitute of material riches or goods

poorly off: unfortunately situated; not well-off

poverty-stricken: suffering from poverty

put to one's last shifts: on the last resources

put to one's shifts: on the last resources

reduced: diminished in standing

scunt: bankrupt, as in marble games

seedy: poor; shabbily dressed

short of cash: without or nearly without money

short of money: without or nearly without money

straitened: pressed with poverty or other necessity

stripped: made destitute; divested of possessions

unable to keep the wolf from the door: incapable of supplying wants

unable to make both ends meet: not able to make income cover expenses

under hatches: in a state of depression or poverty

unmoneyed: not having money

unportioned: not endowed with portion or fortune

without a rap: moneyless; extremely poor

Power—Strongness

able: having competent power, skill, or knowledge to do or accomplish; having intellectual powers

able-bodied: having a strong body

adamantine: too strong to be subdued

adequate: having sufficient power; suitable to the difficulty

all-powerful: having the strength to do everything

almighty: all powerful

Antaean: pertaining to the legendary Antaeus, an invincible wrestler

athletic: strong from exercise

Atlantean: of gigantic strength

bellipotent: powerful in war

brawny: having large and strong muscles

broad-shouldered: having strong and well-developed shoulders

buirdly: stout; strong; well-built

capable: able to comprehend; having mental ability

cervicose: having a strong neck

cogent: convincing in argument or logic

competent: having requisite qualifications to perform

cryptodynamic: pertaining to or having hidden power

cyclopean: very strong and savage

deep-rooted: deep-seated

effective: having power to produce a given effect

effectual: producing an effect

efficacious: producing an intended effect

efficient: producing results; able; competent

endothermic: absorbing energy

equal to: equivalent to in strength or power

exothermic: releasing energy

forcible: possessing force; energetic

galliard: valiant; hardy; sturdy

gigantic: of great and unusual strength

hard: possessing great endurance

hardy: strong to endure fatigue

herculean: of remarkable strength

ignipotent: having power over fire

impregnable: that cannot be influenced by strength

in fine feather: elated on account of the possession of strength

in full force: with unrestrained force

in full swing: with unrestrained force

in high feather: conscious of strength

in the plenitude of power: with the greatest fullness of power

incontestable: too evident to be questioned

indomitable: too strong to be subdued

inextinguishable: too strong to be repressed

influential: having or exerting an influence

invincible: that cannot be overcome by strength

irresistible: that cannot be opposed by strength

like a giant refreshed: with great strength

made of iron: very strong to endure

male: of superior strength

manful: having the strong and courageous nature of a man

manlike: possessing the strength of a man

manly: strong in a manner becoming a man

masculine: strong and vigorous

maximious: of great power

mighty: very forcible

more than a match for: superior in strength

multipotent: having the power to do many things

muscular: having strong muscles

omnipotent: all powerful

overpowering: bearing down by superior strength

overwhelming: crushing with sudden and irresistible force

plenipotent: having full power

potent: having power to accomplish a result

potential: existing in possibility

powerful: possessing great force, energy, or power

productive: having the power of producing or bringing forth

proof against: too strong to be influenced by

puissant: strong and mighty

resistless: too strong to be withstood

robust: having perfect strength

rounceval: large and strong, said of bones

sinewy: strong and vigorous

sound as a roach: perfectly sound

sovereign: possessing the greatest strength

stalwart: strong in frame

sthenic: having great strength and vitality

stout: possessing muscular strength

strapping: physically well-developed

strong: having great physical power

strong as a horse: a figurative expression denoting degree of strength

strong as a lion: a figurative expression denoting degree of strength

strong as brandy: a figurative expression denoting degree of strength

stubborn: obstinately headstrong
sturdy: exhibiting rugged strength
thick-ribbed: having a sturdy constitution
unallayed: not diminished
unconquerable: not to be overcome by force
unexhausted: not having all its strength used up
unquenchable: that cannot be suppressed
unshaken: not weakened in strength
unweakened: not made feeble

unwithered: not having lost its freshness and strength
unworn: having lost none of its strength from use
up to: engaged in; about
valid: based on facts; sound and strong
vigorous: strong in an active and lively manner
virile: strong like a mature male
well-knit: having a strong and compact frame
wight: brave and strong
wiry: thin and strong
yauld: active; strong; vigorous; yald

Predetermination

advised: done with a purpose; counseled
advisedly: deliberately; with conscious intent
aforethought: premeditated
calculated: ascertained or determined by a process of thought
cunning: having craft or forethought
designed: specifically purposed or intended
intended: settled as to the mind upon a purpose; designed
maturely considered: well and carefully considered

predesigned: designed beforehand
predetermined: decided or determined beforehand
premeditated: thought over well beforehand
prepense: considered beforehand
studied: closely examined; premeditated
well-devised: determined after careful consideration
well-laid: determined after careful consideration
well-weighed: determined after careful consideration

Preparation

afloat: in a floating condition; moving
afoot: able to walk
annonary: pertaining to provisions
armed at all points: fully prepared
armed to the teeth: armed from head to foot
at harness: prepared for action
at one's post: ready
booted and spurred: ready for riding
cut and dried: prepared beforehand
elaborate: highly and thoroughly finished
forthcoming: ready to appear
graith: prepared
handy: ready at hand
hatching: producing

highly wrought: well-finished
in agitation: excited
in arms: prepared for war
in battle array: ready for battle
in best bib and tucker: in best attire
in course of preparation: unfinished
in embryo: in progress of growth
in full feather: fully developed
in gear: in working order
in hand: in progress
in harness: at work
in practice: training
in preparation: training
in readiness: prepared
in reserve: prepared for action
in saddle: ready for riding

in store for: ready for use
in training: exercising
in war paint: ready for fighting
in working gear: ready for work
in working order: prepared for work
inchoate: in an imperfect state
labored: earnestly engaged in some labor; thoroughly prepared
made to one's hand: ready for use
mature: completely developed
mellow: ripened
on foot: in progress
on the alert: watchful
on the anvil: ready to be worked on
on the stocks: ready for action
on the table: ready for discussion
practiced: trained
precautionary: having prudent forethought
preliminary: preparatory; antecedent

preparative: serving to make ready
preparatory: serving to make ready
prepared: ready
preparing: making ready
provident: exercising foresight
provisional: provided for a present service
ready: prepared for use or action
ready to one's hand: ready for use
ready-made: fit to be used
ripe: grown to maturity
smelling of the lamp: laboriously prepared, like the orations of Demosthenes
sword in hand: prepared for battle
under consideration: in mental preparation
under revision: in mental preparation; being edited mentally or physically
up in arms: ready to fight
worked up: excited

Presence

anywhen: at any time
commorant: residing
domiciled: provided with a home
endemic: constantly present in an area
full of people: well-populated
inhabited: occupied by people
inhabiting: dwelling
moored: fastened
occupying: holding
omnipresent: present in all places at the same time
peopled: having people

populous: full of people
present: being in a place referred to
resiant: resident
resident: having an abode
residentiary: having a residence
round and square: everywhere
this-worldly: having an interest in the pleasures of the present
ubiquitary: ubiquitous; everywhere present
ubiquitous: being or seeming to be everywhere at once; omnipresent

Prisoner

carceral: pertaining to prison
imprisoned: confined in a prison
in chains: held in captivity by chains
in charge: under the care of
in custody: in the safekeeping of
in durance vile: kept as a prisoner
in limbo: in prison
in prison: confined within the walls of a prison

in quod: in prison
on parole: released on word of honor not to escape
under hatches: confined under the deck of a ship
under lock and key: restrained by lock and key

Privacy

abandoned: left alone
banished: driven from home or country
bye: situated apart or aside
cynical: sneering or criticizing others
delitescent: concealed; in retirement
derelict: deserted or abandoned
deserted: abandoned permanently or without consideration
deserted in one's utmost need: left when help is most needed
desolate: deprived of inhabitants; made lonely
dissocial: not inclined to be social
domestic: pertaining to or liking home duties
estranged: distant in interest; made a stranger
forlorn: without hope; forsaken; lost
friendless: without a friend
homeless: without a home
incommunicative: reserved
inconversable: not conversable
inhospitable: not hospitable
isolated: detached from others
left to shift for oneself: deserted
lonely: deserted by human beings
lonesome: sad because of loneliness
lorn: without kindred or friends; lost; forlorn
out of the way: retired from society
out of the world: retired from society

outcast: rejected as unworthy
private: removed from public view
retired: in privacy
secluded: apart from others
sequestered: withdrawn into obscurity or solitude
single: having no companion
snug: not exposed to notice
solitary: living or being alone; unfrequented by human beings
stay-at-home: not leaving the home
tenantless: without a tenant
the world forgetting; by the world forgot: living in privacy
umbratile: done privately rather than publicly; done indoors
unclubable: not clubable
under a cloud: with an injured reputation
unfrequented: not resorted to or crowded with people
unfriended: not helped by friends
unhabitable: not fit to be inhabited
uninhabited: not dwelt in
unintroduced: not made known to
uninvited: not having had one's presence requested
unsociable: not sociable
unsocial: not social
unvisited: not visited
unwelcome: not welcome

Proffer

conductitious: for hire; hired
disengaged: not occupied; hence, in a state to be offered
for sale: offered to be sold
in the market: in a state to be offered
offered: brought before one for acceptance or refusal

offering: bringing before one for acceptance or refusal
on hire: in a position to be hired
paper: proffered but not fulfilled
proffered: offered for acceptance
tendered: offered
to let: for rent or hire

Progress

advanced: moved forward; promoted; furthered

advancing: progressing; improving
aoristic: indefinite

ascensive: advancing; progressive
elapsing: passing away
évolué: advanced; enlightened; progressive
gradual: slowly progressive

leading: going ahead
marching: progressive
ongoing: being in progress
processive: going forward
progressive: moving forward; advancing

Prohibition

contraband: forbidden by law or treaty
exclusive: having power to shut out; enjoyed to the exclusion of others
forbidding: prohibiting
illegal: not legal
not permitted: not allowed
not to be thought of: out of the question
prohibited: forbidden
prohibitive: that prohibits or forbids

prohibitory: tending to prohibit
proscriptive: relating to proscription
restrictive: tending to restrict or limit
unauthorized: not authorized
under the ban of: not allowed
unlicensed: not licensed
vetitive: having the power to veto; prohibiting

Prolixity

ambagious: characterized by circumlocution
circumlocutory: roundabout
copious: employing more expression and illustration
diffuse: characterized by redundance or prolixity
digressive: given to or characterized by digression
discursive: wandering away from the point or theme
episodic: pertaining to or of the nature of an episode
excursive: disconnected and rambling
exuberant: marked by great plentifulness
flatulent: pretentious without substance or reality
frothy: empty
largiloquent: speaking in an inflated or boastful manner
lengthy: not brief
long: continued to a great length
long-drawn-out: long-winded

longsome: extended in length
long-spun: protracted
long-winded: continuing for a long time in speaking or writing
maundering: incoherent
periphrastic: expressed in a roundabout manner
pleonastic: characterized by the use of superfluous words
profuse: characterized by overabundance
prolix: unduly extended by the use of needless words; pleonastic
prosing: speaking or discoursing prosily or tediously
protracted: to cause to occupy a longer time than is usual
rambling: talking aimlessly
roundabout: characterized by indirect methods
spun out: drawn out to undue length
verbose: containing an unnecessary number of words; prolix
wordy: expressed in many words

Proof

apodictic: showing by argument
apodictical: showing by argument

categorical: absolute
consectary: following necessarily

consequential: following or resulting
crucial: determining absolutely the falsity of a view
decisive: putting an end to uncertainty
deducible: capable of being derived or inferred
demonstrable: able to be demonstrated
demonstrated: proved
demonstrating: proving
demonstrative: convincing; showing clearly
endeictic: demonstrative
evident: manifest or plain
following: to come after in logical order
inferential: that which can be deducible from what is known

irrefragable: not to be overthrown or refuted
irresistible: not to be opposed with success
probative: offering proof; designed to test; probatory
proved: that which has been demonstrated
receptary: accepted as fact, but unproven
unanswerable: not able to be answered or replied to
unanswered: not to be refuted
unconfuted: not confuted; not proved false
unrefuted: unopposed; unassailed

Prophecy

augurial: pertaining to auguries
augurous: full of augury
auspicial: of or pertaining to auspices
auspicious: favorable; promising; of good omen
big with the fate of: showing many signs
Cassandran: foretelling unhappy events
extispicious: relating to the inspection of entrails for prognostication
farseeing: having foresight
farsighted: having foresight
fatidic: prophetic
fatidical: having power to foretell future events
foreseeing: having foresight
ill-boding: promising ill
mantic: pertaining to fortunetelling; prophetic
monitory: conveying warnings
ominous: full of omens
oracular: pertaining to oracles; prophetic

portentous: full of portents or strange happenings
predicting: foretelling
predictive: foretelling; foreboding
pregnant: full of consequence; implying more than is expressed
premonitory: containing premonitions
prescient: foreknowing
prescious: foreknowing
prophetic: pertaining to prophecy
prospective: looking to the future
provident: exercising foresight
sagacious: able to discern and distinguish with wise perception
sibylline: pertaining to the Sibyl; prophetic
significant of: expressive of something beyond the external mark or sign
sponsional: pertaining to a promise, agreement
vaticinal: prophetic
weather-wise: skillful in predicting the state of the weather

Proportion

actinomorphic: having radial symmetry; actinomorphous
balanced: well-proportioned; applied to the mind
beautiful: perfect in form or shaping

coextensive: having equal extent
commensurate: corresponding in amount, extent, magnitude; proportionate
equal: of just proportion and relation

finished: completed; perfected
parallel: essentially alike
proportional: having harmonious dimensions in relation to another; commensurate; eurythmic; proportionate
regular: conforming to the usual rule
severe: exactly conforming to a standard
shapely: well-proportioned in form

symmetrical: having the parts balanced; relatively proportioned
uniform: the same throughout
well-set: having good symmetry of parts
well-shaped: having good form or proportion
zygomorphic: symmetrical on each side

Propriety

acceptable: worthy of being accepted
advisable: agreeing with good sense
applicable: suitable for use
apposite: fitting; suitable; appropriate
as it ought to be: right
as it should be: right
becoming: suitable to the person, occasion
befitting: suitable to the person, occasion
comme il faut: correct; proper
condecent: fit; appropriate; becoming
condign: well-deserved or suitable
convenient: requiring the loss of no time or effort
deserved: accordant with justice
desirable: to be wished for
due: rightly claimed
eligible: worthy of being chosen
evenhanded: impartial; just
expedient: personally advantageous
fair: equitable; just

fit: conforming to a standard of right
fitting: right and proper
good: worthy; righteous
idoneous: suitable; apt
just: impartial; equitable; righteous
justifiable: capable of being justified
lawful: conformable to law; rightful
legitimate: accordant with law; rightful
meet: fit
opportune: coming at the proper time
proper: conforming to usage
proprietary: owned or held as property; having the right to use
reasonable: governed by right reason; just
right: according to the law and will of God or conformity to the standard of truth and justice
rightful: righteous; just
seemly: to be in taste
suitable: agreeable to one's notions
worthwhile: advantageous

Publicity

audiovisual: pertaining to simultaneous use of tape recordings, slides, and video to support pitch, presentation, or display
business-to-business: designating communications or dealings by agencies or between companies
commercial: designating product or service suitable for wide, popular market
current: circulating
divulgate: published
encyclical: intended for general circulation

exoteric: external; public
in circulation: circulating
infamous: notorious
mom-and-pop: having a traditional, rural look in advertisements; designating a small advertising agency
multimedia: involving use of several media simultaneously in single advertisement or campaign
notorious: publicly known, especially unfavorably known to the general public
open: not private; public

promulgatory: spreading from person to person

public: open to all; well-known

publicity-loving: seeking and wanting public recognition

published: made public; promulgated

slice-of-life: denoting advertisement that depicts naturalistic, everyday activities

trumpet-tongued: having a powerful, far-reaching voice or speech

upscale: having a look aimed at the well-to-do urban market

Publishing

clothbound: designating hardbound book with cloth-covered boards

in-print: designating book currently available for sale

mass market: designating small, rack-size paperback book, especially for distribution on newsstands

newsworthy: interesting or important enough to warrant media attention

out-of-print: designating book no longer available from publisher

paperbound: designating paperback book

published: publicly announced or declared; issued to the public

rack-size: describing typical format of paperback for mass market

unabridged: designating complete text of book, story, or article; uncut

uncut: unabridged

unedited: not modified by editorial changes

unpaginated: denoting book, usually brief or for children, with no page numbers

Pungency

acrid: pungent; bitter

acrimonious: full of bitterness; sharp

biting: keen; pungent; nipping

bitter: having a peculiar acrid taste

brackish: somewhat saline

briny: impregnated with salt

escharotic: serving or tending to form an eschar; caustic

full-flavored: abundantly or highly flavored

gamy: having the flavor of game; high-flavored

high-flavored: richly or spicily flavored

high-seasoned: enriched with spice and condiments

high-tasted: having a strong relish; piquant

hot: acrid; biting; pungent

hot as pepper: extremely pungent

meracious: without mixture or adulteration; strong; racy

mordacious: biting; caustic

mordant: biting; caustic

peppery: like pepper; hot; pungent

piperitious: peppery

piquant: stinging; sharp; pungent

pungent: causing a sharp sensation, as of the taste, smell, or feeling

racy: having a strong flavor indicating origin; rich; peculiar and piquant

rough: harsh to the taste

saliferous: containing salt

saline: constituting or consisting of salt; salty

salty: saline; briny

salty as a herring: a figurative expression denoting degree of saltiness

salty as brine: a figurative expression denoting degree of saltiness

salty as Lot's wife: a figurative expression denoting degree of saltiness

seasoned: fitted for taste

sharp: having a stinging pungent taste

spicy: containing, flavored, or fragrant with spices

stinging: pungent; biting

strong: making a keen impression upon the senses; pungent

unsavory: having a disagreeable taste or odor

vellicating: causing to twitch or contract convulsively

Punishment

baculine: pertaining to a rod; punishing with a rod

castigatory: punitive in order to amend

chastened: with a guilty look; shamefaced; sheepish

condemnatory: containing disapproval or censure

condemned: pronounced guilty

damnatory: dooming to damnation

exilic: concerning exile

inflictive: causing the infliction of punishment

nonsuited: adjudged to have abandoned his suit

penal: of or pertaining to punishment, to penalties, or to crimes and offenses

punished: having punishment inflicted

punishing: having punishment inflicted

punitive: tending to punishment

punitory: tending to punishment

self-convicted: convicted by one's own self

Purity

academical: classical

artistic: embodying the principles of art

attic: of the best quality

chaste: pure; undefiled

Ciceronian: polished, fluent, and copious

classical: conforming to the highest standards in art

continent: exercising restraint as to indulgence of passions

correct: faultless

decent: fit; proper; seemly

decorous: becoming; proper; seemly

delicate: pure; chaste

easy: not strained

elegant: having parts well-proportioned

euphemistic: substituting a less offensive term for a more disagreeable one

euphonious: sounding well to the ear

felicitous: enjoying deep and continued happiness

graceful: possessing grace

happy: marked by pointedness

honest: chaste; virtuous

intemerate: completely pure; undefiled

jannock: fair and decent; genuine

meracious: unadulterated; full-strength; pure

modest: characterized by reserve, propriety, or purity

natural: reflecting nature

neat: marked by good order

neatly expressed: cleverly expressed

neatly put: cleverly expressed

numerose: melodious

platonic: purely spiritual or devoid of sensual feeling

polished: freed from coarseness

pristine: from the earliest time or condition; uncorrupted; unsoiled

pure: free from defilement

readable: attractive for reading

rhythmical: having a regular recurrence of accent

Saxon: strong and vigorous in the use of language

smectic: purifying; detergent

tripping: to move lightly and rhythmically

unaffected: not assuming anything unnatural

undefiled: not corrupted as to chastity; unviolated

unlabored: easily executed
virtuous: having moral excellence; chaste; pure

well-put: strongly expressed

Purple

amaranthine: pertaining to the amaranth; reddish purple; everlasting; unfading
aubergine: dark purple; eggplant
cyclamen: of a dark reddish purple
fuchsia: reddish purple or lavender; heliotrope; plum; raspberry
ianthine: violet-colored
lavender: of a very pale purple color
lilac: medium purple; amethyst
livid: of an extremely dark purple color

mauve: bluish purple
modena: deep purple
orchid: light purple; lavender
plum-colored: of a rich reddish purple
porporate: dressed in purple
puce: brownish purple
purple: colored with purple
purpuraceous: purple
purpure: purple
purpurescent: purplish
violet: of a dark blue, inclining to red and not quite purple

Purpose

advised: done with intention and forethought
aimless: without any definite design or intention
at stake: in danger; pledged
autotelic: for its own sake
bent upon: with fixed purpose
bound for: having a definite intention or direction
determinate: determined or resolved upon
effectual: answering a purpose; producing the desired effect
express: intended for a particular purpose
heterotelic: existing for an extraneous purpose

in prospect: in anticipation
in the breast of: in secrecy
in view: in anticipated foresight
intended: purposed to be done
intending: purposed to be done
intentional: with forethought
minded: disposed; inclined
on the anvil: under discussion
on the tapis: on the table; hence, under consideration
prepense: considered beforehand
purposeful: having a meaning or intention
stratagemical: designed as a clever trick
teleological: of or pertaining to teleology, the doctrine of design

Quarrelsomeness

angry: showing marked displeasure
bad-tempered: liable to be passionate
cacochymical: bad-tempered; ill-humored; cacochymic
cantankerous: perverse or malicious
captious: disposed to find fault
choleric: quick to anger
churlish: rude in manners and speech
contentious: fond of contention
cross: angrily peevish
cross as a cat: very cross
cross as a crab: very cross
cross as a dog: very cross
cross as the tongs: very cross
cross as two sticks: very cross
disputatious: inclined to dispute
dissentious: quarrelsome; contentious
edgy: irritable; fractious; testy
exceptious: captious
excitable: easily aroused
fidgety: unable to sit still
fiery: easily provoked; passionate
fractious: inclined to be rebellious
fratchy: quarrelsome
fretful: complaining of small grievances
hasty: quick-tempered
hot: passionate; vehement
huffy: easily offended
ill-tempered: liable to be passionate
in a bad temper: in an angry mood

irascible: prone to anger; hot-tempered; irritable
irritable: easily excited to anger
like tinder: fiery
like touchwood: fiery
moodish: apt to have sullen moods
nettlesome: quarrelsome; short-tempered
on the fret: showing vexation
overhasty: very hot-tempered
oxythymous: quick-tempered
passionate: inclined to strong passion
peevish: feebly fretful and irritable
peppery: quick-tempered
pettish: subject to fits of ill temper
petulant: capriciously passionate
pugnacious: prone to fight; bellicose; belligerent; challenging; combative; provocative; scrappy; truculent
quarrelsome: showing a contentious disposition
querulous: habitually complaining
quick: quick-tempered
resentful: susceptible to offense
resentive: susceptible to offense
restiff: showing restlessness and impatience of control
restive: showing restlessness and impatience of control
shrewish: inclined to nag and scold
snappish: sharp and surly

sudden and quick in quarrel: quick-tempered
sulky: sullenly cross
susceptible: capable of emotional impression
techy: peevishly sensitive
termagant: quarrelsome; scolding
testy: irritable and quick-tempered

tetchy: peevishly sensitive
thin-skinned: sensitive to wrong
touchy: irascible
vindictive: having a tendency to revenge
virulent: spitefully hostile; bitter
warm: slightly passionate
waspish: peevish; irritable; malignant

Quietness

close: silent
close-tongued: cautious in speaking
costive: cold in manner; reserved
curt: short
dumb: unable to speak
inconversable: unsocial; reserved
mum: silent
mute: held from speaking
quiet: without noise; peaceful
reserved: restrained from freedom of words
reticent: inclined to keep silent

silent: not speaking
silent as a post: a figurative expression denoting degree of silence
silent as a stone: a figurative expression denoting degree of silence
silent as the grave: a figurative expression denoting degree of silence
silentious: taciturn
sparing of words: taciturn
taciturn: saying little; naturally or habitually silent; reserved; uncommunicative

Rarity

few: small in number
fine: not coarse; tenuous; subtile
flimsy: having no substantial texture
infrequent: not often
light: lacking density or weight
rare: occurring but seldom; thinly scattered
rare as a blue diamond: exceedingly rare
rarefied: made rare
scarce: rarely occurring
slight: slender in build or construction; delicate

subtile: characterized by rarity; rarefied
tenuous: having little substance, validity, significance; thin; rare
thin: having little body; loose in structure
unfrequent: not happening often
unprecedented: unlike anything that goes before
unsubstantial: having no solid, strong texture; chimerical
virtu: rare or beautiful and of interest to a collector

Rationale—Reason

analytical: resolving into first principles or elements
argumentative: characterized by arguments; given to arguing
Aristotelian: like the reasoning of Aristotle
attributable: able to be attributed
attributed: ascribed
automorphic: patterned after oneself; ascribing one's traits to another
biconditional: pertaining to the relation between two statements that is valid only when both are true or false
cogent: compelling; persuasive; relevant
cognitive: involving the acquisition of knowledge

coherent: logically clear and consistent
controversial: given to controversy
controvertible: capable of being disputed
cumulative: increasing by successive additions; tending to lead to the same conclusion
cut-and-dried: done according to routine, formula, or set plan
debatable: capable of being debated
definitive: conclusive; most reliable or complete
derivable from: known by inference from
dialectic: logical; dialectical
dianoetic: pertaining to logical reasoning

didactic: instructive; pertaining to teaching

discursive: exhibiting the power of connected thought

discursory: discursive

disputatious: eager to enter into disputes

due to: deserving of; meriting

epistemic: concerning knowledge

esemplastic: capable of shaping diverse elements into a unified whole

eudemonistic: pursuing the good life by reason rather than for pleasure; eudaemonistic

facultative: relating to mental activity or capacity

forensic: pertaining to argumentation

hebamic: pertaining to Socratic reasoning

implausible: not particularly believable

irrelevant: not pertinent; immaterial

logical: following the laws of reasoning

lucid: clearly expressed

moot: open to discussion or debate; irrelevant to an issue in debate

noetic: of abstract reasoning

owing to: in consequence of

paralogic: unable to think logically

perspicacious: endowed with keen mental perception

perspicuous: presented in clear and precise manner

polemical: given to polemics

putative: reputed; alleged; supposed

rational: conforming to reason

rationalistic: relying on reason alone

reasonable: endowed with logic, good cause

reasoning: endowed with the power of reasoning

referable: capable of being ascribed

referrible: capable of being ascribed

relevant: suited to the purpose

specious: unsound though appearing to be true

synthetic: constructing wholes from particulars

tenable: defensible; reasonable

thought-out: derived by careful mental consideration

unilateral: one-sided; imbalanced

viable: having likely chance of working

watertight: flawless; having no possibility of evasion or misunderstanding

well-founded: based on sound or valid reasoning

well-grounded: having a sound basis or foundation

well-taken: justified; based in truth or fact

Readiness

bent upon: strongly inclined toward something

content: not disposed to grumble; satisfied; contented

cordial: proceeding from the heart; sincere; affectionate

corrigible: of people, open to correction

disposed: inclined; minded

docile: disposed to be taught; easily managed

eager: ardently desirous; impetuous; vehement

earnest: done with a will; zealous with sincerity

easily persuaded: readily convinced; easily prevailed upon

easygoing: mild-tempered; ease-loving

elozable: open to flattery

facile: ready; quick; expert

fain: well-pleased; glad; eager

favorable: tending to promote or facilitate; friendly

favorably disposed: favorable to

favorably inclined: favorable to

favorably minded: favorable to

forward: ready; prompt; presumptuous

genial: cheering; enlivening

gracious: disposed to show kindness or favor; merciful

gratuitous: free; taken without ground or proof

hearty: willing; energetic; warm; cordial

in the humor: in a pleased state of mind

in the mind: in good spirits

in the mood: in a pleasant frame of mind

in the vein: in a favorable disposition

inclined: having a tendency toward or away from a thing; disposed

minded: disposed; inclined

nothing loth: willing; not reluctant; not backward

persuadable: that may be convinced

persuasible: persuadable; that may be influenced by reasons offered

predisposed: inclined beforehand; adapted previously

propense: leaning forward, in a moral sense; prone

ready: prepared; willing; not reluctant

spontaneous: done without compulsion; voluntary

suasible: easily persuaded

tractable: capable of being easily managed; docile

unasked: unsolicited; not sought by entreaty

unforced: not constrained; not impelled

voluntary: acting from choice; done without compulsion

willing: inclined to anything; ready; consenting

Receptacle—Receiving

camerated: provided with chambers

capsular: like a capsule

cellular: containing cells

concave: curved in

cystic: containing cysts

given: presented as gift

honeycombed: having cells, cavities, or perforations; alveolate; chambered; compartmentalized; faveolate; faviform

locular: having cells or cavities; loculate

marsupial: having a pouch for retaining the young

not given: not received as a gift

polygastric: provided with many stomachs

receptacular: serving as a container or receptacle

received: gotten from any source; acquired

receiving: coming in

recipient: ready to receive

saccular: in the form of a sac

sacculated: provided with sacs

secondhand: received after use by another

siliquose: like a pod

siliquous: like a pod

suscipient: receiving as an effect or influence

unbestowed: not given

vascular: having vessels

ventricular: like a ventricle

vesicular: containing air bladders

Recklessness

adventurous: delighting in adventures or risks

breakneck: extremely hazardous

careless: neglectful of danger or duty

cavalier: high-spirited; gallant

desperate: rendered reckless or heroic by extremity of circumstances

devil-may-care: careless; reckless

fire-eating: having the spirit of a fire-eater

foolhardy: unreasonably daring or bold

free-and-easy: showing little regard for customs or conventionalities

giddy: marked by foolish recklessness; frivolous

harebrained: wild and foolish like the hare

headlong: acting with haste and rashness

headstrong: stubbornly self-willed

heedless: without care or attention

heels over head: in a tumbled or over-turned condition

hot-blooded: quick-tempered; irritable

hot-brained: violent; rash

hotheaded: easily angered

Icarian: like Icarus; reckless

improvident: prodigal; lacking in foresight

imprudent: unadvised; wanting in a due regard for consequences

impulsive: easily aroused; acting on the spur of the moment

incautious: acting without caution

indiscreet: injudicious; lacking good judgment

jaunty: sprightly; putting on airs of care-less ease

madcap: full of wild follies

off one's guard: unprepared; not on the watch

overconfident: too self-reliant

overweening: extremely self-confident; arrogant

precipitate: overhasty; acting with too great eagerness

quixotic: acting like Don Quixote

rakehelly: dissolute; debauched; rash; impetuous; rakehell

rash: characteristic of one who acts with too great haste and too little regard for consequences

reckless: entirely disregarding consequences

temerarious: headstrong; reckless; rash

uncalculating: without properly estimat-ing what the chances are or the conse-quences will be

venturesome: inclined to take risks

venturous: daring; bold

wanton: extravagant; lacking reason and consideration

wild: profligate; highly excited, as with passion

without ballast: without any steadying influence; inconstant

Recurrence

above-mentioned: spoken of before

aforenamed: named before

aforesaid: mentioned before

another: repeated

chiming: repeating in harmony

ever-recurring: coming to view repeatedly

frequent: happening often

habitual: recurring constantly

harping: always talking about

incessant: without ceasing

intervallic: situated at intervals; intervaled

iterative: repeating

mocking: repeating in a jesting or deri-sive manner

monotonous: repeated until tiresome

recrudescent: of something undesirable that abated and then returned

recurrent: occurring again and again; recurring

remeant: returning

remontrant: showing again; reappearing

repeated: done or said over again

repetitional: said over again

repetitionary: repetitional

retaliating: returning like for like

retaliative: returning like for like

retaliatory: returning like for like

retold: repeated or told again

said: aforesaid; above-mentioned

thick-coming: coming rapidly or repeatedly

Red

bloodred: colored with or like blood

blowzed: having a coarsely red or flushed face

blowzy: blowzed; blowsy

blushing: becoming red

brick-colored: of the color of bricks; brownish red

brickdust-colored: brick-colored

buff: a light yellow verging toward pink, gray, or brown

burnt: having the color of that which has been burnt; brownish red

carroty: like a carrot in color; reddish yellow

cerise: medium red; bloodred; cherry; strawberry

cherry-colored: of the color of a cherry

claret: having the color of claret; deep purplish red

coral: yellowish pink; flesh; flesh-colored; peach; seashell

crimson: vivid red; bright red; apple red; cardinal; carmine; cinnabar red; fire-engine red; geranium; lobster red; scarlet; tomato; vermeil; vermilion

erubescent: tending to grow red; blushing

ferruginous: rust-colored, like iron

flame-colored: of the color of a flame

flammeous: flame-colored

flammulated: reddish; ruddy

flesh-colored: having the color of human flesh; carnation

florid: flushed with red

foxy: of the color of a fox; reddish brown

gules: red

hot: fiery red

hot pink: vivid pink; shocking pink

incarnadin: flesh-colored

incarnadine: bloodred or crimson

latericeous: brick red; lateritious

lateritious: of the color of red brick

lurid: giving a ghastly dull-red light

magenta: purplish red; claret; grape; raisin; raspberry

maroon: dark red; burgundy; cranberry; currant; garnet; ruby; wine

murrey: of a dark reddish brown or mulberry color

phenicious: grayish red

poppy: orangish red

puniceous: bright or purplish red

red: having the color of arterial human blood

red as a lobster: a figurative expression denoting degree of redness

red as a turkey-cock: a figurative expression denoting degree of redness

red as blood: a figurative expression denoting degree of redness

red as fire: a figurative expression denoting degree of redness

red as scarlet: a figurative expression denoting degree of redness

reddened: made red

reddish: slightly red

roon: red

roseate: tinged with rose color or red

rose-colored: of the color of a rose

rosy: of the color of the rose; rose red

rubedinous: reddish; rufescent

rubescent: blushing; turning red

rubicund: having a reddened face; flushed

rubiginous: rust-colored; rusty; ferruginous

ruby-colored: of the color of the ruby

ruddy: tinged with red

rufous: brownish red; rust-colored; reddish; burgundy; ferruginous

russet: of a reddish brown color

rutilant: having a reddish glow

salmon-colored: of a reddish yellow or orange color; carnation; rose

sanguine: having the color of blood; red

shell: whitish pink

sorrel: of a reddish or yellowish brown color

stammel: having the color of stammel; of an inferior red color

vinaceous: wine-colored

warm: having predominating tones of red or yellow

Refusal

deaf to: not paying any attention to

impossible: that which cannot come to pass

not to be thought of: not to be considered; refused

not willing to hear of: not willing to pay any attention to

out of the question: not worthy of consideration; impossible

recusant: persistently refusing to conform to authority

refusing: not wishing to yield

restiff: difficult to restrain

restive: difficult to restrain

uncomplying: not yielding

unconsenting: not agreeing with

ungranted: not given

Regard

bareheaded: uncovered from respect

cap in hand: obsequiously; submissively

ceremonious: formally respectful

decorous: suitable for the occasion; becoming

deferential: respectful

emeritus: retired from active service, but retained in an honorary position

in deference to: with respectful submission

in high esteem: regarded as having worth or excellence

in high estimation: regarded as having worth or excellence

obsequious: promptly obedient or submissive; compliant; overly respectful

on one's knees: worshipful

prostrate: to bow in humble reverence

regardful: attentive; respectful

respected: looked upon with respect

respectful: marked by outward civility; courteous

respecting: having regard for

reverenced: regarded with profound respect

reverential: expressing reverence

saving your grace: excepting those present

saving your presence: excepting those present

time-honored: observed or honored from former times

venerable: worthy of the highest respect

with all respect: with a feeling of regard or attention; respectfully

with due respect: with a feeling of regard or attention; respectfully

with the highest respect: with a feeling of regard or attention; respectfully

Regret

contrite: penitent; feeling regret; remorseful; apologetic; repentent

homesick: having a longing for home

lamentable: sorrowful

languorous: sorrowful

much to be regretted: regrettable

oikotropic: homesick

regretful: full of regret

regrettable: causing regret

regretted: feeling sorrow

regretting: feeling regret

unfortunate: unlucky; regrettable

unlucky: unfortunate; regrettable

worse: grievous; regrettable

Regularity

arranged: according to some definite order

businesslike: prompt and orderly

correct: exact; perfectly in order

in apple-pie order: in perfect order
in its proper place: in regular arrangement
in order: in regular arrangement
in trim: in order
methodical: according to method; orderly
neat: well-arranged
orderly: having care for arrangement and method
regular: according to rule
serial: in a sequence or row

shipshape: well-arranged; in good order
symmetrical: well-ordered; in due balancing arrangement
systematic: pertaining to orderly combination or arrangement
tidy: neat; well-arranged
tosh: comfortably neat and orderly
unconfused: not disordered
uniform: harmonious; well-ordered
well-regulated: well-ordered

Relationship

affiliated: intimately associated
attendant: following or accompanying
avuncular: in the manner of an uncle
closely allied: closely connected by blood or marriage
closely related: closely connected by blood or marriage
correlational: related; affiliated; associated; connected; correlated; correlative; interconnected; interlinked; interrelated
distantly allied: connected by blood or marriage
distantly related: connected by blood or marriage
fellow: associated in action, location, or position
fraternal: brotherly
german: related as sisters and brothers
inbred: born of closely related individuals; from the same stock

intimately allied: closely connected by blood or marriage
intimately related: closely connected by blood or marriage
materteral: pertaining to an aunt
nearly allied: of one family
nearly related: of one family
nepotal: pertaining to a nephew
of the blood: related
philoprogenitive: tending to produce offspring
related: connected by blood or marriage
relational: belonging to a human relationship
remotely allied: of the same family
remotely related: of the same family
respective: relating to particular persons or things, each to each
vis-à-vis: in direct relation to; correlative; corresponding; mutual; reciprocal

Reluctance

adverse: acting against or in a contrary direction; opposed
averse: having a repugnance or oppositon of mind; disinclined
backward: unwilling; hesitating; slow
demurring: suspending judgment on account of a doubt or difficulty
disinclined: unwilling; unfavorable
indifferent: having no inclination or interest; apathetic

indisposed: rendered averse or unfavorable; disinclined
involuntary: not proceeding from choice; done unwillingly
laggard: slow; sluggish; backward
loath: unwilling; reluctant; disinclined
loth: filled with disgust or aversion; unwilling
not content: disposed to repine or grumble; dissatisfied

not in the vein: indisposed; not in good humor

reluctant: striving against; disinclined; unwilling

remiss: not attending to duty or engagements; slow; dilatory

repugnant: characterized by opposition; distasteful to a high degree

restiff: unwilling to stir; impatient under restraint; stubborn

restive: unwilling to stir; impatient under restraint; stubborn

scrupulous: hesitating to determine or to act, from a fear of offending

shy of: disinclined to familiar approach; cautious

slack: not earnest or eager; backward; remiss

slow to: not precipitate or hasty; deliberate; forbearing

squeamish: overnice; easily disgusted

unasked: without asking for

unbesought: unasked

unconsenting: not concurring; disagreeing; refusing

unsought: unasked for

unwilling: not willing; disinclined; reluctant

Remedy

abstersive: having cleansing qualities

aesculapian: medical

alexipharmic: serving to counteract poison; antidotal

alexiteric: serving to ward off contagion

alimentary: nutritious

allopathic: relating to remedies that produce different effects from those of the disease

alterative: tending to cause a gradual change

alviducous: purgative

analeptic: restorative; comforting

analgesic: making one feel no pain

anatriptic: pertaining to rubbing as a remedy for disease

anodyne: soothing

anodynic: able to soothe pain or soothe the sensibilities; removing the cares of the world; anodyne

antiorgastic: acting as a sedative

antiphlogistic: reducing inflammation or fever

antipruritic: that which relieves itching

balsamic: having the qualities of balsam

bechic: tending to relieve coughs

bezoardic: used as an antidote

broad-spectrum: describing a drug that is effective against wide variety of microorganisms

chalastic: laxative

chirurgical: relating to surgery

corrective: tending to restore

corroborant: invigorating

curable: susceptible of cure

demulcent: soothing

depuratory: fitted to purify

detergent: having cleansing qualities

detersive: detergent

dietetic: relating to the diet

disinfectant: having power to destroy the germs of infectious disease

emollient: producing a soothing effect

epulotic: having healing qualities; cicatrizing

febrifugal: efficacious against fever

febrifuge: fever-reducing

healing: tending to cure

hypnotic: sleep-producing

intravenous: IV; designating blood transfusion, nutritional solution, or drugs fed directly into vein of patient

lenitive: palliating; soothing

medical: pertaining to medicine or the science of medicine; also possessing curative properties

medicinal: having curative or symptom-relieving properties

mundificant: having cleansing, healing properties

narcotic: stupor-producing

neurotic: efficacious in nervous diseases

nutritious: nourishing
nutritive: having nutritious properties
palliative: giving relief
paregoric: soothing pain
peptic: of aid in digestion
prophylactic: efficacious in warding off disease
recuperative: pertaining to recovery
remediable: curable
remedial: having curative properties
restorative: tending to cure or restore to health
salutiferous: health-giving

sanative: tending to cure or heal
sanatory: health-giving
sedative: having the power of soothing or calming, as the nerves
squinant: very medicinable
stegnotic: stopping diarrhea
therapeutic: curative
theriacal: medicinal; antidotal; therial
tonic: invigorating; bracing
traumatic: efficacious in the cure of wounds
vaccine: connected with vaccination
vulnerary: tending to cure wounds or external injuries

Remembrance

anamnestic: reminiscent; aiding the memory
fresh: in the memory
green: unforgotten
indelible: not to be blotted out
memorable: worthy to be remembered
mindful: regarding with thoughtful care
mnestic: pertaining to memory; mnesic
nepimnemic: of a childhood memory existing in the subconscious
pent up in one's memory: remembered
present to the mind: remembered

remembered: known by memory
remembering: known by memory
retained in the memory: known by memory
revenant: remembering something long forgotten; coming back
tenty: mindful; tentie
unforgotten: remembered
uppermost in one's thoughts: at the forefront of one's thoughts
within one's memory: easily remembered

Remnant

cast-off: thrown off; discarded
exceeding: going beyond; excelling
forby: over and above; besides; forbye
left: remaining after something has been taken away
left behind: remaining after something has been taken away
leftover: remaining after something has been taken away
net: clear of all charges; having no remainder
odd: having a remainder when divided by two

outlying: situated outside; extrinsic
outstanding: standing still; projecting
over and above: leftover
remaining: continuing after others have been removed
remanent: remaining; residual
residual: left over after part is taken
residuary: pertaining to a residue
sedimentary: characterized by sediment; leftover
superfluous: more than is required
surviving: left over alive
unconsumed: left over after a conflagration

Remoteness

antipodean: pertaining to those on the opposite side of the earth
asunder: not near; not with
distal: situated away from the point of origin or attachment
distant: separated
efferent: away from the central motor or nerve system
far: a long way off; remote
faraway: distant
hyperborean: most northern; beyond the frozen north
inaccessible: unapproachable; not to be reached
incontiguous: not in contact; separate
out-of-the-way: secluded; hard to find

remote: distant; far away
stretching to: reaching far out
telescopic: to be seen only by a telescope
tramontane: beyond the mountains
transalpine: beyond the Alps
transatlantic: beyond the Atlantic
transmarine: across the sea
transmontane: across the mountains
ulterior: further; beyond
ultramontane: beyond the mountains
ultramundane: beyond the world
unapproachable: gigantic; awe-inspiring; not to be reached
wide of: far from the mark
yon: at a distance
yonder: at a distance

Removal

decerptible: removable
deracinated: uprooted
displaced: put out of place
effodient: burrowing
fodient: concerning digging
homeless: without a home
houseless: without a house
misplaced: put in a wrong place
out of a situation: without a place
out of its element: out of its proper sphere or condition

out of place: displaced
removable: capable of being removed or moved from one place to another
removing: taking away
unestablished: not settled or fixed
unharbored: unprotected; unsheltered
unhoused: deprived of shelter
unplaced: undetermined as to place
unsettled: not fixed or firm

Renovation

convalescent: recovering health
curable: capable of being cured
curative: tending to cure diseases
erumpent: bursting forth
gentrified: being renewed and rebuilt
in a fair way: convalescing
none the worse: recovered from danger
reappearing: showing forth again
recoverable: able to recover
recrudescent: renewing
recuperative: tending to recovery
redivivous: liable to revive
redivivus: revived; reborn
redux: renewed; revived; brought back

rejuvenescent: making or becoming young again
remediable: capable of being remedied
remedial: intended for a remedy
renascent: revived; reanimated
renascible: capable of being reborn
renovating: renewing
reparative: tending to recover
reparatory: tending to recover
reproducing: bringing forth new life
reproductive: employed in reproduction
restorable: capable of being restored
restorative: tending to restore
restored: made well or strong

restoring: making well or strong
sanable: curable

sanative: sanatory; healing
sanatory: promotive of health

Repentance

conscience-smitten: feeling regret or remorse
conscience-stricken: having a feeling of remorse
contrite: humbly penitent
not hardened: ready to turn from sin
penitent: feeling sorrow on account of sins or offenses
penitential: pertaining to penitence
penitentiary: relating to penance or expressing penitence

reclaimed: freed from sin
repentant: showing sorrow for sin
repenting: expressing sorrow for wrong done
self-accusing: accused by one's conscience
self-convicted: convicted by one's consciousness or acts
unhardened: not confirmed in wickedness

Reputation

at the head of: first
at the top of the tree: most conspicuous
august: inspiring awe or reverence
bright: illustrious or glorious
brilliant: celebrated; illustrious
celebrated: distinguished; known far and wide
conspicuous: very prominent
creditable: deserving credit
deathless: immortal
dignified: stately; majestic
distinguished: noted; eminent
eminent: standing high as compared with those about
famed: spoken of
famous: celebrated; renowned
far-famed: known in many regions
fashionable: conforming to the prevailing form or style
foremost: standing at the head
full-blown: in a state of maturity or perfection
glorious: resplendent with honor or glory
grand: preeminent in ability or character; worthy of the highest respect
great: standing among the foremost; eminent; distinguished
heaven-born: lofty and exalted

heroic: bold; brave; illustrious
high: distinguished; exalted
honorable: worthy of esteem and honor
honored: regarded or treated with honor or reverence
honorific: conferring honor or tending to honor
illustrious: greatly distinguished; full of glory or honor
immortal: of undying fame or renown
imperishable: enduring; immortal
imposing: grandly impressive; commanding
in everyone's mouth: widely spoken of
in favor: esteemed; held in high regard
in good odor: in good esteem
in high favor: noted
in the ascendant: having commanding power or influence
in the front rank: most distinguished
in the zenith: most distinguished
lordly: having the character or mien of a lord; grand; dignified
majestic: exhibiting majesty; stately; grand
never-fading: immortal
noble: exalted in rank or character
notable: worthy of note or regard
noted: well-known; celebrated

notorious: widely known, usually in a bad sense

of note: of reputation or distinction

of the first water: of the first excellence, as a diamond

peerless: without an equal

popular: in favor with the masses

preeminent: standing first

princely: of the highest rank or ability

prominent: of note; attracting attention

proud: worthy of admiration; splendid

psaphonic: planning one's rise to fame

radiant: full of splendor or glory

remarkable: extraordinary; distinguished

renowned: of well-deserved and lasting fame

reputable: of good reputation

respectable: of good reputation; also, of moderate excellence

sacred: worthy of reverence and veneration

solemn: impressive; awe-inspiring

splendid: very good; excellent; brilliant

stately: dignified; majestic

sublime: distinguished by the noblest traits; of solemn grandeur; awe-inspiring

supereminent: highest of all

superior: of higher standing or excellence

talked of: conspicuous

time-honored: claiming veneration because of long observance in the past

to the front: leading

transcendent: very excellent; surpassing

worshipful: worthy of honor or reverence

Rescue

bailed out: rescued from distress or jail

expendible: more easily replaced than rescued

extricable: able to be disentangled

reclaimed: rescued; regained

redeemable: able to be redeemed

rescuable: able to be rescued

retrieved: salvaged; rescued

salvaged: saved

saved: freed from danger

soterial: pertaining to salvation

Resistance

entêté: extremely stubborn

indomitable: unconquerable; stubbornly persistent

inductile: unyielding; inflexible

proof against: unyielding to force

recalcitrant: refusing compliance or submission

refractory: displaying resistance

renitent: offering resistance to any influence or force; resistant; reluctant; recalcitrant

repellent: serving, tending, or having power to repel

repulsive: exciting such feelings that one is repelled

resistant: having the power of resistance

resisting: having the power of resistance

resistive: having the power of resistance

stubborn: inflexible in resistance; intractable

unconquerable: not to be conquered

unconquered: not overcome

unyielding: not yielding; of persistent resistance

up in arms: in armed resistance

Resonance

amphoric: having a hollow sound similar to that produced by blowing across the mouth of a bottle

armisonant: resounding like clashing weapons

clinquant: tinkling; clinking

crepitating: crackling; clattering; rasping

deep-mouthed: having a loud and sonorous voice

deep-sounding: low and bass

deep-toned: of a low tone

fluctisonant: having the sound of rolling waves

grandisonant: great-sounding; grand in sound

gruff: having or giving forth a rough sound

hissing: making a hissing sound

hollow: resembling the sound reverberated from a cavity

libratory: oscillating; balancing

like a bee in a bottle: buzzing

megalophonous: having an imposing sound

oscillating: moving to and fro

oscillatory: moving like a pendulum

pendulous: moving like a pendulum

plangent: of sounds with loud reverberation

pulsatory: in a pulsating manner

reboantic: reverberating; reboant

resonant: tending to prolong and reinforce sound by sympathetic vibration

resounding: ringing

rolling: emitting full, swelling tones

sepulchral: unnaturally low or hollow in tone

sibilant: making a hissing sound

sibilous: hissing

stridulous: making a whistling sound during breathing

tinnient: emitting a clear tinkling sound

tintinnabulary: ringing or sounding like a bell

undulating: rising and falling like waves

unundulating: not undulating; not wavelike

vibratile: vibratory

vibratory: moving to and fro

wheezy: making a whistling sound

Rest

at a loose ends: free from labor and care

at a stand: dormant; stopped

at a standstill: dormant; stopped

at anchor: fastened with an anchor; without motion

at leisure: free from labor and care

at one's ease: free from labor and care

at rest: without motion

becalmed: made quiet because of lack of wind, as a ship

calm: unmoved; at rest; motionless; quiet

cataleptic: pertaining to a disease in which consciousness is lost and the muscles become rigid

cubatory: reclining; resting

deliberate: slow; leisurely

fixed: made firm or solid; immovable

hypnagogic: causing sleep

immovable: fixed; not movable

leisurely: not hasty

lodged: reposing

mawmsey: sleepy; stupid from need of rest

motionless: at perfect rest

moveless: not to be moved

picktooth: leisurely

quiescent: dormant; at rest; inactive

quiet: at rest; unmoving; in repose

recumbent: reclining in comfort; resting; idle; couchant; supine

reposing: in a state of complete rest

restful: at rest; in a state of repose

semisomnous: half-asleep

silent: without sound; still

sleeping: pertaining to slumber, rest, or inactivity

slow: not quick; undisturbed

somnifugous: driving away sleep

stagnant: at rest; without motion

standing still: motionless

stationary: not moving; unchanging; at rest

still: silent; without motion

still as a mouse: without motion

still as a post: without motion

still as a statue: without motion

still as death: without motion

stock-still: entirely motionless
undisturbed: not disturbed; inactive
unmoved: not to be moved; still

unruffled: not discomposed or agitated
unstrained: not strained
untraveled: not passed over

Retrogression

crablike: moving backwards
reactionary: tending toward a former or opposite state
receding: withdrawing, as from a claim; moving back
recidivous: liable to backslide
reflex: turned or thrown backwards; bent back

refluent: flowing or rushing back
regressive: passing back; retroactive
resilient: having the quality of resilience
retrograde: going, moving, or tending backwards; declining toward a worse state of character
retrogressive: going or moving backwards; declining

Revenge

avenging: disposed to avenge
immitigable: not to be mitigated
implacable: not to be appeased
inexorable: not to be moved by entreaty
pitiless: hard-hearted; cruel
rancorous: bitter vindictive enmity
rankling: irritating
remorseless: without mercy

revengeful: vindictive in mind
rigorous: severe and exacting
ruthless: cruel
stonyhearted: pitiless or implacable
talionic: pertaining to revenge
unforgiving: not disposed to forgive
unrelenting: inexorable
vengeful: disposed to take revenge
vindictive: disposed to take revenge

Rhetoric—Prose

allegorical: describing by resemblances
anapestic: composed of anapests
dactylic: pertaining to a foot consisting of a long followed by two short syllables
descriptive: affording description
dialectic: relating to a given and provincial mode of speech
elliptical: shortened
humorous: suited to excite laughter or amusement
hyperbolic: pertaining to rhetorical exaggeration; exaggerating
iambic: of a foot having a short followed by a long syllable
interrogative: denoting inquiry
ironical: covertly sarcastic
metaphorical: figurative

narrative: given to narration
ornamental: serving to adorn
prosaic: pertaining to prose
rhetorical: eloquently expressed; expressed to persuade
rhythmical: pertaining to rhythm
sarcastic: relating to taunting and contemptuous language
symbolic: pertaining to something that serves to represent another thing
synonymous: being similar or equivalent in meaning or force
tautologic: pleonastic; redundant
trochaic: relating to a foot consisting of a long followed by a short syllable or an accented followed by an unaccented
witty: good at repartee; having humor

Roughness

asperous: rough; uneven; rugged

bearded: having a beard

befringed: fringed

bullate: puckered; bulliform

bushy: like a bush

calcified: rocky; petrous

callused: having worn-looking fingers, hands; chapped; coarse; rough

chaetigerous: having bristles; chaetophorous; setigerous

ciliated: having movable hairlike processes

coriaceous: leatherlike; tough

cragged: having many crags

craggy: having many crags

crankling: bent; twisted

crinite: having or like long weak hairs

crinose: hairy

crisp: having waves or curls

dumose: bushy

echinate: prickly; bristled; echinated

feathery: like or having feathers

filamentous: like or having threads or filaments

fimbriate: fringed; fimbriated

fimbriated: having a fringe

fringed: furnished with a fringe

gnarled: full of knots

hairy: covered with or like hair

hirsute: covered with hairs or bristles

hispid: rough with bristles

horripilating: bristling; shuddering (as with goose bumps)

irrefrangible: unbreakable; inviolable

kerasine: horny; corneous

knotted: having knots

laciniate: fringed

lanate: woolly; lanose

lanuginose: woolly or downy

lanuginous: woolly or downy

leafy: full of leaves

like quills upon the fretful porcupine: covered with long sharp quills

lined: having wrinkles; furrowed; wizened; wrinkled

ondoyant: having a wavy surface

pachydermatous: pertaining to the elephant or rhinoceros

pappous: having down; pappose

pilous: hairy

plumigerous: furnished with plumage

plumose: bearing plumes or processes

prickly: having prickles

rough: having an uneven, irregular surface

rough as a bear: a figurative expression denoting degree of roughness

rough as a nutmeg grater: a figurative expression denoting degree of roughness

rough-hewn: roughly shaped

rugate: wrinkled

rugged: having a surface full of points or bristles

rugose: corrugated with wrinkles

rugous: full of wrinkles

salebrous: rugged; uneven; rough

scabrous: roughened with little points

scored: having surface cuts or nicks; abraded; scarred; scraped; scratched; scuffed

scraggly: irregular in form; rough; scraggy

scraggy: rough with irregular points

scrobiculate: with numerous shallow depressions; pitted

setaceous: covered with or like setae or bristles; hispid; spiny

setose: having stiff hairs

setous: having stiff hairs

shagged: covered with a coarse, thick growth

shrunk: drawn up into wrinkles

Sotadic: characterized by coarseness; Sotadean

suberose: appearing to be chewed, like cork

tomentous: covered with matted woolly hairs

tufted: having a tuft or crest

uneven: not even

unpolished: rough

unsmooth: rough

unsnod: rough, not smooth; in disorder

vermiculated: worm-eaten; with worm holes; resembling the tracks of worms; vermiculate

verrucose: warty

villous: covered with short, soft hair

weathered: having a face expressive of weariness; haggard; weather-beaten

well-wooded: thickly covered with trees

wizened: shriveled

woolly: covered with or like wool

wrinkled: having wrinkles; crinkled; crinkly; crispate; rugose

Rule

abdicant: pertaining to one who abdicates

absolute: having no limitations; unrestricted

accredited to: bearing a warrant to deal with

administrative: capable of carrying into effect

arbitrary: acting according to one's own will; despotic

aristocratic: of or pertaining to an aristocracy; haughty

at one's command: under one's rule

at the head: ruling

aulic: pertaining to a royal court

authoritative: having authority; exercising power

authorized: commanded; sanctioned

autocratic: pertaining to a government by one person of unlimited powers

basilic: royal; kingly

bicameral: having two legislative houses in government

bipartisan: pertaining to both major parties

classified: secret

clothed with authority: invested with power

commanding: ordering

communistic: pertaining to communism

compulsory: of that which must be done; required by rules; enforced

cruel: governing so as to inflict injury upon the governed

cunctipotent: omnipotent; all-powerful

decretal: pertaining to a decree

decretive: determining

decretory: established by a decree

designate: used following title it modifies to indicate that person has been selected for office but not yet installed, as in ambassador-designate

despotic: ruling like an absolute monarch

directing: that directs; governing the actions of

dirigent: guiding; directive

ditionary: under rule or domination

domestic: pertaining to internal affairs of state

dominant: exercising chief power; predominant

dynastic: pertaining or concerned in a dynasty

executive: carrying into effect; charged with execution

exousiastic: pertaining to authority

fetial: ambassadorial; fecial

feudal: relating to a fee, founded on tenures by military service

gavel-to-gavel: designating entire period from opening of legislative session to adjournment

global: pertaining to entire world

gubernatorial: of or concerning a governor

hegemonic: ruling; guiding

hegemonical: hegemonic

high-handed: governing in an arbitrary and overbearing manner

imperative: containing a demand; positive

imperatorial: pertaining to an imperator; commanding

imperial: pertaining to an emperor; having power

imperious: given to commanding in an arrogant manner; haughty

in one's grasp: under one's authority

in one's power: under one's authority

in the ascendant: ruling

inexpugnable: incapable of being overthrown

influential: having influence; controlling

interaulic: existing between two royal families

international: that which involves two or more sovereign states

irresponsible: careless of the responsibilities of government

kingly: like a king

masterful: showing mastery

mediatized: reduced from a sovereign position, as a prince

monarchical: pertaining to a monarchy; regal; imperial

most-favored-nation: pertaining to treaty signatory that is accorded most-favorable commercial benefits by another nation

municipal: pertaining to local self-government

official: given with authority; authoritative

old-line: conservative; established; having seniority

oligarchic: pertaining to a government in the hands of a few

overruling: ruling over; predominating

paramount: superior to all; preeminent; superior in authority

peremptory: not admitting of debate or question; final in opinion; dogmatic

plenary: having full, absolute powers

popular: representative of majority of people

predominant: superior in power

preponderant: overcoming

princely: having the qualities of a prince

puissant: powerful; authoritative

regal: belonging to a king; royal

reginal: queenly

regnant: ruling

republican: suitable to a republic; harmonious to the principle of a republic

royal: pertaining to a king; kingly

royalist: favoring monarchy

ruling: exercising authority; governing

rumbustical: boisterous; overbearing

sovereign: supreme in power or authority; imperial

stringent: exact in the exercise of power; severe

supreme: highest in anything

tricameral: having three legislative houses or chambers in government

tyrannical: like a tyrant

tyrannous: in the manner of a tyrant

unconstitutional: in violation of constitutional principles

undemocratic: not in accord with democratic principles, especially totalitarian

under control: governed; under an authority

unicameral: having a single legislative chamber in government

viceregal: pertaining to a viceroy

Ruthlessness

breme: fierce; cruel

cruel: disposed to inflict pain or suffering; merciless

dowelless: having no pity

fell: cruel; ruthless; destructive; savage

harsh: crabbed; abusive

inclement: wanting in a kind and gentle temper

incompassionate: destitute of pity or tenderness

inexorable: that cannot be moved by entreaty or prayer; unyielding

merciless: without mercy; cruel

pitiless: destitute of pity

ruthless: void of ruth; pitiless

uncompassionate: not compassionate

unmerciful: not merciful

unpitying: not pitying

unrelenting: rigid; cruel; stern

Sale

emporeutic: pertaining to merchandise	**pignorate:** pawned; pignoratitious
emptional: buyable	**purchased:** bought
for sale: to be bought or sold	**salable:** that may be sold; marketable
in the market: on hand; for sale	**unbought:** not bought; not sold
marketable: fit to be offered for sale in a market; salable	**under the hammer:** at auction
nundinal: pertaining to a fair or market	**unpurchased:** unbought; not sold
on one's hands: in one's possession, care, or management	**unsalable:** not salable; unmerchantable
	vendible: capable of being vended or sold; salable

Sameness—Uniformity

according to rule: uniformly	**identical:** precisely the same
coalescent: agreeing	**ilk:** identical
coincident: occurring at identically the same time	**indistinguishable:** showing no difference
coinciding: having identically the same condition or quality	**invariable:** absolutely uniform in occurrence
connatural: having a uniform nature	**monotonous:** uniform in a tiresome manner
consistent: characterized by harmony between things or statements	**much of a muchness:** very similar
constant: remaining unchanged or invariable	**much the same:** identical in many respects
cotidal: indicating simultaneity in tides	**of a piece:** of the same sort
customary: established by common usage	**one:** identical
equivalent: identical in value	**regular:** conformed to a rule
even: free from great roughness	**same:** just like something else
homogeneous: composed of uniform material	**self:** identical
	selfsame: the very same
homologous: composed of similar material	**steady:** regular; constant; uniform

symphronistic: identical intellectually

tautoousian: having absolutely the same essence; tautoousious

the same: the identical

unaltered: not modified

uniform: having always the same form, manner, or character

Saneness

in one's right mind: having power to think rightly

in one's sober senses: free from mental derangement

in possession of one's faculties: having power to think

of sound mind: not enfeebled or deranged

rational: having the power of reasoning

reasonable: having the faculty of reasoning

resipiscent: restored to sanity; having learned from experience

sane: having power to reason; mentally sound

self-possessed: in control of one's faculties

sober: not swayed by excitement or passion

sober-minded: having a cool, dispassionate mind

sound: having the faculties of the mind in normal action and relation

sound-minded: of such degree of mental capacity as makes one responsible for one's acts

Scattering

adrift: floating about

broadcast: scattered widely

diffugient: scattering

disheveled: thrown into disorder, as the hair

dispersed: strewed or distributed widely

disspread: widely diffused

disseminated: scattered; diffused; dispersed; strewn

epidemic: affecting great numbers

scattered: dispersed to different areas

sparse: thinly scattered

sporadic: occurring irregularly

stray: having wandered from the way

streaming: flowing abundantly

unassembled: not called into same place

widespread: very generally distributed

Sculpture

anaglyptic: pertaining to an anaglyph, or figure in relief

anastatic: raised; embossed; having raised characters

ceramic: pertaining to pottery

ceroplastic: pertaining to wax molding

engraved: having a surface that is cut into, marked by incisions; incised; tooled

in relief: raised above the background

marble: made of marble

Parian: like the marble statuary of Paros, an island in the Aegean Sea

relief: having a raised surface; embossed; in relief

repoussé: raised or beaten into relief

ridged: having raised lengthwise strips

sculptured: carved or decorated

stylagalmaic: of a caryatid or pillar shaped like a woman

Xanthian: relating to Xanthus, a town in Lycia, famous for the sculptures found there

Secrecy

abditive: concealing

alphanumeric: utilizing both numbers and letters, especially designating such a code or cipher

arcane: secret; hidden

auricular: spoken secretly so as to be heard only by the ears intended for

backdoor: indirect, concealed, or devious

backstage: secretly or in private

backstairs: secret or furtive; scandalous

behind a screen: hidden away

behind-the-scenes: working in secret

buried: concealed by being covered

buttoned-up: concealed by closing up

cabalistic: concealed under mystery

clancular: secret; private; underhand

clandestine: done in secret; surreptitious

classified: designating information not to be revealed publicly, especially for reasons of national security

close: hidden by being enclosed

close as wax: secretive

clouded: hidden by being obscured

concealed: hidden

confidential: secret

covert: concealed for a purpose, often evil; hidden; undercover; veiled

cryptic: intentionally obscure; used to conceal

cryptical: not plainly evident

dark: hidden by a lack of light

doggo: lying in hiding, especially concealed at a distance

esoteric: understood by or designed for only a few

evasive: escaping ready apprehension

feline: stealthy like a cat

furtive: sly or shifty; obtained by stealth

hidden: put out of sight

hole-and-corner: hiding to promote evil

hush-hush: highly secret

in a cloud: beclouded

in a dark corner: out of sight

in a fog: out of sight

in a haze: indistinctly visible

in a mist: hidden

in ambush: hidden in order to attack without warning

in disguise: hidden under an unusual costume

in hiding: in an unknown place

in petto: not yet made public

in the dark: out of sight

in the shade: indistinctly visible

incognito: having one's identity concealed

invisible: that cannot be seen

irrevealable: that may not be brought from concealment

low-profile: in a deliberately inconspicuous or anonymous manner; without attracting attention

mum: silent; kept secret

mysterious: hidden in mystery

mystic: hidden from human observation

not to be spoken of: out of mind

oblique: indirect, devious, or underhanded; obscure

obreptitious: with secrecy or by concealment of the truth

obscure: dim, concealed from view, or unclear; oblique

occult: hidden from observation or knowledge

private: not to be generally disseminated; out of public view or knowledge

privy: hidden in seclusion

recondite: hidden from easy perception

reserved: kept back for the present

reticent: habitually concealing by silence

secluded: hidden from others

secret: hidden from view or knowledge; hidden; obscure

secretive: having a tendency to hide

skulking: hiding from an evil motive

sly: clever in doing things in a hidden manner

stealthy: acting in a hidden manner

sub rosa: secretly; sub-rosa

subterranean: operating secretly outside normal society

surreptitious: accomplished by secret means; clandestine

taciturn: habitually silent

top secret: designating secret information, the revelation of which would pose grave danger to authority or security

ulterior: beyond what is shown or avowed; intentionally kept concealed

uncommunicative: not inclined to talk

under an eclipse: secret

undercover: acting in secret; engaged in spying; covert

underground: deeply hidden

underhand: done in a treacherous and hidden manner

underhanded: secretive or deceptive; sly; dishonest

under-the-counter: clandestine, usually involving illicit transaction or merchandise

under-the-table: secret; underhanded; as a bribe

undisclosed: not explained or exposed

untold: not revealed

wise: possessing inside information

wrapped in clouds: clouded

Security

above water: out of danger

Achillean: invulnerable, like Achilles

at anchor: secure from injury

bailable: able to be bailed

clavigerous: guarding; custodial

defensible: capable of being defended

fireproof: incapable of being destroyed by fire

guardian: charged with the duty of guarding

harmless: incapable of inflicting injury

high and dry: out of harm's way

imperdible: that cannot be destroyed

impregnable: that cannot be injured by attack

in safety: free from danger

in security: free from danger

inexpugnable: that cannot be successfully attacked

insurable: capable of being insured

invulnerable: incapable of being wounded

not dangerous: free from danger

on sure ground: free from harm or danger

on the safe side: free from harm or danger

out of danger: free from harm or danger

out of harm's way: free from harm or danger

out of the meshes: out of danger of being caught; out of the net

panoplied: completely protected, as by armor

preservative: able to preserve

proof against: capable of resisting

protected: rendered safe

protecting: able to protect

safe: in a position where harm cannot be done

safe and sound: free from all harm or injury

salvific: promoting safety

scathless: unharmed

seaworthy: capable of successfully resisting the dangers of the sea

secure: not liable to be exposed to injury or attack

snug: closely protected

sure: certainly protected

tenable: that can be defended

trustworthy: that can be depended upon

tutelary: having guardianship over

unassailable: that cannot be assailed

unattackable: that cannot be successfully attacked

under lock and key: protected by lock and key

under the shade of: under the protection of

under the shadow of one's wing: under the careful protection of

under the shield of: in one's charge or care

under the wing of: in one's charge or care
undercover: protected
unhazarded: not placed in danger of loss or injury
unmolested: not disturbed or attacked

unthreatened: not in the way of danger
waterproof: that cannot be injured by water
weatherproof: that cannot be harmed by destructive force of weather

Self-Indulgence

Apician: epicurean
bred in the lap of luxury: reared luxuriously
brutish: of the nature of a brute; gross; carnal
cade: pampered; spoiled
centered in self: narrow; prejudiced
cosseted: coddled; pampered
covetous: greedy
crapulous: ill by intemperance
debauched: given to intemperance
dissolute: given to vice and intemperance
earthly: material; gross
earthly-minded: limited to earthly things
egotistic: pertaining to self-love
egotistical: pertaining to self-love
epicurean: one given to sensual pleasures
fast: dissipated; intemperate
full-fed: fed to fullness
illiberal: not generous
inabstinent: wanting in abstinence
indulged: humored to excess
intemperate: given to excessive use of alcoholic drinks
interested: biased; caring for self only
licentious: intemperate in sensual indulgences
luxurious: pertaining to luxury
mean: low; stingy
mercenary: greedy for gain; closefisted
mundane: worldly

narrow-minded: unsympathetic; bigoted
nursed in the lap of luxury: addicted to luxury
pampered: indulged intemperately
Paphian: pertaining to Paphos, a city sacred to Aphrodite; hence belonging to Aphrodite or her rites
piggish: acting like a pig; greedy
self-indulgent: indulging one's desires, appetites
self-interested: self-centered
selfish: considering only one's own comfort and advantage
self-seeking: seeking self-interest
sensual: intemperate in the animal nature
swinish: greedy, like swine; gross
sybaritical: luxurious
timeserving: changing one's opinions according to one's advantage
ungenerous: not generous; illiberal
unspiritual: carnal-minded
venal: capable of being bought for money
voluptuous: pertaining to sensual pleasures
wild: intemperate in conduct
worldly: worldly-minded; worldly-wise
worldly-minded: caring for present gain and enjoyment
worldly-wise: caring for present gain and enjoyment
wrapped up: altogether devoted to

Sensitiveness

alive to: attentive; open to impressions
enthusiastic: having the feelings or sympathies intensely aroused in approval
excitable: capable of having the feelings greatly agitated; very nervous

expressive: give forcible expression to the feelings
fastidious: hard to please; oversensitive
gushing: weakly sentimental
high-flying: extravagant in feelings and action

impassionable: capable of being strongly affected by passion

impressible: capable of being affected by an impression

impressionable: susceptible or subject to impression

lively: full of animation or feeling

maudlin: very emotional or sentimental

mettlesome: high-spirited

mobile: easy or slow of expression of feeling

oversensitive: too sensitive

romantic: inspiring imaginary or ideal thoughts

sensible: capable of sensation or emotion

sensitive: easily touched to emotion; impressionable

sentimental: given to or inspiring tender or extravagant emotions

soft: foolishly sentimental or impressible

softhearted: pitiful

spirited: having considerable spirit or vivacity

susceptible: capable of being influenced

susceptive: that receives or tends to receive an impression

tender as a chicken: very tender

tenderhearted: easily moved to pity

thin-skinned: very easily affected or impressed

tremblingly alive: sensible to even the slightest influence

vivacious: full of lively spirit and feeling

warmhearted: sympathetic

without skin: very sensitive

Sensuality

adducent: drawing or binding together

adductive: drawing or binding together

agreeable: pleasant to the senses

allicient: attracting; alluring

amphierotic: sexually attracted to either sex

at ease: comfortable

attracting: causing to draw near

attractive: having the quality of attracting

attrahent: drawing to or toward something; attracting

basial: pertaining to kissing

comfortable: affording comfort

comforting: enjoying

cordial: tending to revive or invigorate

cosy: comfortable; easy

cozy: comfortable; easy

enjoying: delighting in

epithumetic: sensual

fragrant: having a sweet smell

genial: contributing to the enjoyment of life

grateful: giving pleasure to the senses

illecebrous: alluring

in comfort: at ease

lovely: delightful

lovertine: addicted to lovemaking

luxurious: relating to luxury; voluptuous

melodious: pleasant to the senses by a sweet succession of sounds

palatable: pleasant to the taste

refreshing: reanimating

rompworthy: sexually desirable

sensual: given to the pleasures of sense and appetite

sensuous: pertaining to the senses

snug: convenient or comfortable

sweet: having a pleasant taste; agreeable to the senses

voluptuous: given to the enjoyment of luxury and pleasure; excessively indulgent in sensual gratifications

Sequence

after: later in time

after-dinner: postprandial

alternate: of two things, each succeeding the other in turn

antepenultimate: third from the end, as a syllable

collateral: corresponding, especially in parallel sequence; secondary

consecutive: following in regular order; resulting as a consequence
consequent: following as a natural result
continuous: of things, connected or unbroken
correlative: related as reciprocal proofs
enneatic: every ninth of a series
go/no-go: requiring a decision to continue or halt
interlocking: connected; interrelated
latter: coming or happening after something else
linear: proceeding logically or sequentially in a straight line
next: following directly after
posterior: toward the rear
proximate: lying next to; nearest

random: without order or sequence
reciprocal: shared by or affecting both sides equally
relative: associated; relevant; referring or connected to another thing
sequacious: inclined to follow; logically following in a series
sequent: following; succeeding
sequential: in an order; following an order
step-by-step: taken in proper sequence; one at a time
subsequent: coming or being after something else
succeeding: following in regular order
syndetic: connective; interconnected
well-ordered: organized into logical and coherent form

Sexuality

AC/DC: bisexual
age-differentiated: designating homosexuality involving usually bisexual adult male and sexually passive young boy prized for his androgynous qualities, predominant in Islamic world, ancient Greece, and preindustrial Europe
androgynous: having both male and female characteristics
asexual: having no sexual orientation
astride: taking a dominant position during penetration
bent: homosexual
bisexual: attracted to and sexually active with both males and females
butch: designating a masculine-appearing or -behaving female; designating a masculine-behaving male homosexual
buxom: describing woman having large breasts and full body
callipygian: having shapely buttocks
carnal: relating to physical desire
Circean: dangerously or fatally attractive
cold: sexually unresponsive
deviant: departing from the norm; considered perverse or unnatural

easy: available for indiscriminate sex
effeminate: not masculine in appearance or behavior, said especially of homosexuals
epicene: with characteristics of both sexes; sexless; neither male nor female
erogenous: designating areas of body that are sensitive to sexual stimulation; erotogenic
erotic: pertaining to sexual love; strongly sexual
erotogenic: erogenous
fast: easily available for sex
feminine: characteristic of women; female
flaming: blatantly or outlandishly gay
frigid: sexually unresponsive, said especially of women
gay: homosexual, either male or female, sometimes restricted to males only
gender-differentiated: designating homosexuality involving fixed sexual roles in which one partner is passive and the other active-penetrative
gynandrous: having physical characteristics of both sexes
hard-core: graphic and explicit in pornographic content

horny: craving sex; sexually aroused

hot: sexy; aroused; stimulated

hung: having a large penis

impotent: unable to achieve erection for sexual intercourse

ithyphallic: lewd; obscene; displaying an erect penis

kinky: perverse, decadent, or unusual in one's sexual habits

lascivious: lustful; lewd

latent: in popular usage, designating one who appears heterosexual while repressing unconscious homosexual tendencies

lewd: lustful; lecherous; obscene in desires

liberated: without sexual inhibition

lusty: filled with sexual desire

macho: overly assertive, virile, and domineering

male: characteristic of men

mammary: pertaining to woman's breasts

manly: virile; macho

masculine: characteristic of men; male

nellie: designating an effeminate male; designating a homosexual male

neuter: having no sex

nubile: ready for marriage, said especially of young women

off-color: somewhat offensive; indecent

oversexed: having excessive sexual interest and energy

phallic: pertaining to the penis

priapic: pertaining to the penis

pubic: pertaining to or situated in area of pubis

pudibund: prudish

pure: chaste

racy: spirited; sexually zestful

raunchy: coarse; earthy

ruttish: salacious; lustful

salacious: lewd; lascivious

salt-and-pepper: designating interracial couple

scabrous: risqué; obscene

sensual: carnal; devoted to sensory pleasure

sexual: concerned with sex or sexual acts

situational: designating homosexuality that occurs in sex-segregated situations, such as prisons, ships, or boarding schools, where heterosexuals are deprived of contact with the opposite sex, usually temporary and without homosexual self-identity

soft-core: having borderline pornographic content

stacked: having voluptuous, sexually appealing body, especially large breasts

stag: designating all-male event, especially with lewd entertainment

steamy: sexually arousing

sterile: barren; incapable of procreating

straight: heterosexual

sucked dry: fellated with great passion

sultry: characterized by or arousing passion

supermacho: given to extreme displays of virility

taboo: forbidden due to indecency or bad taste

throbbing: pulsing with sexual arousal

transsexual: sexually oriented as if one's body were of the opposite sex

undersexed: having inadequate sexual interest and energy

unisexual: of one sex

unsexual: not sexual

virile: manly; masculine

voluptuous: devoted to sensual gratification

wanton: loose; lewd; promiscuous; immoral

well-hung: having a large penis

X-rated: pornographic, used especially of a book or film

Shallowness

ankle-deep: of a depth sufficient to cover the ankle
depthless: shallow; superficial
ebb: shallow; not deep
eurybathic: capable of living on the bottom of shallow or deep water
flat: wide and shallow
just enough to wet one's feet: shallow
knee-deep: of a depth sufficient to cover the knee

neritic: relating to the shallow water along a seacoast
shallow: not deep
shoal: shallow
shoaly: full of shoals
skin-deep: going only through the skin
superficial: lying on the surface

Shape

acicular: needle-shaped
acinaciform: scimitar-shaped
aciniform: formed like a grape cluster
actiniform: radial
aculeiform: thorn-shaped
acuminate: tapering to a slender point
acute: of an angle of less than 90 degrees
aliform: wing-shaped
allantoid: sausage-shaped; botuliform
almond-eyed: having eyes shaped like almonds, as Asians often do
alphabetiform: alphabet-like
amentiform: catkin-shaped
amoebiform: amoeba-shaped; amoeboid
ampullaceous: bottle-shaped; shaped like a two-handled bottle; ampulliform; utriculate; utriculoid
amygdaloid: almond-shaped; amygdaliform
anguiform: snake-shaped
anguilliform: eel-shaped
angular: sharp-cornered; having points from which two lines diverge
ankyroid: hook-shaped; aduncate; ancistroid; hamiform; unciform; uncinate
annular: ring-shaped
antenniform: antenna-shaped
apical: narrowing to a pointed tip
apsidal: apse-shaped
arboriform: tree-shaped; dendriform; dendritic; dendritiform; dendroid
arciform: arch-shaped
arcuate: curved like a bow

ascidiform: shaped like a pitcher
asteriated: having starlike rays
astroid: star-shaped; actinoid; stellar; stellate; stelliform; stellular
asymmetrical: lacking balance; not the same on both sides of central axis
attenuated: tapering to long, slender point
auriform: ear-shaped; auriculate
aveniform: oat-shaped
awry: turned or twisted from a central axis
baccate: berry-shaped; bacciform
bacillary: rod-shaped
baculiform: rod-shaped
balanoid: acorn-shaped
belemnoid: dart-shaped
beloid: arrow-shaped
biconcave: concave on both sides
biconical: of two cones placed base to base
biconvex: convex on both sides
bifurcate: divided into two branches
bilateral: two-sided; symmetrical on both sides of an axis
biradial: having both bilateral and radial symmetry
botuliform: sausage-shaped
botryoidal: formed like a grape cluster; aciniform
botryose: like a grape cluster; aciniform
brachial: arm-shaped
branchiform: gill-shaped

branching: forming subdivisions like a tree
bulbous: round like a bulb
bulliform: bubblelike
bursiform: pouch-shaped
cactiform: shaped like cactus
calamiform: reedlike
calathiform: cup-shaped
calceiform: slipper-shaped; soleiform
calciform: pebble-shaped; calculiform
campanulate: bell-shaped
canaliform: canal-like
cancriform: crab-shaped
cannular: tube-shaped
capitate: enlarged at the head and spherical; forming a head
capitellate: having a knob at one end
carbunculoid: shaped like a large boil
cardioid: heart-shaped
carinate: keel-shaped; cariniform
caudiform: tail-like
cauliform: stemlike
celliform: cell-like
celtiform: shaped like a celt
cerebriform: brainlike
cheliform: pincer-shaped
cingular: ring-shaped
circinate: ringlike; annular; cingular
circular: circle-shaped
cirriform: curl-like
clavate: club-shaped and thicker at one end; claviform
claviform: club-shaped; clavate
clithridiate: keyhole-shaped
clothoid: tear-shaped loop
cochleariform: spoon-shaped
cochleate: shaped like a snail's shell; cochleiform
coextensive: having the same shape or boundaries
colliform: necklike
colubriform: snake-shaped; anguiform
columnar: arranged in vertical rows
compass: curved; forming a curve or an arc
concave: hollowed, rounded, or curved inward
concavo-convex: concave on one side

and convex on the other, especially with greater curvature on concave side; convexo-concave
conchiform: shaped like half a bivalve shell; conchate
conglobulate: ball-shaped
conical: having a circular base that tapers to another point; cone-shaped; conic; funnel-shaped
conoid: conelike or nearly conelike; conoidal
convex: curved or rounded outward, as with exterior of sphere or circle
convexo-concave: concavo-convex, especially with greater curvature on convex side
convoluted: twisted; coiled
corbiculate: shaped like a small basket
cordate: heart-shaped; cordiform
cordated: heart-shaped
cordiform: heart-shaped; cordate
corniform: horn-shaped; cornute
coroniform: having the shape of a crown
corticiform: barklike
crenate: having margin or surface cut into scallops or notches
crenulate: scalloped or notched; having an irregular wave or outline; crenulated
cribriform: sievelike
cristiform: crest-shaped
cruciate: cross-shaped; cruciform
cruciform: cross-shaped
cubic: solid with six square faces
cubical: cube-shaped
cubiform: cube-shaped
cuboid: somewhat cubic; cuboidal
cucullate: hood-shaped; cuculliform
cucumiform: shaped like a cucumber
cucurbitaceous: resembling a cucumber or squash
cuneal: wedge-shaped
cuneate: triangular at base and tapering toward a point; cuneal
cupulate: shaped like a cupule; cupuliform
cuspidate: terminating in a point
cyathiform: cup-shaped

cylindrical: having an elongated round shape; cylinder-shaped; columnal; columnar; pillarlike

cylindriform: cylinder-shaped

dactyloid: fingerlike; digitate; digitiform

decagonal: ten-sided

decurved: curved or bent downward

decussate: X-shaped

deltoid: triangular

dendriform: tree-shaped; dendroid

dendroid: tree-shaped; dendriform

dentiform: tooth-shaped

disciform: disk-shaped; discoid

discoid: disk-shaped

dodecagonal: twelve-sided

dolabriform: ax-shaped; axiniform; dolabrate; securiform

dolioform: shaped like a barrel

drepanoid: sickle-shaped; drepaniform

elliptic: ellipse-shaped; elliptical

elongate: stretched out

embryoniform: embryo-like

ensiform: sword-shaped

eruciform: like a caterpillar

fabiform: bean-shaped; fabaceous

falcate: hooked or curved like a sickle; falciform

falciform: sickle-shaped; falcate

fastigiate: narrowing toward the top; having upright clustered branches

filiciform: fern-shaped

filiform: thread-shaped; filariform; fililose

flabellate: fan-shaped; flabelliform; rhipidate

foliate: branching, especially into leaves

foraminous: in the shape of a foramina

forcipiform: like a forceps

forciform: shaped like scissors

forficate: forked; furcate

forficiform: shaped like a pair of scissors

fructiform: fruit-shaped

fundiform: in a loop or sling shape

fungiform: mushroom-shaped; agariciform

fungoid: funguslike in form

funiform: cord- or ropelike

furcal: branched; furcate

furcating: forking; furcated

furcellate: branched slightly

furciferous: fork-shaped

fusiform: spindle-shaped; tapering at each end

galeated: helmet-shaped; hooded; galeate; cassideous

galeiform: resembling a shark

geometric: having a simple plane shape

glandiform: acorn-shaped; glanduliform

globose: globular

globular: globe-shaped; spherical; globose

guttiform: shaped like a drop; lacrimiform; stilliform

guttulous: shaped like small drops

hamiform: hook-shaped

harengiform: herring-shaped

hastate: triangular or arrow-shaped with two spreading lobes at base

hederiform: shaped like ivy

helical: spiral; helix-shaped

helicoid: screw-shaped

hemihedral: having half the number of planes required by symmetry

heptagonal: having seven angles and seven sides

herpetiform: in the shape or character of a reptile

hexagonal: having six angles and six sides

hippocrepiform: horseshoe-shaped

holohedral: having all the symmetrical faces possible

hominiform: human-shaped

homogeneous: having parts of similar form and arrangement

hordeiform: in the shape of a grain of barley

hyoid: U-shaped; hippocrepiform; parabolic

ichthyomorphic: fish-shaped

infundibuliform: funnel- or cone-shaped

interfacial: formed by two faces of a polyhedron

involute: curled or spiraling inward

irregular: having an unconventional or uneven shape; bumpy; contorted; de-

formed; grotesque; lumpy; malformed; misshapen

isomorphic: being of the same shape and general appearance

isomorphous: similar in form

labial: lip-shaped; labellate; labelloid

lambdoid: shaped like a lambda

lamelliform: shaped like a thin plate

lanceolate: narrow and tapering at one end, like the head of a lance

leguminose: pod-shaped; leguminiform

ligulate: strap-shaped

liliform: shaped like a lily

linear: narrow and elongated

linguiform: tongue-shaped

lobate: lobe-shaped; lobiform; lobular

lotiform: shaped like a lotus petal

lozenge-shaped: having four equal sides and two acute and two obtuse angles; diamond; lozengelike

lunate: half-moon-shaped; bicorn; bicornuate; bicornuous; lunulate

malleiform: shaped like a hammer

mammiform: shaped like breasts

mammilloid: nipple-shaped; mammilliform

mammose: breast-shaped

maniform: hand-shaped; palmate

manubrial: handle-shaped; ansate

mitrate: miter-shaped; mitriform

moline: having the end of each arm forked and recurved

moniliform: with regular segments, like string of beads; monilioid

moriform: mulberry-shaped

morphic: of or pertaining to a form or shape; morphologic; morphological

morphous: having a definite form

mummiform: mummylike

muscariform: brush-shaped; aspergilliform; scopiform; scopulate; scopuliform

napiform: globular at top and tapering off gradually; parsnip- or carrot-shaped; rapaceous

nariform: nostril-like

nasiform: noselike; nasutiform

natiform: resembling the buttocks

nodiform: shaped like a knot or node

nodose: knobbly; knotty

nodular: in shape of rounded or irregular mass

nonagonal: nine-sided

notched: having V-shaped or rounded indentation, especially at edge

nubiform: cloud-shaped

nummiform: coin-shaped; nummular

nummular: coin-shaped; nummiform

obclavate: club-shaped with the thick part at the base

obcordate: heart-shaped with the attachment on the pointed end; obcordiform

obcuneate: inversely triangular or wedge-shaped, with the thin end at the base; obdeltoid

obeliscoid: shaped like an obelisk; obeliskoid

oblate: flattened or depressed at poles

oblique: inclined; neither parallel nor perpendicular; having no right angle

obovate: ovate with narrower end at base

obovoid: somewhat egg-shaped, with the broader end outward; obovate

obtuse: being an angle of more than 90 degrees but less than 180 degrees

obverse: having base narrower than top

octagonal: having eight angles and eight sides

oculiform: eye-shaped

odontoid: tooth-shaped; dentiform

ogival: having the form of a pointed (Gothic) arch; curving to a point with a dip inward on each side of the apex

omegoid: shaped like an omega

ophidiform: resembling snakes

orbicular: spherical; circular

oriform: mouth-shaped

ostreiform: shaped like an oyster; ostreoid; ostriform

oval: broadly elliptical; egg-shaped

ovate: shaped like longitudinal section of an egg with basal end broader

ovoid: egg-shaped; ovate

palaceous: shovel-shaped

palmate: shaped like the human hand

with fingers spread; palmatiform; palmiform

pandurate: fiddle-shaped

panduriform: shaped like a violin; pandurate

papillary: round or cone-shaped like a bud or nipple

papyriform: papyrus-shaped

parabolic: parabola-shaped; bowl-shaped

parallelepipedal: prismatic with parallelograms at the ends

parted: divided into distinct portions by deep, lengthwise cuts

pateriform: saucer-shaped; acetabuliform

peaked: coming to a point at top

pectinate: comb-shaped; having comb-like teeth

pediform: foot-shaped; pedate

peltate: shield-shaped

pelviform: basin-shaped

pemphigoid: bubble-shaped; bubblelike

penciliform: shaped like a pencil

pennate: wing- or feather-shaped; alate

penniform: having the form of a feather

pentagonal: having five angles and five sides

petaliform: petal-shaped

phalliform: shaped like a phallus

phylliform: leaf-shaped; foliiform

pineal: pineapple-shaped

pinnate: resembling a feather, with similar parts arranged on opposite sides of an axis

pinniform: shaped like a fin or feather

pisiform: shaped like a pea or peas

plano-concave: flat on one side, concave on the other

plano-convex: flat on one side, convex on the other

plasmic: giving form; capable of being molded

plastic: giving form; capable of being molded

pociliform: shaped like a little cup; poculiform

poculiform: cup-shaped

polygonal: shaped like a plane bounded by three or more straight lines

polyhedral: having many faces or sides; polyhedric

pomiform: apple-shaped; maliform

prismatoidal: polyhedral with all vertices in two parallel planes

prismoidal: prismatoidal with parallel bases having the same number of sides

prolate: elongated in direction of a line joining poles

pulvilliform: padlike; cushion-shaped; pulvillar; pulvinate

pyramidal: triangular with the large end as the base

pyriform: pear-shaped

quadrangular: quadrilateral-shaped

ramiform: branching off; branch-shaped

reclivate: having an S-shape

rectangular: rectangle-shaped

rectilinear: forming a straight line

regular: having a shape with equal sides or angles

remiform: oar-shaped

reniform: kidney-shaped

resofincular: resembling a wire hanger

retiary: netlike; weblike; entangling; of making a web

retroflex: turned or bent abruptly inward

retuse: having apex that is rounded or obtuse with a slight notch

rhipidate: fan-shaped

rhombohedral: being a solid figure bounded by six equal rhombuses

rhomboid: rhombus-shaped

rostrate: beak-shaped; rhamphoid; rostriform

rostriform: bill-shaped; rhamphoid; rostrate

rotiform: wheel-shaped; rotate

round: circular; ring- or ball-shaped

sacciform: bag-shaped; bursiform; scrotiform

sagittate: shaped like an arrowhead; sagittiform

samariform: shaped like a winged seed pod

sandaliform: sandal-shaped

scalloped: having a border formed by a continuous series of circle segments or angular projections
scalpriform: chisel-shaped
scaphoid: boat-shaped; navicular
scopiform: broom-shaped
scrotiform: pouch-shaped
scutate: shield-shaped; clypeate
scutiform: shield-shaped; aspidate; clypeate; clypeiform; elytriform; peltate; peltiform; scutatiform
scyphate: cup-shaped; calathiform; calicular; caliculate; cyathiform; scyphiform
sectoral: pie-shaped
securiform: axe-shaped; axiniform; dolabriform
selachostomous: shark-mouthed
selliform: saddle-shaped
semilunar: in the form of a half-moon; demilune
serrate: notched or toothed along edge
shaped: having a shape or form; configured; conformed; fashioned; formed
sigmate: S-shaped; sigmoid
sigmoid: S-shaped; annotated
siliquiform: shaped like a small pod or husk
similiform: having a similar form; conforming; equiform
soleiform: slipper-shaped
spatulate: shaped like a spatula; thin and flat
sphenic: triangle- or delta-shaped; triangular
sphenoid: wedge-shaped
spherical: sphere-shaped
spicate: arranged in the form of a spike
spiciform: spike-shaped; spicate
spiral: winding around a fixed line in a series of planes; coiling around a center while receding from or approaching it; helical
squaliform: shaped like a shark; selachian; squaloid
square: having four equal sides and four right angles in plane figure
stapedial: shaped like a stirrup

stapediform: stirrup-shaped
stellate: star-shaped
stelliform: star-shaped
stirious: resembling icicles
styliform: bristle-shaped
subulate: awl-shaped; subulated; subuliform
sudiform: stake-shaped
sycosiform: fig-shaped
symmetrical: having an axially balanced shape
tapering: becoming narrower at one end than the other
tauriform: bull-shaped
tectiform: rooflike or tent-shaped; used as a cover
tentiform: tent-shaped
terete: cylindrical but tapering at one or both ends; cigar- or torpedo-shaped
ternate: arranged in threes
tetartohedral: having one-fourth the number of planes needed for symmetry
toothed: having series of notches resembling teeth
toroidal: torus-shaped
torous: doughnut-shaped
trapezial: having four sides with no parallel sides; trapeziform
trapezoidal: having four sides, with two sides parallel; irregularly quadrilateral; antiparallelogrammatic
triangular: three-sided and plane
trifoliate: like a cloverleaf; trefoil; trifoliated
trifurcate: branching into three
trihedral: having three faces
trilateral: having three sides
trochlear: pulley-shaped; pulleylike
trochleiform: shaped like a pulley
truncated: having the end square or even
tubiform: tube-shaped; fistuliform
tubular: narrow and cylindrical; tube-shaped; tubulate
turriculate: turret-shaped; turriculated
turriform: tower-shaped; pyrgoidal; turrical; turricular
umbraculiform: shaped like an umbrella

unciform: J-shaped
uncinate: bent at the tip like a hook
undecagonal: having eleven sides
unguiform: claw- or nail-shaped
urceiform: like a one-handled jug
urceolate: pitcher-shaped
ursiform: bear-shaped
utriform: shaped like a leather bottle
valviform: valve-shaped
vasculiform: shaped like a flowerpot
vermiculate: having irregular, thin, wavy lines like the trail of a worm
verruciform: wart-shaped
villiform: closely set and resembling bristles or velvet pile

virgate: wand-shaped; long and slender
virgulate: rod-shaped; bacillary; bacilliform; baculiform; vergiform
volute: spiral- or scroll-shaped
vulviform: V-shaped
winding: describing a line that is curved, sinuous, or irregular
ypsiliform: Y-shaped; shaped like an upsilon; ypsiloid
zeppelinistic: resembling a zeppelin in shape
zosteriform: girdle-shaped
zygal: H-shaped
zygomorphous: yoke-shaped

Sharpness

acanaceous: prickly
acicular: with sharp points like a needle; needle-shaped
aciform: needle-shaped; acerose; acicular; aciculate; styloid
acuate: sharp-pointed
aculeated: having a sharp point; armed with prickles
acuminate: pointed; tapering to a fine point
acuminated: brought to a point
acute: coming to a point; having a sharply tapered point; acuate; acuminate; mucronate; pointed
ansal: two-edged; cutting both ways
arrowheaded: pointed like an arrow
arrowy: sharp like an arrow
barbed: having sharp projections
belonoid: needle-shaped
briery: covered with briers
bristling: standing like or appearing as if covered with bristles
conical: shaped like a cone
corniculate: having horns or projections like small horns
cornute: having or shaped like horns
cornuted: cornute
craggy: with numerous crags
cusped: furnished with cusps
cuspidate: having a sharp end like the point of a spear

cuspidated: cuspidate
cutting: adapted to cut
denticulated: notched into small toothlike projections
dentiform: tooth-shaped
digitated: having fingerlike processes
ensiform: sword-shaped
forficate: scissorlike; deeply forked
fusiform: spindle-shaped
gladiate: sword-shaped; ensate; ensiform; xiphiiform; xiphoid
glockamoid: shaped like an arrow point
hastate: shaped like a spear- or arrowhead
inermous: without thorns or prickers
keen: with fine edge or point
keen as a razor: very keen
knife-edged: with an edge like a knife
lanceolate: tapered to a point at either end, like some leaves; lanciform
mucronate: ending abruptly in a sharp point
mucronated: mucronate
muricate: having sharp points; prickly
muricated: full of sharp points
needle-pointed: pointed like a needle
needle-shaped: pointed like a needle
odontoid: toothlike
oxyacanthous: having sharp thorns, spines
peaked: ending in a point from a wider base

pectinated: having narrow divisions arranged like the teeth of a comb
pointed: having or coming to a point; acuate; acuminate; mucronate; pronged; spiked
prickly: covered with prickles
pyramidal: in the form of a pyramid
salient: standing out prominently; projecting
sharp: having a thin edge or acute point capable of cutting or piercing
sharp as a needle: very sharp
sharp as a razor: very sharp
sharp-edged: keen; cutting
sharpened: made to have a point or edge
snaggy: full of snags
spiculed: spiked
spiked: furnished with spikes
spiky: like a spike; having sharp points or spikes
spindle-shaped: thick in the middle and tapering to both ends

spinous: having spines; prickly
spiny: full of spines
spurred: furnished with spurs; having shoots like spurs
starlike: having points like a star
stellated: pointed like a star
stelliform: star-shaped
studded: filled with studs or little points
tapering: becoming gradually smaller toward one end
thistly: full of or resembling thistles
thorny: rough with or like thorns; barbed; echinated; prickly; spiny
toothed: having teeth or teethlike notches; crenelated; dentate; dentelated; dentellated; denticulate; notched; saw-toothed; serrated; serried; serrulate
two-edged: having two edges
xiphoid: sword-shaped
xyresic: razor-sharp

Shortness

brachyskelic: short-legged
brief: short; not long
commatic: brief; in short sentences or phrases
compact: brief; not diffuse
compendious: abridged; shortened
concise: short; brief; compendious
curt: short
curtailed of its fair proportion: having part broken off
dumpy: short and thick
fubsy: short and stout
improcerous: short in stature
little: not large; small
oblate: flattened at the poles
pug: short and thickset
runtish: having a short body; bantam; runty

scrimp: short
shorn: cut off by shears
short: not long; limited in extent
short by: not sufficiently long
short-waisted: having a proportionately short upper body
spuddy: thickset
squab: fat and thick
squabbish: thick; fat; heavy
squabby: fat and thick
squat: short and thick
stubbed: short and thick
stubby: short and thick
stumpy: short and thickset
summary: reduced into a narrow compass
thickset: having a short, thick body
undersized: shorter in one dimension

Sickness

afflicted with illness: stricken with illness
ailing: affected with pain or illness

anorectic: having no appetite, usually over a long period of time
azotic: incapable of supporting life

bedridden: confined to bed by disease or age

broken-winded: disordered respiration

cankered: having an unkind or malignant temper

carious: having ulcered and decayed bones

catching: infectious

chlorotic: affected with or like to the disease that causes the skin to become of a greenish hue

clonic: spastic; convulsing

confined: kept in bed by sickness

congenital: of a disease or defect existing from birth

conspurcated: corrupted; defiled

contagious: liable to be communicated by contact

contaminated: corrupted; tarnished

crample-hamm'd: having stiff lower joints

cranky: rickety

cresty: having hemorrhoids

crippled: deprived of limbs, strength, or activity

cronk: ill; ailing

cryptogenic: of a disease of unknown or obscure origin

deadly: causing death

decayed: having become weak, corrupted, or disintegrated

decrepit: broken down and weakened by old age

deleterious: destructive or unwholesome

diseased: ill; not well

donsie: slightly sick; donsy

drooping: growing weak or faint

dysepulotic: not healing quickly or easily

dyspeptic: afflicted with or pertaining to dyspepsia

emphysematous: concerning emphysema

emunctory: pertaining to nose-blowing

endemic: pertaining to a disease peculiar to a locality

envenomed: infused with venom

epidemic: of a disease, spreading rapidly through a group; infecting many people simultaneously

epizootic: affecting a large number of animals

febrifacient: producing fever; febriferous

flagging: growing weak or faint

flatulent: affected with flatus or gases generated in the alimentary canal; windy

furuncular: having boils or carbuncles

gasping: laboring for breath or respiring convulsively

halting: tending to stop the progress

healthless: without health

helminthous: infested with intestinal worms

iatrogenic: of an illness caused by a doctor's diagnosis or treatment

ill: not well; not in a normal condition of health

ill of: sick of

in a bad way: seriously ill

in danger: in a state of exposure to injury, pain, or disease

in declining health: in failing health

in hospital: sick; ill

incurable: not to be made well

indigestible: incapable of being converted into food

indisposed: slightly out of health

infectious: easily communicable by contact or otherwise; liable to transmit disease

infirm: weak; not strong

innutritious: not nourishing

insalubrious: not conducive to good health; unhealthy

insanable: incurable

invaletudinary: unhealthy

invalided: made like an invalid

laid up: unable to work or be about

lame: crippled or disabled in limb

lazarous: leprous

lectual: bedridden

leprous: afflicted with or pertaining to leprosy

loimic: pertaining to the plague

luetic: having syphilis

maliferous: unhealthy

mangy: infected with mange, a skin disease

mephitic: having the quality of mephitis; exhaling poison

morbid: not sound or healthful; abnormal

morbiferous: developing disease

morbific: causing disease

morbillous: pertaining to measles

moribund: at the point of death

morose: of a sour, ill-natured temper

narcotic: producing insensibility or stupor

nauseous: causing or experiencing nausea

neuromimetic: psychosomatic

noisome: offensive and injurious; noxious

nosocomial: of a disease originating in a hospital; pertaining to a hospital

nosopoetic: producing disease; unhygienic

noxious: liable to cause injury to health

on the sick list: among the sick

out of health: ill; not well

out of sorts: unwell

palsied: affected with palsy

paralytic: afflicted with paralysis

peccant: morbid; not healthy

peracute: of diseases, very acute or severe

pestiferous: bringing pestilence or disease

pestilent: engendering malignant disease

pestilential: having the nature of a pestilence

phanerogenic: of a disease of obvious origin

phthisic: concerning lung disease

poisoned: infected with poison; made corrupt

poisonous: containing or having the effect of poison

poorly: indisposed; slightly unwell

prodromal: concerning the first signs of disease

prosodemic: spread by personal contact

prostrate: deprived of strength

purulent: containing or discharging pus

qualmish: nauseated

rabid: infected with rabies

rotten: decaying; unsound

rotten at the core: unsound at the most important part

rotten to the core: completely unsound

sanable: able to be cured, remedied, healed

scorbutic: pertaining to scurvy

seasick: sick from the motion of a ship

seedy: old and worn out

seized with: invaded with suddenly

septic: causing putrefaction

sick: affected with disease; ill

sickly: unhealthy; not well

squeamish: having a stomach that is easily turned

stuporous: being in a stupor; stuporose

tabid: wasted by disease

tainted: corrupted; spoiled

taken ill: become ill

taking: catching

tenesmic: pertaining to inability to urinate or defecate

theriodic: malignant

touched in the wind: short of breath

toxic: poisonous

tussive: pertaining to a cough

ulcerated: having sores or lesions; broken

unbraced: loosened; relaxed

uncongenial: not suited to one's temperament

ungenial: not imparting life and health

unhealthy: not in good health; not producing good health

unsound: not strong

unwell: somewhat ill; indisposed

unwholesome: not producing or promoting good health

valetudinary: infirm; weak; sickly

variolate: having lesions, as in smallpox

venomous: containing or having effect of venom; poisonous

virulent: exceedingly poisonous

vitiated: injured; spoiled

weakened: made less in strength

weakly: with little strength

withered: dried up; passing away

zymotic: pertaining to infectious disease; contagious

Sight

amaurotic: pertaining to loss of eyesight with no external change to the eye
argus-eyed: hundred-eyed; watchful
bedroom: having sexy eyes
bright-eyed: having lively eyes; beaming; flashing; luminous
centoculated: having a hundred eyes
clear-sighted: of keen physical or intellectual vision
cockeyed: having squinty eyes; squinting
deep-set: having sunken eyes; hollow-eyed
dewy: having moist eyes; aqueous; glistening; watery
eagle-eyed: farsighted and keen-sighted
eidetic: able to visualize something previously seen
goggle-eyed: having staring eyes
gooseberry-eyed: having large round eyes
hawkeyed: having piercing eyes
heavy-lidded: having half-closed or large-lidded eyes; sleepy-eyed; slumberous; slumbrous
keen-eyed: sharp-sighted

lynx-eyed: having acute sight; lyncean
macromeritic: visible to the naked eye
macroscopic: large enough to be visible to the naked eye
ocular: pertaining to the eye
ophthalmic: of or pertaining to the organ of vision
optic: of or pertaining to the eye
optical: of or pertaining to the science of optics
presbyopic: farsighted
scopic: visual
seeing: having knowledge by the eye
sighted: having sight of a specified kind
specious: pleasing to the view
strabismic: squinting; strabismal
subvisible: not visible to the unaided eye
twenty-twenty: having normal visual acuity
visible: capable of being seen
visual: connected with the sense of sight
wide-eyed: having large eyes; fish-eyed; saucer-eyed
wide-set: having far-apart eyes
winking: closing and opening the eye suddenly

Sign

armorial: relating to heraldry
characteristic: distinguishing; marking
connotative: implying something added to a definition, so that it will apply to fewer objects
curiological: pertaining to hieroglyphics; depicting by images instead of symbolically; curiologic
demonstrative: having the power to indicate
denotable: capable of being indicated
denotative: marking off, designating objects to which a definition is to apply
diacritical: that distinguishes; distinctive
diagnostic: indicating the nature of a disease
emblematic: serving as a sign or emblem

exponential: relating to exponents
indelible: that cannot be removed or blotted out
indicated: pointed out
indicating: marking out
indicative: pointing out; giving intimation
indicatory: serving to show; indicating
individual: indicating singleness
jolloped: in heraldry, depicted with a wattle
known by: indicated or distinguished by
marked: designated; indicated
pantomimic: representing by dumb show
pathognomonic: indicating a disease with certainty

pointed: marked by a point or points, as to designate the pauses in a sentence
recognizable by: capable of being recognized by, as by a mark or sign
representative: indicative of a class
signal: serving as a sign

symbolic: indicating by a symbol
symptomatic: indicating the existence of something other than itself
typical: representing something by a sign, model, form

Silence

awful: inspiring or manifesting awe
conticent: quiet; hushed
deathlike: silent, like the silence of death
harpocratic: concerning silence
hushed: made quiet
inaudible: incapable of being heard
mute: uttering no word or sound
noiseless: without noise
obmutescent: becoming or staying silent, often out of obstinance

silent: making no sound; not speaking; still
silent as the grave: silent, like the silence of death
soft: not loud or harsh
solemn: impressive; awe-inspiring
soundless: without sound
still: making no sound; silent
stilly: still; subdued in sound
sub silentio: in silence

Similarity

akin to: related by blood to; of similar nature with
alike: differing either not at all or not in a marked degree; of the same essential form
allied to: morphologically related
analogical: containing or involving analogy
analogous: bearing analogy or resemblance, as to form, relation
approximate: nearly resembling
as like as it can stare: exactly alike
as like as two peas: exactly alike
au pied de la lettre: literally; exactly
cast in the same mold: alike in form or disposition
close: very similar
congener: of the same stock, group, kind
congenerous: of the same kind; alike in nature or character
connatural: having the same nature
enantiomorphic: having a mirror image; enantiomorphous
exact: precisely and perfectly conformed to a certain standard
faithful: true in detail or representation

for all the world like: having a very close resemblance
lifelike: having the exact appearance of a living being
like: nearly identical in appearance and characteristics
mock: merely imitating the real
much the same: having many characteristics in common
near: closely related or similar
of a piece: of the same kind
parallel: conforming to something in character and form
pedestrian: undistinguished; dull
representing: to present a likeness of
resembling: exhibiting similarity to
ridiculously like: so much alike that not to see the difference is ridiculous
similar: bearing resemblance to each other or to something else; like, but not completely identical
simulating: have a mere appearance of; without reality
so: of a like degree or manner
something like: bearing only a partial resemblance

such as: similar to
such like: similar to
the picture of: very like
the very image of: very like

true to life: exactly portraying
true to nature: exactly portraying
twin: resembling, like twins; being one of twins

Simplicity

ascetic: given to severe self-denial
austere: severe; grave; stern
bald: free from all adornment
chaste: pure
dry: void of that which interests or amuses; plain
dull: not bright; obscure
exoteric: ordinary; simple
flat: without gloss
free from affectation: without artificiality or decoration
free from ornament: without artificiality or decoration
homely: not pretentious; plain; unpolished
homespun: plain and simple in character
inornate: not decorated or embellished
monotonous: wanting in change or variety
neat: free from that which is unbecoming or inappropriate

ordinary: usual; common
overreligious: excessively religious
plain: unpretentious; unadorned
pure: unmixed; clear; simple
puritanical: rigid
Saxon: pertaining to the Anglo-Saxon language
severe: rigidly adherent to a standard
simple: free from affectation; natural
simplistic: of excessive simplification
unadorned: not embellished
unaffected: simple and unpretentious in manner
unarrayed: without decoration
undecked: without decoration
ungarnished: without decoration
unornamented: without decoration; plain
untrimmed: without decoration
unvaried: monotonous
unvarnished: without embellishment

Skepticism

aporetic: skeptical
cynical: inclined to moral skepticism
distrustful: lacking in confidence
ephectic: skeptical; unconvinced; reserving judgment
inconvincible: not capable of being convinced
incredulous: showing disbelief; skeptical; astonished; surprised

nullifidian: skeptical
Pyrrhonic: skeptical
scrupulous: inclined to hesitate for fear of doing wrong
skeptical: disbelieving in a God
suspicious: apt to be continually suspecting something
unbelieving: not believing

Skill

a good hand at: having some skill in
able: having sufficient or superior power
accomplished: having accomplishments
adroit: skillful in use of bodily or mental powers
affabrous: workmanlike

alive to: understanding thoroughly
ambidextral: able to use both hands with equal skill
ambidextrous: skillful in both hands
apt: especially fitted; quick to learn
artistic: showing taste or skill

at home in: thoroughly familiar with

businesslike: like one who transacts business well

capable: possessing adequate power; fully competent

clever: possessing quick, active intellect

competent: fulfilling all requirements; qualified

conversant: having precise and familiar knowledge

crack: of superior excellence

cunning: knowing and skillful

cut out for: specially adapted to

dab: skillful

Daedalian: ingenious, like Daedalus

dedal: ingenious; highly skilled; intricate; daedal

deft: apt; fit; neat

dexterous: skillful with hands or body, especially the right hand

discreet: having excellent powers of discernment

efficient: fully qualified and able to perform successfully

endowed: furnished with endowments

experienced: skillful from experience

expert: taught by practice; very skillful

fabrile: pertaining to an artisan or skilled mechanic

felicitous: characterized by felicity

fine-fingered: skillful in the use of the fingers

finished: of the highest degree of perfection

fit for: adapted to; ready for

fitted: qualified

fitted for: able to do

gain: suitable; dexterous

gifted: having many gifts

good at: skillful in doing

habile: able; skillful

hackneyed: much used

hand-minded: preferring or more adept at manual activities

handy: skillful in use of the hand

in practice: used

in proper cue: in practice

ingenious: characterized by ingenuity

initiated: instructed in first principles

inventive: quick at contriving

master of: having attained great skill in

masterful: showing mastery

masterly: having thorough knowledge and superior skill

neat-handed: skillful with hands

not to be caught with chaff: to have skill or experience

practiced: experienced

prepared: made suitable; qualified

primed: instructed beforehand

proficient: possessed of considerable skill; well-advanced in knowledge

qualified: having the necessary qualifications

quick: of acute, active capabilities

ready: quick in action; expert

scientific: well-versed in science; remarkably skilled

sharp: of keen discernment and excellent skill

shipshape: well-arranged

shrewd: able and clever in practice

skilled: having knowledge and dexterity in applying

skillful: characterized by skill

smart: accomplishing quick results; efficient

statesmanlike: having the wisdom of a statesman

surefooted: not liable to err

talented: having many talents

technical: skilled in mechanical and useful arts

thoroughbred: of long and thorough practice

trained: well taught by practice

up in: informed about; versed in

up to: prepared for; able to perform

up to snuff: knowing; acute

up to the mark: fulfilling the requirements

well up in: skilled

workmanlike: having the characteristics of a good workman

Sleepiness

asleep: in sleep
comatose: in the state of coma
dead asleep: in a deep sleep
dormant: inactive; sleeping
dozy: inclined to doze
drowsy: disposed to sleep
fast asleep: in a state of slumber
heavy with sleep: overcome by sleep
hypnotic: pertaining to hypnotism
in a sound sleep: completely asleep
in the arms of Morpheus: asleep
in the lap of Morpheus: asleep
napping: inclined to take short sleeps
quiescent: in a state of repose
sleepful: full of sleep

sleepy: inclined to sleep
somnial: pertaining to sleep or dreams
somniferous: bringing sleep
somnific: causing sleep
somnolent: inclined to sleep; sleepy; drowsy
soporiferous: tending to cause sleep
soporific: producing sleep
soporous: causing sleep
sound as a top: asleep
sound asleep: completely overcome by sleep
torpid: in a comatose state
unawakened: not roused from sleep; not active
unwaked: not stirred from sleep

Slope—Tendency

abrupt: broken off suddenly; steep; broken
acclivous: sloping upward
ajee: turned to one side; awry; agee
anticlinal: inclining in two directions
antiparallel: parallel, but in different directions
ascending: moving upward
askew: in an inclining manner; awry
aslant: in a slanting position
athwart: in a transverse manner; across
awry: to one side; atwist
battered: sloping backwards vertically or upward
bevel: sloping off; oblique
breakneck: dangerously steep
canted: angled; sloping; aslant; oblique; raked; tilted
clinal: inclining
conducive: tending toward a result
crooked: bent; not straight, as in conduct
curved: having no angles or corners
declining: bending downward
declivous: opposed to acclivous
descending: moving downward and in a sloping manner
devex: bending downward

diagonal: drawn obliquely; passing from corner to opposite corner
downhill: sloping down
falling: going from higher to lower spot; descending
in a fair way to: tending fairly toward
inclined: leaning forward; biased
indirect: not direct; crooked; oblique
knock-kneed: having the knees sagging together
loxotic: distorted; slanting
oblique: leaning from the vertical; indirect
out of the perpendicular: oblique
plagihedral: having an oblique spiral arrangement of planes
precipitous: sloping greatly; steep
raked back: slanted
recumbent: lying back; leaning
rising: moving upward; ascending
skew: shaped in an oblique manner
skygodlin: diagonally
slant: inclined from a straight line; sloping
slantindicular: indirect; aslant; oblique
sloping: inclined to the horizontal
steep: greatly sloping; precipitous

subservient: tending toward some end or purpose

tilted: pushed forward; raised at one end; out of the horizontal

transversal: running crosswise

transverse: lying in an athwart position

uphill: moving up; ascending

wry: twisted to one side; distorted

Slowness

bradypeptic: slow to digest

costive: slow

creeping: proceeding on hands and knees

deliberative: of or pertaining to being slow and careful in decision

dilatory: slow in doing something; procrastinating

easy: causing no disquiet or discomfort

gentle: moderate in action

gradual: moving slowly and regularly

imperceptible: that cannot be perceived

insensible: that cannot be perceived

languid: indisposition to physical exertion

latrede: slow; tardy

leisurely: not hasty; deliberate

phlegmatic: slow; lumbering; laggard; lethargic; snail-like

slack: retarded

slow: having relatively small velocity

slow-paced: moving or walking slowly

sluggish: having little power of motion

snail-like: having a slow or sluggish movement

tardigrade: walking slowly, sluggishly

tardive: habitually slow in development

tardy: having a slow movement

testudineous: slow, like a tortoise; concerning tortoises; testudinal

Smallness

acervuline: resembling small heaps

at a low ebb: small in degree

bare: not more than just sufficient

beady-eyed: having small eyes; ferretlike; ferrety

below par: of smaller value than the face

below the mark: smaller than the average

blebby: full of blebs, small swellings or blisters

boxy: somewhat small and square

diminutive: of relatively small size

evanescent: small to the point of passing away

exiguous: scanty; meager

faint: slight

few: not many; small in number

few and far between: widely scattered

halfway: intermediate

hardly any: very few

homeopathic: extremely small in quantity

inappreciable: too small to be estimated

inconsiderable: too small to be worthy of notice

infinitesimal: infinitely small

infrequent: at large or distant intervals

lapilliform: like a small stone

light: bounded within small limits

littlemeal: little by little

low: small in height

meager: small in fullness

mere: such and no more

micro: small in quantity, size, number

microcephalous: small-headed; microcephalic

middling: neither small nor large

minute: exceedingly small

minutissimic: very minute

moderate: fairly small

modest: not unduly large

nanoid: having an abnormally small body

near ruin: almost destroyed

no great shakes: of little consequence

paltry: of little worth

petite: very small; infinitesimal

pindling: small and ill-nourished, as an animal

puisne: small; insignificant; petty
rare: occurring at distant intervals
reduced: made less
scant: scarcely enough
scanty: small in quantity
scarcely any: very few; hardly any
sheer: having no modifying conditions
simple: too small for consideration
slender: small in diameter
slight: of small significance
small: having little size
so-so: paltry
sparing: scarce

stark: utterly
subtle: nicely discriminating
tender: lacking strength
thin: not crowded
to be counted on one's fingers: few in number
tolerable: moderately good
two-by-twice: small in floor area
under par: of smaller value than the face
under the mark: smaller than the average
unrepeated: not recurring
very small: very much less than the standard
wiry: having a small, supple body

Smell

anosmatic: having virtually no sense of smell
anosmic: having complete or partial loss of sense of smell
aosmic: odorless
deodorized: made inodorous
deodorizing: made inodorous
fresh: well-ventilated and airy
gamy: having the tangy, slightly tainted odor of uncooked game
graveolent: having a strong or rank scent or odor
halituous: concerning the breath
heady: intoxicating and exhilarating to the sense of smell
hircine: goatlike; having a goatlike odor; capric; caprine; culiciform; hircinous
inodorate: without smell or odor; smell-less
inodorous: without smell or odor; odorless
moschate: having a musky smell
nasal: pertaining to the nose or nostrils

noctuolent: smelling strongest at night
odoriferous: yielding or diffusing an odor
odorous: having an odor
olfactory: pertaining to the sense of smell
osmagogue: stimulating the sense of smell
osphretic: smellable; olfactory
pungent: sharp or stinging to the sense
quick-scented: acute of smell
rosiny: like or having the smell of pine tree resin
scentless: without scent
smelling: odorous; smelly
strong-scented: having a very perceptible odor
stuffy: poorly ventilated; stale; lacking fresh air
unscented: having no smell; without scent or odor added
wanting smell: not to be perceived by the sense of smell
without smell: not to be perceived by the sense of smell; scentless

Smoothness

bombycine: pertaining to silk
downy: covered with down
erugate: unwrinkled; smooth
even: wihout irregularities in surface
glabrate: slightly smooth; glabrescent
glabrous: smooth; bald

glassy: like glass
glenoid: possessing the form of a smooth depression
glossy: smooth and bright
lanate: woolly
level: smooth

lubricous: smooth and slippery
lustrous: smooth and shiny; buffed; burnished; glassy; glazed; gleaming; glistening; glossy; lacquered; polished; shellacked; varnished
oily: like oil
plane: flat
polished: made smooth or glossy
sericeous: consisting of silk; silky; satiny
silken: made of silk
silky: like silk
sleek: with a bright and even surface
slippery: causing anything to slip; hard to adhere to
slippery as an eel: very hard to hold
smock-faced: having a pale smooth face; effeminate-looking

smooth: having an even regular surface
smooth as glass: a figurative expression denoting degree of smoothness
smooth as ice: a figurative expression denoting degree of smoothness
smooth as oil: a figurative expression denoting degree of smoothness
smooth as velvet: a figurative expression denoting degree of smoothness
soft: yielding to the touch
uniform: smooth; even; glabrous; levigate
unwrinkled: without furrows
velutinous: velvety; smooth
velvety: like velvet
villiform: like the nap of velvet

Sociability

accubitus: lying together in the same bed
acquainted: personally known; having mutual knowledge
amadelphous: gregarious; sociable
antisocial: unfriendly; inimical
chatty: familiar and gossipy
clubable: liking club life and able to play a part in it
companionable: capable of being or inclined to be a pleasing companion
conversable: disposed to converse
conversational: given to conversation
convivial: devoted to feasting; jovial
cozy: contented and sociable; cosy; cosey
ectovalent: capable of having sex only in a place other than home
entertained: treated as a guest
familiar: having intimate knowledge
festal: pertaining to a festival or feast; merry; festive
festive: pertaining to a feast; joyous
free and easy: at home
gregal: gregarious
gregarious: sociable

hail-fellow-well-met: on very familiar or cordial terms
homiletical: conversable
hospitable: entertaining pleasantly
international: pertaining to two or more nations
jolly: full of or expressing life and mirth
jovial: possessing or expressing mirth and good-fellowship
neighborly: disposed to cultivate acquaintance
on visiting terms: acquainted
peraffable: very easy to talk to
psychosocial: pertaining to both psychological and sociological considerations
rumorous: having the nature of a rumor
sociable: inclined to seek society; agreeable in company
social: pertaining to society; sociable
sociosexual: pertaining to the social or interpersonal aspects of sexual relations
welcome: cordially received
welcome as a rose in May: well-received
xenodochial: hospitable

Society

à la mode: according to a certain fashion
admissible in society: fit for good society
admitted in society: fit for good society
civil: observant of the proprieties of speech and manner
conventional: growing out of custom
courtly: having the refinement becoming to a court
dashing: showy and gay
de rigueur: required by fashion or custom
en grand tenue: in full dress
fashionable: according to the fashion
fast: given up to extravagant and sensuous pleasures
focative: pertaining to a concubine
genteel: suited to the station of a gentleman
gentlemanlike: becoming a well-bred man
gentlemanly: becoming a well-bred man
in fashion: according to style
in full dress: dressed properly for formal, social occasions
janty: showy and at ease
jaunty: showy and at ease
ladylike: becoming to a woman of good breeding

modish: fashionable
newfangled: new and novel
polished: possessing the elegancies of speech and manners
polite: observing the proprieties and careful of the comfort of others
presentable: fit for society
pschutt: overly chic
refined: devoid of anything coarse; cultivated
semple: born to a low social or political rank
sexist: assuming conventional differences between the sexes
societal: concerned with social matters; societary
stylish: according to approved style
thoroughbred: showing the qualities of good breeding
unembarrassed: not disturbed in the presence of others
well-behaved: conducting oneself properly
well-bred: trained to good manners
well-mannered: well-bred
well-spoken: cultivated in speech

Sociology

anthropocentric: regarding human beings as center of the universe
antinuke: opposed to development and use of nuclear weapons or energy
antisocial: holding beliefs or taking actions harmful to well-being of society
apolitical: having no interest in politics
biracial: involving or including two races
blue-collar: pertaining to class of workers who perform manual and unskilled labor or factory work
chic: pertaining to elegance and up-to-date style
classless: free from social class distinctions
conventional: conforming to accepted social standards

designer: originally designed by and carrying label of fashion designer, now used to describe various products considered unique or superior
hard-line: uncompromising or unyielding in adherence to a dogma or plan, especially in politics
heterogeneous: composed of varied elements
homogeneous: composed of similar elements
horse-and-buggy: old-fashioned
indigenous: native to a specific society or region
industrial: related to industry; nonagricultural
life-care: designed to provide for basic

needs of elderly residents, usually in return for a regular fee

lily-white: exclusive of all nonwhites

lonely hearts: pertaining to persons seeking companionship or love

middle-of-the-road: favoring a point of view midway between extremes

nomothetic: involving study or formulation of general or universal laws

old-world: pertaining to traditional European customs and values

politically correct: marked by or conforming to typically progressive, orthodox views such as environmentalism, pacifism, and social equality for those outside the white male power structure and Western, Judeo-Christian tradition

pro-choice: supporting the right to legal abortion

pro-life: opposing the right to legal abortion

pronuclear: supporting the development and use of nuclear energy

psychosocial: relating psychological development to social environment

right-to-life: pertaining to opposition to right to legal abortion based on belief that fetus is a person

right-to-work: pertaining to right of

workers to employment regardless of labor union status

ritualistic: performed according to a rigidly prescribed order

rural: lying outside developed cities; in the countryside

sociological: pertaining to the study of society or social questions

substandard: beneath legal or acceptable levels

technetronic: influenced or characterized by advances in technology and electronics applied to social problems

ticky-tacky: relating to dull uniformity of style, especially in housing development

trendy: following the latest fashion

un-American: opposed to or inconsistent with the accepted notion of American ideals and institutions

underage: below legal age, usually for drinking or sex

underdeveloped: designating poor countries of Third World

underprivileged: socially and economically deprived

unfashionable: out-of-date

universal: held by everyone

unskilled: having no job training or vocation

up-to-date: conforming to latest styles and beliefs

urban: relating to cities

Softness

argillaceous: clayey; of the nature of clay

doughy: like dough

downy: like down

ductile: capable of being drawn out; tractable; pliable

edematous: like the puffiness of the skin arising from dropsy

extensile: capable of being extended

flabby: lacking firmness

flaccid: flabby

fleecy: soft like nap, down; lanuginose; lanuginous

flexible: capable of being bent

flexile: flexible

flimsy: of thin texture

flocculent: like flakes; woolly

frush: flabby

inelastic: not elastic

lenitive: softening

limber: limp; without stiffness

limbered: in a condition of limberness

limp: limber

lissom: supple; flexible; lithe; agile; limber

lithe: supple; bending easily

lithesome: somewhat lithe

malacodermous: having soft skin
malleable: capable of being rolled or hammered into a thin plate
malmy: mellow; soft
medullary: pertaining to the marrow
mellow: soft; friable
mollescent: softening; becoming soft
mollipilose: downy; fluffy
mollitious: sensuous; softening
mome: soft and smooth
nesh: soft; delicate; prissy
pannose: feltlike
pinnate: featherlike; pennaceous; penniform; pinniform; plumaceous; plumiform
plastic: capable of being molded
pliable: capable of being bent
pliant: pliable
pulvinar: cushionlike

remollient: softening
sectile: capable of being easily cut by a knife
sequacious: ductile; pliable
soft: not hard; impressible
soft as butter: very soft
soft as down: very soft
soft as silk: very soft
spongy: of spongelike consistency
supple: flexible; easily bent
tender: soft; not tough; delicate
tender as a chicken: having softness or gentleness of spirit
tractable: not showing a refractory spirit
tractile: ductile
wangary: soft and flabby
withy: flexible and tough
yielding: pliable; bending
yielding as wax: as soft as wax

Solidity

close: dense; compact
coherent: clinging firmly together
cohesive: clinging firmly together
compact: molecules not far apart
concrete: hard and firm
constipated: pressed together or condensed
crystalline: like crystal; hard
crystallizable: able to be reduced to crystal forms
dense: closely crowded; firm; solid
gnarled: full of knots or hard protuberances
grumous: thick; concrete; clotted
heavy-built: of solid build; beefy
impenetrable: that cannot be penetrated
impermeable: not permitting passage through
imporous: destitute of pores
incompressible: that cannot be pressed together
indiscerptible: that cannot be separated into parts
indissoluble: not capable of being reduced to a liquid state

indissolvable: that cannot be separated into parts
indivisible: not to be divided
infrangible: not able to be broken
infusible: not capable of melting
insoluble: not to be dissolved
knotted: full of knots
knotty: gnarled; full of hard protuberances
lumpish: heavy; bulky
massive: huge; weighty
serried: compacted, as in rows
solid: hard and firm
solidified: rendered hard
stuffy: strong; hard to breathe
substantial: solid; firm; stable; concrete; dense
thick: closely put together; strong
thickset: closely put together; strong
undissolved: not dissolved
unliquefied: not reduced to a liquid state
unmelted: not melted
unthawed: not changed from a frozen state to a liquid state

Solitude

alone: without company
apart: by itself
azygous: occuring singly
burd-alane: alone and friendless
compact: united closely together
desolate: made solitary by violent means
dreary: solitary in a forlorn manner
first and last: alone
indiscerptible: that cannot be deprived of its unity by separation of parts
individual: single
insecable: incapable of being divided by a cutting instrument
inseverable: incapable of being divided by force
insular: standing alone
irresolvable: that cannot be divided into its constituent parts
isolated: placed in a detached position
kithless: alone; without kindred
lone: without any thing or person possessing similar qualities
lonely: alone from lack of company
lonesome: wanting the society of human beings
odd: without a like
one: being a unit
single: separated from others
single-handed: alone; without assistance
singular: confined to one
sole: being the only one
solitary: lacking life or society
solus: sole
unaccompanied: having no companions
unattended: having not attendants
unique: without another of the same kind
unky: lonesome
unrepeated: not done again

Sorrow

bathed in tears: shedding tears profusely
begrutten: having a swollen face from crying
blatant: bawling out like a beast
curkling: crying like a quail
dacryagogous: stimulating tears
dissolved in tears: entirely overcome with grief
elegiac: sad or plaintive
epiphoric: pertaining to a great shedding of tears
flebile: tearful; doleful
illachrymable: unable to cry
in mourning: wearing visible signs of mourning
in sackcloth and ashes: sorrowful; repentent
in tears: weeping
lachrymal: tearful; weeping; lachrymose
lachrymose: given to shedding tears
lamenting: mourning; expressing grief
larmoyant: tearful
like Niobe, all tears: shedding tears profusely, like the stone into which Niobe was turned
mournful: oppressed with grief
mugient: lowing
plaintful: given to expressing sorrow
plaintive: given to or characterized by expressions of subdued sadness
querimonious: querulous; whining; complaining
querulous: complaining; peevish
remugient: bellowing or lowing again
sorrowful: expressing deep sorrow; sorrowing
tearful: shedding tears
Trophonian: unable to smile again
weeping-ripe: ready to cry
with moistened eyes: ready to cry
with moisture in one's eyes: ready to cry
with tears in one's eyes: weeping
with watery eyes: crying

Sound

acoustic: pertaining to the sense or organs of hearing or to sound

altitonant: thundering from above

amphorous: hollow-sounding

anechoic: completely absorbing sound waves, therefore free from echoes

assonant: pertaining to a similarity of sound or a messed-up rhyme

audible: capable of being heard

audio: pertaining to transmission, reception, or reproduction of sound

auditory: pertaining to hearing, sense of hearing, or organs of hearing; perceived through the sense of hearing

aural: pertaining to the ear or sense of hearing; auricular

auricular: perceived by the ear; aural

borborygmic: concerning a rumbling noise in the stomach

buccinal: like a trumpet in sound or shape

cacuminal: of sounds produced with the tip of the tongue curled up toward the mouth palate

closed-captioned: designating television program broadcast with captions visible with use of a decoder, intended for the hearing-impaired

dead: nonresonant

deaf: partially or wholly deprived of sense of hearing

distinct: clearly and easily heard

dumb: mute

faint: lacking loudness

foudroyant: striking or thundering, as lightning; sudden and terrifying

glad-warbling: singing or walking joyfully

hard-of-hearing: hearing-impaired

inaudible: incapable of being heard

isacoustic: concerning equal intensity of sound

loud: designating a sound or tone having exceptional volume; noisy or clamorous

monophonic: designating sound recording having single transmission path

mum: silent

mute: silent, especially refraining from speech; not emitting sound; incapable of speech; dumb

noisy: making much noise; loud

nonresonant: without the quality of sending back or prolonging sound

phonetic: relating to or representing articulate sounds or speech

quadraphonic: designating sound reproduction system using four speakers, usually set in four corners of room

quiet: making little or no sound or noise; silent

rataplan: making a repetitive beating or rapping sound, like a drum roll

raucous: hoarse

reel-to-reel: of or pertaining to a system using large, open spools of tape: quarter-inch, half-inch, or three-quarter inch

resonant: sending back or capable of sending back or of prolonging sound; sonorous

rouped: hoarse

roupy: hoarse; husky

singultous: concerning hiccups

soft: designating sound or tone having very little volume; low or subdued in noise level

sonant: sounding; having sound

sonic: having to do with sound waves; equal to or being speed of sound in air

soniferous: producing or conducting sound

sonorific: producing sound

sonorous: loud and full-sounding

sounding: giving forth a sound

soundproof: impervious to sound

stereophonic: designating sound recording having two transmission paths

stertorous: having a snoring sound

still: free from sound or noise; silent; subdued or hushed in sound
stone-deaf: totally deaf
subsonic: less than speed of sound
supersonic: greater than speed of sound
throaty: having a gruff, husky voice;

gravelly; guttural; hoarse; raspy; roupy; scratchy
tone-deaf: unable to distinguish differences in pitch in musical tones
ululant: making a howling sound

Speech

affected: having artificial or pretentious speech
alieniloquent: speaking discursively or straying from the point
alliterative: containing alliteration
altiloquent: pertaining to superior or lofty speech; grandiloquent; magniloquent
antithetical: having opposition of words or sentiments
babblative: tending to babble, prattle
blandiloquent: speaking in a flattering or mildly ingratiating way
bombastic: characterized by bombast
breviloquent: speaking briefly
chrysostomatic: richly eloquent
colloquial: peculiar to common speech as distinguished from literary
communicate: ready to impart or talk
communicative: inclined to be talkative
concionative: pertaining to public speaking or preaching
declamatory: given to speaking in a rhetorical style
demegoric: pertaining to public speaking
diversiloquent: speaking in different ways
doctiloquent: speaking as an expert on some subject
drawling: having a slow, prolonged speech
elocutionary: pertaining to the art of public speaking
eloquent: having the power of expressing strong emotions in an elevated and effective manner
enunciative: definite in statement
euphuistic: of writing or speaking in an affected style

explicit: fully and clearly expressed
expressive: conveying meaning
facund: eloquent
fallaciloquent: speaking deceitfully
fatiloquent: speaking prophetically
flaming: very ardent
flexiloquent: speaking evasively or ambiguously
frothy: empty
fustian: pompous; inflated
glossal: pertaining to the tongue
glossoepiglottic: pertaining to the root of the tongue
gnomologic: sententious; pithy; gnomological
grandiloquent: given to speaking in a pompous manner
grandiose: marked by affectation of grandeur
high-sounding: ostentatious
hyblaean: smooth-talking
inaniloquent: talkative; speaking foolishly; inaniloquous
Johnsonian: resembling the style of Dr. Johnson; pompous
lingual: pertaining to the use of the tongue in speaking
longiloquent: extremely long-winded
magniloquent: speaking in a lofty style
melliloquent: honey-tongued
mendaciloquent: speaking lies
meropic: able to speak
mincing: having affectedly elegant or dainty speech
mouthy: loquacious
multiloquent: talking a great deal; multiloquous; multiloquious
not written: spoken
nuncupatory: oral

omniloquent: talking about everything

oral: uttered by the mouth

oratorical: becoming an eloquent public speaker

orotund: having a pompous speaking or writing style

outspoken: expressing a decided opinion for or against

parrhesiastic: speaking freely or boldly

peripatetic: of speech, rambling

periphrastic: of roundabout speech; circumlocutory

phatic: speaking to socialize, not communicate ideas

phemic: pertaining to speech

phonetic: pertaining to the articulate sounds made by the human voice

phoniatric: specializing in speech defects

plainspoken: straightforward; blunt

planiloquent: straight-talking; speaking plainly

platitudinarian: speaking platitudes

pleniloquent: full of talk

polyloquent: talking about many things

procacious: impudent; outspoken

published: announced to the public

renable: fluent; eloquent

rhetorical: emphasizing style at the expense of thought; of writing or speaking as means of communication or persuasion often with special concern for literary effect; grandiloquent; magniloquent

sanctiloquent: speaking solemnly or of sacred things

sententious: terse and pithy in expression

sesquipedalian: using very long words

sialoquent: spraying saliva when speaking

singsong: having a monotonously rising and falling voice

slangous: using slang; like slang

soliloquacious: prone to soliloquize

soliloqual: talking to oneself

soliloquizing: talking to oneself; speaking a soliloquy

somniloquacious: talking in one's sleep; somniloquent

sonorous: high-sounding

spadish: blunt-spoken

speaking: expressing thoughts in words

spoken: by word of mouth

stammering: hesitating in speech

stilted: pompous

stultiloquent: given to foolish talk or babbling

stuttering: having broken or stammering speech

suaviloquent: speaking in an urbane, sophisticated manner

talkable: capable of being talked about; inclined to friendly talk

talkative: given to talking a great deal

tolutiloquent: speaking glibly, fluently

tremulous: unsteady in speech

tub-thumping: of ranting, impassioned speech

tumid: high-sounding; pompous

unlarded: of speech, unembellished and not mixed with interjection

unwritten: spoken

vaniloquent: speaking vainly or egotistically

ventose: prone to vain, empty talk

veriloquent: speaking only the truth; veriloquous

Spirituality

anagogic: having spiritual meaning or sense; arising from or striving toward lofty ideals

animastic: spiritual

asomatous: without a material body; incorporeal

astral: relating to the stars; denoting a supersensible substance held in theosophy to pervade all space and survive the individual after death

clear: free of mundane, worldly matters, enabling one to see the spiritual essence of things as they are; at the highest state of enlightenment

disembodied: divested of a body

ectoplasmic: pertaining to a spiritual emanation

extramundane: beyond the material world

farseeing: visionary; prophetic

holistic: emphasizing organic or functional relation between parts and whole

hylic: material; concerning matter

immaterial: not consisting of matter

immateriate: not consisting of matter

imponderable: beyond exact measurement or evaluation

incarnate: in a physical form; within a body

incomprehensible: lying beyond reach of human mind; unfathomable

incorporal: not having a material body or form

incorporeal: not having a material body or form

indescribable: too vague, extreme, or far beyond experience to be accurately described

inexplicable: incapable of being explained or accounted for

inherent: essential or intrinsic to something

innate: belonging to essential character of something; originating in the mind rather than experience

innominate: unnamed or of unknown name; unnameable

integral: inherent; essential to completeness

material: corporeal or bodily; the opposite of spiritual

moral: ethically good; principled; conforming to or acting on inner conviction of what is right

organic: forming an inherent vital part; composed of, using, or grown only with animal or vegetable matter

personal: applying to character of conduct

pneumatoscopic: spirit-seeing

realized: spiritually enlightened; in harmony with oneself

revealed: pertaining to truths based on intuition or divine inspiration

spiritual: consisting of spirit; not material

subjective: relating to the mind or the intellectual world

timeless: eternal; everlasting; beyond measurement in time

unearthly: not of the earth; spiritual

unembodied: existing only in spirit

unextended: being without dimensions

universal: present in all spheres of human life

unspeakable: beyond verbal description; that may not or cannot be uttered

unspoken: tacit; silent but understood

unwritten: of truths known and passed on orally

Stability

aground: stranded; set in the ground

anchored: held fast, as by an anchor

astatic: not stable or steady

at anchor: when a ship is tied up or anchored

balanced: settled and adjusted, as an account

confirmed: strengthened; fixed

constant: not liable to change

deep-rooted: solid

durable: lasting

established: already in place; secure

fadeless: not liable to fade

fast: not loose or unstable

firm: stable in opinion or position

firm as a rock: solid

firmly established: securely in place

firmly seated: solid

fixed: immovable

high and dry: out of water; stranded

immovable: not movable

immutable: not liable to change

imperishable: not liable to decay

incommutable: not capable of being interchanged

incontrovertible: too clear to admit of dispute

indeciduous: lasting

indeclinable: not altered by terminations

indefeasible: not voidable; not to be defeated

indelible: incapable of being blotted out, lost, or forgotten

indestructible: not liable to be decomposed

indissoluble: perpetually binding

indissolvable: incapable of being dissolved

ineradicable: not capable of being rooted out

inextinguishable: incapable of being destroyed

insusceptible: not capable of being affected

intransmutable: incapable of being changed into another substance

invariable: not liable to change

inveterate: firmly established because of long continuance

irreducible: not capable of being reduced

irremovable: incapable of being removed

irresoluble: not capable of being dissolved or released

irretrievable: not capable of recovery or repair

irreversible: not capable of being reversed, repealed, or annulled

irrevocable: not capable of being revoked or recalled

moored: confined or fastened, as by cables or anchors

obstinate: stubborning adhering to an attitude, opinion, etc.

on a rock: on a solid foundation

perennial: appearing yearly or on continual basis

permanent: lasting or remaining without change

reverseless: not to be reversed

riveted: firmly fastened; clinched

rooted: firmly fixed

settled: permanently fixed, placed, or adjusted

stable: unwavering; durable

steadfast: firmly established; constant

steady: firm; regular

stereotyped: formed in an unchangeable manner

stranded: driven or run aground

stuck fast: immovable

tethered: confined to certain limits by means of a rope or chain

transfixed: pierced through, as with a dart or spear

unalterable: not to be altered

unaltered: not altered

unchangeable: incapable of being changed

undeviating: regular in rule, principle, or purpose

undying: immortal

unmitigated: not changed; absolute

unsusceptible of change: unchangeable

valid: forceful

vested: fixed; not dependent on contingencies

Stench

bad: unpleasant in smell

caprylic: having a strong unpleasant odor

corky: having a spoiled scent, especially from tainted cork

empyreumatic: pertaining to empyreuma

feculent: stinking; foul; turbid

fetid: having a strong offensive smell; olid; stinking

foul: unpleasant smelling

frowzy: having a musty smell

fulsome: sickening or disgusting to the senses

fusty: musty; moldy

graveolent: stinking strongly
halitotic: having bad breath
high: tainted; said of meat
jumentous: having a strong animal odor, like horse urine
maleolent: bad-smelling
malodorous: foul-smelling
mephitic: stinking; noxious; poisonous; mephitical
miasmatic: noxious; miasmic
mucid: moldy; musty
musty: having the smell of mold or old age
nidorous: smelling like burning or decaying animal matter
noisome: very disagreeable to sense of smell
offensive: causing disgust
olid: stinking; fetid
olidous: of a strong, disagreeable smell
putrescent: becoming putrid; undergoing putrefaction

putrid: in state of foul decay and decomposition with accompanying odor of rot
rafty: rancid; stale; musty
rammish: bad-smelling or -tasting; strongly scented
rancid: having an unpleasant, stale smell
rank: having an offensive, foul smell or taste; strong and disagreeable
reasty: rancid, as of bacon
saprostomous: having bad breath
smelling: being disagreeable to the sense of smell
smelly: having or emitting a strong unpleasant odor
stenchful: smelling offensive; stinking
stinking: foul-smelling
stinky: foul-smelling
strong: disagreeable
strong-smelling: disagreeable
suffocating: so strong as to make breathing difficult
tainted: smelling as if slighty decayed

Sterility

acarpous: fruitless; sterile; agennesic; anandrious; apogenous
addled: spoiled and unproductive, as addled eggs
agennesic: sterile; impotent; acarpous; anandrious; apogenous
anandrious: sterile; acarpous; agennesic; apogenous
apogenous: sterile; impotent; acarpous; agennesic; anandrious
arid: parched and dry; barren
barren: incapable of producing anything; sterile
fallow: plowed and unseeded; uncultivated
fruitless: without fruit or result

infecund: not producing young
inoperative: producing no effect; not active
issueless: without issue; unable to have issue
null and void: inoperative
of no effect: inoperative
sterile: having no productive power; barren
teemless: barren
unfertile: not rich or productive
unfruitful: not producing abundant results
unproductive: not productive
unprofitable: not profitable
unprolific: not producing offspring or fruit

Storage

aggerose: in heaps
barrelled: stored in barrels
binned: of wine bottles stored in tiers
bottled: stored in bottles

cellared: stored in a cellar
concatervate: heaped up
funded: stored up
heaped: accumulated

in ordinary: stored up for constant service
in reserve: held back for future use
in store: in readiness for use
spare: held back for use or need; additional

stored: heaped up; kept
supernumerary: more than is needed at the present time

Straightness

direct: leading only to one place
even: free from abrupt changes in direction
in a line: straight
inflexible: not to be bent
parallel: of straight lines in the same plane
plat: exactly straight
rectilinear: straight

right: mathematically straight
straight: not crooked
straight as an arrow: completely straight
true: exact
unbent: not bent
undeviating: not deviating
undistorted: not distorted
unswerving: not moving from the right course
unturned: not turned

Subjection

a slave to: under complete control of, as a Slav to a German master
anaclitic: overly dependent on another
at one's beck and call: servilely obedient
at the feet of: in submission of
at the mercy of: in the power of
chicken-pecked: under the rule of a child (as henpecked is under the rule of a woman)
constrained: hindered in movement
dependent: subject to
downtrodden: oppressed
enslaved: conquered; held in slavery
feudal: pertaining to feudalism
feudatory: pertaining to feudalism
henpecked: domineered over by a wife
in harness: in subjection
in leading strings: under control of another's will
in subjection to: under the power of
in the clutches of: controlled by
in the hands of: controlled by
in the power of: controlled by
led by the nose: controlled by the will of another, like a bull or boar
liable: bound by law
liberticidal: destroying liberty

mancipated: enslaved
on the hip: in one's power, as the wrestler's
overborne: crushed
overwhelmed: crushed
parasitical: living upon another
prochnial: concerning kneeling or submission
procrustean: concerning conformity or forcing submission
stipendiary: receiving a stipend
subject: yielding obedience to an authority
subordinate: inferior in classification
sycophantic: subservient; servile; craven; obsequious; toadying
the plaything of: completely controlled by
the puppet of: completely controlled by
the sport of: completely controlled by
under control: in a manageable condition
under one's command: subordinate to
under one's orders: subordinate to
under one's thumb: completely in one's power
under the lash: in slavery
uxorious: inordinately submissive to one's wife

Subordinacy

deficient: below what is required

diminished: reduced in degree, quantity, etc.

inferior: lower in rank or quality

least: in the lowest or smallest degree

less: of slighter consequence

lesser: of slighter consequence

lower/lowest: having less than the usual rate, amount, etc.

minor: less in importance or value

minus: deprived of; lacking

not fit to hold a candle to: greatly inferior to

noteless: not noted; undistinguished

reduced: brought to an inferior state

secondary: not of greatest importance

second-rate: second in size, rank, etc.

small: of little importance

smaller/smallest: of little consequence

sub: secondary

subaltern: inferior in rank or position; subordinate

sublunary: inferior; subordinate; sublunar

subordinate: belonging to an inferior order in classification

thrown into the shade: eclipsed

unimportant: not important

weighed in the balance and found wanting: not up to a standard

Success

crowned with success: rewarded with success

effective: producing effect

epinician: celebrating victory

felicitous: happy in operation or effect

flushed with success: animated or elated by success

in full swing: in full operation

in the ascendant: dominant in influence or power

prosperous: succeeding in efforts to gain what is desirable

setup: caused to develop

succeeding: accomplishing one's object

successful: enjoying success

triumphant: gloriously victorious

unbeaten: always successful

victorious: having gained a victory

well-spent: so as to produce results

Support

ancillary: in a supporting role

bearing: supporting a weight; bearable

bracing: supporting; bearing; bolstering; buttressing; girding; suspensory; underpinning

brooking: bearing

buttressing: bracing; supporting

cantilevered: having supports that project from the wall

exposed: having the supports or underpinnings visible

fulcible: able to be supported

fundamental: pertaining to a foundation; essential

offering secours: offering support

supported: kept from falling

supporting: holding up

Supremacy

beyond compare: easily first, highest, or best

beyond comparison: easily first, highest, or best

crowning: completing; most perfect

culminating: arriving at its highest point

dioristically: in a distinguishing manner

distinguished: having a reputation

egregious: exceptional

enlarged: made larger

exceeding: greater than what is usual or sufficient

exemplary: serving as an example, especially a good one

eximious: most distinguished; excellent

first-rate: of the best kind or class

foremost: first in place, rank, or dignity

great: powerful; uncommonly gifted

greater: more powerful

greatest: most powerful

higher: more advanced

incomparable: beyond compare

increased: made larger

inexsuperable: insurmountable; impassable

inimitable: beyond imitation

invictive: unbeatable

major: greater in number, quantity, or extent

matchless: without equal

more than a match for: superior to

nonesuch: incomparable

nonpareil: unequaled; peerless

palmary: superior; prizeworthy

paramount: of highest consideration, value, dignity, or rank

peerless: matchless

preeminent: distinguished above others of eminence

pukka: superior; pucka

ratherest: most of all

second to none: first

signate: marked; designated; distinguished

skookum: first-rate

sovereign: efficacious in the highest degree

superior: surpassing in quantity, quality, or degree

superlative: the very highest

supreme: highest, greatest, or most excellent

transcendent: superior in excellence

transcendental: superior in excellence

ultra: exceeding moderation or propriety; extreme

unapproached: far superior

unequaled: not to be compared with

unparagoned: without equal; peerless

unparalleled: without a similar case

unrivaled: without a rival

unsurpassed: not overcome

utmost: in the highest degree

vaulting: surpassing

without parallel: unparalleled

Surprise

anoetic: unthinkable

blutterbunged: confounded; completely surprised

ferly: sudden; surprising or unusual to the sight; ferlie

gloppened: surprised

imprevisible: unforeseeable

inattentive: not on the lookout

inopinate: unexpected; inopine

mirific: working wonders; wonderful; mirificent

serendipitous: pertaining to happy and unexpected discoveries by accident

startling: causing one to start

struck-comical: rendered speechless or bewildered by surprise or terror

subitaneous: sudden; hasty; unexpected

sudden: coming at an unexpected time

surprised: affected with surprise

unanticipated: not anticipated

unaware: not aware

unexpected: not expected

unforeseen: not seen beforehand

unwarned: not warned

Suspension

beetling: overhanging; jutting; over-hung; pensile; projecting

caudate: having a tail

cernuous: hanging down, like a flower

crapaudine: swinging from top and bottom pivots, like a door

dependent: hanging down; relying upon; unable to exist without something else

flowing: floating loosely, like hair

funipendulous: hanging from a rope

hanging: fastened to something else

having a peduncle: having a stem

loose: not fastened; swinging

low-slung: hanging close to the ground

nutant: having hanging skin; droopy; pendulous

patibulary: pertaining to hanging or a gallows

pedunculate: having a peduncle

pendent: hanging downward and fastened by one end; dangling; dependent; pendulant; suspensory

penduline: pendulous, as a hanging nest

pendulous: hanging; swinging

pensile: pendent and hanging

slack-jawed: having a hanging lower jaw

slaunchwise: hanging down loosely

superposed: placed above

suspended: hanging by one end

tailed: having a tail

Swamp

boggy: having the nature of a bog

fenny: having the nature of a fen

marshy: having the nature of a marsh

moorish: having the nature of a moor

moory: having the nature of a moor

muddy: soft and wet

paludal: marshy; boggy; paludose; paludous; palustral; palustrian; palustrine; quaggy; swampy

palustrine: dwelling in marshes; helobious; paludicolous; paludous

plashy: soft and wet

poachy: soft and wet

quaggy: marshy; boggy; flaccid; irresilient

sloppy: soft and wet

soft: soft and wet

squashy: soft and wet

swampy: having the nature of a swamp

uliginose: muddy; swampy; growing in muddy or swampy places; uliginous

Sweetness

candied: conserved into sugar

cloying: having overly sweet speech; ingratiating; saccharine

dulcet: having a delicate, luscious taste

edulcorant: sweetening

honeyed: sweet

luscious: excessively sweet

lush: full of juice

melliferous: producing honey; flowing with honey

nectareous: of the nature of nectar; delicious

sacchariferous: making or containing sugar

saccharine: pertaining to or like sugar

sweet: pleasant to the taste; tasting like sugar

sweet as a nut: a figurative expression denoting degree of sweetness

sweet as honey: a figurative expression denoting degree of sweetness

sweet as sugar: a figurative expression denoting degree of sweetness

sweetened: with sweetening added

Swiftness

active: quick

agile: able to move or act quickly

au grand galop: at full tilt or gallop

eagle-winged: having an eagle's wings

eagly: swift as an eagle

electric: spirited

expeditious: accomplished with energy and speed

express: pertaining to quick or special conveyance; quick

fast: that moves or acts rapidly

fleet: moving or capable of moving swiftly

flying: intended or adapted to swift or easy motion

galloping: progressing rapidly

gleg: quick to perceive or act

light of heel: nimble in running

light-footed: nimble in running or dancing

light-legged: swift of foot

lish: nimble; quick

mercurial: swift, like Mercury

nimble: showing easy quickness

nimble-footed: able to run swiftly

quick: characterized by rapidity of movement or action

quick as lightning: very rapid

quick as thought: very rapid

rapid: having great speed

speedy: moving swiftly

swack: agile

swift: moving with high velocity

swift as a thought: momentary

swift as an arrow: very swift

telegraphic: pertaining to the telegraph; swift, as by telegraph

winged: passed swiftly

Taking

bereft: lost
parasitic: living on another, and taking nourishment therefrom
predaceous: living by prey
predal: plundering; pillaging
predatorial: pillaging
predatory: pillaging
prehensile: seizing; adapted to grasp
privative: of something that causes loss
rapacious: greedy; grasping; given to plundering
raptorial: seizing
ravenous: hungry to rage
retractile: capable of drawing in
taking: alluring; attracting

Talkativeness

aeolistic: long-winded
chattering: talking idly and rapidly
chatty: talkative
declamatory: pretentious and rhetorical
flippant: having a voluble tongue
fluent: ready in the use of words; flowing
garrulous: talkative
glib: smooth; voluble
largiloquent: speaking in a boastful manner
linguacious: talkative; loquacious
long-tongued: given to gossip
long-winded: tedious in speech or argument
loquacious: given to continual talking
multiloquent: very talkative
openmouthed: clamorous
talkative: given to much talking
voluble: moving with ease in speaking; talkative; loquacious

Technology

alphanumeric: consisting of both alphabetic and numeric characters
Boolean: describing systems in which variable values are restricted to true and false
coin-operated: describing public telephone requiring insertion of coin to place call
compatible: able to use same programs or hardware, especially matched to major brand but manufactured by smaller company

conversational: designating computer systems that engage user in two-way dialogue

corrupted: designating a file, etc., in which data is jumbled or has been lost

dead: having no dial tone on the line; nonfunctioning

dedicated: designed for specific application or function

dial-up: pertaining to a service, account, etc., accessed via modem

down: not operational; said of a computer network or system

drag-and-drop: allowing movement of icons, etc., to another area on the screen via mouse control

dual-processor: designating computer system with two CPUs performing different operations simultaneously

duplex: designating a telecommunications system capable of simultaneous transmission of messages in opposite directions on one channel

front-end: designating software that provides a user interface for access to an application

fuzzy: approximate; not precise; used to describe search or operation that generates a set whose members lie across a spectrum of values approximating a central value

hardwired: built into hardware, as through electronic circuits, rather than functioning through software

Hayes-compatible: designating a modem that utilizes the control commands of Hayes modems, the industry standard

hierarchical: describing any vertical pyramidal organization of information in related levels and sublevels

IBM-compatible: designating computer system that can interface with IBM hardware or software designed for IBM machines

interactive: designating any program or system that has a dialogue with the human user and responds to input

machine-readable: encoded in or translated into form suitable for processing, such as ASCII

menu-driven: run by choosing from presented options rather than by entering commands

multiuser: describing operating system that permits several users to share access to computer

octal: of or pertaining to a base-eight number system, sometimes used to encode data, employing numerals 0 through 7

off-line: designating equipment not directly linked to central computer or CPU

on-line: designating equipment directly linked to central computer or CPU

on-screen: designating data displayed on video terminal

PC-compatible: designating a device, application, etc., designed to run on a PC

plug-and-play: designating a peripheral device, etc., designed for easy, nontechnical installation and use

rack-mountable: designating equipment designed for installation in standard nineteen-inch metal rack

relational: describing development of database as large matrix

stand-alone: designating self-contained software program or computer system that operates independently

station-to-station: designating operator-assisted call to anyone answering number dialed or any direct dial call

technetronic: pertaining to, shaped, or influenced by technological changes in society such as telecommunications and computers

technical: pertaining to the mechanical or industrial arts

technological: pertaining to practical, mechanical, or industrial arts

toll-free: requiring no additional fee beyond basic service charge

up: functioning properly

user-friendly: easy for user to understand and execute without extensive training
write-protect: designating notch on 5¼-inch disk that, when covered, prevents inadvertent writing-over of stored information; designating similarly functioning mechanical switch on 3½-inch disk

Terseness

brief: in few words
close: concise; to the point
compact: consolidated
compendious: abridged
concise: expressed in few words
crisp: short
curt: characterized by brevity
elliptical: having a part omitted
epigrammatic: concise; pointed
exact: precisely or definitely conceived or stated
laconic: expressing much in a few words
neat: free from admixture
pithy: having concentrated force and energy
pregnant: implying more than expressed
quaint: prim
short: brief
snippety: unpleasantly curt
succinct: characterized by pithiness and brevity
summary: condensed to the utmost practicable degree
terse: free of superfluous words
to the point: spoken directly
trenchant: effective; penetrating

Texture

airy-fairy: delicate; visionary; fairylike
anatomic: pertaining to anatomy
anatomical: pertaining to anatomy
coarse: of rough structure
coarse-grained: composed of large or rough structural elements
delicate: of fine, light texture
distressed: beaten to simulate age and use
filmy: of gauzy, unsubstantial texture
fine: of light and delicate texture
fine-grained: composed of fine and light structural elements
gossamery: of fine and filmy substance
grainy: having a grainlike texture; branny; coarse-grained; granular; granulated; gritty; rough-grained
graniform: grainlike
granuliform: granule-like
homespun: spun at home; hence, coarse and rough
ligneous: woody in texture
organic: consisting of organs
papuliferous: pimply; eruptive
pimpled: having small rounded protuberances
pitted: having small depressions; cavernulous; cuppy; foveate; pocked; pockmarked
rimulose: having small chinks or fissures
sandy: having a sandlike texture; arenaceous; arenarious; sabulous; tophaceous
scobiform: like sawdust; scobicular
structural: pertaining to the structure
studded: having small hard protuberances
subtile: of very fine texture
textile: formed by weaving
textural: of or pertaining to texture
tumulose: characterized by mounds, small hills; tumulous
woofy: of dense texture

Thanks

beholden: owing gratitude
forgotten: treated with ingratitude
grateful: full of gratitude
ill-requited: treated with ingratitude when some recompense was deserved
indebted to: full of gratitude toward for a service rendered
ingrate: ungrateful, so as to return evil for good
insensible of benefits: naturally devoid of gratitude
obliged: pleased in a grateful manner
thankful: full of thanks
thankless: not feeling or expressing gratitude

unacknowledged: not having received thanks
under obligation: owing gratitude to
ungrateful: not feeling gratitude
unmindful: not keeping benefits in mind with gratitude
unrequited: not having received any recompense of gratitude
unrewarded: not having received the due reward of gratitude
unthanked: having received no expression of gratitude
unthankful: not possessing or expressing gratitude
wanting in gratitude: lacking in gratitude

Theft

backberend: caught with stolen goods
burglarious: surreptitious; in the manner of a burglar
furacious: thievish; stealing
furtive: stealing
handhabend: posessing stolen goods; handhaving
kleptic: thievish
lestobiotic: living by stealing food
light-fingered: adept at picking pockets
piratical: pertaining to piracy

predaceous: living by preying upon others
predal: practicing robbery
predatorial: thieving
predatory: characterized by plundering
raptorial: adapted for seizing prey
reft: robbed; bereft of something
stolen: taken by theft
theftuous: thievish
thieving: taking without permission
thievish: inclined to thieve, take without permission

Thought

alembicated: overly subtle or refined in thought or expression
catoptric: mirroring in thought
cogitabund: meditative
contemplative: given to thoughtful consideration
deep-musing: contemplative; lost in thought
deliberative: pertaining to deliberation or careful consideration
idiotropic: introspective
in the mind: in thought
introspective: looking within

lost in thought: absentminded
meditative: disposed to meditation or contemplative thought; thoughtful; reflective; deliberative; pensive; ruminative
museful: deeply thoughtful
pensive: thoughtful; sad
philosophastering: acting the philosopher
philosophical: belonging to philosophy
platonic: pertaining to the Greek philosopher Plato; purely spiritual
reflective: meditative

refrangible: capable of being refracted; refringent
sedate: calm; sober; contemplative
specular: pertaining to a mirrored thought
speculative: given to speculation
studious: given to earnest study
subvocal: thought but not articulated
thinking: reviewing in mind

thought of: considered
thoughtful: given to thought; meditative
under consideration: in the thought of
uppermost in the mind: holding the most important position in one's thoughts
wistful: marked by earnest thought

Three

hypertridimensional: having more than three dimensions
passant: in heraldry, having three paws on the ground and one raised
runcible: curved, with three broad tines
terdiurnal: three times a day
tern: threefold
ternary: proceeding by threes
ternate: ordered in groups of threes
tertiary: third in number
third: the ordinal of three
three: consisting of one more than two; a cardinal number
threefold: made up of three
thrice: three times
treble: multiplied by three

trebly: in a threefold manner or quantity
triangular: having three sides or angles; cuneate; cuneiform; deltoid; trigonal; trigonous; trilateral; wedge-shaped
trichotomous: divided into threes
trifid: three-cleft
triform: having a triple form
trilogistic: made up of a series of three dramas
trinoctial: lasting three nights
trinomial: consisting of three terms
triplasian: three; threefold
triple: increased threefold
triplicate: made thrice as much
triquetrous: having three acute angles
triune: three in one

Time

actual: existing at the present time
ago: time past
ahead of time: early
ancient: of very great age
antiquated: of great age; obsolete
antique: very old; belonging to bygone age
aoristic: expressing completed action without any limitation
aperiodic: not periodic; with no regular recurrence
archaic: old-fashioned; of an earlier time
asynchronous: not concurrent
atemporal: outside of time
belated: delayed; too late
brief: very short duration
by turns: alternately
chronic: constant; continuing over time

chronogrammatical: concerning or containing a chronogram
chronological: arranged in order of time
chronometrical: pertaining to or measured by a chronometer
coeval: of the same age
concurrent: at the same time
constant: perpetual; occurring continually
contemporaneous: existing at the same time
contemporary: at the same time; belonging to the same or current time period
continual: chronic; constant; unceasing; uninterrupted
continuous: without break or interruption

current: belonging to the present time or passing period

dated: antiquated; old enough to be out of fashion

dendrochronological: dated via tree rings

dominical: concerning Sundays

ephemeral: lasting for one day; short-lived

erstwhile: some time ago

existing: being or continuing to be

fore: coming first; prior to

former: prior; earlier; preceding in time

frequent: often

fugitive: not durable; transient

gnomonic: relating to the pointer shaft of a sundial

immediate: without delay or interval; next

imminent: about to occur; impending

impermanent: temporary; lasting for a limited time

infrequent: seldom; not often

instant: now passing; current

instantaneous: happening and concluding in an instant; without duration

interim: temporary

intermediate: in an intervening time

isochronal: occurring at regular intervals

last: final; time immediately prior to the present

late: after the appointed or usual time; tardy

new: not existing prior to this moment; of recent origin

occasional: occurring infrequently or irregularly

off-peak: pertaining to time period of less than maximum use, frequency, or duration

old: having lived or existed for a long period of time

ongoing: enduring or continuing

part-time: lasting fewer hours than full-time, usually said of employment

permanent: continuing without change; not temporary

preceding: going before

preliminary: preceding; before

preprandial: relating to time just before dinner

present: occurring in the present period; current

previous: before; preceding; former

primeval: from original time; ancient; primal

prior: before; preceding; previous to

rare: not frequent

recent: pertaining to the near past; lately; new

recurrent: returning periodically

remote: distant

retrospective: directed toward looking backwards

sciatheric: pertaining to a sundial; sciatherical

seely: punctual; timely

semipermanent: lasting, but not permanent; durable

simultaneous: occurring at same moment

sometime: having been formerly

sporadic: happening in scattered instances

spur-of-the-moment: impromptu; occurring without planning or rehearsal

stoundmeal: now and then; from time to time; gradually

subsequent: following; later

successive: following in order

sudden: abrupt; happening unexpectedly; quick

summary: quickly done; without delay

tardy: late; slow

temporal: pertaining to, defined by, or limited by time; transitory

temporary: of certain limited duration; not permanent

terminal: final; occurring at the end

that is: now

thitherto: up to that time

time-consuming: requiring or taking up a great deal of time

time-honored: esteemed due to age or longstanding use

timeless: outside limits of time; unrestricted by time period or era; undated; eternal; with no beginning or end

timely: early, seasonal, opportune, or executed on time

time-tested: having effectiveness proved over a long period of time

transitory: temporary; fleeting

unceasing: continuous; without interruption

untimely: premature; unseasonable; occurring at improper time

upcoming: about to occur; coming to pass

up-to-the-minute: extending to the present moment; new; modern

urgent: requiring immediate attention

vestigial: relating to or indicating something formerly present

vintage: old; antique

well-timed: propitious

Time Period

acronical: happening at sunset or twilight; acronichal; acronycal; acronychal

all-day: lasting from morning to evening

all-night: lasting from evening to morning

alternate: following each other in succession of time

annual: coming once a year

Aprilian: pertaining or similar to April

around-the-clock: at all times of day and night

autumnal: pertaining to or occurring in autumn

biannual: occurring twice a year; occurring every two years; semiannual

bicentennial: occurring every two hundred years or lasting two hundred years

biennial: taking place once in two years

bimensal: bimonthly

bimillenary: lasting two thousand years

bimonthly: occurring every two months; twice a month; bimensal; semimonthly

bissextile: pertaining to leap day, February 29, or to leap year

biweekly: occurring twice a week or once every two weeks; semiweekly

canicular: pertaining to the dog days of July or August

centennial: coming once in a hundred years

circadian: occurring in twenty-four-hour cycles

cyclical: moving in cycles

daily: occurring once a day or occurring each day

decennial: occurring every ten years

diurnal: recurring each day; daily

duodecennial: occurring every twelve years

enneaeteric: occurring every nine years

equinoctial: pertaining to equinoxes

estival: pertaining to summer

eternal: lasting forever

etesian: every summer; periodic; annual

everlasting: endless; unceasing; eternal

every other: alternate

fortnightly: occurring once every two weeks

genethliac: pertaining to birthdays

hebdomadal: weekly; lasting or occurring every seven days

hebdomadary: happening every seven days

hebetic: occurring at puberty

hibernal: occurring in winter

hodiernal: pertaining to today

horal: hourly

horary: happening once an hour; hourly

hourly: occurring once an hour

immemorial: extending beyond memory

intercalary: inserted into calendar, as with leap year's added day

intermittent: starting and stopping at intervals

last-ditch: done in final moment out of desperation

lasting: enduring; unending

last-minute: done when time is running out

Lenten: relating to the fast called Lent

lifelong: for the duration of one's life

long-drawn-out: lasting or seeming to last a very long time

long-run: extended over a long period of time

long-standing: of great duration or age

long-term: of extensive duration

lustral: occurring every five years; quinquennial

matin: pertaining to the morning

matinal: pertaining to morning

matutinal: early; pertaining to morning

menstrual: monthly

millenary: lasting one thousand years

monthly: done once a month or performed in a month

natalitious: pertaining to a birthday; natalitial

Neolithic: designating period of cultural development from about 10,000 to 3000 B.C.

night and day: all the time; at all hours

nine-to-five: pertaining to standard working day in forty-hour week

noctidial: comprising a night and a day

nocturnal: pertaining to night; nightly

on time: punctual; at the specified time

paschal: relating to the paschal feast or Easter

penteteric: occurring every five years

periodic: happening at stated intervals

periodical: happening at stated intervals

perpetual: eternal; everlasting

plurennial: lasting for several years

postpartum: of the time immediately following birth

prehistoric: pertaining to period before written history

present-day: contemporary; modern

prevernal: of winter changing into spring

primaveral: pertaining to early spring

protracted: extended over time; drawn out

punctual: performed at the exact time; prompt; on time

quadrennial: occurring once every four years or lasting four years

quarterly: occurring four times per year

quincentennial: pertaining to a five-hundred-year period or anniversary

quindecennial: pertaining to a fifteen-year period or anniversary

quinquennial: occurring every five years

quotennial: annual; yearly

quotidian: daily; mundane; everyday

recurrent: returning from time to time

recurring: following in succession

regular: pursued with uniformity

regular as clockwork: very steady

remittent: having remissions

rhythmical: pertaining to rhythm

round-the-clock: at all hours of the day or night

seasonal: occurring regularly during a specific season

secular: relating to an age

semiannual: occurring every half year or twice a year; semiyearly

semicentennial: occurring every fifty years

semidiurnal: occurring every half day or twice a day

semimonthly: occurring every half month or twice a month

semiweekly: occurring every half week or twice a week

semiyearly: semiannual

sempiternal: eternal; perpetual

septennial: occurring every seven years

septimanal: weekly

serial: appearing in successive parts

serotinal: pertaining to late summer

short-run: occurring over a short span of time

steady: regular; constant

tertian: occurring every third day

time-lapse: designating photography in which very slow process is made to appear rapid by taking multiple exposures over time

tricennial: occurring every thirty years

triennial: occurring every three years; continuing or persisting for three years

trieteric: occurring every other year

trimonthly: occurring every three months

triweekly: occurring every three weeks; occurring three times a week

vernal: of or pertaining to spring; early; vertumnal

vertumnal: pertaining to spring; vernal

vicennial: occurring every twenty years

weekly: occurring once a week

yearly: occurring once a year

Timidity—Modesty

afraid: somewhat impressed with fear

afraid of one's own shadow: needlessly or excessively afraid

aghast: stupefied with sudden horror or fright

alarming: causing apprehension of danger

apprehensive: fearful of or expecting danger

argh: timid; cowardly

awe-inspiring: filling with awe

awestricken: impressed with awe

awestruck: impressed with awe

awful: frightful; horrible

bashful: modest to excess

blushing: showing reddish color upon the cheeks

breathless: out of breath, as from fright or violent exercise

constrained: held in check by timidity

coy: reserved through shyness

Daphnean: shy; bashful

demure: modest and reserved in manner or behavior

diffident: not self-reliant or self-confident; modest; timid

dire: horrible; dreadful; dismal

direful: dreadful; terrible

dread: exciting apprehension or great fear

dreadful: inspiring dread or fear

fainthearted: not courageous; timorous

fearful: inspiring horror or fear

fearing: being filled with fear

fearsome: easily frightened; timid

fell: fierce; barbarous

fidgety: restless; nervous; uneasy

formidable: adapted to cause fear or shrinking from

frightened: excited by fright

frightened to death: very much frightened

ghastly: horrible; shocking; dreadful

haunted with the fear of: continually fearing something

horrible: inspiring horror

horrid: disagreeable; horrible

horrific: causing horror

horror-stricken: impressed with horror

horror-struck: impressed with horror

humble: not assuming

in a fright: frightened

in fear: fearing

in hysterics: in a state of excessive nervous excitement, as hysteria

inspiring fear: causing or filling with fear

mim: timid; modest

modest: unpretentious

more frightened than hurt: very much frightened, but little hurt

nervous: easily disturbed

out of countenance: abashed

overmodest: very bashful

pale as a ghost: thoroughly overcome by fright

pale as ashes: thoroughly overcome by fright

pale as death: thoroughly overcome by fright

panic-stricken: impressed or filled with panic

panic-struck: impressed or filled with panic

pavid: frightened

perilous: full of risk; dangerous

poor in spirit: humble

portentous: foreshadowing ill
pudibund: bashful; modest; prudish
pusillanimous: timid; wishy-washy; irritatingly indecisive
redoubtable: formidable; dreadful
reserved: keeping one's thoughts to oneself
restless: uneasy; disturbed
reticent: shy; reluctant
revolting: shocking; offensive
shaky: trembling
shamefaced: easily confused
sheepish: awkwardly diffident
shocking: striking with horror
shy: bashful
skittish: timid; shy
terrible: exciting terror; dreadful
terrific: adapted to excite great fear or dread

terror-stricken: impressed with terror
terror-struck: impressed with terror
timid: shrinking from publicity; easily frightened
timorous: shy
tremendous: adapted to excite dread or fear
tremulous: shaking; quivering
trepid: fearful; afraid
unaspiring: unambitious
unassuming: modest
unboastful: not inclined to brag
unobtrusive: not tending to obtrude
unostentatious: not showy
unpretending: without pretense; modest
unpretentious: not characterized by pretension
verecund: modest; shy; bashful
white as a sheet: pale from fear

Toil

amain: with violent effort; vehemently
elaborate: done or prepared with great pains
energetic: active
epitonic: very strained
faffle: concerning work that occupies time but with results not equivalent to the amount of time and labor
hard at work: laboring
hardscrabble: concerning making a living the hard way
hard-working: making great efforts
herculean: requiring great strength
industrious: zealous in laboring
insudate: causing sweating; laborious
laboriferous: painstaking; persevering
laboring: burdened, or moving with difficulty or pain
laborious: requiring a great amount of labor

laboristic: pertaining to policies favoring labor
moliminous: painstaking; laborious
on the stretch: at work
operose: diligent; hardworking; industrious
painstaking: working with care
palestric: pertaining to exercises
panurgic: ready to do any type of work
strained: exerted to the limit of endurance
strenuous: vigorous and persevering
toilsome: marked by toil
troublesome: attended with trouble
trusatile: worked by pushing
uphill: requiring unceasing efforts
wearisome: making weary
womanfully: working or struggling like a woman

Top

apical: at the tip, point, apex; topmost
besprent: sprinkled over
capital: first in importance
culminating: attaining the highest point

head: pertaining to what is at the head of
highest: the topmost
meridian: at the highest point

meridional: relating to meridians
polar: pertaining to the axile extremities of the earth
supernal: pertaining to heavenly regions or things
supreme: highest, greatest, or most excellent

tip-top: highest; best
top: pertaining to the top
topgallant: between the topmast and the royal mast
topmost: pertaining to the very top
uppermost: the highest

Touch

attingent: touching or in contact with
close to: in contact with
contactual: in contact with; tangential
conterminous: having common limits or boundaries
contiguous: touching or joining at the edge or boundary
end-to-end: contiguous
hand-to-hand: in close union; within touch
haptic: pertaining to the sense of touch; tactile
in contact: touching physically
intractible: imperceptible to touch
itching: tingling

lambent: touching lightly
libant: touching lightly; tasting
osculatory: pertaining to close contact; kissing
palpable: perceptible by touch or feeling
pertingent: touching
tactile: of or pertaining to touch
tactual: tangible
tangential: of, pertaining to, or moving in the direction of a tangent
tangible: perceptible by touch or the sense; capable of being possessed
touching: physically in contact
with no interval: having no space between

Transfer

alienable: capable of being alienated or transferred
contagious: transferable by contact
cruciferous: bearing or carrying a cross
drifted: carried along gently or unconsciously
efferent: carrying outward
gerent: carrying; bearing
mastigophoric: carrying a whip or lash; mastigophorous
movable: capable of being transferred
onerary: suitable for carrying freight
portable: readily removed from one place to another
portative: capable of carrying
prehensile: capable of gripping and carrying

smittlish: infectious; contagious
superlunar: beyond the moon; heavenly; celestial
surpassing: going beyond
transanimating: transferring a soul from one body to another
transferred: removed to another place
transmundane: beyond or outside the world
transnational: beyond national boundaries
tursable: portable
ultra vires: beyond one's powers or authority
ultramontane: beyond the mountains; situated beyond
ultramundane: beyond or outside this world

Transientness

ad interim: temporary
brief: short; transitory
brisk: quick; lively; active
cursory: hasty; desultory
deciduous: falling off; shedding yearly
ephemeral: short-lived
evanescent: vanishing or likely to vanish
extemporaneous: on the spur of the moment; impromptu
fleeting: swift; rapid; quick
flying: passing through the air, as a bird
fugacious: transitory; temporary; tendency to flee
fugitive: escaping by stealth, especially, from justice
impermanent: not lasting; changeable; unstable
momentary: lasting a very short while
mortal: fatally vulnerable
passing: relating to the act of passing or going

perishable: subject to decay
picaresque: of a situation, transitory or impermanent
precarious: uncertain; risky
pressed for time: in a hurry
preterient: transient
provisional: suited for the time being; set up for the present
provisory: conditional; dependent
quick: speedy; swift; hasty; alive
shifting: moving from place to place
short-lived: of short duration
slippery: liable to fall away
spasmodic: impulsive; transitory
sudden: quickly; unexpected
summary: rapidly performed
temporal: pertaining to the present
temporary: limited; not permanent
transient: passing before the sight or perception and then disappearing
transitive: not lasting or durable
transitory: continuing only for a short time

Transport

abeam: directly outward from or at right angle to fore-and-aft line of ship
aboard: on board a vessel
adrift: floating freely without being steered; not at anchor
aerostatic: pertaining to aerial navigation
afloat: floating on surface of water
aft: toward the stern or tail; behind
airborne: carried through air by aerodynamic forces
air-to-air: designating weapon launched from aircraft and directed at airborne object
airworthy: safe and fit for flying
amphibious: used on both land and sea
antiknock: relating to any fuel additive that helps resist engine knocking
automotive: self-propelled on land, sea, or air, usually referring to land vehicles
aweigh: designating anchor coming up

bumped: refused seating on flight for which one has reservation
bumper-to-bumper: describing long line of slow-moving traffic
cherry: describing older car in excellent condition
coasting: sailing along the coast
crank: unstable; liable to capsize
dirigible: capable of being directed; steerable
fast: secured, tied, fastened, or arranged, especially of lines
fore: toward the nose or bow; ahead
fore-and-aft: having no square sails; running lengthwise
full-rigged: designating sailing vessel with three or more square-rigged masts
head-on: describing direct collision with car moving in opposite direction

hit-and-run: describing accident in which driver flees the scene

hypersonic: designating supersonic speeds of Mach 5 and above

inboard: close or closest to fuselage or body of aircraft

in-flight: done or occurring while aircraft is airborne

jerkwater: designating small town at which train draws water from track pan without stopping

leeward: at side of vessel away from wind

loaded: having many optional features

loxodromic: of sailing obliquely

maritime: pertaining to the sea

midship: in or at middle of vessel

mothball: designating vessel not in current use or held in reserve, often older vessel

naufragous: causing shipwreck

nautical: of or pertaining to ships, sailors, or navigation

naval: pertaining to ships or navy

navicular: boatlike; cymbiform; hysteriform; hysterioid; nautiform; naviculiform; naviform; scaphoid

navigable: capable of navigation; passable

off-line: designating travel on carrier other than one that sold ticket

off-peak: designating noncommuting hours with reduced passenger fare

omniphibious: able to land on water, land, snow, ice

onboard: inside aircraft cabin, cockpit, or cargo hold

outboard: far or farthest from fuselage or body of aircraft

over-the-top: indicating position of aircraft above cloud layer or other obscuring phenomena forming ceiling

plaustral: pertaining to a wagon or cart

polar: having directional setting at north magnetic pole

pteric: pertaining to wings

raked: describing car, especially hot rod, with lowered front end

revehent: carrying back

sailing: that which sails

seafaring: following the sea

seagoing: made for use in open sea

seaworthy: fit to travel on the open sea

shipboard: aboard ship

shipshape: having everything in good order

sonic: designating speed of sound at given altitude

souped-up: customized for increased power and speed; stroked

square-rigged: having square sails as principal sails

stock: designating standard design, parts, and color of factory-manufactured automobile

stroked: souped-up, especially by lengthening piston stroke for greater power

supersonic: greater than speed of sound at given altitude

tender: riding too high in water, therefore unstable; tending to heel excessively under sail

transonic: just below or just above speed of sound

transportable: capable of being carried or conveyed from one place to another

upwind: sailing toward direction of wind

velivolant: underway with full sail

volant: flying

volitorial: pertaining to flying; able to fly

windward: at side of vessel facing wind

Traveling

ambulatory: pertaining to walking

bumper-to-bumper: marked by heavy traffic with long rows of slow-moving cars

circumforanean: journeying from house to house

circumforaneous: journeying from house to house or place to place

discursive: journeying from the point; digressive
gadding: roaming about idly
itinerant: journeying from place to place
jeepable: of a road able to be traversed by jeeps or four-wheel-drive vehicles
locomotive: moving from place to place
migratory: roving; wandering
mundivagant: wandering over the world
noctivagant: night-wandering
nomadic: pertaining to nomads
peripatetic: moving from place to place; itinerant
rambling: aimlessly moving

round-the-world: designating ticket for passage or trip around the world
roving: wandering
solivagant: wandering alone
touristy: typical of or intended for tourists, therefore often tasteless or banal
traveling: journeying
travel-stained: soiled by travel
travel-tainted: fatigued from travel
vagrant: wandering from place to place
viable: traversable
viatic: traveling
wayfaring: journeying
wayworn: fatigued by journeying

Trial—Testing

analytic: pertaining to an analysis
cut-and-try: experimental
docimastic: proving by experiments
empirical: based on experiment without regard to science
essaying: making weak attempts
experimental: pertaining to experiments
on one's trial: undergoing a test
peirastic: experimental; tentative
probationary: undergoing trial

probative: serving for trial
probatory: serving for trial
provisional: tentative; dependent on conditions
tentative: of the nature of an experiment or hypothesis; provisional
testable: able to be tried or tested; capable of being empirically tested
trial: prepared for testing; able to be tested or experimented with
under probation: on trial

Truth

accurate: conforming exactly to truth
actual: something real or actually existing
apodictic: clearly and undeniably true
as good as one's word: reliable; possessing quality of keeping a promise
authentic: according with the facts; trustworthy; reliable
bona fide: in good faith; without deceit
candid: sincere in speech; straightforward; clear; white
categorically true: true without qualification
certain: established as fact or truth
constant: steady in purpose; faithful
correct: in accordance with what is true
curious: eager for information
definite: having precise limits; known with exactness

delicate: nice in discrimination
exact: strictly observant of truth
faithful: firmly adhering to the truth
fine: excellent or admirable in quality, character, form, or appearance
frank: free from concealment; open in manner
genuine: belonging to the original or true stock
guileless: free from guile; artless; frank
honest: free from fraud; equitable; fair
in its true colors: as it truly is
ingenuous: free from reserve, disguise, equivocation, or dissimulation
just: agreeing with a required standard; true
legitimate: having the sanction of law or custom

literal: true as to fact or detail

mathematical: demonstrably true or correct

natural: true to nature

nice: fitted or adjusted exactly true; accurate

official: pertaining to an office or public trust

open: without reserve or false pretense

openhearted: showing the thoughts and intentions plainly

orthodox: holding the faith commonly accepted as true

ostensible: presented as real or true; avowed

outspoken: plainspoken; frank; speaking out freely and frankly

particular: exact in performance or requirement

precise: strictly accurate

punctual: exact as to appointed time

pure: free from defilement; truly genuine

real: being in true accordance to appearance or claim; genuine

realistic: conformable to the principles and methods of realism

religiously exact: conscientiously observant of truth

right: according to fact or truth

rigid: strict; exact

rigorous: exacting; logically accurate

scientific: agreeing with the rules or principles of science; hence accurate; exact

scrupulous: exact; precise

simplehearted: open; sincere

sincere: acting and speaking the truth; without alloy

solid: characterized by reality; substantial or satisfactory

sound: founded in truth

sterling: true; genuine

straightforward: free from prevarication or concealment

strict: exacting; rigidly observed

substantial: of true worth and importance

substantially true: essentially true

tangible: perceptible by touch or by the senses

true: conformable to reality or fact

true as gospel: absolutely truthful

true to the letter: true in every particular

true-blue: of uncompromising principles

truehearted: loyal; faithful; honest; sincere

trustworthy: worthy of confidence

truthful: habitually speaking the truth

unadulterated: genuine; pure

unaffected: not showing affectation; sincere; real

uncolored: true; without prejudice or exaggeration

unconfuted: not confuted or proved false; hence, true

undisguised: not covered with a disguise; hence, open, frank, truthful

undissembling: true

undistorted: not distorted, as by falsehood

unerring: certain; of true insight

unexaggerated: not exaggerated; hence, truthful

unfeigned: not hypocritical; real

unflattering: not coloring the truth to please

unideal: not ideal; real

unimagined: not imagined, conceived, or formed in idea

unimpeachable: not capable of being impeached or called in question

unperjured: free from perjury; not forsworn

unrefuted: not capable of being refuted; hence, truthful

unreserved: holding nothing back; frank

unsophisticated: simple; pure

unvarnished: not artfully embellished; plain

valid: sufficiently supported by fact

veracious: habitually disposed to speak the truth

veridical: truth-telling; veracious

veritable: agreeable to truth

well-defined: having the precise limit well-marked

well-founded: founded on good and true reasons

well-grounded: founded on good and true reasons

Two

⟨◇⟩⟨◇⟩⟨◇⟩⟨◇⟩⟨◇⟩⟨◇⟩⟨◇⟩⟨◇⟩⟨◇⟩⟨◇⟩⟨◇⟩⟨◇⟩⟨◇⟩⟨◇⟩⟨◇⟩⟨◇⟩⟨◇⟩⟨◇⟩⟨◇⟩

aliquot: that measures or divides exactly

ancipital: having two edges

bicipital: having two heads

biconjugate: twice paired

bicrural: having two legs

bicuspid: double pointed, like bicuspid teeth

bidentate: having only two teeth

biduous: lasting two days

bifacial: having two faces

bifarious: arranged in two parallel rows

bifid: cleft in the middle

bifold: twofold; of two kinds, degrees

biform: having two bodies, shapes, or forms

bifurcate: divided into two parts

bifurcous: having two forks

bigential: having two races

bilateral: having two sides; relating to two sides, questions, parties

bimanal: having two hands

bimanual: requiring the use of two hands

binary: found in pairs

binomial: an expression of two terms

biparous: bringing forth two at the same birth

bipartite: divided into two parts

bisected: divided into two parts

biserial: arranged in two rows, ranks

bivious: leading two ways

both: including two at the same time

cleft: rent in two by force

cloven: divided; pertaining to cloven feet

conduplicate: state of being folded lengthwise; twofold

conjugate: joined together; combined in pairs

couple: united

demi-: half

dicerous: having two antennae, tentacles, or horns

didymous: in pairs; twin

dimidiate: divided into two equal parts

dioscuric: twin

dipterous: having two wings

dirhinous: with paired nostrils

double: twice as much in size, number, etc.

doubled: twice as much in size, number, etc.

double-faced: of two faces to perform the same work; deceitful; hypocritical

dual: composed of two

dualistic: consisting of two

duplex: having two folds; having two parts

duplicate: being a copy of another

dyadic: relative to two parts

fissile: fissionable; capable of being split along natural lines

gemeled: coupled; paired

hemi-: half

janiform: having two faces

jugate: paired; jumelle

jumelle: paired; jugate

second: next to the first; subordinate; inferior in rank

semi-: half

twain: of two

twin: being one of a pair

two: being one plus one

twofold: double

two-sided: folded as to have two parts

Ugliness

awkward: lacking grace in bearing
bald: devoid of hair
beautiless: lacking beauty
bufoniform: like a toad
cadaverous: looking like a human corpse
clumsy: devoid of grace or dexterity
crooked: not straight
deathlike: looking like death
dingy: dusky in color
discolored: changed in color
disfigured: marred as to figure
dumpy: short and thick
evil-favored: not having a good appearance
forbidding: repulsive in appearance
foul: loathsome to the senses
frightful: causing alarm
gaudy: showy
gaunt: emaciated in looks
gawky: ungainly in appearance
ghastly: having a ghostlike appearance
ghostlike: resembling a ghost
graceless: lacking grace
grim: having a forbidding aspect
grim-faced: ugly and dreadful
grim-visaged: ugly and dreadful
grisly: frightful; fear-inspiring
gross: not refined
gruesome: horrid
haggard: having wasted features
hard-favored: not good-looking

hard-featured: possessing unattractive features
hard-visaged: having a harsh expression
hideous: frightful to look upon
homely: not handsome
horrible: exciting fear or dread
horrid: fitted to awaken horror
hulking: clumsy
hulky: clumsy
ill-favored: lacking beauty
ill-looking: ugly
ill-made: not well-formed
ill-proportioned: in bad proportion
ill-shaped: poorly shaped
inartistic: not according to the standards of art
inelegant: not elegant
lumbering: clumsy
lumping: possessing great bulk
lumpish: lacking in motive power
misproportioned: out of proportion
misshapen: badly formed
monstrous: of extraordinary ugliness
not fit to be seen: disgusting or unkempt
odious: exciting disgust
ordinary: undistinguished for beauty
plain: devoid of adornment
repellent: tending to repel
repulsive: exciting dislike, disgust, horror
rickety: shaky; tottering

rough: void of refinement; rude
rude: lacking polish, refinement, or delicacy
rugged: unkempt; disordered
seemless: not becoming
shapeless: void of regular form
shocking: very repulsive
sightless: repulsive to the eye
slouching: having an ungainly manner
squalid: loathsome to the sight on account of filth
stiff: starched; constrained
ugglesome: horrible; frightful
ugly: not beautiful
ugly as a dead monkey: extremely ugly
ugly as a scarecrow: extremely ugly
ugly as a toad: extremely ugly

ugly as sin: extremely ugly
unbeauteous: not beauteous
unbeautiful: lacking beauty
uncanny: devoid of pleasing qualities
uncomely: not comely
uncouth: characterized by awkwardness
ungainly: lacking dexterity or skill
ungraceful: not graceful
unlovely: exciting dislike
unornamental: not ornamental
unprepossessing: not inviting favor or confidence
unseemly: not becoming
unshapely: having a bad form
unsightly: not pleasing to the sight
unwieldy: not easily managed on account of bulk

Undress

bald: destitute of hair or natural clothing
bald as a coot: figurative expression for very bald, the common coot having a bald forehead
bare: devoid of covering or dress; naked
bare as the back of one's hand: figurative expression for bare
barefoot: with feet bare
callow: not yet feathered out; unfledged; hairless
defrocked: deprived of priestly garb; silenced
discalceate: barefooted; discalced
dishabille: loosely or partly dressed
divested: stripped, as of clothes
exposed: laid bare or open
hairless: without hair; bald
in a state of nature: naked as when born
in birthday suit: nude
in buff: naked
in dishabille: having on a loose, negligent dress
in native buff: naked as when born

in nature's garb: naked
leafless: having no leafage
naked: having no clothes on; bare; stripped
napless: made without a nap; threadbare
nude: destitute of clothing or covering; naked
out at elbows: with coat worn through at the elbows; shabby
ragged: worn-out; wearing frayed or shabby garments
roofless: having no roof; destitute of shelter
scuddy: naked
stark naked: wholly naked; quite bare
threadbare: worn so that the threads show; clad in garments worn so that the threads show
undraped: stripped of drapery; uncovered
undressed: divested of clothes; stripped; disrobed
with nothing on: naked; nude; stripped

Universality

all: the whole number or quantity of anything
allover: generally distributed

besetting: generally troubling
broad: general in scope
catholic: general in the widest sense

catholical: general in the widest sense
collective: gathered into a general mass
common: general in occurrence
comprehensive: of general application
covered with: overspread with
customary: according to general usage
ecumenical: generally applying to the habitable earth
encyclopedical: including the entire circle of knowledge and information; encyclopedic
epidemic: generally prevailing
every: each individual of a whole collection
general: wide in meaning or scope
generic: having a general comprehension or application

impersonal: not relating to a particular person or thing
panharmonic: accompanied by universal consent
prevailing: very general
prevalent: most generally current
rife: of general abundance
sweeping: general in comprehension
transcendental: very high in degree
universal: relating to the universe in general
unspecified: not mentioned particularly
widespread: general over a great area
worldwide: general throughout the world

Unlikelihood

antilogous: contrary; inconsistent
autistic: pertaining to imagining oneself in pleasant but unlikely or impossible circumstances
contrary to all reasonable expectations: improbable
improbable: not likely to happen
inconceivable: not conceivable; contrary to reason
incredible: unbelievable

inimaginable: unimaginable
rare: infrequently occurring
Scheherazadian: fanciful; incredible; interest-holding
unheard-of: improbable; obscure
unimaginable: not capable of being imagined
unlikely: not likely; not probable
untrowable: incredible

Unlikeness

anomalous: abnormal; deviating from the normal or common
as different as chalk from cheese: wholly unlike
as different as Macedon and Monmouth: wholly unlike
as like a dock as a daisy: very different
cast in a different mold: very different
disparate: that cannot be compared; entirely different
dissimilar: not similar
diversified: made essentially different in various parts or characteristics
far from it: very different
new: having no counterpart; recently come into existence

no such thing: very different
nothing of the kind: very different
novel: of recent origin; strange and unusual
of a different kind: of a differing type or class
original: not produced by imitation; able to produce without imitating
quite another thing: different
unique: the only one of its kind
unlike: not like
unmatched: with an equal or similar one either not found or not in existence
unprecedented: preceded by no similar case or example

Unpalatableness

acrid: having a biting, burning taste

acrimonious: very bitter

apositic: without appetite; anorectous; anorectic

bitter: having a biting, unpleasant taste, as of gall or aloes

bitter as gall: bitter, like gall

flat: lacking taste

gustless: without taste

illepid: unpleasant

ill-flavored: not having a good taste

inesculent: tasteless; inedible

ingustable: tasteless

ingustible: having no taste

insapory: tasteless

insipid: tasteless

loath: filled with disgust or aversion

loathfulsome: causing an intense feeling of dislike

mawkish: disgusting; insipid

mild: having little taste

milk-and-water: weak-tasting

nasty: disgusting to the sense of taste

nauseous: causing sickness of the stomach

offensive: extremely unpleasant

rancid: having an unpleasant, stale taste

rank: having an offensive, foul taste

repulsive: causing extreme dislike for

savorless: tasteless

scabrous: unpleasant; repulsive; indecent

sickening: revolting; disgusting

stale: old to the taste

tasteless: without a particular flavor

unpalatable: unpleasant to the taste

unpleasant: disliked

unsavory: without taste

unsweet: bitter or sour

untasted: not having been tasted

vapid: insipid

void of taste: tasteless

weak: defective in stimulative properties

wishy-washy: very much diluted and weak to the taste

Unselfishness

chivalrous: sacrificing; self-denying; knightly

disinterested: free from selfish motives

elevated: noble minded

exalted: noble-minded

generous: liberal in giving

great: philanthropic; largehearted

handsome: noble; exhibiting a feeling of generosity

heroic: brave; courteous; unselfish

high: exalted in action

high-minded: of lofty purpose

largehearted: full of brotherly sympathy

liberal: broad in views or sympathies

lofty: elevated in purpose

magnanimous: raised above what is low, mean, or ungenerous; great-minded

noble: grand; having a contempt for everything mean

noble-minded: honorable; magnanimous

princely: exercising the qualities of a prince

self-denying: giving up one's own desires for the good of others

self-devoted: unselfish

self-sacrificing: losing or suffering for another

spirited: bold; courageous

stoical: indifferent to pain or pleasure

sublime: lofty; noble

unbought: not influenced by bribery or favor

unbribed: full of integrity; upright

uncorrupted: above the influences of bribes

unselfish: free from the feeling or regard for one's own comfort of advantage alone

Unskillfulness

adrift: in a confused state
ambilevous: clumsy
ambisinistrous: clumsy; maladroit; ambisinister
at fault: in the wrong
awkward: not skillful or graceful in action
blunderly: badly made; clumsily constructed
bungling: inclined to bungle
clodpolish: awkward
clumsy: lacking dexterity and grace
cow-handed: awkward
disqualified: not having the necessary qualifications
foolish: wholly lacking in ability or intelligence
gauche: awkward and tactless
gawky: very awkward
giddy: lacking judgment
green: lacking knowledge from experience
heavy-handed: clumsy
ill-advised: badly advised
ill-conducted: poorly managed
ill-contrived: badly planned
ill-devised: unskillfully planned
ill-imagined: not well-planned
ill-judged: not well-planned
ill-qualified: not fitted for
inactive: not active
inapt: unhandy
incompetent: unfit
inconsiderate: regardless of what should be considered
inexperienced: without practice
inexpert: unskillful
infelicitous: not felicitous; lacking in fitness; unlucky

inhabile: incompetent; unskillful
jackleg: incompetent
kitthoge: left-handed; awkward
left-handed: clumsy
lubberly: like a lubber
maladroit: lacking adroitness; awkward; bungling; clumsy
misadvised: wrongly advised
misconducted: badly led
misguided: badly led
out of practice: untrained to
penny-wise and pound-foolish: careful in small matters, careless in important affairs
quackish: characterized by quackery
raw: of no experience
rusty: having lost skill for want of practice
shiftless: wanting in energy or ability
slatternly: untidy; slovenly
slovenly: negligent and disorderly
stupid: lacking intelligence and skill
unaccustomed: not familiar
unadvised: not advised
unapt: not fitted for
unconversant: unable to carry on a conversation
unfit: not adapted to
unguided: without a leader or example
unhandy: that cannot be well used
uninitiated: not trained to
unqualified: unable to do
unskillful: without special ability
unstatesmanlike: without the characteristics of a statesman
unteachable: that cannot be taught
untractable: that cannot be trained
untrained: without practice
unused: not familiar
wild: untrained; careless

Unsuitableness

dyslogistic: unfavorable; antagonistic; dislogistic
ill-timed: poorly timed
improper: not suitable

inauspicious: unfortunate; unlucky; unfavorable
inexpedient: not expedient
infelicitous: inappropriate; unfortunate

inopportune: unfavorable
intempestive: untimely; inopportune
intrusive: coming without invitation
melancounterous: poorly timed
misbecoming: unbecoming
mistimed: poorly timed or judged
not the thing: unsuited; out of place
out of the question: not to be asked for
out-of-date: obsolete
out-of-season: at an unfavorable time
premature: done before time; untimely
preposterous: absurd; monstrous
seemless: unseemly

timeless: done at an improper time
too late for: at the wrong time
too soon for: at the wrong time
unfavorable: not propitious
unfortunate: having ill fortune
unlucky: unfortunate
unpropitious: not advantageous; unfavorable
unpunctual: not on time
unseasonable: not in proper season
unsuited: unfitted; unsuitable
untimely: unpropitious; ill-timed
untoward: unfavorable; annoying
would-be: pretentious; presumptuous

Usefulness

adaptable: capable of being adjusted to some use
adequate: equal to what is required
advantageous: affording utility
applicable: capable of being brought into actual use
at hand: available for immediate use
available: capable of being used
commodious: well suited to the purpose for which made
conducive: tending to be useful
effective: producing a decided consequence
effectual: capable of producing an effect
efficacious: possessing the quality of being efficient
efficient: actively operative
expedient: useful in promoting a desired end
functional: serving a simple purpose
gainful: producing profit
good for: useful for
handy: convenient for use
in use: made use of at the present time
instrumental: serving as a means to an end
intarissable: incapable of being used up; inexhaustible

intermediate: occupying a middle place in some action
intervening: coming between other influences in the course of action
mechanical: operated by the action of forces without a directing intelligence
mediatorial: pertaining to intervening for the purpose of reconciling
ministerial: pertaining to ministering to
of all work: adapted for all kinds of work
of use: advantageous
polychrestic: useful for many reasons
proficuous: proficient or useful
profitable: producing profit
prolific: producing in abundance
qua: as; in the capacity or role of
remunerative: making a proper profit
serviceable: that can be used for a purpose
subservient: serving some purpose
subsidiary: giving aid in an inferior capacity
tangible: capable of being possessed or realized
useful: serving a use or purpose
valuable: possessing qualities that are useful
well-trodden: much used
well-worn: much used
worth one's salt: of some service or advantage

Uselessness

abortive: brought forth prematurely

bootless: useless; without result or gain

dear at any price: of little value or use

disused: not used

done with: finished

effete: worn-out and incapable of further use

empty: without force or use

fit for the dust hole: useless enough to be thrown away

flag-fallen: unemployed

fruitless: unproductive of good results

frustraneous: vain; useless

futile: of no avail

gainless: producing no profit

good-for-nothing: of absolutely no use

ill-spent: spent to no advantage

improficuous: unprofitable

inadequate: not sufficient for use

inane: wanting in understanding

incompetent: unable to do what is required

ineffectual: not productive of effect

inefficacious: not capable of producing the desired or proper effect

inefficient: not capable of effective action

inept: not suitable for a purpose

inoperative: not acting so as to produce an effect

inservient: useless

inutile: useless

kokshut: worn-out; used up

leading to no end: without any aim

misembodied: put into the wrong body

misused: devoted to wrong use

not required: unnecessary

not used: not in service

not worth a straw: entirely useless

not worth having: entirely useless

not worth powder and shot: not worth an effort

obsolete: gone out of general use

of no avail: useless

of no earthly use: entirely worthless

otiant: unemployed; dormant

otiose: sterile; futile; useless; not required; superfluous

past work: useless from exertion in the past

priceless: useless because of great price

profitless: void of gain or advantage

stale, flat, and unprofitable: quite useless

strange-achieved: gained by wrong means; gained in foreign lands

subservient: useful in an inferior capacity

superfluous: more than is useful

thrown away: of too little value to have been kept

unapplied: not used according to the intention

unavailing: not having the desired effect

uncalled-for: not required or needed

unculled: not gathered

undisposed of: not distributed or bestowed

unemployed: not used for any purpose

unessayed: unattempted

unexceeded: not surpassed

unexercised: not yet put into use

ungathered: not collected

unnecessary: not required under the circumstances

unproductive: of no use in bringing forth

unprofitable: producing no improvement or advantage

unsalable: not capable of being sold

unserviceable: not capable of being put to service

unservient: useless

unspent: not wasted by use

unsubservient: not of use in an inferior capacity

untouched: not meddled with

untrodden: not used by people in walking

useless: having no use; having no value

vain: having no useful results

valueless: of so little use as to have no value

worthless: without any value

Vacillation

ambidextrous: two-sided; double-faced; with two right hands

at a loss: doubtful

capricious: characterized by whim

changeful: given to alteration

coquetting: trifling

cowardly: of a timid, fainthearted disposition

double-minded: unsettled; unstable

ductile: easily led

dwaible: unstable; dwaibly

easygoing: taking things without concern

facile: easily moved or influenced

fast and loose: inconstant; uncertain

feebleminded: of weak will; lacking decision

fickle: characterized by erratic changeableness

fidgety: changing about in a nervous fashion

frail: easily influenced or led astray

frothy: unsubstantial; trivial

giddy: inconstant to foolishness; having the head swim

halfhearted: timid; hesitating

hesitating: pausing in uncertainty

infirm of purpose: unsure of purpose

irresolute: not fixed or constant in carrying out a purpose; indecisive; hesitating

light: not serious or resolute

light-minded: lacking seriousness or strength of mind

lightsome: of a cheerful disposition

off one's balance: uncertain

reactionary: pertaining to the tendency to return to a former state

reversible: capable of being changed

revocable: capable of being repealed or reversed

revocatory: rescinding

shilly-shally: of a vacillating, trifling nature

slippery as an eel: ready to use evasions

timeserving: servile; complying with ruling powers

timid: hesitant

tremulous: of a timid and irresolute nature; trembling

trimming: fluctuating

unable to say no: like an assentator; easily persuaded

undecided: not having the mind made up

undetermined: not having the mind made up

unjaundiced: free of prejudice

unresolved: not having the mind made up

unsteadfast: not to be depended upon

unsteady: inconstant

vacillating: swinging indecisively from
one thing to another
volatile: easily affected; changeable
weak: lacking firmness and energy of
character

without ballast: unsteady, like an unbal-
lasted ship

Valuation

appraised: having had a value set
depreciated: lowered in worth
depreciating: losing in value
nugatory: of no value; insubstantial;
pointless
overestimated: rated too highly
oversensitive: too easily affected

pretentious: claiming to be more than
one's true value
trumpery: of comparatively little worth
unprized: without prize
unvalued: without value; having no
value

Variegation

barred: marked with bars of colors
bicolored: of two colors
blotched: having irregular spots; blotchy
brindled: of a gray or tawny color with
streaks of a darker hue; brind; brided
brocked: mottled with black and white
checkered: marked with alternate
squares of different colors
clouded: variegated with colors
cymophanous: having a wavy light
daedal: changeful
dappled: marked with spots of different
shades of color
dichromatic: having two colors
divers-colored: of many colors
embroidered: ornamented with
needlework
fernticled: freckled
flea-bitten: of a horse, white flecked with
minute spots of bay or sorrel
flecked: streaked; speckled
fleckered: streaked; speckled
freckled: marked with small discolored
spots
grizzled: sprinkled or mixed with gray
iridescent: having colors like the rainbow
irrorate: speckled; flecked; freckled;
specked; speckled; stippled
kaleidoscopic: variegated
lentiginous: having a lot of freckles
listed: striped

liturate: spotted; maculate; mottled
many-colored: showing a variety of
colors
many-hued: showing a variety of colors
marbled: variegated, stained, or veined
in color like marble
menald: spotted; speckled; dappled;
flecked; macular; maculose; pardine;
speckled; spotted
mosaic: formed by uniting pieces of different colors
motley: consisting of different colors
mottled: spotted
nacreous: like mother-of-pearl
ocellate: having eyelike spots
of all manner of colors: having very
many different colors
of all the colors of the rainbow: having
very many different colors
opalescent: having changeable colors like
those of the opal
opaline: having changeable colors like
those of the opal
paned: provided with panes, as of different colors
party-colored: colored with different
tints; parti-color; parti-colored
pearlescent: resembling mother-of-pearl
pearly: showing changeable colors as a
pearl

VIGOR

pepper-and-salt: sprinkled with white and dark spots; salt-and-pepper
piebald: having spots and patches of black and white
pied: variegated with spots of different colors
plaid: checkered or marked with bars or stripes
polychromatic: many-colored
powdered: sprinkled, as with powder
punctuated: dotted with spots
shot: woven as to produce an effect of variable tints
speckled: marked with small spots of a different color from that of the rest of the surface

spotted: marked with spots
spotty: marked with spots
striated: marked with fine lines of color
studded: set thickly, as with studs
tabby: diversified in color
tesselated: formed of little squares of different colors
tortoiseshell: of variegated colors
tricolored: three-colored
variegated: having marks or patches of different colors; having a varied pattern
veined: streaked
venous: marked with veins
versicolored: of different colors
watered: diversified with wavelike lines

Vigor

active: lively
acute: sharp in perception and understanding
brisk: moving, acting, or taking place with quickness
caustic: spitefully sharp; burning
corrosive: rusting
deep-dyed: of great intensity
double-distilled: purified twice
double-edged: having two edges
double-shotted: heavily loaded, as a gun
drastic: acting with vigor; purging
energetic: acting with force
escharotic: destructive to human tissues
forcible: possessing force
harsh: severe

incisive: cutting
intense: violent
irritating: tending to provoke anger
keen: penetrating
mordant: biting
poignant: painful to the spirit
potent: having power
racy: striking and pleasing
rousing: stirring to action
severe: merciless
sharp: cutting
stringent: severe in operation
strong: having strength
trenchant: cutting deeply
vigorous: being strong and active
virulent: exhibiting envenomed hostility
vivid: intense

Viscidity—Pulpiness

agglutinative: sticky
albuminous: like albumen; thick and oily
amylaceous: like starch
clammy: viscous and sticky
clotted: coagulated or thickened, as blood
colletic: pertaining to glue
colloidal: jellylike
congealed: clotted; coagulated
curdled: changed into a curd, as milk; thickened

doughy: yielding; claylike; pulpy; pultaceous
emulsive: like or capable of making like emulsion
gelatine: like gelatin; similar to jelly; jellylike
gelatiniform: jellylike
gelatinous: like gelatin; similar to jelly; jellylike
gleety: oozy

glutinous: resembling glue; viscid and sticky
grumous: resembling a thick, sticky fluid; clotted
half-frozen: half-solid
half-melted: half-solid
incrassate: thickened
inspissate: of a thick consistency; thickened; inspissated
lacteal: pertaining to or resembling milk
lactean: pertaining to or resembling milk
lacteous: milklike
lactescent: having a milky consistency
lactiferous: containing or producing milk or a milky fluid
lentous: tenacious and viscid
lutaceous: muddy; thick
lutulent: muddy; thick
mastic: sticky and adhesive
milky: made of, containing, or resembling milk
mucid: mucilaginous; slimy
mucilaginous: like mucilage; sticky and soft; mucid; muculent; gooey; gummy
mucopurulent: consisting of mucus and pus
mucous: like mucus; slimy; viscous
muculent: resembling mucus; slimy
muddy: containing mud; thick
myxoid: pertaining to mucus

papescent: containing or having the qualities of pap
pitchy: sticky
pituitous: pertaining to a body secreting mucus; like mucus
plumeopician: consisting of tar and feathers
pulpous: pulpy
pulpy: like pulp; soft; succulent
pultaceous: macerated; softened; semifluid
resinous: of the nature of resin
ropy: stringy and viscous
semifluid: fluid, but thick and viscous
semiliquid: fluid, but thick and viscous
slab: mucilaginous
slabby: thick; viscous
slithy: slimy and lithe
spissated: thickened
sticky: adhering to a surface; thick and adhesive
succulent: juicy; specifically, of plants
tarry: like tar; covered with tar
thick: having considerable density or thickness
tremellose: gelatinous; shaking like jelly
uliginous: slimy; miry
viscid: adhesive; semifluid; viscous; gooey
viscous: having a glutinous consistency; viscid

Vocalization

affricative: of speech or music, characterized by a stop followed by a release
alto: having a low voice; deep; honey-voiced
articulate: clearly enunciated
audible: having a clear voice; articulated; crisp; distinct
balbutient: stuttering
big-sounding: talking loudly or pretentiously
breathy: having a very soft voice; modulated; muted; silken; whispery
bubbly: having a happy voice; chirpy; chirrupy

buccal: pertaining to sounds made in cavity of cheeks
catarrhal: having a nasal voice; asthmatic
chunnering: muttering; murmuring
close: designating vowel produced with tongue close to roof of mouth
closed: designating syllable ending with consonant
coronal: articulated with blade, or front, of tongue raised
crassilingual: thick-tongued
di petto: in singing, from the chest
distinct: clear

egressive: generated with exhalation of breath from lungs

ejaculatory: exclamatory

euphonious: well-sounding

excrescent: designating sound inserted in word due to articulation but without grammatical or etymological justification

fortis: designating consonant sound characterized by relatively strong forceful breath or effort

gingival: pronounced with the tip of the tongue near the upper gum

glottal: articulated in opening at upper part of larynx, between vocal cords

guttural: articulated in back of mouth or throat or with tongue against soft palate

hirrient: of a strongly trilled letter, especially *r* or *n*

hypsophonous: having a high, clear voice

inarticulate: with no distinction of syllables

ingressive: produced with air taken into mouth

intrusive: designating speech sound inserted in connected speech where it is not present in the spelling

laryngeal: articulated in the larynx

lax: designating vowel pronounced with muscles relatively relaxed

lenis: designating consonant sound characterized by relatively weak muscular tension and breath pressure

malacophonous: having a soft voice

melodious: having a pleasing voice; dulcet; euphonious; honey-voiced; mellifluous; rich

monotonous: pronouncing without intonation

mouillé: pronounced as a palatal or palatized sound, as the sounds spelled *ll* and *ñ* in Spanish

nasal: pronounced through the nose

open: designating vowel produced with relatively large opening above the tongue; designating syllable ending with vowel

oral: uttered through the mouth

peroral: through the mouth

phonetic: belonging or relating to sounds made by the human voice or articulate sounds

plummy: having deep, refined articulation

quavering: having a nervous voice; edge; quavery

retroflex: designating speech sound made with tip of tongue curled up and back toward hard palate

rhonchisonant: snoring; snorting

rounded: designating speech sound pronounced with rounded lips

sibilant: pronouncing *s* sounds heavily; hissing

soprano: having a high voice; shrill; treble

sotto voce: in an undertone; in one's lowest voice

stentorophonous: having an abnormally loud voice; speaking very loudly; stentorophonic

stertorious: accompanied by a snoring sound; stertorous

surd: voiceless; unvoiced

tense: designating vowel pronounced with muscles relatively tense

trenchant: sharply perceptive; penetrating; articulate

unstressed: pronounced without stress or emphasis

unvoiced: voiceless; surd

vocal: pertaining or relating to the voice or oral utterance

vocalic: relating to or containing a vowel or vowels

voiced: produced with vibration of vocal cords

voiceless: produced without vibration of vocal cords; unvoiced; surd

whimpering: having a whiny voice; puling

Volatilization

dampish: vaporous; foggy; misty
evaporable: capable of being made into vapor
flichtered: volatile; flighty
fugacious: volatile
fumid: fuming; vaporous
mercurial: volatile

reeking: giving off a strong unpleasant odor
vaporizable: capable of being turned into vapor
vaporous: composed of steam
volatile: easily passing into vapor
volatilized: readily creating vapor, steam

Volition

abulic: pertaining to a lack of will power; aboulic
autocratic: having absolute power; irresponsible
discretional: left to the control of one's own judgment
discretionary: left to the control of one's own judgment
free: having liberty to follow one's own inclinations or choice
intended: purposed to be done
minded: having an inclination; disposed
optional: depending on choice; elective
original: produced by one's own mind or thought

prepense: considered beforehand; premeditated
spontaneous: acting of one's own accord; done without compulsion
unbidden: not commanded; unsought; not invited
volitient: exercising free will
volitional: pertaining to willing or choosing
voluntary: done with deliberation and purpose
willful: done by design; governed by the will

Vulgarity

affected: pretending to possess what is not natural
alabandical: barbarous
awkward: ungraceful in bearing
barbaric: uncivilized; crude
barbarous: uncultivated; rude
bedizened: vulgarly adorned
blackguard: befitting a blackguard
boorish: vulgar; clownish
brutish: resembling brutes in nature
clownish: with the vulgarity and rudeness of a clown
coarse: low and vulgar
countrified: rustic-mannered
doggerel: versified vulgarly in sense or rhythm
dowdy: vulgar-looking
extravagant: beyond the limits of good taste

fescennine: vulgar
gaudy: beyond good taste
gingerbread: too fancifully made
Gothic: having the vulgar manners of a Goth
gross: coarse; indelicate; vulgar
heathenish: rude; uncivilized
heavy: slow; dull; inanimate
homebred: plain; rude; lacking the polish of travel
homely: plain; rude; coarse
homespun: homely; rude
horrid: exciting horror; hideous; frightful
ill-bred: badly brought up or trained
ill-mannered: of vulgar manners
in bad taste: in violation of good taste
incondite: rude; unpolished
indecorous: violating good manners

low: below the standard of good taste

meretricious: vulgar; tawdry

monstrous: inspiring disgust

newfangled: novel in a depreciative sense

obsolete: out of use

obtrusive: tending to thrust into undue prominence

odd: peculiar; not in good taste

outlandish: of strange and vulgar action

particular: odd; singular

provincial: showing the vulgar manners of a province

raffish: flashy; tawdry; gaudy; nonconformist

ribald: low; vulgar; base

rowdy: vulgarly showy and pretentious

rudas: foulmouthed

rude: lacking good taste

rustic: rude; unpolished; countrified

savage: beastly; cruel; barbarous; living in the woods

shabby-genteel: trying vulgarly to achieve gentility

shocking: obnoxious to good taste

slovenly: vulgarly neglectful and untidy

snobbish: making a vulgar pretension to gentility

spurcidical: foulmouthed

tawdry: vulgarly showy

tramontane: lying beyond the mountains; hence, foreign and vulgar

tricked out: vulgarly overdressed

unbeseeming: not fitting to good taste

uncivil: of vulgar manners

unclassical: not of classic taste

uncombed: with hair vulgarly neglected

uncourtly: not pleasing to court taste

uncouth: awkward; ungainly

underbred: of vulgar manners

unfashionable: not in fashionable taste

unfeminine: not feminine in manner

ungenteel: impolite; vulgar

ungentlemanlike: not becoming a gentleman's good taste

ungentlemanly: not becoming a gentleman's good taste

ungraceful: without form or beauty

unkempt: uncombed; rough; offensive to good taste

unladylike: not becoming a lady's good taste

unlicked: ungainly; unpolished

unpolished: of vulgar manners; without refinement

unpresentable: not fit for presentation

unrefined: of vulgar manners

unseemly: not becoming to good taste

untamed: not domesticated

vulgar: unrefined; coarse; rude

Water

adlittoral: pertaining to the shallow water near the shore
aquatic: living in, on, or near the water
aqueous: watery; pertaining to water
balneal: pertaining to a bath
brashy: pertaining to a cloudburst
cloacal: pertaining to sewers, sewage; cloacinal
diluent: weakening the strength of by mixing with water; diluting
diluted: made thinner or weaker
drenching: soaking; wetting thoroughly
eupotamic: capable of living and growing in still and flowing water
grandinous: pertaining to hail
hydrodynamic: pertaining to water power
hyetal: rainy; concerning rain
interlacustrine: between lakes
lacuscular: concerning pools, small lakes
lacustrine: concerning lakes
lenitic: living in quiet waters
lentic: dwelling in still, slow-moving water

limnal: pertaining to lakes
lymphate: diluted with water
lymphatic: pertaining to lymph; absorbent
moiré: resembling watered silk
phreatic: pertaining to underground water or wells; of water reachable by drilling
pluvial: of or pertaining to rain
pluvious: rainy
rainy: abounding with rain
showery: abounding with frequent showers of rain
stagnicolous: living in stagnant water
stillicidous: falling in drops
subriguous: watered from underneath
undigenous: generated by water
vadose: found or located above the water table
watery: containing a great deal of water
weak: feeble; yielding to pressure
wet: damp; rainy; saturated with a liquid

Weakness

adynamic: weak as a result of disease
aidless: weak from want of assistance
amyous: without strength
armless: without arms; deprived of dcfense

asthenic: weak from general debility
bald: without embellishments or elegance; pointless
broken: having one's strength seriously impaired

careless: not carefully done or performed

childish: immature; puerile

cold: having little or no liveliness, ardor, or enthusiasm

cranky: aged and feeble

crazy: mentally weak

creachy: old and weak; craichy

crippled: deprived of the use of limbs; having the power of impaired

dead beat: thoroughly defeated or overcome

debile: weak in the vital functions

decayed: reduced in strength

decrepit: weak from old age

defenseless: without strength to ward off danger

demoralized: having weakened the morals of

diffuse: characterized by redundance or prolixity

disabled: deprived of or impaired in power

disjointed: unconnected

disqualified: not having the necessary qualities

docile: meek; weak-kneed

done up: exhausted; done in

drooping: growing faint from any cause

dry: lacking interest

dull: not pleasing, bright, or spirited

effeminate: marked by womanly weakness

effete: worn-out with age

elumbated: weak in the loins

emasculate: deprived of manly virility

evanid: too weak to be permanent

exhausted: drawn off; weakened

faint: lacking vigor

faintish: somewhat faint

fatherless: without a father

feeble: lacking force, energy, or vigor

feminate: weak as a woman

flaccid: unnaturally soft and weak

flatulent: full of pretense without substance or reality

flimsy: showy and weak

forcible-feeble: seeming vigorous but really weak

fragile: easily broken

frail: too weak to resist external influences

frigid: lacking in warmth of feeling

gimcrack: showy and worthless

gingerbread: unstable

good-for-nothing: absolutely worthless

graveled: embarrassed

harmless: disabled

helpless: disabled

hypophrenic: mentally weak; feebleminded

hyposthenic: physically weak

imbecile: having weak mental faculties

impotent: having no power or energy

improcreant: impotent

inadequate: not having sufficient power, ability

inapt: unsuitable

incapable: lacking capability or adequate ability

incompetent: not able to fulfil the duties

indefensible: not defensible; not maintainable

ineffective: having no effect

ineffectual: not producing the intended effect

inefficacious: not having the requisite power to produce a designed effect

inefficient: not producing the required effect; habitually indisposed to activity

inept: unfit; silly; foolish

inexact: not exact, accurate, or true

infirm: not sound or stable

inoperative: not active or producing an effect

irrelevant: not pertinent

jejune: weak; insubstantial; unsatisfying

laid low: overcome, as by disease

laid on one's back: rendered powerless

laid on the shelf: useless

lame: weakened by an injury

languid: wanting in interest or animation; weak from listlessness

languishing: having lost strength and animation

lax: wanting preciseness of meaning or application

loose: not precise or exact; vague; indefinite

lustless: lacking vigor

marrowless: without marrow; without vigor

meable: easily penetrated

meager: deficient in or destitute of quantity or quality

monotonous: tiresomely unvarying in any respect

nerveless: without nerves; wanting in vigor

nervous: having weak nerves

nugatory: having no force or meaning

null and void: having no effect

on its last legs: about to fail entirely

palsied: not able to control one's movements

paralytic: affected with or tending to paralysis

paralyzed: deprived of the power of moving or acting

parvipotent: having little power

pithless: feeble

poor: lacking in good qualities or the qualities that render a thing valuable

powerless: too weak to produce an effect; impotent

pregnable: incapable of resisting an attack

prosaic: lacking in those qualities that impart animation or interest

prosing: dull and tedious in minuteness of writing or speaking

prosy: commonplace; tiresome; prosaic

puerile: childish; immature; juvenile

pulled down: weakened in vigor

queachy: feeble; shaky

radiolucent: permeable to radiation

rambling: showing absence of plan or system

relaxed: having become weak in energy

rickety: weak enough to fall from lack of stability

rotten: weak and untrustworthy

rudderless: having no guide or rudder

sapless: lacking spirit and energy

seedy: worn-out

shaken: having the strength impaired

shaky: of doubtful strength

shattered: broken in pieces; destroyed as to power

shattery: liable to be shattered

short-winded: affected with shortness of breath

sickly: liable to be affected by disease

sinewless: without sinews; nerveless; weak

sketchy: given roughly or suggestively without detail or finish

slack: too weak to be active

slight: of small importance or significance

slipshod: slovenly

slip-shop: slouchy; slipshod

soft: lacking courage and manliness

spent: exhausted

strengthless: weak

tame: lacking in interest or animation; vapid

the worse for wear: worn-out

tottering: about to fall

trashy: consisting of or like trash; worthless

unable: not able

unaided: weak; with no other strength to depend on

unapt: inapt

unarmed: harmless

unassisted: weak; with no other strength to depend on

unconducing: not tending to bring about as a result

unconducive: not contributing to an end

unconducting to: not leading to

unendowed: not gifted by nature

unfit: not fit by nature

unfitted: made unfit

unfortified: not fortified; weak against attacks

unfriended: wanting friends; unsupported

unhinged: off of hinge; unsteady; nervous

uninfluential: not having the power of influence

unnerved: deprived of nerve, force, or strength

unqualified: not having the requisite qualities

unstrengthened: made weak

unstrung: relaxed

unsubstantial: having no real strength

unsupported: not upheld

untenable: not to be held or maintained

unvaried: monotonous

vapid: lacking life and animation; dull; mawkish

vincible: able to be conquered

washy: lacking substance and strength; feeble

wasted: weakened by constant loss

waterlogged: soaked with water; useless and unmanageable

weak: lacking in power or force

weak as a baby: quite weak; also weak as a cat, weak as gingerbread, weak as milk and water

weakly: inclined to be weak

weaponless: without weapons

weather-beaten: weakened by exposure

wishy-washy: lacking in solidity or vigor; forceless; unsubstantial

withered: having lost freshness and power

without a leg to stand upon: unsupported; powerless

womanly: weak as a woman

wommacky: weak and shaky, as in convalescence

worn: weakened by continuous use

Weariness

altered: changed; tired

anhelose: short-breathed

arid: dry; uninteresting; wearisome

bald: bare; literal; wearisome

battered: worn-out

blown: winded from overexertion

breathless: panting

broken-winded: having disordered respiration

devoid of interest: lacking interest; wearisome

disgusting: exciting aversion or loathing

dog weary: very weary

done up: used up; done in

drooping: having little vigor left

dry: lacking interest

dull: depressing; sad; wearisome; not active or bright

effete: lacking in vitality; worn-out

exhausted: unable to do further work for a time

faint: inclined to swoon

fatigued: painfully tired

fatiguing: tiring

flagging: running out of energy; becoming spiritless or tired

flat: uninteresting; monotonous

footsore: having sore feet from walking

forfoughten: worn out from fighting; forfouchen; forfoughen

forjeskit: worn out from work; forjesket

forswunk: completely worn out from hard labor

gravedinous: drowsy

haggard: gaunt and careworn

hoined: fatigued; oppressed

humdrum: tedious; uninteresting

irksome: wearisome; tiresome; vexatious

knocked up: greatly fatigued

languescent: becoming tired

larbar: exhausted; worn-out

lassate: tired; weary

life-weary: weary of life

monotonous: wearisomely uniform

more dead than alive: utterly exhausted

mortal: long and wearisome

on one's last legs: almost exhausted

out of breath: breathless

out of wind: breathless

overfatigued: greatly fatigued

overspent: greatly fatigued

overtired: fatigued

played out: tired

prosing: speaking or writing in a wearisome or prosy way

prostrate: weary; thrown down

puffing and blowing: breathless

pulled down: in poor health from continued strain

quanked: overcome by fatigue

ramfeezled: worn-out; exhausted

ready to drop: too weary to stand

seedy: old and worn-out

shattered: broken in health

short of breath: breathless

short of wind: breathless

short-breathed: affected with anhelation

short-winded: affected with anhelation

sick of: tired of; disgusted with

slow: dull; tedious

somniferous: producing sleep; wearisome

soporific: causing sleep; tiresome

spent: exhausted

stupefying: inducing stupor

stupid: lacking apprehension or understanding; dull

surbated: harassed

tedious: producing weariness; slow

tired: wearied; fatigued; jaded

tired to death: exhausted

tiresome: wearisome; tedious

toilworn: haggard

trying: hard to endure

unenjoyed: unsatisfying; not affording enjoyment; wearisome

uninterested: having no interest in; bored; wearied

uninteresting: not of interest; not engaging the attention

unrefreshed: not recovered from fatigue

unrestored: not recovered from fatigue

used up: tired out; exhausted to weariness

walked off one's legs: unable to walk farther

wayworn: wearied by traveling

weariable: capable of becoming weary

wearisome: causing weariness from regularity or repetition

weary: worn out by toil, endurance, or vexation

weary of life: tired of living; life-weary

wearying: tiring; making weary

weather-beaten: weathered; weary

windless: breathless

worn: gaunt and spiritless

worn-out: exhausted; wearied

Whim

arbitrary: done according to one's own will or caprice

autoschediastic: impromptu; on the spur of the moment

capricious: subject to whim; erratic

captious: given to finding fault

contrary: given to opposition

crotchety: subject to whims or caprices

eccentric: deviating from the usual course; odd

erratic: departing from the common course in conduct or opinion

extemporaneous: spoken without preparation

fanciful: guided by fancy rather than reason or experience

fantastical: whimsical or capricious

fickle: having a very changeable mind

fitful: characterized by fits or variableness

freakish: given to sudden changes of mind

frivolous: marked by trifling

full of whims: changeable

giddy: unstable; fickle; heedless

humorsome: whimsical or moody

hysterical: affected with hysteria

imperseverant: not persistent

improvisate: unpremeditated

improvisatory: pertaining to improvisation

improvised: devised on the spur of the moment

impulsive: having the power to move

with an impulse; actuated by impulse and not thought

inconsistent: not uniform in opinion or action

indeliberate: done without thought or reflection

instinctive: acting without the assistance or direction of instruction or experience; spontaneous

ismy: switching from one faddish belief to another

maggoty: full of caprices or whims

natural: not acquired; given by nature

particular: concerned with details; fastidious

penny-wise and pound-foolish: saving small sums while losing larger ones

skittish: changeable; humorsome

sleeveless: lacking a pretext; unreasonable

spontaneous: done without special determination of the will

unconformable: not consistent

unguarded: done or said with carelessness

unguided: without guides or restraints

unmeditated: not thought over

unpremeditated: not thought over beforehand

unprompted: not excited to activity or exertion; not assisted by another in the action

vagarious: whimsical; capricious; erratic

volage: inattentive; changeable; fickle; flighty

volatile: changeable; fickle

wanton: straying from moral rectitude

wayward: disobedient; perverse

whimsical: full of whims

without rhyme or reason: without sound or sense

White

achlorophyllaceous: colorless

alabaster: bluish white; creamy; milky; pearl; porcelain; translucent

albescent: becoming white; whitish

argent: silver or white

argentine: pertaining to silver; silvery

auricomous: golden-haired; blond; blonde

blanched: colorless

blonde: fair; of a light yellow; blond

bone white: translucently white

candent: glowing white

candid: white; sincere; frank

canescent: tending to become white

chalky: like chalk

creamy: like or full of cream

eburnean: pertaining to ivory

eggshell: yellowish white; ivory; cream

fair: free from any dark hue; spotless

hoar: white or gray with age; grayish white

hoary: white or gray with age; grayish white; frosty; rimy

leucous: very white; blond

light: not dark or obscure; whitish

like ivory: having the color of ivory

milk white: white as milk

niveous: snowy; resembling snow

off-white: not quite white; grayish white

pearly: like pearls

silvery: having a silverlike luster

snow-white: white as snow

snowy: white; like snow

white: having the hue or color of pure snow

white as a lily: expression signifying a high degree of whiteness

white as driven snow: expression signifying a high degree of whiteness

white as silver: expression signifying a high degree of whiteness

whitish: white in a moderate degree

Winding

anfractuous: full of windings and turn-
ings, twists and turns
anguilliform: in the form of an eel
buckled: bent; curled
circinate: curled in ringlets
circling: moving around
circuitous: running around in a circuit
circumfluent: flowing around
circumforaneous: going from place to
place; strolling about
coiled: wound around in the form of
rings
complicated: folded or twisted together
contortuplicate: twisted; entangled
convoluted: curved or rolled together;
convolved; whorled
crispate: curled in ringlets
Daedalian: artistically worked, as by
mythic Daedalus of Crete
flexuous: winding; bending
frizzly: curled or crisped
helical: of, or relating to, a helix
indirect: deviating from a straight line or
course
intricate: having numerous windings and
confused involutions
involved: wound around; rolled up
labyrinthian: winding; perplexed
labyrinthine: like a labyrinth
mazelike: having a complex network;
labyrinthine; mazy; plexiform
mazy: confusing with turns and windings
pampiniform: like a tendril
peristaltic: contracting in successive
circles
perplexed: confused
raveled: tangled
rivulose: having irregular wormlike lines
roundabout: circuitous

serpentiform: shaped like a serpent
sigmoidal: curved in two directions
sinuous: abounding in bends, turns, or
curves; winding in and out; anfractuous; bending; meandering; serpentine; tortuous; twisting; undulant; undulating; wavy; winding
snakelike: like a snake
snaky: winding like a snake
spiral: winding around; forming a succession of curves; cochleate; cork-
screw; curlicued; gyral; helical; helici-
form; spirulate; tortile
spirated: shaped like a screw
torquated: like a twisted chain
tortile: twisted; coiled
tortive: wreathed; twisted
tortuous: winding; convoluted; bent in
different directions
turbinate: spiraled
turbinated: whirling; winding
turning: bending, curving, or rotating
twisted: winding or coiling
undated: rising and falling in waves to-
wards the margin, as a leaf
undée: wavy; damascened; undé
undulatory: resembling or pertaining to
the motion of waves
vermicular: undulating; sinuous; wavy
(like a worm)
vermiform: having the shape of a worm
volute: spiraled; scrolled; forming a spiral
curve; voluted
wavy: full of waves
whorled: having coils, spirals
winding: wrapping or encircling in a series of coils; curving or twisting
wreathy: twisted; spiral
zigzag: having short, sharp turns or
angles

Wittiness

cocket: saucy; lively; flirtatious
comic: relating to comedy; raising mirth
epigrammatic: pertaining to epigram;
witty; pointed

facetious: sprightly with wit and good
humor; gay
full of point: very witty or humorous;
full of stinging epigrams

humorous: fitted to excite laughter; fanciful

jocose: given to jokes and jesting; merry; sportive

jocoserious: combining funny and serious

jocular: being in a joking mood; making jokes; humorous

merry and wise: laughingly discreet and judicious

nimble-witted: having a ready wit; quick-witted

nipperty-tipperty: silly

Pantagruelian: satiric and ribald

playful: full of play; sportive

pleasant: conducive to merriment; gay; lively

quick-witted: having a keen and sharp discernment; sharp-witted

smart: impertinently or pretentiously witty

sparkling: brilliant; vivacious; lively

sprightly: lively; brisk; animated; gay

staumrel: silly

waggish: mischievous in sport; frolicsome

whimsical: full of odd fancies; capricious

witty: having or displaying wit; droll; facetious

Writing

allonymous: ghosted; ghostwritten

anepigraphous: without an inscription; anepigraphic

anonymous: published with no author's name; written by unknown author

anopisthographic: having writing or printing on one side only

Apollonian: emphasizing formal elements and rationality

Attic: emphasizing clear, lucid, elegant prose

auctorial: of or like an author

battological: pertaining to unnecessarily repetitive writing or speech

bibliophagic: book-devouring

bucolic: pertaining to descriptions of an idyllic, rural life

Byronic: characterized by romantic melancholy and melodrama, as in the works of Lord Byron

classical: pertaining to a style with great scope, depth, clarity, and elegance; pertaining to Greek and Roman classics

cuneiform: wedge-shaped; said of cuneiform letters; cuneal

demotic: simplified form of the Egyptian hieroglyphic characters

Elizabethan: of or pertaining to drama and literature of the reign of Elizabeth I of England including the works of Shakespeare (late 16th c.)

epistolary: pertaining to letters

erotographomanic: loving the writing of love letters

graphic: pertaining to writing or drawing

heroic: dealing with or describing the deeds and attributes of heroes

hieroglyphical: expressive of some meaning by pictures or figures

in black and white: in writing or print

in prose: without regard to rhythm

in type: ready to print

in writing: in printed form

Jacobean: of or pertaining to the literary style characteristic of the age of James I of England (early 17th c.)

macaronic: composed of Latin words mixed with vernacular words or non-Latin words given Latin endings

melic: pertaining to an elaborate form of lyric poetry (ancient Greece)

mock-heroic: of or pertaining to a form of satire in which trivial subjects, characters, and events are treated in the heroic style

not in verse: in prose

onomastic: of the signature of someone who did not write the signed document

onymous: bearing the author's name

out-of-print: no longer on sale, the edition being exhausted

Parnassian: denoting school of poets who emphasized form over emotion (France, late 19th c.)

phat: of printed copy that can be set easily and quickly

printed: impressed with letters

printless: bearing no print or impression

prosaic: pertaining to prose; unimaginative

prosy: having the nature of prose; dull; commonplace

Rabelaisian: characterized by coarse, broad humor, suggestive of the work of François Rabelais

Renaissance: designating literature marked by the humanistic revival of classical influence in Europe (14th–17th c.)

rhymeless: without rhymes

runic: pertaining to rune or runes

scribaceous: fond of writing

scribblative: of writing that is hasty, disorganized

scripturient: having a passion for writing

stylized: conforming to established, conventional pattern of style rather than natural style

tabellarious: pertaining to a letter carrier

tête-bêche: of a stamp printed upside down relevant to the next stamp

typographical: pertaining to the art of printing

uncial: pertaining to uncial letters

under one's hand: attested or confirmed by writing one's name

unpoetical: not having the characteristics of poetry

unrecorded: not preserved in writing

unregistered: not entered in the register

unrhymed: not rhymed

unwritten: not put down in writing

Victorian: denoting writing often associated with strict moral standards and conduct in Britain during reign of Queen Victoria (late 19th c.)

writing: in recorded form

written: reduced to writing

Yellow

amber-colored: of a semitransparent yellow; like amber

apricot: pinkish yellow; nectarine; peach

ash blond: having pale grayish blond hair

aureate: of a golden yellow

aurulent: golden in color

blonde: having yellow hair; blond; flaxen; straw-colored

canary: light yellow

champagne: orangish yellow

chrysal: golden; yellow

citrine: green-yellow, like a citron

citron: greenish yellow; chartreuse; lemon; lime; mustard

cream-colored: rich yellow, as cream

creamy: of a rich yellow color; resembling cream

fallow: of a pale brownish yellow color, like a fallow deer

flavescent: yellowish; yellowing; flavid

flavicomous: having yellow hair

flavous: bright yellow

fulvid: reddish yellow; fulvous

gold-colored: yellow; of the color of gold

golden: yellow; of a color resembling gold

goldenrod: vivid yellow; bright yellow; daffodil; sun

honey: golden yellow; brownish yellow; amber; buff; gold

jaundiced: made sickly yellow by the jaundice

lemon-colored: bright yellow, as a lemon

luteous: of a muddy-yellow color

lutescent: yellowing

oatmeal: grayish yellow; buckskin; chamois; parchment

primrose-colored: of a pale greenish yellow color

saffron-colored: of a deep reddish yellow color

sallow: of an unhealthy yellowish color

straw: pale yellow; flaxen; ocher; primrose

sulfur: pale yellow

sunshine: bright yellow, like the sun

tawny: brownish yellow

xanthic: of a predominantly yellow color

xanthodont: having yellow teeth; xanthodontous

xanthous: yellow-skinned

yellow: of the color of the spectrum between green and orange

yellow as a crow's foot: figurative expression for degree of yellowness

yellow as a guinea: figurative expression for degree of yellowness

yellow as a quince: figurative expression for degree of yellowness

Yielding

concessive: yielding

down on one's marrowbones: extremely humble

downtrodden: unjustly and cruelly oppressed

givy: relaxed; yielding; giving; givey

humble: given to habitual submission

indefensible: that cannot be defended

nonresisting: submitting to everything

on one's bending knee: humble and suppliant

pliant: submitting easily

resigned: given to acquiescing without resistance

self-effacing: humble

stoopgallant: humbling

submissive: given to yielding to the will of others

surrendering: relinquishing possession or control

undefended: having no means of protection against others

unresisting: yielding without the slightest opposition

untenable: that cannot be upheld

yielding: giving way to something else

Zoology

acerous: having no horns

aculeate: of animals, equipped with a sting

agonistic: displaying fighting behavior

allocryptic: using imitative colors or markings for concealment

altricial: having the young hatched in such an immature condition that extra care is required for some time

amphibious: capable of living on land and in water

apterous: wingless

aquatic: water-dwelling

arboreal: tree-dwelling

bicaudate: two-tailed

caudate: having a tail

cold-blooded: having body temperature that varies with the environment, as fish and reptiles; poikilothermal

colonial: of species that occupy a habitat in groups

corniculate: having horns

dimeric: in zoology, having two sides; bilateral

dioecious: in zoology, having two sexes

erostrate: without a beak

eutherian: of placental mammals

flightless: not adapted to flying

impennous: wingless

in utero: unborn and developing in uterus

in vitro: unborn and developing in isolation, as in test tube

latebricole: in zoology, living or hiding in holes

latirostrous: broad-beaked

moil: hornless

nidificant: nest-building

oligotokous: laying four or fewer eggs

oviparous: egg-laying

ovoviviparous: having membrane-enclosed eggs that remain in the female until hatching

palmigrade: plantigrade

placoid: in zoology, having horny scales

plataleiform: spoon-billed

polyped: multifooted

pseudaposematic: of an animal colored to look like its surroundings or its prey

quadruped: four-footed; tetrapod

raptorial: living on prey; pertaining to birds of prey; raptatorial

remiped: having feet or legs used as oars, as some crustaceans and insects

rhipipterous: relating to a minute insect that undergoes structural changes in stages between molts

skewbald: of animals, having patches of white and another color

statant: upright; standing; of an animal, standing with four feet on the ground

struthian: having a flat breastbone, as ostriches and emus; struthious

therianthropic: combining human and animal in form

viviparous: producing live young, not eggs

warm-blooded: having relatively constant body temperature; homoiothermal

zoological: pertaining to the study of animals and animal life

zoomorphic: taking the shape of an animal

ADDENDUM

Quick Word Finder

Active—Passive

Active

acrobatic
active
adroit
aggressive
agile
alert
alive
ambulatory
animated
athletic
attentive
avid
awake
bouncy
breezy
bright-eyed
brisk
bubbly
bustling
busy
buxom
catalytic
chipper
crisp
curious
deft
diligent
dynamic
eager
effervescent
elusive
energetic
energized
enterprising
errant
exhilarated
exuberant
fecund
feisty
fervent
fleet
fleet-footed
fluent
fluid

footloose
forceful
free
fresh
frisky
frolicsome
galvanic
go-go
gung ho
gymnastic
hale
high-spirited
high-strung
hurried
industrious
intense
interested
intrigued
irrepressible
itinerant
jaunty
jingly
kinetic
lambent
liberated
light
limber
lissome
lithe
lively
lyric
mercurial
mobile
motile
moving
nimble
nomadic
operating
operose
outdoorsy
peppy
peripatetic
perky
productive
prolific

prompt
quick
quicksilver
rambunctious
rapid
raring to go
ready
reborn
renascent
salutatory
sassy
saucy
sentient
sinuous
skittish
snappy
speedy
spirited
sprightly
springy
spruce
spry
strenuous
supple
swift
switched-on
sylphlike
tireless
unencumbered
up-and-coming
vibrant
vigilant
vigorous
vital
vivacious
volant
volatile
wakeful
whippy
wide-awake
wide-eyed
willowy
zappy
zestful
zesty

zingy
zippy

Passive

abstracted
aged
apathetic
asleep
atrophied
barren
beat
benumbed
blank
blasé
bored
bovine
bushed
cadaverous
comatose
complacent
dazed
dead
delitescent
dilatory
disinterested
docile
doltish
dopey
dormant
draggy
dreamy
drooping
droopy
drowsy
drugged
dull
dulled
emotionless
empty
enervated
exhausted
fallow
fatigued
flat
floppy

glassy
glassy-eyed
groggy
haggard
hazy
hoary
hypnotic
hypnotized
idle
immobile
impassive
impervious
inactive
inanimate
inattentive
incapacitated
indifferent
indolent
inert
insensate
insipid
jaded
kaput
lackadaisical

languid
languorous
late
latent
lazy
leaden
lethargic
lifeless
listless
logy
lymphatic
malingering
moribund
mute
nonresistant
numb
otiose
overripe
paralyzed
passive
phlegmatic
placid
pococurante
poky
porcine

punch-drunk
punchy
resigned
rusty
sagging
sapped
satiated
sedentary
semicomatose
semiconscious
senseless
shiftless
shot
slack
sleepy
slothful
slow
sluggish
sodden
somnolent
spaced-out
spent
spiritless
stagnant
static

stiff
stuporous
submissive
supine
tardy
tepid
tired
torpid
truant
unassertive
unemotional
uninterested
unmindful
unmotivated
unresponsive
vacant
vacuous
weary
wizened
world-weary
worn-out
yawning
yielding
zomboid
zonked

Angry—Calm

Angry

aggravated
aggressive
aghast
agitated
angered
angry
annoyed
antsy
argumentative
bellicose
belligerent
berserk
blooming
boiling
brash
breathless
choleric
combative
competitive

contentious
defiant
disturbed
dramatic
edgy
effusive
emotional
engagé
enraged
excitable
excited
explosive
ferocious
feverish
fierce
fiery
fire-eating
flighty
flustered
frazzled

free-swinging
frenzied
fuming
furious
galled
harried
hassled
henpecked
hepped up
het up
high-keyed
high-pressure
high-strung
hostile
hot
hot-blooded
hotheaded
huffy
hungry
hyper

hysterical
impassioned
impetuous
impulsive
incensed
indignant
inflamed
inflammatory
infuriated
intemperate
intensive
intent
irascible
irate
irked
irrepressible
irritated
jealous
livid
lusty

mad
manic
miffed
militant
militaristic
overwrought
overzealous
passionate
peeved
peppery
perfervid
piqued
pissed
pissed off
provoked
pugnacious
pushy
quarrelsome
rabid
raddled
raging
rambunctious
rash
resentful
restive
restless
ruffled
rumbustious
scrappy
seething
self-indulgent
sensuous
short
short-tempered
sick and tired
snappish
sore
soulful
spontaneous

steaming
stewing
sthenic
stir-crazy
stirred up
stormy
strained
subjective
sulfurous
sultry
temperamental
tempestuous
tense
testy
ticked
ticked off
ticklish
torrid
touchy
trigger-happy
troubled
truculent
tumultuous
turbulent
turned-on
unglued
unreasonable
unreconciled
unremitting
unrestrained
unsettled
unstable
upset
vehement
Vesuvian
vexed
violent
visceral
volcanic
warm-blooded
white-hot

worked up
wound up
wrathful
wroth
wrought up
zealous

Calm
Apollonian
calm
casual
collected
composed
constrained
cool
coolheaded
dégagé
demure
dewy
dispassionate
dry-eyed
easygoing
emollient
even
even-tempered
gentle
imperturbable
laconic
laid-back
lenient
levelheaded
low-key
low-pressure
matutinal
meditative
mellow
mild
muted
neutral

nonchalant
nonviolent
objective
pacific
pacifistic
passive
patient
peaceful
placid
poised
quiet
relaxed
restrained
reticent
sedate
self-disciplined
self-possessed
serene
soft
staid
steady
stoical
subdued
taciturn
tame
temperate
tempered
tranquil
unbothered
unemotional
unflappable
unforced
unhassled
unhurried
unnervous
unruffled
unstirred
untroubled

Appealing—Unappealing

Appealing
adorable
affluent
alluring
appealing
appetizing

aristocratic
arresting
attractive
beautiful
becoming
beguiling

bewitching
breathtaking
caparisoned
captivating
charismatic
charming

chic
Circean
classy
clean
clubby
couth

crisp
cuddly
dandy
dapper
dashing
dazzling
dear
debonair
decorous
delightful
desirable
devastating
dignified
elegant
enchanting
engaging
enticing
entrancing
exquisite
fancy
fashionable
fetching
finished
flowery
flush
foxy
galluptious
glamorous
glorious
graceful
gracious
handsome
healthy
highborn
hygienic
immaculate
impeccable
imperial
ingratiating
interesting
intoxicating
inviting
irresistible
kempt
kingly
knobby
lardy-dardy
lavish

lovely
lush
luxuriant
luxurious
magnetic
mellifluous
mod
modish
natty
neat
nifty
nubile
opulent
ornate
patrician
photogenic
picturesque
plush
plushy
polished
posh
prepossessing
pretty
princely
privileged
prosperous
redolent
refined
regal
resplendent
rich
ritzy
riveting
royal
sanitary
sartorial
scrumptious
seducing
seductive
select
sexy
silk-stocking
slick
smart
smooth
snazzy
soigné
sophisticated

spanking
spellbinding
spiffy
splashy
splendid
spotless
spruce
stainless
stately
sterling
striking
stunning
stylish
suave
sumptuous
surefooted
sure-handed
svelte
swank
swanky
swell
swish
tantalizing
tasty
thrilling
tidy
trendy
trig
trim
ultrachic
ultramodern
ultrarich
voguish
wealthy
well
well-groomed
well-heeled
well-off
winning
winsome
yummy

Unappealing
abysmal
accident-prone
all thumbs
angular
askew

awkward
awry
blowsy
cadaverous
clumsy
contaminated
crumpled
déclassé
decrepit
derelict
destitute
dingy
disagreeable
disfigured
disgusting
dowdy
down-and-out
drippy
dumpy
fiddle-footed
filthy
frightful
frowzy
funky
gaudy
gawky
geeky
ghastly
gnarly
graceless
grisly
grotesque
gruesome
hard up
heavy-footed
hideous
homely
horrid
horrific
icky
imperfect
impoverished
impure
incondite
incongruous
indecorous
indigent
inelegant

infelicitous
insolvent
lowborn
lowly
macabre
malodorous
meretricious
messy
monstrous
odious
oily
oleaginous
overdressed
penniless
penurious
plain
poor
putrescent
putrid
ragged
ragtag
rancid

ratty
repellent
repugnant
repulsive
revolting
rough
rugged
scabrous
scandalous
scraggly
scummy
scuzzy
seedy
shabby
shaggy
shocking
shoddy
sickening
simian
slatternly
slavering
sleazy

slimy
slobbery
sloppy
slovenly
slummy
sordid
squalid
stinky
subhuman
tacky
tatty
tawdry
tenth-rate
thunderous
tousled
ugly
ulcerous
unappealing
unattractive
unbecoming
unclean
uncoordinated

uncouth
underprivileged
undesirable
undignified
unfashionable
unfit
unhandy
unhealthy
uninviting
unkempt
unpleasant
unpleasing
unpolished
unsanitary
unsavory
unsightly
untidy
unvarnished
unwashed
weather-beaten
woolly
yucky

Beautiful—Ugly

Beautiful

adorable
agreeable
alluring
angelic
appealing
appetizing
attractive
beaming
beauteous
beautiful
becoming
beguiling
bewitching
bonny
breathtaking
bright
built
callipygian
captivating
catching
charismatic
charming

classic
clear
clear-eyed
come-hither
comely
coquettish
curvaceous
cute
dainty
dashing
delectable
delicate
delicious
delightful
desirable
devastating
dimpled
divine
doll-like
elegant
enchanting
engaging
enticing

entrancing
enviable
exotic
exquisite
eye-catching
fair
fancy
fascinating
fetching
fine
flawless
glamorous
glorious
glossy
good-looking
gorgeous
graceful
great-looking
handsome
heavenly
hot
hunky
hypnotic

immaculate
intoxicating
intriguing
inviting
irresistible
killer
light
lovable
lovely
luscious
lustrous
magnetic
magnificent
mignon
moon-eyed
mouthwatering
nifty
ornamental
perfect
photogenic
picturesque
pleasing
precious

prepossessing
pretty
provocative
redolent
regular
resplendent
scrumptious
sculptured
seductive
sell-set
sensuous
sexy
shapely
showy
silky
slick
slight
smiling
spellbinding
spotless
stacked
statuesque
streamlined
striking
stunning
sublime
sumptuous
symmetrical
taking
tantalizing
tasty
tempting
titillating
toylike
voluptuous
well-built
well-conditioned
well-favored
well-formed
well-groomed
well-made
well-proportioned
winning
winsome

Ugly
angular
askew

awful
awkward
bandy-legged
beetle-browed
bent
blemished
blimpish
bloated
blowsy
blubbery
bovine
bucktoothed
bug-eyed
cadaverous
chalky
clammy
cleft
clumsy
crippled
crooked
cross eyed
cumbersome
defaced
deformed
disfigured
disgusting
disheveled
dreadful
droopy
dumpy
elephantine
emaciated
farinaceous
fat
foul
frightful
frowzy
fubsy
gap-toothed
gawky
geeky
ghastly
gnarled
goggle-eyed
graceless
grim-faced
grimy
grisly

grizzled
grotesque
grubby
gruesome
grungy
halt
harelipped
hatchet-faced
heavy-footed
hideous
homely
horrent
horrible
hulking
hunched
ill-formed
ill-looking
ill-made
inelegant
irregular
jagged
leprous
loathsome
lopsided
lumpish
macabre
malformed
malodorous
mangy
marred
mealy
misshapen
moldering
monstrous
musty
nasty
offensive
oleaginous
pasty
pendulous
pitted
plain
pocked
ponderous
porcine
putrescent
putrid
ragged

repellent
repugnant
repulsive
revolting
rickety
rumpled
rumply
runty
sallow
scabby
scabrous
scaly
sclerotic
scorbutic
scraggy
scrawny
scrofulous
scruffy
shabby
shaggy
shapeless
sickening
simian
skew-eyed
sneering
splotchy
spoiled
spongy
squat
squinched
stooped
straggly
stumpy
stunted
sunken
swaybacked
swollen
tabescent
terrible
tubercular
ugly
unappealing
unattractive
unbecoming
ungainly
unhandsome
unprepossessing
unsavory

unsightly	walleyed	wasted	withered
unwieldy	washed-out	waxen	

Black

black	ink black	piceous	raven
blue-black	inklike	pitch	sable
Brunswick black	jet	pitch-black	soot
carbon black	lampblack	pitch-dark	sooty
coal black	noir	pitchy	swarthy
ebony	onyx	pure black	tar

Blue

Alice blue	cyan blue	lapis lazuli	royal blue
aquamarine	cyaneous	light blue	sapphire
azure	cyanic	lucerne	sapphirine
azure-colored	dark blue	lupine	saxe blue
baby blue	deep blue	marine blue	sea blue
beryl blue	delft blue	mazarine blue	sky blue
blue	Dresden blue	midnight blue	slate blue
blueberry	electric blue	Milori blue	smalt
bluebonnet	flag blue	Napoleon blue	steel blue
blue-green	gentian blue	navy blue	teal blue
bluish	greenish blue	Nile blue	Thenard's blue
brittany blue	Havana lake	pale blue	true blue
calamine blue	Helvetia blue	pavonine	turquoise
cerulean	huckleberry	peacock blue	ultramarine
cerulescent	hydrangea blue	pearl blue	Venetian blue
china blue	ice blue	powder blue	water blue
cobalt blue	indanthrone	Prussian blue	Wedgwood blue
copenhagen blue	indigo	purple-blue	wisteria
cornflower	jouvence blue	reddish blue	woad
cyan	king's blue	robin's-egg blue	zaffer

Brown

acorn	brick	burnt umber	cinnamon
amber	brindle	butternut	cocoa
anthracene brown	bronze	butterscotch	coffee
auburn	brown	café au lait	coffee-colored
autumn leaf	brunet	camel	Cologne brown
baize	brunette	caramel	copper
bay	buff	Cassel brown	cordovan
beige	burgundy	Cassel earth	dark brown
biscuit	burnt almond	Castilian brown	doeskin brown
bistre	burnt ocher	chestnut	Dresden brown
breen	burnt sienna	chocolate	dun

earth
ecru
fallow
fawn
fox
fulvous
ginger
hazel
henna
khaki
leather
light brown
light red-brown
liver
mahogany

manila
maple sugar
Mars brown
mink
mocha
nougat
nut brown
nutmeg
nutria
ocher
old gold
otter
oxblood
peppercorn
picclipasso

pongee
putty
raffia
raw sienna
raw umber
reddish brown
roan
russet
rust
sand
sandalwood
seal
seal brown
sedge
sepia

sienna
sorrel
tan
tanaura
tawny
terra-cotta
titian
toast
topaz
umber
Vandyke brown
Venetian red
walnut

Conjunctives

according as
afore
after
against
albeit
also
although
an
and
and also
and/or
as
as far as
as how
as if
as long as
as though
as well as
because
before
being
both
but
considering
directly
either
ere
ergo
except

excepting
for
forasmuch as
fore
gin
how
howbeit
howe'er
however
if
immediately
inasmuch as
insofar as
insomuch as
instantly
lest
like
much as
neither
nor
notwithstanding
now
once
only
or
otherwise
plus
provided
providing
save

saving
seeing
since
sith
so
so long as
sobeit
still
supposing
syne
than
that
then
tho
though
till
unless
unlike
until
well
what
when
whence
whencesoever
whene'er
whenever
whensoever
where
whereabout
whereabouts

whereas
whereat
whereby
where'er
wherefore
wherefrom
wherein
whereinto
whereof
whereon
whereso
wheresoe'er
wheresoever
wherethrough
whereto
whereunder
whereunto
whereupon
wherever
wherewith
whether
while
whiles
whilst
whither
whithersoever
why
without
yet

Direction

aligned
ascending
askew
aslant
aslope
asymmetrical
atilt
awry
back-and-forth
backwards
bearing
beeline
bidirectional
bilateral
bi-level
bisect
circuitous
circumambient
circumference
clockwise
coast-to-coast
counterclockwise
dangling
descending
dextral
diagonal
directional

downriver
downstream
downwind
east
eastward
edgewise
encircling
equiangular
equilateral
facedown
faceup
falling
far and wide
forward
frontal
frontward
geocentric
geodesic
heading
high
high and low
horizontal
inclined
indirect
infinite
inward
isometric
latitudinal

left
lengthways
lengthwise
longitudinal
multilateral
north
northeast
northward
northwest
opposite
outward
outwardly
parallel
plumb
prone
prolate
protracted
radial
radiating
radius
range
ray
rearward
rectilinear
retroflex
retrograde
reverse
right

rising
rotary
seesaw
sideways
sinistral
slanted
slope
south
southeast
southward
southwest
straight
straightforward
stratified
symmetrical
tabular
tangential
three-dimensional
tilt
to-and-fro
unidirectional
unilateral
up-and-down
upright
vertical
west
westward

Dominant—Submissive

Dominant
abusive
adamant
ascendant
assuming
assured
authoritative
autocratic
bossy
bullheaded
bumptious
certain
cock-a-hoop
cocksure
cocky

commanding
compelling
conclusive
confident
controlling
contumacious
decisive
determined
direct
directed
dogged
dogmatic
dominant
domineering
do-or-die

egoistic
egotistic
emphatic
enduring
entitled
entrenched
firm
fixed
focused
forceful
formidable
governing
grandiose
hard-assed
hard-bitten

hard-boiled
hard-edged
hardened
hardheaded
headstrong
hell-bent
high-and-mighty
high-flown
high-handed
high-powered
immovable
impenetrable
imperative
imperious
impervious

implacable
impregnable
independent
indestructible
indomitable
inexorable
inflated
inflexible
insistent
insuperable
intent
intimidating
intractable
intransigent
invincible
invulnerable
ironbound
ironclad
irresistible
lordly
macho
magisterial
magistral
messianic
mighty
militaristic
mulish
obdurate
obstinate
omnipotent
one-sided
opinionated
orgulous
orotund
ossified
overweening
overwhelming
persistent
persuasive
pertinacious
pervicacious
pigheaded
poised
portentous
possessive
predominant
preeminent
preponderant

presumptuous
prevailing
prevalent
prideful
prodigious
proprietary
proud
purposeful
pushy
ramrod
recalcitrant
redoubtable
refractory
relentless
renitent
resolute
rigid
ruling
secure
self-assured
self-confident
self-important
self-involved
self-possessed
self-righteous
self-satisfied
self-seeking
single-minded
smug
stiff
strident
strong-minded
strong-willed
stubborn
superior
supreme
sure
swaggering
swashbuckling
swellheaded
take-charge
tenacious
territorial
thick-skinned
turgid
unassailable
unbending
undaunted

unfaltering
unflagging
unflinching
unreceptive
unregenerate
unrelenting
unstinting
unstoppable
unswerving
unwary
unwieldy
unwilling
unyielding
vain
vainglorious
vehement
volative
whole-hog
willful

Submissive

abject
accommodating
acquiescent
adaptable
ambivalent
amenable
apologetic
apprehensive
assailable
awkward
balky
chameleonic
changeable
chary
chivvied
compliant
complying
concessive
conciliatory
culpable
cursory
dainty
deferential
dependent
different
docile
doubtful

downtrodden
dubious
ductile
dutiful
effeminate
equivocal
exposed
fatalistic
fawning
flexible
flimsy
gentle
halfhearted
halting
haphazard
harmless
hesitant
humble
humiliated
ill at ease
impalpable
inconclusive
inconstant
incredulous
indecisive
indirect
inoffensive
insecure
irresolute
labile
lambent
loath
lost
malleable
masochistic
mealymouthed
meek
mousy
mutable
noncommittal
nonresistant
nude
obedient
obeisant
obeying
obsequious
passive
penitent

phlegmatic
plastic
pliable
pliant
prostrate
protean
qualmish
queasy
questioning
quizzical
receptive
reconciled
reluctant

repentant
reserved
resigned
respectful
self-abnegating
self-denying
sequacious
serviceable
servile
shackled
slavish
soft
solicitous

squishy
subdued
submissive
subservient
suggestible
supple
suppliant
susceptible
sycophantic
tentative
tenuous
thin-skinned
timid

tongue-tied
tractable
tremulous
unresisting
vacillating
vague
vulnerable
wavering
wishy-washy
yielding

Emphasis

a lot
above
after all
again
all
all of
all told
all-around
also
altogether
and how
as well
awfully
beside
besides
big deal
by far
decidedly
either

especially
even
ever so
evermore so
exceedingly
expressly
far and away
fine
further
furthermore
in detail
in particular
in the main
increasingly
indeed
just
just so
lastly
mainly
mighty
more than ever

moreover
mostly
namely
no matter
not to mention
notably
obviously
on top of
over
over and above
particular
particularly
plus
primarily
pronounced
quite
real
really
resounding

respective
right
simply
singularly
so
specially
still
strong
such
tall order
telling
terribly
to boot
to say nothing of
to say the least
too
up
very
well
whopping

Extroverted—Introverted

Extroverted
ambitious
assertive
atwitter
blatant
bloviating
blustering
boisterous
bold

bombastic
brash
brazen
breathy
chatty
choleric
congenial
cordial
defiant

demonstrative
dramatic
emphatic
evangelical
excited
exhibitionistic
expansive
expressive
extemporaneous

extroverted
exuberant
flagrant
flamboyant
flashy
flirtatious
forward
freewheeling
friendly

garrulous
grandiloquent
gregarious
gushy
high-profile
histrionic
immodest
indiscreet
intrusive
jabbering
lippy
logorrheic
loquacious
loud
loudmouthed
madcap
malapert
meteoric
militant
multiloquious
noisy
obstreperous
obtrusive
orotund
outgoing
outspoken
overbearing
overt
overweening
personable
pert
petulant
presumptuous
prolix
protrusive
protuberant
public
pugnacious
pushy
rah-rah
raucous
red-hot
rousing
shrill
sociable
sonorous
spectacular
splashy

stagestruck
stagy
stentorian
strident
stridulous
swinging
switched-on
talkative
theatrical
throaty
turgid
uninhibited
unreserved
unselfconscious
uproarious
verbose
visible
vitriolic
vocal
vociferous
voluble
wordy

Introverted
abashed
alien
alienated
alone
aloof
anonymous
antisocial
ascetic
asocial
austere
autonomous
awkward
bashful
cautious
chary
clannish
claustral
cloistered
cloistral
collected
concealed
confidential
cool
covert

coy
crafty
delitescent
demure
detached
discreet
distant
elliptical
elusive
enigmatic
eremitic
estranged
ghostly
guarded
hermitic
incommunicado
indirect
inhibited
inner-directed
inscrutable
insular
introspective
introverted
invisible
inward
isolated
laconic
latent
lone
lonely
low-profile
misty
misunderstood
modest
monastic
monkish
mum
mute
mysterious
nebulous
nonverbal
oblique
obscure
occult
paradoxical
passive
phantom
private

quiescent
quiet
reclusive
reluctant
remote
repressed
reserved
restrained
reticent
retiring
secluded
secretive
self-absorbed
self-conscious
self-effacing
sensitive
sequestered
shadowy
shamefaced
sheepish
short-spoken
shy
silent
smoky
sneaky
soft-spoken
solitary
solo
spectral
sphinxlike
spooky
standoffish
stay-at-home
stealthy
still
stolid
strange
sub-rosa
subterranean
surreptitious
suspicious
taciturn
tactful
tight-lipped
tiptoe
ultracool
unapproachable
unassertive

unassuming
unclear
uncommunicative
undemonstrative
understated

unexpressive
unfathomable
unobtrusive
unsociable
vanishing

veiled
voiceless
wary
watchful
wistful

withdrawn
wordless
wraithlike
xenophobic

Generality

a few
a little
a lot
about
after all
again
all in all
any
anyhow
anyway
apparently
approximately
around
as a rule
as a whole
as it were
as much as
at all events
at any rate
at large
aught
ballpark
be that as it may
before long
belike
borderline

broadly
by and large
circa
close
close to
collectively
commonly
comparatively
en masse
essentially
ever
fairly
for all that
for that matter
for the most part
generally
here and there
in a way
in all
in any case
in any event
in general
in short
just about
just the same
kind of
lately

latterly
like
long and short of it
mainly
más o menos
mezzo-mezzo
more or less
much
near
neither here nor
    there
now and then
often
on the whole
only just
overall
possibly
primarily
probably
proportionately
relatively
reputedly
roughly
roundly
say
seeming
seemingly

simply
so to speak
some
sometimes
somewhat
somewhere
somewhere near
soon
sooner or later
sort of
so-so
such and such
sundry
then again
thereabouts
to a degree
to an extent
to the tune of
truth of the
    matter
virtually
what have you
whatever
whatnot
wherever

Giving/Innocent—Taking/Demanding

Giving/
Innocent
accessible
accommodating
adaptable
approving
artless
beatific
believing
candid

careless
childlike
complaisant
compliant
credulous
democratic
dewy-eyed
doting
dulcet
easy

faithful
frank
free
game
generous
giving
good-natured
gracious
grateful
guileless

gullible
hopeful
humble
impressionable
inconsistent
indiscriminate
indulgent
ingenious
innocent
insouciant

instinctive
intuitive
lax
liberal
naïve
natural
obliging
open
permissive
rapt
reciprocating
saccharine
selfless
simple
sugary
sweet
syrupy
tender
tolerant
transparent
trustful
trusting
ultraliberal
unabashed
uncritical
understanding
undesigning
unguarded
unquestioning
unsophisticated
unsparing
unsullied
unsuspecting
unwitting
virginal
young

Taking/
Demanding
abrasive
accusatory
acerbic
acidic
acquisitive
admonishing
agnostic
anal
aporetic

arbitrary
arrogant
assiduous
assumptive
atheistic
attentive
biting
blameful
bumptious
cagey
calculating
captious
carping
categorical
caustic
caviling
censorious
challenging
cheap
chiding
choosy
clinical
compulsive
conceited
condescending
constipated
contemptuous
contradictory
contrary
costive
covetous
crafty
critical
cryptic
cutting
definite
deliberate
demanding
deprecatory
derogatory
dictatorial
didactic
disabused
disapproving
disbelieving
disciplined
discriminating
disdainful

disparaging
distrustful
doctrinaire
dogmatic
edacious
egocentric
exacting
exigent
facetious
fastidious
fault-finding
fussy
gluttonous
grabby
greedy
guarded
hard
harsh
high-and-mighty
hubristic
huffy
hypercritical
impatient
incisive
insistent
ironic
judgmental
logical
materialistic
measured
methodical
meticulous
mocking
mordacious
mordant
narcissistic
niggling
obsessive
omnivorous
opinionated
opportunistic
painstaking
particular
patronizing
pejorative
peremptory
perseverant
persistent

pertinacious
picky
pointed
political
precise
precocious
querulous
ravenous
rebuking
reproving
Rhadamanthine
rigorous
sanctimonious
sarcastic
sardonic
satiric
satirical
scolding
scornful
scrimping
scrupulous
sedulous
selective
self-centered
selfish
self-serving
self-willed
set
sharp
sharp-edged
skeptical
slashing
specific
supercilious
superior
systematic
tactical
tendentious
thorough
tireless
trenchant
ultracritical
unbelieving
ungenerous
unrelenting
unstinting
uppish
uppity

| usurious | vituperative | withholding | wry |
| vain | voracious | wolfish | |

Good—Bad

Good	incorruptible	wholesome	devilish
aboveboard	irreproachable	worthy	devious
admirable	judicious		diabolical
angelic	just	*Bad*	disgraced
authentic	loving	accursed	dishonest
benevolent	loyal	adulterous	disingenuous
bona fide	magnanimous	affected	disloyal
candid	moral	amoral	dissembling
capital	natural	apocryphal	duplicitous
choice	noble	apostate	egregious
conscientious	organic	arch	ersatz
constant	prelapsarian	artificial	evasive
dear	principled	awful	evil
decent	pure	backhanded	execrable
deserving	real	bad	fake
devout	reliable	baleful	fallen
direct	respectable	baneful	false
earnest	reverent	barefaced	fatuous
ethical	righteous	base	feigned
exemplary	right-minded	bent	fell
fair	scrupulous	bloodthirsty	fiendish
fair-minded	selfless	bogus	flagitious
fine	seraphic	calumnious	flagrant
first-rate	simon-pure	canting	foul
forthcoming	sincere	casuistic	foxy
forthright	sound	contemptible	fraudulent
foursquare	straightforward	corrupt	fulsome
frank	sublime	counterfeit	furtive
free	true	crafty	guileful
genuine	true-blue	criminal	hangdog
God-fearing	truthful	crooked	heinous
good	uncorrupted	cunning	heretical
guileless	unimpeachable	cursed	hexed
guiltless	untainted	damned	high-sounding
harmonious	up-and-up	debased	hollow
high-minded	up-front	deceitful	hypocritical
holy	upright	deceptive	ignoble
honest	upstanding	delinquent	ignominious
honorable	veracious	delusive	immoral
humane	veridical	demoniacal	infamous
idealistic	vestal	demonic	infernal
impartial	virtuous	despicable	insidious
incorrupt	wholehearted	detestable	insincere

irredeemable
Janus-faced
jive
loathsome
lowdown
malefic
malevolent
malignant
mealymouthed
mendacious
mischievous
miscreant
misleading
mock
monstrous
moralistic
murderous
nefarious
odious
ostentatious
perfidious

pernicious
perverse
pharisaic
phony
piacular
predatory
pretentious
pseudo
purulent
recreant
reprobate
rotten
sanctimonious
satanic
scurvy
selfish
serpentine
shady
sham
shameful
shifty
sinful
sinister

slanderous
slippery
sly
smarmy
sneaky
sophistic
sorcerous
sordid
specious
spurious
stealthy
synthetic
tainted
terrible
traitorous
treacherous
two-faced
unashamed
unconscionable
unctuous
underhanded

unfair
ungodly
unholy
unjust
unpardonable
unprincipled
unscrupulous
untruthful
unworthy
vain
venal
venomous
vicious
vile
villainous
viperous
virtueless
vulpine
wicked
wily
worthless

Gray

ash
ash-colored
ash gray
battleship gray
charcoal
cinder
cinerous
cloud gray
dapple-gray
dark gray

dove colored
flint gray
granite
gray
greige
grizzly
iron gray
lead
light gray
merle

mole gray
moleskin
mouse
mushroom
neutral
obsidian
Oxford gray
pale gray
pelican
pearl gray

plumbago gray
salt-and-pepper
silver gray
slate
smoke
steel gray
tattletale gray
taupe

Green

absinthe
apple green
aqua
avocado
beryl green
bice green
biscay green
blue-green
bottle green
Brazilian emerald

breen
brewster green
Brunswick green
cadmium green
celadon
chartreuse
chrome green
clair de lune
cobalt green
corbeau

cucumber
cypress
dark green
drake
emerald
emerald green
fairy green
fir green
forest green
grass

grass green
gray-green
green
holly
Hooker's green
hunter green
jade
kelly green
Kendal green
leaf

leek green
light green
lime
Lincoln green
lizard
loden
lotus
malachite green
marine green
mint

moss green
myrtle
Niagara green
Nile green
olive
olive green
pale green
Paris green
parrot green
patina green

pea green
pistachio green
reseda
sage green
sea green
serpentine
shamrock
spruce
teal
terre verte

tourmaline
turquoise
turquoise green
verdigris
viridian
willow green
yellow-green
yew green
zinc green

Happy—Sad

Happy

agrin
airy
amazed
amused
amusing
astonished
beatific
bemused
blessed
blissful
blithe
bonhomous
buoyant
carefree
cavalier
cheerful
cheery
chipper
content
contented
convivial
delighted
devil-may-care
droll
ebullient
ecstatic
elated
enchanted
enraptured
enthusiastic
espiègle
euphoric
exhilarated
expectant

exuberant
exultant
fanciful
fancy-free
felicitous
festive
flying
frolicsome
fulfilled
fun-loving
funny
gamesome
gay
gemutlich
giddy
giggly
glad
gleeful
glowing
gratified
happy
happy-go-lucky
harmonious
hilarious
hopeful
humorous
impish
infectious
jaunty
jocose
jocular
jocund
jolly
jovial
joyful

joyous
jubilant
laughing
lighthearted
lilting
lively
lucid
merry
mirthful
mischievous
optimistic
overjoyed
perky
playful
pleased
psyched
puckish
radiant
rapturous
ravished
relieved
rhapsodic
riant
risible
roguish
roseate
rosy
sanguine
sated
satisfied
silly
sky-high
spirited
sportive
starry-eyed

stoked
sunny
thankful
thrilled
triumphant
up
upbeat
waggish
whimsical
winsome
wishful

Sad

abject
absorbed
abysmal
achy
afflicted
aggrieved
agonizing
anguished
beleaguered
bereaved
bereft
bitter
bleak
blue
brokenhearted
brooding
bummed
bummed out
chagrined
cheerless
contrite
crestfallen

crushed
dark
dejected
demure
depressed
deprived
desolate
despairing
despondent
disconsolate
discontented
discouraged
disenchanted
disgusted
disillusioned
dismal
dissatisfied
distraught
distressed
disturbed
doleful
dolorous
doomed
dour
down
down-at-heel
downbeat
downcast
downhearted
elegiac
embittered
fatalistic
forlorn
fretful

funereal
gloomy
glum
grave
grief-stricken
grieved
grieving
grievous
grim
grouchy
grum
grumpy
guilt-ridden
guilty
hapless
harried
heartbroken
heavyhearted
homesick
hopeless
humorless
hurt
hurting
inconsolable
indisposed
injured
joyless
lachrymose
languishing
lonely
lonesome
lovesick
low
low-spirited
lugubrious
maudlin

melancholy
miserable
misty-eyed
moody
mopey
morbid
morose
mournful
nostalgic
oppressed
out-of-sorts
owlish
pained
pathetic
pensive
perturbed
pessimistic
pining
pitiable
pitiful
plaintive
plangent
poignant
pouty
pungent
regretful
remorseful
repentant
rueful
ruthful
sad
saturnine
serious
severe

sober
solemn
somber
soppy
sorrowful
sorry
stern
stricken
Stygian
subdued
suffering
suicidal
sulky
sullen
surly
teary
teary-eyed
tortured
tragic
troubled
trustful
unfortunate
unfulfilled
unhappy
unlucky
wailful
weepy
wishful
woebegone
woeful
wounded
wrecked
wretched
wronged

Healthy—Sickly

Healthy
able-bodied
active
agile
athletic
beaming
blooming
blushing
bouncing
bright

bright-eyed
bursting
bushy-tailed
chipper
clean
clear-eyed
dexterous
elastic
energetic
exercised

firm
fit
fit as a fiddle
florid
flush
full of life and
    vigor
glossy
glowing
hale

hardy
healthful
healthy
hearty
in fine fettle
in good health
in good shape
in shape
in the pink
light-footed

limber
lissome
lithe
lively
lusty
mighty
muscular
peppy
perky
physically fit
pink-cheeked
pliable
radiant
red
ripe
robust
rosy
ruddy
rugged
scrubbed
shapely
shining
shiny
shipshape
sinuous
sleek
sound
spare
sparkling
spry
square-
    shouldered
stalwart
staunch
steady
stout
strapping
streamlined
strong
sturdy
sunny
supple

svelte
toned
trim
twenty-twenty
twinkling
vigorous
vital
well
well-fed
wholesome
youthful

Sickly
aged
ailing
anemic
attenuated
bedridden
below par
bent
blanched
bleary-eyed
blind
bloated
bloodshot
cadaverous
chalky
corpselike
crippled
debilitated
decrepit
delicate
disabled
diseased
doddering
down
droopy
dull
emaciated
enfeebled
etiolated
faint

farsighted
feeble
feverish
flabby
flaccid
flimsy
flushed
fossilized
fragile
frail
gaunt
glassy-eyed
haggard
hollow-eyed
humpbacked
ill
in poor health
incontinent
indisposed
infirm
lame
limp
lumpish
lurid
mute
myopic
nearsighted
obese
off-color
out of action
out of shape
out of whack
overweight
pale
pallid
palsied
paltry
peaked
peg-legged
phthisic
pigeon-toed
pinched

pursy
run-down
scorbutic
shaky
shriveled
shrunken
sick
sickly
skeletal
skinny
slack
soft
sparse
spindle-legged
starved
stone-blind
stone-deaf
strabismic
sunken
swollen
tabetic
tottering
tubercular
under the weather
underfed
undernourished
underweight
unhealthy
unwell
walleyed
wan
washed-out
wasted
waxen
waxy
weak
web-footed
wispy
withered
wizened
wraithlike
wrinkled

Helpful—Troublesome

Helpful
accessory
accommodating

advantageous
aggrandizing
altruistic

amenable
amicable
attached

avuncular
beneficent
beneficial

benevolent
benign
bighearted
brotherly
caring
charitable
chivalrous
civic-minded
clement
compassionate
concerned
conciliatory
conducive
conscientious
considerate
constructive
cooperative
dutiful
eager
equable
equitable
faithful
fatherly
favorable
felicitous
fortunate
fraternal
good-hearted
helpful
heroic
humane
humanitarian
hunky-dory
indulgent
instructive
instrumental
intimate
large
lenient
loving
loyal
magnanimous
maternal
merciful
motherly
munificent
neighborly
nice

obliging
paternal
patriotic
philanthropic
pleasant
positive
pragmatic
progressive
propitiatory
propitious
protective
provident
reliable
responsible
responsive
selfless
self-sacrificing
sensitive
sharing
sisterly
social
social-minded
solicitous
soothing
sunny
supportive
sympathetic
tender
thoughtful
tonic
tried-and-true
trustworthy
trusty
unfailing
unselfish
upbeat
usable
useful
valuable
voluntary
well-intentioned
well-meaning
wholesome
worthwhile

Troublesome
abrasive
abusive

acrid
acrimonious
annoying
antagonistic
arch
argumentative
avaricious
averse
balky
baneful
bilious
bitter
bothersome
bullying
burdensome
cagey
capricious
carking
challenging
cloying
comminatory
complaining
covetous
crafty
crappy
creepy
crotchety
crummy
cutthroat
dangerous
demanding
designing
destructive
difficult
discontented
disquieting
disturbing
divisive
dour
downbeat
envious
fearsome
feral
fickle
fierce
foxy
fractious
harsh

horrendous
horrible
horrid
horrific
importunate
incompatible
inconvenient
infamous
inhumane
invidious
irksome
irreconcilable
irresponsible
irritating
jackleg
jangly
jaundiced
libelous
lousy
lupine
maddening
maladjusted
manipulative
mean
meddlesome
menacing
minatory
nagging
nauseating
negative
negligent
nerve-racking
nettlesome
nihilistic
nosy
notorious
noxious
objectionable
obnoxious
odious
offensive
officious
ominous
onerous
oppressive
parlous
pernicious
pesky

pestilent
pesty
petulant
polypragmatic
pompous
prankish
preachy
prickly
provocative
pugnacious
querulous
rancid
rancorous
rapacious
rascally
remorseless
renitent
reprehensible
restrictive
rivalrous
roguish

sacrilegious
savage
scary
scathing
scurrilous
seditious
self-destructive
severe
sharp
sick
slanderous
slashing
slinking
sly
small
smirking
snide
sniffish
sniffy
snobbish
snoopy

snotty
sordid
sour
spiteful
spleenful
stickly
stressful
stroppy
stuck-up
subversive
terrifying
thorny
thoughtless
toxic
treacly
tricky
troublesome
troublous
truculent
trying
unconcerned

undependable
unfaithful
ungrateful
unpleasant
unsympathetic
useless
venomous
vicious
vindictive
virulent
vitriolic
vituperative
vulpine
wayward
wearisome
wily
worrisome
wrongheaded

Intelligent—Ignorant

Intelligent
able
abreast
accurate
acute
analytical
apt
argute
articulate
astute
au fait
authoritative
bookish
brainy
bright
brilliant
broad-ranging
canny
cerebral
clear
clearheaded
clear-sighted
clever
cogent

cognizant
coherent
comprehending
comprehensive
concise
conscious
conversant
cunning
discerning
donnish
droll
educated
erudite
expert
facile
fluent
gifted
glib
heads-up
heady
highbrow
high-minded
hip
imaginative

incisive
informed
ingenious
innovative
inquiring
inquisitive
insightful
intellectual
intelligent
interpretive
inventive
keen
knowing
knowledgeable
learned
limpid
literate
logical
lucid
luminous
mental
observant
omnilegent
omniscient

organized
pawky
pedagogic
penetrating
perceptive
percipient
perspicacious
piercing
pithy
precocious
prescient
proficient
profound
quick-witted
rational
recondite
reflective
resourceful
retentive
right
ruminant
savvy
serious-minded
sharp

sharp-witted
shrewd
silver-tongued
smart
smooth-tongued
subtle
succinct
terse
thinking
trenchant
tuned-in
ultrasmart
uncanny
understanding
unerring
urbane
versed
well-advised
well-informed
well-read
well-rounded
well-spoken
wise
with-it
witty
worldly
worldly-wise

Ignorant
absentminded
abstracted
addlebrained
addled
agog
amnesiac
backward
baffled
befogged

befuddled
benighted
besotted
bewildered
blithering
bovine
confounded
confused
cretinous
dense
dim
dim-witted
disorganized
disoriented
doltish
dull
dumb
dumbfounded
duncical
empty-headed
erroneous
fallible
fatuous
fat-witted
feebleminded
foggy
fuzzy
hazy
idiotic
ignorant
illiterate
imbecilic
inarticulate
incognizant
incoherent
incompetently
inconscient
inept

inexperienced
lumpish
maundering
mindless
misinformed
mixed-up
moronic
muddled
muddleheaded
myopic
mystified
nescient
not bright
numb
oblivious
obtuse
opaque
perplexed
preoccupied
purblind
puzzled
rambling
rattled
retarded
scatterbrained
senile
simple
simpleminded
slaphappy
slow
slow-witted
sophomoric
spaced
spaced-out
spacey
speechless
stunned
stunted

stupefied
stupid
stuporous
subliterate
subnormal
thick
thickheaded
thick-witted
turbid
unaware
unclear
unconscious
undiscerning
uneducated
unfocused
uninformed
unintellectual
unintelligent
unknowing
unlearned
unlettered
unmindful
unorganized
unread
unschooled
unskilled
untaught
untutored
unversed
unwise
vacant
vacuous
witless
woodenheaded
woozy
wrong
zoned out
zonked-out

Interjections

ah
alack
alas
alleluia
amen
and how
avast

aw, shucks
aye
banzai
big deal
boy
bravo
by jingo

cheerio
cheers
chop-chop
dear
dear me
ditto
egads

eh
eureka
fiddlesticks
fore
forsooth
gadzooks
gee

gee whillikers
gee whiz
gesundheit
giddap
giddyap
giddyup
golly
golly gee
golly whillikers
good-bye
good golly
good gracious
goody
gracious
gracious me
hallelujah
hark
heads up
hear, hear
hear ye, hear ye
heave ho
heavens
heavens to Betsy
hello
hey
hi
hip
holy cow
holy mackerel
holy moly

holy Toledo
hooray
hosanna
hurrah
huzzah
jeepers
jeez
lackaday
lo and behold
mama mia
marry
my gracious
my, my
my stars
my word
nah
nay
nerts
no
nope
nuts
oh
oh boy
oh dear
oh, my
okay
okeydoke
okeydokey
olé
oops
oopsy-daisy

order arms
ouch
oy
oyez
peekaboo
phew
pooh
pop
prithee
prosit
rah
rah-rah
roger
rot
salud
scram
shaddup
shucks
shush
skoal
sure thing
surely
ta-da
tallyho
ten-four
there, there
timber
toodle-oo
touch
tsk tsk
tush

tut-tut
uh-huh
uh-oh
uh-uh
viva
voilà
well
what
whatever
whew
whoa
whoop-de-do
whoopee
whoops
why
woe is me
wow
wowie
wowie-zowie
yea
yeah
yep
yes
yippee
yo mama
yup
zap
zooks
zounds
zut

Limitations

a bit
a breath
a couple
a few
a little
a mite
a trifle
additionally
admitting
albeit
all but
all the same
all things
    considered

alone
although
as far as
as good as
as is
as it is
as long as
as soon as
as the case may be
as well
aside from
at all
at best
at least

at most
at worst
au contraire
barely
barring
be that as it may
below
besides
bit by bit
briefly
but
by any chance
by any means
by chance

by degrees
by hook or by
    crook
by no means
by the same token
catch
circumstantially
conceivably
conditionally
considering
contingent on
cursory
decreasingly
demi-

depending
discounting
else
even
even so
even still
even though
even with
ever less
everything being
     equal
except
except for
except that
excepting
excluding
exclusive of
exempting
expressly
faintly
few
for all one knows
for all that
for aught one
     knows
for my part
for the most part
formerly
God willing
gradually
grain of salt
granting
half
halfway
handful
hardly
hardly any
hardly ever
hedged
hemi-
hen's teeth
hereby
how
howbeit
however
howsoever
if
if and only if

if and when
if at all
if it so happens
if not
if only
if possible
if then
ill
in
in a way
in addition
in any case
in any way
in brief
in case
in no way
in part
in some measure
in spite of
in that case
infrequently
insofar as
insufficient
iota
irregardless
just
just in case
just so
just the same
kicker
kind of
latter
least
leastways
leastwise
leaving aside
less
less and less
less than
let alone
like
limited
little by little
maybe
mayhap
meager
mere
merely
midway

might
mildly
mini-
minimus
minus
minutely
mite
moderately
modestly
modicum
momentary
namely
nary
nay, rather
needless
negligible
neither
never
nevertheless
no less than
no more than
nohow
nominal
nonetheless
nor
not hardly
not in the least
not much
not often
notwithstanding
nowhere near
null
occasionally
off
on balance
on condition that
on the whole
once
only
only if
otherwise
overly
overmuch
part by part
partial
partially
partly
partway
passing

pending
pennyworth
perchance
perhaps
personally
picayune
piddling
piecemeal
pittance
possibly
pretty
pretty much
provided
providing
provisionally
purely
qualifying
quasi
quite the contrary
rare
rarely
rather
regardless
relatively
remote
restricting
restrictive
sans
satisfactory
save
saving
scarcely
seldom
semi-
several
short of
slightly
sliver
smattering
smidgen
so as
so far
so long as
sobeit
some
somehow
somehow or other
someway

somewhat
soon
sort of
soupçon
sparely
sparsely
speck
sporadically
spot
step by step
still
still and all
stipulated
strings
subject to

submarginal
tad
temporary
that being said
that being so
that is to say
thin
though
thumbnail
tittle
to
to a certain point
to a degree
to some degree
to some extent
token
trace

uncommon
under
under par
under the
circumstances
unless
up to
upon my word
verge
videlicet
viz.
waiving
warning
wee
well

were it not
when
whereof
whichever
whit
with a catch
with reservations
with strings
with the proviso
with the
stipulation
withal
without
worse
yet

Moderate—Excessive

Moderate
abstemious
abstinent
adjusted
assiduous
balanced
bearable
businesslike
buttoned-down
careful
cautious
celibate
chary
circumspect
clocklike
closemouthed
collected
composed
compromising
concise
concrete
conscientious
conservative
consistent
constant
controlled
conventional
coolheaded
diplomatic

down-to-earth
equitable
factual
frugal
gentle
gingerly
gradual
inveterate
judicious
laconic
levelheaded
matter-of-fact
measured
mediocre
middle-of-the-
road
middling
mild
moderate
modest
no-nonsense
objective
obsolete
old-fashioned
orderly
orthodox
ossified
outdated
outmoded

passé
penny-wise
pious
practical
pragmatic
prudent
rational
reasonable
regimented
regular
restrained
safe
sane
sensible
sober
sound
sparing
square
stable
standardized
standpat
steady
stick-in-the-mud
sticky
stodgy
straitlaced
stringent
studied
superannuated

tactful
temperate
tepid
though-minded
thrifty
ultraconservative
utilitarian
workmanlike

Excessive
aberrant
abnormal
addictive
alcoholic
amok
anarchic
anarchistic
apoplectic
avaricious
berserk
brash
chaotic
crazed
crazy
daffy
daft
delirious
demoniacal
deranged

deviant	headlong	off	spasmodic
dizzy	hedonistic	off-the-wall	strange
dotty	heedless	overabundant	streaky
dysfunctional	hog-wild	overdone	surreal
eldritch	homicidal	overkill	sybaritic
epicurean	hyper	overwrought	temerarious
erratic	hysterical	perfervid	ultra
esurient	immodest	phrenetic	ultraist
exaggerated	incendiary	pixilated	unbalanced
excessive	indulgent	potty	unbridled
extravagant	inordinate	prodigal	unconventional
extreme	insane	profuse	uncurbed
fanatic	insatiable	psycho	unfettered
fanatical	irrational	psychotic	unhinged
febrile	kamikaze	quirky	unrestrained
fey	kooky	rabid	voracious
flagrant	loco	radical	wacky
flaky	lunatic	raging	warped
florid	mad	rakish	wasteful
frantic	madcap	rapacious	way out
freakish	maniacal	rash	wiggy
frenetic	monomaniacal	ravening	wild-eyed
frenzied	nihilistic	raving	wired
gonzo	obsessive	reckless	zany
greedy	odd	screwy	zooey

Silly-Sounding Words

artsy-craftsy	heebie-jeebies	niminy-piminy	teensy
bleep	ho-hum	okeydoke	teensy-weensy
burry-scurry	hoity-toity	okeydokey	thingamabob
chichi	hugger-mugger	oodles	thingamajig
cockoo	hunky-dory	palsy-walsy	ticky-tacky
comfy	hurly-burly	pell-mell	tutti-frutti
coo	itsy-bitsy	raggle-taggle	whim-wham
cutesy	itty-bitty	razzle-dazzle	willy-nilly
gaga	lardy-dardy	rinky-dink	wishy-washy
gizmo	namby-pamby	screaming	
harum-scarum	newfangled	meemies	

Orange

apricot	carotene	hyacinth red	ocher
aurora	carrot	international	old gold
burnt ocher	chrome orange	orange	orange
burnt orange	copper	mandarin	pale orange
cadmium orange	dark orange	marigold	pastel orange
cantaloupe	helianthin	mikado	peach

pumpkin	red-orange	Spanish ocher	yellow-orange
realgar orange	Rubens' madder	tangerine	
reddish yellow	salmon	terra-cotta	

Physical Attributes

almond-eyed	dolichocephalic	limping	shovel-nosed
ample	domed	long-faced	show-footed
androgynous	downy	loose-jointed	sinewy
aquiline	eagle-eyed	loose-limbed	sinuous
bald	erect	male	skinny
barefoot	exophthalmic	microcephalic	slanted
bearded	fat	mongoloid	slant-eyed
black	feline	muscular	slim
blank	female	mute	sloe-eyed
blind	flat-footed	naked	small
blond	flattened	oblong	smirking
blonde	flossy	open-eyed	smooth
blue-eyed	fluffy	pigeon-toed	sneering
bosomy	flushed	pinched	snub-nosed
bowlegged	freckled	plump	speckled
brachycephalic	freckle-faced	poker-faced	spindle-legged
bristling	full-figured	popeyed	splayfooted
brown	fullmouthed	pouty	squinty
brown-eyed	fuzzy	puckered	straight-faced
brunette	goggle-eyed	pug-nosed	stubbly
bucktoothed	grimacing	pursed	sulky
busty	grinning	pursy	swarthy
buxom	gummy	rawboned	swivel-hipped
chip-toothed	hairless	redheaded	taliped
chubby	hairy	retroussé	tanned
clean-shaven	hewn	right-handed	throaty
clubfooted	hirsute	robust	toothy
cross-legged	horny	roundheaded	unshaven
curled lip	horrent	round-shouldered	vacuous
curvaceous	irregular	rubicund	varicose-veined
curvy	jowly	saurian	voluptuous
dark	knock-kneed	scowling	wavy
deadpan	lambent	setaceous	whiskered
deaf	lanky	shaggy	white
dewy-eyed	large	sharp-nosed	wide-eyed
doe-eyed	leathery	shorn	widemouthed
	left-handed		
	life-size		

Pink

begonia	carnation	deep pink	flush
blush	casino pink	fiesta	fuchsia
cameo pink	coral	flamingo	hot pink

hunter's pink
incarnadine
livid pink
mallow pink
melon
moonlight

nymph pink
orchid rose
pale pink
peach
peachblow
petal pink

pink
reddish pink
rose
rose pink
roseate
royal pink

salmon
shell pink
shocking pink
tea rose

Positiveness

above all
absolutely
actually
after all
all
all along
all out
all over
all the while
altogether
always
as a matter of
    course
as a matter of fact
at any cost
at first
at last
at long last
at that
bar none
by all means
cap-a-pie
categorically
certainly
clean
clearly
complete
completely
conclusively
dead on
decidedly
decisively
definitely
doubtless
entirely
even
eventually
exactly
expressly

finally
first
first and foremost
first of all
first things
firstly
for good
for keeps
for sure
forever
forever and ever
forevermore
forsooth
full-out
fully
granting
hands down
head to toe
identically
immeasurably
in a word
in all respects
in conclusion
in fact
in full
in no way
in particular
in point of fact
in reality
in the first place
in the long run
in toto
indeed
indubitably
inevitably
infinitely
invariably
irrespective of
just

just so
lastly
literally
literatim
lock, stock, and
    barrel
minimus
naught
necessarily
needless to say
never
nil
nix
no ifs, ands, or
    buts
no more
no strings
    attached
no two ways
    about it
no way
nohow
not a bit
not a whit
not at all
now and forever
nowise
null
null and void
of course
once
once and for all
once for all
only
out-and-out
outright
par excellence
paramount
perfectly

plain
plenary
plumb
positively
precisely
premier
prime
primo
principal
proper
purely
quite
really
right
right-on
same
selfsame
sheer
simply
smack-dab
so much as
solely
solid
squarely
stark
stock-still
stone
supreme
sure
sure enough
sure thing
surely
thoroughly
through and
    through
to a tee
to the limit
to the utmost
topflight

topnotch
total
totally
truly
ultimately
unadulterated
unconditional
unconditionally
undeniably
under no
    circumstance

unlimited
unmistakably
unqualified
unquestionably
unreservedly
uppermost
utmost
utter
utterly
uttermost
verbatim

verily
veritably
versal
void
well
whatever
whatsoever
wherever
whole
whole hog
wholly

wide
without exception
word-for-word
world
worst
zero
zilch

Prepositions

a
a la
abaft
aboard
about
above
absent
according to
across
across from
adown
afore
after
against
agin
ahead of
aloft
along
along with
alongside
amid
amidst
among
amongst
an
anent
apart from
après
around
as
as for
as of
as to
aside

aside from
aslant
astraddle
astride
at
athwart
away from
bar
barring
bathing
because
because of
bedside
before
behind
below
beneath
beside
besides
between
betwixt
beyond
but
by
by means of
chez
circa
close to
concerning
considering
contra
contrary to
cum
depending on

despite
down
due to
during
ere
ex
except
except for
excepting
excluding
failing
following
for
forby
fore
forth
forward of
frae
from
hear
in
in between
in favor of
in front of
in lieu of
in spite of
including
inside
instead of
into
irrespective of
less
like
maugre

mid
midst
minus
'mongst
near
near to
neath
next
next to
nigh
notwithstanding
o'
o'er
of
off
on
on account of
on board
on top of
onto
opposite
opposite to
or
other than
out
out of
outside
outside of
over
owing to
pace
past
pending
per

plus	sith	together with	up until
preparatory to	syne	touching	upon
prior to	than	toward	versus
re	thanks to	towards	via
regarding	thorough	under	vice
regardless of	thro	underneath	vis-à-vis
respecting	through	unless	wanting
round	throughout	unlike	while
sans	thru	until	with
save	thwart	unto	withal
save for	till	up	within
saving	times	up against	without
since	to	up to	worth

Proper—Vulgar

Proper	effete	moralistic	right-thinking
acceptable	elitist	nice	rigid
aesthetic	established	obedient	safe
applicable	esthetic	official	sanctimonious
appropriate	ethical	orthodox	seemly
apt	fastidious	pietistic	self-righteous
auspicious	felicitous	polite	smooth
becoming	finicky	pompous	smug
befitting	fitting	precious	snobbish
ceremonious	formal	presentable	snooty
chaste	fussy	priggish	soapy
citified	gallant	prim	sporting
civil	genteel	prissy	sportsmanlike
civilized	gentlemanly	pristine	squeamish
classical	gracious	professional	stable
clubby	hoity-toity	proper	staid
conforming	holier-than-thou	prudent	starchy
conventional	honorable	prudish	stiff
correct	ingratiating	pudibund	stilted
courteous	in-line	punctilious	straight
courtly	irreproachable	punctual	straight-arrow
couth	Ivy League	puritanical	straitlaced
cultivated	kosher	qualified	strict
cultured	law-abiding	refined	stuffy
decent	legitimate	religious	suave
decorous	maidenly	reputable	suitable
delicate	mannered	respectable	suited
demure	mannerly	respectful	tactful
desired	matronly	rhetorical	tasteful
dignified	modern	righteous	taut
diplomatic	modest	rightful	tight-assed
discreet	moral	rightly	too-too

traditional
tweedy
unflappable
upright
uptight
urbane
Victorian
well bred
well-behaved
well-mannered
white
white-bread

Vulgar

abandoned
aberrant
abnormal
abominable
aboriginal
abusive
animalistic
anomalous
atavistic
barbaric
base
bawdy
beastly
bibulous
bizarre
blasphemous
blooey
blunt
boorish
brash
brazen
brutish
caddish
cannibalistic
carnal
cheap
cheeky
coarse
common
concupiscent
contemptible
coquettish
crass
crude

debauched
decadent
degenerate
depraved
deviant
dirty
dirty-minded
discourteous
disgusting
disobedient
disorderly
disreputable
dissipated
dissolute
egregious
erotic
farouche
feral
filthy
flatulent
flip
flippant
flooey
foul
fresh
garish
gauche
gross
heathenish
heteroclite
heterodox
hoggish
hokey
ill-bred
illicit
ill-mannered
immoderate
immoral
impertinent
impolite
impolitic
improper
impudent
inappropriate
incestuous
incongruous
indecent
indecorous

indelicate
inexcusable
insolent
intoxicated
irregular
irreverent
kinky
knockabout
lascivious
lawless
lecherous
lewd
libertine
libidinous
licentious
loose
loud
loutish
low
lowbred
lowbrow
lubricious
lustful
mannerless
meretricious
native
naughty
non-U
obscene
obstreperous
offbeat
off-color
offensive
offhand
opprobrious
outlandish
outrageous
outré
overdressed
perverted
plebeian
pornographic
primitive
profane
profligate
promiscuous
prurient
prying

purple
queer
Rabelaisian
racy
raffish
rakish
rambunctious
randy
rank
raucous
raunchy
raw
rebellious
recherché
refractory
repulsive
revolutionary
ribald
riotous
ripped
rip-roaring
risqué
roily
rough
rough-and-
    tumble
rough-hewn
rowdy
rowdydowdy
rude
rumbustious
rustic
ruttish
salacious
sassy
savage
scabrous
scandalous
scurrilous
self-abandoned
shameless
showy
slutty
smutty
steamy
swinish
tactless
tasteless

tawdry
tipsy
trashy
unbecoming
unblushing
uncivil
uncivilized
uncontrollable

unconventional
uncool
uncouth
uncultivated
uncultured
undiplomatic
ungracious
unmanageable

unmannered
unmannerly
unnatural
unrefined
unruly
unseemly
unsportsmanlike
untamed

untoward
vulgar
wanton
weird
whorish
wild
X-rated

Purple

amaranth
amaranthine
amethyst
argyle purple
aubergine
bishop's violet
blue-violet
bluish purple
bluish red
bokhara
campanula violet
clematis
cobalt violet
dahlia

damson
deep purple
eggplant
fuchsia
grape
gridelin
heliotrope
hyacinth
imperial purple
lavender
light purple
lilac
magenta
manganese violet

Mars violet
mauve
monsignor
mulberry
orchid
pale purple
pansy
periwinkle
perse
phlox
plum
prune
puce
purple

purplish
purpure
raisin
raspberry
reddish blue
reddish purple
royal purple
rubine
solferino
Tyrian purple
violet
violetta

Red

Adrianople red
alizarin
alizarin crimson
alpenglow
anchsin
annatto
bloodred
blush
bois de rose
Bordeaux
bougainvillea
brick red
brownish red
burgundy
cadmium red
cardinal
carmine
carnelian
Castilian red
cerise

cherry
cherry red
Chinese red
chrome red
cinnabar
claret
cochineal
Congo red
cranberry
crimson
crimson lake
damask
dark red
English red
faded rose
fire red
fire-engine red
fuchsia
garnet
geranium

grenadine
gules
Harrison red
high-colored
Indian red
iron red
jockey
Levant red
light red
lobster red
madder lake
magenta
maroon
Mars red
murrey
orange-red
oxblood red
paprika
peach
Persian red

pimento
pinkish red
Pompeian red
ponceau
poppy
Prussian red
puce
red
rhodamine
rose
rose madder
roseate
ruby
ruddy
rust
scarlet
signal red
stammel
strawberry
tile red

| Turkey red | vermilion | wine |
| Venetian red | wild cherry | wine-colored |

Small—Large

Small

bantam	puny	weeny	enormous
bareboned	pygmy	willowy	excessive
bitty	reedlike	wiry	exorbitant
bony	reedy	wispy	extensive
compact	runty		fat
cramped	sawed-off	**Large**	fleshy
dainty	scant	abundant	fubsy
diminutive	scanty	adipose	full
dinky	scarce	Amazonian	full-grown
dwarfish	scraggy	ample	gargantuan
elfin	scrawny	Antaean	generous
flat-chested	scrubby	barrel-chested	giant
gangling	short	beefy	gigantic
gawky	shrimpy	behemoth	goliath
half pint	shriveled	big	grand
inadequate	shrunken	big-bellied	grandiose
infinitesimal	sinewy	booming	great
insubstantial	skinny	boundless	gross
itsy-bitsy	slender	bovine	heavy
itty-bitty	slight	brawny	hefty
lanky	slim	broad	Herculean
lean	slinky	broad of beam	huge
lilliputian	small	Brobdignagian	hulking
little	small-scale	brutish	humongous
meager	spindly	bulky	hunky
measly	spiny	bull-necked	husky
micro	squat	burly	immeasurable
microscopic	string bean	buxom	immense
midget	stringy	capacious	imposing
mini	stubby	chubby	jumbo
miniature	stumpy	chunky	Junoesque
minimal	stunted	clumpish	king-size
minuscule	teensy-weensy	colossal	large
minute	teeny	considerable	leggy
narrow	teeny-weeny	corpulent	leviathan
negligible	thin	cumbersome	limitless
nipped	tiny	cyclopean	long
paltry	undergrown	distended	long-legged
peewee	undersized	dumpy	long-limbed
petite	underweight	elephantine	lumbering
pint-sized	wasp-waisted	elongated	lumpish
pocket-sized	wee	embonpoint	mammoth
	weedy	endomorphic	massive

mastodonic	paunchy	rotund	thickset
meaty	plump	sizable	titanic
mesomorphic	podgy	spacious	top-heavy
mighty	ponderous	squat	towering
monumental	porcine	squdgy	unwieldy
muscle-bound	portly	stacked	vast
obese	potbellied	stocky	voluminous
overblown	prodigious	stout	voluptuous
overdeveloped	pudgy	strapping	wide
overgrown	pursy	substantial	whopping
oversized	rangy	swollen	zaftig
overstuffed	roly-poly	tall	
overweight	roomy	thick	

Smell/Odor

ambrosial	fulsome	olfactory	savory
anosmic	gamy	olid	scented
aromatic	graveolent	osmatic	smelly
balmy	heady	perfumed	stinking
balsamic	malodorous	pungent	stinky
corky	mephitic	putrescent	stuffy
fetid	moschate	putrid	sweet
foul	nasal	rancid	sweet-scented
fragrant	nidorous	rank	sweet-smelling
fresh	odoriferous	redolent	unscented

Sounds/Sound Effects

aaaa	bash	bleed	bot
aargh	ba-wrooo	bleeed	bounce
aarrgh	bawww	bllom	boyng
achoo	bdlm	blm	bradada
ack	bdmp	blodom	brat
ahh	beep	blog	brrrram
ak	bi-eech	blom	brrt
arf	biff	bloo	bsss
arp	bilam	blop	bsssboom
baa	bing	blouw	burble
babrom	birashh	blug	burp
bada	birr	boing	buzz
ba-da-bam	blahhhh	bom	bzzzz
badow	blaff	bong	caw
baff	blam	bonk	cheep
bam	blamma	boo	chink
bam bam	blang	boom	chirp
bammm	blap	boom-da-doom	chirr
bang	blat	bop	chirrup

chomp	drivit	hnf	nyaaooo
chonk	dzzzz	honk	oink
chop	ech	hoo	oof
chsh	eeeeeee	howwow	oop
chugalug	eeeeek	hrf	ooze
churr	eeeeep	huf	oww
clak	eek	huh	paf
claket	eep	hum	panting
clang	ert	humph	pat
clank	feh	hurrah	peaaaa
clap	fizz	ick	ping
clash	flink	inng	pit-a-pat
click	floom	jab	pitter-patter
cli-clip	floosh	kaf	plink
clik	foomf	kchow	plip
clikety-cirrash	fooosh	kchunk	plonk
cling	foosh	klakkety	ploosh
clink	froosh	klek	plu
clinkety-clank	fsst	klink	plunk
clip	fwadoom	klomp	pok
clomp	gag	klop	poof
clonk	gah	kneek	poom
clop	gasp	kortch	poot
clop-clop	ge-boom	kpow	pop
clunk	gha	krak	pow
coff	ghaaaa	kree	punt
coo	giggle	kreet	purr
crack	gik	krk	quack
crackle	gleh	krr-oomf	rap
crak	glig	kr-rumf	rat
crash	glook	krumf	rat-a-tat
creak	glub	kruuugg	rat-tat
crunch	glug	ktak	rattle
cuckoo	gong	kweeg	ring
cut	goo	lick	ring-a-ling
dang-a-lang	gop	meow	riprap
dangling	gring	mew	room
dep	grinngg	mewl	rowl
dia-bom	grrr	mf	rrinng
dig	hack	mff	rrip
ding	ha-ho	mhf	r-rip
ding-a-ling	haw	moo	rrooaar
ding-dong	heart thump	nf	rrowr
dinggg	hem	nfs	runch
dlmp	hf	nggg	salump
dong	hiccup	ngs	schplivartz
doof	hiss	nod	scree
drinnggg	hmf	nok	screech

screee
shmek
shomp
shoop
shriek
shuffling feet
skee
skloorgle
skntch
skramm
skrotch
skwee
slam
slap
slap-ap-ap
slash
slep
slosh
smak
smash
smcccccr
smek
smesh
smooch
snap
snf
snick
sniff
sniffle
snore
snuff
sob
spa-bam
spla-poom
splash

splat
splinter
splish
sploog
sploosh
splow
splush
spong
sponggg
spung
sput
squeak
squeee
squish
srelikk
stomp
stung
stweeeenz
swish
swok
swoosh
swop
ta-da
tantara
tap
tat
thud
thunk
tick
ticktock
tilt
ting
ting-a-ling
tinkle
toot
treee

tromp
trompitty
tsktwang
twee
tweep
tweet
twerp
ugh
umph
ung
vaaaagglum
varoom
vash
va-va-voom
voof
voom
vroom
vrrumm
waa
waaah
waf
wak
wee
weooooeeeoooee
wham
whap
whirl
whirr
whish
whisper
whom
whomp
whoopee
whoosh
whuf
wobble

wok
woof
woop
wow
wrraammmm
wurf
yahoo
yap
yappa
yatata
yayter
yeeeaaakkyhaaa
yikes
yip
yitti
yo
yoo-hoo
yoop
yotter
youch
yow
yyp
zaaaa
zap
zeta
zing
zip
zok
zop
zot
zzap
zzip
zzz
zzzz

Special—Ordinary

Special
ablaze
able
acclaimed
accomplished
adept
admirable
admired
ageless
aglow

all-around
amazing
ambidextrous
anointed
artful
artistic
arty
atypical
auspicious
avant-garde

bedazzling
best
blessed
bodacious
breathtaking
bright
brilliant
capable
celebrated
charismatic

choice
colorful
competent
conspicuous
consummate
controversial
coordinated
corking
creative
creditable

dazzling
different
distinct
distinctive
distinguished
divine
earmarked
eccentric
efficient
effulgent
eminent
esteemed
estimable
excellent
exceptional
exclusive
exemplary
exotic
extraordinary
famous
fascinating
favored
fine
first-class
first-rate
flashing
foremost
fortunate
glimmering
glittering
glorious
glossy
glowing
grand
great
handy
heavenly
hip
honored
iconoclastic
idiosyncratic
illuminated
illustrious
imaginative
imperial
important
imposing
impressive

incandescent
incomparable
incredible
individual
indubitable
inimitable
inspiring
invaluable
inviolate
iridescent
jazzy
light
lucky
luminous
lustrous
magical
magnificent
main
majestic
major
marquee
marvelous
masterful
matchless
momentous
nonpareil
notable
noted
noteworthy
novel
original
otherworldly
out of the
ordinary
outstanding
peculiar
peerless
perfect
phenomenal
praiseworthy
preeminent
prepared
prestigious
priceless
primary
Promethean
prominent
protean

proverbial
quaint
qualified
quality
radiant
rare
refulgent
remarkable
renowned
resourceful
respected
resplendent
reverential
ripe
sacred
saintly
scintillating
select
sensational
serendipitous
sexy
shining
signal
significant
singular
skillful
sole
sovereign
sparkling
special
spicy
splendid
startling
stellar
storied
stupendous
sublime
successful
super
superb
superhuman
superior
superlative
sure-handed
talented
terrific
tip-top
titled

together
top
topflight
topnotch
top-of-the-line
tops
towering
transfigured
uncommon
unconventional
unequaled
unexcelled
unique
unmatched
unorthodox
unprecedented
unusual
unwonted
utopian
valuable
valued
varied
vast
versatile
victorious
vintage
vivid
well-known
well-spoken
well-thought-of
whiz-bang
wonderful
wondrous
worthwhile
worthy

Ordinary
adequate
automatic
average
banal
bland
blank
boring
bourgeois
characterless
colorless
common

commonplace
conventional
cursory
customary
dated
derivative
dim
dingy
dismal
down-to-earth
drab
dreary
dull
empty
established
everyday
expressionless
faded
fair
fallible
familiar
faulty
flat
garden-variety
general
generic
glib
gratuitous
habitual
hackneyed
homespun
humble
humdrum

imitative
inartistic
inconclusive
inconspicuous
indifferent
indistinctive
inefficient
inept
inferior
inglorious
innocuous
insignificant
insipid
jejune
lackluster
lifeless
low-class
lowly
low-quality
lukewarm
lusterless
matter-of-fact
mean
mediocre
menial
middling
mild
minor
modest
mortal
mundane
musty
negligible
nondescript
normal

obvious
okay
one-dimensional
ordinary
passable
pedestrian
perfunctory
petit bourgeois
proletarian
prosaic
prototypical
regular
repetitive
rinky-dink
routine
run-of-the-mill
secondary
second-class
second-rate
shoddy
simple
small-time
soggy
soporific
spare
stagnant
stale
standard
stereotypical
sterile
stock
stripped-down
subordinate

superficial
superfluous
tarnished
tasteless
tedious
tepid
terrestrial
timeworn
tiresome
tolerable
traditional
trite
typical
unadorned
unassuming
undistinguished
unexceptional
unhip
unimaginative
uninspiring
uninteresting
unprepared
unpretentious
unqualified
unsung
untalented
untitled
useless
usual
vapid
workaday
working-class
would-be

Speech Reference/Reflection

according
according to
accordingly
aforementioned
again
against
all the same
all things
considered
allowing for
along

along with
amid
amidst
among
amongst
and so
and so forth
and so on
anent
apart
apparently

arguably
around
as
as a result
as being
as far as
as if
as they say
as though
as to
as well as

asunder
at the same time
attended by
because
because of
between
betwixt
by
by and by
by dint of
by the way

by virtue of
by way of
concerning
conjointly
consequently
considering
contrary to
correspondingly
counter to
coupled with
ditto
due to
either
else
elsewise
equally
ergo
et cetera
evidently
finally
for each
for example
for instance
for that reason
for this reason
given
hence
henceforth
henceforward
hereat
hereby
herein
hereinabove
hereinafter
hereinbefore
hereinbelow
hereon
heretofore
hereunder
hereunto
hereupon
herewith
hither
hitherto

how come
ibid.
imprimis
in addition to
in conjunction
in keeping with
in lieu of
in line with
in other respects
in other words
in passing
in re
in relation to
in return
in the matter of
in turn
in twain
in two
in view of
inasmuch as
incidental to
incidentally
including
indeed
insofar as
insomuch as
instead
instead of
intro-
irrespective
jointly
loc. cit.
midst
'mongst
much as
much less
mutually
natch
naturally
naturellement
of
of course
on account of
on that account
on the other hand
only

op. cit.
or
or else
other than
otherwise
outwardly
penultimate
per
peripheral
qua
re
readily
regarding
respecting
respectively
secondary
seeing that
selectively
self-styled
separately
severally
side
since
snap
so
so as
so far as
so forth
so much
so on
soever
specified
spotty
square
stated
subsidiary
such
supposed
supra
surfeit
tacit
that is to say
then again
thence

thereat
thereby
therefore
thereinafter
thereof
thereon
thereto
theretofore
thereunder
thereupon
thus
thus and so
thusly
together with
uncommon
undue
unduly
unusual
unusually
upon
variable
various
variously
veritable
vice
virtual
what for
what if
whence
where
whereat
wherefor
wherefrom
whereinto
whereon
wheresoever
whereupon
whichever
while
why
with
with regard to
with relation to
with respect to
yet

Strong—Weak

Strong

able-bodied
adventuresome
adventurous
all-powerful
athletic
audacious
ballsy
belligerent
bluff
blunt
bold
brash
brave
brawny
burly
clutched
courageous
daring
dauntless
decisive
doughty
durable
effective
energetic
fearless
firm
fit
flinty
forbidding
forceful
formidable
full-blooded
gritty
gutsy
gutty
hale
hard-assed
hard-nosed
hardy
healthy
hearty
heavy
hell-for-leather
Herculean

indestructible
inexhaustible
intrepid
lionhearted
lusty
manly
massive
mettlesome
mighty
militant
motivated
muscular
nervy
oppressive
physical
plucky
potent
powerful
ready
red-blooded
reliant
resilient
robust
rocky
rough
rugged
ruthless
scrappy
self-made
self-reliant
self-sufficient
self-supporting
self-sustaining
skookum
solid
sound
spartan
spirited
spunky
stalwart
staunch
steadfast
steely
stout
stouthearted

strapping
street-smart
streetwise
strong
sturdy
substantial
thriving
tough
truculent
unblinking
valiant
valorous
venturesome
vigorous
warlike
well-built
yeomanly

Weak

abashed
afraid
ailing
alarmed
anemic
anxious
apprehensive
ashamed
asthmatic
bedridden
bloodless
brittle
candy-assed
clinging
consumptive
cowardly
craven
creaky
cringing
debilitated
decrepit
delicate
desperate
dilute
disconcerted
doddering

effete
emasculated
enervated
exhausted
faint
fainthearted
faltering
fearful
feckless
feeble
fidgety
fitful
flimsy
fragile
frail
frangible
frightened
futile
gimpy
gutless
hagridden
helpless
horrified
horror-struck
humbled
humiliated
hung up
ill
impotent
impoverished
impuissant
inadequate
incapacitated
ineffective
inept
infirm
insecure
insufficient
jittery
lame
lily-livered
limp
limp-wristed
mawkish
meager

milk-livered
mortified
namby-pamby
needy
nervous
neurotic
oversensitive
overwhelmed
pale
pallid
paltry
panicked
panic-stricken
paranoid
pathetic
pavid
petrified
phthisic
pitiful
plaintive

poor-spirited
powder-puff
powerless
punchless
puny
pusillanimous
recreant
scared
shaky
sheepish
short-winded
shrinking
sickly
simpering
skimpy
skittish
slight
sniveling
snuffling
spasmodic
spineless
spooked

squeamish
stressed
stressed-out
sulky
terrified
timid
timorous
toothless
tottering
trapped
trembling
tremulous
uncomfortable
undernourished
uneasy
unmanly
unnerved
unsound
unwell
uptight

vertiginous
wan
wary
washed-out
washy
wasted
watery
weak
weakhearted
weak-kneed
weakly
wet
whining
whiny
white
white-livered
wimpy
wispy
wormy
yellow

Superlatives

a lot
a sight
all
all along
all get-out
all over
all-embracing
all-inclusive
always
aplenty
at length
best
chiefly
chock-full
commonly
considerable
copious
decidedly
ever
evermore
every
exceedingly
extremely
far

far and away
farthest
foremost
galore
great
head and
    shoulders
head over heels
hook, line, and
    sinker
hyper
ideally
jillion
large
lickety-split
likely
lots
major
many
maxi-
mighty
more and more
most
much

myriad
nth
numerous
oft
often
oftentimes
plenteous
plentiful
premium
radically
rattling
real
rife
rip-roaring
roaring
smashing
socko
spanking
staggering
stiff
strong
super-duper
supreme
surpassing

sweeping
thumping
thundering
tip-top
top
ultra-
umpteen
unbounded
unbridled
unmitigated
unremitting
unrivaled
untold
vast
vaulting
walloping
waxing
way
whacking
whopping
wide-ranging
widespread
withering
zillion

Tastes

acerbic
acidic
acrid
aftertaste
ambrosial
appealing
appetizing
astringent
biting
bitter
brackish
briny
caustic
choice
delectable
delicious
divine
dry

dulcet
dulcified
flavored
flavorful
flavoring
flavorsome
fruity
full-bodied
gamy
gustatory
harsh
heavenly
honey
hot
juicy
luscious
mouthwatering
nectarous
palatable
peppery

pickled
piquant
pungent
rancid
rank
rich
saccharine
saline
salt
salty
saporific
saporous
savory
scrumptious
sec
sharp
sour
spicy

strong
succulent
sugary
sweet
sweet-and-sour
sweetened
syrupy
tang
tart
tasteful
tasteless
tasting
tasty
toothsome
treacly
unsweetened
vinegary
yummy
zesty

Warmth—Coldness (personal)

Warmth
adoring
affable
affectionate
agreeable
all heart
amatory
amenable
amiable
amicable
amorous
appreciative
approachable
ardent
avuncular
benevolent
charitable
chummy
companionable
compassionate
congenial
convivial
cordial
devoted

disarming
earthy
empathic
familiar
favorable
fond
forgiving
friendly
genial
good-hearted
good-humored
good-natured
gracious
gregarious
heartfelt
heartwarming
hearty
hospitable
ingratiating
intimate
kind
kindhearted
kindly
kindred

largehearted
likable
lovable
loving
merciful
neighborly
open
openhearted
pally
palsy-walsy
personable
polite
reverent
romantic
sensitive
sensual
sentimental
sociable
soft
softhearted
summery
sympathetic
tender
tenderhearted

thoughtful
touching
understanding
warm
warmhearted
well-disposed
worshipful

Coldness
abrupt
alien
aloof
arctic
arid
asexual
ashen
astringent
atrabilious
austere
bad-tempered
bilious
bitter
bleak
bloody

blunt
brusque
brutal
callous
cantankerous
catty
cheap
chilly
chintzy
chippy
churlish
closed
cold
cold-blooded
coldhearted
cool
contemptuous
crabby
cranky
cross
crotchety
cruel
crusty
cryptic
curmudgeonly
cursed
curt
cussed
cutthroat
cynical
dispassionate
distant
domineering
dour
draconian
dry
dyspeptic
egocentric
empty
envious
forbidding
formidable
freezing

frigid
frosty
gelid
glacial
glowering
gray
greedy
grouchy
grudging
gruff
grumpy
hard-boiled
hardened
hard-hearted
hateful
haughty
heartless
hollow
huffish
humiliating
icy
ignoble
ill-humored
ill-natured
ill-tempered
impersonal
inconsiderate
indifferent
inhospitable
insensitive
insulting
insusceptible
intolerant
inured
irreconcilable
irritable
jealous
liverish
malevolent
matter-of-fact
mean
mechanical
merciless
misanthropic
miserly

nasty
niggardly
nippy
obdurate
ornery
parched
parsimonious
paw
peevish
penurious
persnickety
petty
piercing
pinchbeck
pitiless
procrustean
psychopathic
puckish
reactionary
remorseless
remote
ruthless
sadistic
salty
savage
self-serving
sere
sexless
sharp-tongued
shrewish
snappish
snarly
snippety
snippy
snitty
snotty
sour
spiteful
spleenful
splenetic
stark
steely
stern

stiff
stingy
stoical
stony
stonyhearted
strict
surly
suspicious
testy
tetchy
thick-skinned
tight
tightfisted
touchy
troglodytic
truculent
tyrannical
uncaring
uncharitable
uncommunicative
uncompassionate
uncongenial
unemotional
unfeeling
unforgiving
unfriendly
ungrateful
unkind
unkindly
unmerciful
unmoved
unsympathetic
vengeful
venomous
vexatious
vicious
vitriolic
waspish
wintry
withholding
wizened
wooden
wrongheaded

Weather

antarctic
arctic
arid

azure
balmy
biting

bitter
blistering
blustery

boreal
breezy
brisk

calm
chilly
clammy
clear
close
clouded
cloudless
cloudy
cold
considerable
cloudiness
cool
crisp
dark
dismal
dreary
dry
fair
foggy

foul
freezing
frigid
frosty
frozen
gelid
glacial
gloomy
gray
gusty
hazy
hot
humid
icy
inclement
lowering
mild
misty
moist

mostly clear
mostly cloudy
mostly sunny
muggy
murky
nippy
oppressive
overcast
partly cloudy
partly sunny
rainy
seasonable
shady
shiny
smoggy
snowing
snowy
soaking
soggy

soupy
stormy
stuffy
subzero
sultry
sunless
sunny
sweltering
swirling
temperate
torrid
tropical
turbulent
warm
wet
windy

White

achromatic
alabaster
argent
blond
blonde
bone
chalk
chalky
Chinese white
clown white

dove
eggshell
flake white
gauze
ivory
ivory white
lily-white
milk white
milky
nacre

off-white
oyster
pasty
pearl
pearly
pearly white
platinum
pure white
putty
silver

snow
snow-white
tattletale gray
tin-white
titanium white
white
zinc white

Wise—Foolish

Wise
actualized
acute
adult
all-knowing
all-seeing
astute
august
aware
awesome
balanced
broad
broad-minded

calculating
centered
clear
clear-sighted
clever
cogent
coherent
complex
contemplative
crafty
cunning
deep
discerning

discriminating
disinterested
dispassionate
educated
eloquent
enlightened
ethereal
exalted
experienced
farseeing
farsighted
focused
foresighted

grand
grown-up
immortal
impartial
infallible
infinite
influential
informed
insightful
integrated
intelligent
intuitive
judicious

just
keen
knowing
knowledgeable
large-minded
learned
levelheaded
lofty
lucid
magisterial
majestic
mantic
masterful
masterly
mature
metaphysical
mystical
noble
old
Olympian
omnipresent
omniscient
open-minded
orbicular
oriented
patriarchal
perceptive
perfect
philosophical
practiced
prescient
profound
prophetic
prudent
psychic
realized
reasonable
resonant
sacred
sacrosanct
sagacious
sage
sapient
scholarly
sensible
serene
sharp
smart

sophisticated
spiritual
sublime
supernal
supreme
sybilline
telepathic
unassailable
unbiased
understanding
universal
vatic
venerable
veteran
visionary
weathered
weighty
well-advised
well-informed
wise
wizardly

Foolish
abstract
absurd
adolescent
affected
amateurish
anthropocentric
anti-intellectual
artless
artsy
asinine
awestruck
balmy
barmy
bathetic
bedazzled
biased
bigoted
bird-brained
blind
boneheaded
brainless
bumble-headed
bumbling
callow
capricious

careless
childish
clownish
clumpish
cockamamy
comical
corny
crackbrained
cretinous
cute
cutesy
daffy
daft
dippy
distracted
dopey
ethnocentric
farcical
fatheaded
featherbrained
flabbergasted
flatulent
flighty
foolhardy
foolish
foppish
frivolous
frothy
garrulous
gibbering
giddy
goofy
half-assed
half-baked
half-cocked
half-witted
harebrained
harum-scarum
hasty
highfalutin
homophobic
idiotic
ill-advised
imbecilic
immature
impetuous
impractical
imprudent

in the clouds
inane
indiscreet
inexperienced
infantile
injudicious
insane
irrational
juvenile
kooky
la-di-da
laughable
light-headed
long-winded
loony
loquacious
ludicrous
lunatic
mad
melodramatic
mincing
minor
misanthropic
misogynous
moronic
mushy-headed
muzzy
naïf
naïve
narrow
narrow-minded
nattering
nerdy
nonplussed
nonsensical
nutty
parochial
pedantic
petty
picayune
piddling
pinchbeck
pinheaded
prejudiced
preposterous
pretentious
prolix
provincial

pubescent
puerile
quixotic
quizzical
rash
rattlebrained
redundant
repetitious
ridiculous
sappy
sectarian
senseless

sententious
shallow
shortsighted
sightless
silly
simpleminded
singsong
skin-deep
small-minded
small-time
softheaded
sophistic

speechless
spoony
stupid
superficial
superstitious
trifling
trivial
unfledged
ungrounded
unintelligent
unrealistic
unwise

unworldly
verdant
waggish
wide-eyed
windy
woolly-headed
yeasty
youthful
zany

Yellow

amber
auramine
aureolin
azo yellow
barium yellow
blond
blonde
brass
brazilin
buff
butter
cadmium yellow
calendula
canary
canary yellow
Cassel yellow
chalcedony
yellow

chamois
champagne
chrome yellow
citron
corn
corn-colored
crazen
cream
crocus
dandelion
flax
flaxen
gamboge
gold
golden
goldenrod
green-yellow
Hansa yellow

honey
Indian yellow
jonquil
lemon
lemon yellow
linen
maize
Mars yellow
mustard
Naples yellow
old gold
orange-yellow
orpiment
pale yellow
palomino
pear
primrose
purree

quince yellow
reed yellow
saffron
sallow
sand
snapdragon
straw
straw color
sulphur yellow
sunflower
sunny
tawny
wheaten
yellow
yellow ochre
yolk yellow

Get More of the Best Writing Instruction From Writer's Digest Books!

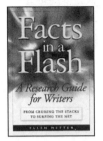